*Speech Handicapped School Children*

# Speech Handicapped School Children

## REVISED EDITION

*Wendell Johnson, Ph.D.*
Professor of Speech Pathology and Psychology,
University of Iowa

*Spencer J. Brown, M.D., Ph.D.*
Medical Consultant in Speech Pathology
Rehabilitation Center for the Physically Handicapped,
Stamford, Connecticut.

*James J. Curtis, Ph.D.*
Professor of Speech; Chairman, Council on Speech Pathology and Audiology,
University of Iowa

*Clarence W. Edney, Ph.D.*
Professor and Head, Department of Speech
Florida State University

*Jacqueline Keaster, M.S.*
Chief Audiologist, Hearing and Speech Clinic
Children's Hospital Society of Los Angeles

HARPER & ROW, PUBLISHERS
NEW YORK AND EVANSTON

*Library of Congress Catalog card number: 56-6096*

*To our students, in partial payment*

*of the debt we owe our teachers*

# CONTENTS

wwwwwwwwwwwwwwwwwwwwwwwwwwwwwwwwwwwwwwwwwwwwwwwwwwwwwwwwwwwwwwwwwwwwwwww

# PREFACE

wwwwwwwwwwwwwwwwwwwwwwwwwwwwwwwwwwwwwwwwwwwwwwwwwwwwwwwwwwwwwwwwwwwwww

This is a book for students who are being trained to work with speech handicapped school children, either as speech correctionists or as classroom teachers. It is particularly designed to prepare the remedial speech instructor and the classroom teacher to work together effectively in the best interests of children with speech difficulties. In part, therefore, it is addressed to the classroom teacher as a "letter of introduction" to the speech correctionist. As such, it is intended to tell the teacher what to do until the speech correctionist comes, after he arrives, and while he is away. At the same time, it is addressed to the speech correctionist as a "letter of introduction" to the classroom teacher, as a means of fostering the perspective and the broad sympathies that make for good working relationships for all concerned.

Fundamentally the book deals with three major questions: (1) What kinds of speech disorders are found among school children? (2) What can the classroom teacher do about them, on her own or in coöperation with a speech correctionist? (3) What are the basic examination methods and remedial approaches of the speech correctionist in dealing with these problems?

This is a text that is designed for use, therefore, in beginning courses for speech correction majors and in speech correction courses—required or optional—for students who are preparing to become classroom teachers. It is particularly adaptable to the textbook needs of an introductory course with a mixed enrollment made up of students whose major interests are distributed among speech correction, education, general speech, psychology, child welfare, premedicine, predentistry, and other areas. It is to be taken for granted, of course, that speech correction majors will undergo specialized training beyond the foundation course for which this book is intended.

In this rapidly shrinking world, speech may not be taken for granted. It is coming to be more and more widely recognized that speech training for all children, including speech correction for the many who need it, is fully as essential to sound present-day education as training in the three R's. Today we know that, for the children who need it—five to ten out of every hundred—our schools have little to offer that is more important than speech correction. And we know, as well, that for all our children, handicapped or not, there is little we have to give them that can enrich their lives more fully than clear, effective, pleasant speech.

As a matter of fact, every teacher, by design or unwittingly, does something about the speech problems of her pupils. Every school administrator and supervisor determines policies that necessarily affect speech handicapped children. There is no question as to *whether* the schools are doing, or should be doing, something for or about pupils who have speech disorders. They cannot avoid doing something. The only question is concerned with *what* they might best be doing. That is what this book is about.

It is quite clear that anything which makes education more rewarding for speech handicapped pupils must necessarily benefit all other school children as well. The kind of education that is best for the speech handicapped child involves an educational philosophy, a general school policy, a type of teaching, and a kind of teacher that combine to make for very effective education in a broad sense. That kind of education, therefore, is also what this book is about.

Most of the forty-eight states now have laws which recognize the special needs of speech handicapped school children. Remedial speech teachers are employed in a very considerable number of school systems, and the rapidly growing demand for qualified speech correctionists far exceeds the available supply. In fact, the demand is not likely to be fully met for many years to come. Until there is an adequate number of professionally qualified speech correctionists, a large proportion of the 5 to 10 percent of school children who have impaired speech must necessarily be dealt with by the regular teachers in most schools, with speech correctionists serving as consultants, or even without any speech correction services at all.

In some states this situation is being faced frankly and constructively. Speech correction is being included among the courses required for teacher certification, and so a need for a new kind of textbook has arisen. This is a need, moreover, that is felt not only by those responsible for the training of classroom teachers, but also by those who are charged with the responsibility of preparing students to function effectively as speech correctionists in the schools and under circumstances in which they need not only the good will but also the active coöperation and actual assistance of the classroom teachers. The authors have kept this specific need in mind in planning and writing this book. They have presented the speech handicapped child as he must be dealt with in the classroom as well as in the clinic.

Many of the principles and methods of speech correction can be applied with good effect by classroom teachers, and a knowledge of them will enable administrators and teachers generally to see much more clearly how they can work hand in hand with the speech correctionist. It is the purpose of this book to help the entire school staff to become more understanding and effective so far as boys and girls with speech difficulties are concerned. Because this is that kind of book, it is also necessarily designed in a somewhat new way to acquaint the professional speech correction worker with the full extent of his opportunities and responsibilities as a specialized instructor and a consultant, and as a co-worker with the administrator, supervisor, and classroom teacher.

A book of this kind is also to be expected to find its way into the hands of many readers in addition to those so far indicated, a fact which the authors have taken duly into account. They have had in mind, particularly, those educators who discharge major responsibilities at the college and university level—professors, deans, and presidents—as well as directors of foundations, commissions, and state and federal programs. These educational leaders will find here an informative statement of a great and pervasive need in American education, together with a basic philosophy and practical recommendations for meeting the need on the level of educational statesmanship.

The book may be expected to have value, as well, for physicians, dentists, public health nurses, social workers, child psychologists and clinical psychologists, parent education workers, and parents. Adults who have speech disorders may also find it of interest and practical value. Finally, it is designed to meet the needs of parent teacher associations, in-service training programs for teachers and child welfare workers, and child study and parent education groups interested in becoming acquainted with the problems of speech handicapped children.

The several authors have worked together to present a unified and comprehensive treatment of the problems under consideration. All of them have contributed their general knowledge and judgment to the overall integrity of the book, and the specific chapters for which each has been chiefly responsible are as follows:

Spencer F. Brown: Chapter VI, "Retarded Speech Development," and Chapter VII, "Cleft Palate; Cerebral Palsy."

James F. Curtis: Chapter III, "Disorders of Articulation," and Chapter IV, "Disorders of Voice."

Clarence W. Edney: Chapter IX, "The Public School Remedial Speech Program."

Jacqueline Keaster: Chapter VIII, "Impaired Hearing."

Wendell Johnson: Chapter I, "Speech Disorders and Speech Correction," Chapter II, "The Clinical Point of View in Education," and Chapter V, "Stuttering." In addition, Professor Johnson has served as general editor.

The authors are indebted to others in ways much too complex to be acknowledged completely. They owe their professional knowledge to the scholars and scientists who have preceded them and to their own teachers, colleagues, and students. They are grateful to the institutions in which they have been privileged to study and work, and as present or past members of the faculty of the University of Iowa they want particularly to acknowledge the fact that for over a quarter of a century the administration of the University—presidents, deans, and department heads—have given constant encouragement and support to the program centering around the speech clinic. In paying special tribute to the pioneering vision of the late Dean Carl E. Seashore, the professional leadership of Professor Lee Edward Travis from 1924 to 1938, and the devoted stewardship of the late Professor E. C. Mabie, the authors are joined by all the other administrative officers, past and present, who have shared in the steady and continuing growth of the program.

In the preparation of this revised edition of *Speech Handicapped School Children* the authors have had the advantage of the reactions of instructors and students who have used the first edition, and for these reactions they are very grateful. Mr. Oliver Skalbeck and Drs. Frederick L. Darley, Earl Schubert, and D. C. Spriestersbach have each read parts of the manuscript, and their comments and suggestions have been extremely valuable. The authors are most appreciative of their painstaking evaluations. Dr. Dorothy Sherman has played an important part in the design and direction of several of the recent experimental studies at the University of Iowa, particularly those concerned with stuttering, upon which certain sections of this book are based. Many others will know that they, too, have helped, directly and indirectly, in the production of this book, and they will understand that the authors, individually and as a group, feel indebted to them and wish that it might be possible to make specific and adequate acknowledgment to each of them personally.

Acknowledgment and appreciation of permission to use specific materials are due each of the following:

American Speech and Hearing Association; Commonwealth Fund; Delta Kappa Gamma Society; Harper & Brothers;

Longmans, Green and Company; The Macmillan Company; John J. Morgenstern, Ph.D.; the National Society for the Study of Education; Office of Education, U.S. Department of Health, Education and Welfare; Psychological Monographs; Speech Association of America; the University of Minnesota Press.

Certain aspects of the recent research at the University of Iowa on the onset of stuttering and on the problem of speech fluency, upon which portions of this text have been based, have been carried on under a grant from the Louis W. and Maud Hill Family Foundation. It is a pleasure to acknowledge with appreciation the enlightened support of Mr. A. A. Hickman, Executive Director, and the Board of Directors of the Foundation.

Special appreciation is to be expressed to Mrs. Mildred Schubert for her extraordinary competence in preparing the bulk of the manuscript for publication. Portions of the manuscript were typed by Mrs. Jayne Zeman and Mrs. Barbara Miller; Mrs. Christina Sturdevant, Mrs. Carol Strange, and Mrs. Ann Laursen assisted with the reading of proof. To all of these the authors are pleased to extend their thanks.

The authors are particularly grateful to their families for the patience and moral support, and for the great deal that eludes even the finest of verbal nets, without which this book would not have been written in the first place nor revised for this edition.

*Speech Handicapped School Children*

# CHAPTER I

~~~~~~~~~~~~~~~~~~~~~~~~~~~~~~~~~~~~~~~~~~~~~~~~~~~~~~~~~~~~~~~~~~~~~~~~~~~~~~~~~~~~

# Speech Disorders and Speech Correction

If all the children of school age in the United States who are handicapped in speech were to be brought together in one place they would make a city the size of Los Angeles. Their number, approximately two million, equals or exceeds the respective populations of twenty-four of the forty-eight states.[1] They make up our largest group of exceptional children. Dr. Romaine P. Mackie, Chief of the Division of Exceptional Children and Youth, United States Office of Education, and Dr. Lloyd M. Dunn have reported that in 1952-53 approximately 307,000 speech handicapped children received special educational services in the public elementary and secondary schools of this country. They wrote, "There are, in fact, more than twice as many children with speech defects being served as there are any other type of handicapped child."[2] Even so, it is to be noted and

[1] American Speech and Hearing Association Committee on the Mid-century White House Conference, "Speech Disorders and Speech Correction," *Journal of Speech and Hearing Disorders* (1952), 17:129-137. The Committee estimated that in an assumed population of 40,000,000 individuals in the United States between the ages of 5 and 21 years there were 2,000,000 with speech handicaps.

[2] Romaine P. Mackie, and Lloyd M. Dunn, *State Certification Requirements for Teachers of Exceptional Children*, Bulletin 1954, No. 1, Office of Education, U.S. Department of Health, Education, and Welfare, p. 39.

1

duly stressed that all the figures here cited indicate that scarcely more than one out of six speech handicapped children of school age is receiving remedial speech instruction.

The substantial progress achieved in recent years in public school speech correction has been made in response to a growing consciousness of need. The great need for speech correction exists not only because the number of speech handicapped children is so large, as handicapped groups go, but also because the distinctive mark of humanity is speech, and the impairment of speech is, therefore, a distinctively human impairment. The number of persons who understand this in a clearly conscious and articulate fashion is becoming ever greater in this highly verbal age of incessant world-wide communication. And it is universally understood on the level of unspoken feeling. We know as though by instinct that speech gives wings to the human spirit, and those whose wings are weak or unnimble command our sympathetic attention and our will to help.

Noticing more and more the need that exists, we become increasingly aware of the shortage of speech correctionists adequately trained to meet the need. The most recent directory of the American Speech and Hearing Association indicates a total membership of nearly 3,700, with about one-third holding either basic or advanced clinical certification in the areas of speech or hearing.[3] The 1954 report of the Association's Committee on Planning revealed that there were state organizations of speech and hearing therapists in twenty-nine states, with combined memberships of 2,132.[4] According to a United States Office of Education survey, there were 2,256 speech correction

---

[3] American Speech and Hearing Association, *Annual Directory*, Supplement, *Journal of Speech and Hearing Disorders*, September, 1955. See p. 3 for essential information about requirements for clinical certification. Further discussion is to be found on pp. 15-16 of the present chapter. For a full statement see "Clinical Certification Requirements of the American Speech and Hearing Association," *Journal of Speech and Hearing Disorders* (1952), 17:249-254, and pp. 15-24 of 1955 *Annual Directory*, cited above.

[4] American Speech and Hearing Association, "Report of the Convention, St. Louis, Missouri, October 23-27, 1954," *Journal of Speech and Hearing Disorders* (1955), 20:94-127. See "Extract from the Report of the Committee on Association Planning," pp. 120-124.

teachers in the public schools of this country in 1952-53.[5] Allowing for overlapping among these figures, one may conclude that there is an approximate maximum total of 5,000 persons working as speech correctionists in the United States. The range of differences probably represented by these individuals with respect to degree of professional qualification is to be duly considered, of course. The extent of the need for trained personnel in the field has been stated in the following terms:

A complete program for the United States would require about 15,000 speech correctionists; this would be one to every 10,000 persons of all ages. . . . Mortality due to death, reaching of retirement age, marriage, and other reasons for retirement probably runs to 10 percent at the very least, and just possibly to 20 percent of the active working force annually. Replacement, therefore, requires from 100 to 200 new trainees each year per 1,000 active workers in the field. This means that when a relatively full working force of 15,000 speech correctionists has been achieved, from 1,500 to 3,000 new recruits per year must be trained just to maintain the personnel supply.[6]

With a current working force of 5,000 speech correction teachers, it is requiring from 500 to 1,000 new correctionists annually to maintain the supply so far achieved, according to these basic estimates. According to the United States Office of Education, 955 students were graduated with majors in "speech correction" or in "speech and hearing" by 92 reporting colleges and universities in the calendar year of 1953; 462 of these received the Bachelor's degree, 260 the Master's degree, and 33 the Doctor's degree.[7] This total number of graduates is scarcely large enough to provide for more than the maintenance of the

[5] Mabel C. Rice and Arthur S. Hill, *Statistics of Special Education for Exceptional Children 1952-53*, Chapter 5 (published as a separate bulletin) of *Biennial Survey of Education in the United States, 1952-54*, Office of Education, U.S. Department of Health, Education, and Welfare, 1954. See Table 1, p. 19.

[6] American Speech and Hearing Association Committee on the Midcentury White House Conference, *op. cit.*, p. 133.

[7] Romaine P. Mackie and Lloyd M. Dunn, *College and University Programs for the Preparation of Teachers of Exceptional Children.* Bulletin 1954, No. 13. Office of Education, U.S. Department of Health, Education, and Welfare. See Table 4, p. 44.

present supply of speech correction teachers in our schools. It is clearly important, therefore, that everything possible be done to increase the number of well qualified speech correctionists. At the same time, it is essential that the classroom teachers in our schools be prepared as well as they can be to work effectively in partnership with the speech correctionists who are available, and to be as helpful as possible to the speech handicapped pupils in their classes when there is no remedial speech instructor at hand.[8]

The basic fact is that every classroom teacher teaches speech. Wittingly or unwittingly, she favors certain standards of speech, voice, and language. Both as speaker and as listener she sets an example and creates an atmosphere in some measure favorable or unfavorable to the best development of each child's speech. Above all, from a speech correction point of view, she creates each day a situation in which the child with a speech difficulty tends to be either demoralized or helped not only to improve his speech but also to live gracefully with his problem so long as it persists and to grow as a person through the experiences he has with it. The administrators of our schools also determine in countless ways by their policies and practices whether the youngster who stutters or lisps shall gain or lose by participation in the great American adventure of education for all. The educational leaders, teachers, and speech correctionists of this nation exercise, individually and all together, an influence of fateful importance in the lives of our speech handicapped school children.

WHAT IS A SPEECH DEFECT OR IMPAIRMENT OR DISTURBANCE?

A straightforward general answer to this question is that a child's speech is defective or presents a problem when most listeners pay as much attention, or more, to how he speaks as to what he says.

[8] A provocative study of the facts and possibilities relevant to the problem of coöperation between speech correctionists and classroom teachers has been reported by Gretchen Wright Lloyd and Stanley Ainsworth in "The Classroom Teacher's Activities and Attitudes Relating to Speech Correction," *Journal of Speech and Hearing Disorders* (1954), 19:244-249.

This answer covers a great deal of ground, not all of which is equally important to us. The definition given here will be refined and developed throughout the book. It is important at this stage to make two basic points:

1. A working definition of defective or impaired speech should be, for classroom purposes, neither too inclusive nor too exclusive. That is, as much harm is done by having speech standards that are too high as by having standards that are too low. A teacher's ears, so to speak, can be too long or too short. She can pay too much attention to a child's speech or too little. A good general rule to follow is that a difference to be a difference has to make a difference. The main purposes of speech are satisfying self-expression and effective communication. If a child is achieving these purposes passably well, his speech does not present a problem in any very important sense, regardless of how he speaks. On the other hand, if he could plainly achieve these purposes more fully with improved speech, then, even though his speech may seem to be reasonably normal, there is something to be gained by him through speech correction. Generally speaking, the kinds of speech imperfections described in later chapters are the ones that will be found to "make a difference" in the classroom as well as outside the school.

2. It is important not to confuse speech defects with certain other types of problems and disabilities. In the case of any particular child, the basic question in this connection is: Is it the child's manner of speaking, as such, that is the chief problem, or is the apparent speech difficulty mainly incidental to something else?

There are four major types of answer to this question:

a. The speech difficulty is the main or even the only problem.

b. The speech difficulty is incidental to, or independent of, some other problem, but solving the other problem will not remove the speech difficulty completely or in any degree.

c. The speech difficulty is incidental to some other problem, and will disappear if the other problem is adequately handled.

d. There is no speech difficulty. Something else has been mistaken for a speech impairment.

Among the other problems that are sometimes confused with speech difficulties, as such, are the following:

a. Improper grammar.
b. Incorrect pronunciation.
c. Substandard ability to read, silently or orally.
d. More or less habitual lack of preparation for class recitations.
e. Certain types of personality maladjustment.
f. Mental subnormality.

Speech impairments may be, and frequently are, related to these conditions. Sometimes they are found in association with one or more of the conditions listed but are not importantly related to them. For example, a child may stutter and also be given to poor grammar, with little if any relationship existing between the two characteristics. Some of these conditions, particularly personality maladjustment or the habitual lack of preparation for class recitation, may be in some cases mainly results of a speech defect, in the sense that a child who finds speaking embarrassing or demoralizing may seek to avoid speaking situations or become discouraged by classroom humiliations. The resulting maladjustments are made more complex by the youngster's rationalizations in defense of his lack of preparation and of his avoidance of situations in which the other children meet and talk with one another. In still other cases, what is thought to be a speech defect may not be at all. It sometimes happens, for example, that a child is referred to a speech clinic, where he is found actually to have quite normal speech but is discovered to be having difficulty with reading or to be using language rather ungrammatically. The habit of saying "ain't" does not constitute a speech defect or difficulty, as these terms are generally used. The habit of saying "ith not" does.

Speech problems of certain kinds may be and often are associated with mental subnormality. Correcting the speech behavior, assuming this is possible to an important degree, will not, of course, remove the low mentality, which will remain as the fundamental problem. (In some cases, it is true, the I.Q. may be raised, usually slightly, by the marked alleviation of a particularly disabling speech impairment.) Referring a mentally subnormal child to a speech correctionist is not anything like a satisfactory solution of his total problem, although speech correction may be very valuable to him. In any event, the classroom teacher cannot deal as well as she might with a mentally deficient pupil by regarding him simply as a "speech defective."

The fundamental consideration is this: If the related condition is removed, will the speech deficiency clear up? If not, the child needs speech correction. If the speech problem is relieved, will the other condition clear up? If not, the child plainly needs special attention in addition to speech correction. The speech condition, and the results to be achieved through speech correction, are to be viewed in relation to the child as a whole and to his other problems, needs, and types of training or special care.

From the point of view of the classroom teacher, any particular child is to be regarded, in this connection, in terms of the following specific questions:

Does the child have a *speech* deficiency?

Does he need speech correction *or* some other type of special help?

Does he need speech correction *and* some other type of special help?

In view of the answers to these questions, what should the classroom teacher do and what can she do?

What should she avoid doing?

This book contains the types of information needed by the classroom teacher as well as the speech correctionist if they are to deal efficiently with these questions separately or together, as members of a team.

WHAT ARE THE DIFFERENT TYPES OF SPEECH DEFICIENCY OR IMPAIRMENT?

In Chapters III through VIII the following speech problems are considered:

1. Problems of articulation.
2. Problems of voice.
3. Stuttering.

4. Retarded speech development.

5. Speech disturbances associated with cleft palate and cerebral palsy.

6. Speech disturbances associated with impaired hearing.

Problems of *articulation* take three main forms:

1. Omission of sounds: a speech sound may be more or less habitually omitted, as in saying *pay* for *play*, or *shovuh* for *shovel*.

2. Distortion of sounds: a particular speech sound may be slighted, articulated too lightly to be heard clearly; a sound may be overarticulated, as in the case of a "whistling" *s*; a sound may be "mushed," as in the case of an *s* that sounds much but not quite like an *sh*.

3. Sound substitution: as in *wun* for *run* (substitution of *w* for *r*), or *thither* for *sister* (substitution of *th* for *s*).

A child with an articulatory defect may make one or more of these types of error. He may make the errors he does only in articulating one particular sound, or two or more sounds may be affected. One sound may be affected more than another. The same sound may be misarticulated more consistently when it occurs at the beginning of a word, in the middle of a word, or at the end. A sound that is produced correctly in one word may be articulated incorrectly in others.

Errors in articulation may be caused, at least in part, by such organic conditions as missing teeth, misarranged teeth, a high and narrow hard palate, a tongue that is sluggish or too large, and the like. The same errors, however, may, and usually do, occur in the absence of any such organic irregularity so far as can be determined. Even when the above conditions are present in some degree they are usually not very important; they may play little or no part in the production of the specific sounds that are improperly formed.

Most articulatory defects in school children are not due to organic causes. They may be thought of as having resulted from faulty training or faulty learning. It is to be emphasized that the great majority of these cases cannot be helped sufficiently, if at all, by referring them to dentists or physicians or by giving them tongue exercises. Every child should have adequate dental and medical care, of course, but that is a consideration quite apart from the main specific need of the children under discussion, so far as their speech is concerned. They need speech correction specifically suited to their particular speech characteristics.

Most speech defects are of the articulatory type. From 70 to 85 percent of the children instructed by public school correctionists have problems of articulation. About 50 percent of them, moreover, experience difficulty with the *s* sound, although many of them also misarticulate other sounds too. As has been shown in great detail by Professor Orvis C. Irwin of the Iowa Child Welfare Research Station, the process of mastering the correct production of speech sounds can be traced from the birth cry through infancy and well into the later years of childhood.[9] Dr. Mildred Templin of the Institute of Child Welfare at the University of Minnesota has reviewed data which indicate that three-year-olds demonstrate mastery of 90 percent of the vowels and diphthongs, about two thirds of the consonants, one half of the two-consonant blends and one third of the three-consonant blends. "By four years of age approximately 80 per cent of correct utterance is attained for consonants, 70 per cent for two-consonant blends, and 60 per cent for three-consonant blends; at six years of age, 90, 80 and 70 per cent; and by seven all are at the 90 per cent level. . . . In the cross-sectional study at eight years only 14 of the 176 sound elements measured were not uttered correctly by at least 90 per cent of the children."[10]

[9] During the past fifteen years or so Professor Irwin has published a substantial series of reports on his studies of speech sound development during infancy. Many of these reports are to be found in the *Journal of Speech and Hearing Disorders.* One that summarizes many of the main findings and indicates the effects of such factors as age, sex, race, intelligence, brain damage, and so forth, is "Speech Development in the Young Child: 2. Some Factors Related to the Speech Development of the Infant and Young Child," *Journal of Speech and Hearing Disorders* (1952), 17:269-279. See also, by the same author, "Infant Speech," *Scientific American* (1949), 181:22-25.

[10] Mildred C. Templin, "Speech Development in the Young Child: 3. The Development of Certain Language Skills in Children," *Journal of Speech and Hearing Disorders* (1952), 17:280-285.

On the basis of speech correction experience in the schools, there is fairly general agreement that 2 to 3 percent of elementary school children have serious articulatory problems, another 2 to 3 percent have less severe difficulties which definitely require special attention, and still another 3 to 5 percent would profit from speech correction although their imperfections are comparatively mild or inconsequential for most ordinary purposes.

*Problems of voice* are mainly classified in terms of the primary attributes of voice. These are pitch, loudness, and quality. Pitch can be too high, too low, or monotonous. The voice may be too loud, too weak, or monotonous with respect to loudness. The chief quality deviations are nasality, hoarseness, harshness, and breathiness. Chronic voice disturbances are not very common among school children.[11] The so-called change of voice occasions some difficulty, of course, at roughly the junior high school level and beyond. Many of the voice difficulties in children are associated with the common cold, laryngitis, or enlarged adenoids.

*Stuttering*, which affects approximately six to ten out of every thousand school children, is, from many points of view, the most challenging of all speech problems, not only to the speech correctionist but also to the classroom teacher. It is not to be defined glibly. While it is a disturbance in the rhythm or fluency of speech, consisting of pauses or hesitancies, repeated or prolonged sounds, and extraneous sounds, it is definitely much more than these surface manifestations. The stutterer feels both tense and apprehensive. His problem is at bottom a psychological one. That is, when a child stutters to his mother, his teacher, or to a playmate, he is *responding* to this other person hesitantly, with some conflict as to whether to respond or not, or whether to respond in one way or another, and with a degree and kind of tension that signalizes this conflict and expresses some measure of fear and insecurity with respect to how the other person will react. It is in some such terms that the stuttering child's difficulty

[11] Two children per thousand is the estimate given by the American Speech and Hearing Association Committee on the Midcentury White House Conference in 1952. *Op. cit.*

is to be appreciated and dealt with, as will be indicated more fully in Chapter V.

*Retarded speech development* is best understood with reference to the various aspects of speech in which development can be seen. Most normal children begin to say words, for example, at about the age of twelve to fifteen months; a child who has not begun to speak in simple words by the age of two to three years needs special attention. Age norms of this kind should not be interpreted strictly; any particular child is not to be compared with the specific accomplishments and chracteristics of the *average* child, but with the general range of abilities and tendencies of the *majority* of children. There are not only wide differences among children, but also great variations in the conditions or environments by which children are affected. A sufficiently unfavorable environment can retard the speech development of a definitely normal child.

Among the more common factors which tend to make for delayed speech development are (1) mental subnormality; (2) illness and physical impairment, such as paralyzing conditions; (3) lack of sufficient speech stimulation, as in homes in which no one coos or babbles or chatters to the baby, or in which the members of the family talk very little among themselves; (4) impaired hearing of a degree sufficient to interfere with the child's ability to recognize clearly the sounds and words and speech patterns to be imitated and learned; (5) inadequate or disturbingly inconsistent rewards—even a certain amount of misplaced punishment—for the child's early attempts at speech. While it is not among the more common factors responsible for retarded speech development, intense shock, fright, or shame, experienced over a sustained period or on one or more crucial occasions, is a possibility which the speech examiner must consider in some cases.[12]

The aspects of speech in which retarded development may be particularly evident are (1) amount of vocalization and babbling

---

[12] A review of studies dealing with the relation of emotional and social maladjustment to certain aspects of speech retardation is presented by Dorothea McCarthy in "Language Disorders and Parent-Child Relationships," *Journal of Speech and Hearing Disorders* (1954), *19*:514-523.

during infancy, (2) age at which single words and sentences are first spoken, (3) correctness of articulation of the various speech sounds, (4) general average length of speech response, (5) amount of speaking, and (6) vocabulary. Retardation with respect to these aspects of speech is, of course, a relative matter. According to the American Speech and Hearing Association Committee of the Midcentury White House Conference, three out of every thousand school children present retarded speech development.[13]

*Speech problems associated with cleft palate and cerebral palsy* are to be described in terms of imperfections in voice, articulation, and fluency or rate. In cases of cleft palate the structures which normally form the roof of the mouth have failed to join properly. As a result, air passes freely between the oral and nasal chambers. Moreover, the action of the tongue and the velar and pharyngeal structures, and the associated variations in size and shape of the oral cavity, tend to be influenced in ways that affect speech. The speech tends particularly to be nasalized. There is also difficulty in building up breath pressure for the stop-plosive sounds (*p, b, t, d, k,* and *g*); the effort to produce these sounds may result, therefore, in what may be called a "nasal snort." Other sounds, too, can be affected, of course.

The cleft may affect only the hard palate; it may be a slight or an extensive cleft. It sometimes extends through the gum ridge at the front of the mouth; it may involve the lip (harelip). In some cases it extends back to the soft palate and velum; the soft palate may be short, divided, or absent. Harelip is commonly repaired by surgery soon after birth or in early infancy. Surgery

---

[13] *Op. cit.* See also Irwin and Templin, *op. cit.*, for information concerning details of speech development. For a systematic procedure for evaluating speech development in individual cases and for appraising factors possibly related to speech retardation, see W. Johnson, Frederic L. Darley, and D. C. Spriestersbach, *Diagnostic Manual in Speech Correction,* New York, Harper & Brothers, 1952, pp. 95-114. A case of retarded speech associated with blindness and cerebral palsy but illustrating several important principles that apply in children not so affected organically is decribed by George O. Egland in "An Analysis of an Exceptional Case of Retarded Speech," *Journal of Speech Disorders* (1954), *19*:239-243.

is commonly used also to repair clefts of the hard and soft palates. When surgery is inadvisable, impractical, or unsuccessful, appliances called obturators, roughly resembling "false plates," are often used to shut off the nasal from the oral passage. This means that school children with cleft palates may have (1) surgically repaired clefts, (2) unsuccessfully repaired clefts (with or without obturators), and (3) unrepaired clefts (with or without obturators). Neither surgical repair nor an obturator is sufficient, except in very rare cases, to eliminate the imperfection in speech; speech correction is necessary in practically every case. Meanwhile, the general adjustment of a child who has a cleft palate or a harelip can be importantly affected by the classroom teacher. Roughly one in every 800 children is born with a cleft palate.

Cerebral palsy is a general term which covers a variety of conditions caused by damage to certain areas in the brain. The most common forms are the spastic, the athetotic, and the ataxic (these are explained in Chapter VII). It is probable that from 250,000 to 400,000 persons in the United States are affected by this condition. Speech is influenced in about 70 percent of cases of cerebral palsy.

In general, the speech of cerebral palsied children is labored, slow, and jerky, the voice tends to be monotonous and relatively uncontrolled, and the articulation suffers because of the impaired muscular coördination. Cerebral palsied speech is a problem for the professional speech correctionist, but the classroom teacher plays a vital role in determining the opportunities which the cerebral palsied child will have in making the most of the training given him by the speech correctionist and by other specialists.

*Speech problems associated with impaired hearing* are revealed chiefly in certain distortions of articulation and voice. The hard of hearing child cannot hear the speech of others well enough to imitate accurately the finer qualities of voice and speech, particularly with respect to the articulation of certain sounds. Moreover, such a child cannot always hear his own voice sufficiently well to know that he is making particular errors or that he is not controlling his vocal inflections normally. The degree to which speech is affected depends generally upon the mannner and degree to which hearing is impaired, and whether the impairment has been present since before, or occurred after, the age when speech would normally have been acquired. The various types of hearing loss, and the practical significance of different degrees of loss, so far as speech is concerned, are discussed in Chapter VIII. Approximately 3 percent of school children have educationally significant hearing losses, and another 5 percent at least have losses that call for proper medical attention and that may affect speech in some cases.

These, then, are the speech and voice problems with which this book is concerned—and it is concerned with them from the special point of view of the general classroom teacher and of the speech correctionist who works as a teammate with her.

WHAT IS SPEECH CORRECTION?

In general, a speech correctionist examines and diagnoses or evaluates the speech, voice, and language behavior of children and adults who experience difficulty with these functions, and provides remedial instruction and counseling for them according to their respective needs. In the United States most speech correction work is carried on in the elementary and secondary schools. It is also done in hospitals, of course, including government hospitals, and in special agencies, such as mental hygiene, child guidance, psychological and community clinics. There are also private speech clinics. Today most of the larger universities and colleges, and many of the smaller ones, maintain speech clinics. These university clinics not only provide student and community speech correction services but are also important as professional training and research centers.

A practical distinction is commonly made between the scientific study of speech disorders, which is known as speech pathology, and corrective work with persons who have speech difficulties or disorders which is known variously as speech correction, speech rehabilitation, and speech reëducation. Speech pathology and speech correction together constitute a professional field which has developed rapidly, particularly since World War I, in response to a growing realization of the impressive incidence of speech disturbances, the seriousness of their effects, the degree to which they are remediable, and the fact that none of the other established professions is prepared to deal with them either comprehensively or specifically. As a profession it has drawn for its special needs from a wide variety of fields, such as the medical sciences—particularly anatomy, physiology, and neurology—education, and child welfare and psychology, to build upon a base made up chiefly of phonetics and speech science and the psychology of personal adjustment. Within this framework, speech pathologists have developed new investigative and scientific procedures with which to amass a growing body of knowledge and theory concerning speech disorders, and this knowledge and theory form the basis of the practical art of speech correction.

The qualifications of a speech correctionist can be described in a particularly meaningful way in terms of the clinical certification regulations of the American Speech and Hearing Association, the recognized organization of scientists, teachers, and clinicians in this field.[14] The Association has two classes of membership, Member and Associate. Members may apply for any of four certificates of clinical competence, Basic and Advanced in Speech and Basic and Advanced in Hearing. The distinctions between levels of certification are made in terms of amount of professional training and experience. Members who have made distinguished scientific, clinical, and scholarly contributions to the profession may be nominated and elected to the class of Fellow.

Not all speech correctionists belong to the American Speech and Hearing Association, although membership in it and certification by it are coming to be recognized generally as basic evidence of professional qualification for work in the field. Public school speech correctionists must also hold proper certification credentials from their respective state departments of

[14] See the *Journal of Speech and Hearing Disorders*, June, 1952.

public instruction. Many states have special certificates for speech correction teachers.[15]

In general the speech correction teacher in a school system serves as supervisor and consultant as well as teacher and clinician. It is her responsibility to identify, by suitable survey or examination procedures, those pupils who are in need of speech correction. Having found them, she divides them into groups according to type and severity of problem and with reference to grade level. Those whose problems can be dealt with adequately by their classroom teachers are left in their regular classes; the speech correctionist, of course, confers with each child's teacher, clarifies his speech difficulty, explains and demonstrates the special procedures and policies that are indicated, and arranges for periodic review of the problem. The children who require the personal attention of the speech correctionist are divided into two general groups: those who must be given individual instruction and those who can or should be handled in small classes, grouped according to similarities in age, grade level, and type of speech problem. The groups may overlap, of course; a particular child may be given both individual and group therapy or instruction.

The speech correction teacher coördinates her schedule of meetings for these children with the general school program and works at all times in close coöperation with the pupils' classroom teachers. It is also essential or desirable in many cases that she work with the parents and that she be instrumental in securing for certain children the medical, dental, psychological, or other types of special attention which they require.

What all this means to the classroom teacher is that she can be most helpful to the speech handicapped children in her classroom by working in coöperation with the speech correctionist, if there is one in her school system. This book is so constructed that the teacher can get from each chapter, dealing with a particular type of speech problem, the information that

[15] See Romaine P. Mackie and Lloyd M. Dunn, *State Certification Requirements for Teachers of Exceptional Children*, Washington, D.C., U.S. Department of Health, Education, and Welfare, Office of Education, Bulletin 1954, No. 1.

will be especially helpful to her in working with the speech correctionist. For the teacher who is on her own, so to speak, with no speech correctionist available, the attempt is made in each chapter to provide the kind of information particularly useful in such a situation.

It is tremendously encouraging to learn of the extremely effective ways in which many teachers have dealt with speech handicapped children in their classrooms. Such teachers and their constructive work come to the attention of speech correction workers regularly in all parts of the country. A case which illustrates very well what can be done, even by a beginning teacher in a rural school, and with a difficult problem, was communicated to the authors by Mrs. Frances Reicken of the Minneapolis Public Schools, formerly speech clinician for the Crippled Children's Services in Minnesota.

In the course of her state-wide activities Mrs. Reicken was informed by a county nurse that one of the rural teachers in her county wished to have her see a thirteen-year-old stuttering boy. The teacher had emphasized—and this is important—that she would prefer to have the appointment at a time when she might accompany the boy. She was not "sending him"; she wanted to "bring him." A day was set for the conference, and advance arrangements were made for the county nurse to obtain a brief case history by interviewing the boy, his parents, and the teacher. The nurse reported back to Mrs. Reicken that in her judgment it would indeed be desirable to make sure that the teacher accompany the boy to the conference because she had found her most coöperative.

The nurse had known the boy's previous teacher and described her as an unfriendly sort of person, with many unrecognized and unsolved personal problems of her own. At the close of the previous school year the boy had expressed the wish that he could suddenly become sixteen years old so he "could leave school for good." The new teacher, inexperienced and just out of teachers' college, had been patient and kind from the start. Her friendliness toward all the children had been evident to the nurse during her visit to the school. It was of special significance that she had assigned certain nonspeech duties to the boy who stuttered. He kept the blackboards washed and did two or three other such tasks—"Not too many," as the teacher put it, "but enough to make him feel that he was doing the sort of things the others were doing and that what he did was important."

The new teacher had been in the school about three months. Already the boy was responding in a decidedly wholesome way to her positive approach. He was even arriving at school earlier than usual, and was willing to stay late in order to improve his work. His parents reported that he was asking them to help him with his studies at home, whereas formerly he had never done this. In fact, there had been many days when they had had to insist that he go to school.

After the conference with Mrs. Reicken the teacher continued to encourage and help the boy in every way she could. His stuttering in the classroom was markedly lessened, and it was Mrs. Reicken's considered professional judgment that the improvement in speech itself was largely due to the teacher's warm, human feeling for all her pupils. She did not "cure" the boy's stuttering, of course; no informed and reasonable person would have expected such a result. She did, however, contribute to a worth-while improvement in his speech, and she gave him a strong desire to continue his schooling. By doing so she reduced his handicap greatly and made life much richer for him than it would have been without her understanding and friendly encouragement. This young rural teacher was not a speech correctionist and did not pretend to be one, but what she was able to do, just by being the kind of teacher she was, added up to a very large share of all that could have been accomplished by a good speech correctionist.

Another inspiring story is related by Miss Jacqueline Keaster, one of the authors of this book. As speech correctionist for the Davenport, Iowa, schools a number of years ago, Miss Keaster was called on the second day of school one September by the principal of one of the junior high schools. He told her about a new pupil, Evelyn, a transfer from a country school, who had almost unintelligible speech. The story is best told in Miss Keaster's own words:

He wanted me to come immediately. I found a tall, thin thirteen-year-old girl with what appeared to be a severe functional articulation disorder. All of the consonants were distorted to a greater or lesser degree. The speech was almost impossible to understand. The girl appeared to be intelligent—her grades from the country school were higher than average—and this impression was later borne out by objective tests. The principal of the school in which Evelyn was now enrolled was extremely interested in her problem. His interest was contagious. All of her classroom teachers became interested and asked how they could help. The girl herself reacted by becoming highly motivated in her desire to improve her speech.

Throughout her grade school career this youngster had kept up by writing everything—she was different from the others. Her feeling of being different permeated her whole being. She walked with her head down, her shoulders slumped. She didn't know how to chatter and laugh with other girls. Mr. R., the principal, called in the president of the Girl Reserve and asked her to see that Evelyn was invited to join. The physical education instructor helped her with game skills at noon and after school. Her fellow students were helped to an awareness of the problem in such a way that it was not infrequent for a student, a stranger to me, to stop me in the hall to report with some pride on one of Evelyn's accomplishments. During all of this she was correcting on an average of one sound every two weeks—by sheer hard work.

Her head came up, her shoulders straightened. By the coöperative efforts of an entire junior high school a transformation was brought about.

Evelyn went to the big senior high school the next fall and took a course in fundamentals of speech with a teacher who was willing that it be a practice hour for the fixing of new speech habits.

Three years later she graduated among the top ten in a class of more than three hundred—a girl who had not wanted to come to high school because of her poor speech, but who continued her education because of the understanding helpfulness of a school principal, who inspired all her teachers and even her classmates by his human feeling for Evelyn's difficulties and his respect for her as a person. He knew where to turn for help, but he also knew that there was more to the problem than the mere correction of specific speech sounds. To him

Evelyn was not just a "speech defective" or a "problem child." She was a young girl, unhappy and handicapped, in whose drawn face and averted eyes he saw the potential smile and sparkle of an attractive woman. It was an exciting experience to be one of the team of teachers and school children that formed spontaneously under this principal's compelling leadership to win the game wth Evelyn.

The place of speech correction in the school and classroom comes alive in stories such as these, and is further indicated throughout this book. It is to be considered, of course, that the classroom teacher cannot be expected to undertake time-consuming tasks on behalf of individual pupils which would distract her attention from her main job. What the classroom teacher may find practical and desirable to do, from a speech correction point of view, need be neither time-consuming nor distracting, as the representative instances sketched above so clearly show. For the greater part, in fact, what is to be recommended is a philosophy of teaching, a classroom atmosphere, general instructional methods, and a few simple things to be done in the course of the classroom routine, or as time can be "made" for them, most of which will be beneficial not only to the children with speech difficulties but to all the other pupils as well. The kind of classroom or school or teacher that is good for a child who stutters or lisps is good for any other child too, generally speaking.

In Chapter II more detailed consideration will be given to the place of speech correction in the classroom—or, better perhaps, the place of the classroom, and of the classroom teacher, in speech correction.

# CHAPTER II

~~~~~~~~~~~~~~~~~~~~~~~~~~~~~~~~~~~~~~~~~~~~~~~~~~~~~~~~~~~~~~~~~~~~~~~~

# *The Clinical Point of View in Education*

Inherent in the philosophy of democracy is the doctrine that every child is entitled to an education to the limit of his capacity. . . . The education of exceptional children represents an attempt on the part of the school to furnish equal opportunity to individuals who differ in physical, mental, and social characteristics. . . . All [children] have an equal right to life's satisfactions. And it is the responsibility of public education to see that they get what they need.

The objectives of the education of exceptional children must be in accord with these principles of democracy. They do not differ from the general objectives of education for all children. Exceptional children, like others, must become well-adjusted members of the family and the community, must participate in the activities of the work-a-day world, and must assume responsibilities in keeping with their capacities as citizens in a democracy.[1]

The basic policies and objectives of education for exceptional children, including those handicapped in speech, are well stated in this pronouncement of a national committee of educational

[1] Committee on the Education of Exceptional Children (Harry G. Baker, W. W. Charters, Elise H. Martens, Edward H. Stullken, and Samuel A. Kirk, Chairman) of the National Society for the Study of Education, *The Forty-Ninth Yearbook of the National Society for the Study of Education, Part II, The Education of Exceptional Children,* ed. Nelson B. Henry, Chicago: University of Chicago Press, 1950, pp. 3-4.

leaders. In delineating the historical background of these policies and objectives the authors point up the substantial growth in special education in the United States since its beginnings in the early years of the present century: "By 1930, sixteen states had enacted laws authorizing reimbursement to local school districts for the excess cost of the education of exceptional children. . . . By 1948, forty-one states had enacted laws authorizing or requiring local school districts to make special provisions for one or more types of exceptional children. Thirty-four of these states have provided funds to help the local districts finance the program."[2] Another indication of the vitality of this growth is to be seen in the increase in recent years in the number of colleges and universities offering teacher preparation programs in special education. The 122 institutions offering such training programs in the academic year 1953-54 represented a 58 percent increase over the number providing comparable programs in 1949.[3]

The greatest relative growth has taken place in the specific area of speech correction. Rice and Hill[4] present the following statistics as indicative of development in public school speech correction in this country between 1947–48 and 1952–53:

1. Number of states reporting speech correction in schools: 1947-48, 40; 1952-53, 49 (the survey included the District of Columbia).

2. Number of school districts reporting speech correction: 1947-48, 450; 1952-53, 1,087.

3. Children enrolled in speech correction programs, 1947-48: in elementary schools, 173,246; in secondary schools, 9,062; total, 182,308; 1952-53, in elementary schools, 254,179; in secondary schools, 52,568; total, 306,747.

---

[2] *Ibid.,* pp. 9-10.

[3] Romaine P. Mackie and Lloyd M. Dunn, *College and University Programs for the Preparation of Teachers of Exceptional Children,* Bulletin 1954, No. 13, Office of Education, U.S. Department of Health, Education, and Welfare, p. 10.

[4] Mabel C. Rice and Arthur S. Hill, *Statistics of Special Education for Exceptional Children 1952-53,* Chapter 5 (printed as separate bulletin) of *Biennial Survey of Education in the United States, 1952-54,* Office of Education, U.S. Department of Health, Education, and Welfare, 1954. See Table 1, p. 19.

4. Number of speech correction teachers: 1947-48, 1,256; 1952-53, 2,256.

While the number of children who need remedial speech services still exceeds by far the number who are receiving them, the development in this field in recent years has been impressive, and it is instructive to inquire into the reasons for this and into its more important consequences. In the early beginnings of special education, it was indeed thought of as special and the children for whom it was intended were decidedly regarded as exceptional. The first significant work of this kind was done, in fact, not in the regular schools but in special institutions, such as the American School for the Deaf, a private agency, established in 1817 in Hartford, Connecticut. Gradually public philosophy with regard to the relevant responsibilities of the schools underwent a change. Mackie and Dunn state:

Toward the latter part of the nineteenth century there were some efforts to educate exceptional children in local communities, but most of these were somewhat experimental. Such special educational projects were usually undertaken by, or in cooperation with, private agencies, and encouraged educators to enlarge their concept of the function of the school to include the handicapped. . . .

It was not until the beginning of the present century that school systems began to assume responsibility for atypical children in any organized fashion. Even as late as 1920, little was done by local school systems except in a few of the large cities. These efforts were mainly on behalf of the crippled, the partially seeing, the mentally retarded, and the socially maladjusted. As the values of these day school programs became recognized, special classes and services were added for the hard-of-hearing, the speech handicapped, and for children with cardiac and other special health problems. Some cities inaugurated day school classes for the blind and the deaf, and a few local schools began experimenting with special classes for the gifted. This movement to extend educational services to *all* children has grown, until today, more than 500,000 exceptional children are reported to be enrolled [in special programs] in local school systems.[5]

[5] Romaine P. Mackie and Lloyd M. Dunn, *State Certification Requirements for Teachers of Exceptional Children*, Bulletin 1954, No. 1, Office of Education, U.S. Department of Health, Education, and Welfare, p. 3.

Among the major factors responsible for the increasing public attention to the needs of the handicapped are to be listed the influence of organized religion in modern times, the rise of the scientific method and outlook, and the revolutionary movements of the past two centuries, still continuing, that have fostered democratic principles of government and a corresponding official respect and concern for the common man and for the children of the common people. One of the most fundamental of the effects of the rise of democracy has been the phenomenal expansion of our systems of public education, as such. Medicine has changed and expanded greatly under the impact of scientific method, and our modern conceptions of public health have made a definite impression on policies and practices in school administration. Stressing the fundamental importance of due regard for health in relation to education, a recent publication of the United States Office of Education contains these statements: "Basic to all other needs . . . desirable and essential for secondary-school age youth is health. . . . Physical, mental, and emotional health are the very warp and woof of satisfactory home and family life, and the expressed rights and privileges of citizenship are little more than hollow platitudes unless the individual is fit to defend and enjoy them."[6]

An increasingly systematic school health program could only lead to a heightened appreciation of the problems and the potentialities of children requiring medical attention. Added to this was the fact that since the last two decades of the nineteenth century, when Sigmund Freud and William James, Ivan Pavlov and E. L. Thorndike, and other scientific investigators of human behavior laid the foundations of modern psychology and psychiatry, there has been a remarkable advance in public enlightenment with respect to mental, emotional, and behavioral problems, particularly those of children. One of the specific consequences of the advances made in the behavioral sciences has been the

[6] Galen Jones and Raymond W. Gregory, *Life Adjustment Education for Every Youth*, Bulletin 1951, No. 22, Office of Education, Federal Security Agency, p. 70. For a discussion of the historical relationship between speech pathology and medicine, see Charles R. Strother, "Trends in Speech Pathology," *Quarterly Journal of Speech* (1943), 29:76-80.

introduction of diagnostic testing programs in our schools. "With the increased development and use of educational statistics, testing techniques, and community surveys, schoolmen learned more about the significance of individual differences, rate of maturation, and rate of learning. They learned that psychological and social endowments were not the same for all, and realized the folly of treating children and youth as if these differences did not exist."[7]

Moreover, in the past two generations or so, we have become more and more conscious of the wonders and the hazards of human language and speech, largely through the influence of the new and vigorous college and university programs in speech and the burgeoning of the science and the means of communication since Alexander Graham Bell's epochal invention of the telephone in 1875 and the more recent fantastic developments in radio, sound photography, electronic recording, and television. The science of communication is rapidly becoming one of the most exciting, comprehensive, sophisticated, and socially important of all our many scientific disciplines, and such new and recently strange words as cybernetics, semantics, and feedback are coming to be part of our common vocabulary.[8] There is

[7] Commission on Life Adjustment Education for Youth (Benjamin C. Willis, Chairman), *Vitalizing Secondary Education,* Bulletin 1951, No. 3, Office of Education, Federal Security Agency, p. 9.

[8] The literature concerned with these matters is becoming relatively vast; the following references provide orientation to the field: George A. Miller, *Language and Communication,* New York, McGraw-Hill Book Co., 1951; John W. Black and Wilbur E. Moore, *Speech: Code, Meaning and Communication,* New York, McGraw-Hill Book Co., 1955; Stuart Chase, *The Power of Words,* New York, Harcourt, Brace & Co., 1954; S. I. Hayakawa, *Language in Thought and Action,* New York, Harcourt, Brace & Co., 1949; J. Z. Young, *Doubt and Certainty in Science,* New York, Oxford University Press, Inc., 1951; Wendell Johnson, *Your Most Enchanted Listener,* New York, Harper & Brothers, 1956. For a comprehensive historical treatment of the field of speech in its various aspects see Karl R. Wallace, ed., *History of Speech Education in America,* New York, Appleton-Century-Crofts, Inc., 1954; see particularly Chapter 13, "Speech Education in Nineteenth-Century Schools," by Gladys L. Borchers and Lillian R. Wagner; Chapter 16, "The Rise of Experimental Phonetics," by James F. Curtis; Chapter 18, "Developmen of Education in Speech and Hearing to 1920," by Clarence T. Simon; Chapter 21, "Speech Education in Twentieth-Century Public Schools," by Halbert E. Gulley and Hugh Seabury. The beginnings of speech correction

today a widespread consciousness of speech that is indeed new under the sun, and one of the most important aspects of it is our heightened awareness of speech disorders and our general acceptance of the view that the study and treatment of speech disorders are matters of great individual and public concern.

This list of factors is by no means exhaustive, but it does serve to suggest the very great substantiality of the philosophical, scientific, political, and social trends that have given rise to special education in general and to speech correction in particular, as we know them today. Special education is no longer as "special" as it used to be, and exceptional children are far less "exceptional" than they once were. Professor Samual Kirk and his Committee have said of the so-called exceptional child that he "has fundamental motives and drives common to children in general; but along with those common characteristics there is in each case a specific handicap or exceptional condition that requires an adjustment or special service in his educational program. That program should be designed with full recognition of (a) his likeness to normal children and (b) his special needs. This, in brief, constitutes the modern approach to the education of exceptional children."[9]

The rise of special education has had a great influence on our entire educational program. Professor Kirk and his associates have put it this way:

All children in a school system profit from the special services provided for exceptional children. . . . Some pioneer educators, such as Montessori, Decroly, and Horace Mann, who began their educational work with exceptional children, found that the techniques which they developed were of great advantage to others. The activity movement, for example, in which it was emphasized that the mentally defective could learn best "through doing," was later advocated as a general educational procedure. Programs for exceptional children have thus provided laboratory situations leading to the development of new

---

in the public schools is delineated in Paul Moore and Dorothy G. Kester, "Historical Notes on Speech Correction in the Pre-Association Era," *Journal of Speech and Hearing Disorders* (1953), 18:48-53.

[9] *Forty-Ninth Yearbook of the National Society for the Study of Education, Part II, The Education of Exceptional Children, op. cit.,* p. 10.

philosophies and methods, which in many cases have a universal school application.[10]

We may sum up many of the "philosophies and methods" that special education has contributed to our educational system as a whole in what we may call the clinical point of view in education—the point of view that each child is an individual, and that the best education for him is that which strives constructively to adapt the school to his individuality in the process of training him to adjust his individuality in creative ways to the school. A dynamic concept of personality and adjustment is embodied in this philosophy of education, a concept that has grown out of the experience of workers in special education, psychology, social work, speech correction, and other clinical or related fields. It is distinctive of the clinical approach that it brings the individual human being into sharp focus, and that in doing so it tends always to lead to the crucial revelation that the individual has essential relationships with other persons. So it is that we have learned that we can best serve a speech handicapped child not by placing him in a program that isolates him from his peers, but by training him always with a clear recognition of the fact that speaking is something that he must do to and with others, and that through speech he must *relate himself* as an individual to others. The clinical point of view, as it pervades our schools, fosters an emphasis upon the differences that make each child a distinctive personality and upon the social settings or contexts —the patterns of interpersonal relationships—in which these individual differences come alive with meaning.

Most children with speech handicaps profit from working in groups, even though they must be examined and evaluated one by one—and no two will ever turn out to be the same. It is beneficial for a speech impaired child to share his experiences with others, to gain perspective from forming relationships with other children who have problems more or less similar to his own or very different from his own—and with those who may seem to him to have no problems at all. He gains motivation to improve

[10] *Ibid.*, pp. 5-6.

by sharing the morale of the group and by contributing to it. And the naturalness of the speaking experiences that come about in group work and in normal school situations is a factor that contributes to the carryover of improvement achieved in the school or clinic into everyday speaking experiences in home and neighborhood.

Examination procedures and certain aspects of treatment or remedial speech instruction must always be individualized, of course. More and more, however, speech correction is emerging from its cubicle to become integrated with the general school program. It is being carried beyond the school and into the home where speech difficulties nearly always begin and where many of the reasons for their persistence are to be found. Speech correction is becoming more "lifelike"—and so is education generally, more slowly than some would wish, more rapidly than others feel it should. One of the many reasons for this is that speech correctionists and other special teachers in the schools, from the time of Horace Mann to our own day, have inevitably demonstrated, simply by serving each exceptional child as best they could, that what is good for the exceptional youngster is nearly always good for all the other children too.

The future historian of education, as he evaluates all this, is likely to conclude that the most importnat consequence of "the rise of the handicapped child" was that it had a good effect on the schools themselves. It is good for teachers to be good to individual youngsters, not only because it is good for the children but also because it is good for the teachers. The handicapped child has done the entire educational system the great service of stimulating his teachers to be good to him—and of persuading them into the bargain that what is good for him is good for all their other pupils as well. The way to be a good teacher of arithmetic is to be a good teacher for the child who, for some special reason, finds arithmetic extremely difficult. The way to conduct oral work in social studies so that none of the pupils will suffer stage fright is to conduct it so that even a stuttering pupil can be at ease and enjoy his own part in the discussion.

One of the most essential requirements for effective teaching of this sort is sufficient knowledge about the problem that a particular child has, and about the physical equipment and the personality of the child who has the problem. This book is about the problems of children whose difficulties center in their speech, and so we shall begin, in the remaining pages of this chapter, to apply the clinical point of view in the education of speech handicapped children by presenting essential information about speech and its impairments, and about the relationship between speech problems and personality. In the light of this information, the types of school policies, teaching procedures, and teacher-child relationships that are good for speech handicapped children, and that are bad for them, will be discussed. In relation to the rest of the book, this is the chapter that deals with "the common denominator" in the responsibilities and opportunities of the classroom teacher in ministering to the needs of children with speech difficulties. It is this "common denominator" that speech correction as a profession has to contribute to the advancement of education for all our children—in a kind of ever continuing reinvestment in the indispensable good that the grand community of the school contributes to the well-being of speech handicapped children.

## *Physiological Aspects of Speech*

### THERE ARE NO SPEECH ORGANS

One of the basic facts that helps us to appreciate the hazards to which speech is subject is that there are no organs of speech, as such.[11] Each of the organs used for speech serves other functions with which speech has to compete. Under certain conditions it competes at a disadvantage. You can appreciate this clearly if you will try to carry on a conversation while lifting one end of a heavy desk. An important function of the vocal cords or folds is that of assisting in maintaining breath pressure in the chest cavity during the act of lifting or similar types of

[11] Classic statements of this general point of view are to be found in Lee Edward Travis, *Speech Pathology*, New York, D. Appleton Co., 1931, and in Edward Sapir, *Language*, New York, Harcourt, Brace, 1921.

muscular exertion. In performing this function the vocal folds come together, or close, and while they are in this position it is not possible to use them for producing vocal tones for speech.

The vocal folds also serve to keep foreign material out of the lungs. That is why one cannot speak and swallow at the same time; during swallowing the vocal folds come together and thus keep the liquid or food being swallowed from going down the "windpipe," or trachea. Likewise, while coughing, hiccoughing, and retching it is practically true that one has no "voice box"; the vocal folds are simply not functioning at such times as *vocal* folds, as a mechanism for producing speech tones. In a literal sense, an essential part of one's co-called speech mechanism is functionally missing. Only when the functions mentioned, which are biologically more vital than speech, are not being performed are the vocal folds and the related parts of the tone-producing mechanism available for purposes of speech.

What is true in this sense of the vocal folds is true also of the organs of breathing, the lungs, diaphragm, muscles of the chest walls, and nasal passages. Breathing and the vitalizing functions which it serves are more important than talking, so far as the life processes of the human body are concerned. This explains why we are able to speak only in a meager fashion or not at all while sneezing, yawning, sighing, gasping for air, or breathing deeply as a result of vigorous exercise. No one is a good conversationalist during a two-mile run.

Moreover, the lips, tongue, teeth, cheek muscles, soft palate, and muscles of the throat were not designed primarily for speech. We use them for speaking only when they are not otherwise engaged. These bodily parts are decidedly engaged when, for example, the infant is feeding or the adult is taking a drink of water. During such acts there are, for the moment, no *speech* organs.

PRACTICAL IMPLICATIONS

The greater share of the time, of course, we get along so well speaking with "borrowed tools" that we are not conscious of any problems arising from this circumstance. Occasionally we may be dimly aware of being frustrated in talking at the dinner table, particularly when the main dish is Italian spaghetti or un-boned fish, but we seldom, if ever, become reflective about it. As bedtime nears it sometimes becomes difficult to read aloud, but for the most part we take yawning for granted and think nothing of it.

There are some important considerations in this connection, however. One of them is that good speech development depends, in part, upon normally vigorous sucking and chewing activities during infancy and early childhood. An implication of this fact, which has perhaps a minor significance in the classroom, is that occasionally the speech correctionist advises a child to chew gum in order to strengthen tongue and jaw muscles that have not been sufficiently exercised. In fact, the use of chewing exercises in certain aspects of speech correction has been developed by Froeschels[12] and Palmer[13] to a degree that is likely to seem surprising to one who has never considered the possible rela-tionships between chewing and speaking.

A further practical consideration is that the interests of good speech are served by the dental hygiene programs in our schools. True, the only teeth that are extremely important for speech are the two upper front ones (provided enough of the others are also present), but the general alignment of the teeth, and especially the position of the upper front teeth in relation to the lower front teeth, are of some significance. Good chewing habits, plus ade-quate dental care, are to be urged for these reasons in the interests of proper speech development.

Another point of some interest is that vigorous crying during infancy is not without value. The weak, passive baby whose voice never rises above a whimper is at least getting off to a slow start in generating the vocal potential and the lung power needed in a modern auditorium.

Breathing exercises were at one time taken for granted as an

[12] Emil Froeschels and Auguste Jellinek, *Practice of Voice and Speech Therapy*, Boston, The Expression Co., 1941.

[13] Martin F. Palmer, "Studies in Clinical Techniques: II. Normalizing of Chewing, Sucking and Swallowing Reflexes in Cerebral Palsy: A Home Program," *Journal of Speech Disorders* (1947), 12:415-418.

important part of almost any speech correction procedure, and although they have been largely abandoned so far as most types of cases are concerned, the part played by normal respiration in good speech is not to be ignored. In certain types of voice training breathing exercises are commonly used. Most children, including speech handicapped children, breathe normally, but occasionally one encounters a case in which the breathing is "shallow," or jerky, or otherwise unsuitable for the demands of sustained normal speech. Teachers sometimes inquire as to the correct manner of breathing. About the only defensible answer is that, while practically everyone "breathes with" the diaphragm *and* the chest, nevertheless, so far as a distinction can be made, both "diaphragmatic" and "chest" breathing are normal. Occasionally one finds a child who gives the appearance of being an "upper chest" breather, and usually such a child's breathing habits might advisedly be retrained.[14]

Mouth breathing, which is ordinarily due to adenoids or other types of nasal obstruction, is in some measure detrimental to good speech habits. It is to be given due attention, of course, for other reasons as well; children who breathe through their mouths to any marked extent should be referred to a physician as a matter of general policy.

The main reason why the speech correctionist is interested in respiration, however, is that it serves as an index of emotional adjustment to the speaking situation. It is in this connection that we see one of the most important consequences of the fact that there are no speech organs as such. In speaking we are dependent upon the smooth functioning of the breathing mechanism, and this mechanism happens to be one of the body's most sensitive indicators of emotion. Perhaps the most striking consequence of this arrangement is to be seen in the common tendency of the stutterer to hold his breath during those moments when his fear of speaking is greatest. The relationship in such a case between

[14] For current information and views on breathing in relation to speech and voice see Virgil Anderson, *Training the Speaking Voice*, New York, Oxford University Press, Inc., 1942; Friedrich S. Brodnitz, *Keep Your Voice Healthy*, New York, Harper & Brothers, 1953; Grant Fairbanks, *Voice and Articulation Drillbook*, New York, Harper & Brothers, 1940.

the disturbance in breathing and the disturbance in speech is complex, but certainly one gains some appreciation of what is happening from a knowledge of the fact that the organs which the stutterer is using for speech are, in part, actually designed basically for respiration. How well they serve for purposes of speech at a moment of emotional disturbance depends, therefore, on how their vital function, respiration, is affected by the emotional disturbance. Most of us are sufficiently poised during most of our speaking to show no important vocal effects of such minor breathing disturbances as may occur. In cases of excessive shyness, stage fright, or stuttering, however, the vocal effects are sometimes striking, since the emotional reactions and the consequent breathing disturbances are so marked. And in cases of cerebral palsy, or other conditions involving paralysis or incoördination, the vocal effects of emotionally caused breathing disturbances are aggravated. It is in dealing with such cases that one realizes most clearly the practical significance of the dependence of the speech function on organs which serve primarily other and generally more vital and "assertive" bodily processes.

## Speech as Learned Behavior

### CHILDREN MUST BE TAUGHT TO SPEAK

Another basic consideration is that speech is a form of behavior that has to be learned. The learning of it is part and parcel of the general acquisition of behavior patterns. Professor E. R. Hilgard has presented a summary of the various types of learning theory.[15] An intriguing discussion of the learning of speech by the child is that of Professor O. H. Mowrer.[16] Comparing the "speech learning" of "talking birds" and human babies, he stresses the role of the association of sounds spoken by a kindly trainer

[15] E. R. Hilgard, *Theories of Learning*, New York, Appleton-Century-Crofts, Inc., 1948.

[16] See O. H. Mowrer, *Learning Theory and Personality Dynamics*, New York, the Ronald Press Company, 1950, Chapters 23 and 24, particularly pp. 685-687 and 698-700. For a charming book on speech development addressed to lay readers, especially parents, see Charles Van Riper, *Teaching Your Child to Talk*, New York, Harper & Brothers, 1950.

or affectionate parent, as the case may be, with feeding or other comforting and pleasant experiences. Given this fundamental association the baby (or bird) tends, in Mowrer's view, to find satisfaction in producing the sounds thus associated with pleasure. Moreover, he stresses the probable importance of imitation *by the parent* of sounds uttered by the baby as a factor in stimulating further vocalization and also as an influence in leading the infant to approximate more and more closely the standard speech sounds of the parents.

There are other theories, of course, and Professor Mowrer reviews many of them, but certainly in one way or another children have to be *taught* to speak. Indeed, if a person aspires to become a speaker of artistic distinction, intensive and prolonged training is essential. Meanwhile most children and adults are a bit surprised upon being told that they have *learned* to speak. So long as a child speaks normally and well, it is fortunate that he takes his speech for granted. He has nothing to gain, as we shall see presently, by becoming too speech-conscious. In fact, one of the characteristics of good speech is that it is spontaneous, practically automatic, and performed with almost no conscious attention to the specific manner in which it is done.

NORMAL SPEECH IS LARGELY AUTOMATIC

One of the fundamental reasons for the relatively automatic nature of speech is the one we have discussed above: speech is performed with organs designed primarily for other functions. Most of these other functions are reflex-like, or nearly so. Breathing, for example, while subject to some degree of conscious control, is ordinarily quite involuntary. Normally it is practically as automatic during speech as it is at other times. This is obviously a large part of the reason why most of us tend to feel that speech, under ordinary conditions, is "as natural as breathing." It is also an important reason why good speech must be essentially automatic—in order to control speech consciously to any great extent one would have to control breathing consciously to a degree that would tend to make for a definite disturbance in speech.

Another reason why too much speech-consciousness is detrimental is to be seen by watching an x-ray sound film of the speech act. The number of moving parts, the rates of their movements, the variations in these rates from second to second, the complex ways in which the many parts move in relationship to one another, the precise adjustment and the rapid succession in which they occur all combine to give one a thoroughly convincing impression that the centipede in walking has nothing on the human being in talking. If one were to stop to figure out whether the larynx should be elevated before the tongue is to be depressed, or vice versa, at any point in saying a simple sentence, one would certainly be as disturbed as would a centipede who paused to reflect on just which leg to lift next in crossing a crack in the sidewalk. The tone-producing mechanism, or larynx, particularly—with the vocal folds vibrating hundreds of times per second, for example—is not something to be operated with any highly conscious "hunt-and-peck" system. The speech organs are best "played by ear," so to speak.

Even the tongue, jaws and lips, which are subject to more conscious control than the other so-called speech organs, function best for speech purposes when they work freely along the smoothly worn grooves of habit. Just what do you do with your tongue in saying "Boston, Massachusetts"? If you are an ordinarily good normal speaker, you can't answer this question. That is a substantial part of the reason why you are a good speaker. If you can answer it in any detail the chances are that either you are a speech pathologist or else you need to see one.

The fine details of the speech act, the multitudinous individual muscular movements involved in it, are normally reflex-like for all practical purposes. That is why you can talk in your sleep. In fact, some persons with impaired speech, such as stutterers and certain psychological voice cases, usually talk better in their sleep than they do when they are wide awake. And we all talk better when we are free from self-consciousness, enjoying ourselves with good friends, and paying no attention to *how* we are speaking.

All these considerations, supported by a great mass of scientific data, have one very important implication: in speech training and in speech correction the goal is good speech that is habitual, automatic, and spontaneous. It is all right, it is frequently essential, in fact, to be highly conscious of *what* one says, but it is most desirable to be as unconscious as possible of *how* one says it. In the correction of speech defects, and in certain details of the training of normal or artistic speech, it is necessary for the speaker to attend closely to how a sound or a word or a certain vocal inflection is best produced, but this is only a means to an end. The end, or goal, is speech in which the basic breathing, phonating, and articulating activities are almost completely automatic.

TWO COMMON MISCONCEPTIONS

In view of what has been said, we can more fully appreciate the significance of two common misconceptions regarding speech training and speech correction. The one is seen in the frequently heard exhortation that people should become more speech-conscious. Parents are often urged to become more speech-conscious, and so are teachers, and they are earnestly advised to make their children or pupils more speech-conscious. It is a term that can lead to policies in the home and in the classroom that can have very undesirable effects. Speech-consciousness can be a particularly harmful form of self-consciousness. To be aware of one's language, one's words, to watch what one says, to strive for effective verbal statements that are accurate, dependable, and constructive or pleasing in their effects is one thing, and most commendable. To be acutely conscious of one's speech, one's breathing, phonating, and articulating activities, to attend intently to them, and to try everlastingly to "control" them is definitely something else again. It is advisable to make children language-conscious. This is practically essential to their good judgment, moral character, and even their sanity. It is not advisable to make children highly speech-conscious except in some cases, for specific speech correction purposes, as a means to an end, and under supervision.

This suggests the other common misconception. It is that speech improvement requires "control." Such expressions as "breath control," "voice control," and "speech control" are probably tossed about too thoughtlessly for the public good. What we probably mean, as a rule, by "speech control"—the production of clear, understandable, pleasing speech—is best achieved indirectly. That is, one can best learn to speak well, not by trying directly to regulate every articulatory movement, but by cultivating a discriminating ear, a desire to communicate, and a proper attitude toward the listener.[17] Generally speaking, the less we know about our soft palates, for example, the better—unless we are physicians, speech pathologists, or persons with cleft palates learning to direct sound out through the mouth instead of the nose.

## THE IMPORTANCE OF REWARD AND PRACTICE

With these words of essential information and caution, we may now give further attention to the fact that speech is a form of behavior that has to be learned. We learn best to do those things that are most rewarded. Part of the reason for this is that the more they are rewarded the more we do them, and the more we do them—practice them, that is—the better we learn them. The kinds of behavior that are most satisfying to us are, therefore, the ones we are mostly likely to persist in cultivating. For our present purposes this suggests that the most important rule in speech training is that speaking should be fun. If speech is made satisfying and rewarding for a child, he will like speaking and will do more of it than he would otherwise.

The amount of speaking a child does is the first concern of the teacher who is interested in his speech development. The babies who show the most rapid speech development are the ones who coo and babble the most, and who are the most rewarded for it by parental smiles and fondling—and cooing. The old idea that children should be seen and not heard is certainly contrary to the best principles of speech training. It is a fairly

[17] Dr. Robert L. Milisen has developed a theory of speech learning essentially similar in many respects to the one presented in these pages, which has contributed its influence to the thinking represented in the present text. See particularly Chapter 1 of Robert L. Milisen and Associates, "The Disorder of Articulation: A Systematic Clinical and Experimental Approach," *Journal of Speech and Hearing Disorders* (1954), Monograph Supplement 4.

reliable rule that superior adult speakers not only like to talk because they are good at it, but what is more important, they are good at it and tend to get better at it because they enjoy talking. The more they enjoy it, the more they practice it. The teacher who wants to encourage a child to improve his speech will do everything she can, therefore, to get him to talk as much as possible and to make the speaking he does thoroughly enjoyable for him.

There are certain things that such a teacher will be careful to do and not to do. She will not criticize a pupil's speech in such a way as to embarrass him. In case of doubt, she will give him a smile, a friendly pat, or a word of praise for the speaking he does. Instead of putting her threatening finger on the things he does incorrectly or poorly, she will single out something in his recitation, or in his manner of speaking, that she can commend. "Gold stars" are much better than "black marks" for the purpose of stimulating interest in improving the performances for which they are received. This is especially true for the child who does not excel or who is deficient in speech. Even at best, he is not likely to get the enjoyment from speaking that he needs in order to have sufficient motivation for improvement. He is likely to be rather quiet, to refrain from asking questions, and to make his answers brief—even to say, "I don't know," when he does know, in order to avoid talking. This is indeed a common classroom response of stutterers.

One of the first signs of success in speech correction, and almost always an important one, is an increase in the talkativeness of the child. It is not important that this increased speech be clear and distinct, or fluent. One of our own cases was a young boy— we shall call him Jerry—who hardly spoke at all when he first came to the clinic. He was not only silent but seemed to have a generalized fear of people, and these two facts were definitely related. The only important objective during the first few weeks was to get Jerry to talk—jabber would be a better word, since it was almost impossible to understand anything he did say. We were delighted when he finally began to flood the clinic with his chatter; the fact that we were unable to make head or tail of it didn't matter in the least at that stage. We wanted him to enjoy his chattering, and we were generous, to a point just safely short of absurdity, in our praise, compliments, smiles, and eager desires to hear more. We were simply applying the principle of reward which psychologists have so abundantly demonstrated to be essential to learning. Until we got Jerry to speak, there was simply no speech on which to work. When we did get him to the point where he was speaking and enjoying it sufficiently, it was possible to proceed with the systematic correction of his errors.

## WHAT IS GOOD FOR THE HANDICAPPED IS GOOD FOR THE "NORMAL"

This sort of case serves the purposes of a microscope, as it were. It is not always easy to see the value of rewarding generously the attempts which children make to share their feelings, to seek and give information, and to establish good relationships with others through speech. In Jerry, however, the crying need for such reward was so striking that hardly anyone could have missed it. Moreover, the demoralizing effects of criticism, demerits, rebuke, and rejection often go unnoticed almost entirely when seen in the children whom we glibly call "normal." The effects, as Jerry showed them, were not only clear but pathetic. And the important thing to notice as we look through the "microscope" which the Jerrys provide for us is that the kind of criticism that is bad for them and the kind of rewards that are good for them are also bad and good, respectively, for all other children. Most of the "special" attention we give, or should give, to speech handicapped children should be given also to the pupils who do not have speech disorders.

As has been pointed out by Professor Lee Edward Travis, Director of the Speech Clinic at the University of Southern California, it is curious that parents who have been advised to improve the psychological care of their children frequently react by asking how soon they can go back to treating their children "normally"! Just as many of us tend to look upon a healthful diet as a form of "medical treatment," so all too often we feel somehow that the psychological practices that make for enriching personal development are something "special," to be used only during crises or with "exceptional" children or adults. Generally speaking, the best physical hygiene measures, the best mental health practices, and the best educational methods have been developed in the interests of the sick, the maladjusted, and the handicapped, and we have been slower than need be in making them fully available to everyone.

It is particularly important to heed the obvious lesson that these remarks are intended to point up as we consider a bewildering problem, one that has dogged our efforts to work out adequate educational programs for the handicapped. All too often any attempt to single out the hard of hearing, the "behavior problem" children, or the speech handicapped, in order to give them the care and training they need, has resulted in their being stigmatized. It happens to be true that we can sometimes do as much harm by applying derogatory labels to children as we can by outright physical attempts to maim them; and the most painstaking discrimination, ethics, and tact are to be expected of those who make surveys of the handicapped children in our schools. At the same time, some children do have speech difficulties and other handicaps, and there is neither wisdom nor kindness in pretending that they don't have these conditions. One of the most sound and practical ways—if not the only way —to avoid stigmatizing them is to apply to all children the same good principles of physical and mental hygiene, and of education, that are now in many instances reserved for the handicapped. After all, it is as difficult to defend the point of view that the handicapped should be treated better than the so-called normals as it is to uphold the proposition that they should be treated worse. There is no more reason for confining the best educational practices to "special rooms" than for restricting the best dietary measures to hospitals.

## THE IMPORTANCE OF "CLASSROOM DEMOCRACY"

In order to create the sort of classroom atmosphere that will encourage speech and make it enjoyable, a certain degree of warmth and good cheer and informality is clearly essential. It is a cardinal principle, which child psychologists and speech correctionists long ago learned to take for granted, that one must establish good rapport with a child before anything can be accomplished with him so far as retraining is concerned. What is meant by "good rapport" is mainly a good relationship between teacher and child. If a speech correction teacher—or any other kind of teacher—is unable to get children to like her, it doesn't matter a great deal how much she knows about the technical aspects of her craft. She simply has to be the sort of person to whom children respond warmly and eagerly. Children must love to be with her, to talk to her, to work with her. To say that a teacher is the sort of person to whom children react in such ways is to say that she establishes good rapport with her pupils. And teachers of this kind are friendly and rather informal with children.

This does not mean at all that they are frivolous, or lax in classroom management, or that they waste time and let the pupils get out of hand. Children like to have rules so long as they are administered justly—and set aside or amended when it would be unfair to enforce them as they stand—especially if they have a voice in making them. They like clear instructions. They want to know rather definitely what is to be expected of them. And they want to know "why" and "what for." There is nothing more exciting and satisfying to them than learning, unless they have been seriously conditioned against it. All of which means that there is genuine tragedy in a dull lesson, or a classroom to which children go with dread.

Experimental studies carried out in the Iowa Child Welfare Research Station showed that children preferred and learned better in a democratic atmosphere than in either an autocratic or a laissez faire atmosphere.[18] When the teacher was strict and dictatorial they became sullen, resentful, and discouraged; they worked more slowly, and when the teacher was out of the room,

[18] R. Lippitt, "An Experimental Study of the Effect of Democratic and Authoritarian Group Atmospheres," *University of Iowa Studies in Child Welfare* (1940), Vol. 16, No. 3.

or when her back was turned, they quit working. When, as in the laissez faire program, the teacher played an utterly passive role and followed an "anything goes, do as you please" policy, the children indulged in horseplay, picked on each other, and didn't accomplish much. It was the democratic teacher who got the best results, as determined by this investigation, in which teachers and pupils were taken into the laboratory and subjected to scientific study. The democratic teacher was friendly, but she was there to instruct. The pupils were allowed a certain leeway in what they were to do and how they were to do it, but the teacher took a lively interest in what they did, told them the best ways to do it, showed them, worked with them, shared their pleasures in accomplishment, sympathized with their disappointments, enjoyed their jokes, helped them understand their mistakes, did not gloss over her own errors, and complimented them for their successes. She was, in the language of adolescents, a good egg. And discipline was almost completely taken care of by the strong sense of fair play generated by the compelling morale of a group working together with a democratic leader whom they appreciated and liked. Seldom, if ever, have the basic principles of good teaching been more dramatically or convincingly demonstrated.

Again, the *general* value of these policies is to be appreciated. The point is that while these are good principles to follow in providing a classroom atmosphere favorable for speech handicapped pupils, they are to be recommended just as urgently on behalf of all other school children. It is only one of their many benefits that they make for the sort of classroom atmosphere that encourages speaking and makes it enjoyable. This specific value, however, is our main concern here.

### ORAL RECITATION AND CLASSROOM DISCUSSION

Any speaking that children do in classrooms, everything from roll call[19] to book reports, is of special importance in this con-

[19] It is not merely roll call, as such, to which attention is to be directed here. On such special occasions as the first day of school, or in the checking of committee members, the assigning of children to cars or buses for picnics or excursions, and so forth, teachers sometimes require children to give

nection. Should pupils with speech difficulties be excused from oral recitations? Should special allowances be made for them with regard to oral work, and if so what sorts of allowances should be made? What are the arguments in favor of their full participation in oral work?

There appear to be two basic answers to all these questions. They have been emphasized in the preceding discussion. The first is that speech handicapped pupils should be encouraged to speak as much as possible. The other is that the speaking they do should be made enjoyable. These are general statements; some elaboration is in order.

It is to be considered that all youngsters who have speech problems are not alike. Their individual needs and abilities should be taken into account. Two facts about stuttering, for example, are of outstanding importance in connection with oral work. The first is that stuttering is especially likely to occur whenever the child is required to say a specific word, such as "Present," or "Washington," to a person in authority (a teacher), with a premium on promptness, in the presence of an audience, and under such conditions that failure to respond properly is more or less embarrassing. Stuttering does not occur at random; it occurs more often on certain words, or sounds, or in speaking to particular listeners, or in certain situations. That is, it becomes more or less conditioned to particular cues or stimuli. Because of the conditions under which roll call is answered, for example, stuttering is particularly likely to become associated

---

their names or respond in some way when their names are called. Stutterers and hard of hearing children, especially, may find this distressing or may present the teacher in charge with momentary difficulties. Obviously, if a deafened child does not answer roll, it is essential to realize that he may not have heard. From the point of view of a stutterer who is particularly bothered by his speech difficulty, any method of "silent roll taking" is vastly different from a method requiring him to respond orally if he is greatly disturbed by stuttering severely in trying to say his name. It is desirable to help such a child to achieve the poise and maturity that will make it possible for him to experience difficulties like these calmly and graciously. Any child who can stutter without excessive distress should have the opportunity to answer roll call when necessary and to do any other speaking that he might reasonably attempt. The treatment of stuttering is discussed in Chapter V.

with the attempt to say "Present," or "Here," or whatever word is customary. If, by chance, the pupils are required to say their own names, as perhaps they might be on the opening day of school, the difficulty is aggravated, since most stutterers are especially prone to stutter in saying their own names. Adult stutterers have actually been known to go through the legal procedure of changing their names. It doesn't help long.

The other fact about stuttering to be especially noted in this connection is that it is essentially an anxiety or fear response. One of the important things about anxiety is that it tends to mount under conditions of suspense. Fiction writers make the most of this fact, of course. The well-worn stories about expectant fathers illustrate the point elaborately. Now, one of the reasons why reciting in certain classrooms is so distressing to many stutterers is simply that it proceeds alphabetically, and the farther down the list from "A" the stutterer's name comes, the longer he has to worry about whether or not he will be able to answer—and the longer he worries, the greater his doubts and fears become and the more likely he is to stutter when his name is finally called. Pity the stuttering child whose name begins with Z!

It is to be realized, of course, that some stutterers have little or no difficulty under such conditions; no two stutterers are alike in detail, and the individual differences among them not only are very great but appear at times to be contradictory and illogical as well. Any pupil who stutters or who has any other kind of impaired speech should participate in classroom speaking if he can do so with a reasonable degree of ease and comfort. For those who cannot, certain modifications in procedure can be made. These are presented in the following section.

MODIFICATIONS OF ORAL RECITATION AND CLASSROOM DISCUSSION

First of all, a rough distinction is to be made between short and long speaking performances. Practically all children with speech disturbances or deviations can give yes and no answers; even in the most extreme cases such an answer can be given by a proper movement of the head. This is actually very important, because one of the chief motivations any pupil has for preparing his lessons is the desire to be able to respond properly if called upon to recite. This motivation holds good even if the child—a tense stutterer or a severely cerebral-palsied child, for example—knows that all he will ever have to do in class is give yes and no answers, orally if he possibly can, of course, but at least by head gestures. To excuse such a child *completely* from responding in class, as is sometimes done, is to remove one of his prime reasons for studying. Moreover, it is a policy hardly calculated to improve his speech; we shall see in the chapter on stuttering why it tends to increase the severity of this particular speech disorder. The difficulties that might sometimes arise because the other children notice and react to the fact that the speech handicapped child does not recite as much as they do, or that he recites in ways that are different, are part and parcel of his overall problem of classroom adjustment. This problem is treated from many angles throughout this chapter.

To the extent that a child's participation in class discussion is reduced, he should be given opportunities whenever possible to make up for it. Such opportunities are to be found in written work, blackboard exercises, and map drill, to select obvious examples. In such classes as shop, art, music, and physical training there is usually little difficulty in getting speech handicapped pupils to participate fully in class activities, since bodily or manual performance is stressed much more heavily than speech. The general principle to be emphasized is that of encouraging participation in the classroom program. This should include as much oral recitation as is wise for any specific child, and any reduction in it should be made up in other ways.

Although practically all speech handicapped pupils can do something so far as short recitations are concerned, some of them may find longer speech performances more or less impractical. For some they will be too upsetting or distressing to be advisable. In others speech may be so unintelligible that their oral book reports, for example, may not accomplish any significant purpose for them or for the rest of the class. If there is a speech correctionist in the school system it will be her objective to prepare such children for fuller participation in oral classwork, either by improving the speech sufficiently or by training them to speak with a stutter or other disorder in ways that involve less emotional turmoil. In the meantime allowance should be made in some cases with respect to longer types of oral activity.

Practical adjustments of longer oral performances for speech handicapped pupils are the following:

1. The pupil may be entirely excused from longer oral activities. This is not advisable except in definitely exceptional cases. Even when it is done, the policy should be regarded as a temporary expedient, and everything possible should be done to prepare the pupil to speak or read aloud in the classroom. In some cases this must be done chiefly through speech correction. In other instances it is primarily a matter of helping the child to achieve a less disturbed reaction to the speaking situations which confront him in the classroom. Possible changes in general classroom management are to be considered, as well as particular measures that might be attempted with the individual pupil. Possible measures will be discussed in the next section of this chapter. In any case, when the pupil is completely excused from longer oral recitations, he should be permitted to do additional written work, notebook exercises, outside reading, and the like to maintain his interest and to permit him to demonstrate his ability to learn.

2. The pupil may be excused only from certain types of speaking or oral reading. The best example for which this could be a practical policy is the stuttering pupil who is greatly disturbed by having to read aloud but does much better in giving an oral report, or vice versa. As has been pointed out several times previously, stutterers differ in ways that sometimes seem puzzling. Some of them can read aloud with little or no difficulty; some find oral reading especially distressing; others can recite memorized material easily; still others stutter with unusual severity in reciting memorized material. It is essential, therefore, that the teacher talk freely and fully with the pupil about the matter and find out whether any types of speaking are especially easy or difficult for him. If there are, usually some feasible plan of oral recitation can be arranged that will serve to avoid undesirable ordeals

while providing as much beneficial speaking experience as possible for the stutterer. By making the most of his relatively successful speaking, rewarding him well for it, it is often possible to give the pupil sufficient self-confidence to enable him to attempt with decreased dread and discomfort the types of speaking that are more difficult for him.

3. The pupil may be asked to participate in all oral work, although with the reasonable provision that he may make such modifications of the usual procedure as seem advisable or advantageous for him. These modifications will fall generally into three classifications.

a. *Topic.* It is a usually dependable rule that a speech handicapped youngster will speak better when talking about a subject he understands well and likes to talk about than when talking "over his head" or about something he is reluctant to discuss, either because he is not interested in it or because he feels "silly" or "out of character" when talking about it. It is extremely important, therefore, that so far as possible topics be not too rigidly assigned for class discussion, speeches, and reports. When one topic for a theme is assigned to all the pupils in a class, and the themes are to be read aloud, there is a fair chance that any speech handicapped pupils in the group will be distressed somewhat more than they would be if given some freedom of choice in selecting their topics. This will tend to be true for the other pupils, too, of course. It is desirable, as has been stressed, that the speaking, or oral reading, done by a speech handicapped child be made as enjoyable as possible. One obvious way to make speech experiences enjoyable for a child is to allow him to choose subjects about which he enjoys speaking. There is a clear advantage, therefore, in encouraging pupils to choose subjects according to this principle—or to assign topics with an eye to each pupil's individual interests. If interests are encouraged they grow and broaden; they can be directed considerably into related areas if the proper rewards are skillfully used. Thus, advantages are gained not only from a speech standpoint but also from a broad educational point of view.

Especially where it can be done in coöperation with an experienced speech corectionist, much can be accomplished in certain cases by having the pupil give a report or two on the subject of his own speech problem. In some colleges and universities, it is rather common practice for students who have speech difficulties, particularly stuttering, to make short speeches before the various sections of the communication skills course, the introductory psychology course, and the speech correction course. They describe their own speech problems, giving important items of personal history, explaining the clinical work they are doing, and in general discussing their speech differences and experiences and their feelings about them in ways that result in a more objective and understanding attitude on the part of other students and the instructors—and of themselves, of course. This is simply part of the total program of training designed to make them more frank and objective about their problems. The result tends to be better personal and social adjustment and a more effective attack on speech improvement as such.

We have had high school stutterers also make personal talks of this kind at appropriate times in some of their classes. A good time for this is when other pupils are reporting on their hobbies or on special projects in which they are engaged. The topic, "How I Spent the Summer," gives the speech handicapped pupil a chance to tell about the summer speech clinic he attended— if he was so fortunate. Themes to be read aloud sometimes provide good opportunities.

The method was used very effectively with one of our cases, a girl, who had a slight lisp. Actually the lisp was hardly noticeable, but the girl was overly sensitive about her speech. It proved very beneficial to her to write a short paper in which she described her speech difference in objective terms, recounted frankly some of the unsatisfactory ways in which she had reacted personally to it and told about the speech correction work she was doing in an effort to overcome it and to modify her poor adjustment to speaking situations. She began by reading the paper aloud a few times to her speech clinician. Then she read it to a small group of students in the clinic with whom she had much in common. After that she read it to a class of university students. The reactions she got from her listeners were those of interest and acceptance. In the process she gained a more mature perspective and a much better understanding of her lisp and her previous reactions to it. As a result, she worked on its correction in a more businesslike manner and came through the entire experience with significantly improved speech and a more adequate personality.

Such a procedure represents considerably more, of course, than the mere selection of a particular topic—one's own problem—for a theme or speech. It amounts to a forthright application of mental hygiene principles, adapted to problems centering around a speech difficulty and carried out in actual speaking situations. Professor Bryng Bryngelson, of the University of Minnesota, has developed this general type of approach to the problems of the speech handicapped in many significant ways and often with gratifying results.[20] It is used in one form or another and in various degrees of elaboration by many speech correction workers.[21] It is one rather substantial speech correction procedure that can be adapted at least in limited ways to many classroom situations.

The classroom teacher is to be cautioned, however, that the technique is not always as simple as it may seem. One would never attempt it with a pupil before getting to know him well and establishing good rapport. Ideally, the teacher should have the coöperation, and preferably the supervision, of a speech correctionist, although every public school speech correctionist might not care to use the procedure. In any event, the teacher should arrange for the pupil to give the speech to her alone before having him deliver it to the class. This will give her an opportunity to judge his reaction to the assignment, and it will permit the pupil to get used to the experience before appearing before the group. In case of doubt, the assignment should not be made. The spirit of frankness and friendly understanding which the

[20] Bryng Bryngelson, "The Interpretative Symbol," *Quarterly Journal of Speech* (1938), 24:569-573 and "Unaccustomed as I Am—," *Hygeia*, November, 1938.

[21] See especially Ollie Backus and Jane Beasley, *Speech Therapy with Children,* Boston, Houghton Mifflin Co., 1951.

project is designed to foster, however, is to be cultivated by the teacher, as well as by the speech handicapped pupil, in all the ways that seem practical. This point will be elaborated later in the discussion of speech in relation to personality.

b. *Reduction in Length of Oral Performances.* One of the obvious modifications of the usual recitation routine is that of arranging for the pupil with a speech problem to speak for a shorter period of time than is customary for the others. This is often a good practice in helping some speech handicapped children to undertake certain kinds of oral activity which they have previously avoided. It is better for them to make a brief current events report, for example, than to say nothing at all. Later, after they have become used to making a particular type of performance, it may be feasible to increase the length of it.

c. *Manner of Participating in Oral Work.* It has already been remarked that a certain degree of informality in the classroom is desirable. This is especially important so far as speech activities are concerned. A child who would dread standing at the front of the room to make a speech according to prescribed rules of formal delivery might have no hesitancy whatever in saying something spontaneously in the course of a thoroughly informal class discussion. Such informal and spontaneous discussion is much better, from the speech handicapped youngster's point of view, than more sedate and regulated recitation and discussion procedures.

Most pupils, particularly if they have speech problems, are likely to speak more often, and to enjoy speaking more, if they can remain seated than if they are required to stand. If they are asked to stand, they feel less conspicuous standing beside their desks than in front of the class. And if they are required to speak from the front of the room, they usually feel better standing in front of the platform (if there is one) than on it. Moreover, most of them prefer some freedom in moving about to standing perfectly still. Modern teachers of public speaking place heavy emphasis on naturalness and conversational ease. What used to be known as "elocution" has fortunately fallen into disrepute. Children should be informed early and fully that making a book report, for example, has nothing whatever to do with "oratory." A conversational manner should be encouraged in all oral work, including the types pupils think of as "making a speech." Good speakers talk *with*, not *at*, their listeners.

So far as possible, in the interests of pupils for whom speaking is difficult or unnerving, emphasis should be placed on informal, casual, spontaneous, conversational speech in the classroom. Where hand-raising can be dispensed with, there will almost always be advantages in discouraging it. In quizzing, an irregular order in calling on pupils will usually be advisable, and if the quizzing can be broken up a bit with some give-and-take discussion, it is all to the good. Letting children volunteer answers is probably a better general practice than encouraging them to refrain from speaking unless called upon. Allowing the pupils to remain seated during recitations and discussions and to assume comfortable postures (short of slouching, of course) are recommendations that are usually sound—although training in the more formal types of speaking and oral reading is by no means to be entirely neglected.

And running through all these suggestions is the fundamental implication that the teacher's own speech manner is tremendously important. If she speaks with friendly ease, conversing more with her pupils than lecturing at them—or talking past them, to use Professor Irving Lee's apt phrase[22]—exploring with them the subjects they are studying rather than simply "telling" them or quizzing them, the children will learn much about good speech from her example. Speech will become for them more and more a pleasant and stimulating sharing of experience, which is speech at its best.

## THE SCHOOL ENVIRONMENT AND SPEECH DEVELOPMENT

To what extent does a child's speech improve merely as a result of school attendance?

[22] Irving J. Lee, *How to Talk with People*, New York, Harper & Brothers, 1953. In this book the author reports the problems he observed in two hundred meetings of boards and committees and presents practical suggestions for dealing with such problems. It is a very enlightening book for any teacher.

One of the most pointed answers to this question—although admittedly it is not the whole answer—is given by the findings of Roe and Milisen[23] in a study made of nearly 2,000 children in the first six grades in nine Indiana cities and towns. There was no speech correction program in any of the schools surveyed. The speech development noted was presumably due to school attendance, plus any effects of increasing age or "maturation." Only one aspect of speech was studied, that of articulation. The consonant sounds and many consonant blends were tested. The number of articulation errors made on the test by the average child in each of the first six grades was as follows: first, 13.3; second, 10; third, 8.9; fourth, 7.6; fifth, 7.6; sixth, 8.

Upon entering first grade the average child makes a considerable number of errors in producing English speech sounds. If he misarticulates every sound included in the test (in the initial, medial, and final positions in the word), he makes 66 errors. The average child in the above study made approximately 13 errors; he articulated incorrectly roughly 20 percent of the time. This does not mean that the average first-grader is a speech defective; in this situation we may reasonably regard the average as normal.

A good deal of improvement occurs in the articulation of speech sounds between the first and second grades. There is less improvement between the second and third grades, and very little between the third and fourth. For practical purposes there is no improvement after the fourth grade, in the absence of a speech correction program. It is possible, of course, that the children surveyed by Roe and Milisen would have shown just as much speech development if they had never gone to school. The investigation was not designed to show whether the improvement was due to school attendance, as such. Roe and Milisen did not rule out the factor of "maturation." It is probably safe to assume, however, that the enriched speech environment provided by the school had some effect.

Nevertheless, considering the amount of improvement that *could have occurred,* the amount that *did occur,* and the fact that

[23] V. Roe and R. L. Milisen, "Effect of Maturation upon Defective Articulation in Elementary Grades," *Journal of Speech Disorders* (1942), 7:37-50.

virtually no improvement was evident after the fourth grade, we may best view the findings from this study as evidence of an opportunity that we may take advantage of even more fully than we have in the past. Speech does improve in the school environment during the early grades, especially first grade, even when presumably no special attention is given to it. This is encouraging. Under more favorable conditions for speech learning, it should improve still more. There is no good reason why it should not continue to improve beyond the fourth grade. After all, speech correction produces gratifying results right up through high school and into college and adult age levels. There is no age at which learning must stop, and this holds for speech as well as for other kinds of behavior or skill.

Indeed, we may take much encouragement from the data reported by Roe and Milisen. If the schools can do as well as the data indicate, even "without trying," surely a great deal more can be accomplished if we put our minds to it and provide in the fullest possible measure the stimulation, the rewards, and the opportunities for speech that make for more and better learning of speech skill.

Milisen summarizes twenty years of clinical experience and laboratory research in the following basic concept concerning articulatory disorders:

> It makes no difference whether the infant's failure to develop the skills and attitudes necessary for speech with good articulation was due largely to his limitations or those of the environment, the difficulties could have been overcome and the child could have had adequate articulation if the environment had been trained to begin early in creating a desire as well as a medium of communication. . . . Conditions which precipitate and maintain articulation defects after the child has begun to speak are only an extension of the conditions which limited the production and differentiation of sounds and which interfered with the development of a communication attitude before he began to speak.[24]

These clear generalizations point to the importance of surrounding children in home and in school with environmental

[24] *Op. cit.,* p. 8.

conditions that arouse in them a desire to speak, that stimulate them with good speech patterns, and that make good speech rewarding and pleasurable. The effects of stimulating a child with good speech patterns are particularly impressive. Milisen, for example, outlines a retraining procedure for youngsters who misarticulate some of their sounds, in which the key feature is what he calls integral stimulation, forceful and vivid presentation by the instructor to the attentive child of the correct production of a sound. He says, "Children are able to improve as many as 85 percent of their misarticulated sounds after receiving only a *few* integral stimulations."[25] There can be little serious question of the value of systematic speech correction. And speech correction is in large part a carefully designed intensification of ordinary stimulation of the child by means of good speech on the part of his parents, teachers, and other persons, the encouragement of clear and adequate speech by the child, and the maintenance in general of an environment favorable to the learning and the profitable employment of good speech on the part of the child.

The psychology of speech development is, at bottom, the psychology of learning. In reward and performance—or, better, rewarded performance—is to be found the basic key to better speech in the classroom and elsewhere.

## Speech in Relation to Personality

### WHAT IS PERSONALITY?

A brief discussion of personality, as it relates to speech and speech disorders, will help point up some of the more important facts which the classroom teacher will want to take into account in dealing with speech handicapped children.

Personality may be defined in a practical way in terms of certain basic "dimensions." We may think of a dimension by picturing a line divided into degrees like the tube in a mercury thermometer. Temperature is a dimension, ranging by degrees from "below zero," through "zero," "freezing," up to "boiling" and beyond. Just so we may think, for example, of a dimension ranging

[25] *Ibid.,* p. 14.

from wholesome self-confidence to distressing feelings of inferiority—the confidence continuum, or dimension, or graduated scale.

The point to be noted here is that there are not simply two kinds of individuals in this respect, the self-confident and those with inferiority complexes. There are "all kinds"; some are very confident of themselves, some are not fully as self-confident, most are more or less average, some are inclined to lack confidence, a few suffer from extreme degrees of what we call an inferiority complex. Moreover, any one person varies along this scale, or continuum, feeling more or less confident at some times than at others. When we say that a particular person is very self-confident we mean "as we know him," or "in the situations in which we see him," or "on the average," or "usually," or "according to what we are told," and so on. Not only is it difficult to make a specific statement about people in general; it is not even easy to make a general statement about a specific person. Individuals differ, and a person varies. That is why we speak of personality dimensions, or continua, or degrees of difference, rather than personality types, or rigid categories. A person is not one thing or another; he is more one thing than another depending on the situation, purposes, risks, or rewards, and who is judging him.

We shall discuss personality, therefore, in terms of those dimensions which we might use in making important judgments about ourselves and others. Some of these dimensions are concerned with self-adjustment or maladjustment—how we feel about ourselves, our "inner" states. Other dimensions have to do with our social adjustment or maladjustment—how we feel toward others, how we react to them, the kinds of relationships we have with them. The main dimensions we shall consider are the following:

1. Dimensions of self-adjustment.
    a. Self-confidence . . . feelings of inferiority, anxieties.
    b. Self-esteem . . . feelings of unworthiness or guilt.
    c. Gratification, happiness . . . disappointment, depression.
    d. Enthusiasm, interestedness . . . boredom, apathy.

2. Dimensions of social adjustment: attitudes and reactions toward others.
   a. Acceptance . . . awe, fear, contempt, rejection.
   b. Friendliness . . . antagonism, aggression.
   c. Coöperativeness . . . competitiveness.
   d. Belongingness, responsiveness . . . loneliness, withdrawal from others.

In each case, the left-hand extreme of the continuum, or dimension, represents very good adjustment, and the right-hand extreme represents very poor adjustment. In other words, the very well-adjusted school child (or teacher) is happy, enthusiastic, and self-confident, with a good opinion of himself; he accepts others on their own merits, is friendly and responsive toward them, and is inclined to coöperate with them whenever possible. The poorly adjusted school child (or teacher) is bored, apathetic, worried, and depressed, with feelings of inferiority and unworthiness; he erects barriers of undue awe or contempt between himself and others, is antagonistic and competitive toward them, and tends to withdraw either physically (stays by himself) or psychologically (does not get well acquainted with others or confide in them).

One point in this connection to be noted with special care is that maladjustment among school children—and adults too, for that matter—is seen not only in boisterous misbehavior but also, and more importantly, in shy, withdrawing, "lone wolf" tendencies, anxieties and tensions, and general unhappiness. In his famous study of teachers' attitudes toward classroom behavior problems, Wickman[26] found impressive disagreement between teachers and mental hygiene authorities as to the relative seriousness of various forms of misbehavior. Wickman summarized his main findings in these restrained words: "Teachers stress the importance of problems relating to sex, dishonesty, disobedience, disorderliness, and failure to learn. For them, the problems that indicate withdrawing, recessive characteristics in children are of comparatively little significance. Mental

[26] E. K. Wickman, *Children's Behavior and Teachers' Attitudes*, Sixth Printing, New York, The Commonwealth Fund, 1937.

hygienists, on the other hand, consider these unsocial forms of behavior most serious, and discount the stress which teachers lay on anti-social conduct."

In a follow-up and extension of the Wickman study Sparks[27] found that even when asked to rate the Wickman list of behavior problems as to the seriousness of their effects on the future adjustment of the child, rather than with reference to their effects on the orderliness of the classroom, teachers still did not agree very well with psychologists and mental hygienists in their ratings.

What the Wickman and Sparks studies seem to make fairly clear is that teachers, as compared with mental hygienists, tend to place more value on conformity to classroom rules and academic standards. For this reason they may sometimes overlook serious maladjustments in the quiet, docile, and excessively obedient child. By the same token, they may be overly impressed by the disturbing exuberance of the pupil who is "naughty in a normal sort of way" because it interferes with efforts to keep the class "in order." Stroud makes the very fundamental point that by frowning officially upon normal childhood behavior in the classroom we put "the teacher in the unfavorable position of having to keep order . . . When the teacher is charged with the responsibility of keeping order at all times and at all costs she cannot take an objective attitude toward pupils who misbehave. She is really not free to try to get at the underlying causes or to plan a long-range course of action."[28]

That mental hygiene principles are coming to be more and more widely recognized and accepted is indicated in the following statements made by W. Carson Ryan in reporting his observations during an extended study of American schools:

In at least two important fields—the nursery school and parent education—mental hygiene principles have definitely taken hold; and in work with younger children generally there is an encouraging trend

[27] J. N. Sparks, "Teachers' Attitudes Toward the Behavior Problems of Children," *Journal of Educational Psychology* (1952), 43:284-291.

[28] James B. Stroud, *Psychology in Education*, Sec. Ed. Rev., New York, Longmans, Green & Co., Inc., 1956, Chapter 15.

toward conditions and practices that make for mental good health. In many schools of today one finds an atmosphere of friendliness and happy activity. Much of the traditional formality, the forced silence, the tension, the marching, is gone. Children's voices are heard in the halls and "classrooms." The younger children come gaily down the stairways (if stairways there are), natural and relatively unrestrained; the older boys and girls throng the corridors or outside walks, making their way to schoolrooms, shops, studios, libraries, laboratories, and playing fields—to tasks that mean something to them, that make demands upon their energies and their imagination, that often involve hard, difficult work, but work that they recognize as creative. Beauty of surroundings is considered a first requirement in these schools— there are flowers about, brightly colored murals painted by the children, attractive, informal workrooms for the various groups. In many of these schools art and music have begun to play the role that belongs to them as fundamentals in education and in life.

There are, moreover, an increasing number of schools, particularly for young children, where teachers are not only friendly but understanding, especially with regard to what are ordinarily known as "the emotions"; where care is taken to find out for every child his needs and possibilities and to try to meet these needs—quite as much for the so-called "normal" children as for the more noticeably "subnormal" or "difficult." In a small but growing number of school organizations, special aid is also available from child guidance clinics, visiting teacher staff, or similar services, to assist the school in applying . . . some of the knowledge derived from modern sciences with respect to human behavior.[29]

Since this book is concerned with speech disorders and speech correction, problems of personality will be considered in relation to these basic interests. No attempt will be made to cover systematically and in detail the various types and causes of personality disorders and the methods of psychotherapy or personality reëducation.[30] In discussing personality we shall

[29] W. Carson Ryan, *Mental Health Through Education,* New York, The Commonwealth Fund, 1938, pp. v-vii.

[30] The student interested in a substantial text in the clinical aspects of psychology and behavior would do well to read Norman Cameron, *The Psychology of Behavior Disorders,* Boston, Houghton Mifflin Co., 1947. A philosophically rich and fascinating treatment of the problem of personal adjustment is to be found in Harry Stack Sullivan, *The Psychiatric Interview* (ed. Helen Swick Perry and Mary Ladd Gawel), New York, W. W.

keep constantly in mind (1) the speech handicapped school child and (2) his classroom teacher. Our aim is simply to make such a child and his speech difficulties as understandable as possible and to point out practical ways in which his teachers can be helpful to him.

Remembering, then, the dimensions of personality mentioned above, the first question to be considered has to do with the difference that a speech disorder makes to a child so far as his personal and social adjustment is concerned.

THE EFFECTS OF SPEECH DISORDERS ON PERSONALITY

The psychology of the handicapped is basically the psychology of frustration. The handicap of impaired speech is no exception to this general rule. In fact, there is hardly anything more frustrating, in ways that matter deeply, than something that constantly interferes with our relationships to other people. And few things are more significant in this respect than impaired speech. In the relationship between parent and child there is scarcely anything more intimate than the speech which passes between them. It conveys and reinforces feelings that can range from love to hate, from the nourishing warmth of affection to the drying chilliness of indifference and rejection.

Everything about it, from the vocabulary to the faintest vocal inflection and the most casual gesture, contributes its mite or mountain to the personality of the child and the parent and the eventual consequences in home, school, and society.

The relationship between speech and personality is, therefore, a two-way affair. They affect each other. And the effect is not only circular, but also cumulative. The more we snarl, the more we snarl. The more we purr, the more we purr. Also, and with special significance, the more we stutter, the more we stutter. In other words, speech characteristics, once created, tend to affect the personality in ways that insure their further develop-

Norton & Company, Inc., 1954. Teachers have a great deal indeed to gain from books such as these which deal with basic life problems as viewed by wise men whose experience in observing human behavior in its clinically significant forms has been extensive and remarkable.

ment. Having begun to speak hesitantly, even a little hesitantly, a child meets with reactions from others that make it likely that he will speak still more hesitantly next time. On the other hand, a child who starts early in life to speak with a ready smile in his voice will be responded to in ways that will make the smile grow. What all this means is that once speech has come to be regarded, by the child or his listeners, as "defective," the impaired social relationships arising from this evaluation serve to inhibit and distort speech increasingly by small degrees; and the more disturbed or inhibited speech becomes, the more do the child's social relationships become impaired. It is the sort of vicious circle by which the child is whirled farther and farther away from the center of his social group.

Through a proper understanding of this vicious circle we can do much to reverse its expanding course. We may with profit, therefore, examine a bit more closely the specific ways in which a speech disorder affects a child's personal and social adjustments.

*Confidence.*    In general, speech difficulties tend to make for impaired self-confidence. Anyone who would like to grasp securely the vital meaning of this can do so by carrying out a simple exercise. It is to be urgently recommended for all teachers and prospective teachers. It consists merely of pretending to stutter, or to lisp, in three or four situations. It can be done, for example, by going to a department store to buy "thome fathe powder" or "thun tan oil," or by going into a restaurant and ordering " huh huh huh ham and eggs with c . . . . . offee." There should be no explanations, and the whole thing should be carried off with a straight face, as though the speech difficulty were real. The act should be convincing to the listener. There is little need to specify the observations to be made. The feelings and the listener reactions that will inevitably be observed are the ones that will help to make the opening sentence of this paragraph come alive with meaning.

Confidence can be defined as a feeling that one can do well, or at least well enough, whatever is expected or necessary. A moment's reflection will make it plain that confidence depends, therefore, on how one's goals or aspirations compare with one's ability. Feelings of confidence come from the experience of achieving one's goals. Of course, one has to want to achieve them, to place some value on doing so, to feel that it matters at least a little. Confidence can be developed, therefore, in three ways:

1. By increasing one's ability.

2. By making one's goals low enough to reach and clearly defined enough to be able to tell that they have been reached.

3. By placing a proper value on reaching the goals so that achieving them is a stimulating experience, while not achieving them is not utterly catastrophic.

It follows that the classroom teacher can help the speech handicapped pupil to develop and maintain self-confidence, particularly confidence in his speaking ability, by:

1. Helping him to improve his speech, not only by her own efforts, but also by seeing to it that he is referred to a speech correction teacher in the school system or outside it.

2. Expecting no better speech from him than he is capable of producing at any given time. This means accepting his speech as it is, with the realization that until he is given speech correction it is unreasonable to expect him to speak as though he had already had it, and with the understanding that even if he is being given speech correction, improvement takes time and may never be "complete."

When a child says that the capital of Wode Island is Pwovidence, the teacher who is trying to build up his speech confidence will smile and say, "That's fine. Providence is the capital of Rhode Island." She will not toss the *r*'s at his tender and unsuspecting ears too hard, but with a friendly and approving smile. She will combine a bit of helpful speech sound stimulation (see Chapter III) with the reassurance the youngster needs in order to feel a little glow of success in having answered correctly and a bit more confidence in his ability to speak up again with similar pleasant results.

When a stuttering child gasps once or twice, shifts his tense little body about in the seat, and grinds out, "S . . . even times n . . . ine is six-six-sixty-three," the understanding teacher will be pleased, and show it. She will realize that there is no good reason why he should not have stuttered. What will matter to her is that in spite of the difficulty he had, he made the attempt and stuck it out. He answered correctly, and deserves to feel good about it. "That's fine!" will not only reassure him, but will also be as constructive an object lesson as his classmates could be given. If the teacher approves of Willie, they will tend to approve of him, too. And that will be very good for Willie—and for his speech. All of which will make everything easier, and more rewarding, for the teacher too.

This is not to say that a speech handicapped child should be greeted with a great show of approval even when he gives wrong answers. He deserves to be treated like the other pupils in this respect. The main point is that when he gives the right answer he should not be penalized for lisping it, or stuttering it, or giving it in nasal tones. He should be rewarded for giving the right answer. And if he is, he will get from the reward added encouragement so far as his speech is concerned. He does not expect to be praised *for lisping*, but he would be distressed by being disapproved *for lisping*. What he needs is confidence that if he measures up in other respects, he need feel no hesitancy in *speaking*. His impaired speech should not be reflected unfavorably in his marks and grade placements any more than it should be permitted to weigh in his favor. The confidence he needs is a confidence that he can hold his own in fair competition, without fear of penalty because he doesn't happen to speak with normal fluency, or sound his *l*'s, or because he sounds his vowels through his nose because his soft palate is too short. He can be fairly held responsible no more for such things than for the color of his hair, or his skin, or the patches on his clothes. He can be fairly held responsible only for the best he can do, or a bit less.

3. Instilling in him a sense of accomplishment in speaking, and a desire to speak as well as he reasonably can. Confidence, if it means anything vital, is not merely a sense of one's ability but a feeling of pride as well. The speech handicapped child not only should feel confident that he can speak and be accepted,

but he should also feel good about it. He needs the sort of confidence that creates a desire to speak. The child rather expects to be penalized or disapproved for speaking incorrectly. Just to realize that he will not be penalized, just to know that it is all right to go ahead and speak, even though he does sound his *r*'s like *w*'s, or even though he does stutter, is tremendously stimulating to such a child. It makes him want to talk—now. So long as he feels that his speech has to be normal before it will be acceptable, he may want to talk ever so much, but not now, not yet. Convincing him that you like to have him talk the way he now talks is like opening the gates of a great dam holding back a flood of desire.

Not only does this give the pupil speech goals that mean something to him, but it also keeps him from setting his goals too high. The importance of this was pointed out in the preceding section. Against the added background of what has just been said, the question of goals should be more closely examined. The crucial consideration is that there is a more or less standard pattern of personal maladjustment, whether it is found in youngsters with speech problems or in other children—and adults too. It consists of a tense striving to achieve goals, or ideals, that are out of reach, resulting in continual or repeated feelings of failure, leading to eventual and increasing demoralization. We may call it the IFD pattern: from idealism to frustration to demoralization.[31]

It is important to recognize the fact that there is no failure in nature, nor any success. Failure and success are feelings, or judgments, about our performances. Failure is the minus difference and success the plus difference between what we strive for and what we achieve, between our goals and our accomplishments. This means simply that whether we feel that we have failed or succeeded depends on (1) our goals, what we are aiming at, and (2) how well, or how much, we actually did. Feelings of failure, and an eventual inferiority complex, may be prevented, therefore, not only by developing a higher degree of skill, but

[31] See Chapter I of W. Johnson, *People in Quandaries: The Semantics of Personal Adjustment*, New York, Harper & Brothers, 1946.

also by keeping our goals realistic, holding them down, keeping them low enough to insure our achieving them. By reaching our goals we enable ourselves to experience the successes from which we gain feelings of confidence.

The speech handicapped child, therefore, should be encouraged to gain, from the kind of speaking he *now does,* the feelings of success that are so essential to his self-confidence. He should not be disapproved because of his speech difficulty, as such. Just as importantly, he should not be praised specifically for not stuttering, or for not lisping, for example.[32] Praise for *not* stuttering is, to the child, just another form of disapproval of his stuttering. To say to a child who can't help stuttering, "That's fine. You didn't stutter at all that time. That's the way I like to hear you speak," is the same as saying to him when he does stutter, "You stuttered that time. I don't like to hear you stutter." Compliments for the wrong things, or at the wrong times, can have precisely the same effects as demoralizing criticisms. There are two ways to say, "I don't like you." One way is to say it. The other is to say, "I like you when you are different."

This point is so very important that if it is not thoroughly understood, and constantly acted upon, almost nothing the teacher can do will build the child's confidence. To dismiss this as an overstatement is to miss the point it is intended to highlight. It is generally true that we hurt many more feelings and cause far more distress by thoughtless and misplaced compliments than by well-meant criticisms. More personalities are injured by glancing implications, so to speak, than by direct verbal fire. The reason is plain. We almost never *mean* to hurt anyone. We are almost always considerate enough to avoid making unkind remarks, or unwise criticisms, intentionally. We are far more likely to try to say something neutral, reassuring, or presumably

---

[32] The only safe exception to this would be a case in which the child is receiving definite speech correction instruction and has reached a stage where it is clearly possible for him to speak without the difficulty, at least in certain situations. In such a case, praise *for consciously cultivated improvement* is in order, of course. That is clearly quite different from compliments for chance moments or periods of good speech, over which the child has no appreciable control.

complimentary. That is why the verbal tool we use the most in trying to repair damaged feelings is: "I'm sorry. I didn't mean it *that* way." Almost always the words that do the damage are the ones we didn't know were loaded.

The speech handicapped child simply has to be accepted on his own merits and approved, speech disorder and all, if he is to be able to develop any significant self-confidence. And without confidence he does not have the will to do his best because he is overwhelmed with the feeling that his best is not good enough. Under such conditions he feels there is no use to try very often or very hard. If speaking is not satisfying or rewarding to him, why should he do any more of it than he has to? And the only speech that can be rewarding for him is the speech he has. If it is to be rewarding, it must not be disapproved. He must not be penalized for his speech impairment even by being praised when it happens to be momentarily absent.

If the speech handicapped child is to gain the fullest possible measure of confidence he must (1) be helped to improve his speech as much as he can, (2) be encouraged to keep his goals realistic, to feel no necessity for speaking better than he can at any given time, and (3) be made to feel that the best speaking he can do—or something a bit less than that—is, for him, successful, rewarding, and decidedly worth doing. In a thousand ways, day in and day out, the classroom teacher can work toward these objectives without working overtime and without adding the tasks of a professional speech correctionist to her other duties. Moreover, she will be making her teaching practices generally more effective and her classroom more stimulating for all her pupils.

*Other Dimensions of Personality.* The influence of impaired speech on personal and social adjustment can be further indicated in terms of the other personality dimensions listed previously. In general, speech disorders tend to make for some degree of difficulty in achieving good personality adjustment. This is not to be overstressed, however. The personality adjustments of persons with speech difficulties are, on the average, not *strikingly* different from those of normal speakers. Most children and adults have some degree of stage fright, at least a mild inferiority complex, a touch of shyness, a few anxieties or fears, tensions, and what they call "problems." Those who have speech deviations tend, on the average, to have just a bit more of these common varieties of "not quite ideal" adjustment.

To begin with, speech handicapped children are, after all, children. Aside from their speech problems, they have the same reasons other children have for being unhappy, discouraged, shy, or worried. It would be unrealistic to expect them to be consistently clear-eyed, zestful, happy, outgoing youngsters, with or without their speech difficulties. One of our most common mistakes—it is made sometimes even by speech correctionists— is to take for granted that every sign of maladjustment in a speech handicapped child is due to his speech deviation or that the speech deviation is due entirely to the maladjustment. Some of the most important questions to be asked about any child with a speech problem are these: If the speech problem were removed *now, today,* what difference would it make? What changes in the child's behavior, interests, attitudes, aptitudes, characteristic moods, and social reactions would be likely to occur immediately? What problems would persist despite the normal speech? Why?

If a teacher wants to gain a good understanding of a speech handicapped child she should ask these questions about him and answer them very carefully. Two things will usually be discovered: (1) The child's whole personality would be improved by effective speech correction. (2) The child needs more than speech correction only.

With these words of caution we may say that, generally speaking, impaired speech tends to make for a decrease in the following qualities:

1. Confidence.
2. Self-esteem.
3. Enthusiasm.
4. Happiness.
5. Acceptance and understanding of others.
6. Friendliness toward others.

7. Coöperativeness.

8. Responsiveness toward others; feelings of belongingness.

It tends to increase the following qualities:

1. Feelings of inferiority.
2. Unworthiness.
3. Apathy.
4. Disappointment; discouragement.
5. Awe, contempt, or rejection of others.
6. Antagonism toward others.
7. Competitiveness.
8. Withdrawing tendencies, loneliness.

These effects of impaired speech give meaning to the statement made several pages back that the psychology of the handicapped is at bottom the psychology of frustration.

Certainly what such children need, above everything else, so far as common day-by-day living with them is concerned, is *reassurance*. They need to be met a bit more than halfway—sometimes they have to be "gone and fetched"—if they are to build friendships, gain confidence, and cultivate the personal qualities that make themselves unmistakably evident in quick smiles and happy laughter. They need help in learning to speak as well as they can and to feel proud of the best they can do.

## The School as a Mental Hygiene Agency

Any careful examination of the possible ways in which the school can contribute to the mental health or personal and social adjustment of children reveals certain crucial factors which necessarily play important roles in this connection. Among these factors are:

1. Teachers' personalities.
2. Disciplinary policies and practices.
3. Marking or grading systems and examinations.
4. Extracurricular activities.
5. Special services, such as speech correction, psychological guidance, visiting teachers, etc.

THE PERSONALITY OF THE TEACHER

In his splendid study of our nation's schools, *Mental Health through Education,* Professor W. Carson Ryan devotes a substantial part of his discussion to the teacher's personality.[33] Pointing up what he has to say on this matter, he quotes the following incisive words of the great mental hygienist, William H. Burnham: "A healthy school atmosphere can only be created by teachers who are themselves mentally healthy and who have an abiding interest in children and a real respect for the personality of each child."

It is much too easy to read sentences like this. As our eyes leap lightly from phrase to phrase, we encounter no strange words to give us pause, no jarring single idea to bring us up short in a posture of reflectiveness. We experience the unfortunate illusion of easy and complete comprehension. In the meantime, almost any mathematical or chemical formula is simplicity itself compared with Dr. Burnham's smoothly flowing sentence, when comprehensively examined and understood to the point of effectively carrying out the actions it prescribes. Any teacher who grasps *and acts upon* what Dr. Burnham means by *only, created, mentally healthy, abiding interest in children, respect,* and *each* will be well on the way to providing a *healthy school atmosphere* for her pupils.

One of the authorities in the field of mental health who has done most to make clear just how a teacher might express "an abiding interest in children and a real respect for each child" is Professor Ralph H. Ojemann of the Iowa Child Welfare Research Station. Professor Ojemann has been concerned for many years with what he terms preventive psychiatry, the ways and means of preventing mental and emotional disorders. In the vast amount of work he has done with school children and their teachers, he has emphasized the basic notion that good

[33] *Op. cit.,* pp. 11-27. The student is to be urged to consult also Fritz Redl and W. W. Wattenberg, *Mental Hygiene in Teaching,* New York, Harcourt, Brace & Co., 1951, particularly Part C, "Classroom Application," which consists of Chapter 8 through 17. Chapter 10 deals specifically with "The Psychological Roles of Teachers."

mental health is fostered by an appreciation of the causes of behavior in ourselves and in others. He distinguishes between a "surface" approach and a "causal" approach to the understanding of behavior. "Some years ago," Professor Ojemann wrote in 1953, "while we were making observations of parental and teacher behavior toward children, it appeared that these adults tended to deal with child behavior as a surface phenomenon instead of taking account of the factors underlying or producing behavior. It also seemed that such an approach tended to favor the development of conflict and emotional strains in both child and adult."[34]

Studies by Ojemann and his associates have yielded very considerable objective evidence of the soundness of his fundamental hypothesis that a "causal" approach to our own reactions and to the behavior of others is more conducive to understanding, coöperation, and good adjustment generally than is a "surface" approach. Professor Ojemann has stated that "as teachers acquire more understanding of the backgrounds, ambitions and worries of their pupils, conflict between teacher and pupil will tend to lessen and the pupils' attitudes toward school tend to take on a more favorable aspect."[35]

The impressively simple and heartening implication of Ojemann's findings is that when teachers are trained in an understanding of the reasons underlying the behavior of children they tend to become the kind of teachers Dr. Burnham was talking about nearly a half-century ago. Ojemann has shown, moreover, that they become able then to do far more than they could before to train their pupils in turn to exercise an appreciation of the motives and circumstances responsible for

[34] Ralph H. Ojemann, "An Integrated Plan for Education in Human Relations and Mental Health," *Journal of the National Association of Deans of Women* (1953), 16:101-108. See also, by Ojemann, "Research in Planned Learning Programs and the Science of Behavior," *Journal of Educational Research* (1948), 42:96-104; *Personality Adjustment of Individual Children,* Washington, National Education Association and American Educational Research Association, 1954; and, with Eugene E. Levitt, "The Aims of Preventive Psychiatry and Causality as a Personality Pattern," *Journal of Psychology* (1953), 36:393-400.
[35] *Ibid.*

their own actions and for those of their classmates—and even for the reactions of their teachers. The consequences are pervasively constructive and wholesome.

What all this means is that it is good for children to be understood by their teachers, and it is good for their teachers to be understanding of them. It seems superfluous to add that this is true for speech handicapped children and their teachers as well as for other children and for teachers generally. If there is any difference—and there isn't always—it is that some youngsters who feel frustrated and stricken by difficulties in speech have a special need for teachers who "have an abiding interest" in them and "a real respect" for their individual personalities.

DISCIPLINARY POLICIES AND PRACTICES

There is probably no educator of substantial stature who would defend today the view that physical punishment is to be tolerated as a method of classroom discipline. True, in the files of the University of Iowa Speech Clinic—and this is probably so of any clinic in which a large number of cases have been examined—there are a few recorded cases of children, mostly stutterers, who have been physically mistreated for "not speaking properly." Dr. Hildred Schuell tells of a severe stutterer who "had for several years had his ears boxed in the classroom whenever he stuttered."[36] Few teachers, however, need to be reminded that no child should ever, under any circumstances, be punished for having impaired speech.[37]

What is less well appreciated, however, is the fact that punishment in the form of "psychological whipping" can be as damaging as corporal punishment. As a matter of fact, it can often be far more devastating in its long-term effects. The undesirability of sarcasm is, of course, generally recognized and need not be labored. Nor does any teacher have to be told that it is bad for a speech

[36] Hildred Schuell, *Differences Which Matter: A Study of Boys and Girls*, Austin, Texas, Delta Kappa Gamma Society, National Office, p. 9.

[37] A particularly informative and stimulating treatment of the matter of school discipline is to be found in Geodge V. Sheviakov and Fritz Redl, *Discipline for Today's Children and Youth*, Washington: National Education Association, Department of Supervision and Curriculum Development, 1944.

handicapped child to be ridiculed, teased, or belittled for his speech impairment. What even the best teachers need to be reminded of occasionally, however, is the sometimes demoralizing effect of unintentional inconsiderateness and rejection. Absent-mindedly "shushing" a youngster, especially a speech handicapped child, who comes bounding into the classroom late, excitedly eager to share with teacher and classmates the unique adventure of a traffic accident that prevented his getting to school on time, can deflect regrettably the course of the child's growing affection for the teacher. Not listening—nothing so positive as outright rebuke, just not listening—to children when they feel warm and friendly and want to talk to us is sometimes, as the child sees it and feels it, a bewildering unkindness. And this is particularly to be appreciated if the child has impaired speech and is quick to feel that he is being rejected on that account.

After all, the kind of discipline that is most important is self-discipline. It is the discipline that a youngster displays when he is proud of having done the best he could—proud not because he has escaped punishment, but because he has gained the positive rewards of a teacher's warm smile and a freckled class-mate's friendly wink, rewards that live on and grow within himself as the kind of self-esteem which is reflected in confidence, zest, and kindness. It is the kind of self-discipline that is seen in a set of motives and a sense of values that can be trusted to go on doing their constructive work when the teacher's back is turned and after school is out. It is the kind of self-discipline that is learned by example from a teacher who lives it herself and lends it a compelling glamour.

## MARKING OR GRADING SYSTEMS AND EXAMINATIONS

Most teachers of the handicapped, including speech correc-tionists, since they are necessarily imbued with a mental hygiene point of view, probably yearn, in their moments of unrestrained idealism, for schools in which there would be no "grade levels," just coöperative groups of students with common interests; no "marks," simply constructive and helpful evaluations of pupils as individuals; no "promotions," just progress toward meaningful goals for wholesomely motivated children; no "examinations," but friendly, conscientious efforts day in and day out to understand each child's specific difficulties and needs and to provide effective counsel and action for dealing with them. In their realistic workaday fashion, however, these teachers combine a practical respect for actualities with an alert watchfulness for opportunities to make the most of them.

There is no question that tests, quizzes, and marks do tend to make for a certain amount of anxiety, tension, and dissatisfaction. A professor of education has complained of certain grading practices in these words:

> A competitive marking system is not only psychologically unsound, it is also very undemocratic. . . . The old argument that all people compete for the essentials of adult living, and that competition in schools is good preparation for later life, ignores the heterogeneous nature of a school population. Any ninth grade class may include future doctors, dentists, teachers, farmers, clerks, and day laborers. People in these different vocations certainly do not compete with individuals in other vocations in adult life. There is no logic in forcing such competition in public schools. There are many opportunities for a more legitimate use of competition in public schools than in determining school marks.[38]

In general, grading systems and examinations that bring teacher and child into closer rapport, and that make for a more understanding and constructive evaluation by the teacher of each child's motives and inner needs as well as the surface manifestations of his performance, are clearly to be preferred.

As has already been stressed, for example, a child who has a speech problem should never be graded either down or up specifically because of his disturbed speech. In any class in which grades depend in part on speaking or oral reading, the teacher should make a conscientious effort to determine precisely in what respects and to what extent deviations in articulation, voice, or fluency are affecting the quality or amount of the pupil's performance. Then she should grade him fairly in allowance of the effect of the speech handicap. If, aside from the lisp or

[38] Paul E. Kambly, "Marking and Reporting," in *The American Secondary School,* ed. Paul B. Jacobson, New York, Prentice-Hall, Inc., 1952, p. 388.

stutter or nasality and its frustrating effects, he is doing B work, he should receive a B, instead of the C, D, or even F that he might receive if no allowance were made for the speech impairment. Moreover, it should be made clear to him, again and again if need be, that this is the kind of treatment he is to expect. Even one day of anxiety is most undesirable if it can be avoided.

There may be severe cases in which no speaking or oral reading should be expected of the child; grades, if they cannot be dispensed with in such cases, should be fairly based on written and other evidence of work done, improvement, and general mastery. Grades for "deportment," if they have not been abandoned, should take into account, in a constructive spirit of mental hygiene, the reactions to frustration normally to be expected of many speech handicapped children. You would not stand on a child's toes and then grade him down in "deportment" if he were to yell or kick. From the stuttering child's point of view it is as though somebody were "standing on his tongue." Grading him down for not smiling simply grinds the heel down more harshly.

As far as examinations, tests, and quizzes are concerned, every effort should be made to make them fair, to give due and reassuring warning, and to promote so far as possible a relaxed and confident attitude toward them. In every way possible the teacher should take the children into her confidence, make her motives in testing them understandable and reasonable, and take pains to explain the reasons for low grades and to help the pupils who receive them to understand their shortcomings and to find ways and motives for correcting them. Examinations should be given as a means of obtaining information about the individual children that is to be used as a basis for improving the instruction they are receiving, not merely as a means of grading and classifying them. From a clinical or mental hygiene point of view, they should be administered in such a manner as to keep worry and tension down to the lowest possible minimum.

Finally, it is to be remembered that speech impairments, particularly speech retardation (see Chapter VI) and difficulties associated with hearing loss (Chapter VIII), sometimes imply a degree of *general language handicap.* To the extent that this is true, the pupil who has a speech problem will be affected adversely in written as well as oral work. The alert teacher will keep this well in mind in evaluating the papers and tests of pupils whose speech is impaired.

### EXTRACURRICULAR ACTIVITIES

To the teacher who is interested in the general school adjustment of speech handicapped children, extracurricular activities are of tremendous importance. In some cases they are so important that one can only wonder why they are called "extracurricular." True, they can be overdone, and there is real danger in this, but wisely employed they can make a gratifying difference in the handicapped child's total school experience.

Special attention should be given by the classroom teacher to every pupil with a speech problem, with a view to finding for him some means of participating in the athletic, musical, dramatic, and other school programs, formal and informal. These children need exhilarating group activity and recognition, oftentimes even more than other pupils do, and it is usually more difficult for them to satisfy their needs in this connection within the classroom. A stuttering child who can sit with the school orchestra and play a violin in front of "all those people" is much better off than one who has no ready means of gaining similar satisfactions. A high school boy who speaks with a nasal twang but can run for touchdowns can even be a school hero instead of merely the butt of thoughtless jibes. If a lisper cannot qualify for a part in the school play, at least he can be on the stage crew and enjoy hours of happy companionship and worth-while accomplishment. Every child can do something that will draw him closer to the eddies of friendship and warming recognition that make any school as memorable as it ever becomes in the lives of its children.

Certain words of warning are in order. As has already been mentioned, extracurricular activities, so called, can be overdone. A child can have too much of them just as he can have too much homework. He can be kept in a state of near exhaustion, not only from physical exertion but from emotional overstimulation also. The wise teacher will of course be as sensible about this matter as she will about "curricular" activities.

Contests, generally speaking, are not as good from a mental hygiene point of view as "no decision" activities. Playing the piano for the fun of it, for the self-expression it affords, and for the gayer party it makes is better for a child than playing the piano before a music festival judge. It may enhance the glory of the school to win a music festival award, but for every child who runs home glowing with victory there are dozens who leave the platform disappointed and more discouraged than challenged. Trophies, medals, and ribbons can do to extracurricular activities what grades and marks have done to the three R's—they can turn them into ordeals instead of adventures in learning, something the child does for the school and the town instead of for his own enriching pleasure, sources of worry and tension instead of gaiety and relaxation. The mental health of all our children and adult citizens depends in some measure upon our fencing off certain areas of experience as recreational preserves with signs around reading, "No Winning or Losing Allowed."

SPECIAL SERVICES

Obviously one of the most direct ways in which the classroom teacher can contribute to the personal and social adjustment of speech handicapped pupils is in seeing to it that the special resources of the school and community are brought effectively to bear upon each child's needs. Youngsters with impaired speech often need more than speech correction: they sometimes require dental care, medical attention, special tutoring, vocational counseling, the sort of personality reëducation that a good school psychologist can provide, and other special services. The classroom teacher is often the person who can do most to see that such a child is not neglected and that the services from which he might benefit are obtained for him. A proper study of the following chapters will contribute toward the teacher's preparation so that she will be more helpful in this connection than she otherwise could be.

Practically every community—town, city, county, state—has many private and public agencies, from service clubs and Junior Leagues to state departments of social welfare and crippled children's services, to which the teacher can turn for help and even for funds with which to obtain needed hearing aids, glasses, social service care, or medical attention for children who are being allowed to drift, through ignorance or for other reasons, without benefit of the services which are rightfully theirs in our democratic society. The classroom teacher has not only the right but the obligation to take the initiative in bringing these services to any pupil who needs them—and some, at least, of her speech handicapped pupils do need them.

Speech correction is, of course, the chief one of the special services which should be secured for every child who has a speech problem. The rest of this book is devoted specifically to a consideration of the ways in which the classroom teacher can coöperate with the speech correctionist in her school, or provide some measure of counsel and instruction herself for her own speech handicapped pupils. For the present it is in order only to point up the principles of personality adjustment which are of special value to the classroom teacher in doing what she can about the adjustments of pupils who have speech difficulties. This will be done in the following section.

## Principles of Personality Adjustment for Speech Handicapped Children

### THE CHILD AS A WHOLE

The fundamental principles and objectives of mental hygiene, or personality training, are essentially the same for everyone. They are to be adapted, however, to every individual for whom they are employed. We shall consider how they can best be adapted to the specific adjustment problems and needs of speech handicapped children.

First of all, it is essential that the child as a whole be kept constantly in mind. Several years ago Professor Lee Edward

Travis emphasized this with unusual effectiveness: "A speech disorder is a disorder of the person as well as a disorder in the movements of the speech organs. It is not enough to know what sort of a speech defect a person has. In addition, one should know what kind of a person has a speech defect. . . . We are not interested in speech defects, but in speech defectives."[39]

Dr. Kenneth Wood, Director of the Speech Clinic at the University of Oregon, has supplemented Professor Travis' dictum in a provocative statement: "All forms of human behavior are associated with language or come to be. . . . A child learns speech, then, as a part of the whole process of organizing his behavior and learning to adjust to his environment."[40]

In a basic sense, as these statements clearly remind us, a speech disturbance is a kind of response which the child is making to his teachers, classmates, parents, and other persons in his environment. And it is in turn a stimulus for these other persons, to which they respond. They tend, however, to overrespond. Too often, the response they make presumably only to the child's unusual speech is actually a response they make to *the child*. In the meantime, the kind of speech he has is only one of his characteristics. He is not just a stutterer, a lisper, a cleft palate case, or a spastic. He is a child who sometimes makes a particular type of speech error but who does many other things too, and who possesses a whole host of personal qualities which have to be taken into account in making a fair evaluation of him. Moreover, his environment has to be considered—his family, neighborhood, playmates or lack of them, the teachers he has had, the opportunities or lack of them that his environment provides and has provided.

TWO BASIC OBJECTIVES

Keeping in clear focus, then, *the child* who has the speech problem, we can readily recognize that there are two basic objectives to be pursued.

[39] Lee Edward Travis, "A Point of View in Speech Correction," *Quarterly Journal of Speech* (1936), 22:57-61.

[40] Kenneth Scott Wood, "Parental Maladjustment and Functional Articulatory Defects in Children," *Journal of Speech Disorders* (1946), 11:255-275.

1. Improving the speech as much as possible is clearly desirable from a mental hygiene standpoint. The more the frustration arising from indistinct, labored, or blocked speech can be decreased, the more will the common maladjustive reactions to frustration be diminished. Specific speech correction measures are presented in succeeding chapters and will not be dealt with here.

2. Training the child to live gracefully and effectively with his speech impairment, so long as it persists, is the other basic objective. While much of the preceding discussion in this chapter is relevant to this objective, it will pay us to emphasize certain of the more crucial considerations.

### ACCEPTING THE BEST ONE CAN DO

Living gracefully with one's shortcomings is largely a matter of accepting one's best without resentment and without apology. The word "best" is to be stressed. The lame boy should be taught to dance as well as he can, to walk with the greatest comfort and grace possible, and helped to feel glad that he can dance and walk the best he can. No self-esteem is gained by giving up and accepting less than the best one might reasonably achieve. It is, to be emphasized just as definitely that the goal should be no higher than the best one can reasonably accomplish. A child whose speech is impaired should be everlastingly at the job of learning to speak as well as possible, with no sense of disappointment that he cannot do better than "possible." He need feel no urge to apologize for the way he speaks so long as he is doing what he can to improve. But it is not to be overlooked that he cannot even be expected to make an effort to improve unless he is given the necessary encouragement and understanding of his problem and ways of coping with it. That is where the classroom teacher comes in. She is in a strategic position to give the child the incentives he needs and at least some measure of the information so essential in dispelling the mystery of his difficulty and in building the hopefulness he must have if he is to make a "reasonable" effort to cultivate better speech.

## THE IMPORTANCE OF PERSPECTIVE

Living gracefully with one's shortcomings is also a matter of placing them in a proper perspective. This is done chiefly by making the most of one's assets. The classroom teacher can do a lot of good for any speech handicapped child by finding out what his talents are and encouraging him to develop them. If he can learn to tap dance, play ping-pong, blow a trumpet, or do card tricks, he forces others to see him as a more complete person rather than as just "a speech defective." Not only should he develop his talents, but he should also play them up in assuming his place in his social group and in thinking about himself.

A man once came to the University of Iowa Speech Clinic and announced himself as a "stutterer." It is true that he did stutter slightly and occasionally. He was one of the mildest cases we had ever seen. In his own eyes, however, he was a "stutterer." What else was he? He managed a very successful brokerage office, spending much of his time on the long-distance telephone transacting business. He had once defeated Walter Hagen at golf. He had a cultivated singing voice, was personally acquainted with many opera stars who respected his vocal talent, and frequently sang over the radio. He had a degree from one of the nation's finest universities, a lovely home, and a charming wife. But he thought of himself as a "stutterer." Clinical "treatment" for this very superior cultivated individual consisted almost entirely in getting him acquainted with himself, in helping him to see how unimportant his slight stuttering was in relation to all his unusual abilities and fine personal qualities, in providing him with an abiding good opinion of himself. About the only thing he needed that he didn't have was a sense of proportion about his stuttering. And when he got it his stuttering tended to decrease, although there was not much improvement for the excellent reason that there was almost no room for improvement in the first place. The total clinical result, however, viewing the case not just as a "speech defect" but as a man, was very gratifying.

This case is not typical, but it is a good one for making a

point, even so. One need not have as mild a speech imperfection or possess as many unusual abilities as this man did in order to profit from the kind of counseling he was given. Any speech handicapped child would profit from much the same instruction and counseling. He was instructed to be more frank and objective about his speech peculiarity and to talk to his friends about it, not as though it were a sin and a shame, but as though it were an interesting aspect of his individuality which he was trying matter-of-factly to do something about. He was to treat it lightly in discussing it and thinking about it, much as he might treat a tendency to muff an occasional golf shot, and he was to work on it, not with grim determination, but with reasonable persistence and moderate seriousness of purpose.

He was asked to write letters regularly to his clinician, in which he was to tell about his accomplishments. The letters were supposed to be a sort of self-elevating diary, but shared with another person and not kept secretly. In other words, he was given training in talking about himself, without boasting and without apologizing either. He was simply encouraged to give due weight to the good things about himself, his assets. Toward this same end, he was asked to keep a scrapbook in which he pasted news stories about himself, congratulatory letters he received, and other evidences of his abilities and achievements. And a considerable amount of talking went on between him and his clinician in order to provide motivation for all this, an understanding of the job to be accomplished, and a reinforcement of the gains made week by week.

By such means any person with a speech problem, child as well as grownup, can be helped to gain a better perspective with regard to his impaired speech and to make the most of his assets in the interests of better personal and social adjustment. Included in any psychologically sound "Children's Charter" should be the provision that every child, handicapped or not— but especially if handicapped—has the right to a good opinion of himself, feelings of success and personal worthiness, the reasonably full development of his assets, and encouragement to feel and to express a justifiable pride in his capabilities and accomplishments. Added to this should be a due recognition of the fact that one of the important signs of maturity and good adjustment is the ability to receive and enjoy compliments, and to give them with easy grace and genuine feeling. Awkwardness in this respect is an almost sure index of inner insecurity. To the remark, "That's a lovely new dress you have on this morning, Sally," the secure, well-adjusted child will reply frankly, "Thank you. I like it, too."

The poorly adjusted person tends to respond to compliments with an inner glow of pleasure, perhaps, but with an outward reaction of befuddlement or even outright apology. The secure public speaker with a good personality responds to "That was a fine speech," not by protesting that "It was nothing," or "I really should have had more time to prepare it," or "I wasn't quite up to par tonight, you should have heard me last Friday," but with "Thank you, I'm glad you liked it. I enjoyed giving it." This sort of adjustment to one's successes usually begins in early childhood; at least, the longer its cultivation is postponed the less likely it is to be well developed. We all go through adult life dragging the nineteen tails of our childhood, and it is easier to keep them gracefully up if we start holding them that way before they get too heavy.

One practical point in this connection deserves special mention. We have developed an attitude in our schools that is most unfortunate from a mental hygiene point of view—the traditional attitude toward what we regrettably call "apple polishing." Because of this ill-advised name for what should, and almost always could, be a sincerely friendly gesture of warmth and appreciation, school children have an almost universal sense of guilt about their wholesome tendencies to like their teachers. The term "apple polishing" and the whole sadly distorted point of view that it symbolizes is a sorry, telltale indication of the impaired teacher-child relationships that have come to be accepted as "right and natural" in all too many schools. For what good reason should a child hesitate to give his teacher an apple, so to speak? For what sound reason should the teacher feel uncomfortable when given an apple? What is wrong with pupils liking their teachers, and saying so, and what is wrong with the teachers frankly showing that it pleases them to be liked by their pupils? There is nothing wrong with this. On the contrary, it is highly desirable from the point of view of the personality growth of both pupils and teachers.

Generally speaking, scientific students of human behavior would doubtless agree that we place too great a premium on modesty. A little cockiness never hurt any child, or any grownup. Freely sharing one's joys and triumphs with others is one of the finest experiences in life. "I done it and I'm glad!" as a response to an achievement might startle one's English teacher, but it would be regarded by a psychologist as a good healthy reaction.

To the extent that the classroom teacher can cultivate this point of view and develop it in her pupils, particularly those who are handicapped in speech or otherwise, she will be doing something for them for which they will be forever grateful to her.

### VERBALIZING ONE'S PROBLEMS

Helping a child to live gracefully with a speech impairment involves training him in one other important aspect of personality growth. This is the ability to talk about his problem impersonally, objectively, and as intelligently as possible—the ability to put his worst foot forward without losing his balance. The common anxiety about always putting one's better foot forward is a sad miscarriage of psychology. You can't get ahead very fast on just one foot, better or worse. The only good first impressions that do not boomerang are the ones that can be maintained, either by living up to them or by leaving town soon enough.

It is almost always necessary for the teacher to take the initiative in getting the speech handicapped child to talk freely about his problem. As soon as she discovers that a pupil has a speech difficulty, she should make it a point to find a little time for discussing it with him. The common fear that such a child is made self-conscious by having his speech peculiarities mentioned is unfortunate, at least with respect to impairments that are severe. It is not a question of making the child self-conscious about a marked speech disorder. He *is* self-conscious already—or if he isn't the problem is to keep him from becoming so. The question is not *whether* the teacher should talk to the child, but *how* she should go about it.

There is no set talk to be made to any and every speech handicapped child on the second day of school. The procedure will vary all the way from saying nothing to carrying out a long-term comprehensive campaign. If the speech problem is very mild, and the youngster seems unaware of it or unconcerned about it, there will usually be no point in saying anything to him about it. In such a case practically the only reason for speaking about it would be to tell him either that you are going to refer him to the speech correctionist, and why, and what she will do for him, or that you are going to teach him how to form his *l*'s or *r*'s better —or whatever else you are going to teach him.

Whether the speech difficulty is mild, average, or severe, the child young or more advanced, shy or outspoken, almost always the best approach will be to tell the pupil simply that you have noticed something about his speech that interests you. You believe he would get a lot of satisfaction from working on it a bit. You think you might be able to help him or to get some help for him. You have studied speech problems in a course you took in college, and really there is a lot that can be done about them. Has he ever thought much about it? Has he ever had any speech lessons or exercises? Do his parents ever try to help him with his speech? What do they do? You'd like to talk to his mother about it as soon as you can find time for it. Would he mind if you did that? You'd like him to tell you more about it. Is there anything he'd like you to keep in mind in the classroom—when to call on him or when not to, for instance? Does he mind reciting? Is it easier to speak or to read? Does he like to sing? Would he like to sing in the glee club? Does he like athletics? Would he like to learn how to play a musical instrument? Does he have a paper route? Would he like to have one? Is he a Boy Scout? Would he like to be one? Tell him about your own interests, what you like to do in your spare time, where you spend your vacations, your speech courses in college, any persons with speech problems you know who have overcome their speech difficulties or have succeeded in some lifework in spite of them. (Don't use the term "speech *defect*" in talking to the child, and don't refer to him as a speech *defective* in talking about him to his parents or others with whom his problem and his possibilities should be discussed.) If you have or have had any personal handicaps that can be talked about in words that would have meaning for him, it will do much to establish a bond with him if you will talk a bit about them. You are trying to arouse his interest, his hope, and a desire to do something, to bring the problem out into the open, to talk about it and work on it. He can be thinking about it. It's going to be fine working with him. He's to be sure to come and talk with you any time he wants to. Maybe you'll be busy sometimes, but you're sure he'll understand that, and you'll always be glad to sneak a minute out of the day any time you can to talk some more.

There are few children who will long resist this sort of friendly human approach. From such a beginning most children will proceed to an increasingly frank attitude toward their speech problems and a growing desire to work objectively on them if only they are given the essential information, methods, and encouragement.

TEASING

Finally, there is the problem of teasing. The teacher who proceeds according to the above suggestions and the principles presented throughout this chapter is not likely to have much trouble so far as teasing is concerned. Teasing flourishes where the speech difficulty is coyly avoided, hushed up, and treated with a false philosophy of misguided pretense that it doesn't exist. There is no other target for teasing quite as inviting as an ostrich with its head in the sand. Teasing withers and decays when met with frankness, a matter-of-fact admission of imperfection, and a hopeful attitude that something should, can, and will be done to improve the situation. The teacher who can get this across to the speech handicapped child—and a teacher who is frank and objective about her own personal characteristics can do it better than one who is not—will provide him with the most effective weapon against teasing that he could have.

Should the teacher ever talk to the class about a particular child's speech difficulty? If she does, should she do it when the child is present? The teacher who views her job as that of developing the whole child, rather than teaching a specific skill or subject, will find these questions more or less pointless. Dozens of times a month such a teacher will go off onto little philosophizing tangents, indulge in reflective comments on happenings in and out of the classroom, and in general teach wisdom and character along with arithmetic or geography. In the course of "teaching herself" in this way it would be strange if she were to avoid entirely any reference to her own and the pupils' problems and shortcomings, the attitudes that might be taken toward them, and things that might wisely be done about them. Of course she will speak now and then to the class about speech problems, usually speech problems in general, as well as other handicaps and difficulties in general, and occasionally, if there is anything kindly or helpful to be achieved by doing so, she will refer directly to Wilbur's lisp, Jane's nasal quality, or Bill's stutter. She will find this to be a particularly effective way to build good group morale, to give the children a reassuring sense of what they have in common, and to get the class behind Wilbur and Jane and Bill in their efforts to be more comfortable with their speech deviations and to work toward improvement.

In addition to this the teacher will find, perhaps, that it will pay now and then to single out the ringleader in a class that tends to tease a particular child and to talk with this ringleader, not as though he were a scoundrel, but as though he were what he is in fact, a leader. As a leader, he is in a position—which he enjoys and from which he gains a feeling of responsibility—to be more helpful to the speech handicapped child than any other single pupil in the class. By arousing his sense of obligation and protectiveness, the teacher can kill two prize birds with one stone. She will be adding materially to the ringleader's training for leadership, and she will be making it practically certain—

if the speech handicapped child is psychologically able to coöperate at all—that the teasing will be stopped.

## HOW TO REACT TO A CHILD IN DIFFICULTY

All that has been said in this section can best be concluded
by summarizing it in the form of a brief decisive answer to the
question that is probably asked by teachers more often than any
other where speech handicapped children are concerned: What
should one do when a child speaks so indistinctly he cannot be
understood, or when he stutters so badly that it seems he just
can't go on?

If the child knows that your feeling about him as a person is
not good, it doesn't matter what you do. It will be wrong. If
the child knows that your feeling about him as a person is good,
it doesn't make any difference what you do. It will be right.
Children can seldom if ever be deceived about our deeper attitudes toward them. They are as sensitive as puppies to postural
tensions and tones of voice. The teacher who has grasped
thoroughly what this chapter contains, and who has made it part
and parcel of her reflex behavior, will have attitudes toward
speech handicapped youngsters that will show through in
friendly facial expressions and vocal intonations. In responding
to a child's difficult speech and wavering poise, she can trust
herself to do "the right thing" without consulting a handbook.

## The Clinical Point of View

What has been presented in this chapter may well be thought
of as the clinical point of view in education. It is the point of view
that in various forms and degrees is representative of practically
all special education teachers, child psychologists, speech correctionists, and others who are driven by the very nature of their
work to focus attention on individual children and to view each
child in relation to all the forces within himself and in his
environment that are creating his problems or keeping open the
door of hope for him. Surely, this point of view with all its
heartening consequences is the greatest single contribution of
speech correction and the other varieties of special education to

the American school system as a whole. To the extent that the clinical point of view is functioning in the nation's classrooms, speech correctionists and their fellow workers for the handicapped have enriched American education at all its levels and in all its branches.

Seldom, if ever, has the clinical point of view in education been more crisply and eloquently expressed than in the following passage from *Differences Which Matter: A Study of Boys and Girls,* by Dr. Hildred Schuell. The author is an unusually effective teacher, with an extensive background of classroom experience as well as clinical work, and with doctorate-level training in speech correction. She is uniquely qualified to make the statement which follows concerning the clinical point of view and its place in classroom teaching:

The clinical point of view can be stated simply. Our schools have failed too many children. When we dismiss a child with a label—a misfit, or a failure—we are making him a potentially costly and dangerous member of society. When deviations occur from acceptable forms of behavior, from normal school progress, or even when a child fails to perform at the level of his ability, it is necessary to find out the contributing conditions—the inhibiting factors or sources of conflict. Punishing the child is seldom an answer—never the complete answer. Indifference, lassitude, school failure, and undesirable "conduct" are symptoms that something is wrong for the child; they are pleas to adults for understanding and help. They are evidence that the child himself has not been able to find adequate ways to satisfy his needs for security, affection, and social approval. He is in trouble, and the situation will become graver, more serious, if he does not receive help. There is nothing new in this statement. It is fortunate for society that this is and has been a thing which good teachers everywhere have instinctively known, and which has consciously or subconsciously guided them in their associations with children. But sadly, it is not a universal point of view, and to the extent that it is not, education fails to perform both its individual and its larger social functions.

Accordingly many earnest and conscientious parents and teachers engage in a never-ending conflict with the young. With sincerity, good intentions, and zeal they go about the business of detecting lapses and errors, bringing them triumphantly to light, forcing confessions, tearful admissions or defiance, and promises which can never be kept. And they feel that they have won a sort of moral victory over a confused and bewildered child whose problems they have not even attempted to understand. The child feels ashamed and resentful, and what he understands is that the adult is his enemy. He goes out bruised, his confidence and self-respect shaken. He will be more evasive in the future or he will retaliate in whatever way he can.

The findings of clinical psychologists regarding conditions which favor growth and adjustment, and the findings of experimental psychologists regarding the conditions under which learning tends to take place are either unknown or disregarded by thousands of well-meaning teachers and educators who have lost sight of the child in their thinking. Their attention is fixed upon a course of study or a set of rules. They set standards which are unrealistic or meaningless to the child. They assign absolute and arbitrary values to success and failure, intelligence and stupidity, industry and laziness, even to worth and worthlessness, and categorize pupils in these terms. They deal out criticisms, disparagements, and penalties righteously, and although they might, it would seem, by their own experience or observation become aware of the frustration which is the chief consequence of such methods, continue to expect pupils to find them salutary. It would seem that all their education has not given them the ability to make observations or evaluate experience; more probably they have not been encouraged to do so. In some situations it might even be a dangerous thing for a teacher to do, if she were concerned about keeping her job. This in itself may well be considered a disturbing commentary on our educational procedures.

Whatever she may say, the teacher whose main objective is uniformity of discipline or standardized achievement does not really like children and should not be teaching. Any teacher who considers her pupils inferior in worth to herself for any reason—social position, "cultural" background, intellectual capacity, or any other artificial standard, is herself so limited, so immature in her thinking, or so personally maladjusted that she should not be considered for a teaching position. It is not through such individuals that a democracy can function, or that the tolerance, mutual understanding, and good will essential to the democratic way of life can be demonstrated. It is only the teacher who knows that washed or unwashed, black, white, brown, or yellow, whole or crippled, from whichever side of the tracks and whatever kind of homes, her pupils are human beings with infinite potentialities for good, which must be discovered and nurtured, who can realize her function as an educator.

Rapport is just as important in the classroom as in the clinic. The pupil must know that he is accepted as he is, that he is respected and appreciated as an individual, his individuality recognized, whatever his social standing or academic record, before he can trust an adult. Unless the teacher has this basic trust she cannot reach him, and nothing that she can say or do will be of any use. The pupil will read her expression, her inflections, and make comparisons; by these means he will know whether or not she is his friend. If he feels himself rejected, defensiveness rather than responsiveness will follow, and damage that may be irreparable and have far-reaching consequences is done to the individual, and through him to society.

When cases are cited, a common response is, "But that is an unusual case." To some degree this is often true. Each case is an individual one, and so to some extent unique. But the numbers of children referred yearly to school psychologists, behavior clinics, reading clinics, child welfare stations, psychological clinics, or institutes for juvenile research are not inconsiderable. In fact they are staggering. These are, moreover, the hopeful cases, the ones for whom help was available, and, for the most part, for whom it was sought while there was still a good chance that it might be effective in preventing the development of more serious maladjustments. If you add to these the gifted children whose abilities were never challenged, grade failures, pupils who leave school when they have passed the age of compulsory school attendance, those referred to juvenile courts and committed to corrective institutions, and those who appear before criminal courts or enter mental hospitals as adults with histories of maladjustments stemming from childhood, the figures are disheartening. No one who has dealt with these cases, or who has any information about the kinds of conditions under which these maladjustments tend to develop, can be so naïve as to suppose "correction" to be of more use than aspirin for a headache whose cause remains undetermined and unaltered.

The brief reports of cases which are cited are offered not as any kind of conclusive evidence, but with the hope that the thoughtful teacher may be led to search for their counterparts among the boys and girls whose lives are influenced by the attitudes she holds.

## CASE 1

Miss A brought a small nondescript girl from her classroom to the speech correctionist. Thrusting the child forward she stated that she thought the little girl stuttered. She added that she wouldn't waste much time with Emily, however, because she belonged to the Blank family, and everyone knew what they were.

Miss A considered herself a woman of refinement and culture. She had a reputation for being a thorough and conscientious teacher. What personal insecurities and false evaluations led her to make pets of "nice" children and despise the less favored would require further study. Not many teachers would, it is hoped, be guilty of such supreme disregard for a child's sensitivity and personal dignity as Miss A was in this instance, which is admittedly a shocking one. However, if that is the way a teacher reacts to her pupils, if it is the way she really feels, the child will know it anyway, and that teacher is directly and personally responsible for the unhappiness of the child and whatever maladjustments develop from it.

Emily was not a "stutterer," although Miss A was well on the way which might have made her one. Her hesitations and repetitions were merely the expression of her insecurity and anxiety in that classroom. They disappeared when she had a teacher who gave her friendliness and encouragement. A year later the small "stutterer" was chosen for a leading part in a children's play because she "stood so straight and had such a nice low voice." Dressed as a princess and radiant with happiness and pride she was a different person from the abject and cowering little girl of the year before. Miss A herself inquired innocently, "Who was that lovely child?"

## CASE 2

Edward was . . . a new student. He was over-age for the seventh grade and larger than any of his classmates. He scowled, walked with a slouch, seldom raised his head, and usually spoke in monosyllables. When his sponsor teacher discovered that he was failing in several subjects she called him in for an interview. Instead of talking about his grades she asked him what he wanted to do when he left school. She found out that his ambition was to have a farm of his own; that he had a responsible job, earned his clothing and books, helped his mother financially, and had a savings account. He admitted frankly that he hated school because everyone thought he was "dumb." Further inquiry revealed that he had never attended the same school for more than a few months at a time, and had never learned to read beyond a second-grade level. Remedial reading helped him some, although he never caught up with his grade. The real gain was the changed attitudes which came from a re-evaluation of himself, and from finding that authority, as represented by the school, was for him and not against him. When last heard from Edward did not have his farm, but he had made several landings under fire on the beaches of Italy.[41]

Dr. Schuell presents other cases too, and the cases she describes are representative, each in its own way, of thousands upon thousands of children in our schools who are being misunderstood and psychologically wounded over and over again —or who are being strengthened day by day through the wise and gracious kindness of teachers who are themselves enriched by the help they give. Some of these children bring their handicaps with them to the kindergarten or the first grade; others acquire their handicaps after they have entered the schools. Among them are the children with impaired or difficult speech. For these as for all the others, every classroom teacher is not only a teacher of speech but a psychologist as well, whether she means to be or not and for better or for worse. This book is dedicated to the conviction that it can be for the better, in heart-warming measure, better for the children and better for their teachers.

[41] Scheull, *op. cit.*

# CHAPTER III

wwwwwwwwwwwwwwwwwwwwwwwwwwwwwwwwwwwwwwwwwwwwwwwwwwwwwwwwwwwwwwwwwwwwwwwww

# *Disorders of Articulation*

Among the various kinds of speech disorders that the teacher will encounter in her classroom, by far the most common are those which we call disorders of articulation. Speech surveys in the public schools have generally indicated that approximately three out of every four speech problems belong in this group. From the standpoint of numbers, therefore, articulation disorders are deserving of special attention and consideration by the classroom teacher.

## *What Is a Disorder of Articulation?*

Children who have difficulty in articulation do not produce all the speech sounds in the usual accepted manner. Hence, their speech tends to call attention to itself and in severe cases may be very difficult to understand or even unintelligible. The speech errors or misarticulations may take one or more of several forms. Usually, however, all these errors may be conveniently grouped under one or more of the following three classifications: (1) omissions, (2) substitutions, and (3) distortions.

### OMISSIONS

Errors involving the omission of certain sounds occur more commonly in the speech of younger children than of older children. Youngsters who make errors of this type do not necessarily do so consistently. In general, a consonant occurring as the final sound of a word is more likely to be omitted than is the same consonant when it begins a word or occurs in the middle of it. But when two consonants are blended together (such as *s* and *t* in "stop") one of the two may often be omitted, irrespective of the position in the word in which the blend occurs. A small child with badly impaired articulation may have no final consonant sounds at all in the usual sense.[1] But he will generally have a few in the initial and medial positions of words. Whole syllables may be omitted. If his entire consonant repertory consists of only a few sounds, one may get such a pattern of omissions and substitutions as the following: "Ta oo uhta? Me ta, datty dah tittuh tittuh a o" for "Can't you understand? Me say, Jacky got little sister at home." It is apparent that such omissions and substitutions can render a child's speech almost completely unintelligible even to the skilled listener. One does not often see a case as severe as this, but even a few such errors can add considerably to the distorted character of a child's speech.

SUBSTITUTION ERRORS

Substitution errors, like omissions, are relatively common in the speech of small children. The little boy who says, "I thwew a wock at the wabbit," illustrates a common error of substitution. He is substituting the *w* sound for *r*. Some other common substitutions are: *w* for *l*—"Weave me awone, Biwy!" for "Leave me alone, Billy!"; *t* for the voiceless *ch* sound in words like "chew" and *d* for the voiced consonant *j*, as in "Dacky can't cat me!" for "Jacky can't catch me!"; *f* for the voiceless *th* sound of "bath" and *v* for the voiced *th* of "mother," as in "Muvver, I hurt my fumb!" for "Mother, I hurt my thumb!" These by no means exhaust the possibilities. In the speech of some small children many such sound substitutions may occur. Often they are inconsistent; a child may frequently substitute one sound for another which he can produce easily, and then substitute that sound for still a

---

[1] Very young children sometimes substitute a peculiar stoppage of the breath stream by the larynx for certain consonants, both in the medial position and in the final position in words. Although this is not a normally accepted consonant sound in standard spoken English, it tends to be consonant-like in the way it is formed.

third one. In an extreme case a child may have mastered the production of only a few of the consonant sounds, which are then substituted more or less irregularly for all the rest. Substitution errors may also be found in the speech of some older children and adults, but such errors are usually fewer in number and much more consistent. The fifteen-year-old who says "For Peteth thake, ith it thikth o'clock already?" is likely to be consistent in substituting the *th* sound for *s* or *z*.

DISTORTIONS

Distortion errors tend to be somewhat more regular and consistent and to occur with greater relative frequency than omissions in the speech of older children and adults. Whereas a small child may often omit a sound entirely, or substitute another sound for it, an older child will more frequently produce something which approximates the normal sound but which by comparison with the usually acceptable standard would have to be regarded as distorted. One of the most commonly distorted sounds is the consonant *s*. Because the positioning and shaping of the tongue with relation to the palate and teeth are so critical for this sound, it can be distorted in various ways. Some faulty *s* sounds have too much of a hissing component, others have a definite whistling character, while still others, particularly when the air is allowed to escape over the sides of the tongue, have an unpleasant mushy sound, as though the speaker had an excessive amount of saliva in his mouth. The *s* is not the only sound, of course, which can be distorted. The *z* can be altered in much the same manner as the *s*; distorted *sh* and *ch* sounds occur with some frequency; *v* is sometimes produced between the lips, instead of between the lower lip and upper front teeth; and so on.

The above discussion has gone into some detail, not in order to give any sort of complete description of all possible misarticulations, but to provide the reader with a general understanding of the principal types and variations of articulatory errors that he may encounter, and also to make clear the particular sorts of speech faults that are to be considered in this chapter. Not included as articulatory errors are such common speech imperfections as "jist" for "just," "git" for "get," "perty" for "pretty," and so on. These are errors in pronunciation, not articulation. The pupil who makes them can produce the sounds required for correct utterance of the words. Hence he is not a speech handicapped child in the sense in which that term is ordinarily used, and he is not properly to be referred to a speech correctionist.

To summarize, the child with an articulatory problem has difficulty in producing speech sounds. His errors are not always consistent. In fact, they may be highly inconsistent: in certain words and in certain phonetic combinations he may produce acceptably a sound which he fails to produce adequately at other times. His errors may take the form of omissions, substitutions, or distortions, or all three. They may be few or many, ranging from the child who has difficulty with only one sound, and whose speech therefore sounds only a little out of the ordinary, to the child whose whole sound repertory consists of only three or four consonants and a half-dozen vowels, perhaps, and whose speech is almost completely unintelligible. The most important single fact about the speech of such a child is that he is not able to produce consistently and effortlessly the ordinary, accepted sound patterns of speech. Therefore, his speech sounds different from that of the normally speaking child.

## Maturation of Articulatory Skill

In kindergarten and the primary grades an important question arises as to what sound errors are to be regarded as speech disorders. Is the speech of Jacky, age five, to be regarded as needing correction because he habitually says "thish" for "fish," and "thirst" for "first?" What about David, age eight, who still says "wed woses" for "red roses"? At what age should we expect a child to be able to produce acceptably all the speech sounds of the language? Moreover, what is the likelihood that a child whose speech contains such errors will "get over it" without any special attention? Don't many children when starting school make such errors and don't they "outgrow them" or learn better speech habits without the ministrations of a speech correctionist? It is the purpose of this section to provide information which may help to answer these basic questions.

Studies of the speech of young children have shown that there is considerable variability in the age at which complete mastery of sounds occurs. Children who are particularly accelerated in speech development may accomplish complete mastery at three to four years of age. For others the process may not be completed until considerably later. Girls have generally been found to surpass boys slightly in speech development. Even so, one of the most frequently quoted studies[2] found that not until the age of 6.5 years did as many as 50 percent of the girls studied attain relatively complete mastery of all sounds. And the boys were almost a full year older before as many as 50 percent of them attained the same degree of articulatory skill. To the extent that these results are typical, it appears that in grades one and two, as well as in kindergarten, it is the rule rather than the exception to find that a child still has some difficulty in articulating certain speech sounds correctly, at least by adult standards. Roe and Milisen,[3] who applied a strict criterion of correctness of articulation in their study of about 2,000 Indiana school children, found even higher percentages of children making such errors in the primary grades.

In the same study, Roe and Milisen pointed up a second significant fact concerning the articulatory errors of children in the early grades. This is the regular and rather marked decrease in the frequency of such errors through the first three or four grades, even in schools where there is no speech correction program. Both the number of children who are found to make errors and the number of errors per child tend to drop rather markedly during these years, the largest decrease coming during the

[2] Irene Poole, "Genetic Development of Consonant Sounds in Speech," *Elementary English Review* (1934), 2:159-161. Poole's findings have been confirmed by Mildred Templin, "Norms on a Screening Test of Articulation for Ages Three Through Eight," *Journal of Speech and Hearing Disorders* (1953), 18:323-331.

[3] V. Roe and R. Milisen, "The Effect of Maturation upon Defective Articulation in the Elementary Grades," *Journal of Speech Disorders* (1942), 7:37-50.

two-year period from kindergarten to second grade, with a much smaller decrement between the second and fourth grades.

The questions posed at the beginning of this section must therefore be answered by saying that it is common to find children still making such errors as "fank oo" for "thank you," "tootbwush" for "toothbrush," and "Thimple Thimon" for "Simple Simon" in the primary grades, and that they do tend to "get over" many of them. Such children often, though not always, develop completely adequate speech as a consequence of maturation plus the favorable learning environment of the schoolroom without the special help of remedial speech training.

Does this mean that no children of this age group (five to eight years) should be regarded as needing speech correction? Does it mean that the speech correctionist may safely by-pass the primary grades? Some persons, including some educators and even a few speech correctionists, have interpreted these data to mean just that. It is our judgment that the data are better interpreted in another way.

To be sure, a considerable number of these children probably should not be regarded as "speech defectives." Their speech errors are not to be thought unusual or disproportionate for their age group. For them the learning and developmental processes of achieving relatively error-free articulation have just not been completed. On the other hand, some (fortunately a relatively small number) have articulation so faulty that it stands out and seems different even at those grade levels where some articulaton errors tend to be the rule. These children are definitely in need of special help, and the help they need should not be postponed until everyone else of their age level has developed adequate speech by adult standards. Such youngsters are clearly handicapped by their inadequate speech in an educational system which places a premium on oral expression. Such a child is frustrated and embarrassed by difficulty in making himself understood. He may be looked upon as backward by his playmates, the neighbors, sometimes his own parents, and even his teachers. It is small wonder that such a child may have more than average difficulty in learning to read, and that he may become educationally retarded. Indeed, a child so frustrated and handicapped may well develop into a behavior problem in the schoolroom or at home and eventually become a relatively helpless educational misfit. The following case, although admittedly somewhat extreme, may illustrate what must happen in some measure to many such youngsters.

Joe was referred to the speech clinic through a social welfare agency. He had come to the attention of the agency because of persistent truancy. He was reported by his teacher to be incorrigible. Although thirteen years of age, he was in the fourth grade and seemed unable to do the work even at that level. His educational history revealed that he had had trouble in school from the very first and had generally been considered "feeble-minded" by his teachers. His speech had undoubtedly improved since he first entered school, but it was still impaired enough to make him somewhat difficult to understand.

When Joe was first seen at the speech clinic he was given an individual mental test as a part of his routine examinaton. This revealed that instead of being mentally retarded he was very nearly average in intelligence. He was referred to the reading clinic, where examinations indicated that he was barely able to read at a level equivalent to that usually attained at the end of second grade.

Boarding home placement was arranged for Joe, and he was placed in the special room of one of the local elementary schools. Arrangements were made for him to come daily to the speech and reading clinics for special remedial instruction. By the end of one year Joe could make all the speech sounds and his ordinary speech was quite intelligible to anyone, although an occasional error would slip in when he was excited or off guard, because some of the newly learned sounds had not yet become entirely automatic. Reading proficiency had been increased from second-grade level to that of fifth grade. His work in arithmetic, which had been seriously deficient, had markedly improved as a result of the gain in reading and of help from his special room teacher. Although he had tended to be somewhat sullen and aggressive in the early part of the year, at no time did any important behavior problem develop. No single instance of truancy was reported. Although no one can say for sure how much of Joe's problem was an outgrowth of his speech deficiencies, it is virtually certain that they had contributed materially to the erroneous impressions his teachers and others had formed—that here was a backward, "mentally deficient" child with whom it was useless to spend much time. That Joe had reacted to such negative attitudes and neglect in ways which seemed to reinforce and confirm the incorrect diagnosis of his problem is hardly surprising.

Fortunately, this case is unusual, but because it is it spotlights the handicapping consequences which may result from a child's difficulty in communication due to faulty speech. Since most cases of faulty articulation are less severe, their consequences, educationally and socially, are likely to be less dramatic. Nevertheless, some measure of Joe's experiences must be shared by many children who have articulatory problems which fail to receive early and adequate attention.

One of the difficulties in deciding whether or not a given child should be regarded as having defective articulation has been the lack of normative data to which a child's performance could be directly compared. Most studies of speech development have not provided such data in very usable form. Recently, however, Templin[4] has published norms on a fifty-item screening test which can be easily and quickly administered. These normative data were obtained from a sample of 480 children ranging in age from three through eight years of age, carefully selected with respect to sex and socioeconomic group as well as age. There is now available, therefore, a better basis for deciding whether or not the speech of a particular child in this age range needs special attention. However, a word of caution may be in order. In using such a test and such test norms it should always be remembered that scoring on a test of this kind is necessarily far more subjective than on most tests for which we are

[4] Mildred Templin, "Norms on a Screening Test of Articulation for Ages Three Through Eight," *Journal of Speech and Hearing Disorders* (1953), 18:323-331, and "A Non-diagnostic Test of Articulation," *Journal of Speech Disorders* (1947), 12:392-396.

accustomed to using norms. The criteria by which a particular examiner judges various sounds to be faulty or normal play a large part in determining how a child's performance will be evaluated. Studies of agreement among examiners making judgments of this kind tend to show rather high agreement on the average, but the agreement for certain individuals will rather often (approximately fifty percent of the time, if the distribution of figures for agreements on individuals follows the normal law of error) be lower than this average figure and, in a few cases, the agreement may be very low. Hence, although such norms may be helpful, they cannot be applied in any sort of automatic fashion. They can contribute toward a carefully considered clinical judgment, but they cannot be substituted for such a judgment.

## Causes of Articulatory Disorders

Why some children fail to develop good speech at the same age as their playmates is not always easy to explain. In some cases the causes are complex and varied. In others they are so obscure that we cannot always be sure as to exactly which factors have produced the deficiency. However, we do know a considerable amount about some, at least, of the important conditions related to poor articulation. In general, the known causes may be divided into three broad classes: (1) constitutional factors, (2) faulty learning, and (3) emotional maladjustment.

### CONSTITUTIONAL FACTORS

Some of the more severe organic conditions which tend to result in speech disorders, such as cleft palate, cerebral palsy, and impaired hearing, are considered in other chapters in this book. Here we shall consider other constitutional factors of a generally less severe character which may have an adverse effect on articulation.

*Dental Abnormalities.* Good teeth are not only essential to the proper chewing of food and to the winsomeness of a happy smile; they are important also from the standpoint of speech. The normal mode of production of a number of consonant sounds

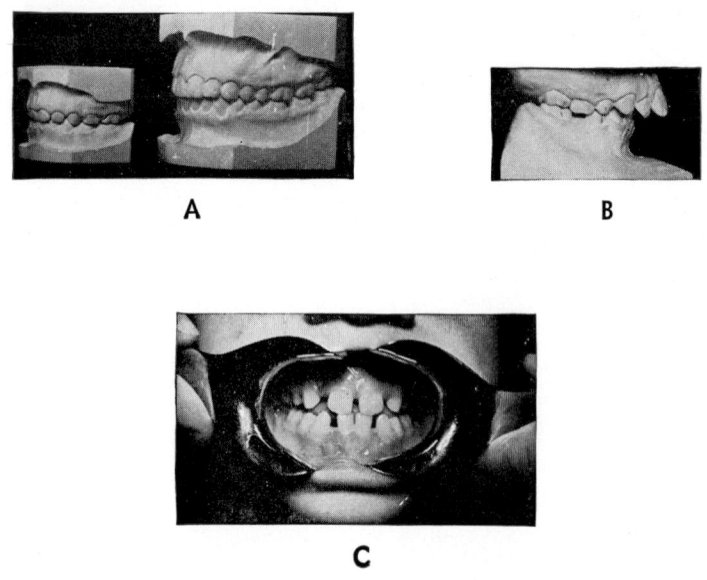

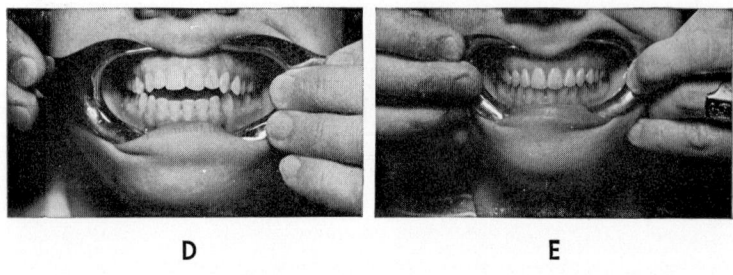

FIGURE 1. Various conditions of dental occlusion. A. Ideal occlusion at 4 years and 19 years of age. B. Severe over-jet with protruding upper anterior teeth and micro-development of the lower jaw. C. Spacing of anterior teeth in 6 year old child. D. Anterior open-bite. E. Same patient as in D after correction of anterior open-bite. (From the collection of Dr. L. B. Higley, College of Dentistry, State University of Iowa.)

requires at least reasonably good dentition.[5] Among these sounds are: *f* and *v*, in which the lower lip is required to make contact with the upper teeth; the two *th* sounds, as in "think" and "these," in which the tongue tip is either thrust slightly between the upper and lower front teeth or placed against the inner surfaces of the upper teeth; and *s, z, ch, sh, zh,* and *j,* which require that the breath be directed across the cutting edges of the teeth in particular ways. If the teeth are badly spaced or misaligned, or if there is poor occlusion (spatial relationship) between the upper and lower dental arches, considerable difficulty in articulation may result. Figure 1 shows some examples of types of dental conditions which may produce difficulty.

Although such dental irregularities do tend to present obstacles to good articulation, one should not conclude that they necessarily make normal speech impossible. Many persons have succeeded in developing adequate and sometimes even superior speech in spite of severe dental abnormalities. The facts are best stated by saying that poor dentition may be a complicating factor which may help to explain why a particular child has difficulty with certain sounds. In a few very extreme cases it may be impossible to produce certain consonants without correction of the dental condition. In the vast majority of cases, however, normal articulation can be achieved in spite of the difficulties imposed by faulty dental structure.

*Other Oral Irregularities.* Although perhaps more common than any other, dental irregularities are not the only deficiencies in the structure or functioning of the speech mechanism that can contribute to articulation difficulties. The roof of the mouth, or hard palate, may also be important in this connection. The tongue must establish contact with it in particular ways to form certain of the speech sounds in the normal manner. If the hard palate is unusually high and very narrow, the tongue may have difficulty

[5] Some knowledge of the physiological mechanics of normal speech sound articulation will assist materially in understanding the possible effects of dental deficiencies and other oral abnormalities on the production of speech sounds. Hence, for the reader who does not already possess such knowledge, a brief discussion of the mechanics of speech sound production has been included in the Appendix.

in making these required contacts in the normal way, and certain speech sounds may be distorted as a consequence.

The tongue is perhaps the most important of all the articulatory structures. It is quite obvious, therefore, that faults of structure or function which interfere with its movements may result in misarticulations. In very rare instances an individual's tongue may be so large in relation to the dental arches that it becomes difficult to make the rapid, precise movements required for good articulation. In a few cases there may be poor muscular coördination. This is sometimes, though not always, the result of a slight paralysis. In such cases the tongue cannot make the necessary movements to the teeth, the gum ridge, and the hard and soft palates which are essential to normal articulation. The individual may also have difficulty in grooving the tongue so as to direct the air stream properly for the *s*, *sh*, and similar consonants. The condition known as "tongue-tie" is probably not as common as was once thought, but it does occur occasionally. In this condition the little web of tissue lying underneath the front part of the tongue, by which the front of the tongue is attached to the floor of the mouth, is either too short or is inserted in the tongue too close to the tip. As a consequence, the movements of the front part of the tongue may be too restricted for purposes of good articulation. Caution should be observed, however, in making such judgments. One needs to avoid the tendency to look too hard for a structural explanation for an articulatory problem. If the child has been able to nurse, can extend his tongue between the teeth, and can touch the upper gum ridge with the tip of his tongue, the judgment that he is "tongue-tied" is probably irrelevant so far as his ability to speak is concerned.

These are the most common, though not all, of the types of mouth condition which may interfere with good articulation. Mouth injuries have been known to cause difficulty. In general, almost any very marked departure from the normal structure and function of the oral mechanism may interfere with speech, although it will not necessarily do so, and if it does it will be in most instances a complicating rather than a disabling factor.

## FAULTY LEARNING

Although constitutional factors, such as those just discussed, may be important in certain instances, in the majority of articulatory cases no significant organic factor can be found. In most cases the articulatory mechanism appears to be entirely normal as to both structure and function. In still others, such deviations as may be found are too slight to account for the speech difficulties. Hence, we must look further for explanatory factors.

Most articulatory deviations seem to be traceable to no other cause than failure to learn the correct patterns of normal speech. In other cases we know that normal rather than faulty speech might have been developed, despite structural deficiencies, if strong enough motivation and a favorable learning environment had been provided. Milisen[6] has stated that, except for cases in which a severe neuromuscular disorder is present, the one basic cause of all articulatory difficulty is a disruption of the normal learning process. Even though one may not subscribe to quite so broad a conclusion, it is doubtless true that the most important single cause of disorders of articulation is the lack of sufficiently favorable conditions for the learning of good speech. For various reasons incorrect speech habits have been formed and have become strongly established. The ordinary environmental pressures of home, community, and school do not seem to have been sufficient to counteract them and replace them with habits involved in normal speech. Children who have "got off to a poor start" in this way tend to persist in making their speech errors long after most of their contemporaries have developed normal articulation. Such children usually require special attention and retraining if they are ever to acquire normal speech.

The specific conditions which can produce this faulty learning are varied and complex. A brief discussion of some of the more common ones will show why, in general, all normal children do not learn to speak correctly.

*Poor Speech Models.* It is well established that speech is

---

[6] Robert Milisen, "A Rationale for Articulation Disorders," *Journal of Speech and Hearing Disorders* (1954), Monograph Supplement 4:5-17.

learned essentially through imitation. Sometimes the speech which the child learns to imitate is itself faulty. Occasionally a parent or older child in the family has impaired speech. The English speech of foreign-born parents, for example, is sometimes inadequately learned and marked by sound substitutions and distortions. A particular foreign language influence may be so strong in a particular locality that the speech of the whole community is affected by it.

An example of faulty learning from a poor speech model was shown in the case of an eleven-year-old whose principal trouble was a substitution for the *r* sound. His father, who had accompanied him to the clinic, started the interview by saying, "I b*w*ought (brought) Danny he*uh* (here) because he can't make his *ah* (r) sounds *w*ight (right). The boys at school *ah* (are) beginning to tease him, and I don't want him laughed at all his life like I have been."

*Lack of Stimulation and Motivation.* Infantile speech habits sometimes seem to persist because there is no motivation to change them, or because there is even positive motivation to retain them. Ordinarily the drive to communicate is so strong, and communication through deficient speech is so unsatisfactory, that the problem of motivation takes care of itself without conscious direction by anyone. Occasionally, however, environmental conditions are not adequate to motivate good speech learning. Sometimes very inadequate speech (by ordinary standards) suffices to meet all the child's needs for communication. Now and then a child is permitted to supplement his inadequate speech with gestures to the extent that he feels no need to develop better speech. Parents and older children, who have learned to understand the youngster's jargon, may act as interpreters for him to such an extent that even the needs to communicate with persons outside the family do not arouse in him any special urge to learn better speech habits. Under these circumstances the development of normal articulation may be so retarded that the child's speech continues to be extremely faulty long after his playmates have sloughed off most of their infantile speech habits.

A somewhat related situation is that in which the child does not receive enough good speech stimulation. He may be so isolated from other children, as well as adults, that he seldom needs to speak to anyone. Moreover, under such conditions he does not hear much speech to imitate. Frequently this lack of speech stimulation is a consequence of parental neglect, more often unintentional than malicious.

A case in point is that of Roger, an only child, age seven, who was brought to the speech clinic with markedly infantile speech. He had been slow in all aspects of speech development, although he seemed physically well developed, and no apparent organic cause for the speech retardation could be found. Nonverbal intelligence tests showed no mental retardation, although he was definitely below average on such verbal items as the vocabulary test of the Stanford-Binet intelligence scale. The interview with the parents revealed that they lived on a farm too large to be managed without hired help. During the war, however—incidentally, the period when Roger was learning to talk—workers had been almost impossible to obtain and, as a consequence, both parents were actively engaged in field work for long hours each day. Even in the evenings, when the day's work was done, they were too tired to give much attention to Roger. Questioning revealed that they had never read stories or nursery rhymes to him and that there was no close companionship between the child and either parent. "Yes, he sometimes tagged after us out to the fields, but there wasn't much chance for talking." The tractor and other machinery made too much noise and besides they were extremely busy. "No, he isn't usually included in conversation at the table." They guessed they just hadn't thought of it. Besides he didn't try to talk much anyway. Most of the care of Roger was entrusted to a grandmother who lived with the family and looked after a large share of the housework. But she was a partial invalid and so had little time to devote to the boy. He had no playmates, since none of the nearby neighbors had children of his age. His sole companions seemed to be his pets, of which he had a plentiful supply. But his dog provided no speech stimulation and was not critical of his infantile substitutions and omissions or lack of vocabulary.

In short, here was a boy whose whole environment was almost devoid of speech, aside from what little was needed to satisfy his simple physical needs and the meager mealtime conversations in which he was not included. It is small wonder that he had made little progress in learning to talk. He was not much better off when he entered school at the age of six. The other children thought him queer, and he didn't know how to play with them, so they left him pretty much to his own devices. The teacher hardly knew what to do with him either. She did, however, take positive steps by talking to the parents and was the main instigator of his trip to the speech clinic.

EMOTIONAL MALADJUSTMENT

Since the emotional conditions which can produce adverse effects on speech development are discussed in other sections of this book, particularly Chapter II and Chapter VI, the discussion of them at this point will be relatively brief. There is a discussion in Chapter VI of the parent-child relationships which may result in refusal of a child to talk. Practically everything said there may be applied also to articulatory deficiencies. The difference is in the degree of the effect produced rather than in the nature of the causal factors.

Much of the evidence for the connection between articulatory problems and unfavorable environmental conditions and parent-child relationships is derived from clinical experience. However, there have been a few systematic investigations of this general problem. In one of the most comprehensive of these studies, Wood[7] collected extensive data for fifty articulatory cases ranging in age from five to fourteen years in which the speech problem could not be attributed to either organic deficiency or low intelligence. Data concerning environmental factors and emotional adjustment of both the children and their parents were obtained by means of psychological tests and extensive case history interviews. In general, the results of this study showed what Wood interpreted as a significant amount of emotional mal-

[7] K. S. Wood, "Parental Maladjustment and Functional Articulatory Defects in Children," *Journal of Speech Disorders* (1946), *11*:255-275.

adjustment among the parents of these fifty children, especially the mothers. Certain salient factors in the homes were also found in a number of cases. Disturbed home membership, as in cases in which both mother and father were working, or in which mother or father had been away from home periodically, or in which the parents had been definitely separated, was found in twenty-four of the fifty cases. Severe child discipline methods were practiced in twenty-two of the homes. Emotional reactions of parents to the child's speech difficulty were found in eighteen cases. Certain effects of these parental maladjustments and environmental influences were indicated by some of the data obtained from the children. Such factors as withdrawing tendencies, sense of frustration, lack of affection, and anxiety-insecurity were discovered in from approximately one third to two thirds of the children tested. To the extent that such conditions affect the learning and normalization of speech, they may be regarded as linkages, as it were, between parental maladjustments and the children's faulty articulation.

The most interesting part of this study was that in which the fifty cases were divided into two matched groups for retraining. For one group of twenty-five, ordinary articulation retraining procedures were employed. For the other twenty-five, the same remedial speech training was given, but in addition extensive counseling of the parents was carried on at the same time. This second group was found to improve significantly more rapidly than the first group.

One should not, of course, overgeneralize from such data. Certainly not in all, and probably not even in most, cases of ordinary faulty articulation are such factors as these extremely important. One should not jump to the conclusion that every child who exhibits a simple sound substitution or distortion, or even two or three such errors, is living in a grossly undesirable home and is being rejected or gravely abused by his parents. Most such children will sing "Home, Sweet Home" with about the same mixed feelings as other youngsters. Yet the classroom teacher will need to be aware of the possible relationship between articulatory problems in children and emotional maladjustment in their parents, at least to the extent of insuring that children who have such problems do not experience still more frustration, anxiety, and disappointment, particularly concerning speech, in the school situation.

### INTELLIGENCE

Before we leave the discussion of causes of articulatory problems a few words should be said concerning low intelligence. Speech imperfections are more frequent among children of low intelligence than among those who are average or above in mental capacity. It is also true that intelligence test scores of children with articulatory deficiencies average slightly lower than those of children with normal speech. Again, however, a word of caution is needed. Such averages can be easily overinterpreted. They do not tell us anything about a particular youngster who has a speech problem. The fact is that impaired speech may be found at any level of intelligence. Unfortunately it is all too easy to set down as mentally subnormal the child whose speech is labored, distorted, or unintelligible. That is perhaps the first reaction of the average uninformed person. The dire consequences of such misdiagnosis can hardly be overemphasized. The writers have known children to be refused admission to school on grounds of "feeble-mindedness" when the only basis for the decision was impaired speech, and where later testing of mental ability showed no basis for classifying the child as mentally retarded. Certainly the informed teacher has a responsibility for combating such misjudgment. Just as a mentally subnormal child cannot be dealt with adequately simply by giving him speech correction, even if he needs it, so a child who lisps cannot be handled adequately as a mentally retarded youngster, even if he is one. And he seldom is one.

## Maintaining and Aggravating Factors

We have seen some of the conditions which tend to produce articulatory disorders. It is the purpose of this section to point out those factors tending to perpetuate such disorders and in some cases to aggravate them. Many of the factors which originally produce the deviations, such as lack of motivation for good speech, structural deficiencies, and the like, tend also to be maintaining factors, unless corrected. What we are concerned with here, however, are conditions besides the original causes which may operate to aggravate and perpetuate the difficulty.

## ANXIETY AND FRUSTRATION IN SPEECH SITUATIONS

Even under the best of circumstances the child with faulty speech is almost certain to experience some frustration and anxiety in speech situations. This may not be evident in the very young child, particularly if there has been a reasonable attitude of tolerance and acceptance of his problems on the part of parents, friends, and playmates. But sooner or later, if the difficulty persists, it is likely to call attention to itself and become a matter of considerable concern to him as well as to others. A certain amount of such concern is of course necessary as motivation for improvement. However, it must not be magnified to the extent that the youngster becomes anxious about all speaking and feels constantly frustrated by his failures.

Conditions which produce such anxiety and frustration tend to increase as the child becomes older. To begin with, speech errors generally become more noticeable as the contrast with the speech of other children of his age group increases. New playmates may not accept his speech as readily as the earlier ones did; they may, in fact, make it an object of ridicule. As the child becomes older parents tend to become increasingly concerned and to show it in numerous ways. Furthermore, unless the teacher is particularly skillful and understanding, the child experiences numerous frustrations and failures in the classroom which are due to his speech —or at least he feels that they are. He may be corrected over and over again by well-meaning parents and teachers, teased by other children, and continually made to feel failure and inferiority in numerous ways.

Such constant frustration and anxiety not only add emotional and behavior difficulties to the already existing speech problems but also tend to maintain the speech problem itself and to increase its severity. No lengthy argument is required to demonstrate that these are not the conditions under which learning takes place easily. The disintegrating effects of anxiety are too well known to require repeating. Moreover, speech is more gravely affected than most other kinds of behavior because it requires such nicety of neuromuscular coördination. The child learns, to be sure, but mainly that each time he opens his mouth to speak he is likely to be hurt in some fashion, that whenever he is required to speak well he can expect to fail. But he does not learn from this how to correct his errors and speak in a more acceptable fashion.

## DISCOURAGEMENT

As a consequence of the despondency which sometimes results from repeated failure and frustration, the speech difficulty tends to be aggravated. One boy known to the authors developed the habit of mumbling his way as rapidly as possible through all speech situations. When he mumbled, his speech errors were not so apparent. Of course, he was very difficult to understand and his speech was anything but communicative. But he seemed to prefer that kind of failure to making his misarticulated sounds unpleasantly prominent. After all, why not? If one is going to fail anyhow, why not take the least unpleasant form of failure?

Danny, the eleven-year-old previously referred to who had trouble with the articulation of *r*, had become thoroughly convinced that it was completely impossible for him to articulate a normal *r* sound. With tears in his eyes he told the examiner that he knew he couldn't learn to say *r* and he didn't see any use in trying. At first he refused even to make an attempt. When the examiner finally succeeded in winning his confidence, so that he would follow directions concerning placement and movement of his tongue, he produced a fairly good *r* after four or five trials. The tears came to Danny's eyes again, but this time there was a smile to go with them.

An eighteen-year-old girl whose speech problem was complicated by bad dental occlusion was astounded when it was pointed out to her that certain errors were not related to her dental condition at all, and that there was no reason why she couldn't learn to produce those sounds with very little difficulty. She had assumed that, because of her crooked teeth and open bite, she could not possibly improve her faulty articulation and had long ago given up the attempt.

## Treatment of Articulatory Problems

GENERAL EXAMINATION PROCEDURES

The first step in treating an articulatory disorder is to become thoroughly familiar with the individual who has the problem and the exact nature of his difficulty. This statement implies that various examination procedures will be employed. Among those routinely used are speech tests, hearing tests, examination of the articulatory mechanism, intelligence tests, and case history interviews. Neither the classroom teacher nor a speech specialist will necessarily be personally equipped to give all these tests. It may be necessary to call on other agencies for mental testing, hearing tests, etc. It may seem desirable to refer the child for medical or dental examination if there are suspected organic complications.

*Objectives of Examining Procedures.* The purpose of these testing procedures is at least threefold: (1) to obtain a careful description of the speech errors and to learn as much as possible about the factors which seem to be related to them as causes or maintaining conditions; (2) to obtain an estimate of the possible improvement that can be expected; and (3) to make possible an intelligent planning of remedial work. The exact procedures employed will vary considerably with the type and degree of difficulty. With many of the simple articulation cases, in which the sounds affected are few in number and there is no reason to suspect anything beyond faulty learning as a cause, all that may be required is a speech test and a rapid inspection of the mouth to determine if there are any dental, palatal, or other oral deviations to be taken into account in planning remedial instruction. It is usually well, however, to obtain some kind of estimate as to whether the child's hearing falls within normal limits, although a formal audiometer test is not necessarily required. In more serious cases all the above examination procedures may be employed. Even then it may not be possible to put one's finger on the particular conditions which gave rise to the disorder. However, one should be able to get enough information to provide a basis for intelligent planning of a retraining program and to make some reasonable preliminary estimate of the probable improvement.

SPEECH TEST

For most of the examining procedures no detailed description will be included in this section. These materials have, however, been compiled for the reader who may be interested.[8] It is appropriate, however, to take time for some discussion of speech testing at this point.

The most usual procedures for examining an individual's articulation are as follows:

1. Eliciting and observing a carefully controlled sample of the person's spontaneous speech.

2. Noting carefully any articulation errors which occur and recording a description of them.

3. Checking the results of this procedure by observing less formal conversational speech.

4. Determining whether or not the person can imitate, as isolated sounds, those sounds on which he habitually makes errors in test words or running speech.

*Material for Articulation Testing.* The controlled sample of speech required for articulation testing can be elicited in one of two ways. If the child can read with some skill, it is possible to use special test sentences, each of which is constructed to include several examples of one particular sound. For nonreaders, or individuals whose reading is so faulty as to make testing of this sort difficult, pictures can be used. The pictures are selected so

---

[8] A systematic and comprehensive presentation of testing procedures is to be found in W. Johnson, F. L. Darley, and D. C. Spriestersbach, *Diagnostic Manual in Speech Correction,* New York, Harper & Brothers, 1952, which may be used to supplement what is said here and at other places throughout this book concerning testing techniques and evaluative methods used in speech correction.

that their names will contain the sounds to be tested. The child is asked to name the pictures.

Several textbooks contain lists of test sentences. Those given in the *Voice and Articulation Drillbook* by Fairbanks[9] are excellent. Fairbanks gives two complete lists: one to be used with older children and adults who have considerable reading skill; a second and easier list, from the standpoint of vocabulary, which is suitable for children with less reading skill. The usual procedure is to have the person being tested read through the sentences one at a time. The examiner notes each error carefully and records a description of it on a specially prepared form keyed to the test sentences. A form which has been found convenient is included in the *Diagnostic Manual in Speech Correction* referred to in Footnote 8.

A number of picture tests have been prepared in printed form. However, many speech correctionists prefer to make up their own tests by cutting pictures from magazines, children's picture books, and similar materials, and mounting them on cards or in scrapbooks. Preferably such pictures should be colorful, and each one should contain a single dominant center of interest. Names of objects shown in the pictures should, of course, be words within the vocabulary of young children. Instructions for making such a test are to be found in the *Diagnostic Manual in Speech Correction* by Johnson, Darley, and Spriestersbach. Lists of words suitable for such picture testing are given by Fairbanks,[10] Van Riper,[11] and West, Kennedy, and Carr.[12] The usual procedure is simply to make a game of having the child name the pictures, or objects and actions shown in them. "Starter" questions may be helpful in getting the child to say the required words.

It has usually been considered better practice to obtain a sample of the child's spontaneous speech by one of the above

[9] Grant Fairbanks, *Voice and Articulation Drillbook*, New York, Harper & Brothers, 1940, pp. xii-xvii.

[10] Grant Fairbanks, *Voice and Articulation Drillbook*, New York, Harper & Brothers, 1940, pp. xii-xvii.

[11] C. Van Riper, *Speech Correction*, Rev. Ed., New York, Prentice-Hall, Inc., 1954, pp. 176-177.

[12] Robert West, Lou Kennedy, and Anna Carr, *The Rehabilitation of Speech*, New York, Harper & Brothers, Rev. Ed., 1947, Appendix D.

described methods than to ask the child to repeat words spoken by the examiner. The notion has been that in repeating words spoken by the examiner the child might imitate the examiner's speech to the extent that test words may not be articulated in the child's habitual way. As a result errors that would ordinarily occur in his spontaneous speech, when his attention is directed less to how he is producing certain words or sounds and more to what he is saying, might be missed. Two studies which have compared these two methods of eliciting samples of speech from children with articulatory problems have shown some disagreement in their conclusions. Templin[13] compared results obtained by the two methods with preschool age children and concluded that there was little difference in the speech elicited when the child repeated words spoken by the examiner compared to speech elicited by using pictures. On the other hand, Snow and Milisen[14] found rather consistent indications that children in grades one and two and grades seven and eight do produce fewer articulatory errors when imitating the examiner's speech than when the speech is more spontaneous. The difference may be that older children such as those tested by Snow and Milisen are more speech conscious than preschool children usually are. At any rate the present writers favor the picture type of testing because it may give a truer estimate of the child's articulatory patterns and because it usually will be more interesting to the child. Moreover, if well planned, it need be no more time consuming.

Whatever method of testing is used, it should be supplemented by observation of the child's connected, continuous speech. A paragraph of material may be read, or the nonreader may be asked to tell a story about one of the pictures, or his speech may be observed in a brief conversation. Such observation enables the examiner to check on the results of the formal testing, to note whether errors not previously observed tend to occur in

[13] Mildred C. Templin, "Spontaneous Versus Imitated Vocalization in Testing Articulation in Pre-school Children," *Journal of Speech Disorders* (1947), *12*:293-300.
[14] Katherine Snow and Robert Milisen, "The Influence of Oral Versus Pictorial Presentation Upon Articulation Testing Results," *Journal of Speech and Hearing Disorders* (1954), Monograph Supplement 4, 30-36.

connected speech, and to see how consistent the errors tend to be. It also provides opportunity for estimating the overall severity of the problem. Such notations as the following are useful in describing one's overall impressions of the child's speech:

Overall frequency of misarticulations:
   Few errors
   Errors rather numerous
   Many errors
General consistency of misarticulations
   All error sounds misarticulated consistently
   Occasional correct articulation of error sounds
   Frequent correct articulations of error sounds
   No consistent errors—general inaccuracy of articulation
Degree of interference with communication
   No interference
   Slight interference—some listeners might react negatively even though speech is easily understood
   Moderate interference—most listeners would react negatively to speech, though it is usually intelligible
   Extreme interference—speech very hard to understand, if not quite unintelligible.

The last step in articulation testing has been called by Milisen[15] the *Stimulability Test*. Its purpose is to discover the extent to which a child is able to modify his misarticulations when he is strongly stimulated by the correct sound patterns spoken by the examiner. An example will illustrate the procedure.

The examiner instructs the youngster being tested as follows: "I am going to make a certain sound several times. While I am saying the sound you are to listen very carefully and try to hear exactly how it sounds. You are also to watch my face very carefully and try to see exactly how I make it. Do not say anything until I give you the signal. Just listen and watch carefully. After I have made the sound a number of times, I will nod to you, and you are then to try to say the sound in exactly the same way that I did. You are to try it just once."

[15] Robert Milisen, "A Rationale for Articulation Disorders," *Journal of Speech and Hearing Disorders* (1954), Monograph Supplement 4, 6-17.

The examiner then produces the sound being tested several times, for example: sss, sss, sss, sss, sss. The signal is then given for the child to attempt it and the examiner records the result of the child's attempt, i.e., (a) whether a correct sound was produced, (b) any modification in the error that the child made in attempting to articulate the sound correctly, or (c) whether the error remained unmodified.

Several such trials should be given on each sound in isolation and the same procedure should be used to test the result of such stimulation with nonsense syllables and words. Every error sound should be tested in this way. Although this may seem like a rather time-consuming procedure, the information gained will be particularly useful in helping to plan the retraining program and in estimating probable progress. Hence, this part of the testing procedure should not be slighted.[16]

*The Interpretation of Results of Articulation Testing.* Obviously one purpose of an articulation test like that just described is to inventory the child's errors and arrive at a general estimate of the severity of the problem. If properly used, however, the testing procedure can also yield valuable information for planning retraining, and help in providing a basis for estimating probable progress. To begin with, one should discover whether the error is consistent or whether normal examples of the sound are sometimes produced. A number of studies have shown that, particularly in young children, the errors are frequently inconsistent. Moreover, the correct sound productions tend to occur somewhat systematically in particular positions of words and under particular phonetic conditions, e.g., in particular sound combinations or blends.[17] Careful observation of such inconsistent errors may therefore yield information which will be useful in planning retraining procedures. Words in which the sound is usually correctly produced can be extremely helpful in showing the youngster that he can really produce the sound correctly. They also enable him to compare his correct and faulty ways of

---

[16] An excellent explanation of this method and its usefulness in guiding retraining procedure is given by Milisen in the article referred to previously.

[17] D. C. Spriestersbach and J. F. Curtis, "Misarticulation and Discrimination of Speech Sounds," *Quarterly Journal of Speech* (1951), 37:483-491.

producing the sound. These words constitute a "nucleus of correct articulation" from which the correct production of the sound may be transferred to other words.

Another important item of information to be gained from the articulation test is an estimate of the relative ease or difficulty the pupil may experience in trying to correct his various errors. The data showing his consistency or inconsistency of errors are useful in making these estimates, since sounds which are correctly produced part of the time should be more easily corrected than those on which errors are always produced. However, the best indications concerning whether the correction of a sound is likely to prove easy or difficult come from the last step in the articulation testing procedure, testing the child's ability to modify his errors when strongly stimulated by the correct patterns. Sounds which can be rather easily imitated should be comparatively easy to master. Sounds for which at least a fair approximation can be produced will probably be less difficult than those which the child is unable to imitate even approximately.

This information on the relative ease or difficulty to be expected in correcting particular sounds is very important in planning a corrective program. One of the basic decisions to be made in such planning concerns the order in which the various misarticulated sounds are to be worked on. There is very good reason for starting with the easier sounds and progressively working toward those that are most difficult. By so doing the child receives maximum reward and reinforcement from his early efforts and is encouraged to greater efforts as the work progresses. Moreover, to the degree that this order speeds up improvement during the early work the handicapping effects of the speech difficulty are more rapidly minimized.

Another important decision that must be made in planning the retraining program concerns the stage at which the work must be begun for each sound. This will be made clear in the next few pages in which the various stages in the retraining procedure are discussed, but it may be pointed out here that for those sounds which can be imitated successfully under strong stimulation certain early stages of retraining can be considerably short-ened, if not eliminated.

In addition, information gained from the articulation test is of prime importance in estimating the rate of probable improve-ment. Lastly, information of this kind may be useful in evaluating the effect of possible causal factors, such as dental and other oral malformations. If the child sometimes produces a particular sound correctly, or if he can imitate the teacher's correct articulation of it, the organic factor can scarcely be important in preventing correct articulation of that sound at least.

### RETRAINING PROCEDURES FOR ARTICULATORY DISORDER

Obviously procedures will vary somewhat from child to child and from sound to sound. For example, if a child is already able to produce a sound correctly in certain words or under certain phonetic conditions, the situation is not the same as it is if the error is consistent. Also, correctionists differ somewhat in the exact procedures they employ, in much the same way that two teachers of reading may be found to proceed somewhat differ-ently. In general, however, the following outline tends to be followed, more or less closely, by almost all speech correction teachers, largely because it results in a set of graded experiences ranging from relatively simple to relatively complex:

1. Eliminate, or minimize the effect of, factors causing the misarticulation.

2. Create vivid auditory impressions which will enable the child to recognize readily both the error and the correct sound, and to discriminate between the two whenever he hears them.

3. Teach correct production of the sound in isolation.

4. Strengthen the correct production of the sound so that it can be produced easily and at will.

5. Secure transfer of the correct sound into connected speech in a small nucleus of commonly used words.

6. Make the production of the correct sound, instead of the error, habitual in all connected speech.

It will be recognized that this is an outline of subgoals to be accomplished rather than of specific procedures for accomplishing them. Various procedures are employed, some of which will be described in the following paragraphs. Even the goals that need to be accomplished will vary somewhat from one case to another. For example, the child who is keenly aware of his error may recognize it readily whenever it occurs. He may also have a distinct auditory impression of the correct sound and be able to discriminate the correct and incorrect sounds without difficulty. But he may still not be able to make the sound correctly. Provided there is no correctable causal factor still operating, the work with him may begin with Point 3 of the outline.

*Eliminating Causal Factors.* Organic factors which contribute to impaired articulation are, fortunately, often remediable. Crooked and spaced teeth can usually be straightened; jaws can sometimes be brought into proper alignment to correct a markedly bad dental occlusion; tongue-tie can be relieved; and misshapen palates can, to some extent, be repaired. Unfortunately, such dental and surgical reconstruction of faulty articulatory structures is usually expensive, and surgeons and dentists trained in such work are not available in all localities. If possible, however, the speech correctionist will seek medical advice concerning the feasibility of remedying such obstacles to good articulation and, if such work is indicated, will recommend that it be done before speech retraining begins. It should be understood that straightening teeth and realigning jaws does not of itself produce good speech. Error habits will still persist, and the speech correctionist will have an important job to do when the dentist or surgeon has completed his work.

Even when it proves impossible to correct the structural defects which have contributed to the problem, the situation is not hopeless. It has already been stated that such conditions are usually contributory causes, rather than disabling factors, with respect to the speech problem. Many individuals have attained excellent speech in spite of marked, and even severe, abnormalities of the articulatory structures, sometimes with no special speech training. The skilled speech correctionist has learned to make an appraisal of the compensatory movements required to produce particular sounds and to plan a program of retraining which will minimize the effects of structural irregularities. Any detailed consideration of such procedures is, however, beyond the scope of this book.

Environmental factors which may contribute to the speech problem are perhaps more difficult to deal with than are the more tangible organic factors. Longstanding behavior patterns of parents and others with whom the child is in daily contact are less easily changed than crooked teeth. We have seen that these factors are certainly important in some cases and that steps to alter unfavorable influences of this sort contribute materially to rapid improvement in speech.

Although the counseling of parents is sometimes difficult, takes considerable time, and may in some cases better be done by a psychiatrist or psychologist than by a speech correction teacher, much can be done which will be helpful in most instances. Some parents may resent what they regard as undue interference, but they will be relatively few. Parents are mostly well-intentioned persons who have a great deal of love and affection for their children. The difficulty is that they sometimes do not understand the problems their children face. Their well-intentioned efforts to help are sometimes misdirected. Moreover, parents are often extremely busy folks. Their time is usually filled with a host of adult activities which keep them on the go from morning till night. Absorbed in their own interests, they are sometimes neglectful or impatient of their children without the slightest intention of being so—indeed, without knowing that they are. The conscientious speech correctionist will, therefore, make a point of seeing the parents of the children with whom she works. If she is skillful she may help them to a much better understanding of the problem, how it came about, and the kind of conditions at home which will be most conducive to improvement. If at all possible, she will enlist their coöperation, because at certain stages of the correction process home coöperation is extremely important in helping the child to establish firmly the new habits he is learning.

*Ear Training.*    In Chapter II it was suggested that the speech

mechanism is an instrument which we learn to "play by ear." If
one were to try to pick out a tune on the piano by ear and had
no clear impression of how it should sound, it would be strange,
indeed, if the result obtained turned out to be faultless. Yet that
is almost exactly the situation of many persons with articulatory
problems. They do not have a clear auditory impression of what
the correct sounds should be or how they differ from their errors.
The little youngster who says, "*One, two, free, . . .*" is often quite
oblivious of the fact that he has made an error. He has no
clear auditory impressions of *f* and *th* as distinct and separate
sounds. That this is true is further demonstrated when he tells
about the "*thish*" he had for lunch. As a matter of fact, these
sounds, along with a number of pairs of other sounds, such as *s*
and *th*, *s* and *f*, *sh* and *ch*, *t* and *k*, and *d* and *g*, are highly similar
in their sound characteristics, so similar that even adults may
confuse them when listening under noisy conditions, or when
their attention is distracted. After all, that is why people sometimes misunderstand what is said to them. It is hardly surprising,
therefore, that the similarities between such sounds seem so striking to the untrained ear of a young child as to obscure the
rather slight differences. It is lack of awareness of this fact
that foredooms to failure many of the efforts of untrained
teachers and parents to correct the child's errors.

"You mustn't say *twick*, Margie," pleads the anxious mother.
"Say quick!" And Margie, who hears no real distinction between
the two, tries again, and says "*Twick*," and is surprised, or
puzzled, or hurt when her mother responds, "No, no, no, not
*twick*. Try it again."

Essentially the same sort of failure to make fine auditory
discriminations may underlie many of the youngster's distortions
and omissions of sound. The distortions sound correct to his ears.
The omissions occur most frequently in positions where the
omitted sounds tend to be obscure anyhow, and to the child's
ear it is possible that no distinctive characteristic of the word
has been lost.

This means that with a large number of cases—some authorities
go so far as to say all—teaching the child to produce the correct

sound must be preceded by some systematic ear training. Before attempting to play, one must get the tune "inside one's head."

The problem is further complicated by the fact that very few people except speech correctionists, phoneticians, and teachers of phonics ever pay much attention to speech sounds as such. We don't listen to a series of connected sounds; we listen to words, or phrases, or sentences. For most of us, adults as well as children, the speech sound is not an entity, a meaningful unit of any sort, and we don't hear it as an entity. Nor do we very often learn it as an entity. What we hear, and what we learn, are words, and the individual speech sounds which make up those words are for the most part somewhat amorphous and un-differentiated pieces of the whole complex auditory pattern.

Hence, the child not only needs to learn to make auditory discriminations which he has never made before, but he needs to learn to break down these word patterns, at least to the extent of being able to recognize, out of the word pattern, those sounds on which he tends to make errors. And eventually he needs to eliminate that error part of his word habit in order that a correctly formed sound may be substituted in its place. The speech correctionist, therefore, spends some time in ear training as one important part of the corrective procedure. The exact amount of time to be spent in such ear training work will vary, of course, for different individuals. The child must attain certain minimum goals before he is prepared to attempt to produce correct sounds.

1. *He should learn to break down the word patterns containing his error, in at least a number of commonly used words, so that the error is recognized and isolated as a distinctive sound unit in those words.*

Among the procedures used for this purpose are the following:

a. Lists of words are read by the teacher. Some contain the difficult sounds and some do not. The child signals each time he hears a word containing the sound. Score may be kept by counting one for each correct recognition of a word containing the sound and subtracting one for each miss. Progress can thus be charted.

b. A scrapbook can be made of pictures of objects whose

names contain the sound. The name, with the difficult sound underlined or printed in red, is written below each picture.

c. A hide-and-seek game may be played in which pictures or objects whose names contain the difficult sound are hidden in the room along with other pictures and objects whose names do not contain the sound. The child is to find as many as he can and place them in separate piles. He is given points for each one found and placed in the proper pile, and points are subtracted for each one placed in the wrong pile.

d. Older children and adults may be assigned to underline all words in a paragraph which contain the difficult sound, to mark all such words in a list, and so forth.

2. *He should learn to recognize and identify the error sound and the correct sound as separate entities, and be able to discriminate between them easily.*

Following are examples of the kinds of procedures used to accomplish this goal.

a. Both the error sound and the correct sound may be given names. For the child the sound can be associated with animals, or objects which make noises, so that *z* may become the buzzing bee sound, *s* may be the punctured tire sound, *r* may be the car starting sound (made by the grinding noise when the starter button is depressed), *ch* may be the train sound, *f* may be the angry cat sound, etc. The main importance of these names is in reinforcing the auditory image of each sound and making it as vivid as possible. Even with older children and adults, names for the sounds seem to facilitate the learning process, so that the *s* lisper may have his error named as the *whistling s* or the *hishing s*, whereas the correct sound is called a *sharp clear s*.

b. If the error is one that the correctionist can simulate (and the skilled correctionist will develop a considerable facility at this), practice can be given in discriminating between the error and correct production of the sound. The teacher reads lists of words, in some of which the error is simulated, or reads a story in which the error is produced part of the time. The child is required to listen carefully for each sound error and signal each time one is heard.

c. If recording equipment is available, the student and the speech correction teacher can record lists of words together, the student reading the word and making his error, and the teacher repeating the same word with the sound made correctly. On playback the student listens carefully and compares the sound of his word with that of the teacher. Older children and adults may be required to write reports of such listening experiences, in which they describe as exactly as possible the characteristics of the two sounds as they heard them and the differences which they were able to hear.

d. Sometimes a child will detect an error in the speech of another child but fail to hear the same error in his own speech. Recordings can prove very helpful in a case of this kind. Both persons who make the error can be recorded, together with the teacher or some other person who produces the sound correctly. When listening to the record the child can hear that he really does make the same error he had noticed in the other person, and how different the speech of both of them sounds from the person whose speech is free of the error.

The above are only a few suggestions to illustrate procedures used in ear training. Throughout the child is constantly stimulated with the correct example of the sound. He hears it and hears it many times. He is learning the tune that he is about to be asked to attempt to play, so to speak. The goal is for him to learn it so well that there will no longer be frustration or puzzlement resulting from uncertainty or confusion as to the result he is trying to produce. This goal may not be completely realized at this stage. Ear training does not terminate with the beginning of the next step. In fact it will permeate the whole retraining process from beginning to end. But a long stride should have been taken before actual correct sound production is attempted.

*Teaching a New Sound.* Before the correct sound can be produced in rapid connected speech, and the old error can be eradicated, the sound must be thoroughly mastered as an isolated element separate and apart from the complex pattern of words. If the child can demonstrate this mastery, then, as we have said, it is a stage in the retraining process that can be correspondingly shortened or eliminated. Otherwise, it will need to be duly emphasized.

At first glance this may seem to be in contradiction to what we have previously said, since it has been pointed out that speech is not ordinarily learned by sound elements, but rather that we learn word patterns as wholes, with no conscious attention to the sound elements from which they are compounded. Nevertheless, the best opinion is that in correcting speech *errors,* the sound must first be taught in isolation, as an entity. Not until the pupil has thoroughly mastered it as a separate sound, so that he can produce it easily and at will, will he be ready to incorporate it into words and connected discourse. So long as a great deal of effort and attention are required to insure the correct production of the sound, it cannot be incorporated in the rapid flow of continuous speech. The child who has to stop and think exactly how to produce a particular sound, before each word containing that sound may be spoken, might indeed be likened to the centipede whose attempt to walk failed utterly because he tried to decide which leg should be moved first. Before the whole tune can be played by ear, the difficult passages must be thoroughly mastered.

An even more compelling reason why sounds need first to be thoroughly learned out of the context of familiar words stems directly from the fact that learning to talk is a matter of learning word habits. Since that is true, we can expect those word habits which have been in the speech repertory of the person for any considerable length of time to be firmly established. Such word patterns are not only unitary auditory wholes; they are, also, strongly established patterns of movement. We cannot expect success in breaking down such strongly entrenched patterns, so that we may extract from the total pattern one of its lesser elements and replace it with a new one, unless the new element is itself thoroughly learned. Even with errors which are produced inconsistently, so that the correct sound is really a part of the individual's speech repertory, some practice on the sound in isolation and in simple syllable combinations may be needed before it can be transferred to words for which a strongly entrenched error habit pattern already exists. In this case, however, the time spent in such practice will as a rule be greatly shortened.

There are a number of different methods for teaching a new sound, of which only a few will be presented. The ones described are the most basic and the most commonly used.

*The Stimulus Method.* The most basic tool in the speech correctionist's kit is the so-called "stimulus method." It is the one method which is always employed. Although the stimulus method has long been used by speech correctionists, only recently has there been any substantial research to evaluate its effectiveness. Milisen and certain of his students have reported a number of experiments in which they tested the general effectiveness of the basic stimulus method as well as certain variations of it.[18] In general their results support the clinical consensus that new speech habits can be effectively taught by the procedures employed in this method. In addition, these studies have demonstrated that, while either auditory stimulation or visual stimulation is effective in some degree, neither is as effective as combined auditory-visual stimulation or, as Milisen prefers to call it, integral stimulation. In the discussion that follows, the stimulus method which will be discussed makes use of this combined auditory-visual stimulation. As a matter of fact, the main essentials of this method have already been described, as the last step

[18] Davis A. Scott and Robert Milisen, "The Effect of Visual, Auditory and Combined Visual-Auditory Stimulation Upon the Speech Responses of Defective Speaking Children," *Journal of Speech and Hearing Disorders* (1954), Supplement 4, 38-43; Davis A. Scott and Robert Milisen, "The Effectiveness of Visual-Auditory Stimulation in Improving Articulation," *loc. cit.*, 52-56; William R. Humphrey and Robert Milisen, "A Study of the Ability to Reproduce Unfamiliar Sounds Which Have Been Presented Orally," *loc. cit.*, 58-69; Edward F. Romans and Robert Milisen, "Effect of Latency Between Stimulation and Response on Reproduction of Sounds," *loc. cit.*, 72-78; Donald B. Rice and Robert Milisen, "The Influence of Increased Stimulation Upon the Production of Unfamiliar Sounds as a Function of Time," *loc. cit.*, 80-86.

in the articulation testing process, where the examiner tests the child's ability to imitate a correct sound when given a strong auditory and visual pattern to follow. The procedure used in training is somewhat as follows:

"All right, Betty, we're going to give you a chance to try to make the new sound. First, I will say it several times and you must watch me very closely and listen as carefully as you can. When I nod my head, you try it once. Remember, you aren't going to make the old 'slurpy *s*' this time. You are going to try to get a sharp, clear *s*. All right, here we go: *sss, sss, sss, sss, sss.*"

Teacher nods and pupil makes an attempt to produce the sound.

In many cases, if the ear training has been adequate, the pupil will need only a few trials to produce a good example of the sound, particularly if there is no complicating organic factor. Each trial should be followed by some comment by the teacher to indicate the degree of success in attaining the desired response. She should keep the pupil encouraged but should not reward, by calling it a success, a sound which is only a fair approximation to the one desired. Such a comment would only confuse the pupil and make him uncertain as to exactly what he is supposed to do. If the ear training has been well done, he will be pretty sure without being told when he has produced a good example.

Throughout this work with the stimulus method the pupil should be kept from becoming tense and trying to force out the sound. He should be encouraged to vary slightly his tongue positions and contacts or other articulatory movements, in an effort to find the correct method of producing the sound, but all attempts should be kept easy and relaxed. At all times attention should be focused both on the auditory result and on the visual cues which can be seen by closely watching the teacher's face. If, following a number of trials, the child does not succeed in making a good sound, or at least a close approximation to one, the attempt should be dropped for the moment, and teacher and pupil should go back and review the ear training work before trying again.

The stimulus method has a number of distinct advantages.

First, it is the simplest and easiest to use. Second, it is the most direct of all the methods. That is, it is a direct attempt at *playing by ear.* The pupil is trying to produce a particular auditory result, without the mediation of some other kinds of cues, such as thinking about what he is doing with his tongue. As a result of this direct auditory approach, the result obtained through the stimulus method is usually more stable, right from the start, than sounds taught by other procedures. Third, no distracting stimuli or irrelevant cues are introduced.

Perhaps the extreme case of such irrelevant cues is found in the method whereby the teacher actually manipulates the articulatory structures. For example, a tooth prop may be used to keep the jaws apart while the teacher guides the movement of the tongue with a wooden tongue blade. It would be hard to conceive of a more artificial method than this of getting a child to produce a sound. No one talks by having his jaw propped open and his tongue shoved around. Even if pupil and teacher succeed in getting a good sound in this way, there is no assurance that the sound can be made when the prop is removed. Moreover, the child's attention is distracted by all manner of irrelevant stimuli—the feel of his jaw propped open, the sensations associated with having his tongue guided or pushed. When he is trying to attend to what happens during production of a sound, he is attending to a whole stimulating situation. If the artificial and irrelevant stimuli from the tooth prop and tongue blade are then removed, the whole stimulating situation is changed. And there is no sound reason to expect that the new stimulus situation, minus tooth prop and tongue blade, will evoke the desired response. For these reasons, such corrective procedures have little place in modern speech correction. Of all methods used, the stimulus method is, perhaps, the most free from such disadvantages.

The stimulus method should be thoroughly mastered by the correctionist for another reason. This is that auditory stimulation, like ear training, permeates all speech correction. Whatever else the correctionist does in an attempt to change the patterns of the child's speech, she continues to bombard his ear with the correct sound. This is of the most fundamental importance because, whatever method may be used to teach the new sound in the beginning, the pupil must, sooner or later, arrive at the stage where he can depend on his ear to tell him whether or not the result has been adequate. Hence the stimulus method is not only the most basic tool in the speech correctionist's kit but also the only one which is used with every case and which is used in one way or another throughout the whole process.

*Phonetic Placement.* As here used, the term "phonetic placement" covers all procedures by which the correctionist directs the attention of the child toward what he is doing with his tongue, lips, jaws, etc. There are many such procedures, but they vary mainly in detail. Underlying all of them is the basic principle of having the student attend to, and consciously attempt to control, the movements and positioning of the articulatory structures. A number of typical phonetic placement procedures are as follows:

1. In mirror work both the pupil and the teacher watch the mirror as they work on the sound. The pupil observes carefully what the teacher does in producing the correct sound and then tries to imitate her.

2. Diagrams or pictures showing tongue, lip, and jaw placement for various sounds may be used to show the child what to do. For young children a drawing of a child with his upper teeth on his lower lip may be called the *f* sound picture or the *v* sound picture. Another picture showing just a little of the tongue between the slightly parted front teeth can be called the *th* picture. Names can be given to the persons in the pictures also, in which the sound is employed; for example, the boy in the *f* picture can be named *Freddy*, while the one in the *th* picture may be *Theodore*.

3. For older children and adults, models as well as diagrams may be employed to show them where to place the tongue.

4. The simplest and most common phonetic placement procedure is a simple verbal instruction as to what to do with the tongue; the student attempts to follow this instruction while he feels, through tactile and kinesthetic cues, what is happening.

5. A special type of phonetic placement technique is that of having the pupil modify slightly the tongue position for sounds that he can already produce. It has been found that some sounds may be more easily produced in certain consonant blends than by themselves. For example, the blends *dr* and *tr* have been found to be produced correctly more often in the speech of young children[19] than is the *r* when it occurs as a single consonant. This suggests that one method of teaching *r* is to have the pupil place his tongue as for *d* and then retract it slightly at the same time dropping the tip. He will, of course, be given auditory stimulation simultaneously. Once he has mastered the *dr*, other blends, such as *tr, thr, kr,* and *gr,* may be tried, and finally the sound by itself after the tongue position has been thoroughly learned in these blends. This is a reversal of the usual procedure of teaching the sound in isolation before attempting it in blends, but it has good research evidence to support it.

Phonetic placement procedures have some of the disadvantages that were discussed a few paragraphs back. That is, they are less direct, because they focus attention on features of the sound other than the auditory pattern, which is a major part of the end result being sought. As a consequence, sounds taught through phonetic placement methods probably tend to be less stable at first than those obtained through the stimulus method alone, and they need to be strengthened and reinforced immediately. However, phonetic placement procedures are essential to the correctionist. By avoiding actual manipulation of the structures, the correctionist will escape most of the serious disadvantages previously mentioned. By using the techniques properly it will sometimes be possible to teach a new sound rather easily by phonetic placement, whereas it would be difficult to do if only auditory stimulation were employed. This is particularly true for the occasional speech handicapped child who seems to have only a few stereotyped tongue movements with which he tries to

[19] M. W. Buck, "A Study of the Misarticulation of [r] in Children from Kindergarten Through Third Grade," M.A. thesis, State University of Iowa, 1948. The findings of this study are summarized and discussed within a comprehensive context of related data and theoretical considerations in Spriestersbach and Curtis, *op. cit.*

produce all sounds. With such a case it is usually necessary to give some actual direction with respect to tongue placement as well as some exercises designed to help him learn to make the desired movements easily.

Another type of case with which phonetic placement procedures are nearly always required is that in which the sounds cannot be produced in the normal fashion because of complicating structural deformities, such as malocclusion. Here compensatory movements may need to be taught. That is, the child may need to learn a method of sound production which compensates or allows for his organic handicap, so that a good sound is produced in spite of it. Such compensatory movements are usually most efficiently taught if the correctionist analyzes carefully the possible ways in which the faulty mechanism can be used to produce the desired auditory result, and then directs the efforts of the pupil accordingly.

Other methods of teaching a new sound that are sometimes used are discussed in the speech correction textbooks listed in the Appendix. However, the above two, stimulus method and phonetic placement, are sufficient for our present purposes, since they are certainly the ones which the public school speech correctionist will employ with almost all cases.

*Reinforcing the New Sound.* In the previous section it was explained that sounds need to be taught as sounds, in isolation, rather than in words. The reason for this is that the child will usually have strongly established word habits, and the error has long been an automatic part of these movement patterns. Such an automatic response cannot be replaced by a new one which is not thoroughly learned.

Not infrequently it is at this point that the parent or teacher who has not had special training becomes too impatient and spoils things because of failure to realize the need to "make haste slowly." Unless gifted with unusual insight into the process that is taking place, it will seem to the untrained parent or teacher that eight-year-old Eddie, who has just said *r-r-r* so clearly, ought now to be able to say "rabbit." And she therefore feels dis-

couraged when she asks him to try, and he obligingly responds
with "wabbit."

The fact is, of course, that the new response has not been
thoroughly enough established as yet to be able to compete on
anything like even terms with the thoroughly overlearned *w*
movement in the whole habit pattern, *wabbit.*

*Practice on Isolated Sounds.* Most trained correctionists, therefore, give every child a substantial amount of practice in producing each new sound in isolation and in nonsense syllables before
any attempt is made to put it into words—unless, of course, the
child is definitely able to do these things sufficiently well. The
youngster is asked to produce the sound many times by itself,
until he can do it easily and consistently, without a great amount
of consciously directed effort. He may be asked to vary the loudness with which he makes the new sound so that he learns to
produce it correctly throughout the whole range from very soft to
very loud. He will be asked to attend carefully to the feel of the
sound. Thus, he uses tactile and kinesthetic sensations of touch
and movement, as well as auditory cues, in forming a clear awareness of the sound. Practice should be strongly motivated. Older
children and adults are motivated, in part at least, by understanding the reason for the practice, but usually learning will be
speeded up by some method of charting progress which will
act as an additional reward. With small children numerous
games can be invented to keep the drill from becoming irk-
some and to provide motivation. One which is in almost every
correctionist's bag of tricks, and which never seems to fail to
challenge a small child, is the "ladder game."

A *speech ladder* is cut from cardboard or drawn on a large
sheet of paper. The child climbs and descends the ladder by
correctly saying the sound on which he is practicing. As the
child speaks the sounds the teacher points with her pencil
to the appropriate rung on the ladder—or the youngster is
allowed to move a button or other object up the ladder—moving
up one rung for each successful production of the sound and
back one rung for each error. The object is, of course, to reach
the top of the ladder, and progress can be charted according to

the number of times the ladder is climbed without having to drop back a single step. This game can be used with isolated sounds or nonsense syllables or words.

*Use of Nonsense Material.* Nonsense syllables make excellent practice material at this stage for two principal reasons: (1) They provide practice material in which the newly learned sound can be combined with other sounds in a rapid sequence of movements, as in ordinary meaningful speech. (2) They do not, however, involve many of the difficulties of words, since they can be kept as simple as may be necessary and *since they are not highly practiced habit patterns in which the new sound will have to compete with a strongly entrenched error.* Nonsense syllables can be built up by combining the newly learned sound (ordinarily a consonant) with any of the common vowels and diphthongs.

The way in which this practice proceeds can be illustrated by nonsense syllables formed with the consonant *s* and the vowel *o*. In this illustration a repeated symbol indicates that the sound is prolonged. Dashes indicate very brief pauses.

1. Consonant in the initial position (preceding the vowel): *ssss–oooo; s–s–s–o; s–o; sssooo; so.*

2. Consonant in the final position (following the vowel): *oooo–ssss; o–s–s; o–s; ooosss; os.*

3. Consonant in the medial position: *ooo–sss–ooo; o–s–s–s–o; o–s–o; ooosssooo; oso.*

It may be seen that the syllables are built up gradually. The sounds are first repeated or prolonged as separate units before the child is asked to blend them together. The last production of each should be spoken rapidly with no more duration for each sound than it would have in normal running speech.

Like the isolated sound practice, this nonsense syllable practice needs to be strongly motivated. The same types of games and other motivational devices can be used for both.

*Negative Practice.* Once the sound is well mastered, so that it can be produced with reasonably good consistency in isolation and in nonsense syllables, a type of drill sometimes called *negative practice* can be very valuable. Negative practice consists in producing the *error* itself, but in such a way that the error habit is weakened, not strengthened, by the process. This weakening will occur if the error is penalized rather than rewarded each time it is spoken. The error will be penalized if the child produces it with full knowledge that the sound he is making is the one that he is to avoid in his ordinary speech. Various devices can be used to reinforce the knowledge that this is the sound to be rejected. The error can be represented in written spelling, or some other symbol, and crossed out with a pencil each time it is produced. A thumbs down-thumbs up game can be played in which the pupil and teacher turn thumbs down each time the error is produced and thumbs up for each production of the correct sound.

Negative practice is usually best used in a drill procedure in which the pupil alternates the production of the correct sound and the error sound. Such voluntary, intentional alternating of the two sounds not only reinforces the auditory discrimination between the two but also provides an opportunity to learn the differences in the way they *feel*. The teacher can focus the pupil's attention on these differences by asking him to describe in his own words the ways in which the two sounds feel different. For sounds like the *th* and *f*, which are easily visible, mirror work may be used to provide visual cues.

As was stated in beginning the discussion of negative practice, its use requires full knowledge on the part of the pupil concerning what he is doing and why he is doing it. The error sound must be produced voluntarily and intentionally, and with the attitude that it is an error which is not to be made in ordinary talking. Practice of the error without such thorough knowledge and understanding of the process is not *negative practice*. Obviously, therefore, the practice must be preceded by a very careful explanation by the teacher of the reasons for using this type of drill. If it is unlikely that the pupil will be able to grasp the purpose and need of the drill, it is probably best not to use it. This will sometimes be true for younger children. If it is used correctly, however, with complete understanding by both teacher and pupil, it is a powerful tool both to strengthen the correct sound and to weaken the error.

*Putting the New Sound into Words.* If the preceding goals have been adequately accomplished, no real difficulty should be experienced in putting the new sound into words. If failures in attempting words are at all numerous, it means that more work must be done to (1) reinforce and strengthen the correct sound habit, (2) weaken the error habit, and (3) establish the essential auditory discrimination. If this should happen, therefore, the speech correction teacher will go back to these earlier stages of the work and provide additional training. As a matter of fact, the skilled speech correction teacher will probably not have stopped the training begun in these earlier meetings with the pupil. Each speech correction period will usually begin with a brief review of the earlier work and further reinforcement of the good habits previously acquired.

Transfer of the new sound to words can be accomplished by the use of word lists or, for the nonreading child, series of pictures whose names contain the sound. The attempt on each word should be preceded by strong stimulation by the teacher. That is, before the pupil attempts the word, the teacher will repeat it several times, using the correct sound, while the pupil watches and listens carefully. And this stimulation should be repeated each time the word is attempted, until the new word pattern has become fairly easy for the child to produce. Failures should be pointed out to the child and successes should be rewarded. Usually following a failure it is well to practice the sound a few times in isolation, or in nonsense syllables, before the word is attempted again.

Practice on words should begin with a few familiar words which the child will have occasion to use over and over again in his daily communication. Tongue twisters may be all right in parlor games but they have no place in speech correction. They usually involve too many productions of a sound, in insufficiently varied phonetic contexts, in rapid succession. Moreover, as word practice goes on new words may be added to the practice lists, but common sense dictates that they should be words included in the pupil's ordinary speaking vocabulary and that unusual words which he will rarely use make poor practice material.

It should be emphasized that the goal of word practice is

easy, effortless production of the sound in each word. Ordinary
speech is a rapid, fleeting thing. In normal speech there is no
slow, labored sound production. Hence, the goal of word practice
has not been reached until the sound has been made a part of
the same effortless, rapid sequence of movements that character-
izes the word in normal patterns of connected speech.

*Transfer to a Few Commonly Used Words in Connected
Speech.* When a few commonly used words have been mastered
so that the correct sound can be produced in them easily and
without hesitation, the transfer to connected speech may be begun. The importance of this stage of the retraining process cannot
be overstressed. All too often the pupil comes to regard speech
work as something he does only in special speech periods and in a
few outside assignments. The goal of this step is to begin to
bridge the gap between the speech that the pupil can and does
produce in his speech correction lessons and what he usually does
in his everyday talking.

Various kinds of assignments can be used to assist in this
process. Some of these will be described. Certain basic ideas
should be kept constantly in mind, however, no matter what
specific assignments may be given.

1. No one, adult or child, can be expected to maintain a constant police watch on his speech throughout all the varied activities of his day. Hence, the assignments used to incorporate new
habits in connected speech should be made for specific periods of
time and for particular situations.

2. No child can make the transfer to all words in his speech
at once. Hence, the emphasis should be on transfer to a few
commonly used words. Later, after these limited objectives are
accomplished, there will be time enough to eradicate the error
whenever and wherever it occurs and replace it with the good
habit.

3. Here, almost more than in any other step of the procedure,
the emphasis on thorough ear training should pay dividends. If
adequate ear training has been distributed throughout the previous work, the pupil should experience little difficulty in distinguishing between his error sound and a correct production

of the sound, even during the rapid flow of connected speech. If he cannot do this, the ear training has been incomplete. If he is to go on to the next step, that of stamping out all occurrences of the error and replacing them with correct sounds, he must be able to detect all occurrences of the error. Hence, ear training does not terminate at this point but is an important part of the entire transfer process.

4. This stage of the speech correction process is where parents and other teachers can begin to be of most direct assistance. The speech correction teacher will ordinarily enlist their coöperation in helping the pupil to carry out assignments and in making reports concerning his success in completing assignments.

*Use of Nucleus Situations.* The use of nucleus situations has been suggested by Van Riper.[20] As was pointed out above, no one can be expected to keep a constant watch on his own speech, nor does he like to have some other person nag at him constantly about his errors. The writers know of one child whose mother interrupted his speech at any and all times to remonstrate concerning an error and to drill him then and there on the correct sound. The boy had become so apprehensive about talking that he had begun to develop some of the straining and forcing characteristics that are associated with stuttering. It is much wiser, at first, to attempt to transfer the new, correct habit into casual speech only in a few situations.

A strong word of caution is necessary, however. Nucleus situations can become highly artificial and very distasteful to the youngsters for whom they are planned. They should not be employed rigidly and unreasonably. If mealtimes are used for speech correction, feeding problems can result. In general, school situations are probably better for the purpose than home situations are. With such cautions as these, the use of nucleus situations for the setting of new speech habits can be advantageous in many cases.

Anyone with a bit of ingenuity can think of a number of situations which can be used for this purpose. For a younger child they can usually be ones in which another person can check on

[20] *Op. cit.*

his success in carrying out the particular assignment of the moment and report back to the speech correction teacher. A few examples of such situations and assignments follow.

1. With a child who has the daily task of helping mother with washing the dishes or getting the family meals, these opportunities for conversation can be used as *good speech* situations, provivided the parent is one who can develop the necessary feeling of relationship with the youngster and understand clearly the objectives and the method. Topics of conversation can be planned by the teacher and pupil, and words or phrases likely to occur can be used as practice material. It will usually be better, also, if some specific assignment is planned. For example, the correctionist and the pupil can plan for him to tell about some interesting happening at school, the telling of which will require the use of two or three words on which they have been practicing. (Or some of the phrases or sentences he will need to use can be made practice material for the day's speech lesson.) A note to the mother may ask her to listen to check on the success the child has in using the particular words on which he is working, and to send back a report.

2. Many families have an evening story hour. Even where that has not been a custom of long standing, parents will probably be willing to start it if they can be shown that it will help their child's speech. This situation will provide many opportunities for speech practice. Stories can be prepared by the child either to be read or to be told. The teacher can help select stories which will provide practice on words and sounds being taught, and can provide practice in the speech period to prepare for the correct use of these sounds when the time actually comes.

3. If the child often goes shopping with the mother another *good speech* situation can be provided, if the mother can be persuaded to allow the child to ask questions of the clerk, check prices, and the like, while she stands by and checks on the use of sounds in words which have been practiced. The various items on the shopping list will provide practice for almost any sound the child may be learning. As before, these words and phrases

should usually be practiced in the speech lesson before an assignment is given involving an actual situation.

4. The schoolroom, as has been suggested, should provide even more and better nucleus speech situations than does the home. How effectively they are utilized will be quite as much up to the classroom teacher as it will be up to the speech correctionist. For example, the classroom teacher can let the speech correctionist know when oral reports are to be given. If she has this information in advance the speech correction teacher can then show the pupil how to use this oral report as a chance to transfer new sound habits to connected speech.

5. If the classroom teacher can inform the speech correctionist when a class discussion is to be held on a particular topic, the speech correctionist may be able to utilize the information by having speech handicapped pupils from this class use, as practice materials, words, phrases, and sentences which are likely to occur in such a discussion.

6. The classroom teacher will usually be kept informed by the speech correctionist concerning sounds and words on which pupils from her class may be working. Many opportunities for practice on these sounds and words, other than those suggested above, will occur in real speaking situations. It is to be remembered, however, that correction of errors should be confined to specific situations in which the pupil knows he is going to be checked. Also, the correction should generally be limited to particular words in which he is learning to establish the new habit.

*Nucleus Words and Phrases.* It has been pointed out that the goals at this stage of the work should be kept limited so that the pupil may reasonably be expected to achieve them. This applies to words as well as situations, as should be clear from some of the specific suggestions for assignments. It is a good rule to try first to secure transfer of the new sound habit to those words and phrases which the child has need to use most often. Not too many should be attempted at one time. Experience has shown that if the correct sound can be firmly established in a relatively few commonly used words, and be rewarded so that satisfaction is derived from this limited success, the good habit will usually spread to other words in which the error had formerly occurred and will generally be used in new words as they are learned. Previous discussion has already indicated some of the ways in which nucleus words may be chosen. Other words and phrases which may be utilized are:

1. Greetings: hello, good morning, good afternoon, how do you do, etc.

2. Phrases used upon leave-taking: good-by, I had a very nice time, etc.

3. Words and phrases used as courtesies: thank you, if you please, you're welcome, yes, please, etc.

4. Names of friends and associates containing the difficult sound.

5. Frequent requests that the child is called on to make (he will have to ask permission for many things every day).

Many of the things just suggested are stereotyped phrases used over and over again by everyone, day in and day out. Hence, they make excellent material with which to begin the transition of a new sound into casual everyday speech.

*Completing Eradication of the Error.*   As has been indicated above, the biggest job in securing transfer of a new sound habit into ordinary speech is to provide situations and practice which will insure its consistent use in a few commonly used words and in a few nucleus situations. If the correct habit, as thus employed, is regularly rewarded, it will tend to spread to other words and other situations. With young children this is often all that is required. With older children, whose errors are usually more strongly entrenched, some assistance to this process is usually given with assignments of the type suggested in the following paragraphs.

*Continued Ear Training.*   It has already been suggested that ear training becomes most important when the pupil must be relied on to maintain a check on his own errors in rapid connected speech. Some ear training techniques are particularly adapted to these connected speech situations.

1. The teacher, or the pupil, can read aloud a paragraph and

the pupil can check or underline every word in which the difficult sound occurs.

2. The teacher can read paragraph material, occasionally imitating the error. The pupil is to check every occurrence of the error.

3. The pupil may be assigned to observe the speech of another person which contains a similar error and record all the errors he hears during a particular time.

4. If a tape recorder is available, recordings can be made during which the pupil is to stop each time he realizes he has made an error, say the word correctly three times, and then go on. On listening to the playback of the record he can check on whether any errors occurred that he was not aware of when he was talking.

5. If no recording equipment is available, somewhat the same sort of practice can be given if the teacher makes a note of all errors that the pupil failed to catch and calls his attention to them at the end. Part of the value of the practice is lost, however, if the pupil cannot hear his own errors, as on playback of a recording.

*Penalizing the Error.* The error will tend to be eradicated more rapidly if it is penalized rather frequently. What is meant here is not that someone should act as a constant proctor of the child's speech and pull him up short each time an error occurs. As has been emphasized, such nagging is to be avoided. Limited doses of checking by parents or teachers may be necessary, but it should be done, if at all, in a genuinely friendly manner. The goal is for the pupil to learn to recognize his own errors and provide the penalties himself. The penalty can be almost any device which will tend to make the occurrence of the error more vivid. Its main function is to increase awareness of the error, which should itself come to act as the real penalty.

1. A pair of toy telephones can be used with which the pupil makes a call to the teacher across the room. If the pupil catches himself in an error he stops, says, "Oh, oh!," corrects the error, and goes on. If the teacher hears an error that the pupil fails to catch, she hangs up.

2. The pupil may be required to carry a card and a pencil during a particular time, and make a mark on the card each time he catches himself in an error.

3. The pupil can be required to collect a list of words on which he either catches himself in an error or someone else catches him in an error, in such nucleus situations as those previously suggested. He can then be assigned to use these words in negative practice assignments in which he deliberately and intentionally makes the error.

*Negative Practice.*    Other uses may be made of negative practice in addition to those suggested above. The pupil may be given an assignment to employ negative practice during the whole of one of the nucleus situations, or with respect to particular words. An older child or adult may be assigned to use negative practice on particular words in a series of assigned telephone conversations, or in visiting stores and asking prices and other information about merchandise. The student should be required to make a definite report on success in carrying out such assignments.

Negative practice assignments like these can be valuable in helping to complete the process of transfer of the new habit to ordinary casual speech. They tend to make the pupil highly aware of his errors so that he can eradicate them. If the pupil understands the purposes of the assignments there is no danger that the error habit will be strengthened rather than weakened.

Probably the only risk in such assignments is that the pupil might find them psychologically disturbing. He may be reluctant to exhibit his error deliberately in public, even though he has made the same error many times before. However, no undue embarrassment should occur if he is carefully prepared for the assignment.

GENERAL CONSIDERATIONS

The preceding pages have presented a rather complete description of the general process of correcting errors of articulation. This description has been mainly organized around goals to be accomplished at various stages of the process. The specific techniques for reaching the goals may vary considerably from one case to another; the ones described are only suggestive, more are presented in Chapter IX, and the ingenious teacher will be able to devise many interesting and worth-while variations and improvements. But the goals stated here are believed to be the basic ones.

In concluding this description of the process of correcting articulatory disorders certain specific questions which have not previously been fully considered will be discussed.

*Order of Teaching Sounds.* One of the questions on which there has been some argument among authorities in speech correction is the question of the most appropriate order for teaching the various sounds which the child misarticulates. A preference has been stated previously for starting with the more easily corrected errors and working progressively toward the more difficult ones. Ways of using information from the articulation test in determining this order were suggested, and although such information is certainly basic in this connection, there are at least two other important considerations.

The first of these is the visibility of the articulatory positions for the various sounds. Sounds which are made with easily visible tongue or lip contacts, such as *f* and *th*, will usually be easier for a child to imitate than are sounds having more hidden articulatory contacts, e.g., *r* and *s*. Although this matter of visibility will usually influence the results of that part of the articulation test in which the child's ability to modify his production of misarticulated sounds is being measured, it is probably important enough to be given separate consideration. This is especially true if the results of the articulation test do not give clear indications as to the specific sounds the child will find most easy to imitate when he is strongly stimulated.

The second factor which should be considered is the possible effect of any complicating structural deviation, such as an oral or dental malformation. In the majority of cases having such structural deviations their complicating effects will be much greater for certain sounds than for others. Oftentimes a speech handicapped child with an organic involvement makes certain articulatory errors which are not at all related to it. Such errors should be relatively easy for the child to correct, and the encouragement and motivation derived from success with one or more such easy sounds are invaluable in establishing rapport between teacher and child and in establishing the interest and confidence essential for effective work on the more difficult sounds.

It seems obvious that no exact order in which sounds should be taught can be prescribed. Too much depends on the individual case. But a careful analysis of the factors mentioned above— cues from the articulation tests, visibility of the sounds, and influence of organic involvement, if any—should enable the speech correctionist to make a reasonably accurate prediction for each child concerning the relative ease or difficulty with which certain sounds will be learned, and, hence, the appropriate order for teaching them in the corrective program.

*Number of Sounds That May Be Taught Simultaneously.* Just as it is not possible to lay down rules concerning the order in which sounds should be taught which will be appropriate for all cases, so one cannot give a universal rule concerning the number of sounds on which to work at one time. Again, too much depends upon the individual—how rapidly he is able to learn, the types of sound errors he makes, how difficult the particular sounds may be for him, etc. However, it is possible to state a few general principles which can be used as guides.

In the first place, it should be emphasized that the general tendency of teachers and parents is to try to hurry the child. Neither thorough nor efficient learning results. As should be clear to the reader who has followed the chapter this far, the process of teaching a sound involves much more than showing the youngster what to do with his tongue or helping him to make the sound a few times in isolation. There are definite goals to be accomplished throughout the process of teaching a sound, and the teacher who gives careful attention to the reasonable attainment of each goal before going on to the next will be rewarded by better progress than if the process is rushed. Progress is sometimes slow, at times almost impercep- tible, but nothing will be gained by skipping a part of the learning process because it is not rapidly accomplished. Indeed, this will almost certainly insure failure at the next step, which depends for its successful completion on the thoroughness of the work that has preceded. Rather than to hurry on when lack of progress is encountered, it is better to go back and to review and learn more thoroughly the steps that have gone before.

By the same token one should not attempt too much at one time. It is far better to teach well one sound at a time than to try for more and encounter defeat. As a general rule, therefore, a speech correction teacher will start work on one sound only. Work on a second sound will usually not be started until the learning process is well along with the first. It would probably be well in most cases to carry the work on the first sound through the stages where the child can produce it easily and effortlessly in at least a few commonly used words before beginning on a new one. The process of completing the transition to connected speech can ordinarily be carried along while the learning of the new sound is in the preliminary stages. As with almost all other rules which apply to human behavior, this one has its exceptions. They should not be made, however, without good reason and careful consideration.

One exception which can often be made safely occurs with respect to the pairs of sounds that we call, phonetically, voiced and voiceless cognates.[21] These are pairs of sounds in which both members are made with the same positions and movements of tongue, jaw, and lips. The only difference between the two members of each pair is that during the production of the voiced sound the vocal cords vibrate; the voiceless sound is produced without any vocal cord vibration. Examples of pairs of voiced and voiceless cognates are: *v* and *f*; *z* and *s*; *b* and *p*; *d* and *t*; *g* and *k*; the *th* in bathe and the *th* in bath. (In each case the voiced sound is given first.) It sometimes happens that a child will make errors on both sounds of one or more of these cognate pairs. Since the two sounds are made so similarly, it is usually possible and more efficient to work on both of them at the same time.

[21] See Appendix V.

Exception to the rule of one sound at a time can also be made sometimes with older children and adults who, because of their stronger motivation, can work more rapidly than younger children and can work on more things simultaneously without becoming confused. However, the rule to "make haste slowly" will still generally apply. Probably at most not more than three sounds should be worked on at the same time, even with an adult.

One other caution may perhaps be in order here. The teacher should never be in such haste to get on with the teaching of a new sound that the transition of the previously learned sound to connected speech is neglected. The learning is not completed until the pupil makes automatic use of it in his ordinary everyday talking. There is small value in just knowing how to make the correct sound. The error must be stamped out. The correct sound must be habituated. And that process cannot be entrusted to the unsupervised efforts of the pupil.

*Group Work vs. Individual Work.* Speech correction is, to a considerable extent, an individual process. Different individuals make errors on different sounds and make them in different ways. The causal factors differ from person to person. Such complicating factors as deficient oral and dental structures are present in some cases and not in others. Moreover, pupils learn at markedly different rates, and so techniques of correcting articulatory errors must always be adapted to the person with whom they are used. Hence, much of the speech correctionist's work must be done on a completely individual basis.

Nevertheless, there are many advantages in group work and it definitely has a place. Children in groups tend to stimulate and motivate one another. A group situation provides opportunities for realistic speaking activities. Many types of speech games can be played in groups which could not be played in individual lesson periods. Group speech correction also has advantages from a mental hygiene point of view. Since each child gets a chance to compare his speech with that of others and find out at first hand that other children also have speech problems, he may not feel so singled out as a child who is slow or different in some undesirable way. All this is apart from and in addition to the fact that group work is, when correctly used, more economical of the speech correction teacher's time. The advantages of group work are sufficiently great so that for most types of cases some of it, in addition to individual lessons, is probably a more desirable arrangement than individual lessons exclusively.

Many of the activities which have previously been discussed can be utilized as group retraining procedures. Ear training games and activities are one example. Much of the practice used to transfer new sound habits to ordinary continuous speech can also be provided. The basic principles for conducting work in groups are the same as those already discussed. Continuous auditory stimulation is just as important and must be provided in group instruction no less than in individual lessons. Constant checking on progress of individuals with special individual attention to successes, near successes, and failures is no less important. The skilled speech correction teacher will never allow group instruction to deteriorate to dull routine drill in which pupils read lists of words or sentences, without adequate attention to the needs of each child, without adequate stimulation with the correct sound, and without adequate attention to the results produced. Such group instruction is not only dull and uninspiring; it literally fails to instruct.

The proportion of time to be spent in group work and in individual work may vary considerably from pupil to pupil. For some children, who present only a few simple sound substitutions of an entirely functional nature, well-planned and executed group work may be enough. Most cases, however, will need some individual lesson periods in addition to the group activity. And for a few severe cases with many errors, and ones which are difficult to correct, especially if there is any extensive organic involvement, practically all of the work may need to be intensive, individual training. It is generally not sufficient, certainly not most desirable, to try to carry on all speech correction instruction with groups.

## What the Classroom Teacher Can Do

IF THERE IS A TRAINED SPEECH CORRECTIONIST IN THE SCHOOL

It should be obvious to any teacher who has thought about the problem that the fact that the school employs a trained speech correctionist does not relieve her of all responsibility toward the special problems of the child with an articulatory problem. In numerous ways she can smooth the way for children with such handicaps.

In Chapter II we have discussed at length the responsibility of the classroom teacher to see that the speech handicapped child has every possible opportunity to develop at his own rate in spite of his handicap.[22] Methods for creating optimum learning conditions have been outlined. Specific ways in which the teacher can insure that the child is not unnecessarily penalized by his handicap, either by the other children or by the teaching methods employed, have been described in detail. This discussion will not be repeated here, except to emphasize the importance of the contribution which the classroom teacher can make. Any experienced public school speech correctionist can testify to the effect of the classroom teacher on the progress of pupils in correcting their speech problems. She has seen at first hand the more rapid progress of pupils fortunate enough to have really excellent teachers.

The foregoing discussion of the process of correcting articulatory errors also suggests many ways in which the classroom teacher can be of direct assistance in the retraining process. The correctionist will need to depend on the classroom teacher for help in having the child carry out assignments aimed at incorporating the new sound habits into running speech. A number of ways in which the classroom teacher can assist in this process have already been suggested. It may be added that the alert classroom teacher who is informed about speech problems, at least to the extent represented by this book, and who keeps posted on the progress of her pupils in their speech

[22] Further discussion along these lines is to be found in Chapter IX.

correction lessons, will be able to devise and suggest to the correctionist ways of being helpful. She, better than the correctionist, will know of occasions for talking and oral recitation in class which can be utilized as nucleus situations for practice in good speech habits. She should of course be guided by the correctionist in rendering such assistance, but the correctionist will welcome her suggestions and offers of coöperation.

The correctionist will also need to depend on the classroom teacher for information about the child which may be important and relevant to his speech problem. The correctionist may therefore ask the classroom teacher to furnish her with information concerning various aspects of the child's behavior, both in the classroom and on the playground. Is he shy and withdrawing? Is he hyperactive and aggressive? Or does he seem well adjusted under most circumstances? Does he tend to be talkative; does he tend to be extremely quiet; or is he average in this respect? Does any refusal to talk seem to result from embarrassment about his speech problem? How does he react to other children? How do they react to him and his speech problem? Are there any circumstances in which his speech problem seems worse than in others, or to cause him more embarrassment? Does he seem to have more difficulty, or show more embarrassment, with adults or with children his own age? What kinds of things interest him most? How is he best motivated? What kinds of rewards and penalties are most effective? Which ones produce undesirable reactions? To these and other similar questions the classroom teacher may be able to help supply answers. In order to do so, however, she will need to become a keen observer of her pupils. She will need to know them intimately as individuals. Her answers will be most useful if based on specific observations and if she can give concrete illustrations of particular matters of behavior.

Beyond these important considerations, there is much else that the classroom teacher can do. In the interests of orderly arrangement, however, the additional things that she can do, if there is a speech correctionist in the school or if there is not, are discussed in the following section. The suggestions made there will have to be adapted, of course, to the situation in which the classroom teacher and the speech correctionist work together.

IF THERE IS NO TRAINED SPEECH CORRECTIONIST IN THE SCHOOL

Faced with this situation, what can the classroom teacher do beyond seeking to understand the child's problem, doing her best to create conditions that will penalize him as little as possible for his impaired speech, and recommending that he be referred to someone with thorough training in speech correction? With certain cases she can do a great deal, provided she is interested, sincerely desires to help, and is endowed with those qualities of understanding, patience, and perserverance necessary to do a job of retraining with speech handicapped youngsters. The teacher who has these qualities and is willing to put out the effort to inform herself as thoroughly as possible—the minimum might be taken as a thorough study of this book—can take positive steps to help some of her pupils correct their articulatory errors.

Does this mean that the classroom teacher can undertake to treat speech disorders herself? Yes, with certain types of cases. Does it mean that the classroom teacher can fill the place of the special speech correction teacher? No, except to a limited extent. There is no substitute for the training and experience possessed by the specialist, if all children with speech disorders are to have their chance. The classroom teacher, however, can partly bridge the gap between what is and what ought to be. No teacher will ever "have the time" to do this, of course. In every school that the writers have ever known, anything about the curriculum was packed to the bulging point. If the teacher is to carry out the suggestions proposed in this section, she will almost literally have to make the time. It may be fifteen minutes two or three times a week before school begins in the morning; it may be a part of the lunch hour; it may be following the close of school in the afternoon. Or the fortunate teacher may be able to schedule her activities within the school day to provide for such activity several times a week. Whenever it is, it will probably require special planning and effort by the teacher to make room for individualized speech correction work for those of her pupils whom she may be able to help. Further practical suggestions will be found in Chapter IX.

Very well, then—specifically what can the classroom teacher do? Most of what she can do has already been fully described in the section of this chapter dealing with remedial procedures. Many of these techniques can be employed by the person without special training, especially with children who have relatively simple articulatory problems, and they will make up the overwhelming majority of the cases. The teacher will need to follow carefully the steps previously described. She can, if she will employ the suggested procedures, provide the necessary ear training work. The stimulus method for teaching new sounds is basically a simple procedure, but it will be found effective enough to secure the desired results with all but a few cases. Phonetic placement techniques require more knowledge of the mechanics of sound production than most persons who are not specialists usually have. But the mirror work type of phonetic placement technique is not extremely difficult to carry out. The other steps in the process of correcting articulatory errors can also be followed by any teacher who will take care to inform herself how they ought to be accomplished. She will need to talk with parents and explain the work that she is doing and enlist their coöperation. Sometimes she will meet with resistance from a parent who refuses to recognize that a son or daughter has a problem requiring special help, but more frequently the response will be an eager desire to coöperate.

The principal risk is that the teacher without special training will attempt too much. As has been indicated, her efforts should usually be confined to the simpler types of cases. Children whose speech problems are complicated by any significant organic involvement will usually be difficult cases, and the correction of their disorders should probably not be undertaken by the nonspecialist. Children whose problems either are due to or have become complicated by emotional maladjustments are probably beyond the scope to which the nonspecialist should confine her efforts unless she can get help and guidance from a specialist. If such guidance and supervision are not available these cases are better referred to a speech clinic, or other special appropriate agency. But even with these more difficult cases excluded there will still be plenty to do. Most of the articulatory problems found at the lower grade levels are rather simple, uncomplicated cases of poor habit formation. They are usually more easily corrected in the early grades than if the faulty habits are allowed to become more firmly set over a longer course of years. Even in the upper grades the majority of cases are primarily the result of faulty learning. What most of these pupils need is someone to show them how to develop better habits and to give them careful guidance during the process. They can be shown how by employing the techniques herein described.

In deciding whether or not a case is suitable for her to work with, the classroom teacher should first look for any obvious structural deviations. Deviations of sufficient severity to be significant will usually be fairly obvious. In case of doubt, professional medical, or dental advice should be sought.

Emotional involvement is not always so easily recognized. However, there will usually be overt signs if the teacher is alert to them. Out-and-out behavior problems are usually overt enough to prevent their escaping anyone's attention. Extreme shyness or withdrawal will also usually be evident enough. The more difficult cases, however, are sometimes those who have learned to throw a protective cloak of diffidence about their sensitiveness concerning their problems. Such seeming diffidence may sometimes cover deep-rooted frustrations and anxieties and present a baffling problem even to the trained specialist.

Cases in which neither significant organic nor emotional involvement is apparent can be considered ones with whom the classroom teacher, with no more training than that provided by this book, can try her hand at speech correction. With these the risk that a person without special training may do more harm than good is almost negligible.

Progress may seem slow at first, for two reasons: first, because the teacher has not developed realistic standards by which to measure progress and may therefore expect too much; and second, because in speech correction work, as in other things, skill is acquired only after a certain amount of practice and experience with the techniques. But progress will usually come if the work is carefully planned and the techniques are properly used. It cannot be overemphasized that the teacher will need constantly to guard against the urge to hurry. That point has been stressed on several occasions in this chapter, but it cannot be made too strong. Haste will almost surely result in slipshod instruction and partial attainment of goals. The resulting half-established good speech habits will never replace errors which have been thoroughly fixed by years of practice. It is better to err on the side of overlearning than to risk failure and frustration because learning has been inadequate.

The teacher who follows the suggestions just given will find herself spending a substantial amount of time at the project she has undertaken. In addition to the time actually passed with pupils, she will have to take time to plan the work, to prepare materials, to devise assignments, to talk with parents, and to study. She is not likely to find that her pay check is fattened thereby at the end of the month. She will, however, find herself engaged in an extremely fascinating and rewarding branch of teaching, that of helping boys and girls with handicaps to become more nearly normal.

# CHAPTER IV

wwwwwwwwwwwwwwwwwwwwwwwwwwwwwwwwwwwwwwwwwwwwwwwwwwwwwwwwwwwwwwwwwwwwwwww

# Disorders of Voice

An excellent voice is an almost universally admired personal characteristic. We comment favorably upon the voices of certain of our acquaintances and perhaps unfavorably about others. We may base our listening preferences for particular radio announcers or newscasters upon how we react to their voices. On the other hand, there is a commonly held idea (which we shall presently see has some basis in fact) that particular vocal characteristics disclose significant clues concerning an individual's personal characteristics, and we tend to form our impressions of people partly on the basis of how we react to their voices. We think of some voices as *effeminate*, others as *whining*, still others as *gruff*, or *coarse*, or *shrill* and *scolding*; we sometimes talk about the little weak voice of a person whom we regard as excessively timid, and so on.

It is apparent, then, that a good voice is a distinct asset and that a poor voice may be an unfortunate handicap. It is the purpose of this chapter to discuss the more common sorts of voice disorders, particularly those that the teacher is likely to find occasionally among the children in her classroom, with a view to seeing what can be done about them.

## An Essential Orientation to Acoustics

It will be easier to understand what happens in various kinds of voice disorders if we first have in mind a few basic ideas con-

154

cerning the normal functioning of the vocal mechanism. This mechanism is primarily a sound generating system, and in order to understand its functions in relation to speech we have need of some fairly clear concepts about sound. We need to know a bit about what sound is and how it is produced. It is essential also that we know about some of the ways in which sound vibrations can vary and how variations in them are related to variations in the ways in which we hear sounds with regard to their pitch, loudness, and tone quality. In this section, then, certain fundamental notions concerning sound are presented in a simple and nontechnical manner. No mathematical formulas are employed and only utterly essential technical terms are used. These are rather carefully defined, with examples. Illustrations are drawn as far as possible from everyday experience. It is our hope that this brief discussion of basic facts and principles concerning sound will serve to make the rest of the chapter much more meaningful.

Almost everyone is familiar with the basic idea that sound is closely associated with vibration. We know by ordinary experience that sound can be created by setting objects into vibration, as the musician does when he causes the string of a violin to vibrate by bowing or plucking it. We know that a radio loud-speaker vibrates when it generates sound. We know also that when columns of air are set into vibration sound is produced, as when we blow across the mouth of a bottle, or when the player of a wind instrument sets its air column into vibration by means of his breath pressure and his vibrating lip.

We are probably also familiar with the idea that sound is transmitted as vibration, that it travels through the air from the source where it is created to the ear of a person, because the air has been set into vibration, and that the person who hears it is able to do so because the receiving mechanism in his ear is set into vibration by the vibrating air.

These vibrations which are so much a part of our everyday experience can be studied, measured, and described in various ways. Let us start by thinking of a sound which is being transmitted through the air. We can view the disturbance which we call the sound wave as a back and forth motion of the particles of the air, and we can describe the way in which the air particles vibrate. For example, we can specify the amplitude (maximum extent) of the to and fro motion of the air particles, or the average velocity of motion of these particles, and so on. For our purposes, however, the most useful single way of thinking about sound vibrations in the air is to consider them as pressure disturbances. We may not be very familiar with the idea, but it is quite accurate to say that when an object vibrates so as to generate a sound, it creates a pressure disturbance (consisting of alternating increases and decreases of pressure) in the surrounding air. The air near the vibrating body passes these pressure variations on to the air farther away, and the listener's eardrum is set into vibration because these pressure variations of the air are transmitted into his ear canal. It is important to emphasize that sound, viewed as a pressure phenomenon, consists of *variations* of pressure. (A more precise though somewhat more technical term is *oscillations* of pressure.) Steady pressures, or gradual increases or decreases of pressure in one direction only, do not constitute sound.

There are certain attributes of these pressure oscillations which it is important to understand. One of these is frequency. Frequency refers to the rate at which the pressure oscillations occur. We call a single complete oscillation—waxing and waning—of pressure a cycle, and frequency is usually expressed in cycles per second. The frequency of a sound is closely related to an important attribute of the way we hear sounds—the perceptual attribute that we call pitch. It is not entirely accurate to say that the pitch of a sound is completely determined by its frequency, because certain other attributes of sound can be shown to have some effect on the pitch that we hear. However, frequency is the principal determiner of perceived pitch, and under most circumstances the higher the frequency of a sound the higher its pitch.

Another important dimension of sound pressure oscillations is their magnitude (amplitude). Sounds of any frequency can vary over a great range of pressure amplitudes, from pressure oscillations so small that the ear cannot detect them to those so large that they produce sensations of tickling, or even pain, in the ear. Variations in pressure amplitude are closely related to the perceptual attribute of sound that we call loudness. Again, it is not entirely accurate to say that the loudness of a sound is completely determined by its pressure amplitude. It is true, however, that changes in the pressure amplitude of a particular sound will usually be heard as changes in its loudness; and increases or decreases in the loudness of a sound will usually be associated with corresponding increases or decreases in pressure amplitude.[1]

Very simple sounds, those that we sometimes call pure tones, consist of only one frequency. Such sounds can be completely described by specifying three dimensions: frequency, intensity (or sound pressure), and duration. Most of the sounds we hear as part of our everyday surroundings, however, are complex sounds, compounds of many frequencies. If this seems hard to understand, because our ears do not usually notice the separate components of the complex sound, it may help to remember that something very similar happens with respect to another kind of vibratory energy to which our sense organs are receptive, namely, light. Nearly all light that we see is a mixture of many different wavelengths (frequencies). Yet we see the mixture of wave lengths as a single shade or hue. We do not detect the colors which correspond to the separate wave lengths. In a somewhat analogous fashion our ears respond to complex sounds by perceiving a unified blend of sound which is the result of all the frequencies which have been compounded to produce the complex sound. To describe a complex sound completey we must specify the fre-

---

[1] The term "intensity" is often used to refer to the dimension which we have called sound pressure amplitude. In the science of acoustics a technical distinction is made between these two terms. Strictly speaking, the intensity of a sound is measured in terms of its power, rather than its pressure variation. However, for most of our discussion, this technical difference is relatively unimportant. For the sounds with which we shall be concerned, there will usually be a simple proportional relationship between sound pressure and intensity. Since "intensity" is often a more convenient term (for example, it is easier to talk about a sound as being more intense or less intense than it is to talk about changes in magnitude of sound pressure), we shall frequently use the term "intensity" in this somewhat broad sense, as a rough equivalent to "sound pressure amplitude."

quencies of all the components which are present in it as well as their amplitudes.

Complex sounds may be conveniently divided into two principal classes, periodic and aperiodic. Periodic complex sounds are those we usually think of as tones, whereas the aperiodic ones have little tonal character and we often refer to them as noises. Examples of periodic sounds are the tones produced by a musical instrument such as a violin or trumpet. Examples of aperiodic sounds are the hiss of escaping steam and the noises produced by the shuffling or rattling of papers. Our speech mechanisms produce both kinds of complex sounds. The tones produced when a vowel sound is spoken or sung are relatively periodic, especially if the sound is sustained as a tone. On the other hand, the voiceless consonant sounds, such as *s* and *f*, are aperiodic noises. Some speech sounds have both periodic and aperiodic components. For example, the voiced consonant sounds have periodic components consisting of the tones produced by the vocal cords. They also have aperiodic components resulting from the friction noises produced as the breath stream is forced through a restriction formed between the tongue and the teeth, the lower lip and the upper teeth, etc. Examples of such sounds are *z*, *v*, and the *th* in *this*.

For our present discussion of voice, we are mainly concerned with periodic sounds, although some voice disorders are characterized by the presence of unpleasant aperiodic components in the vocal tones. Periodic sounds, or tones, are so called because their complex vibrations have a certain pattern which is repeated over and over at a regular rate. This rate (or frequency) at which the complete pattern of the vibration is repeated is spoken of as the fundamental frequency, and it is this frequency of the sound which is its most important characteristic so far as its pitch is concerned. That is, variations in the fundamental frequency will cause us to hear variations in pitch, whereas other frequency components can be changed a great deal with little, if any, effect on our perception of pitch. Usually the fundamental frequency is also the lowest frequency in a complex tone. Musicians usually speak of the higher components of such a tone, those having higher frequencies than the fundamental, as overtones. The relative amplitudes of these overtones have little to do with the pitch of the tone as we hear it, but they do affect other important aspects of our perception of the tone. For one thing, its intensity, and thus the loudness with which we hear it, is the result of adding together all the intensities of the fundamental and the overtones.

In addition to pitch and loudness, there are other attributes of sound to which our ears are responsive. We can tell that there is a difference between two tones, such as those of a flute and a violin, for example, even though they are heard at the same pitch and loudness. We refer to this difference as one of tone quality, or timbre. Distinctions in tone quality are importantly related to the overtone structure of complex tones, because tone quality depends primarily on (a) the particular frequencies of the overtones, and (b) their relative intensities. Another way of stating this is to say that the quality of a tone is closely related to the way the sound intensity is distributed among the fundamental and the overtones. This aspect of complex periodic tones we call wave composition. Tone quality, and hence wave composition, are significant aspects of speech sounds because many of the important distinctions we hear between speech sounds are distinctions of tone quality. We recognize the differences among the various vowel sounds of speech, even when they are uttered with the same fundamental frequency and intensity, because these differences are primarily differences of wave composition. We also recognize tone quality differences among various speakers' voices. We recognize some voice qualities as pleasing, others as displeasing.

To summarize, we can classify sounds as simple, single frequency sounds (pure tones), or as complex sounds having many frequency components. Complex sounds may be further subdivided into periodic sounds (tones) and aperiodic sounds (noises). The important attributes of periodic complex sounds are (1) fundamental frequency, which relates closely to pitch, (2) intensity (total of the respective intensities of all frequency components), which relates closely to loudness, and (3) wave composition (distribution of intensity among the fundamental and overtones), which relates most closely to the tone quality that we hear. Speech sounds and tones are complex in character, some being periodic tones, some aperiodic noises. Vocal tones, however, from which listeners gain their impressions of a person's voice—impressions, that is, of pitch, loudness, and voice quality— are mainly periodic in character.

In order to understand how complex tones, including vocal tones, are generated and given particular characteristics of wave composition, one further matter of acoustics needs brief discussion. That is the phenomenon of resonance.

Most objects which generate tones when set into vibration vibrate in a complex rather than a simple fashion. The result is that a complex tone is produced whose wave composition depends upon the particular complex pattern of motion executed by the vibrating body. This pattern can be changed somewhat by altering the way in which the body is set into vibration. For example, a violin string may be either plucked or bowed and the sound produced will be somewhat different in these two cases. The sound produced can also be changed by altering the characteristics of the body itself. For example, a string may be stretched more or less tightly, or a diaphragm may be clamped more or less rigidly around its edge or at certain points on its surface. Such changes in the vibrating body, or the conditions under which it is made to vibrate, tend to alter its pattern of vibration, and thus the wave composition of the sound that is generated. Some of these variations may also produce changes in fundamental frequency and intensity, but it is the wave composition changes that we are concerned with at the moment. In brief, the wave composition of a periodic complex tone depends, in part, on the particular pattern of motion of the vibrating sound source. Altering the sound source in ways which affect its pattern of vibration is one way of changing the wave composition and, therefore, the tone quality.

There is, however, at least one other way in which wave composition may be modified that is important to our discussion, since it relates closely to the production of vocal sound. Suppose that the sound vibrations which are generated by a vibrating body can reach the surrounding air only by being transmitted through a system of tubes and cavities. This is the case with vocal sounds, since the vibrations originating from the larynx are transmitted to the surrounding air by means of the throat and mouth and, sometimes, the nasal cavities. In a system of this kind the exact pattern of vibration which is radiated into the surrounding air may be affected by the characteristics of this transmission system. If this transmission system has resonance characteristics the wave composition will be changed as a result of the sound vibration having been transmitted through it. We need, therefore, to understand a bit about resonators.

From our point of view, the most important property of a resonator is that it can be set into vibration much more readily at certain frequencies than at others. As a result, it vibrates with greater amplitude at these "resonant" frequencies. That is, a resonator may be considered to be frequency-selective, because its vibratory response is greater for one or more frequencies than for others. Now suppose that the complex pattern of vibration which is being impressed upon a resonant body by a sound generator contains frequency components which match, or almost match, these selected frequencies of the resonator. These frequency components are transmitted to the surrounding air with greater amplitude than are the other frequency components of the generator tone, which do not coincide with the resonant frequencies. As a consequence, the distribution of intensity among the frequency components of the generator tone is changed before it reaches the surrounding air. In other words, the wave composition of the complex tone is modified.

A concrete example may help to clarify what has just been said. As we shall see presently, the particular example chosen bears some resemblance to the human vocal mechanism. Suppose that a diaphragm which can be set into vibration electrically (such as a loud-speaker diaphragm or cone in a radio receiving set) forms the closure at one end of a cylindrical tube. The farther end of this tube is coupled to a second tube of somewhat different cross-sectional area. At its farther end this second tube is open to the surrounding air. Now if the diaphragm is caused to produce a complex tone by means of an appropriate electrical signal, the sound can be transmitted to the surrounding air only through these tubes. However, the sound emitted from the far end of the second tube will not have, in general, the same complex pattern of vibration as that which is generated by the diaphragm. In being transmitted through the tubes, the wave composition of the complex tone will have been altered, because the tubes constitute a resonant system which has a markedly greater response to some frequencies than to others.

Let us suppose further that the tubes which constitute this resonant transmission system are so constructed that their dimensions can be changed. Suppose, then, that the first tube is shortened to half its previous length, while the length of the second tube is increased by 50 percent and at the same time its cross-sectional area is doubled. Now let the membrane which serves as the sound generator of this system be activated again with the same electrical signal as before, so that it generates the same complex vibration. If we now have some means of comparing the tone produced under these conditions with that produced before the tube dimensions were changed, we will find that the two tones are not quite the same, even though the diaphragm is generating the same vibration pattern. They will be different because the changes in the resonant system will have changed its resonant frequencies. As a consequence, a different set of frequencies in the original complex tone now receives the maximal resonating effect of the transmission system, and a different wave-composition results.

## How Voice Is Produced

Let us now proceed to an example which is even more closely analogous to our own vocal mechanism. By means of this example we shall understand better how the few basic principles of sound vibration which we have been discussing actually apply to our own speech sound producing systems. It will also serve as a means of introducing a few additional ideas concerning the way in which our vocal mechanisms function. Such an example is the sound producing system schematically shown in Figure 2. The essential parts of this system are (1) the air pressure generator

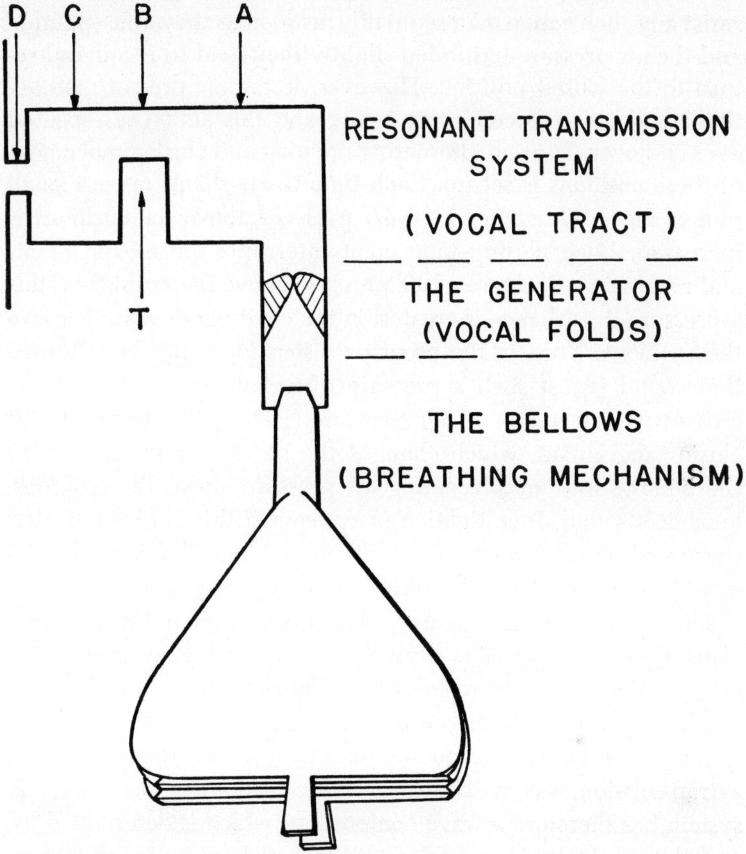

FIGURE 2. Schematic representation of a sound producing system whose principal features are closely analogous to those of the human vocal mechanism.

(represented as a bellows), (2) the sound generator, and (3) the resonant transmission system. The sound generator in this artificial system is represented as two wedge-shaped elastic cushions whose inner edges are in contact, so that no air may move between them unless some force, such as an increase of air pressure from below, causes them to separate. Because they are elastic, they tend to resist any such action. Consequently, as soon as they are separated and the air pressure has fallen slightly they tend to recoil and return to the closed position. However, if the air pressure is continued, they are forced apart again, and this action is repeated over and over. Thus an alternating opening and closing movement of these cushions is set up. Each time the cushions open a small puff of air is released and the air pressure above the cushions is increased. Each closing movement interrupts the escape of air and results in a decrease of air pressure above the cushions. Thus a pressure disturbance is created in the cavity immediately above the cushions. Now, in the previous discussion it has been shown that sound is just such a pressure disturbance consisting of increases and decreases of air pressure. Hence, this opening and closing movement, which changes the steady air pressure from the bellows into an alternating air pressure above the cushions, generates sound. Investigation of systems of this kind shows that the sound which is generated is a complex tone, having a fundamental frequency and a considerable number of overtones.

The upper part of Figure 2 has been labeled the resonant transmission system. The drawing is intended to represent the cross-sectional view of a series of cylindrical tubes connected to one another. As indicated in our previous discussion of sound, a system of this kind is a frequency-selective—that is to say, resonant —transmission system. The tone emitted from the mouth of this system has therefore a wave composition which is determined by (a) the particular frequencies to which the transmission system is most responsive, and (b) the particular wave composition of the tone generated by the cushion vibration. It is of interest that a study by Dunn[2] indicated that a system very much like that represented in the upper part of Figure 2 is acoustically similar in a number of important respects to the human vocal transmission system. Dunn showed that the important dimensions of this system, which determine its resonant frequencies, are the lengths and cross-sectional areas of the cavities represented at A and C

[2] H. K. Dunn, "The Calculation of Vowel Resonances, and an Electrical Vocal Tract," *Journal of the Acoustical Society of America* (1950), 22:740-753.

and of the constrictions represented at *B* and *D*. He further showed that, by appropriate choices of these lengths and areas, this artificial system can be made to produce vowel sounds which are readily recognized by listeners.

It is useful to note some of the similarities between this system and the human vocal transmission tract. The constriction shown at *B* divides the whole tract into two principal cavities, *A* and *C*. In the same fashion the tongue is capable of dividing the human vocal tract into two principal cavities. By changing the location of this constriction, and by increasing or decreasing the height and width of the rectangular bulge labeled *T* in Figure 2, the length and area dimensions of both cavities, and the length and closeness of constriction can be varied over a wide range of possible values. Each such change will produce a characteristic set of resonance conditions for this artificial vocal tract. The resonance characteristics of the system can be varied still further by modifying the constriction labeled *D*. This corresponds to the constriction produced by the lips in a person's vocal system.

The system represented in Figure 2, like that investigated by Dunn, is much more regular in shape, and is more highly schematized and simplified than the acoustical system with which humans are endowed. Dunn could not have carried out his mathematical investigations on a system as complex as the human vocal tract.[3] However, this difference in complexity means primarily that the resonance possibilities of the human vocal transmission system are even more varied than those of the schematized system.

Figure 2 has been presented as a simplified and schematized representation of the human vocal system because it is believed that an understanding of the latter might be more easily approached in this way. We turn now to a discussion of the human sound-producing mechanism.

[3] As a matter of fact, Dunn made a number of simplifications in addition to those involving cavity shaping. Figure 2 contains no cavity corresponding to the nasal passages, nor did Dunn's model. We know that when the nasal cavity is connected into the system certain changes in sound are produced. Another factor not considered by Dunn was the effect of changes in tissues composing the cavity walls. These, however, are believed to be of a minor nature so far as their effects on the resonant frequencies are concerned.

THE BREATHING MECHANISM

The breathing mechanism, like the bellows of Figure 2, plays a key role in the production of voice. It consists of the lungs and windpipe (trachea), the chest cavity in which the lungs are located, and the muscles of the trunk which cause the chest to be expanded and contracted. The function of the breathing mechanism, like that of the bellows in Figure 2, is to furnish the air pressure required to set the vibrating cushions (vocal folds) into motion. It is the modulation of this steady air pressure by the opening and closing motion of the cushion valve which produces the pattern of air pressure variations that constitutes the vocal sound.

There has been much argument about the correct way to breathe for best voice production. Generally this argument has concerned the location at which the maximum expansion and contraction of the torso should take place for proper speech breathing. Some have advocated what has been called thoracic (chest) breathing. Others have insisted on abdominal breathing as the only correct type. Still others have proposed "medial" breathing, which presumably centers the activity midway between the chest and abdomen. Another notion which seems to have had some currency is that considerable lung volume is required for good voice production. At least, many voice training textbooks have contained exercises in deep breathing.

It is not the purpose of the present discussion to take sides in these arguments about the optimum kind of breathing for speech. It does seem desirable, however, to consider the best available facts from research on speech breathing and to present a point of view with respect to them.

One fact which has become apparent in a number of research studies of speech breathing is that speech does not ordinarily require deep breathing. No study, to our knowledge, has shown any relationship between lung volume and good voice. Several studies have shown that speech requires little more volume of air in the lungs than we ordinarily take in during quiet, normal respiration. To produce voice, *adequate breath pressure,* not a *large volume of air*, is the important thing. The intensity of sound that is produced depends much more upon the pressure furnished by the breathing mechanism, and the extent to which that pressure is modulated by the opening-closing movement of the vocal folds, than upon the amount of air expelled from the lungs. In fact, one study, which involved comparisons of breathing movements for various intensity levels of voice,[4] indicated that the greatest movement (also, presumably, the deepest breathing and greatest volume of breath movement) occurred when the subjects were producing a "stage" whisper which had a very low intensity of vocal tone.

On the other hand, there is little doubt that breathing can be too shallow for the production of good voice. A certain minimal inflation of the lungs and expansion of the torso are required, if the necessary breath pressure is to be created and adequately controlled. Probably the breathing of all but very few persons is adequate in this respect, however, and exercises to increase depth of breathing will not often be very useful in improving voice for speech. They are more likely to be of value in the training of the singing voice, a matter that is beyond the scope of this book.

Probably the best studies of the muscle action coördinations involved in speech breathing have been those of Stetson and his associates.[5] These studies have shown that the breathing movements required for speech involve both abdominal and thoracic muscles. In general, the role of the abdominal muscles is preparatory to the breath pressure pulses employed in ordinary connected speech. They contract just slightly before the beginning of speech utterance. Their function seems to be to produce an appropriate posturing of the abdominal walls and rib cage—that is, a posture from which the breath pressure movements can be easily and

[4] E. May Huyek and Kenneth D. A. Allen, "Diaphragmatic Action of Good and Poor Speaking Voices," *Speech Monographs* (1937), 4:101-109.

[5] R. H. Stetson and C. V. Hudgins, "Functions of the Breathing Movements in the Mechanism of Speech," *Archives neerlandaises de Phonetique Experimentale* (1930), 5:1-30.

R. H. Stetson, *Motor Phonetics*, Amsterdam, North-Holland Publishing Co., 1951, Chapter III. This book may be purchased from the Psychology Department, Oberlin College, Oberlin, Ohio.

effectively produced and controlled. In addition to these abdominal posturing movements, which occur at relatively slow rates, there are the more rapid breath pulse movements which are apparently produced by certain muscles of the rib cage. These "chest pulses," as Stetson called them, are the movements which actually produce the air pressure required by the vibratory system in generating vocal tones. Stetson's studies showed that during speech there is a chest pulse for each syllable, whereas a separate contraction of the abdominal muscles, to change the basic posturing of the structures, may occur only once for each several syllables.

It may be inferred that the breathing movements which govern and control the air pressure for voice production are rather intricately coördinated. The abdominal muscle contractions must perform their role in order for the chest pulse movements to occur properly. On the other hand, it is the chest pulse movements which produce, control, and vary the air pressure as required for different intensities of tone, different vocal pitches, and, probably, different vocal qualities. In short, this rather intricate coördination of movements involves many muscles distributed over the whole torso, and it is probably erroneous to talk of different ways or methods of breathing for speech, such as abdominal breathing, or thoracic breathing, or medial breathing. As a matter of fact, about twenty years ago Gray and his students[6] showed that attempts to classify speakers according to "breathing types" as abdominal, thoracic, and medial failed to reveal any relationship to any aspect of good or poor voice production that they were able to observe.

However, one may also infer from Stetson's findings that breathing movement which is restricted to the extreme upper chest region may be inadequate for good voice. Such very restricted movement would seem to be incompatible with the muscular coördinations which Stetson found to be required for speech. Also, it is nearly certain to result in very shallow breathing.

The basic essentials of an adequately functioning breathing

[6] Giles W. Gray (ed.), *Studies in Experimental Phonetics*, Baton Rouge, Louisiana State University Press, 1936.

mechanism for speech may be summarized as follows: (1) It must be able to furnish adequate air pressure to the vocal cords so that they may be set into proper vibration. While this does not require deep breathing or large lung capacity, some inflation of the lungs is needed, and very shallow breathing is probably inefficient. (2) This breath pressure must be under sufficient control so that the necessary variations in the manner of vocal fold vibration, which occur partly as a result of variations in breath pressure, may be produced in a controlled manner. This probably involves sufficient activity of the whole torso so that the natural breathing movement coördinations required for speech, as described by Stetson's studies, are facilitated.

## THE LARYNX AND VOCAL FOLDS

The sound-generating mechanism of the human vocal system consists of the larynx and vocal folds. Its location is indicated in the cross-sectional diagram of Figure 3. However, because it is difficult to show the important features of the larynx and vocal folds in a diagram like Figure 3, no attempt has been made to do so. In Chapter II the fact was mentioned that the larynx serves the biological function of a valve located between the throat and windpipe. The most important parts of this valve are the vocal folds. Although these structures are sometimes called the vocal cords, they are not really shaped like cords, but resemble small, movable fleshy cushions, shaped much like the cushions shown in Figure 2. There is a slit between them, called the glottis. This slit can have a rather wide, triangular shape when the cushions are separated to permit the free passage of air in and out of the lungs. It is narrowed when the vocal folds are brought tightly together to form the valvelike closure. When the vocal folds are closed, or nearly so, and the air pressure beneath them is increased by action of the breathing mechanism, they are set into vibration in a manner very similar to the way in which the cushions of Figure 2 were said to vibrate. That is, they execute a rapid opening and closing motion which has the result of modulating the steady air pressure from the lungs to produce rapid variations of pressure in the air above the glottis, and thus to produce vocal sound.

The nature of the tone produced in the larynx can be changed considerably as a result of internal adjustments within the larynx,

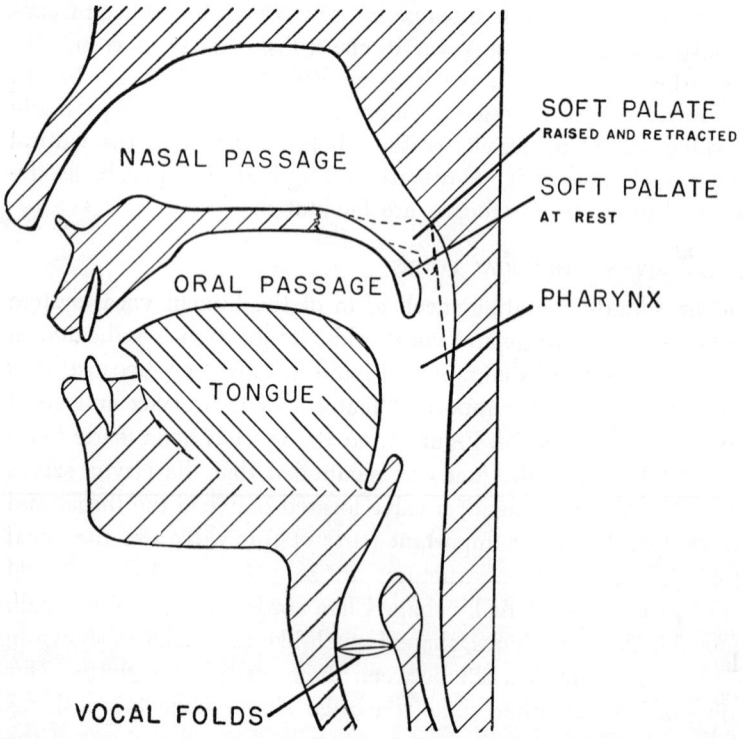

FIGURE 3.   Schematic cross section of the vocal resonance cavities. The dashed line shows the soft palate and pharyngeal wall in the position of velopharyngeal closure, separating the nasal cavities and nasopharynx from the rest of the vocal transmission system.

in conjunction with adjustments of the air pressure produced by the breathing mechanism. For one thing, the rate of the opening-closing movement, which determines the fundamental frequency of the vocal tone, can be varied. This changes the pitch of the vocal tone; the pitch is raised as the rate of vibration is increased, and vice versa. Other adjustments of the larynx and breath pressure can be made to vary the intensity of the tone which is generated. Increase in the intensity of the tone results from muscular adjustments within the larynx which close the folds more tightly and resist more strongly the tendency of the air pressure to blow them apart. When this happens greater air pressure (and a more vigorous chest pulse to produce the greater air pressure) is required to cause them to separate and they tend to recoil and close again more quickly. The result is that they tend to open more suddenly and release each puff of air under greater pressure than when a lower intensity of tone is being produced. They also tend to stay closed for a longer portion of each complete opening-closing movement for a high-intensity tone, as compared to a tone of low intensity. It follows that the pressure variations produced in the air above the glottis have greater amplitude. A third type of variation is also possible. The particular form of the opening-closing motion is somewhat subject to alteration in ways that change the complex pattern of the pressure variations produced in the air above the larynx. In this way the composition of the sound wave—hence the tone quality of the vocal fold tone—can be modified.

To summarize briefly, the vocal folds, as a result of their own elastic closure and the pressure furnished from the breathing mechanism, execute a vibratory opening-closing movement which produces a tone. As a consequence of internal adjustments in the larynx and in the air pressure in the trachea, this tone can be changed so as to raise or lower its pitch, to increase or decrease its loudness, and to modify its tone quality.

THE RESONATING SYSTEM

The third part of the sound-producing system diagrammed in Figure 2, the resonant transmission system, has its counterpart in the throat and the oral and nasal passages of the human vocal mechanism.[7] In the previous discussion of the system shown in Figure 2, we considered the influence of this resonant transmission system on the wave composition of the tone which finally

[7] For simplicity, no tube or cavity corresponding to the nasal passages is included in the diagram in Figure 2.

issues from the mouth of the system. In a similar way the resonant transmission system of the human vocal mechanism is able to modify the wave composition of the tone which is generated by the vocal folds.

The human vocal mechanism is somewhat more complicated than the artificial system of Figure 2, of course, and it is capable of even more variations. Hence, the possibilities for varying the wave composition of the tone, and thus the tone quality, are even greater. The tongue is an extremely mobile organ and can be moved and shaped in many ways. It can be raised or flattened to change the cross-sectional area of the oral tract. It can be humped toward the roof of the mouth, or retracted toward the back wall of the throat, so as to produce a constriction separating the complete vocal tract into two or more divisions having a variety of lengths and cross sections. The throat tube, or pharynx, is likewise a muscular structure and is capable of considerable modification in cross section. The jaw and lip movements can, of course, vary the mouth opening. Each of these possible variations produces a characteristic change in the resonance characteristics of the vocal tract, and hence a distinctive kind of modification of the wave composition of the vocal tone. A wide variation in vocal tone qualities is possible. The nasal cavities are not very modifiable as to size and shape, but they can be coupled into the vocal tract system, or decoupled (shut off) from it, by the action of the soft palate in conjunction with the movements of the walls of the throat. Figure 3 shows how this takes place. The back part of the roof of the mouth, called the soft palate, is muscular and capable of movement. It can either hang down in a relaxed position as represented by the shaded portion of Figure 3, or it can be raised and retracted in the position shown by the dotted line. In the latter position the walls of the pharynx tend to move in to meet it and produce a closure which seals the nasal cavity off from the throat and oral passages. It is thus apparent that the coupling between the nasal cavity and the rest of the vocal tract is quite variable. This variation introduces still further possibilities of variation in the resonance characteristics of the vocal tract.

It is apparent from the preceding discussion that voice production is a function of all three divisions of the vocal mechanism that have been described. The breathing mechanism furnishes the energy in the form of air pressure below the vocal folds. The vocal folds vibrate in a manner which produces a modulation of this breath pressure so that a tone is generated. The possible variations in the frequency and manner of vocal fold vibration determine the pitch, loudness, and to some extent the quality variations of the vocal tone. The resonant transmission system, consisting of the throat and oral and nasal passages through which this tone is transmitted to the surrounding air, also produces modifications of the vocal fold tone which are reflected in additional variations of tone quality. This, in brief summary, is how normal voice is produced. The important disorders of voice are to be viewed and understood against a background of essential knowledge such as this about the normal functioning of the vocal mechanism.

INCIDENCE OF VOICE DISORDERS

Disorders of voice occur less commonly than the disorders of articulation which were considered in the last chapter. This is particularly true among young children. Nevertheless, voice disorders do occur with some frequency at all ages. Although by far the largest number of school age children have reasonably adequate voices, a few do not. Some of these latter have organic conditions which interfere with good voice production. For the rest the structure of the vocal mechanism seems to be all right, but for one reason or another it fails to function adequately. Estimates vary, but probably from 1 to 2 percent of school children present significant voice problems.

## What Is a Voice Disorder?

Before considering what constitutes a voice disorder it is necessary to come to some agreement concerning what constitutes adequate voice. We all know that voices vary widely in pitch, in quality, and even in loudness. We know that the voices of our friends, most of whom, at least, would be considered to have normal voices, differ considerably in these respects. We know that some voices are pleasing, and we like to hear them. Others are not so melodious, and yet we would scarcely call them defective. Apparently any definition of normal voice must allow for considerable latitude. In general, however, we may set down the following requirements for adequate voice:

1. *The voice must be appropriately loud.* The voice must not be so weak that it cannot be heard under ordinary speaking conditions, nor should it be so loud that it calls undesirable attention to itself.

2. *Pitch level must be adequate.* Pitch level must, of course, be considered in terms of the age and sex of the individual. Men and women differ systematically in vocal pitch level, and children differ from adults.

3. *Voice quality must be reasonably pleasant.* This criterion is essentially a negative one implying the absence of such unpleasant qualities as hoarseness, breathiness, harshness, and excessive nasal quality.

4. *Flexibility must be adequate.* Flexibility involves both pitch and loudness. An adequate voice must have sufficient flexibility to express variations in stress, emphasis, and meaning. A voice which has good flexibility is expressive. Flexibility of pitch and flexibility of loudness are not inseparable, but they tend to vary together to a considerable extent.

### CLASSIFICATION OF VOICE DISORDERS

The foregoing requirements for adequate voice imply a possible classification of voice disorders. In what follows in this chapter, therefore, we shall classify disorders of voice as *disorders of pitch, disorders of loudness* (or intensity), *disorders of quality,* and *disorders of flexibility.*

*Disorders of Pitch.* By pitch level of the voice we mean the general highness or lowness of the voice with respect to the musical scale. Some individuals regularly employ pitch levels which are unusual, or inappropriate to their age and sex. The eighteen-year-old who still talks in the high-pitched voice that he used as a preadolescent boy, the young woman whose extremely low-pitched and rather gruff tones almost suggest the voice of a man, and the woman whose high-pitched, shrill voice stands out in unpleasing contrast to the other voices in the room are all examples of persons with pitch disorders.

A person with a disorder of pitch, then, is one who regularly talks with a pitch level which is too high or too low. Constant use of such a pitch level calls unwelcome attention to itself. But there is another consideration that is almost equally important. Such a disagreeable pitch level is often badly suited to the person's vocal mechanism. In fact, if the pitch level regularly employed is really inappropriate the vocal mechanism may not be able to function efficiently in producing adequate loudness or pleasing voice quality. Continuous talking at an inappropriate pitch level may even be accompanied by unusual strain and fatigue. The result is that pitch disorders may be causally related to other types of voice disorders.

*Disorders of Loudness.* Most voices affected by a disorder of loudness are those which are deficient in loudness. We have difficulty hearing them in many ordinary speaking situations. The sound produced lacks adequate intensity. We often say that such voices do not "carry well." The most extreme case of deficiency in loudness is that of the individual who can produce no voice at all. Temporary loss of voice resulting from acute laryngitis is something that we all have known and may perhaps have experienced. Certain kinds of pathological conditions affecting the larynx can result in a more or less permanent loss of voice. In addition, there are persons who are unable to produce voice as a consequence of profound emotional or personality disturbances. These extreme cases are, generally speaking, subjects for medical or psychiatric treatment. They occur relatively infrequently, especially among children, and the classroom teacher will rarely, if ever, have such a case among her pupils.

It can happen, also, that voices are generally too loud. However, most cases of excessive loudness are caused by deficiencies in hearing. These will be considered in Chapter VIII, in which the special speech problems of hard of hearing children are discussed.

Somewhat rarer are cases of uncontrollable loudness. One

young man known to the writer had such difficulty in controlling the loudness in his voice that he would very suddenly find himself shouting, seemingly without any conscious volition. These cases, like those of complete voicelessness, occur infrequently, and the classroom teacher hardly needs to concern herself about them. Her principal concern with respect to loudness disorders will be with students whose voices are just not loud enough so that they can be easily understood.

*Disorders of Voice Quality.* The most frequently occurring voice disorders are those of voice quality. One of the troublesome things about voice qualities is that they tend to be difficult to describe. There are so many of them, for one thing—each person's is relatively unique. Also, there has never been adequate agreement concerning the adjectives which should be used to describe particular sorts of voice qualities. Fortunately, in describing *disorders* of voice quality, we can get along with a fairly small number of these terms without sacrificing any important discriminations. Only four terms will be used, therefore, and these will be defined rather carefully so that we can know what is meant by each of them:

1. *Nasal voice quality* is produced when the resonance characteristics of the vocal tract are modified by coupling the nasal cavities into the vocal system during the production of speech sounds which normally are essentially nonnasal, i.e., all sounds except *m, n,* and *ng.* For these three, of course, the sound must be transmitted through the nose. If, for any reason, the soft palate and walls of the throat do not perform their usual function of shutting off the upper part of the throat and nasal cavities during the production of nonnasal sounds, the voice is excessively nasal in quality. It sounds to us as though the individual were talking through his nose, and he literally is.

2. *Breathy voice quality* is heard in a voice which seems to have a whisper effect added to the usual vocal tone. It reminds one of a stage whisper. It results from the fact that the vocal folds are not brought closely enough together during the production of the voice tone. As a consequence a considerable amount of air rushes out through the larynx without being

modulated by the vibrating vocal folds. This rush of air produces friction noises, not unlike whisper noises, which are superimposed upon the tone resulting from the vibrations of the vocal folds.

3. *Hoarse voice quality* can be heard as a temporary condition in persons who have a bad cold which affects the larynx. We sometimes use the term "husky" to describe the way it sounds. Sometimes a temporary hoarseness may be caused by vocal abuse as, for example, too much shouting at a football game. Such hoarseness results from a temporary condition of inflammation affecting the larynx and vocal folds. More permanent pathological conditions of the vocal folds can produce a permanent condition of hoarse voice. It has also been found that a hoarse voice can result from habitual use of a pitch level unsuited to the vocal mechanism, particularly a pitch level which is too low for the individual.

4. *Harsh voice quality* has an unpleasant, rough, rasping sound. It is often heard in people for whom voice production seems to be a considerable effort or strain. The particular way that a harsh voice sounds to us may vary somewhat with the pitch of the tone. The term "strident" is sometimes used to describe harsh tones of high pitch. Harsh voice is generally considered to be associated with excessive strain and effort in producing voice, as a result of which there is too much muscular tension in the throat and larynx. That there is such excessive tension during voice production in many harsh voice cases has been verified clinically by the fact that these persons sometimes report fatigue if they try to talk for any substantial length of time. Laboratory research has tended to bear out these clinical observations.

Some writers use a considerable number of terms, in addition to those given above, to designate what they regard as voice quality disorders. Most of these can, however, be included within the classifications given here. Those which cannot will usually be found to refer to some other aspect of voice, not voice quality at all. One such term is "shrill," which is usually used to indicate a very loud high-pitched voice. Shrillness is not a matter of voice quality, since the same voice at normal pitch and loudness levels may be found to have entirely acceptable voice quality. Such distinctions may seem fussy, and, indeed, in ordinary casual conversation they would probably not matter. But in the diagnosis of voice disorders such loose use of terms tends to make for loose thinking and may lead to erroneous conclusions.

*Disorders of Flexibility.* Voices said to have a disorder of flexibility may be adequate so far as general pitch level, general loudness, and voice quality are concerned but inadequate because they are defficient in expressiveness to a rather extreme degree. These voices are monotonous; that is, there is very little variation in either pitch or loudness. Pitch monotony and loudness monotony could conceivably occur independently, but the two are so strongly interrelated that they usually do go together. Often this extreme lack of expressiveness is accompanied by a mumbling, indistinct articulation. In such cases, the picture is one of general inexpressiveness—with respect to both voice and articulation. The person seems to lack any real desire to communicate; he seems to mumble to himself without concern as to whether anyone can understand him.

A certain amount of lack of expressiveness is probably a fairly normal matter in untrained children's voices, especially in situations in which they feel self-conscious. But normal youngsters lose their reticence, and with it their lack of vocal expressiveness, in most situations in which they feel any real spontaneity, as when relating an interesting experience. The individuals we are concerned with as having voice problems have so much reticence in all speaking situations that their voices are almost never expressively "alive."

One such case was a university freshman who was referred to the speech clinic by the instructor of his speech class. His speech and voice fitted almost exactly the description given above. That is, it was extremely monotonous and inexpressive, with respect to both loudness and pitch. There was almost no pitch inflection and little emphasis to reinforce the meaning of what he had to say. His articulation was mumbled and indistinct. Investigation revealed that this was true of his typical speech in all situations. This young man had made an outstanding high school record and had scored very near the top of the university freshman placement examinations. His ambition was to study medicine. It is not hard to foresee the handicap which his speech would represent in such a program.

It should be mentioned, too, that his general behavior was excessively withdrawn. His dress and personal appearance were untidy. He seldom shaved or had his hair cut. His clothing was often unkempt. According to his own statement, he had few, if any, friends. He seemed to have none of the normal social interests, and certainly none of the graces, that one would expect in a young man of his age. These facts of personal adjustment— or lack of it—help considerably to explain the associated voice problem.

## Causes of Voice Disorders

Any complete account of the causes of voice disorders would go far beyond the scope of this book. Inadequate voices may result from numerous organic abnormalities which can affect the various parts of the vocal mechanism. Many of these organic conditions are relatively rare. Quite a number are almost entirely confined to adult levels and hence are not of important concern to the classroom teacher. The discussion in this section will be limited to those which are more common among school age children.

### ORGANIC CAUSES

Pathological conditions of the larynx which affect voice in any sort of permanent manner are sufficiently rare, especially among children, that the classroom teacher will seldom have a child with this type of difficulty in her classes. It should be understood, however, that there are a number of pathological conditions of the larynx which may affect voice. In a few such cases the voice symptom may be the first indication that there is anything fundamentally wrong. The usual symptom is a severe chronic hoarseness. If by rare chance, therefore, the classroom teacher should at some time have among her pupils a child with severe and chronic hoarse voice, it would be well to have the child referred to a physician for medical attention. A further word should be said concerning chronic hoarseness. Because it can be the first symptom of a diseased condition of the larynx, no voice retraining should be undertaken until the child has been seen by a physician. If there is a diseased condition, voice retraining may aggravate it and do positive harm. One would not, therefore, begin any voice work until assurance had been given by the physician that no harm was likely to result.

Organic abnormalities of the oral cavity are more likely to have an adverse effect upon articulation than upon voice. One special case which affects the voice very markedly, cleft palate, is of sufficient importance to merit special attention by itself and is considered in Chapter VII.

Perhaps the most commonly occurring case of voice disorder due to organic pathology which the classroom teacher will find among her pupils is that resulting from enlarged adenoids. The child with enlarged adenoids has a great deal of difficulty breathing through his nose because the upper part of his throat tube (pharynx) and the openings at the rear of the nasal cavities, which connect them to the pharynx, are obstructed. This obstruction is caused by an enlarged mass of lymphoid tissue in the upper part of the pharynx, just behind the nasal cavities. The condition has consequences which affect speech. First, since he has difficulty breathing through his nose, the child with enlarged adenoids also has difficulty producing speech sounds which require nasal resonance. That is, he cannot produce the sounds *m, n,* and *ng* adequately. If the condition is not too severe, these sounds may only be weakened. If the obstruction is complete, or nearly so, he may not be able to produce these sounds at all. Instead he tends to substitute a slightly distorted *b* for *m, d* for *n,* and *g* for *ng.* He talks all the time as though he had a severe head cold.

This type of speech is sometimes referred to as *denasality.* Strictly speaking, it is an articulatory rather than a voice problem, since the difficulty is primarily one of producing certain speech sounds—the nasal consonants. However, if the adenoids are removed surgically, a definite voice problem may follow, and in most cases will. This voice problem results from another important consequence of the fact that the enlarged adenoids obstruct the upper pharynx and nasal cavities. Because of the obstruction, the soft palate and walls of the throat do not function normally to close off the upper part of the pharynx which connects with the nasal cavities. This failure of function may result in part from the fact that the enlarged tissue gets in the way of the action of the soft palate and pharyngeal walls, and in part from the fact that the connection with the nasal cavities is already largely obstructed so that the function has become unnecessary. In either case the function is not performed. So far as the voice problem following the operation is concerned, the important thing to understand is that although the surgery removes the obstructing tissue, it does not restore the function of the soft palate and walls of the pharynx. Therefore, when the obstructing adenoids are removed the child is left with an open passageway from the lower part of the throat up into the nasal cavities. He can now breathe normally through his nose and produce normal nasal consonant sounds, but he cannot shut off the upper pharynx and nasal cavities for nonnasal consonant and vowel sounds, especially those consonants requiring air pressure in the mouth. The restoration of this function and correction of the voice are retraining jobs for the speech correctionist.

FUNCTIONAL CAUSES

As was seen to be the case also with articulatory disorders, most voice problems cannot be accounted for in terms of organic causes. For various reasons, the *functioning* of the vocal mechanism may be deficient, and a voice problem may exist, even though the structure is entirely adequate.

*Imitation.* Some voice problems, like some articulatory problems, are the result of poor habits. Bad voice habits are probably most often due to imitation of poor speech models. With respect to voice, as well as articulation, we "play by ear," and we usually play the tunes that we have heard over and over. The child whose parent, or parents, speak with extremely nasal voice quality is apt to develop the same fault through imitation. The girl whose mother's voice is typically high-pitched and shrill may follow suit, and so on. It may not be out of place to point out that the teacher's voice is also sometimes a model which children imitate—a fact every teacher should duly consider.

*Psychological Factors.* Among the more prolific of the causes of voice disorder are psychological disturbances or maladjustments. This statement is especially true if we include adult cases, but it also holds for children. Psychological maladjustments may cover the range from deep-rooted emotional disturbances to the shyness and timidity that seems to be a characteristic of a considerable number of children. We have noted the rather common belief that vocal characteristics reveal personality traits. This belief is substantiated by a rather large accumulation of clinical observation and some systematic research investigation. In the case of the university freshman already cited it was indicated that the lack of flexibility and expressiveness seemed to be related to a general behavior pattern of withdrawal. Cases could also be described to illustrate the relationship of other types of voice problems to personality factors. For example, chronic feelings of anxiety and insecurity may result in excessive bodily tensions which in turn may produce vocal disturbances such as harsh quality or high pitch. Deficient loudness may come from excessive shyness, and so on. In all of these cases the voice disorder is only one symptom of a more general problem. It is often one of the most obvious symptoms and may be of sufficient importance to merit special attention. However, the general emotional or psychological problem is the more basic one and must be resolved in some fashion before any great or lasting improvement in voice can be expected.

*Adolescent Voice Change.* A problem of psychological adjustment with respect to voice which is of particular interest to teachers of children at the upper elementary and secondary school levels occurs in connection with adolescent voice change. As one of the normal pubescent changes during adolescence the larynx undergoes a very rapid growth. In the adolescent male the length of the vocal folds increases considerably in a rather short period of time. The female larynx also increases in size, but the change is much less marked. As a consequence of this development of the larynx the phenomenon of adolescent voice change occurs. The pitch of the voice deepens considerably. In males the change in pitch is approximately one whole octave. In females it is much less—from one to two tones.

During the period of this rapid growth and probably during a period of adjustment to the new characteristics of the vocal mechanism, the individual may experience considerable difficulty in controlling the pitch of his voice. Boys, because of the greater extent of the change, have many more such problems than do girls. The mechanism is no longer adapted to the high-pitched voice of childhood, and the individual has not become accustomed to, or learned to control, the lower pitch level of his adult voice. Hence, to a greater or less degree, the voice becomes temporarily a strange and unmanageable instrument. At times, it may take uncontrollable jumps from the childhood level to the adult level and back again—the phenomenon called "voice breaks." It is almost as though the young man could not make up his mind whether to continue talking like a child or to talk with the voice of a man.

With boys, the adolescent voice change most typically occurs between the ages of fourteen and sixteen. For a few, who are precocious in pubescent development, the phase may begin a year or two earlier. Girls are usually about two years earlier than boys in adolescent development.

Most boys pass through this stage without much difficulty beyond the amusement which their lack of voice control affords their families and friends. In fact, one investigation of the matter indicates that a considerable number of boys have very few, if any, real difficulties in making the adjustment. To some, however, the experience seems to be almost traumatic. It may be that they have more than usual difficulty in learning to control their changed vocal mechanism so that they have more frequent embarrassing voice breaks. Or it may be that the "humorous" jibes of their families and friends are more cruelly barbed; or that they are more sensitive and more easily embarrassed. In any case some few boys do experience more than usual tribulation. Now and then a boy fails to make the adjustment and continues as a young adult to employ the high pitch level of his pre-adolescent voice.

One such case, a university sophomore, finally came to the speech clinic for help. Careful examination of his pitch range revealed that he had a normal baritone range, but his habitual speaking range was at least an octave higher and his higher spoken pitches sounded almost falsetto. With only a little practice he found it possible to speak on the lower pitch level, but this low-pitched voice sounded so strange to him that a considerable period of "getting used to it" was required before he could bring himself to try it on his friends in everyday talking.

One other point should, perhaps, be mentioned in connection with adolescent voice change. Parents, relatives, or friends sometimes have preconceived notions of the voice range (tenor, baritone, or bass) that they would like to have the young man develop. Unfortunately, the growth processes are impervious to such wishes. The boy himself, however, may be inclined to be more pliable, and in attempting to comply with the desires of his well-meaning associates, or with his own notions of what is manly, he may develop voice habits with respect to pitch level which are somewhat out of line with what nature had intended. As we shall see presently, such pitch habits may have undesirable consequences on aspects of voice other than pitch.

*Unsuitable Pitch Level.* Although habitual use of a pitch level which is inappropriate to a person's age and sex and unsuited to his vocal mechanism is, itself, a voice disorder, it may have more far-reaching effects and actually operate as a cause for other types of voice problems. In one study of a considerable number of hoarse voice cases, it was found that a large proportion of the individuals were employing pitch levels which were too low.[8] Another study showed that long continued

[8] A. B. Williamson, "Diagnosis and Treatment of Seventy-two Cases of Hoarse Voice," *Quarterly Journal of Speech* (1945), 31:189-202.

use of such improper pitch levels may even produce organic changes of a pathological nature in the larynx.[9] The explanation seems to be that constant and habitual use of a pitch level that is ill-suited to the vocal mechanism tends to place this mechanism, especially the larynx, under a great deal of strain. As a consequence the voice may be adversely affected in various ways. This effect seems to be more often the result of a pitch level that is too low than one that is too high. This seems reasonable when one becomes aware of how difficult it is to produce very loud tones at the lowest pitches of one's vocal range. If, then, such a low pitch level is habitually employed, it may take considerably more effort, and place a good deal of excess strain upon the vocal mechanism, to produce voice of even the ordinary loudness required for everyday conversation and communication.

Other studies and clinical observations have indicated a possible relation between such abnormally low pitch levels and both deficient loudness and inadequate flexibility. It appears, therefore, that a pitch level properly adjusted to the capabilities of one's vocal mechanism is not only desirable in itself but a prerequisite of good voice in general.

*Poor Breathing Habits.* As we have noted previously, the proper way to breathe for good voice production occupies a large place in the literature on speech and singing. A considerable amount of what has been written has been based on opinions that have not been verified by careful observation. Moreover, it has been shown that good speech breathing is not a highly specialized matter requiring a great deal of specific training. Nevertheless, bad breathing habits can exist and they can contribute to voice disorders.

We have seen that the breathing mechanism supplies the energy for voice by creating pressure in the trachea below the vocal folds. Although the performance of this function does not require deep breathing, very shallow breathing can be inadequate. When a person tries to talk without a certain minimum amount of air

[9] Georgianna Peacher, "Contact Ulcer of the Larynx: III, Etiological Factors; IV, A Clinical Study of Vocal Re-education," *Journal of Speech Disorders* (1947), *12*:173-190.

in his lungs, a great deal of effort and strain is required. Even then the resulting voice may be weak and have poor quality.

Breathing for speech should be almost as easy and as relaxed a process as ordinary breathing during silence. But occasionally a person is found who seems to make hard work of it, involving an excessive amount of muscular tension and strain. Neither very shallow breathing nor breathing which involves excessive tension is likely to furnish the controlled air pressure at the vocal folds which will make possible good voice quality, adequate loudness, and easily controlled flexibility of pitch and loudness.

An occasional person has a particular type of shallow breathing which contributes to poor voice production. Almost the whole of the expansion and contraction of the torso is restricted to the extreme upper part of the chest. This type of breathing is undesirable, not only because it is shallow, but also because it fails to bring into play the musculature needed for adequate regulation and control of the air pressures required for speech.

There are other types of peculiar breathing faults which may interfere with voice production, but they occur more rarely. Now and then a person is found who tries to talk on inspiration rather than during expiration. The breathing movements of an occasional person are found to be jerky, almost spastic. Cases have been reported who took deep sudden inhalations and then wasted most of them by preceding speech with a gasp or sigh, so that very little air was left in the lungs with which to speak. All these conditions can obviously interfere with good voice. Most of the latter ones, however, occur only in unusual cases.

## Treatment of Voice Disorders

### CONVINCING THE PERSON THAT HE HAS A PROBLEM

A rather important problem in treatment which frequently arises with respect to voice disorders is that of convincing the person that he really has a problem about which he needs to do something. This sometimes presents itself with respect to the articulatory disorders discussed in the last chapter, too, but less frequently. A person is likely to be conscious of faulty articulation,

whereas he may not be aware of a nasal voice or a high pitch level
and the unpleasant effects that it has on his listeners. If the speech
correctionist has access to recording equipment, so that the pupil
can get a more accurate notion of how his voice sounds to others
by listening to a recording, this problem is frequently solved rather
simply. Without some means of enabling the pupil to "hear himself as others hear him" the problem of motivating him to attempt
correction may not be so easy. Right here the classroom teacher
can be of substantial assistance. Since she is better acquainted
with the pupil and is more likely to have his confidence than is
a comparative stranger, she is in a more strategic position to be
persuasive. Moreover, she may be able to provide specific motivation in the way of rewards for honest effort, such as an opportunity to have a place on a program or a role in a dramatic skit
which is being planned, if the pupil will try to overcome his
voice problem. Care should be taken that the goal to be attained
before the reward is earned is not placed too high, so that a failure
occurs in spite of hard work—simply because too much was
expected.

This is, perhaps, a good place for another word of caution. The
diagnosis of a disorder of any kind should not be made unless
one is reasonably sure that the diagnosis fits. This is just as true
of voice disorders as it is of any other kind. One's ears should not
be "too long." And it is very easy to be hypercritical of voice.
Personal preferences vary. The reader is reminded that in our
definition of normal voice wide latitude was allowed for variation
within what we may think of as "the normal range." A disorder of
voice should be a definite departure from these limits.

GENERAL REMEDIAL PROCEDURES

*The Goal of Corrective Work.* One can state the goal of corrective work very simply. It is to help the pupil achieve as *good
general voice production and usage as possible.* This statement
seems so obvious that its important meaning may be overlooked.
Too often the tendency is to classify a voice problem as one of
nasal voice, or high pitch, according to its most predominant
single characteristic. Once the voice has been so classified, all

other aspects of good voice usage are forgotten. To the ordinary listener, however, the important thing is the *overall impression* that is created by the voice. He is seldom analytical concerning the particular aspect of voice that he finds pleasant or unpleasant. Moreover, one seldom finds an individual who presents just a pitch problem, or just a voice quality problem, or just a loudness problem, etc. In the greater share of voice cases it will be true that, although one such problem is most prominent, the voice will have deficiencies in other respects also. One does not, therefore, solve the problem by working only on the single most prominent feature. Rather *a general program of voice retraining* is required which will give a proper place to all aspects of good voice production. Furthermore, it sometimes happens that the single most prominent faulty feature of the voice is remediable only within limits. If, in such a case, we stop work when these limits have been reached without taking steps to insure that the voice has been made as adequate as possible in all other respects, we have not done all that we can and should do to help the person. In other words, all aspects of voice production and usage should be regarded as alterable features of the person's vocal condition. To the extent that there is less than complete adequacy with respect to any such alterable feature, the problem is increased. We must, therefore, concern ourselves not only with the single most prominent defect but with any alterable feature which may be contributing to the voice condition, considered as a whole.

An illustration may help to clarify what is meant. Martha was a college student whose most prominent vocal fault was a hoarse quality. So far as could be determined by a physician there was no organic pathology of the larynx, so that the difficulty was classified as functional hoarseness. Possibly as a result of embarrassment concerning her poor voice quality, her voice was also deficient in both pitch and loudness flexibility, and was somewhat weak. In spite of rather intensive and prolonged work, she was never able to achieve voice quality that was completely free from hoarseness. If the corrective work had gone no further, she would really have been helped very little. However, at the same time that she had been working on her voice quality, training had been given in improving the flexibility and expressiveness of her voice, and she had learned to increase her general loudness so that she was much easier to hear and understand. Hence, when she was finally dismissed from the speech clinic, she had improved in several respects. Her voice was a much more effective instrument for communication than it formerly had been. The voice quality still left something to be desired, but she had learned to adjust to that, and she could and did talk with animation and expressiveness, at a loudness level that made her speech easily apprehended by her listeners.

What has just been said implies that certain voice improvement procedures will be rather routinely employed with almost all voice cases. The following paragraphs will attempt to make clear the nature of these procedures.

*Adequate Pitch Level.* With voice problems which fall into the classification of pitch disorders, procedures for teaching the pupil to employ a more adequate pitch level are, of course, the core of the treatment. As has been pointed out previously, there are, in addition, pitch levels which are not so deficient as to call particular attention to themselves but which may nevertheless result in poor voice production.

In general, there is for each person's vocal mechanism a general pitch level at which he is able to produce voice most efficiently and effectively. Because this pitch level is determined by his vocal mechanism—length and mass of vocal folds, for one thing— it is sometimes referred to as his *natural pitch level*. The problem is to discover what that pitch level is, and then to make the use of it habitual.

A number of procedures have been suggested for determining natural pitch level. To the writers it seems that the best of these involve a careful determination of the total range of pitches the individual can produce, and of the pitch level most suitable for his voice in terms of that range. Such procedures have a definite rationale, since the best general pitch level for an individual's voice must almost certainly be some function of his pitch range. It must, at least, lie somewhere in the midpart of his easily producible pitch range, since it must allow for pitch inflections both above and below this average level. Furthermore, the general procedure is practical. Except for individuals who have so little pitch sense that they cannot sing a scale, the total pitch range may be reliably determined by anyone who has a reasonably good ear for pitch and has access to a piano. A complete description of the recommended procedure for determining the total pitch range and locating the natural pitch level within this range is given in Appendix VI.

*Good Breathing Habits.* The function of the breathing mechanism in voice production and the untoward effects of bad breathing habits have already been discussed. The general program of training for adequate voice production in all respects will therefore take note of the student's breathing habits for speech.

It has already been mentioned that most persons learn adequate speech breathing without any special training. Even a large proportion of cases with voice disorders will be found to have adequate breathing habits. One cannot assume this, however, so the person's breathing habits should be carefully observed. If the breathing is markedly shallow, is badly controlled, or involves a considerable amount of excessive tension, better breathing habits should be taught. In cases of doubt, it is better to spend some time in building good breathing habits than to neglect the matter.

Training in good breathing habits emphasizes easy expansion and contraction of the whole torso for inhalation and exhalation without excessive muscular tension and effort. It insures that the expansion of the torso in the lower chest and abdominal region is not restricted. It emphasizes easy, effortless, and controlled production of voice during exhalation. Various pitches and loudness levels are employed in this work to make sure that adequate air pressure is produced for the whole range of pitch and loudness required in speech. For reasons already given, in this training one does not waste time on exercises in deep breathing or attempt to teach any special method of breathing.

*Relaxed Tone Production with Unrestricted Throat and Oral Passageways.* There is ample evidence from the experiences of teachers of voice for both singing and speech that good voice is produced without excessive muscular tensions in the speech mechanism and its associated structures. The subject of such tensions in the breathing mechanism has just been discussed. It is generally recognized, in addition, that certain voice disorders, especially harsh voice quality, may be caused by excessive tensions in the muscles of the larynx and throat. In producing good voice one should not be aware of special effort and strain. Pronounced vocal fatigue as a typical experience, which it seems to be in some cases, indicates that something is definitely wrong, either in the vocal mechanism or in the way it is being used.

This matter is considered of such importance by some authorities and teachers that they recommend spending some time on practicing easy, relaxed voice production with all cases. The real goal of such practice is optimum muscle tonus, of course. Good voice production is easy and relaxed in the same way that a good golf swing is easy and relaxed. Whether or not time should be spent on practice to achieve this goal with all cases is a matter on which there is some room for difference of opinion. The writers lean to the view that if the person shows no evidence of excessive effort and strain for voice production, if his voice shows no traces of harshness, or breathiness, or hoarseness, and if he seems to be able to produce an ample amount of loudness rather easily, then such practice has little to recommend it. But with many voice disorders these conditions will not be fulfilled, so practice to achieve easy, effortless tone production will be needed.

Another consideration, which is to some extent related to what we have been talking about, is that of avoiding unnecessary constriction of the throat and mouth passageways during voice production. Singing teachers talk about developing an "open throat" and "open tones." So far as the throat is concerned, the desired result is obtained if the relaxed, easy voice production discussed in the previous paragraph is achieved. However, an open mouth passageway for the sound is not necessarily assured by such practice. Some persons, a large proportion of those with voice problems, habitually speak with narrow mouth openings and inactive jaws and lips. With respect to articulation the possible effects are relatively obvious. It may not be so obvious, however, that such restriction of jaw movement and mouth opening also has a bad effect on voice. It is probably the most important single factor in many cases of functional nasal voice quality. In fact, Williamson[10] found that all but a few of his nasal voice cases achieved good voice quality and eliminated excessive nasal resonance as a consequence of training which emphasized wider mouth and jaw openings and greater jaw and lip activity.

The reason for this is fairly easy to understand if one stops to think about it. If the oral channel for the sound is constricted by a close jaw position or a high tongue position, or both, the opposition to the transmission of sound energy out through the mouth will tend to be increased. The result is that a greater percentage of the total sound energy from the vocal folds will tend to be transmitted into the nasal passages, either through an incomplete closure between the soft palate and pharyngeal walls or through the soft palate acting as a drum membrane. The effect of nasal resonance on the sound produced by the voice is thus increased. In addition, an open oral passageway for the sound is important for adequate loudness of voice and good voice production in general. Hence, as a part of the general program of treatment which can be used to good advantage with most cases of voice disorder, attention is given to developing a normal amount of activity of the jaw and lips, and to eradicating any existing habits of speaking with a very narrow mouth opening.

*Improving Flexibility and Expressiveness.* Training to improve flexibility and expressiveness of voice is the most important single goal for those whose disorder is mainly one of flexibility. What we are talking about here is, therefore, the very heart of the retraining program for such cases. However, most poor voices, whether they be poor with respect to quality, loudness, or pitch, are also somewhat monotonous and inexpressive. It follows that training to overcome this deficiency is an important part of the more *general program of vocal retraining* that is here being discussed.

An extended discussion of techniques for such retraining would

[10] A. B. Williamson, "Diagnosis and Treatment of Eighty-four Cases of Nasality," *Quarterly Journal of Speech* (1944), 30:471-479.

be out of place in this book. Only certain basic principles will be mentioned. The chief requisites of flexibility and expressiveness of voice are something to say and a desire to communicate. Another is that the individual feel sufficiently comfortable and at ease in the speaking situation to allow his voice to express what he wants to say with forcefulness and meaning. These are psychological factors, of course, and, as we have seen, the individual whose voice is extremely deficient in expressiveness usually has important difficulties in adjustment to all kinds of speaking situations. If a deep-seated and serious personality disturbance lies at the root of the difficulty, then the job to be done is beyond the training and knowledge of the speech correctionist or the classroom teacher. On the other hand, quite frequently the difficulty is nothing more than a certain more or less common degree of shyness and timidity, and what the individual needs is merely a little special encouragement and some help in developing a normal amount of self-assurance. In a case of this sort, both the speech correctionist and the classroom teacher can be of considerable assistance. The important ideas and techniques for helping the child with this sort of problem have been thoroughly covered in Chapter II.

A further requisite for overcoming a deficiency in flexibility of voice is for the child to learn to recognize how inflexible and monotonous his voice patterns are, and to develop definite auditory impressions of what good expressive voice usage is. Lastly, he needs practice in developing habits of better expressiveness and in transferring these habits to ordinary speech situations. Oral reading of stories and poetry is frequently used with good results. But the habits must be carried into other types of speaking situations besides that of oral reading, so practice should include the use of discussions and conversation. And the transition of the habit to other situations, in the classroom and outside of it, should be emphasized.

The *general program* of voice retraining which has just been discussed will be adequate to take care of all but a few of the voice disorders ordinarily encountered in the schoolroom. The procedures will need to be adapted to meet the particular problems of each child. But the adaptation will be mainly a matter of emphasis, and the important matters of pitch level, breathing habits, easy, relaxed tone production, and adequate flexibility will need to be considered for each pupil. Retraining with respect to them will be planned according to the particular needs of the individual. There has been little mention in this section of specific exercises and practice materials. An ample amount of material of this sort can be found in the references listed in the Appendix. Among these, the two books by Fairbanks are particularly recommended.

VOICE RETRAINING TECHNIQUES

The preceding discussion has outlined a general program of voice retraining which, if properly carried out, will meet the needs of most pupils having voice problems. Very little was said about techniques for carrying out this program, however, and it is the purpose of this section to suggest the techniques which may be used. As a matter of fact, they are in many respects so similar to those already described in the chapter on articulatory disorders that little more will need to be added here.

*Ear Training.* The child with a voice problem needs ear training just as does the child with an articulatory deficiency, and for much the same reasons. He needs to learn to recognize what it is about his voice that needs correction. He must build up a strong auditory impression of good pitch, or good voice quality, or adequate loudness or flexibility, so that he knows what he is working for. He needs to be able to discriminate readily between good and faulty voice production.

Practice in recognizing and identifying his fault when imitated by the teacher will aid in providing such ear training. Practice in discriminating between good and bad pitch, or quality, as she stimulates him first with one and then the other, will be helpful. Assignments can be given to older pupils to observe the speech of others and to see how many can be found who exhibit similar faulty vocal habits. As with articulatory errors, names can be given to the faulty habits, such as the "talking through the nose voice," the "rusty hinge voice," the "talking to yourself voice," and so on. Care should be taken that these names do not carry connotations which will be injurious to the child's sensitive feelings or will increase his timidity or anxiety about his problem in any way. Recording equipment, if available, is of particular value in this ear training practice.

*Practice with Isolated Vowels.* With some kinds of voice practice, isolated vowels make better practice material than connected speech with which to begin acquisition of the new habit. This is particularly true when practice is first begun on a new pitch level, when practice is being given in easy, relaxed vocalization, or when any new voice quality habit is first being taught. In many respects this is similar to the practice with isolated sounds in teaching a new articulatory habit. It provides a simpler, easier situation in which to teach the new habit.

In teaching a new pitch level the teacher can ask the pupil to sing up or down a scale until the desired pitch is reached. The pupil can then be asked to sustain this pitch as he produces the vowel *ah*, then *oh*, *ee*, and so forth. He should practice it on all vowels, at various loudnesses. He should learn what it feels like and definitely fix in mind the auditory impression of this pitch level. After it has been thus practiced, words can be practiced at the same pitch level, allowing a normal inflection of pitch but maintaining the same general level. Still later, phrases and sentences may be used.

In teaching easy, relaxed voice production, the teacher will nearly always use isolated vowels at the beginning of the work. The pupil, seated in an easy, relaxed position, is asked to sustain a vowel in a very soft voice. Some teachers start with a relaxed sigh and only gradually have the pupil begin to vocalize the sigh. The loudness is increased little by little until a vowel of normal loudness is being sustained. Various vowels are used, though there is perhaps some advantage in starting with a relatively open vowel, such as *ah*. The pitch also is varied, but with easy, relaxed voice production maintained at all times. Later, words, phrases, and sentences can be used, as above.

Teaching a new voice quality involves much the same technique of using isolated sustained vowels. Since the child is usually able to hear and imitate the new quality on isolated vowels more easily than if words or sentences are used, the new quality will be taught first by using vowels and will be reinforced thoroughly before word and sentences are attempted.

*Auditory Stimulation.* Voice habits, like articulatory habits, are learned largely through imitation of what the pupil hears. Auditory stimulation is thus the basic technique for teaching a new voice habit just as it is for teaching the correct articulation of a speech sound. The teacher will bombard the pupil's ear with the model that he is to imitate. He will learn correct loudness through imitation, good flexibility and expressiveness through imitation, the correct pitch level through imitation, etc. Throughout all the voice retraining, as throughout all corrective work in articulation, auditory stimulation is the basic technique used at each stage of training and to supplement any other procedures which may be employed.

*Negative Practice.* Once the student has acquired the new vocal habit to the extent of being able to produce it easily and at will, at least on isolated vowels, negative practice can be very useful. It has the same virtues of weakening the old, faulty habit that were discussed in the preceding chapter. In addition, it seems to give the pupil a considerable sense of having control of the situation if he can produce his old faulty habit or the new good habit at will, and can alternate them as he chooses. Valuable reinforcement to ear training is also provided by this kind of practice.

*Transfer to Ordinary Speech.* The process of transferring the new habit, whether it is one of pitch, voice quality, loudness, or flexibility to ordinary everyday speaking situations will require the use of the same sort of assignments that were suggested for achieving the transfer of a new articulatory habit to connected speech. Nucleus situations may be employed in a very similar manner. The classroom teacher can assist in this stage of the retraining process in much the same way as was indicated in the previous chapter. Goals should be kept limited, at first, so that the pupil has the reward of experiencing success. Later, assignments seeking to eradicate the old habit in all speaking situations can be carried out.

SPECIAL VOICE RETRAINING TECHNIQUES

The program of retraining and the techniques which have been discussed are the fundamentals for the treatment of voice disorders. Very few remediable cases will not yield to such a program. There are, however, a few types of voice disorders which require more specialized techniques. Those that are likely to be encountered in the classroom will be considered in this section.

*After the Adenoids Are Removed.* The problem of the child with enlarged adenoids has already been discussed so far as the organic factors and their relation to his speech are concerned. It was pointed out that removal of the adenoids does not solve the speech problem, but really creates a different one, since the obstruction to the nasal passages is removed but the normal functioning of the soft palate and walls of the pharynx is not restored. Special retraining procedures are required to develop this function again. The child must be able to close off the upper pharynx and nasal cavities so that air pressure can be produced in the mouth for certain consonant sounds, and so that sound can be emitted through the oral cavity without excessive nasal resonance. In this respect the problem is similar to that of the child with a repaired cleft palate. The speech problem of the cleft palate child is discussed in Chapter VII and exercises are suggested there for developing the necessary activity of the soft palate and walls of the throat. These same exercises should be employed with a child whose voice is very nasal following the removel of adenoids. In addition to these exercises, considerable portions of the general program previously outlined in this chapter will be needed. Practice in speaking with good jaw and lip activity and directing the sound out through the mouth will be especially important.

*Other Severely Nasal Voices.* Most cases of functional nasal voice quality will respond to the kind of treatment discussed under the general program of voice retraining. Sometimes children with severely nasal voices are found who for no apparent reason, other than faulty habit formation, seem unable to close the port leading to the upper pharynx and nasal cavities. They have sluggish soft palates. These cases also require special exercises of the types prescribed in the preceding paragraph.

Sometimes it will be noted that certain vowels are produced with little or no excessive nasal resonance, despite the generally nasal character of the voice. These vowels can be used to teach the child what his voice sounds like when it is not nasal, and as "nucleus" sounds from which nonnasal quality may be learned on other vowels.

*The Breathy Voice.*   Breathy voice quality, as previously explained, is a result of excessive escape of air from between the vocal folds during production of voice. It will usually yield to the general program of retraining discussed above, especially if a faulty pitch level or poor breathing habits are found to be related to the quality problem, as they often are. Certain special techniques may often be used to good advantage, however.

One thing that is sometimes helpful is to have the child prolong a vowel sound at a rather loud level. This loud voice will seldom be breathy in quality because the nature of the adjustments required in the larynx make it difficult to produce loud voice which is at the same time breathy. If the pupil then gradually reduces the loudness of this tone while trying to keep out breathiness, he may find that a nonbreathy quality can be produced at ordinary loudness. A successful attempt will need to be reinforced immediately, of course, and the student should listen to it, try to feel what is happening, and get all possible cues which will enable him to learn to produce this quality at will.

Another device is to have the child practice prolonging a tone as long as he can on one breath, or to practice counting as far as possible on a single breath, or to practice reading as long as possible without taking breath. We do not ordinarily do these things when we talk, obviously, but forcing the student to conserve the breath by these devices will frequently help in securing nonbreathy voice. Breathy voice is extremely wasteful of the air supply in the lungs. Practice like that suggested works in the direction of achieving a voice which is less wasteful and hence less breathy.

## What the Classroom Teacher Can Do

TO AID THE SPEECH CORRECTIONIST

Much of what the classroom teacher can do to aid the speech correctionist has already been suggested. Her part in helping the child to realize that he has a voice problem on which he needs to work has been mentioned and only needs to be emphasized here. The importance of this step in the correction process is obvious. Nothing can be accomplished unless the child is motivated to improve. The classroom teacher can be of important assistance in helping to arouse this motivation, without at the same time creating anxiety. Her part in providing encouragement along the way is no less important.

The assistance that the classroom teacher can provide during the stage when new voice habits are being transferred to connected speech is so similar to the assistance needed in transferring new articulatory habits that no additional discussion is required. Because only brief mention of this function is made, it should not be assumed that it is relatively inconsequential, however. The speech correctionist can teach good habits during the speech correction lessons, but she cannot insure that they are made part and parcel of the child's everyday speech without assistance from the classroom teacher. And all her efforts come to naught unless the everyday speaking of the child is improved.

Because many voice cases lack confidence and self-assurance, and because these lacks are often basic to their voice problems, the classroom teacher can be of special help in guiding the child to better adjustment to various social and speaking situations. This is not to suggest that she attempt to operate as a clinical psychologist. The things she can do are, in the main, what good teachers usually do. Counteracting shyness and timidity and encouraging confidence and poise are certainly a part of the teacher's everyday job. The only reason for mentioning them here is to emphasize that voice disorders are sometimes important symptoms of such adjustment problems, and that the child with a voice problem may need a little special attention in this respect.

*When There Is No Speech Correctionist.* Just as the teacher who has a special interest and is willing somehow to "make" the time can help the child with certain types of articulatory problems by undertaking actual corrective work, so can she do much to help children with many sorts of voice disorders. Again it should be emphasized that this is not the ideal or even the desirable answer to problems of children with speech handicaps. At best it is only a partial solution, since there will be disorders with which the classroom teacher is not prepared to deal without considerable additional training. And, of course, she already has a full-time job. But in the absence of the specially trained teacher, the classroom teacher can help to bridge the gap for children with voice problems in the same way that she can for children with articulatory disorders.

The information and procedures given in this chapter provide the main tools, though they will need to be supplemented with exercises and assignments from the references provided in the Appendix, and with assignments of the teacher's own devising.

One other tool is needed by the teacher who attempts voice retraining. She should have a voice which is, itself, adequate in all important respects. The retraining process depends so much on imitation, and the auditory stimulation provided by the teacher is so fundamental, that this requirement is a must for any person who would work with voice problems. Most teachers have good voices and so will have no cause for concern on this point. However, each person undertaking work with voice problems should be aware of its importance.

The voice cases which the classroom teacher without special training can attempt to work with will need to be selected only to the extent of avoiding those in which a profound emotional disturbance may be a complicating factor, and those which may have some active organic condition that would be aggravated by vocal practice. In all cases in which the latter situation is suspected medical consultation should be sought. These latter cases are, however, not common among school age children.

Most, then, of the children with voice problems which the teacher may find in her classroom will be ones she can attempt to help, if she will. The work will require time, energy, and patience. The teacher should not undertake it unless she is prepared to carry through. Only if she begins with a determination to finish what she starts can she expect her efforts to be of any real benefit to the child. Her rewards will be the gratitude of the children with whom she works and her own satisfaction in knowing that she is meeting the needs of her children better. But these will be rich rewards if she is the type of person who ought to attempt to work with children's handicaps at all. To them she can add the thanks and blessings of those of us who are the so-called "experts" in the correction of speech disorders, but who are not yet numerous enough to get around to all the children who need this special kind of training and care.

# CHAPTER V

wwwwwwwwwwwwwwwwwwwwwwwwwwwwwwwwwwwwwwwwwwwwwwwwwwwwwwwwwwwwwwwwwwwww

# *Stuttering*

What is stuttering?[1] Several recent clinical and laboratory studies have served to help us appreciate the complexity of this question. It is a question that takes on great importance particularly at two specific times in the life of any individual who may be concerned. The first of these is the moment at which the individual, usually when he is a child between two and four years of age, is looked upon for the very first time by someone, nearly always his parents, as a stutterer. This is truly a fateful moment and the decision made at this time by the mother or father as to whether the child "is a stutterer" is one that has serious and enduring consequences. The basis on which such parents—any parents, or teachers, or physicians, or any persons whatever— answer for themselves the question "What is stuttering?" is to be scrutinized certainly with all possible care and thoughtfulness. The other time in the life of the individual when the question becomes crucial is when it becomes for him, "Am I no longer a stutterer?" How does one enter into the category of "stutterer" and, having entered, how does one leave? This is the basic and clearly significant question we are asking whenever we ask, "What is stuttering?"

[1] In accordance with prevailing custom in the United States the word "stuttering" is used predominantly and in general preference to "stammering" in this book. The latter term appears to be preferred, however, in England and most other English-speaking parts of the world. It is generally agreed that the two words may be used synonymously.

## The Problem of Definition

The problem of defining stuttering is not to be dismissed in a paragraph or two. During the next several pages we shall give rather detailed consideration to it, and after due examination of the more important aspects of the matter, we shall present a definition. What we are to mean by stuttering, especially in its early childhood forms, is so fundamental to all that we are to say about it and do about it that it will be very much worth our while to give careful attention to the problem of definition.

Although stuttering is commonly defined in dictionaries and textbooks as a disorder in the rhythm or fluency of speech, manifested in repeated sounds, words, or phrases, or in prolonged sounds, pauses, blockages, or hesitancies, this can be only a partial definition, and it is one that turns out to be ambiguous when applied. Among its other shortcomings as a definition, it seems to imply that in normal speech there are no disturbances of rhythm or fluency, no repetitions or prolonged sounds or other hesitancies.

The fact is that speech fluency, or nonfluency, is a statistical matter. That is, persons who do not stutter show a vast range of individual differences with respect to the fluency of their speech. So do persons who stutter. In studies that have been done at the University of Iowa, as yet unpublished as this is being written, objective measurements have been made of nonfluency in the speech of 50 University of Iowa male students, ranging in age from seventeen to twenty-four years, with an average age of slightly over nineteen years, and 50 male stutterers of the same general age level drawn from seven different midwestern colleges.[2] Speech samples were tape-recorded under each of three conditions: (1) Job task: each subject spoke ex-

[2] Speech samples have also been obtained from 50 female nonstutterers of approximately the same age level, and samples are now being accumulated from a group of 50 female stutterers; comparisons of these groups with each other and with the male groups will be made in due time. This research is being done under a grant from the Louis W. and Maud Hill Family Foundation. The investigators who have participated in the study are Richard Boehmler, Forrest Lee Brissey, Robert Duffy, Carolyn Gustafson, James V. Frick, William Trotter, Dean Williams, and the writer.

temporaneously for at least two minutes and not more than three and one-half minutes about a past job or a desired future job; (2) TAT task: each subject responded according to standard instructions to TAT card No. 10;[3] Oral Reading task: each subject read aloud a 300-word passage prepared by Darley.[4] Measures of reading and speaking rate are summarized in Table 1.

Nonfluencies were classified in eight different categories: interjections of syllables, sounds, words, or phrases; repetitions of parts of words; repetitions of whole words; repetitions of phrases; revisions (changes in wording or grammatical structure of a

TABLE 1.  Rate Medians, 90th Percentiles, and Ranges in Words Per Minute for 50 Male Stutterers and 50 Male Nonstutterers of College Age, for Oral Reading and for Each of Two Extemporaneous Speaking Tasks (Talking about Past or Future Job and Responding to a Projective Test Picture Card—TAT Card No. 10)

|  | Range | Median | 90th Percentile |
|---|---|---|---|
| Job Task |  |  |  |
| Stutterers | 15–184 | 97 | 139 |
| Nonstutterers | 42–201 | 136 | 163 |
| TAT Task |  |  |  |
| Stutterers | 13–149 | 83 | 128 |
| Nonstutterers | 72–198 | 117 | 147 |
| Oral Reading[a] |  |  |  |
| Stutterers | 16–200 | 122 | 173 |
| Nonstutterers | 104-217 | 174 | 196 |

[a] Darley, in the study cited in Footnote 4, reported a median rate of 166.1 words per minute for 200 college age nonstuttering subjects. Bloodstein, in "The Relationship between Oral Reading Rate and Severity of Stuttering," *Journal of Speech Disorders* (1944), 9:161-173, reported a median overall oral reading rate of 133.4 words per minute and a median rate for nonstuttered words of 146.1 words per minute for 30 college age stutterers.

[3] H. Murray, *Manual for Thematic Apperception Test,* Cambridge, Harvard University Press, 1943.

[4] F. L. Darley, "A Normative Study of Oral Reading Rate," unpublished M.A. thesis, University of Iowa, 1940. The reading passage is available in published form in Grant Fairbanks, *Voice and Articulation Drillbook,* New York, Harper & Brothers, 1940, p. 144.

phrase, or in pronunciation of a word—e.g., "I was—I am going home"); incomplete phrases (e.g., "She was—and after she got there, he came"); broken words (words not completed or broken as in "I was g(pause)oing home"); prolonged sounds or parts of words. The number of instances of each type of nonfluency per 100 words was computed for each task for each subject, and the total number of instances of all types per 100 words was also determined for each task for each subject. Nonfluency data are summarized in Table 2 in terms of the total number of nonfluencies of all types per 100 words.

TABLE 2. Ranges, Medians, and 90th Percentiles of Speech Fluency Measured in Terms of Number of Nonfluencies of All Types Per 100 Words for Each of 50 Male Stutterers and 50 Male Nonstutterers of College Age, for Oral Reading and for Each of Two Extemporaneous Speaking Tasks (Talking about Past or Future Job and Responding to a Projective Test Picture Card—TAT Card No. 10)

|  | Range | Median | 90th Percentile |
|---|---|---|---|
| **Job Task** |  |  |  |
| Stutterers | 2.7–127.3 | 17.5 | 55.4 |
| Nonstutterers | 0.8– 20.2 | 6.7 | 12.0 |
| **TAT Task** |  |  |  |
| Stutterers | 4.5–135.3 | 21.7 | 61.2 |
| Nonstutterers | 0.7– 19.9 | 6.2 | 11.5 |
| **Oral Reading** |  |  |  |
| Stutterers | 0–141.5 | 7.7 | 34.3 |
| Nonstutterers | 0– 4.0 | 1.0 | 3.0 |

During the speech tasks over three fourths of the stutterers' nonfluencies were interjections (over one third of the total), part-word repetitions (one fourth of the total), and whole word repetitions (slightly less than one sixth of the total); during oral reading part-word repetitions made up nearly 45 percent, prolonged sounds or parts of words comprised 14 percent, and interjections made up nearly 12 percent of the stutterers' nonfluencies. During the two speech tasks approximately 90 percent of the nonstutterers' nonfluencies were interjections (over 55 percent, revisions (over 20 percent), and whole word repetitions (about 12 percent); during oral reading, revisions made up 40 percent of the nonstutterers' nonfluencies, and part-word repetitions made up about 35 percent. In general, while there are considerable group differences, there is at the same time a good deal of overlapping so far as numbers of nonfluencies are concerned. The differences appear to be greater, though still with some similarity, between stutterers and nonstutterers with respect to the kinds of nonfluencies that were more and less frequently observed in their speech.

A particularly striking way to indicate the extent of overlapping or similarity between the groups is to be found in data obtained in a special study made by means of some of the oral reading samples. For each one of the 12 most fluent stutterers during oral reading it was possible to select a nonstutterer who presented approximately the same total number of nonfluencies. The tape-recorded oral reading samples of these 12 stutterers and 12 nonstutterers were presented in random order to a group of 43 speech pathology students, about one third of whom were speech correctionists with job experience, who were instructed to judge each recording as being that of a stutterer or a nonstutterer. The average stuttered sample was classified as such by 14.6 listeners, and the average nonstuttered sample was classified as a stuttered sample by 10.6 of the 43 listeners. (The difference between 14.6 and 10.6 was not statistically significant at the 5 per cent level.) Only seven of the 12 stutterers' samples were so considered by more than 13 of the 43 judges, and no stutterer's recording was so judged by all 43 listeners. Moreover, three of the nonstutterers were considered to be stutterers by more than 13 judges, and only one speech sample was classified as that of a nonstutterer by all 43 judges.

The fact that 43 relatively sophisticated listeners had this much difficulty in trying to tell which of the 24 samples were those of the 12 stutterers indicates that the two groups of speakers were much alike not only with respect to fluency but also with regard to other aspects of their speech. As a matter of fact, it is most thought-provoking that approximately one fourth of a presumably representative sampling of 50 stutterers drawn from seven midwestern colleges should turn out to read orally in such a way that they could be matched for fluency on an objective basis with an equal number of presumably representative nonstutterers of like age. This in itself forces attention to the complexity of the problem involved in defining stuttering as a "disorder of the rhythm of speech." There is evidently no clear and sharp dividing line between the speech of stutterers and that of nonstutterers, certainly not with respect to fluency. It seems to be the case that speakers are distributed along the various dimensions of speech behavior, including fluency, from one extreme to the other, with the great majority to be found somewhere between the extremes.

Meanwhile, if a person is convinced that he stutters, he definitely has a problem even though he may speak quite fluently —and a notable proportion of cases who come to speech clinics as stutterers do speak with relatively slight disturbance so far as fluency is concerned. In drawing due attention to the fact that stuttering and nonfluency are not the same we must not, however, overlook the fact that as a group, particularly beyond the early childhood age level, stutterers are definitely more nonfluent than are persons who are not regarded by themselves or others as stutterers. Due attention is to be given also to the reported differences in the predominating types of nonfluency in the speaking and reading of stutterers and of nonstutterers.

So far we have discussed speech fluency in college age adults. Fluency norms for children between the ages of two and five years, inclusive, have been determined in investigations involving nearly 200 youngsters, unselected except for the fact that they were attending the preschools of the Iowa Child Welfare Research Station in Iowa City. Speech samples were obtained during free-play situations by observers who presumably did not disturb the activities of the children in the preschool setting while securing the samples. Other samples were obtained by means of a specially constructed test designed to elicit speech in response to pictures, toys, and activities. Repetitions of parts of words (generally syllable and sound repetitions), whole words, and phrases (two or more words) were noted and tabulated. There was marked agreement among the findings from five different samplings or studies made at different times by different investigators.[5] In general, counting repetitions of all types during free-play speech, there was an average of 49 instances of repetition per 1,000 running words. Slightly less than one fourth of the words figured in some kind of repetition— either a part of the word in each case was repeated, or the word as a whole was repeated, or the word was part of a repeated phrase. In the speech test situation there was an average of about 36 instances of repetition per 1,000 words, and approximately 10 per cent of the words were involved in repetitions of one sort or another. No child was found who did not repeat at all, and the range, presumably the range for normal speech at this age level, extended up to well beyond 100 instances of repetition per 1,000 words for free-play speech and nearly 90 for the speech test situation. The average amount of repetitiveness declined somewhat with age, within the age limits covered in the various samplings; in the Davis sample of 62 children at 2, 3, and 4 years, in the free-play situation, the average values decreased from 54 instances of repetition per 1,000 words at age 2 to 40 instances at age 4; in the Hughes sample of 39 children, one group age 2 and one age 4, in the test situation, the average number of repetitions per 1,000 words at age 2 was 41 and at age 4 it was 27.

[5] For a detailed account of this research see Margaret E. Branscom, Jeannette Hughes, and Eloise Tupper Oxtoby, "Studies of Nonfluency in the Speech of Preschool Children," in *Stuttering in Children and Adults: Thirty Years of Research at the University of Iowa,* edited by Wendell Johnson and Ralph Leutenegger, Minneapolis, University of Minnesota Press, 1955, Chapter 5. See also Dorothy M. Davis, "The Relation of Repetitions in the Speech of Young Children to Certain Measures of Language Maturity and Situational Factors," *Journal of Speech Disorders* (1939), 4:303-318; (1940), 5:235-246. For discussion of the theoretical and practical implications of the data from these studies see Wendell Johnson, "The Time, the Place, and the Problem," Chapter 1, and "A Study of the Onset and Development of Stuttering," Chapter 3, in *Stuttering in Children and Adults: Thirty Years of Research at the University of Iowa, op. cit.;* and Perceptual and Evaluational Factors in Stuttering," in *Handbook of Speech Pathology,* edited by Lee Edward Travis, New York, Appleton-Century-Crofts, Inc., in press.

Repetition is a normal characteristic of speech from the very beginning, of course. The birth cry itself is typically repeated over and over again. Professor Orvis C. Irwin and his students at the Iowa Child Welfare Research Station have found in their extensive studies of the vocalizing and speech sound production of infants that roughly one third to nearly two thirds (depending on mode of analysis) of the sound elements produced during the first year of life are repeated.[6]

It has so far proved essentially impossible to obtain a set of speech samples from young stutterers at the time of so-called onset of stuttering—that is to say, on the very day of onset or within a few days, or even a few weeks, after the alleged onset. It would be very desirable also, and has not yet proved to be possible, to obtain speech samples from such children a day or so, or a few weeks, before they are first judged to be stuttering. We know from intensive studies of the conditions under which stuttering arises, and the nature of it at time of onset, that once a child has come to be regarded or diagnosed as a stutterer, his speech behavior tends to change, rather slowly in some cases and very quickly in others, so that unless a speech recording is made promptly at the time when someone is just beginning to feel that a specific child is stuttering, it cannot provide a valid sample of the child's speech at "time of onset."[7] Intensive interviewing of parents relatively soon after alleged date of onset of stuttering in their children indicates that, generally speaking, the parents

[6] Relevant data are included in a dissertation by one of Professor Irwin's students, Han Piao Chen, "Speech Sound Development During the First Year of Life, a Quantitative Study," unpublished Ph.D. dissertation, University of Iowa, 1946, pp. 79-87. A further study of these data and additional data covering the second year of life is being made at the present time by H. Winitz under Professor Irwin's direction.

[7] Detailed accounts of investigations of the onset and early development of stuttering have been published by Frederic L. Darley and by the writer, and are to be found in Chapters 3 and 4 of *Stuttering in Children and Adults, op. cit.* An additional comprehensive study of this kind involving 150 stuttering children and their parents, and 150 nonstuttering children and their parents, has been completed by the writer and his associates, under a grant from the Louis W. and Maud Hill Family Foundation, and is scheduled for publication under the title of *The Onset of Stuttering*, probably during 1956, by the University of Minnesota Press.

are the first to make the judgment, or diagnosis, of stuttering in nearly all cases, and that the speech phenomena they take to be stuttering are for the most part the simple, essentially effortless, repetitions of syllables, words, and phrases of the sort that, as we have seen, are to be observed with considerable frequency in the speech of normal children. In Johnson's study of 46 young stutterers, the sole type of speech reaction in 42 cases, and the main type in all 46 cases, that the parents had originally identified as stuttering was the normal repetition we have been considering.[8] In Darley's investigation of 50 stutterers, who were on the whole somewhat older than Johnson's 46 cases, one or both of the parents of 41 of the 50 children reported that the first signs of what they took to be stuttering were solely repetitions of sounds, syllables, words, or phrases, and that in four other cases the only other reactions reported were "hesitations" or prolonged sounds. "At least one parent in each case for forty-four of the children stated that the stuttering was characterized by no tensions whatsoever. In only six cases did the parents agree that the first stuttering was characterized by some tension, and in only two of these cases did the parents agree as to the degree of tension. . . . In the case of only three children did the parents agree that the child seemed aware of a difference."[9]

The basic facts appear to be fairly clear in this connection. So far as the kind of nonfluency is concerned, one can hardly be sure from the known data that there is, *at the moment of original judgment or diagnosis,* any considerable difference— and there may be little or no difference—between the speech of children who are judged by their parents to be stutterers and that of children who are not so judged by their parents. As to the amount of nonfluency, again one can hardly assert as a fact, from known data, that the children whose parents look upon them as stutterers are, *at the moment of original judgment or diagnosis,* more frequently repetitive or nonfluent in their speech than are children whose parents do not classify them as stutterers. Certainly, as we have seen, the norms indicate that in the speech of

[8] *Stuttering in Children and Adults, op. cit.,* Chapter 3.
[9] *Stuttering in Children and Adults, op. cit.,* Chapter 4.

normal or representative youngsters there is a considerable quantity of repetitiveness—roughly 35 to 50 instances of repetition per thousand words on the average. In the close questioning of hundreds of parents of allegedly stuttering children one gets the impression that the nonfluency they are referring to in the speech of their own children was not more than that on the average, *at the moment of diagnosis.* In an impressive number of cases the children do not appear, even at time of interview, to be more nonfluent than the average normal youngster.

Once a child has been diagnosed or classified as a stutterer, however, as has been mentioned, his speech behavior tends to become modified. Darley's findings in this connection are particularly revealing:

In only two cases (in both of which the interview was conducted within one month of onset) had both parents apparently refrained from making any comment to the child about his speech. . . .

In all the other forty-eight cases one parent or both had made suggestions or comments to the child calculated to help him overcome the stuttering. The most frequent suggestions were to "talk more slowly" (made to forty-three children), "stop and start over" (to thirty-six children), "think of what you're going to say" (to thirty-two children), "take it easy" (to twenty-six children), "relax," "take a deep breath," and "repeat." Many parents (at least one for each of twenty-seven children) said the difficult words for the child. Such helps were given at least daily to thirty-five of the children according to at least one of the parents. Eighteen mothers and eleven fathers who had once offered suggestions, stated that more lately they had abandoned such efforts and simply allowed the children to speak as best they could.

Examination of the complete list of suggestions made in this home therapy shows that most of the comments and efforts, though well intended, could have been interpreted by the child involved to mean that the parent was worried about his speech or disapproved of it for some reason. Recalling the facts reviewed in the preceding section concerning the initial lack of awareness on the part of the children of any "difference" in their speech, one can visualize the baffling and frustrating effect of suggestions to speak somehow differently without the children's having a clear idea of why they were to do this or precisely what they were to do. . . .

The mean number of repetitions in current stuttering reported by both mothers and fathers was slightly higher than that reported at onset. The parents judged the current stuttering to be characterized by more tension than the stuttering at onset. At least one parent of each of twenty-five children judged that the child was using "much more force" (manifesting much more tension) than at first, and at least one parent of each of seventeen additional children rated the "force" used in speaking as "somewhat more" than at first. Only fifteen sets of parents agreed exactly as to the degree of tension manifested currently in stuttering.

Twelve of the children were judged by both parents to be free of facial grimaces and bodily movements in their stuttering. At least one parent of each of the other thirty-eight children listed some such behavior as associated with the child's present stuttering.[10]

In research subsequent to Darley's investigation, tape-recorded samples of speech have been obtained from young stutterers and nonstutterers, and as this is being written, the analysis of 84 of these samples, 42 from each group, has been partially completed.[11] The samples have been analyzed with respect to nonfluencies in accordance with the procedure used in the determination of speech fluency norms for adults, which have been described in relation to Table 2. Essential data are summarized in Table 3.

A few words of comment and explanation are in order with reference to the figures presented in Table 3. First of all, to the degree that they are comparable to the median values given in Table 2 for nonfluency measures made of adult speech samples, it is to be inferred that the differences in nonfluency between stuttering and nonstuttering adults are greater than the differences between stuttering and nonstuttering children. This is due chiefly to the difference in fluency between younger and older stutterers; young nonstutters, it is interesting to note, are very nearly as fluent as adults who do not stutter. The figures indicate that within from one to two years after date of onset of stuttering

[10] *Stuttering in Children and Adults, op. cit.,* Chapter 4, pp. 139-141. Quoted by permission of the University of Minnesota Press.

[11] Dr. Richard Boehmler has done most of the analysis of these samples to date. Further work is being done by Mr. Joseph Kools under the direction of Dr. William Trotter and the writer.

—that is, after first being regarded as a stutterer—the average stuttering child has become definitely more nonfluent than the average child of like age who has not been regarded as a stutterer. (The mean time that elapsed between reported date of onset of stuttering and time at which these speech samples were obtained was approximately a year and a half.) Even so, similarities—even lack of any difference—between the stuttering and nonstuttering children with respect to certain specific types of nonfluency, especially interjections, revisions, and broken words, are to be duly noted.

TABLE 3. Average Numbers of Nonfluencies of Specified types per 100 Words in the Speech of 42 Stutterers and 42 Nonstutterers, Matched for Age, Sex, and Socioeconomic Status of Family, with Average Age Approximately Five Years within an Approximate Range of Two to Eight Years.

| Type of Nonfluency[a] | Stutterers | Nonstutterers |
|---|---|---|
| Interjection | 2.9 | 2.7 |
| Part-word repetition | 4.2 | 0.4 |
| Whole-word repetition | 4.5 | 1.2 |
| Phrase repetition | 1.4 | 0.5 |
| Revisions | 1.4 | 1.5 |
| Incomplete phrases | 0.2 | 0.05 |
| Broken words | 0.1 | 0.03 |
| Prolongations | 1.5 | 0.15 |
| Total | 16.1 | 6.53 |

[a] See Table 2 and text accompanying it for essential explanations.

Finally, it is to be recognized that the figures in Table 3 are not fully comparable with those previously reported by Branscom, Hughes, Oxtoby, and Davis (see pp. 207-208). In the first place, the children used in the previously mentioned investigations were on the whole somewhat younger than the ones represented in Table 1. In the second place, conditions under which speech samples were obtained and methods of recording were not the same. The samples summarized in Table 3 were obtained by having each child respond to pictures and converse with the examiner while a tape recording of his speech was being made. In the third place, the categories of nonfluency were different. The repetitions in the earlier studies were comparable to the three types of repetition listed in Table 3, but they probably also included some, though hardly all, of the phenomena listed in Table 3 as interjections and revisions. It will be recalled that the earlier studies showed that the average representative, presumably nonstuttering, child between the ages of two and five years repeated from 35 to 50 times per 1,000 words. Taking only the strictly repetition categories in Table 3, the mean is 21 instances, and including also interjections and revisions, the mean is a total of 63 instances per 1,000 words for the nonstuttering children. While the exact degree of comparability of the different sets of data is not wholly clear, it would appear that in general nonstuttering children in the various studies are more or less alike as to fluency, and so the data from the youngsters represented in Table 3 who had been speaking as "classified stutterers" for a year or two are to be evaluated accordingly on a comparative basis. At that point in the course of their speech problem they were definitely doing more repeating, most particularly perhaps of parts of words. Boehmler has found, in a laboratory study of the ways in which listeners evaluate various kinds of nonfluent speech, that repetitions are definitely more likely to be evaluated as stuttering than are interjections or revisions.[12]

It is to be emphasized again, however, that we have no data derived from speech samples recorded at or near the *moment of original diagnosis of stuttering*, and that we have been discussing the nonfluency characteristic of the speech of children as recorded from one to two years *after* the moment of original diagnosis. It is to be assumed that the records reflect largely or wholly the aggravation of normal nonfluency resulting from the diagnosis and its consequent effects on parental policies and practices and, therefore, on relevant aspects of the parent-child relationship.[13]

[12] Richard M. Boehmler, "A Quantitative Study of the Extensional Definition of Stuttering with Special Reference to the Audible Designata," unpublished Ph.D. dissertation, University of Iowa, 1953.

[13] Additional data relevant to the general problem under discussion have been reported by George O. Egland in Chapter 6, "Repetitions and Pro-

The child may be expected, of course, to react to the fact that he is evaluated as a stutterer, and to such circumstances under which this occurs as may be of emotional significance to him, as well as to the consequent parental attentions to his speech of the types described above by Darley. In general, as Darley has indicated, these reactions by the child appear to be mainly in the direction of a gradually stirring awareness of parental disapproval of his speech—and seemingly, though in a complex way—of himself in a personal sense. With this there comes, usually very subtly at first, a hesitancy in speaking that seems to be related in a special way to the specific fact of disapproval of his speech. In due course slight, and then more pronounced, tensions appear. The simple, easy repetitions gradually give way more or less, not completely, to more tense and more frequently occurring repetitions and to more effortful blocking reactions.

It is extremely difficult to find out from a child what he feels and thinks and what his purposes, conscious or unconscious, are as he repeats sounds or words, holds his breath, presses his lips together, or does the other things that he may do in "having difficulty" speaking. Much can be learned from older persons, however, and what has been learned has been made the subject of much speculation and theorizing. There is not sufficient space in this book to summarize all the pertinent data or to review all the pertinent theorizing, but particular aspects of both will be dealt with here and there as they prove to be relevant.

A DEFINITION OF STUTTERING

On the basis of the foregoing discussion, we may consider the problem of defining stuttering by giving attention to the basic fact that, as the information so far presented implies, there are two major aspects of stuttering: there are the movements or activities which the speaker performs in being nonfluent or hesitant, and there are the feelings or attitudes or motivations—and conflicts among them—with which he anticipates, performs, and

---

longations in the Speech of Stuttering and Nonstuttering Children," and by Mary B. Mann in Chapter 7, "Nonfluencies in the Oral Reading of Stutterers and Nonstutterers of Elementary School Age," in *Stuttering in Children and Adults, op. cit.*

remembers these activities. Beyond all this, there are the inter-personal relationships within which the stutterer does his speaking. And there is the inner life of the stutterer to be considered, his self-feelings, his attitudes toward himself, his moods, aspirations, fears, joys, and discontents, as these come to be conditioned by—and to condition—his stuttering reactions, as such.

The basic fact is that however stuttering comes about, and whatever it may come to be as feeling and overt behavior, it is done by a person. First of all and above all, stutterers are persons. To be a stutterer involves more than talking with a certain type or amount of nonfluency. It involves also, and as a rule more importantly, a way of feeling about the nonfluency, or about certain aspects of it, and a way of feeling about its real and imagined consequences. It involves some kind of self-evaluation and a pattern of interpersonal relationships. And it involves the ways in which the individual behaves while talking, and at other times too, because of the fact that he speaks the way he does and feels the way he does about it.

The writing of a short definition of stuttering is clearly a difficult and hazardous undertaking. Mindful of this, we may proceed nevertheless by stating first of all, and very vaguely, that stuttering appears to be a kind of fear problem. The person who stutters has been influenced by his experiences with speech to be uneasy and concerned about whether he can say the words he wants or needs to say. The tensions and feelings he has experienced accordingly have come to be identified by him as stuttering—and since they are unpleasant and even threatening to his personal status, he has come to have a fear of them. He fears stuttering—and all that it involves and means. So it is that he does not want to stutter—again. And he tries not to whenever he feels that he might. Now—what he does trying not to stutter is his stuttering. A first approximation to a definition might be, then: *stuttering is what a speaker does trying not to stutter again.*

We can elaborate this somewhat and, in the bargain, clarify it a bit, perhaps. Here is a rather more adequate definition: *Stut-*

*tering is an anticipatory, apprehensive, hypertonic avoidance re-action.*

In other words, stuttering is what a speaker does when (1) he expects stuttering to occur, (2) dreads it, and (3) becomes tense in anticipation of it and in (4) trying to avoid doing it. What he does in trying to avoid stuttering amounts to a complete or partial stopping of speech. All this is to say that stuttering consists, as we have considered, in the stutterer's attempt to keep from stuttering again as he has in the past—to prevent the occurrence of something he expects, dreads, and would rather avoid.

An analogy will be helpful. In certain basic respects stuttering consists of behavior much like that of a tightrope walker who is not entirely sure of himself. Much of the time he gets along all right, but now and then he is overtaken by the thought that he might fall off the rope. When that happens he has an "anticipatory, apprehensive, hypertonic avoidance reaction." That is, he (1) expects to fall off the rope, (2) dreads it, and (3) stiffens and becomes unsteady in anticipation of the fall and in (4) trying to avoid it. What he does in trying to avoid it amounts to a complete or partial stopping of his progress along the rope. What he does in falling off the rope consists of his attempt to keep from falling—to prevent the occurrence of something he expects, dreads, and would rather avoid.

No doubt most of us have experienced something like this now and then on the dance floor, or in roller skating, in gymnastic exercises, even in typing and various other complex motor skills. Students of music sometimes complain of similar difficulties. One individual, doubtless representative of thousands of others, claimed to be a good violinist during practice sessions—and this was independently confirmed—but said that he tended to "freeze" in front of an audience. He became concerned lest he make a mistake, and so he lost his relaxed ease and poise, tensed in anticipation of a possible "sour note," particularly when he came to certain "difficult passages," "lost his touch," and played poorly. He was making "anticipatory, apprehensive, hypertonic avoidance reactions."

The fact that this sort of thing is so common should make it possible for all of us to have a fairly good appreciation of what the stuttering child does when he stutters. Stuttering has been regarded traditionally as "mysterious," "unaccountable," "one of mankind's most baffling afflictions," and what not. Actually, how-ever, when we look upon it as just another type of anxiety-tension, and realize that we all experience anxiety-tensions of various kinds and degrees, it is seen to be no more strange or mysterious than much of our other behavior.

In any event, it is certainly highly desirable for anyone, par-ticularly the speech correctionist and the classroom teacher, to feel something in common with the stuttering child. To be able to put oneself "inside his skin" is just about the most important prerequisite to any kindly, wise, and effective approach to the problem of helping him. To be able to say to him, and to mean it, "I know how you feel," is to establish a bond with the child that will work its beneficent magic in a thousand subtle ways day in and day out.

## Incidence

There is considerable variation among published estimates of incidence of stuttering. This variation is probably due to (a) the fact that the proportions of children who stutter vary from school to school and perhaps even from social class to social class and from culture to culture, (b) survey and examination pro-cedures differ from one study to another, and (c) definitions of stuttering, as actually applied, may differ markedly from one investigator to another. The Committee on the Midcentury White House Conference of the American Speech and Hearing Associa-tion estimated the incidence of stuttering among American school children to be seven per thousand, or 0.7 per cent. For an esti-mated 40,000,000 children of school age the total number of stutterers would be 280,000.[14] Other estimates and survey find-

[14] Committee on Midcentury White House Committee, "Speech Disorders and Speech Correction," *Journal of Speech and Hearing Disorders* (1952), 17:129-137. It is interesting to compare the Committee's estimates for the school age population with D. E. Morley's findings for university students. Writing in 1952, Morley reported that of 33,339 incoming and

ings in this country have ranged between percentages of this general order and somewhat higher figures. One of the earliest studies was that of Wallin, who reported in 1916 that 0.7 per cent of 89,057 public school pupils in St. Louis were identified by their teachers as stutterers.[15] In 1942 Mills and Streit reported an incidence of stuttering for the population they surveyed of 1.5 per cent.[16] Reporting in 1955 an analysis of data obtained in a survey of over 20,000 school children in Grades I through XII in five Iowa counties in the period 1939-1942, Schindler indicated that 0.55 per cent were classified as stutterers. The author states, "For a diagnosis of stuttering, corroboration of the examiner's judgment was required. No child was classified as a stutterer unless he was so regarded by his teachers, parents, and associates."[17] A useful generalization would appear to be that in every 100 to 175 children in the United States there is one who stutters.

In a school with an enrollment of 3,500 there are likely to be from 20 to 35 stutterers, a rather heavy load of cases of this type for a speech correctionist. In a state such as Iowa, with approximately 500,000 children of school age, there are from 3,000 to 5,000 stuttering children. There are plainly more of these youngsters than can be adequately served by the present working force of public school speech correctionists, and it is very important, therefore, that their needs be reasonably well appreciated by their classroom teachers. Moreover, the classroom teacher can often do a good share of what most needs to be done for a child with this particular problem.

---

transfer students at the University of Michigan "during the past 10 years," 269, or 0.8 per cent, had been identified as stutterers. See D. E. Morley, "A Ten-Year Survey of Speech Disorders Among University Students," *Journal of Speech and Hearing Disorders* (1952), 17:25-31.

[15] J. E. Wallin, "A Census of Speech Defectives among 89,057 Public-School Pupils—A Preliminary Report," *School and Society* (1916), 3:213-214.

[16] A. W. Mills and H. Streit, "Report of a Speech Survey, Holyoke, Massachusetts," *Journal of Speech Disorders* (1942), 7:161-167.

[17] Mary Dupont Schindler, "A Study of Educational Adjustments of Stuttering and Nonstuttering Children," in *Stuttering in Children and Adults, op. cit.,* Chapter 29.

## CULTURAL AND SOCIOECONOMIC FACTORS

As has been stated, it is probable that the incidence of stuttering varies from culture to culture and perhaps from one socioeconomic level to another within a culture. Substantial indications of this became known in the early forties as a result of studies made among the Bannock and Shoshone Indians of Idaho.[18] No stuttering was found among these tribes and they appeared to have no word for stuttering. Since then other explorations of cultural variations in incidence of stuttering have been made. In a recent doctoral dissertation completed by John J. Morgenstern at the University of Edinburgh, Scotland, information obtained from 258 anthropological field workers in various parts of the world is assembled and analyzed.[19] Dr. Morgenstern lists the following peoples as ones who "do not stammer" and who seem to have no words for this condition:

1. The Wapishianas of British Guiana, 2,500 persons. The informant, a missionary who had lived in the area for 17 years, reported that no children or adults stammer and that they have no word for stammering.

2. The Patamonas, 1,100 persons, and Akawaio, 1,500 persons, in British Guiana. The informant, a physician, reported: "I travel extensively and visit all Amerindian tribes in British Guiana. . . . I have probably met 99% of all Amerindians. I have never encountered a case of stuttering or blocking. I have not had time to make extensive inquiries amongst all tribes, but the Akawaio

---

[18] Wendell Johnson, "The Indians Have No Word For It: Stuttering in Children," *Quarterly Journal of Speech* (1944), 30:330-337; see also by the same author, *People in Quandaries: the Semantics of Personal Adjustment,* New York, Harper & Brothers, 1946, Chapter 17. The Bannock and Shoshone study is also reported and discussed by John Snidecor in "Why the Indian Does Not Stutter," *Quarterly Journal of Speech* (1947), 33:493-495. Relevant information concerning the Navaho Indians, as well as certain Eskimo, Australian, and South Pacific cultures, is to be found in Adelaide K. Bullen, "A Cross-Cultural Approach to the Problem of Stuttering," *Child Development* (1945), 16:1-88.

[19] John J. Morgenstern, "Psychological and Social Factors in Children's Stammering," unpublished Ph.D. dissertation, University of Edinburg, 1953. Permission granted by Dr. Morgenstern to quote from this dissertation is gratefully acknowledged.

and Patamonas do not know the condition, and my imitations caused great amusement. They possess a word for 'dumbness' but that is all."

3. Garia, forty miles west southwest of Madang, Territory of New Guinea. The informant, a physician, reported that he had observed no stuttering among these people. "They do not have a word for it. The problem does not arise."

4. Kelabits, West Borneo. The Curator of the Sarawak Museum reported: "They have no word for it. I have never seen it among children or adults. . . . I really know these people intimately. . . ."

5. Malayan Aborigines (Negrito, Senoi, Aboriginal Malay), Malaya. The Director of Museums, Kuala Lumpur, stated: "Have not observed it among children nor adults. There are some sixteen languages and I have not been able to trace a word in any one. . . . I have . . . some sixty Aborigines from eleven different groups on my staff and none can recall a case amongst themselves although they gleefully told me of Europeans and Malays they had met with this affliction."

6. Sonthals, Bhuyans, and Gatwas (from Behar), Turis and Tantis (from Orissa), Assam, India. The informant, a physician, reported: "No children or adults stammer. . . . The above statement applies only to the labourers and their families employed on the Tea Estates of a British Company in this Central Area of the Assam Valley of the River Brahmaputra. . . . These people are not recent arrivals (new recruits to these parts). Most of them have been here for two or three generations but they have not intermixed with any of the other communities of Assam—such as Hindus, Ahoms, or other original Hill Tribes of Assam. . . . I have not been able to get hold of any word for stammering or stuttering in any of the dialects. . . ." (The report, says Dr. Morgenstern, "goes on to cite quite common stammering among other residents of this area—Hindus, Moslems, Ahoms (Buddhists), particularly among the literate.")

Dr. Morgenstern's study indicated also that many so-called native tribes were found to have a word for stuttering and to have some stutterers among them. Occasionally a word for stuttering was present in the language of a tribe but was used mainly or entirely to refer to the stuttering found among neighboring tribes. It is of special interest that two cultures were found to have an apparently excessive amount of stuttering. Dr. Morgenstern reports that a survey conducted by 13 headmasters of primary schools and 20 Ibo school teachers among 5,618 Ibo school children in Southeast Nigeria resulted in 2.67 per cent being classified as stammerers. Dr. Robert Armstrong, an American anthropologist working among the Idoma people of Nigeria, made the following report to Dr. Morgenstern: "Stammering (in the sense of the spasmodic repetition of the same speech sound) is practically a mass phenomenon here. I have met many dozens of persons who stammer in some degree. . . . Ability to speak well in public is vastly admired in West Africa, and Idoma and Ibo country is no exception to this statement. People make speeches on the slightest pretext—long, narcissistic speeches. . . . There is strong ridicule from the stammerer's age-mates. . . ."

A third culture in which there may be excessive stuttering— there appears to be some question of whether it is stuttering as we know it—is that of the Messiria Arabs of the Baggara Group, Southwest Kordofan, Anglo-Egyptian Sudan.

A related study has been made by Lemert "covering eight reserves of Salish Indians, two Kwakiutl and one Nootka, all located on the coastal mainland of British Columbia and Vancouver Island," supplemented by "interviews from two Haida informants, one Tsimshian and one Nootka who were not living in their respective areas. . . ."[20] Lemert found stuttering in these cultures with incidence rates probably equal to or possibly exceeding our own. He also found words for stuttering in the languages of these cultures. Particularly interesting is the information he reports concerning the peculiar competitive emphasis throughout the cultures of the Northwest Coast. Individuals, and their families at the same time, were strongly penalized socially for abnormalities of speech or of other characteristics. "This made the clan or family particularly sensitive to the deviations of its members and led to exacting educational practices. . . .

[20] Edwin M. Lemert, "Some Indians Who Stutter," *Journal of Speech and Hearing Disorders* (1953), *18*:168-174.

The rigorous child-training procedures held especially when participation in feasts, potlatches and associated rituals was demanded of the individual." Lemert concludes with the statement that "the cultural and sociopsychological prerequisites for the development of stuttering were strongly operative in the Northwest Coast. Thus we have (1) the cultural recognition and symbolizing of stuttering, (2) social penalties for the disorder, (3) specific anxieties about the speech development of children on the part of parents, and (4) internalization of sensitivity about speech in both the child and adult."[21]

In the earlier studies of the Bannock and Shoshone Indians of Idaho, as has been stated, no stutterers were found and no word for suttering could be identified. The cultures of the Bannock and Shoshone Indians seemed to be favorable to freedom from tensions or concern about childhood speech, particularly with respect to child-rearing policies and customs. As Dr. Lemert puts it, in commenting about the Idaho tribes, "In decided contrast to the Northwest Coast culture . . . no interfamily nor interclass relationships complicated the family treatment of abnormal children. Family attitudes are portrayed as kind, helpful, sympathetic, and although protective are not over-protective."[22]

All these studies appear to indicate not only definite variations in incidence of stuttering from culture to culture, but they suggest, moreover, that, as Dr. Morgenstern concludes, "Stammering incidence in a culture is very highly correlated with cultural practices of stigmatization of the stammering, particularly with parental anxiety over the possibility of their children's stammering."[23] In cultures in which stuttering is not observed there appears to be little or no concern over childhood speech, little or no ritualistic or ceremonial speech perfection required of children, no clearly conscious imposition of "norms" of speech development, and an apparent lack of "pressure" or "tension" of the types calculated to result in disturbances of the speech of children. These are tentative conclusions, subject to refinement or

[21] *Ibid.,* p. 173.
[22] *Ibid.,* p. 174.
[23] *Op. cit.*

amendment on the basis of the more extensive and systematic investigations so greatly needed, now that the probable fruitfulness of the cultural approach to the problem of stuttering has been indicated.

The picture so far sketched may be filled in a bit by reference to findings reported by Dr. Darley and again by Dr. Morgenstern. Darley found that 80 per cent of the families of the 50 stuttering children he investigated were from the middle and upper socioeconomic classes, as defined by Warner.[24] Darley regards this as a deviation from the normal distribution of families according to this type of classification. His comparison of parents of stuttering children and parents of nonstuttering children suggests that what is probably more important than socioeconomic class, as such, however, is the degree of "upward mobility" (drive or intensity of determination and effort to rise socioeconomically) of the family. "Upward mobile" families may, as a general rule, be expected to experience to a greater than usual degree the tensions attendant upon competitiveness, and to place a correspondingly high value on absence of defects and on good or superior speech in their children, which they consider important in the competition for status. Darley's data would seem to indicate that there is some such tendency among his "stuttering families."[25]

Dr. Morgenstern surveyed some 35,000 school children in Scotland and reported a notable concentration of stutterers in the socioeconomic class representative of "semiskilled manual wage earners" and a comparatively low stammering incidence among "unskilled labourers, industrial and agricultural." The differences he obtained were shown by him to be statistically significant. He stresses the "upward mobility" factor in making the point that in the region in which he made his survey it is the semiskilled laborer who stands the best chance of "getting ahead"

[24] *Stuttering in Children and Adults, op. cit.,* Chapter 4. For Warner's system of socioeconomic classification see W. L. Warner, M. Meeker, and K. Eels, *Social Class in America,* Chicago, Science Research Associates, 1949.

[25] Generally corroborative data are at hand in the previously mentioned study at the University of Iowa that is similar to Darley's, and that has involved a sample of 150 stuttering children and their families; 70 per cent of this sample were classified as middle or upper class socioeconomically.

into the next higher class through a sufficient show of ambition. The semiskilled laborer is particularly likely, therefore, to be unusually ambitious for his children and to appreciate the advantage of speech fluency to the child in his effort to improve his social and economic status.[26]

With a realization of the need of further research along these lines, one may at this point entertain the definite impression that the more information about stuttering we accumulate the more it takes on the appearance of a disorder of civilization, so to speak. It could well be that it is a part of the price we pay for the particular culture we make for ourselves. We may wisely note the possible importance in individual cases of the indicated competitive and perfectionistic practices and attitudes in the home, the school, the community, and the culture at large.

## Important Common Questions About Stuttering

Some of the more basic questions which the reader is likely to want to ask at this point will be considered. These are also among the more important questions that stutterers and their parents want to have answered, and it will be to the teacher's advantage to be familiar with them.

### IS STUTTERING HEREDITARY?

Not very much is known in scientific detail about *human* heredity, even with respect to physical characteristics, such as eye color, bodily size and shape, dental structures, and so forth. Still less is known about the relation between inherited bodily characteristics and *behavior*. Practically nothing is known about human heredity with respect to such reactions as anxiety or fear, which play so large a role in stuttering.[27]

[26] *Op. cit.*

[27] The implication of many writers who prefer to assume a physical cause of stuttering is that the causal condition is congenital—that is, present at birth. Many of them also apparently assume that it is hereditary—transmitted from parent to offspring. Certain other writers make no clear statement or implication restricting the organic cause to a hereditary or to a congenital condition, and it therefore seems reasonable to assume that for these writers the organic cause in some cases at least may be acquired after birth. In the present discussion the term "organic or physical cause" is used to refer to hereditary, congenital, or acquired organic factors, singly or in combination.

This we do know: each one of us inherits a body. Regardless of whether a child's chin, for example, resembles that of his mother, or of his father, or of neither, he inherited it. He was born with it. The condition of the mother during pregnancy may or may not have modified it somewhat, but our best hypothesis is that essentially the chin the child had at birth was structurally laid down in the genes present at the very beginning of his embryonic development. And the same is to be said of all the other parts of the child's body, and of his body as a structural unit.

Since we can be sure that this is true, it is to be taken into account in any statements we might conceivably make about the "inheritance" of any particular type of *behavior*, such as stuttering. Many physiological, neurological, biochemical, and anatomical studies have been made comparing stutterers and nonstutterers, and the net result of them has been that no specific organic or physical cause of stuttering has been demonstrated. Such would need to be demonstrated before one could make any specific and testable statements about the possible inheritance of any bodily characteristic responsible for stuttering. What a child inherits is a body, and specific bodily parts. If there is some physical characteristic with which some children are born that will cause them to stutter later, then it should be possible to demonstrate the existence of this physical characteristic and so to predict which six to ten infants out of any thousand will stutter sometime after they become old enough to talk. No one is able to make such a prediction, however, by means of any known test or examination procedure. In fact, it is impossible by means of physical examination methods alone to pick out the six to ten stutterers in any chance group of a thousand adults.

IS STUTTERING DUE TO SOME ORGANIC FAULT?

Approximately 2,300 years ago Aristotle allegedly asserted that stuttering was due to a defect of the tongue.[28] The tongue is easy to

[28] For a fascinating historical summary of theories of stuttering, including the interpretation of Aristotle's views that is cited here, see G. M. Klingbeil, "The Historical Background of the Modern Speech Clinic," *Journal of Speech Disorders* (1939), 4:115-32. Dr. Morgenstern, *op. cit.*, and in per-

observe, and as we now know, and as might have been discovered at any time by means of simple observation, stutterers' tongues are normal. Nevertheless, roughly only a century ago some of the leading surgeons of Europe were still treating stuttering by cutting pieces out of stutterers' tongues! This is, of course, only one of the more dramatic bits of evidence that in our general culture there is a powerful tradition of belief to the effect that faulty behavior is caused by faulty physical structure.

Meanwhile, what might be said in a proper spirit of scientific responsibility as to the likelihood of our ever discovering an organic or physical cause for stuttering?

First of all, the facts we now have about stuttering and stutterers do not make obvious, or even slightly apparent, what the precise nature of such a causal condition would be. Moreover, known facts give us no clear clue as to the specific parts of the body in which we are to look. We are hard put, therefore, to decide whether current research methods might or might not be used profitably, or precisely how they are to be modified, for purposes of detecting the character, location, and mode of operation of the organic condition to be sought. In short, we find ourselves at a loss as to the direction in which we are to tell the investigator to go. We are left essentially in the position of having to suggest that he search for a needle no one has ever seen in a haystack we do not know how to find. We can tell him, however, that the needle he is to bring back must possess certain properties.

That is to say, if ever an organic condition is found to be responsible for stuttering, it must be one that will function in certain ways. It must be the kind of organic condition that will operate to produce such effects as these:

1. The average stutterer stutters on about 10 per cent of the words he speaks, and he produces the other 90 per cent normally.

sonal communication to the writer, has expressed strong doubt that stuttering as we understand it was known to the early Greeks; he questions whether Aristotle made reference to stuttering as we know it. The belief in a physical cause of stuttering has been traditional in Western culture for a considerable period, of course. Intensive historical studies of these matters are greatly needed.

The organic condition must account for the 90 per cent fully as well as it does for the 10 per cent.

2. Most stutterings last one or two seconds or less. The organic condition must function as a cause for time periods of this order, and it must not function as a cause of stuttering in the intervening intervals.

3. No two stutterers perform their stuttering in exactly the same way, and any one stutterer varies somewhat, and can be trained to vary markedly, in manner of performance during any given day, or hour, and from week to week and year to year. The organic condition must operate to cause an effect that varies as to form in this fashion.

4. Stuttering begins, in the average case, at about the age of three years. In some cases, however, it begins earlier than this, and in others somewhat later. The physical cause must lie dormant for corresponding average and exceptional periods of time before beginning to function.

5. A considerable number of individuals are reported to have stuttered during some period in their lives and to have "outgrown" the difficulty without undergoing treatment. The physical cause must, therefore, be one that in some cases apparently subsides or atrophies after having flourished for a time.

6. Stuttering has been eliminated in substantial numbers of cases by means involving no recognized changes in the organic condition of the stutterer.[29] The physical cause must be one that ceases to function in such cases in the absence of any intended or known physical alteration of the person.

7. Practically all stutterers can sing, or speak in time to almost any sort of rhythm, or speak without stuttering under conditions created by sufficient intensities of sound or noise fed into the ears while speaking; some can act on the stage, most of them can talk to themselves, or to their pets, or they can whisper, or shout, speak with a dialect, or by using an electrolarynx, and read in chorus with another person, even a fellow stutterer,

[29] For a review of published reports of results of stuttering therapy see Dean E. Williams, "Intensive Clinical Case Studies of Stuttering Therapy," in *Stuttering in Children and Adults, op. cit.,* Chapter 39.

with no stuttering or practically none.[30] The organic cause must be one that—for some reason that is to be identified—operates feebly or not at all under these conditions.

8. More stuttering occurs on words that are nouns, verbs, adjectives, and adverbs; that begin sentences; that are longer than the average word; and that begin with consonants rather than vowels.[31] The organic condition must exhibit a tendency—which, in turn, is to be explained—to vary in systematic relationship to the indicated attributes of words spoken by the individual.

9. Strother and Kriegman[32] found no differences between young adult stutterers and nonstutterers in ability to perform rapid, or rhythmical, movements of the lips, tongue, jaw, and breathing musculature. The authors also reviewed and analyzed data reported by several other investigators whose findings, taken all together, confirmed their own. The organic cause must, therefore, be one that permits the structures used for speech to function normally in performing such rapid, or rhythmical, movements.

10. Ritzman[33] found no significant differences between

[30] Oliver Bloodstein, "Hypothetical Conditions under Which Stuttering is Reduced or Absent," *Journal of Speech and Hearing Disorders* (1950), 15:142-153; Virginia Barber, "Chorus Reading as a Distraction in Stuttering," *Journal of Speech Disorders* (1939), 4:371-383; Virginia Barber, "Rhythm as a Distraction in Stuttering," *Journal of Speech Disorders* (1940), 5:29-42; W. Johnson and L. Rosen, "The Effect of Certain Changes in Speech Pattern upon Frequency of Stuttering," *Journal of Speech Disorders* (1937), 2:105-109; Frederick A. McKenzie, "A Stutterer's Experiences in Using an Electrolarynx," Chapter 41; and Mary Lou Sternberg Shane, "Effect on Stuttering of Alteration in Auditory Feedback," Chapter 22, in *Stuttering in Children and Adults, op. cit.*

[31] Spencer F. Brown, "The Loci of Stutterings in the Speech Sequence," *Journal of Speech Disorders* (1945), 10:181-192.

[32] C. R. Strother and L. S. Kriegman, "Diadochokinesis in Stutterers and Non-Stutterers," *Journal of Speech Disorders* (1943), 8:323-335; "Rhythmokinesis in Stutterers and Non-Stutterers," *Journal of Speech Disorders* (1944), 9:239-244.

[33] Carl Ritzman, "A Comparative Cardiovascular and Metabolic Study of Stutterers and Non-Stutterers," *Journal of Speech Disorders* (1943), 8:161-182. Earlier studies in which different procedures of sampling, testing, and analysis were used were those of L. E. Travis, W. W. Tuttle, and D. W. Cowan, "A Study of Heart Rate During Stuttering," *Journal of Speech*

stutterers and nonstutterers in measurements of heart rate, blood pressure, and basal metabolism. The organic condition must be one that evidently does not unfavorably affect these vital bodily functions.

11. At one time it was suspected that the inner condition being sought had been, or might be, found in handedness, or change of handedness, or the central nervous system organization presumably related to handedness.

In this specific area of investigation, there has been a gradual development of increasingly refined sampling, interviewing, testing, and statistical procedures. The more recent and technically more satisfactory studies have not supported the view that stutterers and nonstutterers are different in any significant sense with respect to handedness.[34] In neither the Johnson nor the Darley samples, totaling 96 stuttering and 96 nonstuttering children, nor in the subsequent research on onset of stuttering involving 150 stuttering children and 150 matched controls have group differences as to handedness been found.[35] The physical condition to be sought, therefore, must be one that apparently does not affect the organism in such a way as to reveal itself in handedness characteristics.

12. Two comprehensive and critical reviews of over 150 physiological and biochemical studies of stuttering have been

*Disorders* (1936), *1*:21; and M. F. Palmer and A. M. Gillette, "Sex Differences in the Cardiac Rhythms of Stutterers," *Journal of Speech Disorders* (1938), *3*:3. Later confirmation of Ritzman's finding of essential similarity between stutterers and nonstutterers is to be found in Arnold J. Golub, "The Heart Rates of Stutterers and Non-Stutterers in Relation to Frequency of Stuttering During a Series of Oral Readings," unpublished Ph.D. dissertation, University of Iowa, 1952.

[34] Harry Heltman, "Contradictory Evidence in Handedness and Stuttering," *Journal of Speech Disorders* (1940), 5:327-332; W. Johnson and A. King, "An Angle Board and Hand Usage Study of Stutterers and Non-Stutterers," *Journal of Experimental Psychology* (1942), 31:293-311; E. J. Spadino, *Writing and Laterality Characteristics of Stuttering Children*, New York, Teachers College, Columbia University, Contributions to Education No. 837, 1941.

[35] *Stuttering in Children and Adults, op. cit.*, Chapters 3 and 4, and research at the University of Iowa scheduled for publication under the title of *The Onset of Stuttering, op. cit.*

published by Hill.[36] In a statement concluding his evaluation of this impressive amount of scientific investigation, Hill says, "An agent in the form of an inner condition . . . is still as distant from discovery as it was four thousand years ago. Advances in theory have only been attained through recognition of situational influences on behavior." The previously mentioned studies of stuttering and nonstuttering children have not revealed any differences between them relevant in this connection. Finkelstein and Weisberger administered the Oseretsky Tests of Motor Proficiency to 15 stuttering and 15 nonstuttering children matched for age, sex, and laterality and found no group differences.[37] The organic condition in question must be sufficiently subtle and elusive to escape detection by means of these tests and the varied and intensive scientific investigations such as those reviewed and evaluated by Hill.

This list is not exhaustive, and so—to return to the metaphor —the needle our investigator is to bring back will have to possess still other properties in addition to those that have been specified. In any event, it is destined to be a needle most certainly out of the ordinary. If only out of curiosity as to what precisely it could look like, one cannot but hope that there might turn out to be such a needle and that it might be found. Meanwhile we are frustrated, of course, by the fact that we cannot tell our investigator where to find the haystack.

DOES STUTTERING RUN IN FAMILIES?

In the Johnson study of stuttering and nonstuttering children there were 44 sets of parents in each group.[38] Of the stutterers'

[36] Harris Hill, "Stuttering: I. A Critical Review and Evaluation of Biochemical Investigations," *Journal of Speech Disorders* (1944), 9:245-261; "Stuttering: II. A Review and Integration of Physiological Data," *Journal of Speech Disorders* (1944), 9:289-324.

[37] Phyllis Finkelstein and Stanley E. Weisberger, "The Motor Proficiency of Stutterers," *Journal of Speech and Hearing Disorders* (1954), 19:52-58. Another study in which no evidence of difference between stutterers and nonstutterers was found with respect to psychomotor coördination or stability was that of Francie L. Ross, "A Comparative Study of Stutterers and Nonstutterers on a Psychomotor Discrimination Task," in *Stuttering in Children and Adults, op. cit.,* Chapter 30.

[38] *Stuttering in Children and Adults, op. cit.,* Chapter 3.

parents, one father and two mothers were stutterers, and four fathers and three mothers had been stutterers; of the non-stutterers' parents, two fathers and no mothers stuttered, and no fathers and one mother had formerly stuttered. Of 58 siblings of the stutterers, nine were stutterers and three were former stutterers; of 36 siblings of the nonstutterers one was a stutterer. Fifteen of the 46 stuttering children and four of the 46 non-stuttering children were said to have one or more stuttering relatives.

In the Darley study of 50 stuttering and 50 nonstuttering children and their families, eight fathers and four mothers of stutterers, and three fathers and one mother of nonstutterers, had once been or were at time of interview considered to be stutterers.[39] Nine of the stutterers' fathers and four of their mothers, and five of the nonstutterers' mothers, reported having stuttering siblings. Of the 50 stuttering children four had one sibling whom one parent thought was a stutterer, and in two of these four cases both parents agreed that the siblings stuttered; one parent, but not the other, regarded a sibling of one of the nonstuttering children as a stutterer. In 26 of the stuttering group families and in 21 of the nonstuttering group families, at least one parent knew of at least one stuttering relative. Other studies also indicate that stutterers tend to have somewhat more stuttering relatives than nonstutterers have.[40]

Such figures do not, in themselves, constitute direct evidence that stuttering is inherited. It is not simply a question, moreover, of how large or small such numbers, or the group differences with respect to them, are found to be. The fact observed is that to a limited extent stuttering does tend to run in families. The question is not simply to what extent, but why to any extent at all?

There are two main reasons, of course, why characteristics run in families. One is biological, genetic, hereditary in a physical

---

[39] *Stuttering in Children and Adults, op. cit.*, Chapter 4.
[40] See Joseph Wepman, "Is Stuttering Inherited?" *Proceedings of the American Speech Correction Association* (1935), 5:39, and Robert West, Severina Nelson, and Mildred Berry, "The Heredity of Stuttering," *Quarterly Journal of Speech* (1939), 25:23-30.

sense of the word. We take for granted that this is the kind of reason which accounts for family resemblances in respect to hair color and texture, eye color, and other bodily features.[41] The other reason is social—custom, tradition, training.[42] For example, the Mormon religion, or the Methodist, or Buddhist, or any other tends to run in families. We understand, of course, that this is not due to heredity in a biological sense, but that it is rather a matter of family tradition, something taught by parents to their children, and passed along in this way from generation to generation. Thus we have family traditions with respect to food preferences and dislikes, occupations, literary tastes, political leanings, psychological reactions to illness, ethical and moral tendencies, and attitudes, beliefs, and evaluations generally.

The reason why stuttering tends to run in families seems to be rather definitely a matter of tradition rather than genes. Parents who stutter, or have stuttered, or who have grown up with stuttering brothers and sisters, or parents, or uncles and aunts, or cousins —such parents when faced with the *normally* hesitant early speech of their own children may be expected, in some cases at least, to react somewhat differently from parents to whom stuttering means little more than an unfamiliar word they have seldom heard or used. And the way they react to the speech of their own children seems to have a great deal to do with determining whether or not their children will develop the self-consciousness about speech, the anxiety-tensions, that make for stuttering. What runs in families (in those cases in which something seems to) appears to be a background of experience with stuttering and therefore a kind of concern, a set of attitudes and a tendency to deal in certain ways with children who are just learning to talk, and with the *normal* imperfections in their speech. It seems a fair conclusion, and a generally useful one, that these attitudes and training policies in turn tend, to a limited extent, to lead

[41] See William C. Boyd, *Genetics and the Races of Man,* Boston, Little, Brown & Co., 1950, for a general treatment of the mechanics of genetics.

[42] See John J. Honigmann, *Culture and Personality,* New York, Harper & Brothers, 1954, for a systematic survey and discussion of the relationship between individuals and their cultures.

to stuttering in the children of the families in which the attitudes and policies have become traditional.[43]

## WHY DO MORE BOYS THAN GIRLS STUTTER?

The ratio of male to female stutterers varies somewhat with age level, from family to family, and so forth, and in general ranges from about two to one to ten to one. The average, for whatever it may be worth, is roughly four to one. The most systematic and comprehensive study of this sex ratio has been done by Schuell.[44] In addition to investigating the stuttering sex ratio itself, she attempted to lay the groundwork for a better understanding of it by exploring a large variety of sex differences in growth and development generally, in personal and social adjustments, in speech and language abilities, in diseases and deficiencies. She also investigated possible differences in school and home attitudes and policies toward boys and girls, and considered the general question as to whether social or cultural influences affect boys and girls differently. The conclusions are best stated in Schuell's own words:

"A sex difference of from two to ten males to one female is found among stutterers, the magnitude of the ratio varying according to the age and educational status of the population studied, and according to methods used in obtaining samples and making surveys. Males tend to experience a more severe form of stuttering than females, and more females than males are found who 'outgrow' stuttering."

Dr. Schuell then summarizes findings available to her to the effect that, generally, in our culture males develop more slowly than females and are more susceptible to a considerable number

[43] For further discussion of this problem and additional data relevant to certain aspects of it see Oliver Bloodstein and Sonja M. Smith, "A Study of the Diagnosis of Stuttering with Special Reference to the Sex Ratio," *Journal of Speech and Hearing Disorders* (1954), *19*:459-466.

[44] Hildred Schuell, "Sex Differences in Relation to Stuttering," *Journal of Speech Disorders* (1946), *11*:277-298; (1947), *12*:23-38. See also, by the same author, *Differences Which Matter: A Study of Boys and Girls,* Austin, Texas, Delta Kappa Gamma Society, National Office, 1947. An interesting aspect of this problem was investigated by Oliver Bloodstein and Sonja M. Smith, *ibid.*

of diseases and handicapping conditions as well as personal and social maladjustments. She concludes:

It is found that teachers, parents, and society generally tend to reward children for submissive and withdrawing behavior (which psychologists and mental hygienists consider indicative of serious maladjustment) and to penalize them for traits of aggressiveness, independence, and assertiveness, which males in our culture are nevertheless expected to develop.

A tenable hypothesis would seem to be that the male child, whose physical, social and language development proceeds at a slower rate than that of the female, encounters more unequal competition, and consequently more frustrations, particularly in relation to language situations, than the female child, and that as a result he exhibits more insecurity, more hesitancy, and more inhibitions in speech. If the frustrating situations are too many, if his speech behavior is compared unfavorably with that of other children, or if he becomes aware of unfavorable reactions toward it on the part of other people, it is conceivable that anxieties and tensions and the overt behavior regarded as stuttering might develop.[45]

## IS STUTTERING A PSYCHONEUROSIS, OR A SYMPTOM OF PERSONALITY MALADJUSTMENT?

Traditionally there have been two major theories of stuttering and of practically every other problem of human behavior. One of these has been that stuttering is a symptom of some sort of physical fault; this is the view we have considered above. The other has been that stuttering is a symptom of some kind of "personality disturbance," or "psychoneurosis," or "personal or social or emotional maladjustment."

In one of the early studies in this area, Johnson employed interviews, written autobiographies, and tests in an exploration of the personal and social adjustments of 80 stutterers.[46] He

[45] Hildred Schuell, "Sex Differences in Relation to Stuttering," *Journal of Speech Disorders* (1946), *12*:194-295. It is to be stressed that there is great need for more research concerning this problem. There are several possible hypotheses—genetic or constitutional, sociocultural, developmental, etc.— by which one might attempt to explain the sex difference in incidence of stuttering. The basic needs at this time are for more data and for the logical and semantic refinement of existing hypotheses.

[46] Wendell Johnson, *The Influence of Stuttering on the Personality,* Iowa City, University of Iowa Studies in Child Welfare, Vol. 5, No. 5, 1932.

concluded that "the adaptations and attitudes of stutterers, especially insofar as they constitute emotional and social maladjustment, have been found to be in many important respects the results of stuttering." As one part of his study, Johnson administered the Woodworth-House Mental Hygiene Inventory to 50 stutterers, 39 male and 11 female, ranging in age from 15 to 34 years with an average age of 21.5 years. He compared their responses with those of 70 diagnosed psychoneurotic individuals, with an average age of 32.5 years, and 400 male college students, with an average age of 19.5 years, at Princeton, Havard, West Point, and four universities in the New York City area tested by House in standardizing the Inventory.[47] Mean Inventory scores for the three groups were as follows: Childhood—stutterers 10.8, House's students 11.9, Houses' psychoneurotics 6.9; Maturity—stutterers 26.2, House's students 25.1, House's pyschoneurotics 38.1. When the groups are compared with respect to the percentages of their problems that were identified by them as extreme, the following figures were obtained: Childhood—stutterers 19.5, students 19.3, psychoneurotics 26.7; Maturity—stutterers 19.3, students 16.1, psychoneurotics 35.9. In general, the stutterers resembled rather closely the presumably normal or representative college students and differed markedly from the psychoneurotics. It is of special interest that ten of the stutterers analyzed their own test responses and judged over half of their problems, 48 per cent of their childhood problems and 58 per cent of their maturity problems, to be due to their stuttering.

Since the time of this study there have been several other investigations in which stutterers and nonstutterers have been compared by means of various procedures for evaluating personality. An interesting study is that in which Walnut used the Minnesota

[47] S. Daniel House, "A Mental Hygiene Inventory: A Contribution to Dynamic Psychology," *Archives of Psychology*, No. 88 (1927). The Inventory consists of 100 statements of personality problems, 30 referring to childhood (up to age 14) and 70 to adulthood (beyond age 14). The score for each part of the test, childhood and maturity, is the number of problems which the individual identifies as his own in either moderate or extreme degree. On the childhood items, House's psychoneurotics, possibly as a function of repression or distortion of memory, scored lower than his normal students.

Multiphasic Personality Inventory (MMPI) as a means of comparing 38 stutterers, 25 crippled subjects, 26 persons with cleft palate, and 52 presumably normal subjects, all groups being of high school age.[48] The author reported mean scores for nine MMPI clinical scales and on all of them all the groups fell within the normal range, approximating the norms for the test. What group differences there were within the normal range were of a kind that indicated that "the specific area of deviation of the stuttering group" was that of speech. That is, the stutterers seemed to be a little more discouraged and unsure of the reactions of other persons in situations where speech was involved.

The MMPI has been used also by Dahlstrom and Craven in a study of 80 male and 20 female stutterers.[49] The authors compared the stutterers' scores with those of 100 presumably normal university freshmen and with data obtained by other investigators from psychiatric cases and university students with adjustment problems of presumably nonpsychiatric grade for which they had sought counseling. No consistent pattern of personality was found to be distinctive of stutterers, and such differences as were found among group means for subscores on the test indicated the stutterers were much better adjusted than the psychiatric patients, tended to show certain resemblances to the students with problems, and so far as they were different from the presumably normal subjects they were a bit more discouraged, socially withdrawn, and uneasy in social situations. Scores on the test were not found to be related to severity of stuttering.

Similar findings were reported by Richardson, who studied differences between 30 adult stutterers and 30 nonstutterers, matched for age, sex, education, and intelligence, by means of the Guilford Inventory of Factors STDCR, the Rorschach ink-blot test, and the Murray Thematic Apperception Test.[50] In the

[48] Francis Walnut, "A Personality Inventory Item Analysis of Individuals Who Stutter and Individuals Who Have Other Handicaps," *Journal of Speech and Hearing Disorders* (1954), *19*:220-227.

[49] W. Grant Dahlstrom and Dorothy Drakesmith Craven, "The Minnesota Multiphasic Inventory and Stuttering Phenomena in Young Adults," abstract, *American Psychologist* (1952), 7:341.

[50] L. H. Richardson, "A Personality Study of Stutterers and Non-stutterers," *Journal of Speech Disorders* (1944), 9:152-160.

Murray test the subject is requested to respond to each of a series of pictures of one or more persons, shown in a more or less undefined setting, by telling what he supposes has happened to the persons in the picture, what is happening, and how it will turn out. The Guilford test indicated that the stutterers were somewhat the more socially introvertive or withdrawing and depressed, and less happy-go-lucky. The Rorschach responses, generally difficult to interpret sharply, seemed to suggest that the stutterers "tended not to recognize their inner promptings" and not to "respond impulsively to outside environment" as much as did the nonstutterers. The Thematic Apperception Test results revealed "no significant differences between the groups in the proportions of needs, reactions to frustrations, themas, attitudes toward environment, adequacy of the central character, and satisfactory or unsatisfactory endings" of the stories made up in response to the pictures.

Using a test of the individual's conformity with group norms with respect to fundamental value judgments, Spriestersbach also found stutterers to differ markedly from psychiatric patients and to show, in comparison with presumably normal nonstutterers, relatively slight degrees of social maladjustment.[51] His group consisted of 50 male stutterers, with a median age of 21.5 years, 183 nonstuttering male university students, with a median age of 20.5 years, and 20 male psychotic patients in a state mental hospital, with a median age of 47 years. Each subject was shown a number of pictures, each of which represented one or more persons engaged in some sort of activity. The subject rated each picture, using a 7-point scale ranging from 1, extremely poor, to 7, extremely good, as an example of persons engaged in *worthwhile* activity, or *good, or peculiar* activity—in all, 15 pictures were used and each was rated by each subject as an example of the kind of activity represented by each of 11 words. In addition to the three words already mentioned, the following were also used: *fun, foolish, funny, interesting, undesirable, unpleasant,*

[51] D. C. Spriestersbach, "An Objective Approach to the Investigation of Social Adjustment of Male Stutterers," *Journal of Speech and Hearing Disorders* (1951), *16*:250-257.

*wholesome, work.* The median ratings of the stutterers and the nonstuttering students were not significantly different, but the median ratings of both of these groups differed very considerably from those of the psychotics. A few more stutterers than non-stuttering students tended to give ratings that were relatively extreme.

In 1955 Staats published a study of the sense of humor in 26 college age male stutterers and 120 nonstuttering male university students.[52] Using a 7-point scale, each subject rated the funniness of each of twenty cartoons, ten of which involved characters with impairments or handicaps and ten of which depicted normal characters in presumably funny situations. No significant difference between the stutterers and nonstutterers was found with respect to ratings of any single cartoon of either type.

The Rosenzweig Picture-Frustration Test was administered by Quarrington to 30 adult stutterers. "No significant differences between stutterers and normals were found on seven test characteristics examined." Quarrington stated that he found no support for the "assertion that suttering is a symptom of a basic character neurosis."[53]

The general conclusion to be drawn from these investigations would appear to be that stutterers differ very considerably from psychoneurotic or psychotic patients, that they differ slightly or not at all, depending on the type of test, from presumably normal nonstutterers, and that whenever stutterers are found to differ from nonstutterers on measures of personality they differ in tending to be a bit more depressed or discouraged, a bit more anxious or uneasy or unresponsive, especially in speech situations, and somewhat more withdrawing socially. The kinds and degrees of difference indicate not a serious personality maladjustment, but rather a normal kind and amount of emotional reaction to the sorts of frustrating, threatening, and unpleasant experience that stuttering involves. If stutterers did not react at all to their

[52] Lorin C. Staats, Jr., "Sense of Humor in Stutterers and Non-stutterers," in *Stuttering in Children and Adults, op. cit.*, Chapter 24.

[53] Bruce Quarrington, "The Performance of Stutterers on the Rosenzweig Picture-Frustration Test," *Journal of Clinical Psychology* (1953), 9:189-192.

stuttering it might perhaps be inferred that they were abnormally bland or lacking in normal affect. They seem on the average to react just about enough and in just about the right ways to indicate that as a group they are emotionally normal.

Moreover, this general impression appears to be borne out by our studies of stuttering and nonstuttering children and their parents, previously discussed, and by our general clinical experience with a considerable and presumably more or less representative sampling of stutterers. In the Darley study cited in Footnote 7 the Roger's Test of Personality Adjustment was used to compare 28 stuttering children and 18 non-stuttering children 14 years old and younger, and no statistically significant differences were found. On the whole, those who stutter seem to be much like those who don't—except that they do stutter and this brings them a certain amount of distress. Some react to this in ways that amount to considerable maladjustment; others react in exceedingly constructive and wholesome ways; the majority lie between these two extremes. Like individuals who don't stutter, stutterers have the usual human reasons for becoming maladjusted and apparently about the same proportion of them as of other persons seek and need psychiatric help and for essentially the same sorts of reasons. In our clinic at the University of Iowa we have worked for about thirty years in close relationship with the Department of Psychiatry. We have referred for psychiatric evaluation probably 3 to 5 per cent of our cases, those who have appeared to be in greatest need of such referral. It is to be fairly estimated that about three fourths of those referred have been sent back by the psychiatrists with the statement that, in effect, they did not have enough need of psychiatric therapy to warrant time being spent, with them in their Department. On the basis of this rather long record of experience, our own clinical observations and impressions, and the data that have been obtained in studies of the sort here reviewed, it does not appear possible to conclude that stuttering is a psychoneurosis or a symptom of a distinctive personality maladjustment. It does seem incontrovertible that in some cases the experience of stuttering produces a certain amount of personality maladjustment, and, in addition to this, there appears to be no ground for assuming that among the population of persons who stutter there would not be the same proportion as of the general population who have the customary kinds and grades of personality maladjustments. By and large, stutterers are people who stutter.

## WHAT ARE THE CONDITIONS UNDER WHICH STUTTERING BEGINS?

Scientific findings to date, considered together with general clinical observations, indicate that stuttering is to be most usefully and meaningfully regarded not as a symptom of a physical flaw or instability nor as a symptom or outward effect of a basic "nervousness" or "neurotic personality structure," but rather as a form of behavior that is learned. So far as we can tell, any child might learn to stutter, provided he is placed in the proper circumstances and handled in such a way as to create in him the necessary specific anxiety tensions. A person may be too paralyzed or too severely brain-injured to stutter, or too drugged or exhausted or psychotic to be sufficiently responsive to other people to stutter to them. In general, aside from such considerations, so far as we know, no particular type of body or personality is essential to stuttering.

It is to be considered, of course, that children may differ with respect to their allegedly congenital or trained "readiness" or "predisposition" to stutter, or their "aptitude" for cultivating the anxiety-tensions peculiar to stuttering, although we must bear in mind that these terms stand for possible and obscure inferences rather than facts that we have observed. The problem is to use such terms in statements that we can test by making observations. In the meantime, with the facts at hand there is much we can say and do that seems advantageous.

Generally speaking, the onset and development of stuttering can be stated as follows. As we have noted in some detail, beginning speech is normally nonfluent. This does not mean that all children stutter. It is simply that all children speak nonfluently in some degree; so do all adults. Stuttering is something else again. To say that all children "go through a stage" in which they speak hesitantly and repetitiously is not entirely right either. Repetition, as we have seen, starts with the birth cry and continues throughout infancy. It does not stop when the child begins to say words. There is really no "stage" that the child goes through. It is simply that speech follows a course of development. Throughout this course there is some amount of nonfluency.

Now, in most homes, particularly those in which no one has had any personal experience with stuttering, the normal nonfluency of beginning speech appears to be almost completely disregarded. Most parents are surprised to learn that the average youngster repeats thirty to fifty times per thousand words; they had not noticed, or do not remember, that their own children ever did repeat sounds or words at all. The fact is not that most children—about 99 percent—are perfectly fluent, never repeating or hesitating otherwise in speaking, but rather that about 99 percent are permitted to develop speech, with all its normal nonfluencies, without being made self conscious about it by parents who are overly concerned and perfectionistic. The basic question is not so much what causes some children to stutter, but rather what causes an occasional parent to cultivate the attitudes and policies that tend to make him dissatisfied with his child's speech fluency, and to worry about it and react to it in ways that influence the child to become uneasy and tense in speaking.

The reasons for the onset of stuttering, then, are not to be sought most significantly within the child or even in the way he speaks, but primarily "inside his parent's head," or, rather, in the parent's attitudes and reactions to the child and especially to the way the child speaks. The point not to be missed is that any child speaks with enough nonfluency to be worried about and diagnosed as "stuttering," provided his parents are prepared, by their conditioned attitudes, beliefs, and standards, to worry enough and to see simple repetitions and hesitancies as danger signals. Parents differ amazingly in this general respect. Any one parent, moreover, fluctuates, sometimes greatly, with regard to the way he evaulates and reacts to the speech of any one of his children, or of his two or more different children. Circumstances vary, competing sources of concern shift about, distractions of all sorts arise and subside, and the total impression made by a child at one time differs markedly, for changing and complex reasons, from the impression made by the same child on the same parent at another time. What may be unnoticed one day may be perceived as "stuttering" the next and disregarded again a week later.

Almost any parent of a supposedly stuttering child will say, sometime during a clinical interview, "He's better sometimes than others. He may go for a day, or even several days, without one bit of stuttering, just talking perfectly, and then he stutters again." One suspects, on the basis of all we know about stuttering, that as a rule and for the most part such a parent is describing not so much his child's fluctuating speech fluency as his own wavering attention to it and concern over it. He is like the man who dozed off and on during a long committee meeting, and then reported later that in his judgment the committee chairman was incompetent and a bit queer to boot: he talked incoherently by fits and starts.

Tuthill[54] has shown how widely individuals differ and how very inconsistent any one person can be in using the word "stuttering" to label actual speech phenomena. He made phonograph and sound film recordings of the speech of stutterers and non-stutterers, and asked listeners to mark, on mimeographed copies of the material, the words which they judged as stuttered. His listeners included laymen, students with training in speech pathology, stutterers, and professional speech pathologists. All groups showed about the same degree of disagreement as to which specific words were stuttered and which were not, and regardless of whether they only heard or both saw and heard the speakers, and the disagreement was indeed astonishing. In fact, there was on the average only about 37 per cent of perfect agreement. Each listener, moreover, heard the recordings twice, about a week apart, and the relatively low average degree of self-agreement

---

[54] Curtis E. Tuthill, "A Quantitative Study of Extensional Meaning with Special Reference to Stuttering," *Speech Monographs*, Vol. 13, No. 2 (1946).

was also impressive. Tuthill's findings, together with all the other available information bearing on the point, make it very plain that what one person would call "stuttering" another might call perfectly normal speech, and that what a particular person would call "normal" at one time he might label "stuttering" at another time.[55]

All this helps greatly to account for the fact that not all children in a given family are regarded as stutterers, and that almost all parents report that what they call stuttering "comes on gradually," "for no apparent reason," and that it tends to "come and go," especially during the early period of its development. According to some parents, of course, it "starts suddenly," and, while the child "has more difficulty sometimes than others," he is "never" entirely free of it.[56] In general, investigation of the onset and early development of stuttering[57] has shown that:

[55] When confronted with a series of 12 two-minute samples of the recorded speech of young stuttering and nonstuttering children, parents who had previously come to regard their own children as stutterers were found by Bloodstein and his students to make more diagnoses of stuttering than parents who had not diagnosed their own children as stutterers. See Oliver Bloodstein, W. Jaeger, and J. Tureen, "A Study of the Diagnosis of Stuttering by Parents of Stutterers and Non-stutterers," *Journal of Speech and Hearing Disorders* (1952), 17:308-315. The problem investigated by Tuthill has been further explored by Richard Boehmler (see Footnote 12).

[56] These statements refer to reports made by parents interviewed soon after they have diagnosed their children as stutterers. It is to be most strongly emphasized that case history data concerning the onset of stuttering, obtained from adult stutterers themselves, or from stutterers' parents, any considerable period of time after the supposed onset of stuttering, are likely to be very unreliable, even extremely and systematically distorted. In the Darley study previously noted the average discrepancy between ages of onset of stuttering as given by mothers and fathers independently was 15 months! Memory for such events, long past, tends to be not only vague but confused, and to reflect the personality conflicts and tendencies of the informant fully as much as the facts themselves. Competent case history interviewers insist upon meticulously detailed time-and-place documentation of any statements about the onset of stuttering, and as a rule such documentation simply cannot be obtained unless the history is taken soon after the onset has occurred.

[57] The statements made here are based for the most part on the Johnson and Darley studies reported in *Stuttering in Children and Adults, op. cit.,* Chapters 3 and 4; W. Johnson and others, *The Onset of Stuttering*, Minneapolis, University of Minnesota Press, in press; A. C. La Follette, "A Study of the Parental Environment of Stuttering Children," unpublished Ph.D.

1. Practically all stutterers are originally diagnosed (regarded as "stutterers," or as "not talking right," or as "having difficulty saying words," and so forth) by laymen, not speech specialists. They are usually diagnosed by their parents, more often than not the mother being the first to become concerned.

2. What these laymen diagnose as stuttering is chiefly the simple, easy, apparently unconscious repetitions of syllables, words, and phrases which we know to be characteristic of normal childhood speech.

3. The age at which most children come to be diagnosed by their parents as stutterers is from two to four years. It is to be considered that this is approximately the age at which the average child begins to talk enough to call attention to what he is saying and how he is saying it. Until then most parents are pleased that the child is "learning to talk," but at around the age of three he "has learned," as the parents sense it, and must henceforth be reckoned with as a speaker. Speech standards, as the parents define them, are then applied, the child is judged and, if found wanting, is so evaluated. And certain parents, nearly 1 per cent, make this evaluation in the form of a diagnosis of "stuttering."

4. Practically all children so diagnosed have spoken for from six months to several years without bing regarded as "defective in speech," or "abnormal," or as "stutterers." Moreover, from birth they have phonated, breathed, suckled, chewed, swallowed, coughed, and cried normally.

5. So-called stuttering children are not different from children not so diagnosed, with respect to birth injuries, other injuries, diseases, and general development as indicated by such indexes as age of beginning speech, sitting and standing without support, and teething. They are not different with regard to intelligence. In general they are normal children.

6. Stuttering children are like nonstuttering children with respect to handedness and handedness development. Moreover, conditions of handedness seem not to be related to the degree of

---

dissertation, University of Denver, 1948; and J. P. Moncur, "Parental Domination in Stuttering," *Journal of Speech and Hearing Disorders* (1952), 17:155-165.

stuttering or of speech improvement observed in stuttering children.[58]

7. What is originally diagnosed as stuttering in the young child is decidedly different from well-developed stuttering in the adult. Stuttering as a definite problem, as an "anticipatory, apprehensive, hypertonic, avoidance reaction," occurs, not before being diagnosed, but *after being diagnosed.* In order to emphasize this finding, the writer has coined the term *diagnosogenic;* stuttering is a diagnosogenic problem in the sense that the diagnosis of stuttering is one of its causes.[59]

What this means essentially is that once the parents have persuaded themselves that the child's speech is disordered, that he is a stutterer, they do not react with calm indifference. Their concern, vague and mild before perhaps, now has a disturbing name, "stuttering" (or any equivalent), and all the alarming and depressing implications of such a name, upon which to feed. Their worry becomes intensified. One who has not dealt intimately with such parents would doubtless find it all but impossible to appreciate the heightened sensitivity with which they sometimes come to listen for any sign of "stuttering" in the child's speech so that even when it is normal by any ordinary standard, to them it is disturbingly "defective." Moreover, they tend to generalize their anxieties beyond the child's speech: in their distress he seems now to be somehow "nervous," "unstable" perhaps, "defective in some way," the "victim of bad heredity." He has "something wrong with him." Maybe he is "run down." And running through it all is a furtive and distracting bewilderment: "Why did this have to happen to *us?*"

Few such parents, of course, show these reactions outwardly in any sort of agitated behavior. Most of them protest that they "never let on to the child." Closely questioned, however, they

[58] Detailed data bearing on this point are included in *Stuttering in Children and Adults, op. cit.,* Chapter 3, pp. 51-62.

[59] A similar concept is presented by Franklin G. Ebaugh and Edward G. Billings in an intriguing article, "The Iatrogenic Factors in Illness," *American Journal of the Medical Sciences* (1948), 215:103-107. An iatrogenic disease or disorder, according to Dorland's *American Illustrated Medical Dictionary,* is one that is "induced in the patient by the physician, based on the physician's examination, manner, or discussion."

reveal, as the previous quotations from the Darley study indicated, that, for all their efforts to "do nothing" and to be outwardly calm, they show their anxieties in countless ways—from postural tensions, facial expressions, vocal inflections, ways of looking or not looking at the child when he speaks; through restrained or casual attempts to help the child, suggestions that he speak slowly, or "take a breath," or "stop and start over," or "take it easy," subtle or outright apologies or "explanations" to guests, relatives, and friends, discussions, guarded or not, about "the difficulty" in the child's presence; to, in occasional instances, sterner measures, rarely brutal of course but always disturbing, in the way of "discipline," varying from insistence upon the child's "not stuttering that way" to punitive actions of various kinds. The effects of all this are seen in the child's slowly developing self-consciousness; in occasional cases, of course, the undesirable effects are sudden and marked, depending upon circumstances and incidents. As the child takes on the parent's anxiety-tensions and begins to react in terms of them, the normal nonfluencies in his speech tend gradually to become transformed into more aggravated and strained hesitations or stoppage reactions.

The more anxious the parents become, the more they hound the child to "go slowly," to "stop and start over," to "make up his mind," to "breathe more deeply," etc., the more fearful and disheartened the child becomes, and the more hesitantly, frantically, and laboriously he speaks—so that the parents, teachers, and others become more worried, appeal more insistently to the child to "talk better," with the result that the child's own evaluations become still more disturbed, and his outward speech behavior becomes more and more disordered.[60]

That, in brief essentials, is how stuttering appears to begin and develop.

DO TENSE PARENT-CHILD RELATIONSHIPS MAKE STUTTERING WORSE?

Any sort of impaired relationship between parent and child, or teacher and child, is detrimental on two counts. First, it tends to create situations in which the child's natural hesitancies in

[60] W. Johnson, *People in Quandaries, op. cit.*, Chapter 17.

speech are aggravated. The most flowing and spontaneous speech of which the child is capable will occur in circumstances in which he is happy and thoroughly accepted, and in which he feels warm and affectionate toward the persons to whom he is speaking. The basic fact is that impaired relationships make for more nonfluent speech, and though even very nonfluent speech is not in itself stuttering, yet parents or teachers might be more likely to regard it as stuttering and to react in unfortunate ways accordingly. Second, once the child has been labeled a stutterer, and the chain reaction of spiraling anxiety-tensions has been set in motion, any relationships between parent and child or teacher and child that are unsatisfactory for whatever reason contribute to an intensification of the child's distress regarding speech.

So far as the prevention of stuttering is concerned, there are two major considerations with respect to parental policy:

1. Conditions and parent-child (and teacher-child) relationships should be maintained in such a way as to keep the normal hesitancies and nonfluencies in the child's speech from becoming excessive or an issue of concern. Nothing is to be gained by making his speech more nonfluent as a result of unnecessary frustrations and disapprovals. Relationships with the child, and circumstances generally, that are conducive to flowing, spontaneous speech are clearly desirable, in the interests not only of good speech development but also good personality development generally.

2. The speech nonfluency that the child does exhibit under the circumstances that are provided for him should be accepted and certainly never disapproved. If the nonfluency seems to be excessive, the conditions outside the child that are presumably to blame should be investigated and changed.

### IS STUTTERING EVER CAUSED BY IMITATION?

Imitation in and of itself does not cause stuttering. For example, teachers need have no worry whatever that if one child in a classroom stutters the other children will "catch it" by imitation or in any other way. If there were any tendency for this to occur there would certainly be vastly more stutterers than there are. Actors have been known to play stuttering roles night after night, with intervening rehearsals, for months on end, with no ill effects whatever. Imitating a stutterer will no more make one talk habitually like a stutterer than imitating the call of a moose will doom one forever to sound like a moose at inopportune times.

What does appear to happen occasionally—very occasionally—is that a parent or teacher, overhearing a youngster imitating a stuttering playmate, descends upon the child and makes such an issue of it that a vivid and unfortunate impression is left in the offending child's consciousness. It is at least conceivable that he might as a consequence develop a preoccupation with the foreboding thought that he might become a stutterer himself because of what he had done. Moreover, a parent or teacher who believed that stuttering could be acquired through imitation might possibly keep a watchful eye on the child who had done the imitating and begin to detect what she might take to be signs of beginning stuttering in the youngster's normal but of course imperfect speech. In other words, if stuttering ever does develop following imitation it does so for the same reasons that it develops in other cases, as explained above, and not because of the imitation as such.

## SHOULD LEFT-HANDED CHILDREN BE TAUGHT TO BE RIGHT-HANDED?

It is in connection with the subject of parent-child relationships that change of handedness may most appropriately be considered. This is a matter of considerable importance to teachers as well as parents. As has been indicated previously, the more recent studies do not support the contention that changing a left-handed child to right-handedness in and of itself produces stuttering. There is this to be said, however: any parent or teacher who would so strongly disapprove of left-handedness as to insist that a child who preferred to use the left hand be made to use the right instead might very well be the sort of parent or teacher to whom it would be difficult for the child to adjust generally. Obviously it takes a person who is rather unreasonable, lacking in appreciation of the child's point of view, or at least given to carrying out policies without thinking them through, to insist that a child who unmistakably prefers to use the left hand should use the right one nevertheless. Changing a child's handedness, per se, will not cause the child to stutter, but a parent or teacher who would do it might.

No one has yet brought forth a good reason why the few nonconformists among us should be forced to learn at great inconvenience to do, awkwardly perhaps, with the right hand what they can do so much more easily and just as well or better with the left. It is clearly better to give them any special instruction they may need in order to develop their left-handed skills to the best possible advantage. For example, the standard right-handed writing manuals used in schools, where penmanship is taught, are decidedly unsatisfactory and definitely handi-capping to the child who is learning to write with the left hand. Dr. Warren Gardner, after intensive study of the problem, produced a handwriting manual for left-handed writers[61] that has proved to be very useful to left-handed school children— and roughly 5 per cent of school children are left-handed. Incidentally, Dr. Gardner found that the sole reason why some left-handed writers "lead with the back of the wrist" and point the writing tip of the pencil toward instead of away from themselves is that those who taught them to write insisted that they place the paper in front of them at the same angle as for right-handed writing! With the paper at that angle the left-handed writer cannot write with his hand below the line of writing and must hold his hand above the line of writing in what seems to be a cramped position. In addition to the writing manual, left-sided arm-rest chairs (if arm-rest chairs are used in the classroom) should be provided for these curiously neglected pupils. They are a large group to be neglected, as they have been for so long with respect to basic handwriting instruction and such necessities as chairs with left-handed writing arms.

Children should be permitted to be left-handed if they want to

[61] Warren H. Gardner, *Left Handed Writing: Instruction Manual,* Danville, Ill., Interstate Publishing Co., 1945.

be, just as they should be allowed any and all other reasonable freedoms to develop their own seemingly natural inclinations.

## ARE THERE OTHER SPEECH PROBLEMS THAT MIGHT BE MISTAKEN FOR STUTTERING?

We have already discussed essential differences between stuttering responses and normal nonfluencies, and the great importance of not mistaking the one for the other. It remains to be noted that there are two types of speech disturbance that are sometimes confused with stuttering. In one of these there is a more or less mechanical speech repetition, without normal affect or emotional reaction, which appears to be due to certain kinds of brain injury. It is sufficient, for purposes of clarification, to point out that such cases are encountered occasionally by brain surgeons and other medical specialists, and that they are not stutterers. Practically nothing that has been said in this chapter applies to them. The other type of disorder, sometimes confused with the speech difficulty we have been discussing, is that commonly called "neurotic stuttering." Superficially it resembles stuttering, but it is basically different in being characterized by sudden onset in adolescence or adult life under conditions of unusual physical or emotional strain. In the military services, particularly under conditions of combat or impending combat, men occasionally suddenly exhibit blocked speech, apparently resembling stuttering as seen in adults. From the standpoint of causation and motivation, conditions of onset, course of development, character, and pattern of variability of the blocked speech reactions, related disturbances, and indicated mode of treatment, this type of disorder is to be differentiated from stuttering. It should be given a distinctive name of its own. What has been said in this chapter about stuttering is not said with reference to psychoneurotically disturbed speech.

## UNDER WHAT CONDITIONS DOES STUTTERING INCREASE AND DECREASE?

Stuttering is like anything else in the sense that, when all is said and done, there are only two kinds of knowledge about it that we can have. In the first place, we can know what it is—

that is, we can recognize it when we see it, we can describe it more or less clearly, and we can tell the difference between it and other things that might be confused with it by an untrained observer. The other kind of knowledge about it that we can have has to do with its variations, with increases and decreases in its amount or severity, and with the conditions under which these variations occur. This latter kind of knowledge about stuttering is particularly useful because "therapy" or remedial training for stutterers reduces, after all, to a matter of bringing about those conditions—psychological, physical, social, semantic, emotional, informational, instructional, or whatever— under which the severity of stuttering decreases.

We may begin by considering whether there are any physiological conditions related to variations in stuttering. We have already referred to the essentially negative findings of the large number of studies reviewed by Hill (Footnote 36) and of several related investigations, but there may be special interest in three other studies not yet mentioned. Curtis found that stuttering does not increase as a result of even extremely fatiguing amounts of muscular activity.[62] He had stutterers read test passages every fifteen minutes under a control condition of rest and an experimental condition in which each stutterer stepped onto and down from a standard stairstep, in time to a metronome, and the total stepping amounted to climbing to the top of the Empire State Building, down again, and halfway up and down again, in an hour and fifteen minutes. The stutterers became very tired indeed, but, contrary to what one would expect on the basis of popular belief, the only change noted in their stuttering was that it decreased slightly.

Love investigated the effects on stuttering of two drugs, nembutal and benzedrine.[63] Under each of two control conditions (no capsule and sugar capsule, or placebo, respectively) and two experimental conditions (capsule containing three grains

[62] James F. Curtis, "A Study of the Effect of Muscular Exercise upon Stuttering," *Speech Monographs* (1942), 9:61-74.
[63] William R. Love, "The Effect of Pentobarbital (nembutal) and Amphetamine Sulphate (benzedrine) on the Severity of Stuttering," in *Stuttering in Children and Adults, op. cit.,* Chapter 23.

of nembutal and capsule containing twenty milligrams of benzedrine, respectively), he noted stuttered words during eight successive readings of a test passage by each stutterer. There were no significant mean differences among the four conditions either with reference to total amount of stuttering or amount of decrease in stuttering during the series of eight readings (adaptation effect).

Four research workers at the University of Toronto Department of Psychiatry subjected to appropriate laboratory test the notion, first set forth by L. J. Meduna, M.D., that the speech of stutterers is affected by the inhalation of carbon dioxide gas.[64] They administered thirty to seventy administrations of gas to each of sixteen stutterers, and their relevant records and observations extended to two months beyond termination of the therapy. No reduction in stuttering was found to result from the gas inhalations.

Stuttering involves varying degrees of muscular tension and at times seeming incoördination, particularly of the muscles directly used in speaking. Various writers in the past have attempted to explain these phenomena by assuming them to be evidence of some sort of "neuromuscular instability," or "stuttering block," or "neural block." A recent study by Williams has yielded information that is fundamental in this connection.[65] Williams recorded action potentials from the jaw muscles of stutterers and nonstutterers during stuttered and nonstuttered speech and noted various types of differences between them. Differences between the potentials from the two sides of the jaw in the stutterers were of particular interest. Then, by instructing the nonstutterers to move their jaws in particular ways, essentially duplicating the jaw movements of the stutterers during stuttering, he was able to record from their jaw muscles the kinds of action potential "abnormalities" occurring during stuttered

[64] R. G. S. Arthurs, D. Cappon, E. Douglass, and B. Quarrington, "Carbon Dioxide Therapy with Stutterers," *Diseases of the Nervous System*, Vol. 15, No. 4 (April, 1954).

[65] Dean Williams, "Masseter Muscle Action Potentials in Stuttered and Non-stuttered Speech," *Journal of Speech and Hearing Disorders* (1955), 20:242-261.

speech, including differences between the right and left sides of the jaw. In other words, the seeming irregularities in the stutterers' records turned out to be indicative, not of "neuro-muscular instability" but merely of the particular movements of the jaw they were making in the act of stuttering. Moreover, by instructing the stutterers to do their stuttering in more simple and easy patterns, Williams was able to obtain from their jaw muscles the same kinds of action potential records that he got from those of the nonstutterers. Such data, along with the many findings of similar implication previously reviewed, suggest strongly that there is no particular reason for assuming that severity changes in stuttering reflect fluctuations in physiological conditions of some sort.

Common sense prescribes physically hygienic living for persons who stutter as well as for those who do not, but scientific data have not indicated that stuttering tends to be made worse or better by any particular physiological factors, as such.

The conditions that have been found to be most clearly and importantly associated with variations in stuttering are in general psychological and evaluational. Reference has been made to Bloodstein's investigations of the conditions under which stuttering is markedly reduced or absent.[66] He obtained data from 204 stutterers concerning their speech experiences under each of 115 types of conditions. He concluded that, in general, stuttering is decreased as anxiety concerning it is reduced, and he classified specific conditions under which such anxiety reduction occurs under six headings: those involving (a) reduced "communicative responsibility" (as when speaking while alone or to an infant), (b) absence of unfavorable listener reactions, (c) reduced need to make a favorable impression, (d) considerable change in speech pattern (as when speaking with a dialect or in a very loud voice), (e) accompanying activity (as when

---

[66] In addition to the previous references to Bloodstein's work, see also Oliver Bloodstein, "A Rating Scale Study of Conditions Under Which Stuttering Is Reduced or Absent," *Journal of Speech and Hearing Disorders* (1950), 15:29-36. The present discussion is based in part on his article, "Hypothetical Conditions Under Which Stuttering Is Reduced or Absent," *Journal of Speech and Hearing Disorders* (1950), 15:142-153.

speaking in time to walking), and (*f*) strong or unusual stimulation (as when reading in chorus with others, or in a noisy environment, or when highly excited). Conditions (*a*), (*b*), and (*c*) would seem to involve factors directly diminishing the level of anxiety concerning anticipated stuttering; conditions (*d*), (*e*), and (*f*) appear to involve marked reductions, largely because of some sort of "distraction," in anticipation of stuttering, with attendant reduction in anxiety, since one does not fear stuttering if one does not expect to stutter.

It is also to be said that if stuttering is expected, then the more anxious or concerned about it the speaker is, the more he will stutter. Moreover, if the speaker has a fear of stuttering, then the more expectation of stuttering he experiences the more he will stutter. We have defined stuttering as what the stutterer does trying not to stutter again, and, more fully, as an "anticipatory, apprehensive, hypertonic avoidance reaction." Any conditions which make for increased anticipation of stuttering, or increased apprehensiveness concerning it, tend to result in correspondingly increased avoidant effort and tension.

The relevant literature is much too extensive to be fully reviewed here. Probably the most fundamental data yielded by the many investigations dealing with variations in stuttering are those which represent the adaptation effect. Several years ago Johnson and Knott and Van Riper and Hull discovered that if stutterers read the same passage several times in succession the average amount of stuttering decreases from reading to reading, and they called this decrease in stuttering the adaptation effect, or adaptation of the stuttering response.[67] The average

[67] The original adaptation data reported by W. Johnson and J. R. Knott are to be found in "The Distribution of Moments of Stuttering in Successive Readings of the Same Material," *Journal of Speech Disorders* (1937), 2:17-19. At about the time of this study C. Van Riper and C. Hull made a similar investigation which went unpublished, however, until 1955 when it was included in *Stuttering in Children and Adults, op. cit.,* Chapter 8, "The Quantitative Measurement of the Effect of Certain Situations on Stuttering." Part IV of *Stuttering in Children and Adults,* consisting of Chapters 8 through 23, pp. 199-310, is made up of reports of studies of adaptation and other aspects of the general problem of stuttering variability. Adaptation of the stuttering response has been found to occur, though apparently not always to the same degree, in the speech as well as

stutterer has about half as many stuttered words in the fifth reading as in the first reading of a passage under ordinary conditions with one listener. Johnson and Knott also found that the stuttering which occurred in later readings tended strongly (in about two thirds of the instances) to involve words previously stuttered in earlier readings; this they called the consistency effect, the tendency for stuttering to occur consistently on the same words or in response to the same cues or stimuli.[68] In later research

in the oral reading of stutterers, in studies by Edwin Cohen, "A Comparison of Oral Reading and Spontaneous Speech of Stutterers with Special Reference to the Adaptation and Consistency Effects," unpublished Ph.D. dissertation, University of Iowa, 1952, and Parley W. Newman, "A Study of Adaptation and Recovery of the Stuttering Response in Self-Formulated Speech," *Journal of Speech and Hearing Disorders* (1954), *19*:450-458. The adaptation effect has been shown in several studies to be greater when the same passage is read several times in succession than when a different passage is used in each of several successive readings; see, for example, Arnold Golub, "The Cumulative Effect of Constant and Varying Reading Material on Stuttering Adaptation," in *Stuttering in Children and Adults, op. cit.,* Chapter 13. Using a modified form of the Lewis-Sherman method of scaling the severity of stuttering, William D. Trotter found that adaptation occurs in successive readings of the same passage, not only as seen in reduced frequency of stuttering, but also in the sense that the stutterings occur in less and less severe form. See William D. Trotter, "The Severity of Stuttering During Successive Readings of the Same Material," *Journal of Speech and Hearing Disorders* (1955), *20*:17-25. Other studies of variation in stuttering are referred to in other footnotes in the present volume. Explorations of phenomena in nonstuttered speech comparable to adaptation in stuttering have been reported by H. B. Starbuck and M. D. Steer in "The Adaptation Effect in Stuttering Speech Behavior and Normal Speech Behavior," *Journal of Speech and Hearing Disorders* (1953), *18*:252-255.

[68] The consistency effect has been demonstrated in a variety of forms. As has been noted previously, the extensive investigations made by Spencer F. Brown have shown that stuttering consistently occurs more frequently with some kinds of sounds and words than others. See reference, Footnote 31. The tendency for stuttering to occur consistently in response to such cues as pencil marks drawn through certain words, the colored border distinguishing a specific reading passage, and other discernible characteristics of words or passages or speech situations has been reported by many investigators; see, for example, Ella Yensen Fierman, "The Role of Cues in Stuttering Adaptation," Chapter 16; Maribel Hopper Connett, "Experimentally Induced Changes in the Relative Frequency of Stuttering on a Specified Speech Sound," Chapter 18; and Naomi Hunt Berwick, "Stuttering in Response to Photographs of Selected Listeners," Chapter 19, in *Stuttering in Children and Adults, op. cit.*

it was also demonstrated that once stuttering has been reduced through adaptation in reading a passage several times in succession, there is a tendency for the severity of the stuttering to return to its former level after a few hours. Wischner has called this the spontaneous recovery of the stuttering response following adaptation, borrowing the term "spontaneous recovery" from the field of the psychology of learning.[69]

These three phenomena—(a) adaptation or decrease in the frequency or severity of the stuttering response during oral reading or speaking, (b) recovery or increase in the frequency or severity of the stuttering response, following adaptation, and (c) the consistency effect, the tendency for stuttering to occur consistently in response to the same words or other stimuli— have come to be recognized as fundamental aspects of stuttering behavior. A large part of the relatively recent and current research on stuttering is concerned with them. It is particularly revealing to note that in the adaptation effect we have a sort of laboratory model of the improvement process, and we can study it to observe whether improvement is retarded or speeded up under specified conditions (the Love study of drugs, Footnote 60, and the Curtis study of fatigue, Footnote 59, are illustrative). Just so, the spontaneous recovery effect serves as a kind of laboratory model of what is recognized in the clinic as a relapse, and we can subject this also to observation under controlled conditions. These two phenomena are, therefore, not only of very great theoretical importance (they strongly suggest that stuttering is a learned response rather than a "neuromuscular disorder"), but they also are of unusually practical value because of the use that can be made of them in studying the basic processes of improvement and relapse, and so the whole matter of therapy or remedial training.

[69] Spontaneous recovery has been the subject of experimentation reported in *Stuttering in Children and Adults, op. cit.,* by E. Leroi Jones, Dorothy Jamison Williams, and James Frick, Chapters 11, 14, and 15, respectively. It has been investigated also by Ralph Leutenegger, "A Study of Adaptation and Recovery in the Oral Reading of Stutterers," unpublished Ph.D. dissertation, University of Iowa, 1954. Parley W. Newman, *op. cit.,* found that recovery of the stuttering response following adaptation is similar in oral reading and in spontaneous speech.

Together with the consistency effect, and the well-documented fact that stutterers experience expectancy of stuttering and anxiety or concern about it in conflict with their urge or drive to speak, these fundamental aspects of stuttering have been the subject of several extremely significant theoretical discussions of stuttering in the past few years. In two articles, Wischner has systematically developed an analogy between stuttering behavior and certain kinds of conditioned and learned responses that have been investigated in both human subjects and animals in the laboratories of learning psychologists.[70]

Utilizing a learning theory frame of reference also, Sheehan has developed in considerable detail a theory in which stuttering is viewed as learned behavior expressive of a conflict between the drive to speak and the drive to avoid expected stuttering.[71] Van Riper has interpreted stuttering in a way that emphasizes the conflict between the urge to speak and the fear of expected stuttering, and the reinforcement of the resultant behavior by virtue of the "release from punishment" involved in finally saying the word.[72] Hill has presented a compact theory embodying features similar to the above, and he has convincingly produced "stutter-like" disturbances in the speech of nonstuttering

[70] George J. Wischner, "Stuttering and Learning: A Preliminary Theoretical Formulation," and "An Experimental Approach to Expectancy and Anxiety in Stuttering Behavior," *Journal of Speech and Hearing Disorders* (1950), *15*:335-345 and (1952), *17*:139-154. Following Mowrer (O. H. Mowrer, "A Stimulus-Response Analysis of Anxiety and Its Role as a Reinforcing Agent," *Psychological Review* (1939), *46*:553-566), Wischner includes as an interesting aspect of his theoretical discussion the hypothesis that one of the reasons why the stuttering response continues to recur is that it is followed, after all, by the utterance of the word with attendant reduction in anxiety and tension and this serves as a kind of "reward" to reinforce the stuttering response that precedes it.

[71] Joseph G. Sheehan, "Theory and Treatment of Stuttering as an Approach-Avoidance Conflict," *Journal of Psychology* (1953), *36*:27-49. Sheehan develops the proposition that the conflict involved in the act of stuttering is resolved by virtue of the fear-reducing effects of actually performing the stuttering after having built up fear in anticipation of stuttering. An earlier version of a conflict theory of stuttering is to be found in W. Johnson and J. R. Knott, "The Moment of Stuttering," *Journal of Genetic Psychology* (1936), *48*:475-480.

[72] Charles Van Riper, *Speech Correction Principles and Methods,* New York, Prentice-Hall, Inc., 3d Ed., 1954. See especially pp. 369-382, Chapter 9.

adults in a laboratory situation designed in accordance with
his theory.[73]

It is clear that the most fruitful research on stuttering to date
has been that concerned with conditions under which stuttering
varies in amount or severity. It has been much too fruitful,
in fact, to be reported fully or even summarized more than very
briefly in an introductory text. With the risk of oversimplification
that brevity involves, it may be said that what we have so far
learned from this research suggests that the more stutterers
talk and read aloud, the better, and the more continuously
they talk the better. The data seem to imply, moreover, that
the stutterer benefits from talking repeatedly to the same or
similar listeners in the same or similar situations until substantial
reduction of stuttering has been achieved. Then he should go
through the same adaptation process in other situations with
other listeners. Some of the data imply that stuttering tends
to be reduced to the degree that the stutterer is ready and willing
to perform his stuttering behavior relatively simply and easily.[74]
Most of the adaptation and recovery studies suggest, too, that
substantial early improvement in any situation is likely to be
followed by slower and more gradual further improvement with
occasional relapses in some degree and inconsistencies in accordance with varying influences of the complex pattern of
relevant conditions. The most important overall generalization
to be made is that reduction in anxiety about stuttering is
attended by reduction in frequency or severity of stuttering, and
that the anxiety is diminished most during speaking.

The writer prefers the theory that stresses anxiety deconfirma-
tion in explaining either the adaptation effect or improvement in
the ordinary sense. That is, the things we anticipate with dread
or uneasiness we tend to exaggerate, so that when we actually
experience them we discover that they are not as bad as we

[73] Harris E. Hill, "An Experimental Study of Disorganization of Speech
and Manual Responses in Normal Subjects," *Journal of Speech and Hearing
Disorders* (1954), *19*:295-305.

[74] This is further discussed in the section of this chapter concerned with
remedial training. Experimental data relevant to this point have been reported by Eloise Tupper Oxtoby in "Frequency of Stuttering in Relation to
Induced Modifications Following Expectancy of Stuttering," *Stuttering in
Children and Adults, op. cit.*, Chapter 10.

expected them to be. Our fear of them is correspondingly "deconfirmed" in some degree and therefore weakened. So it appears to be in the case of stuttering behavior. It is anticipatory. The stutterer nearly always expects more stuttering, more attendant discomfort, and more serious personal and social consequences than he actually experiences. To the degree that the stuttering and its consequences, as experienced, turn out to be less fearful than anticipated, the stutterer's anxiety is deconfirmed. With less intense anxiety, he is subsequently less apprehensive about stuttering on the words he has to say, less concerned about avoiding the stuttering he does anticipate, and so he does less to avoid it and does it with less tension. For this essential reason there is adaptation; that is, more and more talking leads to less and less stuttering because the stutterer gradually learns that in general his expectations are exaggerated and that speaking is nearly always not as bad as he thinks it will be.

Moreover, the writer is inclined to believe that an important effect of this process of anxiety-deconfirmation is the positive increase in satisfaction gained from speaking. To the degree that stuttering involves a conflict between the drive to speak and the drive (because of fear) to avoid stuttering, anxiety-deconfirmation results not only in a relative increase in the drive to speak compared with the fear of stuttering, but an absolute increase as well because the more pleasant and rewarding speech becomes for the stutterer the greater becomes his drive to speak in and of itself. What is more, anxiety-deconfirmation tends to be essentially self-increasing, so that the less afraid of his stuttering the stutterer becomes the less he stutters, quite aside from how much he talks. That is, not only is it true of the stutterer that the more he talks the less he stutters and the less he stutters the more he talks, but also, as a kind of bonus, the more he talks the more he talks and the less he stutters the less he stutters.

### WHAT ARE THE ADVANTAGES AND DISADVANTAGES OF CLASSIFYING A CHILD AS A STUTTERER?

No child should be diagnosed or classified as a stutterer by the classroom teacher, or by his parents or anyone else, merely because he seems to speak hesitantly and with repetitions. As has been emphasized, even very considerable amounts of non-fluency are part and parcel of normal speech. So long as the child shows no anxiety-tension with respect to his speech nonfluencies, certainly nothing is to be gained by placing him under a cloud by calling him a stutterer, and it is clear that doing this can have seriously harmful consequences. So long as the child is accepted by his parents, friends of the family, neighbors, and his own friends and playmates as a normal speaker, one should make no move to disturb this acceptance, which is highly important to the youngster's sound speech development. One should, as a matter of course, attempt to remove or modify any conditions making for aggravated feelings of insecurity and hesitancy in the child's speech. One should do this, however, without aggravating the problem by calling the youngster a stutterer, or encouraging others by any other means to look on him as "abnormal" or "defective" to no point and for no solid scientific reason. An actual case will help to illustrate what is meant.

The . . . case is that of Jimmy, who as a pupil in the grades was regarded as a superior speaker. He won a number of speaking contests and often served as chairman of small groups. Upon entering the ninth grade, he changed to another school. A "speech examiner" saw Jimmy twice during the one year he spent in that school. The first time she made a recording of his speech. The second time she played the record for him, and after listening to it, told him he was a stutterer.

Now, if you have ever tried to speak into a speech recording machine you probably suspect what is true. In the studies to which we have already referred all children who have done this have shown hesitations, repetitions, broken sentences, etc. It is easy to see how the apparently untrained teacher misguided Jimmy who was, after all, a superior speaker as ninth-graders go.

He took the diagnosis to heart, however. The teacher told him to speak slowly, to watch himself, to try to control his speech. Jimmy's parents were quite upset. They looked upon Jimmy's speech as one of his chief talents, and they set about with a will to help him, reminding him of any little slip or hesitation. Jimmy became as self-conscious as the legendary centipede who had been told "how" to walk. He soon developed tense, jerky, hesitant, apprehensive speech—the kind that any speech pathologist would call stuttering of at least average severity.[75]

Before a child is classified as a stutterer full consideration should be given to the purposes to be accomplished by so classifying him. In what way will this be beneficial to the child? For practical purposes of thinking constructively about this matter, it is helpful to group children in the following way.

First, there are children whose speech is normally nonfluent to the degrees and in the ways that we have previously discussed. They exhibit no tensions or signs of uneasiness in their hesitancies, pauses, and repetitions. Nobody is concerned about them. They are not to be usefully thought of as "passing through a stage" of being nonfluent or of "stuttering," and they need not be regarded as "primary stutterers."[76] There appear to be clear advantages in thinking of them as normal children so far as their speech is concerned.

Second, there are occasional youngsters who are noticeably more nonfluent than most other children are, or, though they may not have more frequent hesitancies or repetitions, seem to be somewhat more tense and more "bothered" by them. They are, however, decidedly different from representative adult stutterers as far as the tensions and emotional reactions involved in their nonfluencies are concerned. Moreover, they have not developed definitely fixed and elaborate attitudes, interests, specific habits, and general behavior patterns around the non-fluencies or as a reaction or adjustment to them. They do appear to be on the way to becoming confirmed stutterers, however, largely or solely because their parents, and usually other adults and sometimes children as well, are taking notice of their speech nonfluencies, reacting to them in one way or another,

[75] From "An Open Letter to the Mother of a Stuttering Child," by W. Johnson. See Appendix VII.

[76] Problems centering around the varying usages of the terms "primary" and "secondary" stuttering are dealt with by Philip J. Glasner and Frana Dahl Vermilyea in "An Investigation of the Definition and Use of the Diagnosis, 'Primary Stuttering,' " *Journal of Speech and Hearing Disorders* (1953), *18*:161-167.

having feelings about them, sometimes making unfortunate comments about them, or responding to them by urging the child to talk better, or slow down, say the words over, and so forth. Out of this specific disapproval of the child's speech and worry about it, and out of any other reasons for impaired parent-child or other relationships that may exist, pressures develop. The child's sense of security is weakened by all this. If he is inclined by training to be sensitive to disapproval or to feel insecure generally, he will be all the more likely to react to the issues made over his speech by becoming self-conscious about it, less spontaneous in speaking, more cautious and hesitant, more repetitious, and more and more tensely nonfluent as the conflict between his urge to speak and his concern over disapproval of his speech gradually develops.

Such a child, while not yet possessed of all the characteristics of an adult stutterer, and while still changeable and very responsive to good influences, does present a problem. It may do no good, and it can make matters worse, to call it stuttering. It is not a question of whether the child *is really* stuttering or *really is not* stuttering; it is a question, to be answered as well as possible in each individual case, of what the effects will be of calling the child a stutterer and what they will be of not calling him a stutterer. So far as the facts, judged by common-sense standards, are concerned he can be called a beginning stutterer, or he can be referred to as a child who presents more or less disturbed speech with a considerable probability of becoming a stutterer in a significant clinical sense. One should do, with care, what seems calculated to have the best effects in each given case. Whatever is done about what name to call the problem, certainly someone other than the child, nearly always the parents, are to be given major attention. The problem of counseling parents will be dealt with in a later section of this chapter.

Third, there are children whose speech behavior is clearly different from that of children in either of the two groups we have just discussed. They present considerable nonfluency. Their hesitations and repetitions are tense and accompanied by obvious associated movements or grimaces. They are avoiding certain speech situations, substituting words perhaps, and are in general more like adult stutterers. There are various signs that they themselves have taken on the problem emotionally and are being adversely affected by it. Their parents, relatives, friends, and teachers take for granted that they are stutterers. They think of themselves as stutterers. So far as stuttering is to be defined as a reputation, they have the reputation. It would be plainly impractical, and doubtless confusing to all concerned, including the child, to attempt to say that the youngster is not a stutterer. In such a case the advantage nearly always lies in accepting the label, the reputation, which the child brings with him, and in being matter-of-fact in dealing with the problem as stuttering.

In any case, and particularly any questionable case, the speech correctionist, if one is available, should be consulted as a matter of course, and the question should be thoroughly investigated with his coöperation in order to determine how to classify the child and his speech most helpfully and, if there is a problem, how to deal with it most effectively.

### Remedial Training for Stutterers

A rather useful or practical way of thinking about the general problem of what to do for a child or adult who stutters is to be found in an analysis of the various kinds or dimensions of improvement that are possible and advantageous for him. Once we are fairly clear about the particular kinds of improvement a given stutterer might best try to achieve, we have a good basis for thinking about the procedures that he—and we—might use in order to bring about these particular kinds of improvement. And we can also think clearly then about the basic question of what in general should be done first and what next and what should probably not be attempted until rather late in the retraining program, because some kinds of improvement are basic and tend to make other kinds of improvement more readily attainable.

Moreover, at the same time that we are working out our analysis of the retraining problem in these terms of the possible dimensions of improvement, we shall find it useful to consider that certain of these dimensions or kinds of improvement are as clearly indicated or desirable from one theoretical point of view as from another. For example, whether we believe that the stutterer does whatever he may do as a stutterer out of biological or neurophysiological necessity, or that he does it out of some deep-lying emotional or motivational need, or that he does it because he has learned to do it as a habit—that is, as a conditioned or reinforced response to the cues or stimuli with which the doing of it has come to be associated—doubtless we agree that it is to the stutterer's advantage to improve certain aspects of his personal and social adjustment and to accomplish certain of the specific changes in behavior and attitude that we shall presently be considering. To say that a stutterer might gain by improving his personality adjustment by no means implies that he is now necessarily "maladjusted' or "neurotic." If he were to undertake to sell insurance, for example, he would be likely to be enrolled by the insurance company in a course of training designed in part to "improve his personality" even though he might be "well adjusted" when first employed. Just so, if he is to undertake to acquire better speech behavior, he might very well, no matter how "well adjusted" he may be in a general sense, increase his chances of success if he were to accomplish certain kinds of improvement in adjustment. It will also be clear, of course, that some of the types of improvement we shall be considering are more definitely indicated as necessary or desirable from one theoretical point of view than from another. After all, regardless of how clear or unclear about it we may be in our own minds, we do operate with some theory or other about stuttering, and the particular theory we favor does influence us in the decisions we make as to what to do from moment to moment as we work with stutterers. It would seem desirable, therefore, to be as clear about our theories—our fundamental assumptions about what stuttering involves and what factors or conditions "cause" it or affect the severity of it—as we can be with the dependable knowledge that is currently available to us.

POSSIBLE DIMENSIONS OF IMPROVEMENT

The problem of any particular child or adult who stutters is likely to have several aspects, and some of these will be more severe, or more important, or more susceptible to improvement than certain others will be. The practical significance of this fact is that for any stutterer there are as many kinds of desirable change, as many kinds or dimensions of improvement, as there are notable or significant aspects of his total problem. We shall proceed by listing, with only brief comment, the various aspects of the overall problems that stutterers in general have, and then we shall give attention to (*a*) those kinds of improvement that are of particular interest and practical importance to the classroom teacher and (*b*) those additional dimensions of improvement that are in most instances of specialized interest and significance to the professional speech correctionist.

What follows is a list of eight major aspects of the problem that any stutterer might have, stated in such a way as to indicate corresponding kinds of changes or improvements. The list can be used as an outline in working with a particular stutterer. In using it in this way, the teacher or speech correctionist should attempt to secure the information that will make it possible for her or him to rate each aspect of the problem by underlining one of the five terms (no problem; slight; moderate; marked; very marked problem) alongside each of the eight major headings in the list.[77] This should be done as early in the retraining period as possible, and new ratings should be made for comparative purposes at the end of retraining. Under each major heading there are subheadings which are intended to serve as guides to a further breakdown or analysis; this breakdown, in turn, amounts

[77] The relevant information needed to make these ratings or judgments may be obtained in many ways, of course, some simple, others elaborate, and the thoroughness as well as the precision with which it is obtained must necessarily be adapted to the time available, the technical means at hand, one's training and experience, and the circumstances under which one works. Several interview procedures, tests, and special rating forms are to be found in W. Johnson, F. L. Darley, and D. C. Spriestersbach, *Diagnostic Manual in Speech Correction,* New York, Harper & Brothers, 1952. Ordinary observation, questioning, and gathering of relevant information from parents, teachers, school records, and other available sources are, of course, the main procedures used by teachers and speech correctionists in this connection.

to a listing of the possible changes or kinds of improvement that might be undertaken.[78]

I. Speech (aside from stuttering): No problem; slight; moderate; marked; very marked problem.

    A. Degree to which speaking is enjoyed in general, and in specific situations that occur often or are otherwise important for the particular individual.

    B. Strength of the individual's "communicative drive"; proportion of the individual's experiences in speaking that he evaluates as successful. Degree of the individual's interest in the listeners to whom he is speaking.

    C. Quality of speech aside from stuttering. Correctness of speech sound articulation, quality of voice, and expressiveness.

    D. Degree of interest in, feeling for, or appreciation of good speech. Degree to which the individual admires effective speakers and enjoys listening to them. Tendency to be curious about language and problems of meaning. Degree to which he likes to say things well, to make his statements clear and dependable, and to interpret as best he can the meanings of material that he reads aloud.

    E. Speaking time. In general, is the stutterer very talkative, rather quiet, or about average in comparison with others his own age?[79]

II. Stuttering: No problem; slight; moderate; marked; very marked problem.

    A. Severity of stuttering.[80]

        1. Frequency (percentage of words spoken or read). One can actually count stuttered words during oral reading or in

[78] The very considerable contribution of Dr. William Trotter to the development of this method of analyzing and evaluating a stutterer's problem is gratefully acknowledged.

[79] According to our general observations, the average college student probably talks—solid speaking time, that is—about 45 minutes a day. We try to get stutterers of comparable age to talk at least an hour or so per day. It is to be appreciated that a child's verbal output varies greatly from one situation to another, of course. A speaking-time record form and instructions for its use are to be found in the *Diagnostic Manual in Speech Correction, op. cit.,* pp. 153-154.

[80] Procedures for evaluating severity of stuttering and attitudes toward stuttering are given in *Diagnostic Manual in Speech Correction, op. cit.,* pp. 115-152.

tape-recorded speech, of course, but speech correctionists who are too busy to do this will prefer to estimate the percentage of stuttered words. They should practice marking stuttered words during oral reading, however, before making such estimates in order to avoid the common tendency to overestimate.

2. Degree of tension involved in stuttering reactions.

3. Duration of stutterings.

4. Complexity of stuttering reactions—the number, variety, and patterning of the grimaces, eye-closures, lip-puckerings, extraneous vocalizations, holding of the breath, bodily movements, and so forth.

5. Attitude toward stuttering. This may range from an emotionally charged intolerance of stuttering, a refusal to face it, and a tendency to run away from it, to calm and objective acceptance of it and interest in it as a fact to be observed and understood, and as a problem to be worked on as conscientiously and effectively as possible. The attitude is revealed in degree of willingness to talk about the problem and the sorts of statements made about it. It is shown also in evident degrees of embarrassment, as well as in the strength of the desire to avoid stuttering and to avoid situations and personal relationships that involve or might involve stuttering. It is revealed in the extent to which the stutterer has sought information about stuttering from books, teachers, doctors, and other possible sources of such information, and in his response to opportunities to observe his own stuttering in a mirror or by means of a tape recorder. It is reflected in his sense of humor regarding his stuttering and, of course, in countless other ways as well.

III. Adjustment to others: No problem; slight; moderate; marked; very marked problem.

A. Attitude toward others, with due reference to specific individuals of special importance. The attitude may range from a negative distrust, dislike, or rejection of others to a positive trustfulness, responsiveness, and friendliness toward others.

B. Relationships with others.

1. Number of close friends.

2. Number of acquaintances.

3. Group memberships; number of offices held; extent of active participation.

4. Degree of participation in school activities, including playground activities and sports.

5. Extent of dating; level of social skills, such as dancing; degree of enjoyment of parties.

6. Sharing of hobbies—that is, the stutterer's preference for doing things with others rather than retiring to the basement on the attic, as it were, to pursue his hobbies by himself, is to be evaluated.

IV. Self-adjustment: No problem; slight; moderate; marked; very marked problem.

   A. Attitude toward self. The stutterer's attitude toward himself can range from negative self-rejection, a poor opinion of himself, a feeling of inferiority, to positive self-acceptance and a good opinion of himself that acknowledges his faults and places them in perspective in relation to his assets, with due recognition of his capacity for future growth and improvement.

V. Adjustment to school: No problem; slight; moderate; marked; very marked problem.

   A. Attitude toward school. This attitude may range from negative dislike of school, teachers, schoolmates, studies, and so forth, to positive enjoyment of school and the companionship of the other children, appreciation of the teachers' efforts and of the opportunity to achieve an education, and a lively interest in studies.

   B. Scholastic achievement with reference to specific subjects as well as grade placement.

   C. Special school problems. Problems may involve crowded classroom conditions, questionable school policies or instructional procedures, unfortunate teacher-pupil relations, transportation difficulties, lack of necessary or desirable speech correction or other special services, and so forth. There may be discipline problems of various sorts, personality clashes with classmates, and the like.

VI. Adjustment to home and family: No problem; slight; moderate; marked; very marked problem.

   A. Relationship with parents. This can range from warm, intimate, and secure to cold, noncommunicative, and unstable.

It can range from rejection, through a constructive balance between independence and dependence, to overprotectiveness.

B. Relationship with brothers and sisters, if any. This can range from tense rivalry and ill feeling, through mutual good feeling and coöperativeness, to either overdependence or oversolicitousness.

C. Family problems. These may be of any sort from financial to strained relationships between the parents, including separation and divorce. The cohesiveness and general character of the larger family group, including grandparents and other relatives, are to be considered too.

VII. Physical health: No problem; slight; moderate; marked; very marked problem.

A. Physical condition. General state of nutrition, vitality, and general health. Presence and degree of diseases, insufficiencies, or impairments.

B. Attitude toward physical condition. Tendency to be overconcerned, worrisome, and fussy about health. Unwarranted suspicion, without medical or laboratory evidence, that the stuttering is a sign of physical weakness or deficiency of some sort. Tendency to worry about possible hereditary cause of the stuttering. Unwarranted overconcern about getting enough rest and sleep and "not overdoing."

VIII. Adjustment to remedial training: No problem; slight; moderate; marked; very marked problem.

A. Motivation for doing remedial work. This can range from marked absence of motivation for work, even active resistance to it, to keen interest in learning what might be done to improve and a consistent show of good work habits. Problems can center around the stutterer's expectation of a magical cure, "the pink pill," "the sudden miracle." They can arise from the stutterer's extreme fear of stuttering and speaking and his consequent repertoire of avoidance reactions. The stutterer's willingness and ability to talk freely about his problems are important in this connection. Lack of adequate motivation can be due to a great variety of reasons.

B. Conditions under which remedial training is attempted. There can be difficulties in retraining traceable to the attitudes and practices of the parents. In some instances there is lack of time, or the stutterer is too busy with other things, or there may be transportation difficulties. Illnesses may interfere. The stuttering may be so mild that it is difficult to figure out what changes to attempt that will not intensify the problem. There may be limitations of intelligence. Other problems, physical or psychological, may complicate the picture. There are other such possibilities, of course.

## ASPECTS OF THE STUTTERER'S PROBLEM AND REMEDIAL TRAINING OF SPECIAL CONCERN TO THE CLASSROOM TEACHER

The aspects of the stuttering youngster's total problem that are of chief interest to the classroom teacher are those having to do with his adjustment to school, first of all, and his adjustment to himself and to others. She will be concerned so far as she can be with his adjustment to home and family. There is much that is fundamental that she can do also about the speech aspects of his problem aside from his stuttering, although she can be most effective along this line if she coördinates what she does with what is being done by the speech correctionist. If there is no speech correctionist, the classroom teacher should work on the child's speech, to the extent that she does, with due appreciation of the influence that his stuttering has on the other aspects of his speech behavior. She can do her best to see to it that he receives any medical attention he may require for whatever reason, and that he not be encouraged to worry about his health needlessly. If there is a speech correctionist in the school, the classroom teacher can do much to contribute to the stutterer's adjustment to the remedial program which the speech correctionist is attempting to carry forward with him. What she can do so far as the stuttering aspect of the total problem is concerned, she can best accomplish for the most part through the good effects of her efforts along these other dimensions of improvement, although she can do some things directly.

What the classroom teacher can do in an effort to help the stuttering child improve the various aspects of his adjustment and of his general speech behavior she can do best, as a rule, in the following specific ways:

1. Encourage the child to talk more. In a very basic sense this is the single most important type of improvement for a stutterer to achieve, because his speaking time is his working time. Practically any speech improvement of whatever sort that he is going to accomplish he will have to achieve while he is speaking and through the act of speaking. The stuttering youngster who talks only five full minutes a day or less (and there are many such) can hardly change his speech behavior or his feelings about it at all, because he is not speaking enough to practice anything sufficiently to achieve any significant effect. Talking at least a half-hour to an hour or more a day will not necessarily lead to improvement along other lines, though in and of itself it is likely to have some good effects, but it at least makes various improvements possible that would otherwise not be possible. It brings the child into relationship with the other children and the grown-ups to whom he does his increased talking, and makes possible— and likely—improvement in his attitudes toward them, in their attitudes toward him, and in his social adjustment generally. It tends to make him feel more adequate, to decrease his feelings of inferiority, and to lead to improvement generally along the dimension of self-adjustment. And it is well known that experience in speaking tends to lead to improvement in basic speech skills, expressiveness, and poise, and so an increase in daily speaking time is one of the surest means to improvement in general speech behavior.

The classroom teacher should get to know the child who stutters by talking to him, consulting the school records concerning him, checking with the speech correctionist if there is one and with his other teachers, past and present, and it is desirable that she also talk with his parents. Having become acquainted with him and his problem and his feelings about it, she will be prepared to encourage him in many ways to do more talking. First of all, she will want to get him to do more talking to her, especially outside class hours. Judiciously, she can draw him more often into the talking that goes on in the classroom itself. She can find and make errands for him to run. She can arrange for him to help sell tickets at games, serve on a refreshments committee this week, a cleanup crew next week, see the janitor about the use of a room after school hours, and so on and on until a very considerable increase in speaking is achieved. And more talking leads to more talking, partly because the more persons a child talks to the more persons he knows to whom he will talk again whenever he meets them. The effects of increased speaking tend to be good in many ways and they are cumulative.

In carrying out these suggestions, the teacher should always bear in mind, of course, that, as was pointed out in Chapter II, some stuttering children are so disturbed emotionally by their speech difficulty that it is sometimes advisable to arrange things so that they have little or no speaking to do until they have gained needed self-assurance. A stuttering pupil should never be *forced* to recite or to speak or read aloud. He should be given the opportunity, and rewarded if he takes advantage of it. But he should never be disapproved for being too overcome with fear to speak. The teacher should do anything she can, by her handling of classroom situations generally, and by talking with the child whenever she can find the time for it, to develop his desire to speak.

By doing this, and by following the recommendations made in Chapter II, the teacher can usually help to increase appreciably the stuttering child's desire to talk, his capacity for enjoying speech, and the amount of speaking he does.

2. See to it that the child has as much feeling of success as possible in speaking. The teacher should do all she can to make the speaking the child does as enjoyable and rewarding as possible. Certainly she will not make a point of criticizing him for mistakes in grammar or pronunciation, or for the way he stands when he talks, or for other things about his speech that are not important in relation to the fun and satisfaction he gets from speaking as well as he can. She will associate his speaking with her own pleasantness, with interesting classroom activities, and in general try to see to it that he finds speaking to be something pleasant and fun to do.

It is of great importance to recognize the fact that the relatively young stutterer has not yet developed an elaborate pattern of habits, attitudes, and dread-ridden memories. He is comparatively susceptible to the direct effects of successful speaking experiences. Surely, one of the strongest impressions one receives in becoming acquainted with considerable numbers of young stutterers—at about the age level of first to fourth or fifth grade in school—and in working closely with them, is that they are so very much like other youngsters of their own age who do not stutter and so strikingly unlike severe adult stutterers. In a speech correction camp or a summer clinic at a university the homesick young stutterer or the unsmiling one is very conspicuous in being rare and different from his energetic, darting, grinning, friendly companions who are full of chatter and whose eyes twinkle quite as much as do the eyes of any other group of kids in a camp or school situation. At that age their tensions, even when marked, are not firmly set and the concern and anxiety that motivate them are still fleeting and not yet well enough established to last long in competition with an abundance of the good feelings that come with successful and pleasant speaking. The youngster's memories are short. If he has very good speech experiences on Wednesday their Thursday effects will be strong because he has no overwhelming background of unnerving memories to weaken them or blot them out. Not only is it true, then, that the more speaking the stuttering child does the better, but, in addition—an extremely important addition—the more fun and enjoyment and feeling of success he gets from his speaking the better.

A child is most likely to feel that his speech is successful when he speaks without stuttering, or with what seems to him to be much less stuttering than usual. It is important, therefore, that the teacher find out as much as she can about the kinds of speaking the child does with little or no stuttering. Some stuttering youngsters can read aloud with slight or no difficulty. Others can recite memorized poetry or other material. Many are quite fluent on the playground. Most do better if a classroom discussion becomes lively and "sneaks up on them," so that they are into it before they know it, than they do when it is formal and they are "called upon" by the teacher to say something apart from any verbal give-and-take with the other children. Usually a child talks more freely and fluently with certain friends or classmates—or teachers

—than with others. The teacher should do what she can, and counsel the parents to do what they can, to get the stuttering child to do as much as possible of the kinds of speaking he does best. The more this kind of experience and the good feelings that result from it can be made to outweigh his stuttering experiences and their effects, the more rapidly and fully he is likely to improve. He is not to be criticized for the stuttering he does, of course. As we shall consider in detail presently, it is to the stutterer's advantage to accept his stuttering in a frank and objective manner as a problem to be faced. At the same time, it is also beneficial for him to learn by experience that he is capable of good speech.

The speech correctionist can do a great deal, but the classroom teacher also can usually do enough to be decidedly worth while, in using certain special techniques to bring about successful speech feelings. One of these is that of chorus reading. All stutterers can with a little coaching and practice—and most stutterers can at once with no practice—read or speak in unison with other readers or speakers, as in the case of responsive readings in church, or in the giving of school yells, or the reciting of club rituals in chorus. This can be used to help convince the stuttering child that he is physically able to speak normally, something we shall discuss presently, and this is important in and of itself, but it can be used also to give the youngster an abundance of experience with fluent speech and the feelings that go with it. Here are some representative uses that can be made of this procedure.

*a.* The teacher can read in chorus with the child. After a time she stops reading and he continues alone. When he begins to hold his breath or press his lips tightly together, a little uncomplicated discussion of the fact that he got along better a while ago when he wasn't doing those things might be in order (the teacher will have to judge whether it is or not), and then the teacher can resume reading together with him, stopping again after awhile as before and letting him go on alone as long as he can.

*b.* This general procedure can be followed with two stuttering children reading together.

*c.* A procedure well suited to a group of four to six or more stutterers is what in our clinic we call "hullaballoo." Everyone reads aloud at the same time, each one reading something different. The teacher watches to see if any of them have any difficulty. Most will have none, and it is well to spot the occasional one who does because it may be that his habits are a bit more firmly set or that his feelings of uneasiness about speech are deeper, and so the teacher may want to give him special attention at another time. Stuttering youngsters enjoy a little "hullaballoo" now and then, and it is very important for them to associate fun with speaking, of course.

*d.* The teacher may ask the child his name, age, street address, or anything at all. If he stutters in answering, she can ask him to repeat it in chorus with her. He will probably say it easily, and then some little comment about the difference will usually not be amiss. He can benefit by being reminded that he speaks better and more easily when he doesn't gasp, or open his mouth tensely, or keep his lips together.

Another key to successful speech is to be found in certain practical applications of the adaptation principle. It will be recalled that when stutterers read a passage several times in succession they adapt in the sense that they stutter less and less. The basic adaptation process can be observed in many forms and in many situations. For example, when in common oral recitation a child stutters in saying something like the name of a state capital, if the teacher will ask him to say it again he may say it without stuttering the second time, and the chances for this become even better with the third and the fourth attempts, and so on. When a stuttering child is asked his name and stutters on it, he can be asked—in a friendly and interested manner, of course—to say it again, and on the second or third trial he is likely to say it fluently. Even if he doesn't achieve complete fluency he will nearly always say it with less and less severe stuttering. He should seldom or never be asked to say anything over more than two or three times, and more often two than three. This technique provides the youngster with many more memories of successful speech than he would otherwise store up for himself. Moreover, in line with the theory that the acts involved in stuttering, such as holding the breath, are reinforced by the fact that they are followed immediately by utterance of the word, the practice suggested here is important because it separates the final successful, accepted utterance of the word, or phrase or whole sentence, from the holding of the breath or other stuttering act, and so does not permit it so fully, if at all, to reinforce that act.[81]

Such practices as these should be explained to the child by the teacher before she uses them, so that he will know as well as he can what their purposes are and how he can most effectively coöperate in their use. This sort of talking between teacher and child about the ways in which they can work together on his problem can be in itself very beneficial.

3. Stimulate the stuttering child's interest in good speech and effective speakers. Phonograph recordings made by the world's best tellers of children's stories tend to have the effect of deepening a child's feeling for delightful and emotionally satisfying as well as intellectually challenging speech. Whatever a child appreciates and admires he is likely to want to do himself to some degree at least. In trying to increase the youngster's enjoyment of effective speech the teacher must be sensitive to the possibility of creating the impression that desirable speech is so excellent that he can never attain it. There need be no danger, of course. After all, most youngsters who admire Ted Williams or Willie Mays are driven by their admiration of these superb baseball players to play baseball more rather than less. If a child thinks of speech as something delightful and wonderful he will be likely to do more talking than he would otherwise.

4. Encourage the child to talk about his stuttering and his feelings about it. This suggestion is to be applied, of course, with a generous dash of common sense. There is no point, and there can be undesirable consequences, in trying to get a youngster to talk about "problems" that he honestly doesn't recognize and to ventilate "deep feelings" that he doesn't have. If the teacher is

[81] For laboratory data and theoretical considerations relevant to this point see Joseph G. Sheehan, "The Modification of Stuttering through Nonreinforcement," *Journal of Abnormal and Social Psychology* (1951), *46*: 51-63.

not certain that a child recognizes his speech difficulty as stuttering and that he is bothered by it, she should either do nothing about his "problem" or she should do whatever she does without talking to him about it at all, or at least not in any very serious or intimate way.

If, however, it is obvious that the child feels he has a speech problem and that he is definitely concerned about it in the classroom or elsewhere, it can amount to a kind of neglect not to encourage him to discuss it at least with reference to the most essential decisions that must be made about his participation in class activities. If he can be led to share his concerns and bafflements with others, almost always they will be genuinely interested in trying to help him work out a better understanding of his problem and of what best to do about it. This tends naturally to make for improvement in his relationships with others.

A striking example of the good that can come from this sort of speaking experience has been described by Mrs. Elizabeth Parker Small, a speech therapist in Tasmania. A ten-year-old girl in one of the schools where Mrs. Small was working arrived after some weeks of remedial speech work at the decision to speak to her class about her speech problem and what the class could do to help her learn to speak better. She also demonstrated to them some of the variations in her stuttering. The response was excellent. "She has hardly stuttered since she gave the talk and is now so enthusiastic for her teacher to give her speech assignments [that the teacher has] begun to feel I should discharge her." The pay-off came when she won a speaking contest at the school with an outside judge![82]

Actually, most youngsters who stutter enough to be bothered by it are very responsive to any teacher sufficiently interested to take a friendly sort of initiative in talking about it with them and in trying to be helpful. In general, getting a stuttering child to talk freely about his stuttering, the experiences he has because of it, and the feelings he has about it, is one of the most direct

[82] This information was contained in a personal letter to the writer and is reproduced here with Mrs. Small's permission, which is gratefully acknowledged.

and effective means to the improvement of his personal and social adjustment in school and out.

5. Help the child to develop a more realistic attitude toward his stuttering. In addition to the suggestions that have been made, it is possible in nearly all cases in which it would be judicious to say or do anything at all, to accomplish some good by helping the youngster to place his stuttering in perspective. Stutterers tend to exaggerate the amount of stuttering they do and the seriousness of its consequences. It is not as "shameful" or "disastrous" as they are more or less inclined to think it is. Nearly always it pays to compare notes with the child about the importance of his stuttering and in a forthright manner to talk it out with him in an effort to help him face the problem in its realistic proportions.

6. Help the child to develop a realistically good opinion of himself. A child who stutters comes in time to think of himself as *a stutterer*. It is possible to think of oneself as a stutterer so often and over such a long period and with such preoccupation that one actually fails to notice or else disregards most of the other facts about oneself. It is obviously beneficial to a child who stutters to give due attention and thought to his other characteristics, his good health, his speed as a runner, the fact that his muscles are growing, the good or at least acceptable grades that he makes perhaps, his skills and assets generally, his pet calf, his paper route, his friends, everything that is good about his home and his family, and so on and on well beyond the boundary of discouragement. This is part of the general matter of putting the stuttering in perspective, but it is more than that. It should involve the child's positive, continuous acknowledging and emphasizing of his accomplishments and other reasons for having a good opinion of himself.

If possible, the child's parents should be persuaded to do all they can to make it possible for the child to take lessons in dancing, boxing, golf, music, art, or simply to see that the youngster has time and necessary equipment for developing his abilities along these or other lines. If the child comes from an underprivileged home, an effort should be made to get him in touch with community recreation centers, the neighborhood public library, or social work agencies that might be in a position to expand his opportunities for play, special study, or the exercise of talents which might otherwise be neglected. The teacher will sometimes be able to get help for the pupil from other members of the school staff—the orchestra leader, coaching staff, dramatics instructor, school psychologist, and so forth, depending on the type of school. In some cases, private individuals can be found who will be willing, even delighted, to spend time with the child teaching him to draw cartoons, play the banjo, do sleight of hand tricks, build radios, or what not. The proprietors of any hobby shops in the community are likely to have useful ideas and to know individuals from whom the youngster might learn much that he would otherwise miss.

It is not to be overlooked that in some cases a great deal of good can be done by helping children to learn more about social graces, grooming, what to do at a party or on a date, and in general how to cultivate their good personal qualities. If the teacher has established a good relationship with the stuttering child, she is likely to be pleasantly surprised by the ease with which she can enter into such problems with the youngster without embarrassment or awkwardness. Many a young girl would be forever grateful to any teacher who would show her how to do her hair to the best advantage, how to combine colors effectively, and how in general to conduct herself at a party. It is often not a question of money so much as a matter of making the most of what the child has to work with.

It is sometimes possible to suggest reading material from which a particular child would benefit greatly. A competent librarian, or the school psychologist perhaps, if there is one, can be helpful in this connection. There are many attractive books, genuinely interesting to youngsters, on etiquette, clothes, ideas for parties, and the sensible and effective use of cosmetics. Moreover, many children just do not know much about those distinguished personalities who for most of us serve in some measure as "models." Almost any library contains numerous excellent juvenile biographies of Jane Addams, Madame Curie, Martha Washington, Eleanor Roosevelt, and other outstanding women; Abraham Lincoln, "Teddy" Roosevelt, Thomas Edison, Lou Gehrig Bob Feller, and countless other admirable men. Children like such books and derive tremendous benefits from them. Good material can also be found in children's magazines and other current publications. Much, indeed, can be accomplished through guided reading.

Asking a child frequently to report the things he has done or that have happened to him that he feels good about is one simple technique for encouraging him to keep his justifiable reasons for pride in clear focus. It is not a matter of encouraging boasting or egotism, but only of encouraging desirable self-development and of including in self-evaluation the good things along with the neutral and the not-so-good.

7. Help the child to see the best in others. Good social adjustment depends in large measure on favorable relationships with other people. It is possible for the teacher to do a great deal about this for the stuttering child in a rather direct way as well as by means of the example she sets by her own positive attitudes and reactions toward her pupils and her associates. By talking to the child about his parents, his other teachers, and his classmates in ways that express good will toward them and a lively appreciation of the worth of each individual, the teacher can exert a very considerable influence on the youngster, helping him to be more trustful of others, less afraid of them, less resentful of them for reasons that may be as often imaginary as real. She can influence him to enjoy being with others more, doing more things with them, getting to know them better, talking with them more and more. These effects are nearly certain to contribute to the improvement of his speech.

8. Help the stuttering child to participate more fully in school activities. A child's social adjustment is to an important degree a function of the friendships he forms, the groups with which he identifies himself, and the activities he shares with others. The teacher can often help a child who stutters, and who may for that reason be rather shy and withdrawing, to work and play together with more other children, to join or take a more

active part in clubs suited to his needs or interests, to be a member of the chorus or orchestra, to be a member of a stage crew, and to have more acquaintances and friends and to play a more active part in various other ways in the life of his school. The effect on his speech can hardly be other than good.

9. Encourage the child to enjoy learning and to cultivate worth-while interests. One of the major problems of many adults who stutter is that of adjusting to the world of serious work and the responsibilities of earning a living. Many stutterers carry their avoidance of stuttering to the extreme of avoiding vocations which seem to require very much speaking and the training programs that lead to them. The result is a good deal of vocational mal-adjustment, which amounts in some cases to the most serious aspect of the stutterer's overall problem. The case histories of such stutterers indicate generally a failure during childhood to develop serious and substantial interests and hobbies that might have grown into vocational choices in adulthood. Many of them also indicate that the individual had never been stimulated to see the value of learning and education, to seek pleasure in reading or experimenting or observing or visiting new places and seeing people at work in unfamiliar ways. The teacher of a child who stutters can do much to ward off later vocational maladjustment and to enable the youngster to live a rich life day by day if she will use her ingenuity to help him cultivate a keen appreciation of learning, a liking for reading, a preference for informative and cultural television programs, and a lively interest in the various kinds of work that men and women do to make their livings and to gain their important satisfactions. An active interest in the daily news, in the world and the people in it, in science and politics and business and industry and sports and "everything"—this is a sign of health. It is good insurance against drifting into an unsatisfactory vocation for want of information about the world's wonderful possibilities for useful and rewarding work. It is one of the finest things that a teacher can help a stuttering child to acquire.

This recital of suggestions for the teacher who is in a position to be helpful to a stuttering child serves to underscore again the point that was stressed in Chapter II: that what is good for speech handicapped children is good for other children, too. And it is good for teachers to do these things for children. Everybody gains when anyone is helped to become a better person.

ASPECTS OF THE STUTTERER'S PROBLEM AND REMEDIAL TRAINING OF SPECIAL CONCERN TO THE SPEECH CORRECTIONIST

The preceding section is fully as relevant to the interests of the speech correctionist as to those of the classroom teacher. Everything that the classroom teacher can do to help a child who stutters can be done also by the speech correctionist. When both are present in a situation they will benefit, and so will the child, if they will work closely together. They will both do the same things to a considerable degree, of course. There are some additional things, however, that a speech correctionist is prepared to do, and we shall now consider these.

1. Build the stuttering child's confidence in his physical ability to speak normally. Much that the classroom teacher can do will help to accomplish this purpose, but the speech correctionist is likely to be equipped with more specialized information that is reassuring to the child—and his parents—and to be in a position to work more systematically and for a longer period in an effort to achieve this objective.

As has been stated in the first part of this chapter, no organic cause of stuttering has been demonstrated. It is scientifically unjustifiable, therefore, and clinically undesirable, to allow the child or his parents to persist undisturbed in the vague or confident belief that there is some such organic cause. It is handicapping to the stuttering child to be convinced that he has "something physically wrong" that keeps him from speaking normally. It discourages him. It keeps him from entering hopefully and zestfully into any sustained attempt to improve his speech. There is clearly no advantage in assuming that there are limitations which do not in fact exist.

This general point of view can be translated into action in a very direct way by demonstrating to the stuttering child that he is physically able to speak without stuttering. This can be done as follows:

*a.* Suggest to the child that he find opportunity often to talk to himself (or to his pets, perhaps) with no one near to overhear him. The chances are very great that he will be able to talk to himself with no difficulty. He may of course stutter occasionally, and a rare child will be found who stutters almost as much when alone as at other times. This appears to be due partly to the tendency to visualize or imagine very vividly a particular listener or an audience, so that in a psychological sense the stutterer is not entirely "alone." Also, some stutterers are so convinced that certain sounds or words are very difficult—they are so thoroughly conditioned to reacting with anxiety-tensions to these sounds or words—that even when talking to themselves they sometimes make the usual conditioned responses. It is well to know this, in order to explain to any child who may stutter a bit when alone why he does. The great majority of children, however, will report that they don't stutter when talking to themselves, and they will be hopefully impressed with the clear meaning of this: that their speech organs are normal. Most of them have probably never looked at it that way before. Even if they have, the teacher's reinforcing statements will go far to convince them that they can talk.

*b.* Have the child sing a few songs that he knows. We have yet to see a stutterer who could not do this without stuttering (although it might be possible to find one). Many stutterers we have known have been talented in vocal music.

*c.* Any stutterer can talk in time to almost any rhythm. The child can be expected to speak without stuttering if he says one word to each step while walking, or one word to each tap of his foot, or swing of his arm, or to each flash of a light being turned on and off, or to each tap on his shoulder, and so on. Practically all stutterers can speak in a singsong manner, or with an assumed dialect. Such practices are not to be regarded as "cures," of course. Indeed, there is serious danger in a superficial use of them; in employing them one must be careful not to suggest to the stutterer that he is to avoid stuttering at all cost. This will increase his fear and he will stutter worse than ever as a consequence. The point of rhythm-speaking is to demonstrate to the stutterer that his speech mechanism is in good working order.

The other methods suggested to the classroom teacher for giving the stuttering child successful speech experiences can also be used, of course, by the speech correctionist for the present purpose. And the desired effects of all these procedures can be reinforced considerably by the speech correctionist if she will tell the child in language he can understand the main facts, gained through scientific research, that will enable him to feel more confident of his own physical normality. The speech correctionist is in a strategic position to give this scientific information to the child's parents also, and it will usually be advantageous to do this.

2. Train the stuttering child to observe his stuttering, to view it as his own behavior, and to modify it. Before describing this and the following procedures, we should give attention to a very important consideration which arises at this point. Everything we have covered so far by way of methods of helping children who stutter can appropriately be used with the general run of elementary school age children, and much that has been suggested can also be applied in working with adults, of course. We are now about to consider a number of procedures that are to be adapted in various ways to the special requirements and peculiarities of individual cases, and so they are to be used with discrimination. In general, in working with very young stutterers, those who show definite anxiety-tension reactions but whose habit systems are not well established, it is advisable to make extensive use of the techniques discussed up to this point, giving them a very good trial before electing to employ the methods about to be described. The procedures that we are now going to consider constitute a very intensive direct attack on the stuttering aspect of the problem, and are designed particularly for stutterers in whom the "anticipatory, apprehensive, hypertonic, avoidance reactions" are firmly set and relatively difficult to modify or eliminate. Prospective speech correctionists using this textbook will be professionally concerned with these procedures, of course, and prospective classroom teachers will gain from a knowledge of these methods an

improved preparation for working coöperatively with speech correctionists.

An outstanding characteristic of well-established stuttering behavior is its relative automaticity, its tendency to "go off like a reflex." Stutterers commonly talk about it as though to them it were not really their own behavior, but rather something that "just happens to them." They say they "can't help it." They usually claim to have little or no control over it. For all practical purposes, most of them "don't know how they do it." Moreover, a significant aspect of their strong drive to avoid stuttering is to be seen in their extreme tendency not to observe their own stuttering behavior, to give it no studious attention, to make little or no effort to inform themselves about it. This all tends to mean that, unless the stuttering can be eliminated by means of the indirect methods so far considered (or by other methods not covered in this textbook), the stutterer must attack it directly—and he is not likely to be well oriented to his stuttering as a problem to be faced up to and solved by means of his own efforts to deal with it.

His retraining in this connection can very well be started by having him attempt to observe his stuttering in a mirror and listen to it by means of a tape recorder. As we have previously considered, there is much to be said for the proposition that stuttering is basically a perceptual and evaluative problem rather than a motor speech problem. To the degree that this is the case, the stutterer has a need to retrain his habitual ways of perceiving and evaluating his speech behavior. A particularly direct way for him to undertake this retraining consists of intensive and prolonged observation of his stuttering reactions, while being encouraged and helped to view them as something that he is indeed doing himself, and that he must have some kind of reason for doing, and that he can do more or less differently as he chooses.

It turns out that a practical way for the stutterer to observe his own stuttering behavior is simply to duplicate it on purpose, imitate it, perform it, while watching himself in a mirror. In this way he comes to "get the feel of it." And when finally he "can do it" he experiences a new sense of control over this behavior which always before has seemed to be so automatic and reflex-like as to feel uncontrollable. It helps if he spends a great deal of time also listening to his stuttering on a tape recorder, ideally until it comes to sound commonplace, "old shoe," and absurd in a sense. Through these practices, accompanied by appropriate discussion with the speech correctionist, the stutterer can achieve a very high degree of calm, observant objectivity about his difficulty. He can become able to think about it in a more mature and problem-solving fashion, and to develop a practical "sense of understanding" of it. This means mainly that in time he begins to see some things that he can do about it, certain changes he can make in the way he talks and in the way he does his stuttering— for now he sees it and hears it and feels it as something that he himself does.

It helps too if he is encouraged to learn a new way of talking about it, a more descriptive way made up of statements about the things he *does,* not the blocks he *has,* about the way he *presses* his lips together tensely, not about the tension that *comes and goes* as though he had nothing to do with it. He should try not to talk about his stuttering as though it were a thing, an entity, visited upon him as a disease such as pneumonia might be, and in the face of which he feels not only helpless but irresponsible as well. It will encourage him to do more about it if he talks about it as behavior for which he alone is responsible.

Once the stutterer definitely feels that he has a choice as to how he can do the things that he calls his stuttering behavior, he will begin to ask himself seriously what might be the best things to do. Or he will simply begin to exercise his sense of choice by doing stuttering reactions that are simpler, less tense, and that generally feel or sound or look better to him. The stuttering the individual has done is in general the kind of stuttering that he will anticipate in the future. If it has been very complicated, tense, and distressing his fear of its recurrence will be great, and he will express this fear in a very tense effort to keep the stuttering from occurring again. If, however, the stuttering the individual has done is very simple, effortless, and inconsequential his fear of its recurrence will be slight, and he will express this slight fear in very weak, if any, effort to keep from stuttering again. On this

basis it is to be said that some ways of stuttering are more desirable than others, because they tend to lead to less and less severe,
and so less and less frequent, avoiding stuttering reactions. As the
stutterer finds this out by observing and performing and finally
modifying his stuttering behavior, he comes to feel a preference
for doing his stuttering less and less tensely and more and more
simply.

This type of retraining is not advantageously to be called
"symptomatic therapy," or " superficial therapy." If it is conceived
of in these ways it is very likely to be misapplied. It is a type of
retraining most appropriately carried out with due appreciation
of the depth and extensiveness of the changes in the patterns of
motivation and behavior and feeling that it necessarily involves.
The speech correctionist who has this kind of feeling for what it
involves will be extremely patient with the stutterer as he tries
to carry it on, and very understanding of the difficulties he is
likely to have, the mistakes and bewilderment and discouragement he will probably experience, the slowness and unevenness
of his improvement—and the magnitude of the change in his
stuttering, his general speech behavior, and his overall adjustment
in the event that he substantially succeeds. Most stutterers need,
or at least benefit from, the opportunity to talk out from time to
time with the speech correctionist, or in a group therapy situation,
the problems and experiences they have in carrying on this type
of modification of their stuttering behavior. The speech correctionist can be helpful by being a good listener and by supplying
essential relevant information, instruction, and demonstration, and
a certain amount of counseling with reference to the changes in
feeling and general adjustment that the retraining involves.

The specific instruction which the speech correctionist can
provide is likely to be most effectively directed to two aspects of
the problem. The one is that of eliminating certain mannerisms
associated with the stuttering behavior. The other is that of reducing the degree of tension involved in stuttering. By giving
special attention to these two aspects of the problem involved in
modifying the stuttering behavior it is usually possible to increase
the rate and extent of improvement.

Much of any stuttering child's handicap lies in the grimaces, odd sounds, and seemingly random movements associated with his stuttering. If, for example, a child who tends to turn his head strongly to the right or protrude his tongue whenever he stutters can learn to stutter without doing these things, his speech difficulty can be made much more tolerable for him and more acceptable to his listeners.

There are three things to be done as a rule in sloughing off a mannerism of this kind. First, the specific mannerism to be worked on must be selected. It is best to work on one at a time. The more removed from the speech act, and the more clearly unessential the mannerism is, the more easily will the stutterer be able to deal with it. A tendency to stamp the foot, for example, or to turn the head to one side, would probably be easier to eliminate than a habit of puckering and protruding the lips.

Second, the mannerism should be closely observed in the mirror, studied, analyzed, imitated, practiced, and deliberately modified. If the child does this practicing by himself he is not likely to stutter, of course, or at least not severely enough for the mannerism to occur, and so he will have to imitate his stuttering behavior, including the mannerism, deliberately, in order to practice at all. After a few sessions of such practice with a mirror, he should begin to perform the mannerism on purpose a few times a day in speaking to others. That is, if he is working on an eye-closure, for example, he should now and then deliberately close his eyes when he stutters even though he would not have done so otherwise.

Finally, the child should attempt, in situations where he is most likely to succeed, to do his stuttering for brief periods without the mannerism. With success, these periods can be lengthened and the situations in which the elimination is attempted can be more and more difficult. Meanwhile, the practicing described in the preceding paragraph should be continued. When relatively consistent success has been achieved, so that the mannerism seldom or never occurs, another one may be selected and worked on in a similar way.

The child's parents should be clearly informed and their coöperation assured. The child should be encouraged to tell his classmates what he is doing, and if the classroom atmosphere is what it should be, their most likely reaction will be to help him stick with the task, show pleasure in his successes, and remind him in a friendly way whenever he might forget to practice. The coöperation of the class, and especially of the child's closest friends, should by all means be stimulated in every way possible. It is one of the most important elements in the success to be achieved, just as lack of it is sure to be a substantial factor contributing to failure.

One word of caution is absolutely essential. The child must never get the impression that he is being disapproved for stuttering. That would intensify his fear of stuttering and result in greater tension and generally more severe blocking. He is to be given every assurance that he may stutter as much as he likes. It is simply that he is to do his stuttering without closing his eyes, or stamping his foot, or jerking his head to the right, or whatever the particular mannerism happens to be. In fact, he is to be complimented for stuttering without the mannerism. He should feel a positive glow of success in stuttering without the mannerism. And when he fails, when the mannerism occurs, the attitude should be —well, he needs more practice. The habit is deeply ingrained. Improvement takes time.

The second type of special instruction that might be given by the speech correctionist in connection with modification of the stuttering behavior is concerned with encouraging a lessening of the tension or effortfulness with which the behavior is performed. The stutterer is to be told to go ahead and stutter in his usual way, but with the one difference of doing it as easily as he possibly can. Again, it is a good idea for him to do this while looking in a mirror. Performing the stuttering behavior with less tension is partly a matter of being less frantic and hurried about it, more leisurely, of doing everything involved in the stuttering reaction a little more slowly than usual.[83] It is also partly a matter of just

[83] This does not mean that the stutterer should be instructed to talk more slowly. As we have seen, stutterers talk and read orally more slowly on the average than nonstutterers do. Although stutterers differ considerably, of course, most stutterers probably increase rather than decrease their speaking rates as they improve, largely as a result of becoming less fearful and inhibited and more spontaneous and responsive.

not "pushing" so hard, not holding the breath so doggedly, not puckering the lips quite so tightly, not jamming the tongue so forcefully against the front teeth.

Finally, with sufficient self-observation, enough stuttering in front of mirrors and listening to tape-recorded stuttering, after a certain amount of deliberate performance by the stutterer of his own stuttering behavior, sloughing off of mannerisms, reduction of tension, and development of a sense of control over the stuttering behavior and a sense of choice over how it is to be done—the result tends to be that the stutterer, in performing his stuttering behavior more and more simply and easily, either repeats or prolongs the initial sound or syllable of the stuttered word. These are, generally speaking, the most simple and easy ways there are to perform stuttering behavior. It is better, however, for the stutterer to find this out for himself, by trying to perform his stuttering as simply and easily as possible, than for him to be instructed or "assigned" to do his stuttering in these ways—before he is ready to so far as his own insights, motivations, sense of control, and feelings of preference are concerned.

A great deal of work is essential; regular daily practice is highly advisable. If a stutterer is going to change radically his accustomed manner of stuttering, he must work persistently and diligently over a long period of time. This is not because easy and simple ways of stuttering involve any complex motor skills that are hard to learn. The need for practice arises from two other facts. One is that the habits being replaced are thoroughly established and tend to continue until the new habits have become well set and motivated through frequent and rewarded performance. The other is that, while the motor activities involved in simplified stuttering are easy to do, the objective, nonavoidant, positive-performance attitude required to perform them properly is by no means easy to develop and maintain. Unless this attitude is developed, the attempts to do the simplified and easy stuttering amount to nothing more than pointless and misdirected motions gone through to no purpose. The purpose is always to be kept sharply focused. *It is to reduce anxiety.* The stutterer should sense a growing confidence that if he should stutter he will be able to do it without having to strain and indulge in unpleasant "struggle reactions." Therefore his anxiety about it will be correspondingly reduced. And with less fear of stuttering there will be less avoidant tensions—which means less stuttering.

Anxiety about stuttering is the key problem. There is no point in having the stuttering pupil attempt to change his way of stuttering unless the entire procedure is carried out in such a way that anxiety is reduced. After all, the ultimate objective is to achieve normal speech. Of course, even if the objective were to find the most comfortable way to continue stuttering, there would be something to say for that, too, as an alternative to stuttering in some more distressing manner. But the stutterer might as well aim to go beyond this more modest goal so long as there seems to be a possibility of doing so. And the surest means to normal speech lies in overcoming the fear of stuttering. For in the absence of this fear there is no expectation that stuttering is going to occur, and so there is obviously no active motivation or drive to avoid it. In the absence of the avoidance motivation, the tension or strain through which it is expressed is absent also. All of which is a way of saying that there is no stuttering when there is no fear of stuttering. That is why the basic objective of the procedures described is to reduce, and if possible to eliminate, the fear of stuttering.

In general, psychologists have discovered two rather practical and effective ways to get rid of many undesirable fears. One way is for the individual to become convinced that the thing he fears will never happen—or will never happen again. The other way is for the individual to do the thing he is afraid to do and thereby learn by convincing experience that it is not fearful. Fundamentally, this is what the stutterer is doing when he learns to stutter deliberately in a way of his own choosing. And when he reaches the point where he is no longer afraid to do this, the method has achieved its purpose. For when he no longer is afraid to stutter, he is not afraid that he will stutter, and so he does nothing to avoid it, and thus has no stuttering to do. And when this has come about, he has two reasons for losing his fear of stuttering: he not only has ceased to find it fearful, but now he also has good reason to become convinced that it will never happen again. And these, as we have said, are two practical and effective ways to get rid of fear.

It is to be understood, of course, that although what has been set forth here has been addressed to the problem of working with stuttering children, it is intended to apply to remedial work with stuttering adults as well.

COUNSELING OF PARENTS

In general, there are two kinds of parent-counseling problems that are dealt with by speech correctionists so far as the fluency-anxiety aspects of children's speech are concerned. First, there is the problem of the parents who are beginning to worry about their child's speech, and beginning also to react, even though slightly perhaps, to the youngster's nonfluency, but as yet the problem is theirs rather than the child's. The child may or may not be more nonfluent than most children of his age, and it will usually be the case that he is not apparently aware of any difference and seems to be in no sense bothered by the way he speaks. If he appears conscious of his speech in any relevant way, the evidence of it is likely to be fleeting and generally superficial. Even if at times he reacts with definitely noticeable strain and uneasiness when hesitating in speaking, most of the time he does not do this. There are advantages in proceeding on the assumption that the "patient," or the more important part of the "combined patient," as it were, is the parent rather than the child, and that the child is chiefly or wholly responding to the parent. It is to be assumed further, therefore, that if the parent can be influenced to change his or her mode of evaluating and reacting to the child and his speech, the child will, in turn, change his mode of responding to the parent. There is the problem, then, of counseling the parents so as to effect such changes in their evaluations of the child and his speech and in their relevant policies and practices as will result in the reduction of pressures. The objective is to make speech pleasant and emotionally meaningful and satisfying for the child.

Second, there is the case in which the process has developed to the point at which the child is to an important degree reacting to his own nonfluent speech, but his anxiety-tensions are not yet well established, and he is still relatively very responsive to his parents' feelings and to their practices in dealing with his speech nonfluencies. The child is definitely having difficulty in speaking outside as well as inside the home; he is carrying his own trouble around with him. There is something to be gained by working with him directly, along the lines that have been discussed in the past several pages, but this can best be done with the parents' coöperation. There is the problem, then, of counseling the parents so as to secure their coöperation.

Whether the "patient" is the parent or both the child and the parent, there are in general three major specific objectives of the parent-counseling to be done. The first is that of supplying the parents with the information they need in order to appreciate the nature of normal childhood speech. They are helped by knowing the essential facts about normal speech development, especially so far as fluency is concerned. They are helped, too, by knowing about the more important conditions under which children— and adults for that matter—are more and less fluent in speech. In general, it is beneficial for them to become acquainted with the wide variations in normal speech fluency in different children and in the same children from circumstance to circumstance. This enables them to shift their attention away from the child's mouth, as it were, away from the nonfluencies in his speech, and on to the conditions under which he tends to speak more and less non-fluently.

The conditions that tend to occasion increased nonfluency in young children are, to list only the more common ones: (a) attempts by the child to "talk over his head," to explain things he doesn't understand, or tell about things for which he lacks a ready use vocabulary; (b) speaking to an unresponsive listener— to father engrossed in the evening newspaper, or to mother when she is trying to figure out a new recipe; (c) speaking in competition with others—as at the family dinner table where Junior can hardly get a word in edgewise, and so the best he can do sounds as though he were "having trouble talking"; (d) speaking in situations involving conflict—as when trying to do something other than what his mother, or teacher, or playmate wants him to do, or when trying to get others to do what he wants them to do instead of what they want to do; *(e)* speaking in distracting or disturbing circumstances—while very excited over a game or a new puppy, or while being punished, especially when the reasons are not clear, or under conditions of moving into a new house or neighborhood, going on a bewildering or fatiguing trip, or entering a new play or school situation that seems confusing or threatening; and *(f)* speaking under the conditions involved in generally impaired or insecure parent-child relationships.

To the extent that such conditions are present, and apparently related to excessively hesitant or nonfluent speech of the child, the parents are to be helped to recognize them and to reduce or eliminate them.

In one of our cases, it was learned from the clinical interview and investigation in the home that the child, a four-year-old boy, was doing more than a normal amount of repeating and was beginning to show unmistakable anxiety-tension reactions. The full list of the conditions under which most of the speech difficulty was occurring was very long, owing to the fact that the mother was practically carrying on a "running fight" with the boy. She was arguing with him at the table about the foods he wouldn't eat, and about the way he ate the foods he would eat; in trying to get him to nap she practically wrestled with him nearly every afternoon; bedtime was another battle scene; whenever he ran to the neighbors she called him back, or went and brought him back, usually against lively resistance; and in addition he liked to "pound" the piano, but his father, who was a musician and "couldn't stand it," habitually insisted that he stop it. There were other details.

A program was worked out for changing all this. Eating habits were to be temporarily ignored. The nap was to be discontinued. A story hour was to be instituted at bedtime. (Having the parents read aloud to the child for fifteen minutes to a half-hour at bedtime has proved especially beneficial in a large number of cases and may be accepted as a virtually standard recommendation. It calms the child and the parents, provides a period of close companionship, tends to make the child go to bed willingly, promotes better sleep, provides good speech stimulation, aids in building vocabulary and in the general development of language, gives the child and the parents a wealth of stories and information in common so that they have more to talk about and to be interested in together, and makes for a generally better relationship.)

In this particular case there were other recommendations also. For example, the child was to be allowed much more freedom in going about the neighborhood. The mother was to talk to the neighbors and explain that if he caused inconvenience she would appreciate their calling her; otherwise he was to be free to come and go and play with the other children. Instead of resenting the "pounding," the father was to teach the youngster how to play the piano—an idea that had never occurred to him and which he thought was excellent. Moreover, it actually worked out well and definitely brought the father and son together more closely.

In order to get this whole plan of attack properly launched, it was suggested to the mother that she start it off by spending a day at the city park with the boy. She was to "talk it up" for at least three days, planning with the youngster just how they would go, what they would do when they got there, what things they would take along, what they would carry in the lunch basket, whether to include orangeade or chocolate milk, and so on. Then when the Big Day came they were really to go and stay all day, just the two of them. The youngster was to be allowed to play as he liked to his heart's content. The mother was to watch over his physical safety, of course, but gently and with no scolding whatever. They were to be pals for a day on a grand scale. Then, next morning, as soon as he came down to breakfast, the mother was to start a lively conversation about all the fun they had had the day before, and she was to keep referring to it at every reasonable opportunity. And more good times were to be planned and carried through and talked about at great length.

It was done, and it made a tremendous difference. In this case some clean-cut stuttering had definitely developed. Within two months, however, the mother reported that the speech problem had cleared up, that the boy's behavior—as well as her own— had improved generally, and that "you wouldn't recognize this home as the same place any more."

The second major purpose of parent-counseling is to help the parents, so far as possible, to recognize their own insecurities, their excessive psychological need to have their child speak extremely well and perhaps to excel in other ways too, and, in general, their specific discontents and the reasons for them. Most speech correctionists are not prepared by training and by their professional credentials to go beyond modest limits in this direction. They should be prepared, however, to listen well and to encourage expression of anxieties and other relevant feelings, and to direct the parents to family counselors, mental health centers, child guidance clinics, psychiatrists, or clinical psychologists, to the extent that such are available and suited to the particular needs of specific parents.[84]

Nothing said here is meant to imply that the parents we are discussing are likely to be in unusual need of such services. Such parents are fairly representative of the general population so far as their general adjustment is concerned. They do tend to be overly concerned about the speech, and specifically the speech fluency, of their children. If we are careful to speak a gray language, rather than a black-and-white one, we may also say that they tend to be a bit perfectionistic, to have standards for their children, especially speech standards, and most especially fluency standards, that are somewhat too high. Moreover, once such parents have decided their child is stuttering, they feel that they really do have something to worry about, and if the youngster develops marked anxiety-tensions in speaking, they definitely do have. So we find that they have some degree of anxiety, some tendency to worry about their children, and while this is part of

[84] Inquiries concerning family counseling and mental health services in particular states or communities should be addressed to state departments of health; state universities; the American Medical Association, 535 North Dearborn Street, Chicago 10, Illinois; the American Psychological Association, 1333 Sixteenth Street N.W., Washington 6, D.C.; National Association for Mental Health, Inc., 1790 Broadway, New York 19, N.Y.; or the United States Department of Health, Education, and Welfare, Washington 25, D.C.

the problem they present it hardly means that they are very different from other parents. So far as they stand to gain from referral to counseling agencies, they should be assisted in obtaining the services such agencies have to offer.

The third main objective in counseling parents is to help them to coöperate effectively with the speech correctionist. In part, coöperation is a negative matter: the parents should not make an issue of the child's fluency one way or the other. That is, they should neither be disapproving or dismayed when he is nonfluent nor complimentary or unusually pleased when he is not. With adequate understanding of speech development and of the normal variations in fluency and the common reasons for these variations, most parents are able to reduce greatly or even wholly eliminate their worry and concern about their child's hesitations. They are able then to react to the feelings the child is expressing and to what he is saying rather than to the degree of fluency or nonfluency with which he is saying it.

Coöperation with the speech correctionist is also a matter of reducing tensions in the home so far as this seems desirable, removing unnecessary restrictions on the child's activities, providing consistent and meaningful discipline, and improving basic parent-child relationships in any and all ways that are readily possible. Finally, coöperation involves, in more advanced cases, an appreciation of the methods employed by the speech correctionists and a certain amount of help in reminding the child to do his stuttering more easily and simply, in encouraging him to talk more in a greater variety of situations, and in providing the smiles and pats on the back that are needed by most youngsters in any sustained effort to improve their speech or any other aspect of their behavior.

It is well to use the classroom teacher's list of procedures for helping children who stutter (pages 271-283) as a basis for help-ing the parents to see what they might do to encourage the child to make the most of the possibilities for improving his speech. The ways in which these procedures can be adapted to the home situation will vary, of course, and the speech correctionist will need to exercise judgment according to the relevant facts in particular cases.

There is one very fundamental word of caution to which due attention is to be paid, of course. While there is much that most parents can do as a rule, it is not to be overlooked that parents are individuals too—parents have had parents themselves—and they are not always able to coöperate very well even when they understand what they should do. They cannot always change appreciably the home conditions which they have created for themselves. The reasons for this stem sometimes from personality characteristics that are difficult or impossible to change, and sometimes they are due to conditions beyond the parents' control —the nature of the father's occupation, financial hardship, grandparents or other relatives living in the home, and the like. One parent may be missing for any one of many reasons. After all is said and done, allowance must be made for the fact that to an important degree what parents do to their children is part and parcel of their general way of responding to the world about them. Parents, as well as their speech handicapped children, need to be sympathetically understood by the speech correctionist.

Anyone who makes a vocation of trying to improve the behavior and the circumstances of others has need of a sustaining patience, a mature acceptance of the best one can do, a freedom from cynicism, and a stubborn conviction that progress is man's destiny. Certainly the speech correctionist and the classroom teacher can make good use of these qualities day in and day out—and they tend, of course, to acquire them in ever richer measure. It is hardly to be expected that they might ever do as much good for others as they would want to, but what they are able to do for children who stutter, or who are on the way to becoming stutterers, is tremendous, and turns out often to be more than they could have dared to expect.[85] The freedom to speak has conse-

[85] General experience with young stutterers has been very encouraging, particularly in recent years; in most cases the problem can be greatly reduced or eliminated. See *Stuttering in Children and Adults*, *op. cit.*, Chapter 3, for relevant data. Adults too are justified in taking heart from the sub-

quences often more wonderful than we are wholly prepared to comprehend.

stantial advances achieved in recent years as a consequence of the scientific study of stuttering. As this is being written relevant research at the University of Iowa, being carried on with support from the Louis W. and Maud Hill Family Foundation, is designed to yield a detailed description and comprehensive evaluation of a stuttering therapy program. In general, this research involves the type of therapy described in this chapter, together with certain extensions and modifications suggested by continuing consideration of the data reviewed here which imply the essential physical and psychological normality of persons classified as stutterers. This work is being significantly affected by the clinical and theoretical contributions of Dr. Dean Williams at Indiana University. While he has not yet published an account of these contributions, it may be said that Dr. Williams' clinical approach involves a forthright attempt to replace the speaker's negative assumption that he "is a stutterer," and that the best he can hope for is to "stutter" one way or another, with the more positive assumption that he "is a speaker" and that he can "move forward into speech" even when he "expects to stutter," and so discover for himself through a sort of reality testing that no "stuttering" occurs if only he "moves on into speech." Dr. Williams has approved this statement, but he is not to be held accountable for the failure of the present wording to convey his meaning with full clarity.

Because of the relatively great amount of research and new development going on in this field, students have special need to keep abreast of new books, monographs, and other publications, particularly the *Journal of Speech and Hearing Disorders.*

www

# Retarded Speech Development

In kindergarten and in the primary grades there may occasionally be found a child who is capable of very little speech. Such children are more numerous in nursery schools, where indeed they are often sent in the hope of stimulating the development of speech. These children present some of the most difficult and challenging problems in the whole area of speech pathology.

The difficulty of diagnosing and treating these children is not decreased by the confusion in the literature of speech pathology regarding their problems. One author[1] collected twenty different terms used to refer to children whose speech development is significantly slower than normal, and other terms could be added to his list. In this chapter we shall use the term *retarded speech development* to avoid making dubious assumptions as to the nature or the cause of the condition. As we shall see, there are a number of causes of delay in development of speech.

## Normal Speech Development

The phonetic raw material of speech is heard first in crying, which normally begins at the moment of birth. The physiological function of the birth cry is the expansion of the infant's lungs

[1] William G. Peacher, "Neurological Factors in the Etiology of Delayed Speech," *Journal of Speech and Hearing Disorders* (1949), 14:147-161.

and the commencement of respiration, but it is also the first vocalization. Gurgling and cooing are heard in the early weeks of life. These early vocal sounds are not speech, since they involve no conscious effort to communicate, but rather are reflex responses to internal or external stimuli. Quite early, however, there appear variations in the crying from one situation to another, and crying becomes more than an automatic and undifferentiated response to hunger or pain. The infant also begins to respond to external stimuli, such as his mother's laughing and playing with him, by gurgling and cooing, and he thus achieves a level of communication of the sort that in more elaborate form is found in much adult social life.

By the time the infant is three months old he may be heard to utter six or seven vowels and four or five consonants. At six months the average infant has seven vowels and five consonants. At nine months he has eight vowels and eight consonants in his repertory, and at twelve months he has nine vowels and ten consonants.[2] During the last half of the first year of life the infant's babbling becomes increasingly complicated. Out of this raw material are formed the first words, which appear between ten and fourteen months of age. By the time their first birthday is celebrated for them, most children have two or three words.[3] These may be far from perfect according to adult standards. For example, the infant may say "bah" for *bottle*; he uses this combination consistently to refer in one way or another to the bottle.

[2] These data are derived from studies published by Orvis C. Irwin and his students. Irwin's careful researches have added much precise detail to our knowledge of infant speech development. The figures in the text were taken from H. P. Chen and Orvis C. Irwin, "Infant Speech: Vowel and Consonant Types," *Journal of Speech Disorders* (1946) 11:27-29. See also Irwin, "Development of Speech during Infancy: Curve of Phonemic Frequencies," *Journal of Experimental Psychology* (1947), 37:187-193; "Some Factors Related to the Speech Development of the Infant and Young Child," *Journal of Speech and Hearing Disorders* (1952), 17:269-279.

[3] Arnold Gesell *et al., Biographies of Child Development,* New York, Paul B. Hoeber, 1939, p. 129. "The language norms for the second year of life in the Yale developmental schedules call for two words at twelve months, four at fifteen months, and five or more at eighteen months. Joining of two words is expected by twenty-one months, and combining words in short sentences at two years."

His saying "bah" may in some cases be a demand for food, or it may be simply recognition of the object in question. Other meanings are possible, and variations in facial expression, vocal inflection, gestures, and loudness of utterance help to convey what the child intends to communicate.

During the second year of life the vocabulary grows at first slowly and then with increasing rapidity as the infant approaches his second birthday. During this same period there may be much use of jargon—a flow of jabbering syllables that has the cadence of the sort of speech the child hears. At times a word that the child uses in other situations may be heard embedded in the apparently meaningless and haphazard stream of jargon. A few infants start to use jargon before twelve months. In most instances the child develops jargon between twelve and fifteen months, and may come to spend many and long periods in this vocal activity, especially when in the presence of others. As his vocabulary increases, his use of jargon declines, and as he begins to acquire facility in combining two or more words that are intelligible to others, he rather quickly stops using jargon. At twenty-one to twenty-four months of age the average infant is using combinations of words and simple sentences. More complicated expressions make their appearance later.

The speech of the infant or the young child may be difficult to understand because of his distortion of sounds and substitution of one sound for another. Final consonants are usually omitted in the early stages of speech development; medial consonants may or may not be omitted; one or two consonants may be omitted from blends.[4] Intelligibility gradually improves, however, as the child develops greater skill in speech. By the age of three and a half years the average child is able to speak intelligibly—that is, he can be understood by persons unacquainted with him.

The development of speech in the early years of life can be described in much greater detail than this brief sketch, and

[4] Beth L. Wellman, I. M. Case, I. G. Mengert, and D. E. Bradbury, *Speech Sounds of Young Children,* University of Iowa Studies in Child Welfare (1931), 5: No. 2.

there are many interesting and detailed studies of phonetics, syntax, vocabulary, and other aspects of speech development.[5]

It is often overlooked that speech is an extremely complex skill, probably the most complicated that the average person ever acquires. Because everybody talks we tend to take for granted this amazingly difficult performance. It is only because we begin at birth the vocalizations and the movements of the lips and tongue and jaws that are necessary in speech, and because we practice these endlessly for many months and even years, that we are able gradually to learn to talk and to increase the fluency and the clarity of our speech. It has been pointed out, for example, that the word *church* requires twenty different adjustments of the lips, tongue, larynx, and jaws. These twenty must occur in correct sequence, and each of the delicate adjustments must be made precisely. Yet the word requires less than a quarter of a second to speak, which means that the average time available for each of the twenty necessary movements is barely over 1/100 of a second! Many other impressive examples could be given of the sheerly technical, mechanical requirements of everyday speech. When these almost incredible demands are considered, it is easy to see that the process of *learning* to talk is not a simple one. The word learning is emphasized to indicate the nature of the process—it is in every sense a matter of learning, just as much so as with any subject that is studied in a more formal way in later life.[6]

Not all children achieve two or three words by twelve months of age, nor do they all form simple sentences by twenty-four months. There is much variability even among normal children, with a "normal child" being here defined as one who develops clear and intelligible speech by the time he enters school without any special attention being given to his speech.

[5] An excellent and comprehensive review of early speech development is that of Dorothea McCarthy, "Language Development in Children," Chapter 9 (pp. 492-630), *Manual of Child Psychology, Sed. Ed.* (ed. Leonard Carmichael), New York, John Wiley and Sons, Inc., 1954. The bibliography cited runs to more than 750 items.

[6] A particularly interesting and valuable book dealing with this general problem, a book especially suitable for parents, is Charles Van Riper's *Teaching Your Child to Talk,* New York, Harper & Brothers, 1951.

At what point should a child be regarded as being significantly delayed in his speech development? We have listed several stages in the early development of speech—vocalization, single sounds, babbling, single words, jargon, two-word combinations, simple sentences. Which of these is most important may be debatable. Apart from any theoretical considerations, however, any reasonable definition of retarded speech must be stated in terms that are useful in dealing with children and their parents. Ordinarily parents seeking help for a child whose speech is delayed state their complaint in such terms as "He doesn't talk." When they are asked to give more details, they may say that the child says no words at all or that he has only a few words (which they can readily list). Less often the complaint is stated as "He doesn't talk much," or "He doesn't make sentences." It seems best, therefore, to define speech retardation in terms of the use of single words and word combinations.[7] Although the normal variability makes it difficult to set up a hard and fast criterion, we shall classify as a case of retarded speech development any child whose speech is twelve months behind the standards we have mentioned. That is, if a child is not saying single words by twenty-four months he is significantly retarded in speech development and should be studied to discover the cause of his delay; if he is not using simple sentences by thirty-six months he is again significantly retarded and deserving of study. The problems to be discussed in this chapter will be limited to these two types of delay in speech. Children who are slow in achieving clarity of articulation are considered in the chapter on disorders of articulation (Chapter III).[8]

It may well be that as we increase our knowledge of early

[7] McCarthy (*loc. cit.*) and others have pointed out the difficulties of determining the exact time of appearance of the infant's first word. These difficulties do not invalidate a criterion of delayed speech stated in terms of age of use of single words. Even greater practical difficulties would attend the application of other possible criteria, such as the number of phonemes used in babbling, the amount of jargon, etc.

[8] Various approaches to the measurement of speech development and to the evaluation of factors possibly related to speech retardation in specific cases have been presented systematically by Darley in *Diagnostic Manual in Speech Correction, op. cit.*, pp. 98-114.

patterns of emergence of speech, the maximum delay permitted before a child is considered a candidate for special diagnostic study will be reduced to nine months or even less. Any reasonable standard we set up for a classifying a child as one who has a retarded speech problem will inevitably include some fairly normal children, but even these can profit from suggestions made to their parents as to sound methods of speeding up the rate of speech development.

## Causes of Retarded Speech Development

In seeking the explanation of almost any problem of a child, we must study the child himself and also study his environment. Recognizing the artificiality of any sharp distinction between "intrinsic" and "extrinsic" causes of any problem and particularly one involving communication, we can nevertheless concentrate either on the child or on those around him in our search for the causes of his delayed speech.

### MENTAL RETARDATION

The commonest cause of the slow development of speech skills is mental retardation, or mental deficiency. Speech is a learned process, and if the child finds all learning difficult, he will also find slow going in acquiring the complex skills of speech. In general we find that the degree of speech retardation parallels the degree of mental deficiency. (Indeed, one rough but quite useful classification of mental deficiency is in terms of language usage. The idiot has neither spoken nor written language; the imbecile has spoken but not written language; the moron has both, though he is much more likely to have a speech or reading problem than the person of average intelligence.) Of course, there are many exceptions to this rule. Some children whose intelligence is in the border zone between the low normals and the slightly retarded seem to have great difficulty in learning to talk; others who ultimately turn out to have severe degrees of mental retardation show a pattern of speech development that is not markedly deviant from the normal in the early years of life. However, the exceptions are uncommon, and their occasional occurrence does not disprove the general rule.

The majority of children who are markedly slow in developing speech will be found to be mentally retarded, but in the past much harm has been done by assuming that all children with delayed speech were feeble-minded. Many children of average intelligence or better, whose delayed speech was caused by some other condition, were diagnosed as feeble-minded and placed in institutions. These mistakes were deplorable and caused untold harm and unhappiness to the children. Recently many workers have been making the opposite sort of mistake and have with unwarranted optimism assumed that every child with delayed speech could be made normal or nearly so by speech training. The parents of subnormal children often think that speech training can permit their children to make normal progress in school. These unrealistic notions are understandable in parents, for they rarely have special training in speech or in psychology and are naturally reluctant to accept the seriousness of their child's mental deficiency. Professional personnel in speech, education, medicine, and other fields dealing with retarded children should not fall prey to wishful thinking. Of course, it is possible to improve the speech of a feeble-minded child by intensive training, and it is also possible to improve his intelligence test scores somewhat. Only infrequently, however, are these changes indicative of real improvement in the child's ability to make his own way.

The causes of mental retardation are numerous. Although a detailed discussion of them would be outside the scope of this book, we can mention some of the more important conditions. Injuries to the brain may, in addition to having other effects, sometimes produce mental retardation of some degree. Such injuries may occur before, during, or after birth, and they may be produced by many different agents. Certain illnesses of the mother during pregnancy may cause such injury to the brain of the growing fetus. Brain hemorrhage at birth may have mild or severe ill effects on the baby's potentiality for mental growth. Various illnesses of the infant and certain poisons may affect 'he brain. These are examples of some of the kinds of influences that may produce brain injury resulting in impairment of intelligence. Many—probably most—children with mental retardation have no history suggesting brain injury, and we do not know why their intelligence is markedly subnormal. Serious degrees of feeble-mindedness accompany certain congenital abnormalities of metabolism or of bodily structure.

For the purposes of our discussion here, however, it makes no difference at all what caused the mental retardation producing the delay in speech development. This would not be true if it were possible to treat one or more types of mental retardation and by so doing make possible normal mental growth. There have been many attempts to improve the intelligence of feeble-minded patients by operations, drugs, or other forms of medical treatment, but none has yet been successful. So long as all types of mental retardation resist efforts at correction, the medical diagnosis of the case is not of great importance to the speech correctionist. The degree of retardation is of far more significance, and is usually the most valuable index of the likelihood of improvement.

The existence of a severe degree of mental deficiency in a given child may be obvious to almost anyone. Accurate diagnosis of less marked feeble-mindedness is far from easy and requires trained and experienced persons. Every child with delayed speech development should have a psychological test carried out by a good clinical psychologist. It is, of course, difficult to test a child with little or no speech, but a skillful psychologist can get a valid estimate of the child's intelligence.

A careful and detailed history of all aspects of the child's development is just as important as the psychological test. Often such a history gives unmistakable clues pointing toward mental retardation. There are so many such clues that mention can be made of only a few. Marked delays in rolling over, sitting, standing, and walking are usually important, though they do not always indicate mental retardation. Highly significant is the lack of ability to play with other children. This is usually stated in a positive way by the parents—"He likes to play by himself." A lack of ability in verbal comprehension may go entirely unnoticed by the parents, who often insist that "he understands everything you tell him," and then go on to mention that "he won't sit still for stories." Not every child of two or more who fails to enjoy being read to is mentally retarded, but one must strongly suspect such a possibility in any child who simply refuses to listen to stories. An odd episode in the development of many mentally retarded children is the appearance of a few words which are used for a few days or even several months only to disappear and never return.[9] Why a few words may appear at a nearly normal time and then drop out is not clear, but regression also occurs in other aspects of the behavior of mentally deficient children. Whenever such a history is given, one may be almost certain that the child is seriously retarded mentally.

Not every school system has a clinical psychologist, but it is almost always possible to arrange somehow to have the child tested. In almost every state there are psychologists in the state department of education, and they travel about the state testing children who have been referred to them. There are child guidance clinics in many cities. State universities have facilities for mental testing of school children, especially those with special problems. Many large hospitals have children's clinics or psychiatric clinics which offer diagnostic services.

The diagnosis of mental deficiency is a serious matter with many long-range implications for the child. It may be used by a school system as a basis for exclusion of a child from school as being unable to profit from education or as the basis for assigning him to a special class. The diagnosis should not be made on the basis of an I.Q. alone, and no competent worker puts sole reliance on a test score, valuable as the test is. When a child whose speech is retarded is found to be mentally deficient, the question always arises as to whether he should be given speech therapy. This decision must always be made in the light of all relevant circumstances rather than in terms of rigid rules. If the mental deficiency is extreme, one can scarcely consider seriously giving speech therapy. If the degree of deficiency is slight, and especially

[9] Spencer F. Brown, "A Note on Speech Retardation in Mental Deficiency," *Pediatrics*, (1955), *16*:272-273.

if the child has abilities that make him a potentially useful member of society, it would be hard to refuse to help him. Most trained speech correctionists have such heavy case loads that they are reluctant to include children who seem mentally incapable of profiting from speech correction. The parents of many retarded children are able to work at home on the child's speech with the help of occasional meetings with the speech correctionist. In general it may be said that much the same considerations that govern the placement of the mentally retarded speech handicapped child in school apply to the decision as to whether he should receive speech correction.

### HEARING IMPAIRMENT

For centuries it has been understood that persons who are born deaf do not learn to talk, or at least not without special training. The common term *deaf-mute* recognizes this fact. But it is not always easy to be sure that a child cannot hear. In the experience of many clinicians, at least half the parents of deaf children between the ages of two and two and one-half do not complain that the child does not *hear*—they are concerned because he does not *talk*.

What is particularly confusing to the parents—and often to teachers and others as well—is that the child may hear some sounds and not others. He is often misjudged as being inattentive or uncoöperative. The remark, "He hears perfectly well when he wants to," should immediately make one suspect that a serious hearing loss may be present. In some cases the child hears low-pitched sounds such as the rumble of a truck, the growl of a dog, the low notes on the piano. But he cannot hear the higher-pitched sounds which are necessary for the understanding of speech. Since he cannot understand the speech of others, he does not learn to talk himself. He hears the speech of others only as noise and not as meaningful words.

Every child with delayed speech should have a hearing test. If the child is only two or three years old, it is not easy to test his hearing, but with patience, skill, and proper instruments it can be done. In Chapter VIII there is a description of hearing tests, so we need not describe them here.

Like the psychological test that is equally necessary, the hearing test may be difficult to arrange. If there is no audiometer in the school system and no otologist near at hand, a request to the state department of education may bring aid. Large hospitals and clinics may be able to do the testing.

Chapter VIII discusses in detail the problems and the treatment of children with various types and degrees of hearing losses. It is important to mention here that many of these children come to the attention of the teacher or the speech correctionist because they are retarded in speech development.

MOTOR DIFFICULTIES

In some instances a child with normal intelligence and hearing will fail to talk because of unusual difficulty in controlling his tongue, lips, palate, or other structures used in speech. Such inability to control the speech organs may take the form of a partial or complete paralysis of the palate, for example, or of the muscles of the throat. When throat muscles (constrictors of the pharynx) are paralyzed, there is difficulty in swallowing. Paralysis of the soft palate may produce nasality, or regurgitation of liquids through the nose. There may be no paralysis but rather a serious incoördination, so that the child cannot have any idea what will happen when he tries to move his tongue in a given direction.

We have previously touched on the enormous complexity of the speech act and the extreme delicacy and coördination required to produce normal speech. The sheerly mechanical and physiological difficulties of learning to talk are so great that one sometimes wonders how anyone ever manages it. When these difficulties are greatly multiplied by the handicaps of some degree of paralysis, or severe incoördinaton, or both, it is easy to understand why the child finds that learning to talk is extremely hard. He may stop trying, or he may continue despite the failure of his efforts.

The paralysis and the incoördination are caused by damage to the nervous system, and this may be the result of many factors

Some examples of these were given in the discussion of the brain injuries that may result in mental retardation. Depending on what parts of the brain are affected, injuries may cause mental deficiency, hearing loss, blindness, paralysis, incoördination, behavior disturbance, and other unfortunate results. In some cases the damage is apparently confined to a small area of the brain, and the consequences appear in only one aspect of behavior—in motor ability (paralysis, for example) or in deafness. In other instances the damage is more widespread, and its results are seen in almost every aspect of the child's living. It would be quite possible, therefore, for a brain hemorrhage or a lack of oxygen during and after birth to produce in one child mental retardation, hearing loss, and partial paralysis of the speech organs, any one of which conditions would be sufficient to cause severe speech retardation.

The strength of the drive to communicate verbally is seen in the fact that most children with motor speech difficulties continue to try to talk and generally manage to make considerable progress on their own. They may do well enough that they are never considered to have retarded speech development, though they usually need remedial help with articulation, voice, and possibly other aspects of speech. If they make little or no progress, they fall into the retarded speech group. The existence of deficiencies in intelligence or in hearing complicate the problem and may even produce insuperable difficulties in some cases.

The treatment of the speech retardation of children whose difficulties stem from brain damage is most difficult. It should be undertaken only by persons with advanced training and by them only in consultation with medical specialists. Although this is the ideal arrangement, we must recognize that many of these children cannot get highly specialized clinical help. One cannot endorse attempts at treatment by untrained personnel, no matter how well-intentioned, unless there is supervision by qualified and experienced specialists. In many instances there has been successful remedial work carried out by a mother or a nursery school teacher with monthly visits to a speech clinic for detailed instructions for the next steps in the retraining program. Accurate medical diagnosis, including neurological consultation, is an important prerequisite to proper planning of the speech retraining. The speech techniques that the mother or the teacher will be asked to carry out are in many respects similiar to those described in the chapter on disorders of articulation (Chapter III), but in every case there must be special modifications of the methods to suit the individual child.

These three factors of mental retardation, hearing deficiency, and impaired control of the speech organs must be considered in evaluating every child whose speech development is retarded. Appropriate examinations by qualified persons can almost always be arranged, though often at considerable trouble and expense. Without such studies the diagnosis of any case of speech retardation is a matter of guesswork, luck (often bad), and desperation.

ENVIRONMENTAL CAUSES OF DELAYED SPEECH

In some instances the explanation for delay in speech development lies chiefly in the environment rather than in the child himself. The child posesses normal intelligence (or above), adequate hearing, and normal control and movement of all the structures used in speech. Yet the child has reached the age of two and one half years without being able to speak single words. Or he may be four years old and still unable to form simple sentences. So we turn to a study of his home situation, his play associations, and other factors in an attempt to understand why he is not talking. The techniques here are not standardized tests or electrical instruments, but rather detailed questioning of the parents and other informants. The results are not expressed as numerical scores, but in terms of careful description of the relevant facts.

(It should be made explicit that ordinarily a diagnostic study of a child with retarded speech development does not actually proceed in the order in which the causes of these problems have been discussed in this chapter. We do not first give a psychological test, then evaluate the hearing, then test the mobility and the control of the speech mechanism, and finally take a history of the case. The best practice is precisely the reverse of this order—

first the history is taken, then the child is given careful physical and speech examinations, and finally, in the light of the facts uncovered, various special tests may be administered.)

The questions that are asked of the parents are designed to elicit information about two important aspects of the learning process as it relates to speech—*motivation* and *stimulation*. The process of learning to talk is a long and difficult one, and if it is to take place at a normal rate there must be adequate motivation for this learning. Now the motivation of all learning can be reduced to the basic elements of reward and punishment. We learn in the hope of reward or in the fear of punishment, and often both elements are present. The reward (or the punishment) may be immediate or remote, it may be tangible or not, it may be transient or relatively permanent, it may be reversible or irreversible. There may be many rewards involved in the motivation of a single learning situation and also many punishments.

When we consider that speech learning goes on over a period of many years, with the most rapid and significant learning extending over the first two or three years of life, it is clear that literally thousands of small rewards and punishments must be involved, and it seems hopeless to try to get a clear understanding of the motivational factors. When speech learning has failed markedly, how can we discover whether there has or has not been proper and adequate motivation? There are several facts that help bring at least some elements of order into this complicated confusion. The first is simply that although there are thousands of little episodes involving speech learning, many similarities run through them. What is true of one situation will also be true, not for all the rest, but certainly for many hundred similiar situations. Second, in so far as the parents make conscious attempts to teach their child to talk, the element of reward is of far greater significance than that of punishment. For example, the parents may be trying to get a child of eighteen months, already somewhat slow in his speech development, to say a single word—"mama" or "dada" or whatever. Obviously, it will do no good to punish the child for not saying the word. All they can do is reward the child for whatever attempt he makes. What sort of reward? A smile, a pat on the head, "That's a good boy," a proud glance—whether they are aware of it or not, the parents are importantly rewarding the child by these and a hundred other manifestations of affection. The normal loving relationship between parent and child yields dozens of valuable emotional rewards for the child every day—rewards given spontaneously and unconsciously. Parental disappointment and irritation when weeks and months pass without any words may be a punishment, but these usually are less openly and directly expressed.

Now it is not easy to discover exactly what sort of rewards the parents have used in their efforts to develop speech in the child. Dozens of times a day one parent or the other may be involved in some sort of potential speech learning situation with the child, and the subtleties of these situations usually escape the participants. We can take advantage, however, of the fact that there is another area of family life in which the manipulation of reward and punishment can be studied rather easily—the area of discipline. We make the assumption that if the parents have become badly confused, uncertain, or maladroit in their handling of reward and punishment in this rather clear-cut matter of discipline, they are likely also to be misusing rewards and punishments in other areas, including that of speech learning. If they are handling reward and punishment effectively and consistently in their discipline of the child, they are probably doing so in other areas as well. This assumption seems a reasonable one, and it has proved useful clinically.

A most illuminating case is that of Bruce G., a boy of three years and two months who had a vocabulary of about six words, only one of which he used to any extent. This word was "no." To any and all requests from his parents or others he would answer, "No." He played with several other children of his own age and seemed to get along well with his limited speech, but occasionally would get into disagreements in which his sole response was "No." Bruce had no siblings and lived with his parents in a pleasant small home in a neighborhood of relatively new houses.

When he was examined, he was found to be normal physically, with excellent nutrition and development. He was not negativistic during the speech examination, smiling and pointing to pictures, but neither would he say any words. He coöperated well on the hearing test and gave normal responses. He tested in the bright normal group on the psychological test.

Hearing and psychological tests were done as precautions against overlooking significant information in these areas, but the history had already provided a clue that seemed sufficient to explain the child's failure to talk. Inquiries about discipline brought out that the parents were "always very reasonable" with the child, and "wanted him to understand everything." A typical episode went as follows. The father came home from work, said "Hello," and asked the boy to bring him a broken toy he had promised to fix. Bruce said "No." The father then picked him up and took him on his knee. (Significantly, the child did not resist this.) Then he began a discourse that went something like this: "Look, Bruce, I work hard all day for you. Now when I come home and ask you to do something, you ought to do it. I do things for you. You ought to do things for me. Daddy loves you and wants to do things for you. Don't you see why you ought to do what Daddy asks you? This is why—you see, all day I work hard just for you and Mommy . . ." and so on, for about twenty minutes. All this time the father was patting the boy and showing him great affection. Finally Bruce did what he had been asked to do twenty minutes before. Similar episodes occurred several times a day in relation to all sorts of major and minor matters.

It was pointed out to the parents that unwittingly they had fallen into the error of rewarding Bruce for bad behavior. The long "explanations," almost always conducted with Bruce on the lap of one of the parents and the recipient of frequent physical and verbal demonstrations of affection, were actually very pleasant for the child. All he had to do to touch off such a pleasant scene was to say "No," and stick to it. The suggestion was made that the parents arrange things so that there was no such rewarding of undesirable behavior, and a rather thorough analysis of the family's system of discipline was made to help avoid this error. Other recommendations were minor and included no direct effort to elicit speech in any situation. Within two months the vocabulary had increased amazingly, and in another month sentences appeared.

The inference is that by this indirect approach—by adjusting the badly warped system of rewards in the area of discipline and by discussing the problem of reward and its relation to learning—the parents were enabled to use rewards effectively in motivating Bruce's speech learning.

Few cases present the motivational factor so clearly, but there are many circumstances in which factors of motivation play a part in retarding speech development. If the rewards are inadequate or given inappropriately, speech learning proceeds slowly—and sometimes scarcely proceeds at all.

For example, mention is often made of the "overprotected" child as one who may be slow in speech development. The overprotection referred to consists in anticipating the child's desires and satisfying them so that he "has no need to talk." Such an explanation makes rather naïve assumptions about motivation, and yet it is true that overprotected children may often be delayed in speech. When the behavior of the parents toward the child in areas other than speech is examined, it is apparent that their system of rewards and punishments has become badly confused. Rather, they have no system at all—they reward the child indiscriminately and are reluctant even to consider withholding any reward. The rewards thus lose their effectiveness—in fact they can no longer be classified as rewards. It is hard to prove that the motivational elements in speech learning situations have become confused, but such an assumption seems warranted. If such be the case, then instructing the parents to "Make the child say what he wants," "Don't give it to him till he asks for it," seems ill-advised and irrelevant. Rather, a careful study of rewards and punishments in nonspeech areas, together with systematic efforts to reward any speech efforts made by the child, almost always results in improvement. It is particularly important in dealing with overprotective parents to point out that the rewards to be given consist of warm and accepting approval of the child's efforts at speech, but not exaggerated and overeffusive praise.

The way parents feel is more important than what they say. Non-verbal rewards are more highly motivating than verbal ones.

In a few cases of retarded speech, the most important factor seems to be a marked degree of parental rejection, which seems to affect speech learning adversely—chiefly through depriving the child of proper rewards for his speech efforts. Some rejecting parents are dimly aware of their lack of love for the child, and in an effort to conceal this lack from themselves as well as others, they behave in the smothering, overprotective manner we have just discussed. Other parents are more candid with themselves about their lack of affection for the child. They may neglect him and treat him with a good deal of indifference. Under such circumstance there will probably not be enough rewards for normal speech learning.

Occasionally it is found that the course of speech development comes to a more or less abrupt halt at the time of the birth of a younger sibling. Under the best of circumstances the birth of a new baby constitutes a threat to the older child. The threat is usually not serious, however, and because the parents have ample love for all their children, the problem remains only a potential and temporary one. In every home there are occasional displays of jealousy of the younger child, and all through childhood and adolescence there are bound to be quarrels and conflicts of various sorts. These normally do not cause undue concern to anyone. There are, however, instances in which parents are not able to give the older child the reassuring love he needs when faced with the new competitor. This means that the arrival of the younger sibling is much more than a potential threat. Among other changes that occur rather suddenly, the parents may no longer be able to give the older child enough evidence of love and approval—not enough reward to continue to give incentive to his speech attempts. The result may in rare cases be a sudden stop in speech development and even a regression to earlier stages. Problems of this sort are not encountered in the public schools, of course, and are mentioned briefly here for the sake of completeness. From what has been said it will be clear than an essential part of the approach to any such problem is counseling the parents, and this may be done by a qualified speech correctionist, a psychiatrist, a psychologist, a social worker, or other trained specialist. Speech retraining for the child may or may not be necessary.

The examples which have been given by no means exhaust the types of situations in which a child's learning to talk is impeded because of motivational factors. In considering any case of speech retardation we always need to take into account the matter of reward in speech learning. Sometimes this is the only plausible explanation one can find for the difficulty. In other cases lack of reward acts to intensify the effects of another cause. No matter what other conditions may be present, it is always wise to see if the amount of reward for speech efforts could be increased and to try to improve generally the handling of rewards and punishments by the child's parents. We must also realize that there is tremendous individual variation in the need for rewards and in the effectiveness of them. The motivation may seem to be adequate, but if it can be made still better, one would make a serious mistake if he failed to take advantage of every possible beneficial change. There is no justification for leaving likely stones unturned.

The amount of *speech stimulation* is the other environmental factor of great importance that must always be taken into account. Some of the importance of speech stimulation is generally known and taken for granted. Other aspects are less widely understood.

The child learns to speak the language of his parents because that is the language with which he is constantly stimulated. But when the child is cared for by someone who speaks a different language, he may learn to speak that instead of the language of his parents, depending upon which language he hears most. In many families of American army personnel in Germany since World War II, the children are brought up by German nurses and maids. Cases have been reported of four-year-old children unable to speak English because of their constant association with German maids and lack of contact with their parents. When the parents spend much time with the child, he may learn to speak German and English simultaneously. Children tend to reproduce the dialect, the grammar, and often the individual mannerisms of speech of their parents or other adults with whom they are closely associated. These facts are generally appreciated.

Likewise it is easy to understand that extreme lack of stimulation will result in failure of development of speech. There are a few cases on record of children having been raised by animals— the "Wolf Boy" and other such cases.[10] These children had no speech because they had never heard human speech—to use the terminology of this discussion, they had not had any speech stimulation. Other rather extreme instances may be cited. Mason[11] reports the case of a six-year-old girl who had lived her entire life shut up in an attic with her deaf-mute mother and who had no speech whatsoever except cries and grunts. The lack of speech of the deaf child may be regarded as a special case of lack of speech stimulation.

There are many less spectacular cases in which the normal development of speech is seriously interfered with by insufficient stimulation. An example of such a case is Polly M., a child of thirty-four months who was studied because her speech was confined to only a few single words which she used infrequently. The history disclosed that Polly had been entirely normal in physical development, had walked at thirteen and one-half months, had begun to use her first words at twenty-three months, and had made almost no further speech progress. She had had no serious illness.

When the details of the home situation were studied, it was found that Polly lived with her parents on the second floor of a duplex apartment. She had no siblings. The family who lived downstairs didn't like children and had made complaints to Polly's parents about the noise she made. Since Polly was a quiet child, the parents attributed the complaints to the generally disagreeable nature of their neighbors, but they tried to keep her

[10] See, among others, Arnold Gesell, *Wolf Child and Human Child*, New York, Harper & Brothers, 1940; Jean Marc Gaspard Itard, *The Wild Boy of Aveyon* (1801), translated by George and Muriel Humphrey, New York, D. Appleton-Century, Inc., 1932.

[11] Marie K. Mason, "Learning to Speak after Six and One-Half Years of Silence," *Journal of Speech Disorders* (1942), 7:295-304.

as quiet as they could. The house was set among some business and factory buildings, there were few other houses within a block, and no other children lived in the area. Even if there had been other children, the little girl could not have played in the yard with them, for the downstairs tenants would have objected.

The father worked as an office manager in a busy firm, and his work required him to leave the house every morning before Polly got up. He put in an eleven-hour day at work and got home in the evening after Polly had eaten. Tired and hungry, he had little desire to postpone his dinner by talking or reading to Polly, and the mother tried to hustle the child off to bed soon after she had greeted her father. Since he worked six days a week, Polly's father really saw her only on Sunday, and then church, Sunday School, and visits to grandparents occupied most of the day.

Polly's mother was a slender, tense woman who was proud of the fact that she kept her house spotless despite its smoky industrial surroundings. She cleaned every room in the apartment thoroughly every day. Preoccupied with her meticulous housework, she paid little attention to her quiet, undemanding daughter. It had occurred to her that perhaps she ought to read to Polly, but she had not found time for that in her schedule. Since Polly didn't talk, her mother talked very little to her.

Polly was found to be in good physical condition, aside from being a little underweight. She had normal control of her speech organs. Her psychological test score placed her in the average intelligence group. Her hearing test response was normal.

Polly's parents were told how normal their daughter was on all these tests, and it was pointed out how greatly deficient in speech stimulation her environment was. This had to be done cautiously, for Polly's mother was an intelligent and sensitive woman who had allowed herself to become engrossed in housework, and she was horrified when she realized that her daughter had been so markedly deprived of normal speech stimulation.

It was suggested that the mother start at once to read stories to Polly every day and that the father read her one story in the evening before she went to bed. The amount of reading was to be increased to an hour a day as fast as Polly would accept it (which turned out to be less than two weeks). In addition, the mother was to try to engage in as much talking with her daughter as she could. She was urged to get Polly to "help" her in as many household tasks as possible, and to talk to the child about all the things they were doing together.

New words were heard from Polly within a week after this program was begun, and she made steady improvement thereafter. In less than four months she was using a few simple sentences. In about ten months the family moved to a new house in a neighborhood where there were many children, and though Polly's speech had not caught up to the average for children of her age (forty-five months at the time of moving), she had made enough progress so that she was able to play well with other children and use speech successfully with them. In another eight months her speech was considered to be approximately normal for her age.[12]

This story of Polly is essentially like other stories of hundreds of children who live under circumstances that deprive them of adequate speech stimulation. These children are usually not neglected in the ordinary sense of that term. Their parents are well-meaning people who have not realized the extent to which their preoccupation with other matters is depriving their children of the chance to hear speech and to use it themselves.

There is great individual variation in the amount of speech stimulation different children require, just as we remarked in the matter of motivation. Some children who receive very little speech stimulation during their early years still manage to develop speech at a rate not greatly different from the average. In other cases we may find no apparent reason for delayed speech development; everything seems normal, including the amount of speech the child hears. Yet when a systematic effort is made to increase the amount of stimulation, the child begins to respond almost at once. It is difficult to prove that the increased stimulation deserves the credit for the speech improvement, but there have been many cases in which the relationship seemed clear. Accordingly, a marked increase in speech stimulation is a recommendation

[12] A similar case, that of Roger, is described on p. 105.

that may be made for almost every child with retarded speech development. The presence of some other causative factor must not make us forget that inadequate stimualtion can also be present and aggravate the effects of any other condition.

The prescription of "increased speech stimulation" is far too general. In order to help the child, the suggestions given his parents must be specific. They need to be given many examples of how they can increase the amount of talking they do to the child —not merely in his presence but *to* him. Some parents seem to feel they must wait to talk to the child until he can hold up his end of the conversation. They need to be shown that talking to the child is crucially important, beginning in the earliest days of his life. These earliest days are now long past if the child is considered a retarded speech problem, but explanations of the value of stimulating the very young infant with speech provide an *a fortiori* argument for talking a great deal to the older child. The parents should be instructed to spend much time talking about concrete objects present in the room, since most of the child's own early speech efforts will be concerned with such things.

The importance of reading to the child as a means of speech stimulation needs to be stressed. There are hundreds of excellent, attractively illustrated storybooks for children. Reading such material provides a sort of stimulation which, though not better than conversation, has special values. The child can hear a given story read over and over again. He comes to anticipate almost every word and soon to form the words himself. The pictures and the story are associated, providing increased stimulation. The person doing the reading is likely to be more careful of his speech than when he is engaged in ordinary conversation. Being read to is far from a passive, one-way process for a child. He can, and usually does, interrupt frequently, and his interruptions should not be discouraged.

Listening to the radio or watching television, on the other hand, is a passive and one-way affair. It is inaccurate and unjustified to ascribe to radio or television any intrinsically harmful influence on the course of early speech development, but it is also a mistake to regard either radio or television as a substitute for the other direct forms of speech stimulation we have been discussing. In some cases, sheerly because of time limitations, it is necessary to suggest that the child spend less time watching television and more time listening to his parents read to him.

We can understand the adverse environmental influences on speech development in terms of inadequacy of these two crucial factors, motivation for speech learning and speech stimulation. Certain situations that are sometimes regarded as special problems can be explained in these terms. For example, it has long been noted that children raised in orphanages tend to be somewhat retarded in speech. But conditions of life in an orphanage are such that there could be few effective rewards to serve as incentives for speech learning, and there could also be relatively little speech stimulation, at least on an individual basis. Fortunately, this is no longer as great a problem as formerly for there has been a trend over several decades away from orphanage placement of children and toward placing them in foster homes. Some of the remaining orphanages are more adequately staffed than was formerly the case. Even so, orphanage children still tend to be somewhat slower in speech development.[13]

OTHER CAUSES OF SPEECH RETARDATION

The factors we have been considering in this chapter provide adequate explanation of the retardation in speech development of all but a minute fraction of the cases thus diagnosed. This does not mean that there may not be other causes, but it can safely be said that all other causes taken together are relatively insignificant, whether these other causes be demonstrable facts or theoretical speculations.

One of the minor but demonstrable causes of delayed speech is severe emotional shock. Speech may be developing normally in a child who suffers a harrowing experience, a great fright, the sudden loss of a parent, or some other severe emotional shock.

[13] Many studies have shown the adverse effect on speech development of orphanage or similar environment. See, for example, Arthur J. Brodbeck and Orvis C. Irwin, "The Speech Behaviour of Infants Without Families," *Child Development* (1946), *17*:145-156; William Goldfarb, "Effects of Psychological Deprivation in Infancy and Subsequent Stimulation," *American Journal of Psychiatry* (1945), *102*:18-33.

From that point on the speech fails to continue developing normally and may even regress. This is clearly not exactly the same sort of problem as that of markedly slow development of speech from the beginning, but since retarded speech is a loose category defined in terms of its manifestations and not in terms of cause, perhaps one should not object to the inclusion of some children whose normal development is thus suddenly arrested. It must be pointed out, however, that while severe shock does infrequently have such an effect on speech, its importance is often greatly exaggerated. Children are often brought to speech clinics with the story that their difficulties are due to some severe shock, only to prove to be mentally retarded, deficient in hearing, or lacking in proper environmental factors for good speech learning. Only in rare instances does careful study fail to reveal another and more likely cause for the retarded speech.

Over the past hundred years there have been in journals in the fields of medicine, education, psychology, and speech many reports of children of allegedly normal hearing and intelligence who were markedly retarded in speech development. These have been referred to by many different terms. The assumption is often made that in these children there is some brain injury which intreferes with speech development. This explanation may be plausible but remains unproved in nearly every case. Only a very few of these cases have been adequately studied, and one must often question the claims that subnormal intelligence and impaired hearing could not account for the speech delay. Often little or no study was made of environmental factors. Particularly unfortunate is the use of the term "congenital aphasia" in referring to cases of retarded speech development. Proof is usually entirely lacking that the difficulty is congenital (existing at birth, inborn) or that it bears any relation to what is ordinarily understood by the term aphasia.[14] Sugar has described some of the neurological objections to the term "congenital aphasia."[15] It must be admitted that no satisfactory explanation has been found for the delayed

[14] Aphasia is a complex language disorder which is outside the scope of this book. The term refers to an impairment of symbolic formulation, expression, and reception resulting from injury to the brain.

[15] Oscar Sugar, "Congenital Aphasia: An Anatomical and Physiological Approach," *Journal of Speech and Hearing Disorders* (1952), 17:301-304.

speech development of certain children. More adequate studies of such obscure cases are certainly needed, and pending such clarification it is desirable to use terminology which avoids untestable or possibly fallacious assumptions.

## What the Classroom Teacher Can Do

### COÖPERATING WITH THE SPEECH CORRECTIONIST

Because the faulty speech of many children is "outgrown" without any remedial attention, there is in some schools a policy of confining the work of the school speech correctionist to children in the third grade and above. While such a policy may have something to justify it, there are many children below the third grade for whom exceptions should be made. Children with retarded speech development, almost all of whom will be found in the first grade and kindergarten, certainly warrant such special consideration. Whether or not the remedial speech teacher ordinarily works with youngsters in the kindergarten, during the early weeks of school there will be much for him to do in the way of examining children throughout the grades, setting up schedules, and the like, and in the ordinary course of things it might take several weeks before instruction of a specific child could be started. But during those first weeks of school much valuable time may be lost, or even some harm might be done, if the child with retarded speech gets no help of any sort. It is particularly important that a child with a special problem get off on the right foot in school. Therefore, it is the first responsibility of the classroom teacher to notify the speech correctionist immediately if she discovers such a case, and ask for specific suggestions for dealing with the child until the correctionist is able to see him regularly.

Most of what the teacher will be able to do in these first weeks consists in observing the child, collecting information that will help in identifying the cause of the problem. She can make observations that will throw some light on the possible influence of some of the causal factors that have been mentioned. For example, she can compare his behavior with that of the others in the class with regard to learning ability. How quickly does the child grasp simple instructions? Does he seem to remember what he has been told? Does he seem as mature as most of the other children in the class? Evidences of impaired hearing can be looked for. Does the child watch the face of the speaker carefully, and often misunderstand when he cannot see the speaker's face? Is he less responsive to soft sounds than other children are? The social behavior of the child is important. How does he get along with other children? Does he make any efforts to talk to them? How much does he try to talk in the classroom? If his vocabulary is limited, exactly what words does he say? How clearly does he say them? These and many other similar observations can be furnished the speech correctionist, and will provide valuable clues for the first approaches to the improvement of his speech.

Once the remedial speech instructor is seeing the child regularly, he is likely to ask the classroom teacher for periodic reports on his progress outside the speech correction sessions. These will usually be brief and informal talks, but occasionally the correctionist may wish more detailed information. Often he may ask that the teacher do various things in order to aid the child's speech progress. Such requests will obviously be few and simple, for the classroom teacher is not able to give elaborate attention to all sorts of special problems, much as she might wish to. However, retarded speech development is a most serious thing. There will be few such children in the classes of any kindergarten or primary teacher during her whole teaching career. When one appears, he warrants some measure of special attention. Depending on individual circumstances, the teacher may be asked not to try directly to elicit speech at all for a time. Or she may be asked to call on the youngster as much as possible without seeming to single him out. She may be asked to seat the child as close to her as possible. These and various other relatively simple things may contribute a great deal to the child's progress.

IF THERE IS NO SPEECH CORRECTIONIST

The school's lack of a competent speech correctionist to deal with a child with retarded speech places the classroom teacher in an embarrassing dilemma. She is faced with a child whose disability may be a distracting influence in the classroom. The reactions of his peers to his lack of speech may in some cases be far from tolerant and helpful, and an already serious problem thus may become worse. For the sake of the child and of the others in the class, the teacher wants to do something. But retarded speech development is far more difficult to deal with than are most of the other speech problems a kindergarten teacher may encounter. It is a problem that taxes the skills of the most experienced speech correctionist. Realizing this, the classroom teacher understandably feels hesitant about attempting anything at all with the speech retarded child.

The course of action in this situation will naturally depend on the circumstances, but a few generalizations may be offered. The first and most obvious one is that the classroom teacher can use the suggestions made earlier in this chapter as to ways of getting skillful psychological and hearing testing carried out. Most children with delayed speech are studied for purposes of evaluation and special training by the time they are three or four. If the child is entering kindergarten without ever having received such attention, he deserves to receive it without any further delay. If energetic efforts are made, it ought to be possible to get hearing and psychological tests arranged for in a short time. Physical examination should take much less time, and the teacher should ask that special attention be given to the question of neurological control of the speech organs. Meanwhile, it may be possible for her to visit the child's home and gather a good deal of information regarding environmental factors that might have interfered with speech learning.

If all these lines of approach are carefully pursued, the basis of the speech retardation will nearly always be discovered. The measures to be taken have already been sketched.

It remains to be mentioned that because this book is concerned with speech problems, we have stressed here the speech aspects of the retardation of these children, but many of them have other kinds of language retardation as well. A child who at three or four presents a delay in speech development will often later show marked slowness in learning to read. His ability to express himself in writing may also be found to be poor as he progresses through school. Not all retarded speech development is part of a more general difficulty with language, but this possibility must always be kept in mind and arrangements should be made to have it properly checked. If general language retardation is present, a decreased likelihood of rapid improvement in speech is to be taken duly into account.

# CHAPTER VII

∿∿∿∿∿∿∿∿∿∿∿∿∿∿∿∿∿∿∿∿∿∿∿∿∿∿∿∿∿∿∿∿∿∿∿∿∿∿∿∿∿∿∿∿∿∿∿∿∿∿∿∿∿∿∿∿∿∿∿∿∿∿

# Cleft Palate; Cerebral Palsy

In this chapter we shall discuss children whose speech impairments are associated with certain physical conditions—cleft palate and cerebral palsy. Speech difficulties found in relation to these two problems together constitute a large proportion of the so-called organic speech disorders found in children.

## Cleft Palate

First let us consider children born with cleft palate or cleft lip (harelip). Figures from different parts of the world vary somewhat as to the frequency with which these structural defects occur. Recent studies show a higher incidence than those done several decades ago. Whether this is to be explained in terms of an actual increase in frequency of cleft palate is not wholly clear, though it seems to be the sounder view that no actual increase has taken place. The recent studies have been more carefully done and are based on larger samples and thus probably give a truer picture of the incidence of cleft palate births. Figures from Pennsylvania[1] show that one child in every 800 is born with a cleft of the lip or palate or both, while data from Denmark[2] give a figure of 1 in 665. One fourth of the Danish

[1] L. G. Grace, "Frequency of Occurrence of Cleft Palates and Harelips," *Journal of Dental Research* (1943), 22:495-497.

[2] Paul Fogh-Andersen, *The Inheritance of Harelip and Cleft Palate*, Copenhagen, Nyt Nordisk Forlag-Arnold Busck, 1942, p. 30.

cases had cleft lip only, one fourth had cleft palate only, and one half had clefts of both lip and palate.

To understand the possible reasons why cleft palates occur, we must know something of the development of the embryo. During the early weeks of growth within the uterus, the various parts of the body appear and rapidly assume a form much like that which they will have at birth. At one early stage of development the mouth and nose are one cavity, and there is no upper lip. The upper jaw is lacking except for that portion on the sides of the face back toward the ears. Over a period of several weeks the upper lip and upper jaw are formed by structures growing in from each side and meeting in the midline with a third portion growing downward from the nasal region. In much the same way the roof of the mouth is formed. It consists of the bony hard palate in the front part of the mouth and the soft palate, which is mainly muscle, behind it. The fusion of all these structures starts with the lip and proceeds posteriorly, ending with the soft palate. First evidences of the various parts of the upper lip and hard and soft palate appear about the sixth week of fetal life. By the end of the twelfth or thirteenth week the nasal cavity is separated from the oral cavity by the completely formed hard and soft palate.

If there is a disturbance of development in the face region during the period when fusion of the lip, jaw, and palate is normally occurring, the result will be some sort of incomplete fusion, or cleft. If the disruption of normal growth begins early and lasts throughout the period when fusion should take place, the child will be born with a cleft involving one or both sides of the upper lip and continuing back through the upper jaw and gum ridge, the hard palate, and the soft palate. If the disturbance starts early but lasts only a short time, there will be a cleft lip and a normal palate. If it occurs after the lip is formed there will be a normal lip and a cleft palate. In this latter case the cleft may involve only the soft palate or both the hard and soft palate. The uvula may be split, short, or absent. Babies born with cleft palates are somewhat more likely than normal babies to have other physical abnormalities also. Many of these defects are in the mouth region. Some may be obvious at birth, but others may not appear until years later, when, for example, teeth may fail to grow or may be located in unusual places in the mouth.

The causes of cleft lip and palate have long been sought, and many theories once advanced have been discarded. The most detailed genetic study to date is that of Fogh-Andersen,[3] which indicates that there is an important hereditary factor in cases of cleft lip, whether or not it is associated with cleft palate. Figures from this study show that if either parent has cleft lip (with or without cleft palate) the chances of one of the offspring having the same defect are about 2 percent, as compared with 0.15 percent in the population at large. After one child with cleft lip is born to a parent also having cleft lip, the chances of succeeding children being born with this defect rise to 10-15 percent. Cleft palate without cleft lip, however, seems to occur without any demonstrable hereditary factor in the great majority of cases. It is to be assumed that more satisfactory conclusions must await further research.

In recent years much evidence has accumulated as to the kinds of factors in addition to heredity that may be responsible for congenital anomalies such as cleft palate. It has been shown, for example, that certain deficiencies of vitamins or minerals in the diet of the pregnant mother may result in various defects. Similar defects may come from other substances (selenium, for example) in the diet which act as poisons. Excess or deficiency of hormones in the pregnant mother may result in abnormal offspring. Certain other adverse influences affecting the pregnant mother have been given wide publicity in recent years—radiation (x-ray, radioactive substances) and infectious disease, especially German measles. Reduced atmospheric pressure can also cause defects in the offspring. Mechanical factors such as pressure on the growing embryo may cause deformities but are not now considered as important as formerly. Most of these observations have been made on lower animals and hence cannot be taken to be adequate explanations of human malformations. They are

[3] *Ibid.*

highly suggestive of areas for study, however, and it seems reasonable that similar factors may be causes of anomalies in human infants.[4] It is also of great interest that recent work[5] has shown that it is possible to produce cleft palate in pregnant mice by injecting cortisone into the pregnant mothers at a time after the embryonic palate would normally be closed. This suggests that in some cases cleft palate may be the result of a degenerative change occurring in the embryo rather than a disturbance of development.

It does not require any specialized knowledge to predict that a cleft palate will have many important effects on a child from the moment of birth. Think, for example, of the problem of feeding the infant. If the cleft is small, and especially if the lip is not involved, the baby may be able to nurse fairly efficiently and easily. If the cleft is of considerable size, however, it often prevents the baby's building up enough suction to nurse well. In many cases this can be overcome by enlarging the hole in the nipple, or by means of a plastic obturator fitted to the nursing bottle—a sheet of plastic shaped like a flattened dome which fits into the defect in the palate and closes it well enough to permit nursing. In some cases the baby must be fed by means of a slender rubber tube passed through the mouth and into the stomach. While it is almost always possible to maintain good nutrition in a baby with a cleft palate, this often requires a great deal of careful attention.

Consider now the matter of colds and sore throats in cleft

[4] An excellent review of this subject is that of Josef Warkany, "Etiology of Congenital Malformations," *Advances in Pediatrics*, Vol. 2, New York, Interscience Publishers, 1947, pp. 1-63. Warkany lists as causing cleft palate in lower animals the following: heredity, deficiency of Vitamin A or of riboflavin ($B_2$) in the maternal diet, and exposure of pregnant mother to x-rays on certain days early in gestation.

See also Stuart S. Stevenson *et al.*, "677 Congenitally Malformed Infants and Associated Gestational Characteristics," *Pediatrics* (1950), 6:37-50 and 208-222; Theodore H. Ingalls, *et al.*, "Experimental Production of Congenital Anomalies," *New England Journal of Medicine* (1952), 247:758-768.

[5] F. Clarke Fraser, T. D. Fainstat, and H. Kalter, "The Experimental Production of Congenital Defects with Particular Reference to Cleft Palate," *Etude Neo-natales* (1953), 2:43-58. A preliminary report was published in *Pediatrics* (1951), 8:527-533.

palate babies. These infants seem to be more susceptible to such illnesses than other children. It is easy to understand that when an infection starts in any part of the nose or throat, it can spread farther and faster when a palate that is widely cleft permits open communication between nose and mouth. One of the worst places for such an infection to reach is the ear, and in cleft palate children it frequently lodges there, traveling into the middle ear cavity by means of the Eustachian tube, which connects the middle ear with the upper part of the pharynx. Normally the pharyngeal end of the Eustachian tube is closed by the light contact of folds of mucus membrane; each time swallowing occurs the pull of the muscles of the upper pharynx opens the entrance to the Eustachian tube, thus permitting air to enter. This process equalizes the air pressure on the inner and outer surfaces of the eardrum, and it also aids in maintaining the tissues of the middle ear in a healthy condition. A cleft of the soft palate disrupts the normal muscle functioning of the upper pharynx, and often means that the Eustachian tube is not properly ventilated. Hence the eardrum may be thrust inward by pressure of the outside air, creating an interference with proper functioning of the middle ear. The tissues are also rendered more vulnerable to infection. Repeated infections of the middle ear are the commonest cause of acquired hearing losses in children, and it is not surprising to find that cleft palate children as a group are much more likely than others to have hearing losses.[6] The modern drugs used to treat infections (for example, penicillin) have reduced the number of hearing losses caused by ear infections, but the problem has by no means been conquered.

Although the psychological problems of a person with a cleft palate may seem obvious, they are too often neglected. If the child was born with a cleft lip, the repair may have left a visible scar. The lip may be short and somewhat stiff, so that the facial

[6] Joseph Sataloff and Margaret Fraser, "Hearing Loss in Children with Cleft Palates," *A.M.A. Archives of Otolaryngology* (1952), 55:61-64. Twenty-seven out of 30 cleft palate cases were found to have hearing losses of 15 db. or more for two or more frequencies.

See also Frances P. Gaines, "Frequency and Effect of Hearing Loss in Cleft Palate Cases," *Journal of Speech Disorders* (1940), 5:141-149.

expression may be affected. Modern improvements in plastic surgery tend to result in far better appearance of these patients than was generally achieved with older methods. Even so, many children with cleft palate, especially if the lip is also involved, are self-conscious about their appearance. They are even more self-conscious about their speech impairments, and are often shy and tend to avoid talking.

## CLEFT PALATE SPEECH

Even if one had never seen or heard a person with an untreated cleft palate, it would not be hard to predict that the speech of such an individual would be different from what we refer to as normal speech. Since the nose cannot be shut off from the mouth, we would expect that the voice quality would be nasal, as indeed it almost always is. The nasality, however, is not the penetrating nasal "twang" of the hillbilly singer. Actually the voice has little penetrating quality and does not carry well, but there is a good deal of nasality on almost every word. In nontechnical language this quality might be characterized as that of "snorting."

The cleft palate speaker is difficult to understand because of his numerous faults in articulation. Among various studies in which investigators have tried to define these articulatory disorders, the most recent and most comprehensive is that of Rouse.[7] Twenty-five cleft palate children between the ages of three and eight were given a 176-item articulation test. It was found that the group was generally retarded in the development of articulatory skills as compared with norms established by Templin. Vowels and diphthongs occasioned little difficulty. The consonant giving the least difficulty was *m*, followed in order by *n, h, y,* and *ng*. The consonants most often misarticulated were in order of decreasing difficulty *z*, voiceless *th, s, ch, j,* voiced *th, sh,* and *t*, all of which were incorrectly made more than 60 percent of the

[7] "A Study of the Articulation of a Group of Cleft Palate Children," Unpublished M.A. thesis, University of Iowa, 1955. The study was carried out by Verna Rouse under the direction of D. C. Spriestersbach and Frederic L. Darley. It will probably be published in an appropriate journal in 1956 or 1957.

time. The subjects had significantly less difficulty with voiced than with voiceless consonants. Fricatives caused the greatest difficulty. Consonants appearing as elements of blends were misarticulated oftener than when they appeared singly. There was a good deal of inconsistency in the articulatory errors the cleft palate children made.

The combination of nasal voice quality and distorted articulation produces a characteristic speech pattern that is nearly always instantly recognized, whether the speech be relatively good with excellent intelligibility or almost impossible to understand. This pattern is found in patients whose clefts have been treated, as well as in the relatively small number of untreated cases. Improvements in all phases of treatment should give far better results in the future.

### TREATMENT OF CLEFT PALATE

Enough has been said about the anatomical deviations of cleft lip and palate, and about the effects of such deviations on speech, to indicate that these patients present difficult problems which are made even more difficult by the great differences found from one patient to another. No two cleft palate patients are alike. Consider the diverse factors already mentioned. The cleft may involve only the soft palate or both hard and soft palate; it may extend through the gum ridge; it may also involve the lip; the width of the cleft may vary widely. There may be several different associated abnormalities of the nose. The teeth, when they appear, may be abnormally placed. The number of possible combinations of these factors is great. Then one must also take into account other relevant matters—the possible presence of hearing loss, nutritional problems, level of intelligence, other attendant congenital abnormalities, and certain less tangible factors, such as morale, vocational considerations, and family environment. It would be amazing if we were to find two patients who were alike in all these respects. This great complexity of the cleft palate problem makes it impossible for any one person to deal with all its aspects and make all the decisions that must be made about any given patient. This is a problem that requires a group of specialists working together.

Now it must be made clear that the crux of the problem is speech. It is true that there are other results of the cleft besides the mutilated speech, but these are minor by comparison and are to be looked on as conditions complicating the speech problem. For example, the increased susceptibility of the cleft palate patient to colds has been mentioned, but this is never sufficient reason for subjecting the child and his family to the trouble and expense of treatment directed at the cleft. *The only valid basis for considering surgical or any other treatment is in terms of its predicted effects on the child's speech.*

There are some persons with cleft palates who have achieved nearly normal speech without any special treatment or with the aid of speech training only. They are to be admired and congratulated, but their number is so small that for the purposes of this discussion they may be ignored, except for the fact that their existence serves to indicate that there has been too much emphasis on closing the palatal defect and not enough on speech correction. It may well be that these rare individuals have some compensating condition that permits them to do without repair things that most cases find great difficulty in doing even with repair. At any rate, practically all cleft palate cases need to have the defect in the palate closed in order to make significant improvement in speech. There are two chief methods of doing this.

*Surgical Repair.* If there is a cleft lip, it is always best that it be repaired early unless there is some good medical reason for delaying the operation. The preferred time of operation varies from one surgeon to another, but most surgeons prefer to carry out the repair when the child is between two and four weeks of age. Such early repair restores the normal lip pressure, and this in turn results in closure of a cleft in the gum ridge (if one exists) without other treatment. It may also reduce the width of the cleft in the hard palate.[8] There is no disagreement as to the necessity and desirability of early surgical repair of a cleft

[8] Samuel Pruzansky, "The Role of the Orthodontist in a Cleft Palate Team," *Plastic and Reconstructive Surgery* (1954), *14*:10-29.

lip, whether or not it is associated with cleft palate. The effects on speech of a repaired cleft lip, however, are few. If the repaired lip is short and inflexible, the labial sounds (*p, b, m*) may be distorted, but there is rarely any other effect. In the rest of this discussion, attention will be confined to clefts of the palate.

The purpose of surgical repair of the cleft palate is not merely the filling of the hole. Satisfactory closure of the defect in the hard palate is surely of considerable importance, but of even greater importance is the desired functional result—a palate functionally similar to a normal palate. Whether this aim can be accomplished depends on many factors—the size and shape of the cleft, the thickness of the tissue available, and many other technical details. Every case presents special problems.

In recent years steady advances have been made in the surgery of cleft palate, and results are generally better than those of twenty or more years ago.[9] One of the marked advances is in the reduction of the number of operations planned for a given child. It used to be not uncommon to carry out five or more separate operations on the cleft palate. The results of such surgery, however, were almost invariably bad. Many advances in surgery have made it possible to do only one operation on most patients, though some may need to have a second.

There is much disagreement among surgeons and among speech pathologists as to the best time for surgery. It used to be believed that if the operation were carried out before the child had begun to talk, the speech would be normal and no speech correction would be needed. Accordingly, many surgeons performed the closure of the palate at six to nine months of age. The speech results of this early closure were generally disappointing, and it was also found that early operation resulted in a narrowing

[9] No attempt will be made here to discuss the technicalities of the surgery of cleft palate. The interested reader is referred to the following works: George M. Dorrance, *The Operative Story of Cleft Palate*, Philadelphia, W. B. Saunders Co., 1933; H. S. Vaughan, *Congenital Cleft Lip, Cleft Palate and Associated Nasal Deformities*, Philadelphia, Lea & Febiger, 1940; Richard C. Webster, "Cleft Palate," *Oral Surgery, Oral Medicine, and Oral Pathology* (1948), 1:647-669 and 943-980 and (1949), 2:99-153 and 485-542; W. G. Holdsworth, *Cleft Lip and Palate*, New York, Grune & Stratton, Inc., 1952.

of the upper jaw and interference with facial growth.[10] Hence there has been a rather widespread trend toward deferring the closure. Many surgeons now prefer to operate when the child is four or five years old, since approximately five sixths of the lateral growth of the upper jaw is accomplished by the end of the fourth year.[11] Other surgeons feel they have developed techniques which permit early operation (fourteen to eighteen months) without interference with facial growth. As to the claims that early operation permits speech to develop normally without need for special speech training, it might be pointed out that most of these assertions are made by surgeons who are not specialists in speech correction and are made on the basis of inadequate examination of the child after operation. It is true, however, that in some studies by speech pathologists children have been followed for several years after operation; in some instances speech has been found to develop normally,[12] although this is far from being the rule at present. No generalization is justifiable here except the statement that skillful surgeons of wide experience differ markedly in their opinions as to the best time for operation and in their reasons therefor.

*Prosthetic Appliances.* The other method of closing the defect in the palate involves the use of an artificial palate. Such a device is known as an obturator and is constructed by a dentist. One who specializes in this branch of dentistry is called a prosthodontist. (The term "prosthesis" refers to an artificial substitute made to take the place of a missing part.)

The obturator must be carefully constructed, and it is a painstaking job to design and fit one. It must be made in such a way that it can easily be removed to be cleaned, and yet it must fit firmly when it is in place. It is not possible, of course, to close off the nose completely from the mouth with an obturator,

[10] Benjamin F. Edwards, "Evaluation of Cleft Palate Surgery," *American Journal of Surgery* (1953), 85:638-641.

[11] T. M. Garber, "Craniofacial Morphology in Cleft Palate and Cleft Lip Deformities," *Surgery, Gynecology and Obstetrics* (1949), 88:359-369. See also by the same author, "Changing Philosophies in the Management of Cleft Palate," *Journal of Pediatrics* (1950), 37:400-415.

[12] Muriel E. Morley, *Cleft Palate and Speech*, Sec. Ed., Baltimore, The Williams & Wilkins Co., 1951, p. 74.

for if this were done the patient could not breathe through his nose. A sizable opening must be left between the back part of the obturator and the wall of the throat. During speech this opening is partly or completely closed by action of the muscles of the upper part of the throat so that the voice is not nasal. Some obturators are made with a hinged portion at the rear in an effort to simulate the action of the soft palate. This does not seem to be necessary, however, in order to secure satisfactory results.[13]

Since there are two methods of closure of the palate available, a choice must be made. It is unfortunate if this choice is made without taking both possibilities into account, and without careful consideration of the problems of the particular child by a group of experts in consultation. Too often in the past it has been routinely assumed that surgical closure was the only satisfactory method and that prosthetic closure was to be reserved for cases in which surgery had failed. Actually both methods are equally deserving of consideration. The task of the prosthodontist is obviously made far more difficult by previous surgical failure.

It must be admitted that the ideal of careful study of each cleft palate child by a group of experts is not always realizable. There are not many skilled and experienced cleft palate surgeons outside of large medical centers. Even smaller is the number of prosthodontists who are expert in making obturators for cleft palate patients. As for the speech pathologists, most of them have in the past been consulted only after the work of the surgeon or the dentist was finished. Very few are familiar with evaluation of the speech problems of the child before any dental or surgical treatment is carried out. It is easier to find the other persons who should be included in the board of consultants for cleft palate children. Among these might be mentioned orthodontists, clinical psychologists, pediatricians, and child psychi-

[13] The following references will prove useful as a starting point for those who wish to investigate the matter of cleft palate prosthesis: Cloyd S. Harkins and Herbert Koepp Baker, "Twenty-five Years of Cleft Palate Prosthesis," *Journal of Speech and Hearing Disorders* (1948), 13:23-30; James H. Platt, "History and Principles of Obturator Design," *Journal of Speech Disorders* (1947), 12:111-123.

atrists. It is not nearly so vital that these specialists have great experience with cleft palate children, although as they acquire such experience they will obviously contribute more to the success of the program for each child. As the child grows older, educational specialists, vocational counselors, and others may be of a great deal of help. In certain cities, cleft palate centers with experienced staffs of specialists working together have been set up and are proving the great value of coördinated and carefully planned evaluation of each case. If enough interested people know of such centers, the demand for their services will call more into being. Perhaps it will some day be possible for every cleft palate child to have the benefits that only a small proportion now get.

## SPEECH CORRECTION

Within the last few years a marked change has occurred in the theories and practice of speech correctionists with regard to cleft palate speech. As has been mentioned, the former procedure was to defer special speech training—and even any consultation with the speech correctionist—until the operation had healed or an obturator had been fashioned. Everybody, including the speech correctionist, was bemused by the fact that the child had a hole in the roof of his mouth and was determined to get this closed by one means or another before bothering about anything else. Of course, the cleft in the palate is the source of the child's speech difficulties. But not until recent years has there been due recognition of the fact that much can be done before the cleft is closed to prepare the way for faster and greater progress in speech improvement afterwards. For example, it has been shown [14] that faulty jaw and tongue action are responsible for

[14] Eugene T. McDonald and Herbert Koepp Baker, "Cleft Palate Speech; An Integration of Research and Clinical Observation," *Journal of Speech and Hearing Disorders* (1951), *16*:9-20.

See also McKenzie Buck and Robert Harrington, "Organized Speech Therapy for Cleft Palate Rehabilitation," *Journal of Speech and Hearing Disorders* (1952), *14*:43-52, and McKenzie Buck, "Facial Skeletal Measurement and Tongue Carriage in Subjects with Repaired Cleft Palates," *Journal of Speech and Hearing Disorders* (1953), *18*:121-132.

many of the articulatory and voice difficulties of the cleft palate patient. It is possible to begin to correct these faulty functions in preschool children.

Speech correctionists formerly placed great reliance on blowing exercises in their work with cleft palate cases. Children tooted on whistles and on harmonicas, they puffed bits of paper and cotton, they blew up balloons, the purpose being that of favoring the oral rather than the nasal passageway in the emission of air. These techniques are still in use, but are no longer the mainstay they once were. There is some evidence[15] that blowing exercises may actually be harmful, and in some clinics they are not used at all. The former emphasis on blowing exercises was another evidence of the overconcern with the cleft *per se* and with the fact that it permitted air to escape through the nose during speech. Speech correctionists were inclined to feel that they must take advantage of the obturator or the surgical closure to get the air stream to come out the mouth and that this must be done before other corrective work could be attempted. There is now good evidence that great improvement in speech and in voice quality is possible even though a considerable amount of air continues to escape through the nose. It seems also to be true that nasal emission of air during speech can be effectively reduced by concentrating clinical attention on what is heard rather than on the portal of its emission.

The general principles underlying remedial training for children with all other types of voice and articulation problems apply, of course, to speech correction for children with cleft palate speech. The speech is carefully analyzed to determine as precisely as possible just what faults are present. The child is carefully examined, during speech and at rest, to discover what abnormalities, if any, of structure or function may be causally related to each of the speech imperfections noted. Then, in terms of all these facts, the corrective program is planned. The condition of the palate or the substitute therefor will be one important fact, but not the only one.

[15] McDonald and Baker, *op. cit.*

## WHAT THE CLASSROOM TEACHER CAN DO

*If There Is a Speech Correctionist.* In coöperating with a speech correctionist who is working with the cleft palate child, the classroom teacher can provide a great deal of helpful information about the child's speech in his daily classes. How much is the child talking in school? Does he tend to keep still because his speech is different, or is he willing to talk as much as the others? How does he react when others have trouble understanding him? What sort of relations does he have with other children? These and many other facts can be supplied by the classroom teacher and will be of great help to the speech correctionist.

The correctionist may ask the teacher to carry out some direct work on the child's speech, basing the suggestions in part at least on information supplied by the teacher. This might in the beginning include ear training and sound stimulation. Later the speech correctionist may want the teacher to reinforce and supplement other phases of the remedial program. The precise things the classroom teacher can best do will vary from one child to another, and are limited only by the imagination and resources of both the teacher and the speech correctionist.

Whether or not there is a speech correctionist in the school system, the most important things a classroom teacher can do for the child with a cleft palate are to help him meet some of the psychological problems connected with his condition and to create in the classroom the kind of atmosphere that will minimize these problems. This point has already been made in Chapter II, and it has been repeated several times since with regard to other speech problems. It needs to be said again with regard to children with cleft palates. No teacher is likely to have many cleft palate pupils during a lifetime of teaching. The few she may encounter often have great needs that only a sensitive and understanding teacher can meet.

Some cleft palate children are matter-of-fact about their problem. They may even enjoy taking out their obturators to show them to the other children, or they may like to talk about their operations. More often, however, such a child is embarrassed about his cleft, his obturator, or his operation and is fearful of ridicule. A perceptive and skillful teacher can help him to overcome this embarrassment and fear. She can do much to develop in the child's classmates friendly and understanding feelings toward him rather than feelings that result in rejection and taunts. In order to do this the teacher may need to explain to the other children why the cleft palate child talks as he does. A little frank discussion will usually prevent or remedy difficulties with the other children.

*If There Is No Speech Correctionist.* When no specialized help is available in the school system, there is much the class-room teacher can do by herself. First, of course, she will want to discuss the child's problems with his parents. If he has had no treatment of any sort, the parents should be encouraged to take the child to a cleft palate center such as has previously been described. Information on facilities available in various parts of the country may be had from the American Speech and Hearing Association.[16] Every state has a Crippled Children's Service, supported jointly by the state and federal governments, that can be located through the local medical society or by writing to the nearest university. The exact name varies from one state to another. Cleft palate falls within the definition of childhood crippling conditions cared for by these Crippled Children's Services. These Services will provide surgical and prosthetic treatment, and speech correction is also usually offered.[17] No

[16] Address inquiries to the Secretary, American Speech and Hearing Association, whose address as of 1956 is Wayne University, Detroit 1, Michigan. A usable permanent address is care of the Speech Correction Fund, National Society for Crippled Children and Adults, 11 South LaSalle Street, Chicago 3, Illinois.

[17] As of March, 1955, according to Lucille J. Marsh, M.D., Chief of the Program Services Branch, Division of Health Services, U. S. Children's Bureau, "All States include care for children with cleft lip and/or palate in their programs for crippled children. Surgery is available in all the programs and many of them provide prosthetic and/or orthodontic services also.

"States differ in their use of the means test. All diagnostic service is free. Treatment service which includes surgery, prosthetic treatment and speech therapy may or may not require a means test before being available. Most States have some kind of financial determination before entering on treatment." Personal communication to the writer, March 25, 1955.

cleft palate child from however poor a family in the remotest town need go through life without benefit of skilled treatment if only an interested teacher will tell the right people about him or tell him about the right people.

If the child has already had surgical or prosthetic treatment of his palatal cleft, he is likely also to have had some attention, and perhaps a great deal, from a speech correctionist. For example, in most states a speech correctionist in the Crippled Children's Services sees the child before and after surgery and makes suggestions for a program of exercises at home. The classroom teacher can help carry these out with further suggestions at intervals from the speech correctionist. Even if the surgical or prosthetic treatment was not carried out under the auspices of the Crippled Children's Services, the aid of their speech correctionist is always available. In some way, then, it will usually be possible for the teacher to get expert guidance in any help she tries to give the child.

If such experienced supervision is not available, or if it can be obtained only at such infrequent intervals as to be of little or no help, then the classroom teacher should probably not try to do any intensive work on the child's speech directly. Indirect, supportive help—the right sort of classroom atmosphere and the warm sympathetic understanding of the child's problems—becomes doubly important. But remedial speech training for a child with a cleft palate is a difficult challenge even to the trained and experienced speech correctionist. It is not realistic to expect anyone without special training to accomplish very much in such a case, and it must always be considered that ineffectual efforts over a long period may be seriously detrimental to the morale of the child.

## Cerebral Palsy

The term *cerebral palsy* denotes motor impairment as a result of damage to the brain. Such damage can, of course, occur at any time of life, but as the term is usually applied it refers to cases in which the damage occurred before or during birth or shortly thereafter. One of the best of the many definitions that might be formulated is the following: " A child has cerebral palsy when it has suffered injury to the brain occurring during the period of rapid development from conception to three years, which distorts orderly development and leads to abnormal motor control."[18] The result of such early damage is that the child begins his learning of motor skills—walking, talking, eating—with an organism that is deficient in some way. The practical consequences of this condition are in many ways far different from the consequences of impairment of control occurring after these skills have been acquired. Learning with an impaired mechanism is usually far more difficult than relearning after a previously normal mechanism has been damaged.

We have said that cerebral palsy refers to motor impairment, and several different kinds of impairment may be involved— paralysis, spasticity, incoördination, involuntary movements, tremors, rigidity. The cause is damage to the brain, and this can occur in a number of different ways—hemorrhage, poisons, infections, and various others. Clearly, then, cerebral palsy is not a disease. It is not a unitary condition resulting from a single set of circumstances. It is a group of conditions—a number of different end results of various adverse factors affecting the brain. Though these differences are important, there are marked similarities: social and educational effects on the child, limitation of physical activity, need for special kinds of treatment, and so forth. These similarities justify considering cerebral palsied children as one group.

There are several ways of classifying patients with cerebral palsy. Dr. Meyer Perlstein lists six bases of classification: (1) anatomic site of lesion, (2) clinical evaluation, (3) topographic involvement—muscle groups, portions of body, etc., (4) degree of tonicity, (5) severity of involvement, (6) etiology.[19] Patients are most often classified in terms of the clinical evaluation, which

[18] Bronson Crothers, "Clinical Aspects of Cerebral Palsy," *Quarterly Review of Pediatrics* (1951), 6:142-148.

[19] Meyer A. Perlstein and Eugene T. McDonald, "Nature, Recognition and Management of Neuromuscular Disabilities in Childhood," Round Table Discussion, *Pediatrics* (1953), 11:166-173.

refers to the sort of motor difficulty presented.[20] The number of categories used varies from one authority to another. The classification we shall use here is one of the simplest, and for our purposes it is quite adequate.

First, then, we shall mention the *spastic* group of cases. (The term "spastic" is sometimes incorrectly used to refer to all cerebral palsied children.) Although there is some variation in figures from different studies, it seems clear that this is the largest group of cerebral palsied children. These children make jerky movements of their extremities when trying to perform any voluntary act such as walking, eating, or writing. Some of their muscles become abnormally tense, and any movement involving these muscles is inaccurate, sudden, jerky, excessive, and unsteady. In some cases only one arm or one leg is affected, and the child may have comparatively little handicap. In other instances all four extremities may be spastic and the muscles of the neck and trunk may also be involved, so that in more severe cases the child is unable to walk, talk, sit up, feed himself, or perform any other act for himself. In some cases the spasticity is confined to one side of the body with one arm and the corresponding leg being affected. In other cases the legs are spastic but the arms are normal or nearly so, or the arms may be more spastic than the legs. We need not be concerned here with the technical terms for all these groups of spastics, nor with all their diagnostic criteria, but it is important to know that there are great differences among children within this spastic group.

Many spastic children have difficulty with the swallowing muscles and hence drool. Since the muscles used in swallowing are also important in speech, it is easy to see why speech is often difficult, slow, and indistinct. The lips and tongue may be affected by the spasticity and so may the breathing muscles—the chest muscles and the diaphragm.

The next largest group of cerebral palsied children is the *athetoid* group. These children are characterized by involuntary

[20] For examples of this classification see, among the many publications by Dr. Winthrop M. Phelps, "Description and Differentiation of Types of Cerebral Palsy," *Nervous Child* (1949), 8:107-127. See also John F. Pohl, *Cerebral Palsy*, St. Paul, The Bruce Publishing Co., 1950.

and uncontrollable movements. In rare cases these movements may be confined to one side of the body, but in nearly all cases all four extremities are affected; muscles of the head, neck, and trunk are also usually involved. The movements are purposeless and bizarre and often result in the distortion of any posture the child tries to assume. They are usually quite unpredictable, though some cases may tend to make chiefly writhing movements, for example, or flail-like movements. These movements are increased whenever the child tries to carry out any voluntary act. They are decreased when he is at rest and are greatly decreased or absent during sleep. As with the spastic group, muscles used in speech are usually among those affected, and the occurrence of random movements of the tongue or other structures makes speech laborious and difficult to understand. It is possible to make many subdivisions of the athetoid group, and some twelve or more types of athetosis have been described.[21] Again, for our present purposes the important thing is not terminological elaborateness but a clear recognition of the great differences among athetoid children.

The third group, the *ataxic,* is smaller than either the spastic or the athetoid. The chief symptom of the ataxic type of cerebral palsy is lack of coördination and balance. The child has difficulty walking because of his poor equilibrium and faulty coördination —he walks with legs spread far apart. The legs are usually far more involved than are the arms, but the child may have poor coördination for such activities as writing, feeding himself, and related activities. He may have incoördination—ataxia—of the tongue and speech muscles and thus may have impaired speech.

There are several other kinds of cerebral palsy, but taken together they make up only a small percentage of the total. There is, for example, the *atonic* or flaccid type of child. The involved muscles are weak, flabby, and undeveloped. As with the spastic child, one, two, three, or four extremities may be affected. The types designated as *tremor* and *rigidity* need little explanation. There may also be *mixed* cases in which spasticity and athetosis,

[21] Temple Fay, "Cerebral Palsy," *American Journal of Psychiatry* (1950), 107:180-183.

for example, or spasticity and ataxia are present in one case. These mixed cases are uncommon.[22]

A number of conditions may be listed among the causes of cerebral palsy. In some cases the condition is thought to be hereditary. In other cases the brain may fail to develop properly during embryonic life. It may be deformed, some part may be missing, or the number of nerve cells may be abnormally small. The cause of this faulty development may be an illness of the mother early in her pregnancy. German measles (rubella) is one of the illnesses of the pregnant mother most likely to produce abnormalities in the baby, and among these abnormalities may be brain defects producing cerebral palsy. Erythroblastosis fetalis, resulting from Rh incompatibility between the pregnant mother and her child, results in many cases of cerebral palsy, chiefly of the athetoid type with hearing loss.[23] Certain other conditions or illnesses in the pregnant mother may result in cerebral palsy.

Conditions occurring at the time of birth are responsible for many cases of cerebral palsy. In fact, the term "birth-injured" is sometimes used to refer to a cerebral palsied child, though it is often inappropriate and inexact. Injury in the sense of trauma—physical damage inflicted on the baby's head—is only one of the factors involved here. There may be cerebral hemorrhage from causes other than trauma. There may be inadequate oxygen supply to the infant's brain (cerebral anoxia) for any of a dozen reasons—for example, too deep anesthesia of the mother during delivery, compression of the umbilical cord during breech delivery, maternal hemorrhage just before delivery, and so forth. Various authors have emphasized the great importance of anoxia, which "plays a dual role in causing both primary encephalo-

[22] See works of Phelps and Pohl cited previously. Not all authorities agree, however, and Barnett says that spasticity and athetosis "coexist in approximately 15 to 20% of cases." See Harry E. Barnett, "Orthopedic Surgery in Cerebral Palsy," *Journal of the American Medical Association* (1952), *150:* 1396-1398. A detailed description of procedures that can be used in evaluating specified reflexes in patients with cerebral palsy is presented in K. Bobath and Berta Bobath, "Tonic Reflexes and Righting Reflexes in the Diagnosis and Assessment of Cerebral Palsy," *Cerebral Palsy Review* (1955), *16:*4-10.

[23] Perlstein, *op. cit. supra;* Lassman, *op. cit. infra.*

malacia [softening of the brain as a result of injury to the brain tissue] and secondary vascular hemorrhage."[24] In the early years of life, injury, infections, illness, and poisons are the most frequent causes of brain damage resulting in cerebral palsy. This listing of possible causes of cerebral palsy is by no means complete, but it includes most of the important causes. Certain of the causes cited tend to produce predominantly one type of problem. Thus traumatic injury to the brain or hemorrhage tends to result in spasticity. Anoxia tends to produce athetosis.[25]

The definition of cerebral palsy specifies a motor defect, but injuries to the brain such as have been listed rarely affect only the control of the muscles. Important sensory and perceptual defects may also be present. Hearing deficiencies are frequent and seem to occur more often in the athetoid group. Lassman[26] found that more than one fourth of his athetoid subjects had hearing losses of twenty decibels or more. Others have found hearing losses in spastic and other types of cerebral palsy.[27] Visual defects may frequently occur. It has been said that 40 to 50 percent of cerebral palsied patients have strabismus (cross-eyedness).[28] Nystagmus and other defects interfering with vision are also often found, especially in athetosis.[29] Dolphin and Cruickshank have found cerebral palsied children to be inferior to normals in their visual and tactual motor perception. In both

[24] Eric Denhoff, Victor N. Smirnoff, and Raymond H. Holden, "Cerebral Palsy," New England Journal of Medicine (1951), 245:728-735 and 770-777.
See also Stewart H. Clifford, "Fetal Anoxia at Birth and Cyanosis of the Newborn," American Journal of Diseases of Children (1948), 76:666-685.
[25] Perlstein, op. cit.
[26] Frank M. Lassman, "Clinical Investigation of Some Hearing Deficiences and Possible Etiological Factors in a Group of Cerebral Palsied Individuals," Speech Monographs (1951), 18:130-131.
[27] William G. Hardy, "Testing the Hearing of Cerebral Palsied Children," Proceedings of the Scientific Sessions of the American Academy for Cerebral Palsy, Chicago, Illinois, October 20-21, 1950, 17-23; Martin F. Palmer, "Speech Disorders in Cerebral Palsy," Nervous Child (1949), 8:193-202.
[28] G. P. Guibor, "Eye Defects in Cerebral Palsy," Crippled Child (October, 1950), 30, No. 3: 4-6.
[29] Guibor, op. cit.; D. G. Cogan, Neurology of the Ocular Muscles, Springfield, Illinois, Charles C. Thomas, 1947, pp. 69-73; J. H. Doggart, Diseases of Children's Eyes, St. Louis, Mosby, 1947, pp. 82-85 and 189-192.

sensory modalities, the cerebral palsied children had significantly more difficulty than did the normal controls in distinguishing the figure from the background.[30]

The injury to the brain which results in cerebral palsy may have yet other effects in addition to motor and sensory impairment. Behavior may be noticeably affected. Anoxia, which has been mentioned as a frequent cause of cerebral palsy, has often been found to produce a characteristic behavior pattern consisting of unpredictable variability in mood, hypermotility, impulsiveness, short attention span, fluctuant ability to recall previously learned material, and marked difficulty with arithmetic.[31] Some cerebral palsied children may present such an organically determined behavior pattern. In addition, the existence of motor and sensory handicaps may arouse in the child feelings of fear and guilt which may render him less able to function happily and effectively in society.[32]

In the decades immediately following the first description of cerebral palsy (by Little in 1862), it was too often assumed that all children with this condition were severely retarded mentally, and there were few efforts to provide special treatment and training for them. We now know how tragically wrong such a generalization is, but we also know that many cerebral palsied children have such severe damage to intellectual functions as to be incapable of profiting from any sort of schooling.

The sensory, perceptual, and behavior difficulties already mentioned, added to the motor and speech difficulties of the cerebral palsied child, make the estimation of intelligence extraordinarily difficult. Standardized intelligence tests may unduly penalize the cerebral palsied child and, on the other hand, there are dangers in administering tests in a nonstandard way or in making special

[30] Jane E. Dolphin and William M. Cruickshank, "The Figure-Background Relationship in Children with Cerebral Palsy," *Journal of Clinical Psychology* (1951), 7:228-231; "Tactual Motor Perception of Children with Cerebral Palsy," *Journal of Personality* (1952), 20:466-471.

[31] Geroge B. Rosenfeld and Charles Bradley, "Childhood Behavior Sequelae of Asphyxia in Infancy," *Pediatrics* (1948), 2:74-84.

[32] William M. Cruickshank, "The Relation of Physical Disability to Fear and Guilt Feelings," *Child Development* (1951), 22:291-298.

allowances.[33] Estimates of the frequency of mental retardation among cerebral palsied children are variously given as 26 percent,[34] "over 35 percent,"[35] and 50 percent.[36] Holden has contributed a review of forty-three different studies of this general subject, concluding, in part, that several of the more recent investigations "have indicated an incidence of mental deficiency of from 45 to 50 percent in cerebral palsied children, even when flexible test procedures were utilized." He stresses the need for more refined procedures and further research.[37] Differences in application of testing standards account for some of the variability in the results of these studies, and sampling errors and biased samples may also have influenced the results. But whatever figure is most nearly correct for any given group of cerebral palsied children, there can be no disagreement on the fact that the amount of mental retardation is great.

The high proportion of mental deficiency among cerebral palsied children must not make us lose sight of the fact that many cerebral palsied persons are unusually gifted. There have been many successful scholars, physicians, mathematicians, writers, and others who have succeeded despite the handicap of cerebral palsy. An annual feature of the conventions of the National So-

[33] Many authorities have discussed the special problems involved in the intelligence testing of cerebral palsied children. See, for example, Charles R. Strother, "Evaluating Intelligence of Children Handicapped by Cerebral Palsy," *Crippled Child* (1945), 23:82-83; Else Haeussermann, "Evaluating the Developmental Level of Cerebral Palsy Preschool Children," *Journal of Genetic Psychology* (1950), 80:3-23.

[34] William G. Wolfe, "Comprehensive Evaluation of Fifty Cases of Cerebral Palsy," *Journal of Speech and Hearing Disorders* (1950), 15:234-251; 26 percent of cases judged to be "uneducable."

[35] Meyer A. Perlstein and Harry E. Barnett, "Nature and Recognition of Cerebral Palsy in Infancy," *Journal of the American Medical Association* (1952), 148:1389-1397.

[36] Elsa Miller and George B. Rosenfeld, "Psychologic Evaluation of Children with Cerebral Palsy and Its Implications in Treatment," *Journal of Pediatrics* (1952), 41:613-621.

See also Bessie B. Burgemeister and Lucille H. Blum, "Intellectual Evaluation of a Group of Cerebral Palsied Children," *Nervous Child* (1949), 8:177-180.

[37] Raymond H. Holden, "A Review of Psychological Studies in Cerebral Palsy: 1947 to 1952," *American Journal of Mental Deficiency* (1952), 57:92-99.

ciety for Crippled Children and Adults is a panel of distinguished handicapped persons, which regularly includes one or more cerebral palsied individuals who have achieved outstanding success in one field or another. An accurate appraisal of the cerebral palsied group must include these brilliant intellects as well as those who are average or retarded.[38]

Many teachers have taught for years without ever having had a child with cerebral palsy in their classrooms. Yet the condition is far from being as uncommon as one might judge from the number of such children in the public schools. On the basis of the few available figures on the incidence of cerebral palsy, Phelps has estimated the total number of such cases in the country as between 150,000 and 200,000[39] The number may be much greater. Probably the most thorough study to date of incidence and prevalence of cerebral palsy was completed in Schenectady County, New York, by the New York State Department of Health in 1949-50. The number of cases located indicates an actual prevalence of 152 cases per 100,000 population, which would suggest a national total of approximately 250,000. Perlstein has presented an analysis of relevant data which indicates an incidence of 300,000 or more cerebral palsied cases in the United States today.[40]

## CEREBRAL PALSY SPEECH

Not every child with cerebral palsy has a speech problem, for the muscles involved in speech may be spared or only minimally

[38] Some of the more gifted cerebral palsied persons have written autobiographical accounts of great interest. See, for example, Earl R. Carlson, *Born That Way*, New York, John Day Co., 1941; E. S. Miers, "Gosh, I'm Glad I'm Handicapped," *Crippled Child Magazine* (1953), *31:* No. 4, 4-7; John D. McKee, *Two Legs to Stand On*, New York, Appleton-Century-Crofts, Inc., 1954.

[39] Winthrop M. Phelps, "Cerebral Palsy," in *Textbook of Pediatrics*, Sixth Ed., ed. Waldo E. Nelson, Philadelphia, W. B. Saunders Co., 1954, pp. 1211-1215.

[40] These statements are based on M. A. Perlstein, "Etiology of Cerebral Palsy," *Nervous Child* (1949), 8:128-151. Dr. Perlstein based his remarks concerning the Schenectady County, New York, study on 'New, York State Department of Health, Cerebral Palsy Program Plan, 1949-50,' a mimeographed report from Herman E. Hilleboe, M.D., Commissioner of Health, 1949."

affected. Wolfe found that 70 percent of his cases needed speech correction.[41] The other 30 percent had "substantially normal" speech.

It would be reasonable to expect that children with cerebral palsy would be somewhat slower than others in the development of speech. In discussing the causes of retarded speech development, we have already mentioned motor difficulties as one of the potent causes of retardation (Chapter VI). The child with cerebral palsy has such motor impairments, and he also often presents sensory, perceptual, intellectual, and behavioral difficulties. It would be surprising if cerebral palsied children did not develop speech more slowly than the average child. Irwin[42] has shown that cerebral palsied children present a deficiency of back vowels and of front consonants. At the age of ten years their average status with regard to back vowels was similar to that reached by the average infant at two years. The elimination of the nonstandard glottal consonants required ten years for cerebral palsied children against the norm of two and one-half years. Such measures are important in helping to describe the degree of speech retardation that has generally been observed in cerebral palsied children.

The articulation of the cerebral palsied child is usually faulty and may often be so impaired as to render the speech unintelligible. It is usually stated that the articulation errors of the spastic child tend to be consistent as contrasted with the variable and inconsistent errors of the athetoid.[43] In a recent study Powers[44] obtained results in direct contradiction to this widely accepted dictum; his athetoid subjects were significantly more consistent in their misarticulations than his spastic subjects. Further studies will doubtless clarify the matter, but regardless of which group is more consistent, both have serious articulatory

[41] Wolfe, op. cit.
[42] Orvis C. Irwin, "Phonetic Speech Development in Cerebral Palsied Children," American Journal of Physical Medicine (1955), 34:325-334.
[43] See, for instance, Evans, op. cit. infra.
[44] Max H. Powers, "A Study of the Consistency of Articulation Defects in Cases of Athetoid and Spastic Cerebral Palsy," unpublished M.A. thesis, State University of Iowa, 1953.

problems.[45] Not all the errors of either group are caused by cerebral palsy. There may be "functional" errors which are not caused by spasticity, athetosis, or ataxia. They are of the same kind as are described in Chapter III. In this conection it is interesting to note that Rutherford[46] found the *s* sound to be the one most frequently misarticulated in a group of cerebral palsied children. It is also the most frequently misarticulated sound among normal children.[47]

The voice of the cerebral palsied child may be affected in several ways. It may often be of poor quality, with breathiness, harshness, and nasality being the undesirable qualities most often encountered. It may be weak in intensity. There is often poor control of the use of pitch inflections and intensity shadings, so that the voice impresses the listener as monotonous. These voice characteristics are not found in all cerebral palsied children, nor is there a pattern characteristic of the athetoid group as opposed to the spastic.[48]

There are still other effects of cerebral palsy on speech. The rate is often slow.[49] The rhythm may be jerky. The speech is often labored and effortful. The combination of faulty articulation, monotonous and breathy voice, slow rate, and labored and jerky enunciation is sometimes referred to as "cerebral palsy speech," but Rutherford found no speech pattern that could be called characteristic of cerebral palsied children as a group.

## TREATMENT OF CEREBRAL PALSY

The treatment of cerebral palsy is a complex problem, and the coöperation of a number of persons is needed. The child's physi-

[45] See also Orvis C. Irwin, "Phonetic Equipment of Spastic and Athetoid Children," *Journal of Speech and Hearing Disorders* (1955), 20:54-57. Irwin concludes that "phonetic differences among spastics and athetoids are not statistically significant." He did not study the matter of consistency of errors.

[46] Berneice R. Rutherford, "Frequency of Articulation Substitution in Children Handicapped by Cerebral Palsy," *Journal of Speech Disorders* (1939), 4:285-287.

[47] See Chapter III.

[48] Berneice R. Rutherford, "A Comparative Study of Loudness, Pitch, Rate, Rhythm and Quality of the Speech of Children Handicapped by Cerebral Palsy," *Journal of Speech Disorders* (1944), 9:263-271.

[49] *Ibid.* See also Wolfe, *op. cit.*

cian, of course, should supervise his general health, take care of his illnesses, and make sure he is properly nourished. Cerebral palsy does not in itself make a child more susceptible to illness, but it may make his care more difficult if he becomes ill.

It is desirable that an orthopedic surgeon examine the child as soon as it is suspected that he has cerebral palsy. The orthopedist will advise as to exercise, walking, and many other matters. He will often prescribe treatment to be given by a physical therapist or exercises that can be carried out at home. In some cases braces are used. In others, operations may be advised.

Many other specialists should give advice about various aspects of the problems of a cerebral palsied child, and it is obvious that if their advice is to be of the greatest help it must be given at appropriate stages in the child's life, and there must be effective liaison and consultation among these experts. Among the specialists whose help should be sought in the early years of the child's life are the pediatrician, the neurologist, the psychiatrist, the orthopedist, the speech pathologist, and the clinical psychologist. Beginning early in life there may be need for regular prescribed treatments and training routines to be carried out by the occupational therapist, the physical therapist, and the speech correctionist. As the child arrives at school age, advice and supervision from persons trained in special education are important. Later on there may be need for vocational counseling. From time to time the child may require attention from the dentist, the ophthalmologist, the otolaryngologist, the neurosurgeon, and the audiologist. The time-consuming task of arranging for all these consultations may require the help of a medical social worker, who can also help keep the family informed as to what treatment facilities are available. Certain children may have special problems for which help must be sought from a large number of other specialists not enumerated here.

Although some cerebral palsied children get along quite well with only infrequent assistance from medical or other advisers, the majority need many kinds of help. They are multiply-handicapped persons.[50] They have the motor handicap by which their

[50] "Among all handicaps, cerebral palsy is perhaps the most complex in its origins and in the diversity of its manifestations." Arnold Gesell, "Cerebral

condition is defined and diagnosed, but they also present sensory difficulties and perceptual impairments. They have understandable difficulty in adjusting to their handicaps, in getting through school, and in finding a place in the world. Sometimes the child is emotionally unstable; sometimes he is mentally retarded. The home environments may vary widely. Facilities for treatment may be excellent or nonexistent. Some few cases require permanent institutional care, while most get along best at home with attendance at either a special school or a regular public school. In recent years there has been a great increase in the number and in the quality of facilities for treatment of cerebral palsy. This improvement is due in great measure to the work of the National Society for Crippled Children and Adults[51] and its affiliated Easter Seal organizations throughout the country; more recently the United Cerebral Palsy Association[52] and its local affiliates have offered much help.

The goal of any and all treatment of the cerebral palsied child is that of realizing to the utmost the capacities he has.[53] In many cases this will permit him to achieve ultimately far more than most unhandicapped persons. Improving the child's control of his muscles is a long slow task that may occupy many years. Many drugs have been used in the treatment of cerebral palsy, and all but a few have been abandoned. Those which are in use at the time of this writing do not provide a satisfactory way of attaining better motor control, but they may have a limited value in some stages of the physical therapy program, when combined with proper exercises and other techniques.[54] Likewise surgery

---

Palsy Research and the Preschool Years," *Postgraduate Medicine* (1954), 15:104-108.

[51] Information concerning this organization's publications, educational and consultative activities, and other services, national and local, may be obtained from the National Society for Crippled Children and Adults, Inc., 11 South LaSalle St., Chicago, Illinois.

[52] Address: 50 West 57th Street, New York 19, New York.

[53] See Juliette M. Gratke, *Help Them Help Themselves*, Dallas, Texas Society for Crippled Children and Adults, 1947; Marsee F. Evans, "Problems in Cerebral Palsy," *Journal of Speech Disorders* (1947), 12:87-103.

[54] See, for instance, Perlstein, *op. cit.*; Phelps, chapter in *Textbook of Pediatrics* referred to above; J. P. N. Tizard, "Cerebral Palsy," in *Paediatrics*, Vol. 3, pp. 98-117, ed. Wilfrid Gaisford and Reginald Lightwood, London, Butterworth, 1955.

sometimes has a limited value, but it does not at present provide any general answer to the problems of any cerebral palsied patient.[55]

## WHAT THE CLASSROOM TEACHER CAN DO

The more severely handicapped cases of cerebral palsy will not be found in the regular public school classrooms. Those who are uneducable usually have such severe muscular difficulties that they are never enrolled in school. Many of those with normal intelligence suffer from serious degrees of physical handicap which prevent regular school attendance. (One severely athetoid boy known to the author had to be educated entirely by private tutors and special schools. Finally, after years of physical therapy, he had made enough progress to enter a large state university, where he was regarded as the most brilliant and talented mathematical student in many years. He is now a research scientist.) The cerebral palsied children who are able to attend the public schools are, in general, the less severe cases. This does not mean they are not handicapped, though in the mildest cases the handicap may not be great.

If there is a speech correctionist working in the school the classroom teacher can give the kind of help already mentioned in the section on cleft palate—she can supply information about how much and how well the child is talking in the classroom, about how he gets along with his classmates, and so forth. She can also carry out direct work on the many different aspects of the child's speech problems under the supervision of the remedial speech instructor.[56]

[55] "Orthopedic surgery is largely concerned with the correction of deformities and improvement of muscle and joint mechanical action. . . . The indication for [neurosurgical procedures] is extremely rare." Phelps, *loc. cit.*, footnote 37. See also Barnett, *op. cit.*

[56] The specialized techniques which have been developed for use with cerebral palsied speech cases have been well described by several authors. See, for example, Harold Westlake, "Muscle Training for Cerebral Palsied Speech Cases," *Journal of Speech and Hearing Disorders* (1951), *16*:103-109; Berneice R. Rutherford, *Give Them a Chance to Talk*, Minneapolis, Burgess Publishing Co., 1948. The methods described by these authors, or similar techniques, will form the basis of the special speech training with which the teacher can give much assistance.

If there is no speech correctionist, the classroom teacher may be instrumental in getting the parents to seek help for the child through the state Crippled Children's Services, the state or local Society for Crippled Children and Adults (Easter Seal Society), United Cerebral Palsy, or other agencies offering expert aid to cerebral palsied children. In such a way the child can be brought into touch with a speech correctionist, who may be able to suggest specific ways in which the classroom teacher might help the child improve his speech. If no such expert supervision is to be had, then —as with the cleft palate child—the best advice one can give the classroom teacher is to exercise due prudence in not permitting sympathy and eagerness to help tempt her to try to deal directly with the child's speech.

In any case the classroom teacher should bear in mind two important points. First, the child with cerebral palsy often needs to have things made easy for him physically. In seating arrangements, assignment of classroom duties, and other such matters this fact should be taken into account. He should be permitted to do what he can without fatigue—he will rarely need to be encouraged to do so—but a certain amount of watchfulness and care is necessary. Second, relaxation is one of the child's main problems. At least some of his muscles are nearly always too tense. He will be helped if the classroom routine can be arranged in such a way as to provide him with frequent opportunities to relax. If need be, a special seat should be provided to help him be more comfortable and relaxed in the classroom.

In some instances cerebral palsied children who have been making a fairly good adjustment develop severe problems in adolescence. With their multiple handicaps in locomotion, speech, and the other areas we have mentioned, they find difficulty in developing satisfactory relationships with the opposite sex. While others are going to dances, they must stay at home because they cannot coördinate well enough to learn to dance. It is not surprising that cerebral palsied adolescents are often depressed, discouraged, resentful, and rebellious to a greater degree than most other persons in this usually stormy period of life.

## Understanding the Physically Handicapped

In considering the speech problems of children who have cleft palate or cerebral palsy, we have suggested ways in which the classroom teacher can be of help. None of the things already mentioned is nearly so vital as her intelligent and sympathetic understanding of the child's problems. The teacher may not be able to follow specific suggestions regarding speech. Circumstances may prevent her from carrying out any of the things she would like to do in the way of improving the child's voice and articulation. But no sort of classroom routine or other outside circumstances need prevent her from understanding the sort of difficulties the child is forced to cope with. If she is able to do this to any significant degree, she will do far more to help the child than if she merely paid attention to his speech imperfections. And she will win the child's undying gratitude.

In dealing with any physically handicapped person—and cleft palate and cerebral palsy are good examples of physical handicaps—many people concentrate on the difference, the physical defect. They seem blocked, unable to get beyond the obvious physical difference. They act as if they thought the individual's physical handicap explains and defines all his problems—all his fears and inadequacies and hopes and frustrations. They think of the child as a cleft palate girl or a cerebral palsied boy—or, in other instances, as a clubfooted, blind, deaf, or one-armed child.

All of us tend to fall into this error to some extent. After all, if a physical difference is striking, one cannot help noticing and remembering it. It should be mentioned, too, that physical handicaps are only one of the many stereotypes we use in thinking about others. We often tend to react to others in terms of definitions of some aspect of their behavior, appearance, or vocation. We may react to one person as an "athlete" (hence, strong), to another as a "politician" (likely to be insincere), and to others in terms of many other verbal stereotypes—red-headed (likely to be rash and quick-tempered), or rustic (unpolished, but with a lot of good common sense). Small wonder that we also react to physically handicapped persons in terms of misleading and inaccurate stereotypes.

But having seen the obvious, having noted the physical handicap, the wise and understanding person doesn't stop there; he does more than select the appropriate cliché; he doesn't concentrate on the crippling condition and ignore the rest of the person. He seeks to discover what sort of person it is who is physically handicapped. And as he becomes better acquainted with the person, he assigns the physical condition to its proper place—he neither forgets nor concentrates on the handicap.

Anyone who is thrown into close association with a physically handicapped person will eventually learn more about him than the nature and degree of his disability. How much one learns, the sort of things one learns, and the time required to learn them are good measures of one's sympathy and understanding. Even in a brief meeting, however, something more than the handicap should be impressed on one's memory. Some of us are quick to appreciate the personal qualities of others, some are much slower, and some never manage to understand others well at all. Nearly all of us, though, could improve in the manner in which we respond to those we meet, and especially to persons with handicaps.

To some extent, then, most persons tend to regard the problems of any physically handicapped person as being "organic" or "physical," and some carry this misevaluation to an extreme. We forget that the way the individual feels about his physical difference is just as important as the difference itself—often much more important. Another crucial factor is what the physically handicapped person thinks others are thinking about his difference. Many children with cleft palates, for example, make slow progress because they talk very little— because they feel that others do not like the way they talk. Improving this situation may require some work with the environment as well as with the child. The point is, however, that whether or not the child is correct in his appraisal of the feelings of others toward him, his embarrassment can effectively block improvement. Cerebral palsied children are highly responsive to the way others act toward them. They tend to be excitable, distractable, and self-conscious. It is a serious error to pay attention only to the jerky, poorly coördinated movements and forget that they become much worse when the child is apprehensive or excited. An important part of the treatment of the cerebral palsied child is the development of emotional control, so that the child does not "go to pieces" in each new situation.

The classroom teacher, then, will find that the greatest contribution she can make to the improvement of the child with a cleft palate or cerebral palsy is the creation of an atmosphere in which he can function at his best. Some children with cleft palates are not self-conscious about their speech, and if there is no such problem both the child and the teacher are fortunate. If the child is overly concerned about the reaction of others to his impaired speech, the teacher can discuss the matter with him tactfully. She should let him know that he is appreciated as an individual for any and all talents he has. She should explain that she and his classmates are not unaware of his speech problem, and are glad to be of any help they can. But she should also emphasize that he feels worse about his speech imperfections than he should, for they are not the most important thing about him. It might be well for the teacher to have a talk with the rest of the class in the absence of the child with the cleft palate, in addition to any talking she does to the child—alone or in the presence of the class (see Chapter II, pages 82-86). She should be careful to say nothing that might not be said in the child's presence, for other children may repeat it to him. She might explain to the class how each of us has his own peculiarities and differences, some large and some small, and how everyone tries to do as well as he can despite any flaws or shortcomings he may have. The imperfections of the cleft palate child are merely somewhat more noticeable than most of the differences other members of the class may have. This should not set him apart, though, or make him an object of ridicule.

Such a talk should likewise be given to a class which contains a cerebral palsied child. If the teacher, by such a talk and even more by her constant example, creates a friendly and understanding feeling in her classroom, a good deal of the tension of the cerebral palsied child may be relieved. His problem remains great, but it will not be aggravated by efforts to do more than he is able to do in adjusting to a needlessly difficult situation.

When confronted with a handicapped child, many people have an exaggerated reaction of pity. Some make the mistake of displaying such feelings—of letting the child know by word or act their feelings of pity. It is said that Alec Templeton, the famous blind British pianist, first became aware of his difference when a woman who was a complete stranger rushed up to him and cried, "You poor little blind boy!" Unfortunately one occasionally encounters such persons who obtrude their misguided and warped feelings into the lives of others. Even when there is no such mawkish display, if pity is one's predominant feeling, the child will soon sense this and the effect on him will be destructive.

For no one wants pity. Even when we are depressed and despondent, when we feel that we are having a hard time, the frank expression of pity by another is often most embarrassing. But it is easier to endure being pitied because of temporary bad luck than to go through life receiving frequent misguided pity because of a physical difference. It is tremendously difficult to maintain self-respect and a feeling of personal worth in the face of repeated expressions of pity.

Apart from mawkishness and oversentimentality, pity fails because it stops short. It is natural and entirely commendable to feel a sincere sympathy with another's misfortune. The finest expression of this feeling, however, is behavior which is likely to be helpful in relieving the misfortune. Helpful behavior does not include pitying looks, sentimental sighs, or words of regret. The ways in which one can be most helpful to a person with a physical handicap depend in large measure upon one's special talents and abilities. But no one can be truly helpful who does not make the other feel that he is wholeheartedly accepted.

Often the communication of this feeling is all one can do—and sometimes it is all that needs to be done.

Like everyone else, the physically handicapped individual wants—and needs and *deserves*—to be accepted as a person, if this cliché retains any meaning. He wants his personality to be recognized. He wants to be known for all his abilities and talents, and not just as a cripple. If he has some outstanding skill, it is relatively easy to pay proper attention to it. The high school lad who can score twenty-five points in a basketball game or whip a forward pass to just the right spot is lionized for his achievement, and his disfiguring scar, his stuttering, or his cleft palate is forgotten. But most physically handicapped persons are unable to perform athletically, and many are unable to perform in many other ways. Cerebral palsied children are probably the most thoroughly and dramatically handicapped group. Activities involving muscular skill are outside their abilities—they cannot star in games, play musical instruments with artistic skill, or become crack debaters. Usually their physical disability limits many other things they can do. It is too easy, then, to put them down as cripples—merely that and nothing more.

But the sympathetic and wise teacher sees more than just a cripple, a spastic. She knows, she feels, that here is a person, a personality that yearns for self-expression and for the understanding of others. This cerebral palsied child is an individual. He is different from anyone else who ever lived. Despite all his difficulties he can do many things. He can, and if given human and humane treatment, he will eventually be able to do many more. And so the genuine teacher seeks and finds the person behind the handicap.

What is being said here applies, of course, not only to the physically impaired or the speech handicapped, but to all children—and all adults, for that matter. It is more obviously important in the case of the cerebral palsied child, perhaps, and it may well be true that in seeking to help such a child the teacher will learn also how better to help other children—and herself.

The teacher's wholehearted acceptance and sympathetic understanding of each individual child will almost automatically insure that her classroom is a friendly, warm, comfortable place. There is a healthy, good-humored acceptance of differences of all sorts. There is praise for success and help in case of failure. Each child in the classroom feels a sense of personal security. The teacher's own sense of security is great because in such an atmosphere the children's acceptance of her is unreserved. To the extent that she approaches this ideal—and any classroom teacher can come pretty close—she can make a tremendous contribution to the lasting benefit of any and every child.

# CHAPTER VIII

~~~~~~~~~~~~~~~~~~~~~~~~~~~~~~~~~~~~~~~~~~~~~~~~~~~~~~~~~~~~~~~~~~~~~~~~~~~~~~~~~~~~~~~~~~~~~~~~~~~~~~~

# *Impaired Hearing*

Among the new pupils who enrolled for the fall semester in a large midwestern high school was a small, sallow-complexioned, dark-haired girl named Mary. She seemed to have more trouble than the average student adjusting herself to the new school. One teacher, who was very much interested in the problems of her students, observed the girl rather carefully in order to discover some cause for her apparent lack of adjustment. She noted that Mary did not seem to mingle with the rest of the students as they stood about in groups talking before class, never volunteered when a general question was asked, shook her head negatively when questions were addressed to her, and was generally listless and unresponsive. The classroom teacher began to suspect a rather severe hearing loss. But rather than jump to conclusions she decided to question another of the girl's teachers, who replied, when asked if she thought Mary might have a hearing loss, "I don't know. I just supposed she wasn't very interested. She just sits in the back of the room and says nothing."

This statement served only to corroborate the suspicions of the first teacher, who immediately referred Mary to the school nurse for a hearing test. It was found that Mary did have a hearing loss, so severe that she could hear only about half of what went on in the classroom. The nurse made a home call to inform the parents of the girl's hearing problem and suggested that she be taken immediately to an otolaryngologist (ear, nose, and throat specialist). At school the nurse referred Mary to the speech correctionist for speech and lip reading instruction. In the course of the next few months Mary made rapid improvement. Her seat was changed from the back to the front of the room in all her classes where it seemed advantageous. All her teachers and fellow students were made sympathetically aware of her hearing problem. She learned to speak so that she could be heard in the back of the classroom and, most of all, she was learning to understand others by means of lip reading and a shiny new hearing aid.

In any classroom of thirty-five or forty children there is more than an even chance that there will be a child with as much hearing loss as the youngster just cited.[1] Her observable behavior was rather typical of that of many children who are hard of hearing. Some children, however, instead of exhibiting an almost total lack of response, become belligerent, are continually accused of "picking fights" on the playground, and are seldom seen happily taking part in group activities.

The sense of hearing has two dimensions when considered clinically—quality and quantity. A loss in hearing, when thought of in its relationship to a little boy or girl, must be viewed in addition from the vantage point of its effect upon communication, its duration in the life of the individual, its acceptance both intellectually and emotionally by the child and his parents, and the availability of facilities for rehabilitation in a given community. It is the intent of this chapter to discuss the various aspects of hearing and hearing impairment as they pertain particularly to the school age child, and especially to those children who hear in a normal enough manner with or without a hearing aid to be able to attend a public school for normally hearing children.

Not long ago a mother brought her ten-year-old boy into the Hearing Clinic at the Children's Hospital in Los Angeles because

[1] R. S. Silverman in *Hearing and Deafness, A Guide for Laymen,* ed. H. Davis, New York, Murray Hill Books, Inc., 1947, p. 354.

he had an earache. After the doctor had examined his ears, his hearing was tested by the audiologist and found to be sufficiently impaired to be causing him to have some difficulty in the school-room. The mother commented that she had known of the existence of the hearing loss for some time. When asked if she had ever discussed it with his teacher, she said, "No, she has never complained about him, other than to say that he doesn't pay very good attention in class, but I didn't think that had anything to do with his having a hearing loss." The audiologist explained the probable relationship between the child's behavior and the hearing loss and obtained permission to write a letter of explanation to the teacher. Knowing why this little boy's attention may tend to wander should help the teacher to place him in her classroom so that he can better adjust to the hearing loss. And perhaps the next time the teacher finds a child in her class whose attention often wanders she will be alerted to the possibility of deficient hearing as a cause of the behavior and will refer him for a hearing test and needed counseling.

## Basic Concepts Concerning Sound

Before a hearing loss can readily be understood and appreciated it is essential to understand a few simple facts concerning the nature of sound and how the ear detects it. The reader is to be referred to Chapter IV for a review of the discussion on the subject of sound and sound production. The following brief remarks are presented in the present context in order to relate the acoustic principles explained in Chapter IV to the particular problems of hearing, or sound reception.

### THE NATURE OF SOUND

First of all, we must remind ourselves that sound is vibration.[2] It has its origin in the vibration of a sound source. For example, the vibrating strings of a violin, the vibrations of the loud-speaker of a radio, or the vibrations of the human vocal folds

[2] Hallowell Davis in *Hearing and Deafness, A Guide for Laymen*, ed. H. Davis, New York, Murray Hill Books, Inc., 1947, p. 25; S. S. Stevens and H. Davis, *Hearing*, New York, John Wiley & Sons, Inc., 1938, 1947, p. 3.

create sound. The air itself is set in motion by the sound source and the vibrations of the air are transmitted to the ear. The ear is able to hear sound because its parts are set into vibration by the vibrations of the air.

If we are to understand how the ear functions we must also remember that there are a number of ways in which sounds vary. Sounds differ from each other if their vibrations occur at different rates; that is, some sounds have higher rates of vibration than others. We say, then, that they differ in frequency. The frequencies of sound are measured in cycles per second, which means the number of complete vibrations that occur during each second. The important thing to understand is that sounds of different frequency are heard as different in *pitch*. High-pitched sounds are sounds of high frequency, and low-pitched sounds are sounds of low frequency. A high soprano voice is perceived as high-pitched, and the tones sung by it are tones of high frequency. A deep bass voice is perceived as low-pitched, and the tones that the bass singer produces are low-frequency tones. The sounds which the normal ear can hear extend over an extremely wide range of frequencies—from about 16 cycles per second, or about 4 octaves below middle C, to as much as 16,000 cycles per second.

INTENSITY

Sound is a special kind of energy—vibratory energy. There is more energy in some sounds than in others. Even sounds of exactly the same frequency may differ a great deal in the amount of energy they manifest. The term used to indicate the amount of energy in a sound is *intensity*. The intensity of sound is perceived by the ear as its *loudness*. Sounds which have a great deal of energy, such as the noise of an airplane engine, are sounds of high intensity and to the ear they seem very loud. Sounds which have very little energy, like a low whisper, are sounds of low intensity and they seem very weak as they are heard.

The unit ordinarily used as a measure of how much more intense one sound is than another is the decibel. It is not an

easy unit to define, but it may help to know that the normal ear
is capable of responding to a range of sound intensities of about
100 decibels. If sounds have too little energy the ear cannot
hear them; if they are extremely loud, they will be so intense that
they will cause the ear to tingle or they may actually produce
a feeling of pain. In the middle range of frequencies there is a
difference of about 100 decibels in loudness between sounds
which can just barely be heard and those which cause the ear to
tingle or feel pain.

MOST SOUNDS ARE COMPLEX

Most sounds, including those of speech, as we learned in
Chapter IV, are complex sounds. They contain not one but a
large number of different vibrations occurring together, all of
which vary in frequency. As has been said, frequency is the
measure of the number of times per second a vibrating particle
executes a complete cycle. The engineer further defines a complex
vibration or complexity of vibration by saying that something is
vibrating at several frequencies at the same time. In general,
the larger number of separate frequencies of vibration present
in a sound, the more complex the pattern of vibration. Some
sounds are made up mainly of vibrations of low frequency and
others are made up primarily of vibrations of high frequency.
Some vowel sounds, such as *ah* and *oo*, are mainly composed
of vibrations which are low in frequency. Other kinds of sounds,
for example *s* and *f*, are composed primarily of high-frequency
vibrations. The importance of understanding these latter kinds
of vibrations among speech sounds will become apparent during
the discussion of the way in which different kinds of hearing
losses affect a person's ability to understand and to produce
speech.

### The Anatomy of the Ear

In order to understand how we hear it will be helpful to
consider, in rather broad general terms, the three parts of the
ear and how they work.[3] The ear appears as one of the most
complicated organs in the body when studied in detail. For

[3] S. L. Polyak, G. McHugh, and D. K. Judd, *The Human Ear in Anatomical Transparencies,* New York, T. H. McKenna, Inc., 1946.

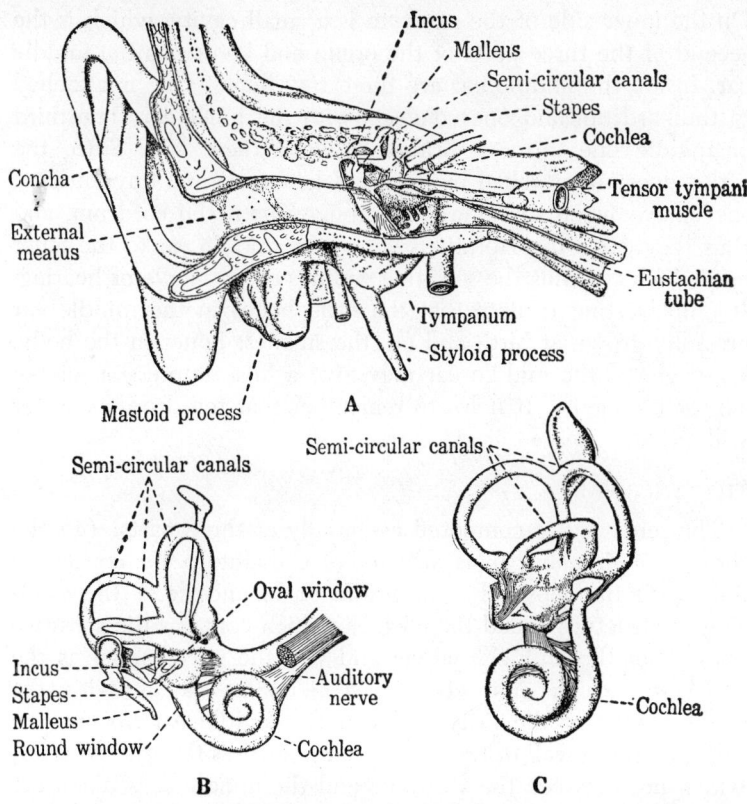

FIGURE 4. Diagram of the ear, showing the inner ear. (From Gray and Wise, *The Bases of Speech,* rev. ed., Harper & Brothers; after Sobotta.)

purposes of this discussion it will be sufficient to understand it only in its three main divisions: the external ear, the middle ear, and the inner ear which is well hidden in the temporal bone of the skull.

### THE EXTERNAL EAR AND THE MIDDLE EAR

The external ear is composed of the appendage on the side of the head that children learn to call "the ear," together with a canal lined with skin, at the inner end of which is the eardrum.

On the inner side of the eardrum is a small cavity, which is the second of the three parts of the organ and known as the middle ear. Inside the middle ear are three tiny bones. One is attached to the eardrum and one connects with the inner ear. The third or middle one forms a bridge between these two. Since the little bones are attached by means of ligaments and tiny muscles, they move when sound waves impinge upon the eardrum, and thus they carry the vibrations across the middle ear to the inner ear, which contains the sensitive endings of the nerve of hearing. It is interesting to note that the little bones in the middle ear are fully grown at birth and are the smallest bones in the body. Diagrams of the middle ear may give a false impression of the size of the cavity. It helps to remember that ten drops of water will fill it.

THE INNER EAR

The inner ear is composed essentially of three parts: (1) the three semicircular canals which are thought to be concerned only with the sense of equilibrium or balance; (2) the snail-shaped structure called the cochlea, which contains the sensitive endings of the auditory nerve; and (3) the part known as the vestibule, which connects the semicircular canals with the cochlea. One of the little bones in the middle ear fits into an opening in the wall of the middle ear known as the oval window, which lies between the vestibule and the middle ear. When the little bone is moved by sound vibrations this sets up corresponding movement of the fluid that fills the vestibule and this in turn excites the nerve endings in the cochlea and causes the sensation known as hearing.

## The Extent of Hearing Impairment

Hearing impairments vary in extent and in type. Speaking only in terms of extent, children with hearing losses might be divided into three groups:[4]

Group I.   Children whose hearing loss is very slight (as much as 20 decibles below normal intensity).

[4] W. Temple in *Foundations of Speech*, ed. J. M. O'Neil, New York, Prentice-Hall, Inc., 1945, p. 188.

Group II. Children whose losses are moderate in severity (as much as 40 decibels below normal intensity).

Group III. Children whose losses are severe (60 decibels or more below normal intensity).

The child whose hearing loss falls in the first group may easily go unnoticed in the regular classroom. He might occasionally ask to have a direction repeated but in all probability he would not do this often enough to attract the attention of the average person. It is because of children in this group particularly that routine hearing tests should be given in every public school system at regularly scheduled intervals. Medical attention aimed at the improvement and conservation of hearing is known to be more effective in early hearing loss in children than in chronic, severe cases. Early detection and diagnosis of hearing losses of children in Group I may help to prevent their joining the ranks of Groups II and III later on in their school careers.

## TYPES OF HEARING LOSS

When an abnormal condition exists in either the external or the middle ear a conductive type of hearing loss sometimes results. In this type of hearing loss there is interference with the passage of sound wave energy from the outer to the inner ear. This may be caused by wax or any hard substance obstructing the outer canal or impacted against the eardrum and restricting its movement; by swelling in the mucous membrane lining of the middle ear cavity; or by pus, scar tissue, or any bony growth which tends to hamper the movement of the little bones, keeping them from conducting sound across the middle ear in normal fashion.

A typical conductive type of loss tends to reduce the loudness of all tones or sounds by an equal amount. That is, a person with a middle ear loss of any consequence tends to hear speech as though he were in the next room with the door closed. By holding your fingers in your ears while someone talks to you, you can get a good idea of this kind of hearing loss. The audiogram shown in Figure 5 illustrates a loss of this type.

Another type of hearing loss is that caused by damage to

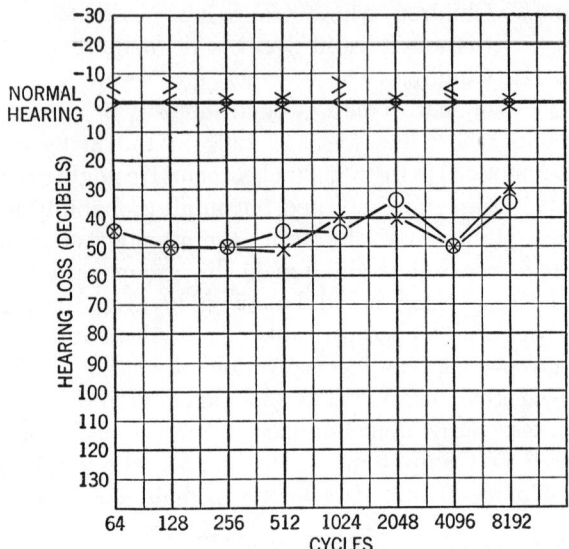

FIGURE 5. This audiogram illustrates a *conductive type of hearing loss*. The circles (0) indicate the intensity at which the child heard each tone by air conduction (A. C.) in the right ear. For example, she heard 64 cycles per second at 45 decibels below normal threshold (marked with a heavy black line). The crosses (−) indicate the intensity required for her to hear each sound in the left ear. For example, she heard 512 cycles per second at 50 decibels below threshold. Bone conduction (B. C.) is indicated by < for the right ear and by > for the left.

the nerve of hearing. This type is known as perceptive or inner ear impairment. Such a loss is sometimes congenital (existent from birth), or it may be due to disease or injury. A hearing loss of nonconductive type typically affects the high-pitched sounds more than the low. That is, a person with inner ear impairment may hear the sound of a whistle an octave higher than middle C at an intensity level no higher than that required by the normal ear, but tones higher in pitch he will hear only when intensity is increased. Some very high-pitched sounds he may not hear at all. Usually the higher the pitch the greater the intensity required for it to be heard by the ear with a nonconductive type of loss. The audiogram in Figure 6 illustrates a rather typical inner ear or nonconductive type of loss.

A third kind of hearing loss is a combination of the first two and is referred to as a mixed type. The conductive mechanism of the middle ear may have become defective through some chronic condition which also has affected the nerve of hearing. A person with this kind of hearing impairment will tend to require more intensity in order to hear the high-pitched sounds than he does to hear the low-pitched sounds.

## Hearing Tests

THE 4-C PHONOGRAPH AUDIOMETER

At the present time the most convenient way of testing objectively the hearing of children in the third grade and beyond is with the 4-C phonograph audiometer.[5] It consists of a phonograph record playback to which are attached forty earphones. The recording used is heard equally well through all the phones. The test record most frequently used is that of a man's or woman's voice repeating pairs of numbers, such as 2, 5; 4, 7; 3, 6; and so forth. At the beginning of the record the voice is easily audible. As the record proceeds the voice is reduced in loudness in controlled steps until at the end the numbers are barely audible to the normal ear. The level of the child's hearing is determined by the lowest level at which he hears the numbers accurately. This test serves very well as a rough screening test, but it does not sift out those children who hear low-pitched sounds normally but who have a hearing loss for high-pitched sounds. The results of the test tell only one thing about a child's hearing and that is at what level of intensity he is able to hear numbers. It tells nothing about whether his hearing deviates more for some pitches or tones than for others and it is important

[5] Loraine A. Dahl, *Public School Audiometry*, Danville, Illinois, The Interstate Press, 1949.

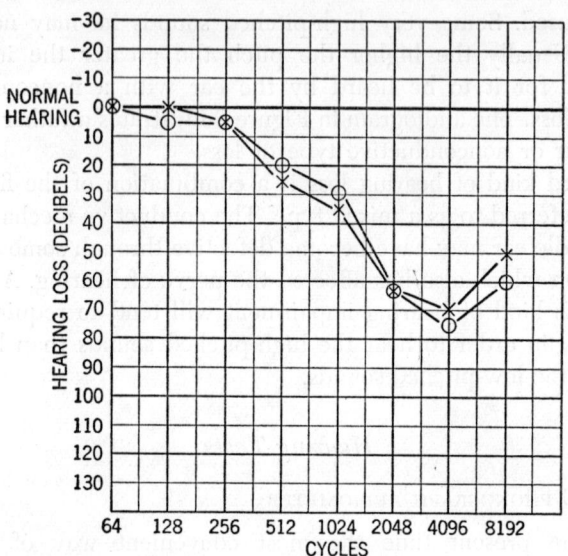

FIGURE 6.   An audiogram illustrating a *non-conductive type of hearing loss.* Bone conduction curves follow approximately those for air conduction in this audiogram.

to know this. Furthermore, the children being tested must be mature enough to be able to write the numbers they hear with a fair amount of reliability. In testing large groups of children it has been found that it is rarely possible to use the phonograph audiometer with children younger than those in the third grade, because writing is still a rather laborious taks for children younger than seven or eight years.

### THE PURE TONE AUDIOMETER

As was said previously, hearing losses differ in two respects: in extent, which is roughly discernible by the test just described, and in type. Both characteristics are testable by another kind of device known as the pure tone or discrete frequency audiometer.[6] This instrument tests only one child at a time. It is an

[6] Ira Hirsch, *The Measurement of Hearing*, New York, McGraw-Hill Book Co., 1952.

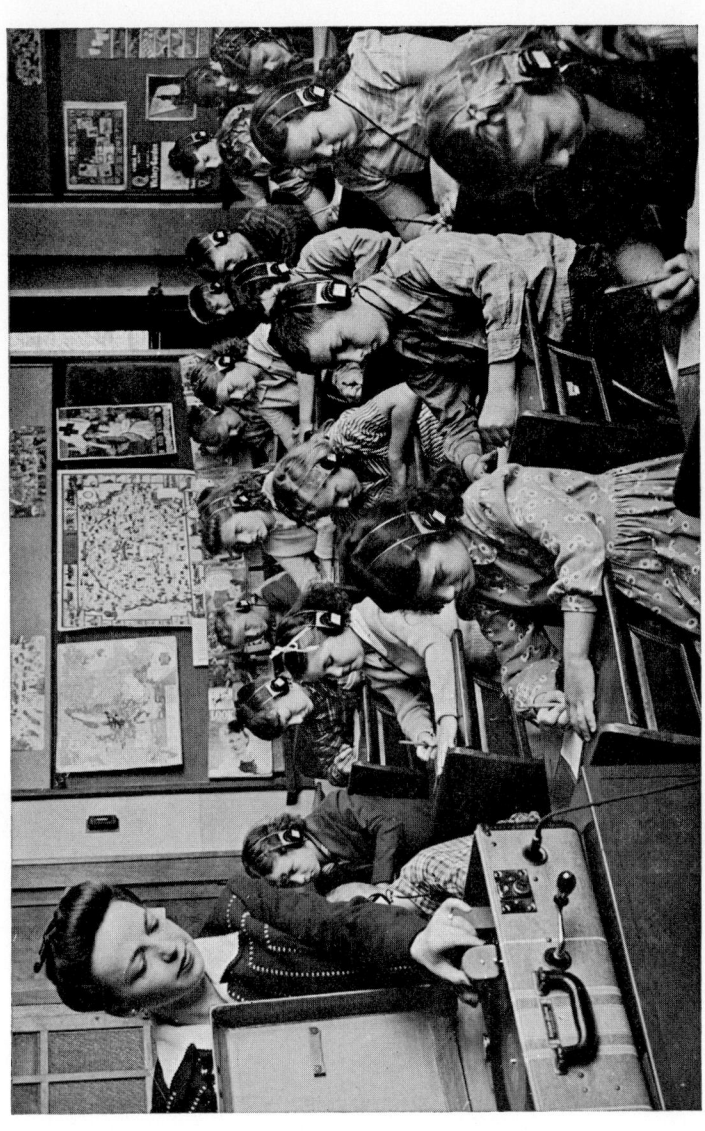

FIGURE 7. A group of elementary school children taking a hearing test with the phonograph audiometer.

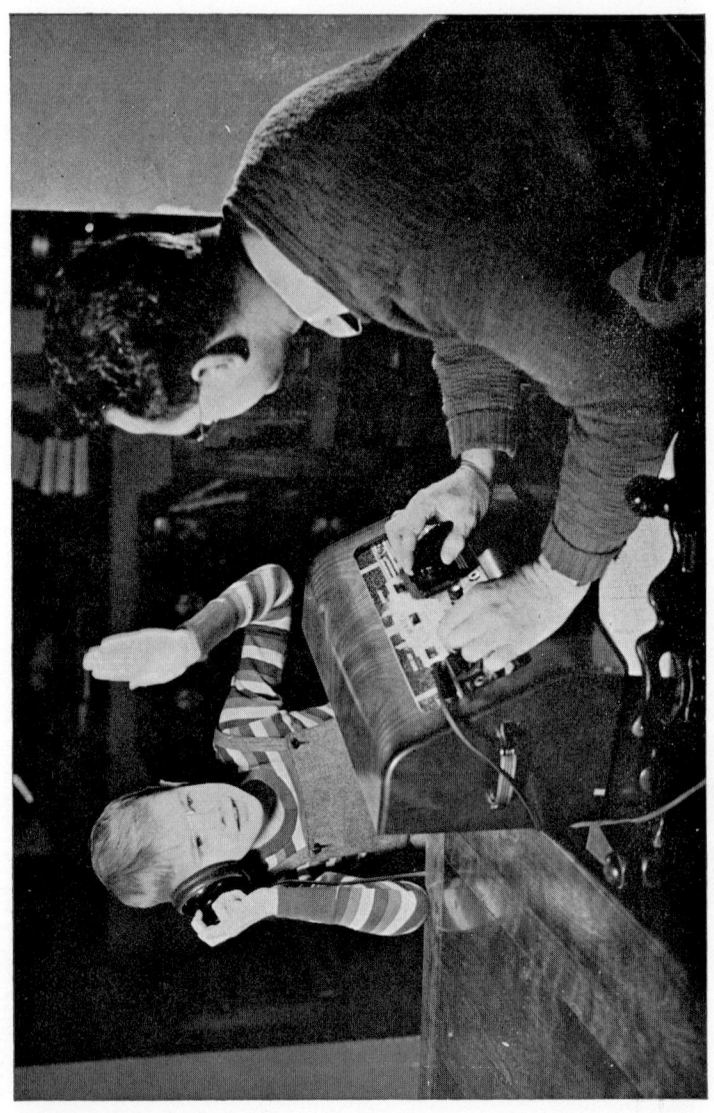

FIGURE 8. A child taking a pure tone audiometer test.

electronic mechanism which produces pure tones with controlled intensity and frequency in the hearing range. Most pure tone audiometers in common use test hearing for tones of 125, 250, 500, 1,000, 2,000, 4,000, 8,000 cycles per second. The intensity of these tones can be varied from below audibility to levels of 70 to 100 decibels above the average threshold of hearing.

This means that the loudness can be varied from a level where a sound is not audible to the average ear to a level where it is as loud as a factory whistle close to the ear. A single earphone which is worn or held by the child is attached to the audiometer, and the child signals in some fashion agreed upon by him and the person giving the test whenever he hears the sound. (See Figure 8.) His responses are recorded on a blank known as the audiogram. By comparing the test results of any child with the accepted norm it can easily be determined how much more intense each tone must be for him to hear it than for the normal ear.

It was said in the preceding section that children below the third-grade level can rarely be given a satisfactory hearing test with the group audiometer. An experienced person, however, can administer an individual pure tone test to children as young as five years of age with reasonably accurate results. The youngest children are, no doubt, the most difficult to test, but by working with them individually it is not impossible to hold their attention during the test.

## THE GROUP PURE TONE AUDIOMETER

A third type of audiometer makes it possible to combine the advantages of both the phonograph group hearing test and the pure tone individual test.[7] Forty earphones may be attached to a specially constructed pure tone audiometer. Sounds that are, respectively, 1 octave, 2 octaves, 3 octaves, and 4 octaves above middle C on the piano (512, 1,024, 2,048, and 4,096 cycles per second) are each presented in 1, 2, 3, or 4 spurts at controlled

[7] This new type of audiometric test has been developed by Dr. Scott N. Reger, Department of Otolaryngology and Oral Surgery, State University of Iowa. See: Scott N. Reger and Hayes A. Newby, "A Group Pure Tone Test," *Journal of Speech Disorders* (1947), 12:61-66.

levels of loudness. The children being tested write down on a specially prepared blank the number of times they hear each tone presented. It is possible with this mechanism to determine the extent of the loss and the tones for which the hearing is deficient. As many as forty children can be tested in about forty-five minutes. The test has been used successfully with children as young as those in the third grade.[8] To test the hearing of first and second graders with any degree of reliability it is necessary to use an individual test. No group test yet devised has been found suitable for children of this age level.

### WATCH TICK AND VOICE TESTS

In some schools where hearing testing equipment is not available it is still common practice to test hearing with a ticking watch or with spoken or whispered voice. If a child cannot hear a forced whisper across the average classroom he is said to have a loss in hearing. Neither the watch tick method nor the test using whispered or spoken voice is accurate enough to give any but the crudest estimate of hearing, because in neither case has the loudness or the pitch of the sound been measured. Such an estimate is of little value.

### OTHER TESTS OF HEARING

Frequently, articles appear in the popular literature about hearing losses and hearing tests. Mention is sometimes made of tests of speech threshold[9] and speech intelligibility[10] and a procedure which employs the use of a conditioned reflex coupled with changes in skin resistance.[11] Both tests have appropriate

[8] Hayes A. Newby, "Group Pure Tone Hearing Testing in the Public School," *Journal of Speech Disorders* (1947), 12:357-362.

[9] C. V. Hudgins, J. E. Hawkins, J. E. Karlin, and S. S. Stevens, "The Development of Recorded Auditory Tests for Measuring Hearing Loss for Speech," *The Laryngoscope* (1947), 57:57.

[10] J. P. Egan, "Articulation Testing Methods," *The Laryngoscope* (1948), 58:955.

J. Keaster, "A Quantitative Method of Measuring the Hearing of Young Children," *Journal of Speech Disorders* (1947), 12:159.

[11] W. G. Hardy and J. E. Bordley, "Special Techniques in Testing the Hearing of Children," *Journal of Speech and Hearing Disorders* (1951), 16:123.

clinical use in an audiological center. Neither can be employed in a public school testing program because of the equipment necessary and the time and skill involved in their use.

Within the next decade hearing conservation programs should be set up in all forty-eight states which will provide screening tests for all school children, individual tests where they are needed, and adequate medical and educational follow-up for any child with a hearing loss.

## Classroom Considerations

Before discussing the speech problems of children with hearing losses, it will be helpful to consider briefly the possible overall behavior characteristics exhibited in the classroom by a child with sufficient hearing loss of any type to cause him to have difficulty following classroom activities, particularly those requiring oral communication. Such a child, as he sits in school, may hear only part of what his teacher says. He may, in consequence, become disinterested in the lesson and try to find other things to do to provide diversion. The pastimes he finds may be very disturbing to the rest of the class. On the other hand, he may make a great effort to hear what is being said. He may hear only part of a question, however, and in attempting to answer it may make a ridiculous statement that is amusing to the rest of the class.

The hard of hearing child, like any other, does not like to be laughed at. In time he will cease to try to recite. Gradually he will tend to withdraw from the group. Either problem— disturbing behavior or withdrawal—develops from a feeling of insecurity, from not quite knowing what is going on around him. The teacher can do a great deal to help him by:

1. Having him sit as near as possible to where she is likely to be most of the time.

2. Allowing him to move freely about the room in order to hear what is going on. For example, if another pupil or the teacher is demonstrating a class project at a desk near the back of the room it will help the hard of hearing child to participate if he may walk quietly back to the center of activity. It is a rare child who will abuse such a privilege.

3. Being sure, when giving a direction, that the hard of hearing child is following what is being said. One effective way to check is to ask him occasionally to stand and repeat the direction to the rest of the class.

4. Finding a time to explain the problem of the hard of hearing child to other pupils. Few children will tease or taunt another child if they know why his reactions are sometimes different from those in the rest of the group. What was said in this connection in Chapter II applies fully to the child with a hearing problem.

5. Helping him to understand and to acknowledge his hearing problem. This is one of the most important aspects of any handicapped child's problem, but it is especially important for the hard of hearing. If a child learns early in life to say when meeting a stranger, "I am hard of hearing and so may not always understand what you say," he will meet people on common ground with no apologies and with nothing to hide. And in consequence he will meet new situations without tension, and so will be able to follow conversation to the limit of his ability.

6. Allowing him to recite and to read orally just like any other member of the class. Some hard of hearing children have speech problems as a result of the hearing loss. This should not be a reason for not allowing them to participate in oral recitations.

7. Seeing to it that he is included in as many extracurricular activities as possible that are participated in by his classmates. Frequently a hard of hearing child is a bystander when a group game is being played simply because he didn't hear the rules and doesn't want to ask. With a little help from the teacher he may be able to become a more active member of the group.

The foregoing suggestions are not merely special techniques for the hard of hearing; rather they are common-sense procedures practiced every day by all good teachers. But any or all of them can be of tremendous assistance in helping a child adjust to a hearing loss.

## Types of Hearing Problems

At the beginning of this chapter it was said that a hearing loss could be described in terms of two properties: first, its extent—mild, moderate, or severe; second, its type—conductive or middle ear loss, nonconductive or inner ear loss, or mixed type. In addition three other terms are sometimes used in speaking of persons with hearing loss: "hard of hearing," "deafened," and "deaf." When these are thought of in relation to the speech process their meaning and proper use become immediately clear. A hard of hearing child or adult is one who has sufficient hearing to learn to produce speech and to understand speech and language naturally by ear. The speech he has may be impaired, though not necessarily, but it serves him for purposes of oral communication. He has some hearing—the loss may range from slight to very severe, but he is not deaf. The deafened child or adult is usually spoken of as one who has learned speech and language naturally by ear but who no longer has sufficient hearing to enable him to hear his own speech or that of others. And, lastly, a deaf child or adult is one who, at the time of life when speech usually develops, did not have sufficient hearing to make its natural acquisition possible. The hard of hearing child is one who will be found most frequently in the public school and so will be discussed first.

THE HARD OF HEARING CHILD

*Middle Ear Type of Hearing Loss.* Frequently one sees children in elementary school who had normal hearing during their preschool years but who now have a mild to moderate middle ear or conductive type of hearing loss as a result of a middle ear infection.[12] This means that their acuity for all pitches is probably reduced a relatively equal amount throughout the range of tones that are important in speech, and that they hear these sounds at normal intensity through bone conduction.

[12] Robert West, Lou Kennedy, and Anna Carr, *Rehabilitation of Speech*, Rev. Ed., New York, Harper & Brothers, 1947, p. 227; J. Keaster in *Speech Problems of Children*, ed. W. Johnson, New York, Grune & Stratton, Inc., 1950, p. 246.

Bone conduction is measured by placing a vibrator, which is attached to the pure tone audiometer, against the mastoid process, the bone back of the ear. The person being tested responds just as he does when air conduction acuity is being tested. If he has a pure middle ear type of loss he will hear sounds at approximately normal intensity through the bones of the skull, which means that the nerve of hearing is in normal working order. A child with a middle ear type of loss in all probability will have normal speech, or at least if he does not, the cause is likely to be found apart from the hearing problem. Such a child was seen recently by the writer. She was seven years old and had a moderately severe middle ear type of hearing loss. She substituted *th* for *s* and *w* for *r*. She was able to produce each sound normally the first time she was asked to imitate it when it was said to her correctly. Neither sound, consequently, was thought to be misarticulated as the result of the hearing loss.

Sometimes a child with a conductive loss, especially if he tends to be a shy, retiring youngster, will talk so softly that he can scarcely be heard in an ordinary classroom. Part of the problem may be shyness and part of it may be due to the fact that he hears his own speech louder than he hears the speech of others. That is because his own voice reaches his ear with normal intensity by bone conduction, while his hearing by air conduction is impaired. His voice sounds much louder to him than it sounds to his listeners. By telling him to "talk louder" or to "speak up" the teacher will not accomplish very much. But if she will take a few minutes now and then to help him recognize the loudness level he should maintain in order for the class to hear him easily she will be doing a great deal for him. She can, in other words, help him to work out his own measuring stick.

In summary, a child with a middle ear impairment will probably have little or no speech problem as a result of his hearing loss—with the exception, perhaps, of a little difficulty in keeping his voice loud enough for his classmates to hear. As has been suggested, the teacher might help him learn to feel the loudness of his voice when it is at a good level for listening.

*Inner Ear Type of Hearing Loss.* The problem of the child with an inner ear impairment, or nonconductive type of hearing loss, is frequently misunderstood. This is partly because at times the child's responses to sound appear to be inconsistent. Sometimes he responds and sometimes he doesn't. He usually responds to his name when it is spoken in an ordinary tone of voice. When asked to do something, however, he frequently will not understand the directions, particularly if it is something that he is not in the habit of doing. His parents and even his teachers accuse him of "not paying attention" and of "hearing only when he wants to." Actually he is probably paying very close attention, but what he hears is just a jumble of sound that doesn't make sense. The jumble of sound makes the most sense to him when the situation shows clearly what is being discussed, or when he is hearing familiar words about activities or things to which he is accustomed. This child will probably have faulty speech directly due to the hearing loss, particularly if the loss has existed from birth or early infancy.

An inner ear impairment typically affects the high-pitched sounds more than the low. A child with such a loss might hear low-pitched sounds at comparatively normal intensity, but tones of higher pitch he will probably hear only when intensity is markedly increased. (See the audiogram in Figure 6.)

There are still a good many questions to be answered about how the human ear hears speech. We do know that the vowels are predominantly low-pitched sounds.[13] From that it can be assumed that a child with essentially normal hearing for low-pitched sounds will hear and be able to produce most vowels normally. His acuity for medium-pitched sounds may be somewhat reduced but he will probably hear such sounds as *m, n, ng,* and *l* with enough clarity to be able to produce them normally. But sounds like *s, sh, ch,* and *j* will probably be distorted or omitted. Such sounds as *f* and voiceless *th, v,* and voiced *th, t,* and *k,* and *d* and *g* will frequently be interchanged. Sounds that

[13] Raymond Carhart in *Hearing and Deafness, A Guide for Laymen,* New York, Murray Hill Books, Inc., 1947, p. 300.

can be imitated visually, such as *p* and *b*, are less likely to be affected than some of the others.

The voice of a child with this type of hearing loss is likely to be abnormally loud and to have a muffled kind of quality which appears to be largely the result of a retracted tongue in the production of such sounds as *t, d,* and *n.* The pitch of the voice is frequently very monotonous. The child with inner ear impairment shows reduced hearing acuity by bone conduction as well as by air conduction. He will sometimes have a tendency almost to shout, therefore, in order to hear his own voice as well as possible.

When a classroom teacher has a pupil with impaired speech and voice comparable to that just described, she should refer him as soon as possible to the person in the school system who gives hearing tests with a pure tone audiometer. The extreme importance of this point is well illustrated by a case which came to our attention only a few weeks ago. A child, age nine, was referred to us by an ear, nose, and throat specialist for an evaluation of her hearing. The father and mother were in disagreement over whether this child actually had a hearing loss. Her sibilant sounds were distorted and she substituted *t* for *k* and *d* for *g* and had a voice quality which sounded as though her mouth might be full. It was almost immediately apparent to the examiner that a hearing loss probably existed. A pure tone audiometer test was done at the outset. She was found to have normal hearing through 500 cycles; a drop to 35 decibels at 1,000 cycles. In one ear, she did not hear 2,000 cycles at all and did not hear it until it reached a volume of 90 decibels in the other ear. She did not respond at 4,000 or 8,000 cycles in either ear. This youngster was in regular public school in the fourth grade and had been making reasonably good progress. The father contended that the child was inattentive when she failed to carry out instructions which he gave her. The mother felt that there might possibly be a hearing loss. The little girl had learned to read quite adequately and was receiving speech instruction in the public school speech correction program. The speech teacher had not made a hearing test. This youngster was having difficulty in school with spelling and was beginning to have some difficulty with reading because of the increasing complexity of the vocabulary. At the present time, placement of the child in a school for hard of hearing children is being considered. The alternative to this placement would be a smaller classroom where she could have more individualized instruction than she receives in a class of forty children. She is an excellent lip reader and carries on very well when a conversation is with one or two persons. This is a clear example of a child who, because she could hear some sounds and not others, caused confusion in the minds of her parents and teachers over the possibility of the existence of a hearing problem. Whenever there is doubt, a child should always be referred to an audiologist for a thorough evaluation.

In order to prevent such instances as this from occurring, it is imperative that children whose responses to sound appear to be inconsistent, whose speech is characterized by the omission or distortion of sibilants, by the interchange of fricatives, by lack of normally nasal resonance, and by a monotonous pitch pattern or undue loudness, be given a pure tone audiometer test as soon as possible, to determine the possibility of the existence of a hearing loss. If after screening tests are completed there is the least question of the existence of hearing impairment, the child should be referred first to an otolaryngologist for an examination of his ears, nose, and throat and to an audiologist for more detailed hearing tests, including especially those that measure threshold for speech and those which measure ability to understand speech. With information thus obtained the teacher can undertake to help the child with his problem.

Most children learn to talk by imitating the speech of the older children and adults around them. Sometimes children reach the age of six or seven years with incorrect sounds in their speech, in spite of the fact that their hearing is normal. In most such cases the faulty sounds can be corrected with added ear training and aural stimulation, as described in Chapter III. Such procedures help very little, however, to correct misarticulations caused by a hearing loss. A child with an inner ear impairment produces speech according to the way he hears it. If he listens intently while the teacher produces a sound he will still hear it incorrectly and will give back approximately what he hears. Consequently he must learn to imitate an acceptable sound by the way it looks on the teacher's mouth, by the approximate tongue position which he has learned from diagrams,[14] and by the way it feels in his own mouth. For example, *f* and *v* sound very much like unvoiced *th* and voiced *th*, respectively, but these pairs of sounds look entirely different. A child can usually learn to produce the *f* sound very quickly by being shown how it looks. He may even be shown how to bite a tiny bit of his lower lip in order to produce it. To add voice for the *v* is a simple matter if the child is asked to place his fingers lightly on the teacher's thyroid cartilage (Adam's apple) as she makes the sound. The unvoiced and voiced *th* can be taught in much the same way. The *t* and the *k*, the *d* and the *g* are hidden sounds, and therefore are very much more difficult to teach. With these pairs of sounds simple diagrams similar to that in Figure 9 are often helpful in showing the relative positions the tongue must take in order to form the *t* and *k* and the *d* and *g* correctly.

Sounds that the child with an inner ear impairment frequently distorts or omits are *s*, *ch*, *sh*, and *j*. To learn to produce these sounds in spite of reduced hearing acuity for high-pitched tones sometimes takes a lot of doing. One of the things that seems to help most is for the teacher to make the sound herself against the back of the child's hand, so that he can feel the contrast between them. The difference between *sh* and *ch* can frequently be taught rather quickly in this way, as the reader will appreciate by making these two sounds close to the back of the hand. Such a technique makes use of cutaneous sensation as a partial substitute for hearing.

Thus far the discussion has been concerned with teaching the child to make the sounds. With a hard of hearing child, even more than with a hearing child, that is just a beginning. After learning to make each sound he must become accustomed to it, just as the hearing youngster does, but he must do it through feeling rather than hearing. Each sound as it is learned must be made a part of the child's speech pattern. This takes many

---

[14] See discussion of phonetic placement techniques, Chapter III.

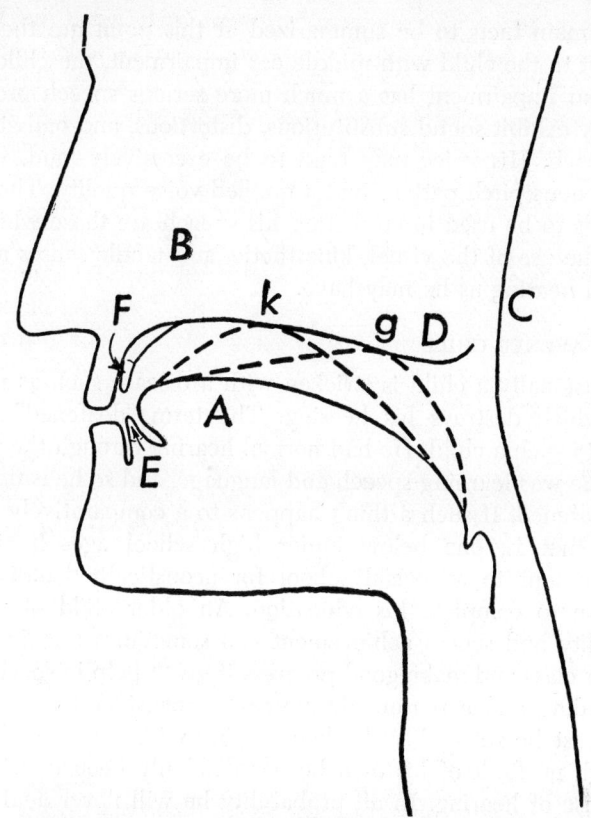

FIGURE 9.  Cross section showing tongue position for *k* and *g*.

A, tongue; *B*, nasal cavity; *C*, wall of throat; *D*, soft palate; *E*, lower front tooth; *F*, upper front tooth.

hours of patient drill. Much of the work that a child with normal hearing does is ear training, learning to recognize the sound when he hears it. After such training he is constantly stimulated by the speech that he hears around him. The hard of hearing child receives little if any such stimulation because of the very nature of his problem. It is necessary, therefore, that he be given a greater than ordinary amount of drill in order to "fix" the sound.

The main facts to be summarized at this point are these: In contrast to the child with middle ear impairment, the child with inner ear impairment has a much more serious speech problem. He may exhibit sound substitutions, distortions, and omissions in his speech. His voice may tend to be excessively loud, with a monotonous pitch pattern and a muffled voice quality. The chief methods to be used in correcting his speech are those which require the use of the visual, kinesthetic, and tactile senses as aids to such hearing as he may have.

### THE DEAFENED CHILD

Occasionally a child is stricken with a disease such as meningitis which destroys his hearing. The term "deafened" would apply to such a child. He had normal hearing through the period when he was learning speech and language, and so he is not deaf but deafened. If such a thing happens to a comparatively young child—that is, one below junior high school age—he is frequently sent to a special school for acoustically handicapped children to complete his education. An older child of normal mentality and school achievement can sometimes remain in his regular class and make good progress if given help in speech and lip reading and a reasonable amount of consideration.

It must be remembered when dealing with such a child that through no fault of his own he has suddenly been deprived of his sense of hearing. In all probability he will never again hear a bird sing or his friend whistle outside the window. He will never hear human speech again. It is difficult to imagine oneself in such a situation even for a day or for an hour—and remember, his will be a lifetime of silence. His adjustment at best will be difficult. The teacher who attempts to help a child who has suddenly lost his hearing will need to have, above all else, an infinite amount of patience and understanding. In order to help him as much as possible, it will be essential to talk with his parents to see how they are accepting the problem. Sometimes, in trying to be kind, a parent will tell a child that the handicap is only temporary, that his hearing will return. If the nerve of hearing has been destroyed or seriously damaged, as is frequently the case when hearing is affected by meningitis, the impairment is *permanent*. It is easier in the long run if a child learns to accept that fact from the beginning.

Recently the writer has seen a number of children who have recovered from tuberculous meningitis but who have, as a residual, a severe or total loss in hearing. Such a child was little Jo. She was four at the time of her illness. The hearing loss, when first discovered, was about 35 decibels in the speech range but became total within about a six-months period. She had better than average speech and language for her age and tested in the superior range on intelligence tests administered after her recovery. When it was discovered that she was losing her hearing, her parents were helped to work with her on their daily visits to the hospital. On her release, she came in for daily work in the Hearing and Speech Clinic, where she had training to preserve her speech and training in lip reading. In addition, she was taught to read as an added means of preserving her language. The father and mother worked very closely with the clinic personnel and learned to deal with this difficult problem in communication in a most effective fashion. This child, because of her normally learned speech and language, was very superior in that respect to a deaf child of comparable age. It was therefore not appropriate that she be placed in a school for deaf children where the first two or three years of their school career are devoted to learning speech and language. She was therefore placed in a regular first grade, more or less on an experimental basis, when she was six years old. Now, three years later, she is completing the fourth grade in that same school for normally hearing children and making excellent progress. This child, from the very beginning, fought the possibility that her hearing would not return. The father and mother accepted the situation readily from an intellectual standpoint and gradually learned to accept it emotionally. The youngster went through a period of very antisocial behavior, which was her way of expressing resentment over her loss in hearing. She still has periods of serious frustration but under the circumstances has made an excellent recovery. To say that it has been accomplished without extreme difficulty, however, would be to underestimate the problem which the family and the school personnel have encountered in helping this very bright child with a sudden, total loss in hearing.

*"Speech Insurance."* It was said previously that a deafened child or adult is one who lost his hearing after he had acquired normal speech and language. With this fact in mind, the need for speech training in such a case may not be immediately evident. We all know that in order to acquire normal speech it is necessary to have hearing. We do not always consider, however, that in order to maintain normal speech it is also necessary to have fairly acute hearing. This does not mean that immediately after a child loses his hearing he will lose his speech—not at all. But it does mean that in order to maintain reasonably intelligible and well-modulated speech over a period of time he will need to learn to "monitor" it by the way it looks and feels rather than by the way it sounds. During World War II many servicemen suffered sudden losses in hearing. The speech training offered to them in Army and Navy rehabilitation programs was sometimes referred to as "speech insurance," a term very descriptive of the kind of help that it was. In a manner of speaking, it did insure that the men taking such training would maintain reasonably intelligible and well-modulated speech in spite of the fact that they could no longer monitor it satisfactorily through auditory means. Speech insurance is a difficult sort of thing to teach and calls for the services of a trained speech correctionist.

When a speech correctionist is not available, however, the classroom teacher can give the deafened child some practical assistance in the following ways:

1. It is very difficult for a child who has suddenly lost his hearing to know whether he is speaking loudly enough for the class to hear. The classroom teacher can help him a great deal by suggesting that he yell with all his might in order to get the feel of an excessively loud voice. After yelling it is to be suggested that he speak very, very softly in order to feel the contrast between the very loud and the very soft voice. Lastly, he should speak at what to him seems to be a fairly normal loudness level between these two extremes. In order to achieve this final

adjustment, he may need some special help from the teacher. If the foregoing procedure is repeated often enough over a sufficiently long period for the feel of various loudness levels to become familiar, the teacher will have helped the deafened child materially in keeping the volume of his voice under control.

2. By somewhat the same sort of procedure, the deafened child can be taught to control the pitch of his voice. Sometimes the voice of the child with a severe hearing impairment will suddenly soar to a pitch so high that it is extremely unpleasant. If, when this happens, the teacher makes note of it, she can in an after-school session help the child to feel excessively high and low pitch levels in much the same way as she taught him to feel loudness levels. Either procedure takes time and painstaking effort but is well worth it when considered from the standpoint of accomplishment.

3. Speech sounds deteriorate rather slowly following loss of hearing, but the deterioration is sure to happen, nevertheless. Many of the so-called sibilant sounds—*s, ch,* and *j*—especially in the final position, seem to become distorted or to be omitted before some of the other sounds. If the teacher will mark one sound throughout a short, familiar passage, calling the child's attention to the feel of it as he reads, some of the sounds which otherwise may be lost from his speech can perhaps be retained.

Many times a teacher must be a supersalesman to convince the deafened child of his need for speech insurance training. At the outset he can see no reason to suppose that his speech won't remain just as it is, and changes that others may be acutely aware of he probably will not hear. Sometimes it takes a good many hours of patient explanation to show him that if he begins immediately, before any change has taken place, his total speech problem will tend to be much less difficult.

THE DEAF CHILD

When a speech correctionist or a teacher of the deaf speaks of a deaf child, she means a child who did not have sufficient hearing at the time when speech normally develops to be able to learn to speak through auditory means.[15] The child may have been born with a total or very severe hearing impairment, or he may have lost his hearing during early infancy. In either case the loss was so profound that he was not able to learn speech through imitating what he heard, and so reached school age without the ability either to articulate or to understand speech. Infrequently a kindergarten or preprimary teacher may have a pupil with such a problem in her classroom. As far as the speech problem per se is concerned, she cannot do much about it because it is a full-time job for a highly trained teacher over a period of a good many years, but in some other ways she can be of tremendous help to the child. In the first place, she can help the parents to understand why the little boy or girl must have special education. The hearing child of fifteen to eighteen months begins to name the objects in his environment, to imitate expressions that he hears other children and adults around him use, and gradually accumulates a vocabulary of some 2,000 words by the time he reaches school age.[16] The deaf child, on the other hand, frequently enters school with no speech at all. Ewing and Ewing point out:

The average deaf child who enters a school for the deaf at the age of five has no vocabulary at all unless he possesses considerable residual capacity to hear or at one time heard speech normally or unless his parents have been helped to understand his needs and through home training have encouraged him to lip read. Even when a deaf child begins to lip read he cannot use all the vocabulary that through lip reading he understands. At best, he only attempts to say approximately a few or comparatively few of the words that he can see on the lips. A child with some hearing may learn to talk a little that way but a severely deaf child cannot do it without much more help than his parents, who are not teachers, can give him. Speech does not serve as an adequate means of communication unless it is spontaneous. It can-

[15] I. R. Ewing and A. W. G. Ewing, *Speech and the Deaf Child,* Washington, D.C., The Volta Bureau, 1954.

Helmer Myklebust, *Auditory Disorders in Children,* New York, Grune & Stratton, Inc., 1954, p. 103.

[16] M. E. Smith, "An Investigation of the Development of the Sentence and the Extent of Vocabulary in Young Children," *University of Iowa Studies in Child Welfare* (1926), Vol. 3.

not be fluent unless words come readily to the lips and it cannot be truly rhythmic unless the speaker expresses his thoughts in connected phrases and sentences. A deaf child's fundamental need therefore is for language and his teachers long-term policy is primarily concerned with its place and growth in his thinking and usage.

During the first two or even three years that he spends in a special school for deaf children, most of his time is spent in acquiring skill in the use of language, and in learning to understand speech visually by means of lip reading. The deaf child in a school for normally hearing children has little or no opportunity for such training. And it is obvious that without language skill of even a rudimentary nature he is just about helpless in a school situation. Frequently parents accept verbally the child's hearing problem but emotionally they are not able to accept it. They convince themselves that the child will be homesick if sent away to school, even that he will not be properly cared for. Actually, they can't bring themselves to part with him. Their next move is to bring him to the kindergarten teacher in the neighborhood school. She, they feel sure, is a kind person who will see their problem and allow their little deaf child to sit in her classroom and get what he can out of what goes on.

Not very long ago the case of a twenty-eight-year-old woman was brought to our attention. When this woman was a little girl her father and mother convinced the teacher of a rural school that he was being kind if he allowed her to sit out her school career in a classroom for hearing children. At twenty-eight she could not speak well enough to be understood nor could she understand the speech of others. Neither did she have a manual means of communication that was understood outside her immediate family. She was able to read and write on little more than a primary level. But the saddest part of all was the fact that tests showed she had normal intelligence and had had, as a small child, potentialities for becoming a functioning member of society if only she had been given the opportunities afforded by proper special education. As it was, she was forced to live out her life as a drudge. The schoolteacher no doubt thought he was being kind.

Had he attempted to help the parents to realize that they were really being selfish in their desire to keep their deaf child at home, he would have done a much greater kindness.[17]

Sometimes parents fail to send a child to a special school because they do not realize that such opportunities for handicapped children exist. Teachers and school administrators can be of great help to these parents by keeping informed of the opportunities offered by the states and communities they serve. Information concerning resident schools for deaf children can be obtained through the Volta Bureau, 1537 35th Street, N. W., Washington 7, D.C. Every state in the union makes some provision for deaf children, either through its own special school or by paying tuition fees to a neighboring state. Increasing numbers of town and city school districts are making provision for the special handling of deaf and severely hard of hearing children within their own schools. In some instances classes for children with impaired hearing are formed within a regular school for normally hearing children. Here the hearing handicapped child receives the special help he needs and at the same time has the social stimulation of normally hearing children. In some large cities there are sufficient numbers of deaf children to make possible the establishment of separate special schools where the entire program is especially designed for the acoustically handicapped. Public School 47 in New York City and the Mary E. Bennet School in Los Angeles are examples of such schools. There are also numerous private and denominational schools in various parts of the country.

Actually the problem here is not with the child himself but with his parents. It is a wise and thoughtful teacher who will take the time and show the patience to help them understand how they can best educate their deaf child. If the teacher passively allows the youngster just to sit in her classroom she is doing him irreparable harm.

[17] The teacher who finds herself confronted by parents similar to those described here might possibly find it helpful to have them read this paragraph. It is assumed that she would be judicious and tactful about it, of course.

## Lip Reading (Speech Reading)

The hard of hearing or deafened child may have no difficulty in producing normal speech, but he may have a great deal of difficulty in understanding the speech of others. He needs to learn to fill in the gaps through lip reading, which has been defined as "the art of understanding a speaker's thought by watching the movements of his lips, his face, and of his entire body."

In many school systems the itinerant speech correction teacher also teaches lip reading. In other schools there are special teachers of lip reading. But the actual practice that the hard of hearing child gets in learning to follow speech with the aid of lip reading is gained in the regular classroom. The teacher can provide an atmosphere conducive to such practice by:

1. Giving instructions, telling stories, and making suggestions or comments so that she is within the hard of hearing child's line of vision. If she addresses him when his back is turned she will put him at a great disadvantage. The importance of this point can be made clear if the next time the teacher is faced with the problem of trying to understand a person with an unfamiliar dialect, she cuts out the visual impression of what he says by closing her eyes or turning her back. She will find that the already difficult speech becomes even less intelligible. She will be putting herself in somewhat the position in which the hard of hearing child finds himself when she speaks to him without facing him properly.

2. Speaking clearly but naturally. It is assumed that any good teacher takes pride in having clear, intelligible speech that can be understood by any child in any part of the classroom. That kind of speech will make lip reading easier for the hard of hearing child. The teacher's speech must not be exaggerated or markedly slow in rate. Like any other child, the hard of hearing youngster can understand best when he is spoken to in an easy, relaxed way.

3. Speaking so that the light is shining on her face rather than in the eyes of the child who is attempting to lip read.

4. Repeating an instruction in the same words only once. If the

child doesn't understand the second time, the teacher should rephrase the instruction in different words. A different set of words frequently helps a child to understand. And more than that, if he does understand he has been helped to succeed, and that is very important. If the teacher in this instance were to go on to the next child with, "Oh, Bob, you do it, John doesn't understand," she would defeat John in such a way that the next time she asked him to do something not only his hearing loss but his sense of failure, too, would keep him from lip reading to the best of his ability.

5. Speaking expressively by means of appropriate vocal inflections, gestures, bodily movements, and so forth. Speech that is highly expressive, as interpreted by pupils with normal hearing, is also correspondingly easy for the hard of hearing child to understand through lip reading and such hearing acuity as he possesses.

### LIP READING TECHNIQUES

Frequently no lip reading teacher is available in small town and rural schools. But there are children in need of such instruction in villages and rural areas just as there are in larger cities with more adequate facilities. It is important, then, to make the most of the idea that simple lip reading instruction can sometimes be provided by the classroom teacher. Lip reading is based on the fact that speech is learned and understood through hearing it, watching it, feeling it, and relating it to the whole situation in which it occurs. As long as hearing is unimpaired the average person is scarcely aware of the visual and kinesthetic (feeling) senses in relation to speech. But when hearing acuity is reduced the visual and kinesthetic impressions come into greater prominence. Lip reading instruction attempts to point up the visual impression of speech as a partial compensation for the hearing loss. There is one method of teaching lip reading which places a great deal of emphasis on the feel of speech (the kinesthetic response) as well.[18] In this discussion, however, emphasis

[18] See Anna Bunger, *Speech Reading: Jena Method*, Danville, Illinois, Interstate Publishing Co., 1945.

will be placed on the use of the visual impression only. This approach is particularly fundamental and it is more practical for the use of the classroom teacher.

Spoken language is made up of a rapid succession of overlapping syllables that are in turn composed of some forty-odd sounds of varying degrees of visibility. The hard of hearing child who is attempting to follow speech with the help of lip reading must be able to recognize instantly all the visible movements and fill in, primarily through context, those that are invisible. Only about 30 percent of the sounds of English are visible; all the other sounds are hidden in the mouth or look like one or two other cognate sounds. For example *p, b,* and *m* sound different one from the other but they look exactly alike. Ideas must be grasped in a fleeting instant; speech is never static. It is a constantly moving change of syllables. No two mouths are alike and no two individual speech patterns are identical. But even with these limitations taken into consideration, some instruction and practice in lip reading can be extremely helpful. To gain practice in lip reading it is necessary that the visual stimuli be isolated and pointed up, at least for a time. That is, in the first stages of instruction auditory stimuli should be eliminated. In order to accomplish this, several lip reading practice techniques have been developed which make use of silent moving pictures. Since such materials are almost never available to the average teacher, she must make use of the next best thing, which is, in our opinion, voiceless speech. A teacher can train herself to speak in a natural way without voice by practicing in front of a mirror until her speech has a normal feel as well as a normal look. Some authorities advocate the use of voice soft enough to be below the level of the hearing of the children with whom the teacher is working. This can be a satisfactory approach if the teacher is willing to try out different levels of loudness in each lip reading practice period. This is necessary because in some cases hearing acuity tends to fluctuate, the noise level of even the same room will vary from time to time, and the children may not always be at the same distance from the teacher.

The second very important consideration as far as the teacher's speech is concerned is that she should always speak with what is, for her, a normal amount of lip movement and at a normal rate of utterance. The hard of hearing child, when he leaves this classroom, will be called upon to read the speech of the grocer, the baker, and the bookseller as well as other teachers and his friends and classmates. If he learns in his lip reading practice periods to read speech which is not exaggerated or abnormally slow in rate he will be able to read with much greater ease the speech of the people with whom he comes in daily contact.

The lip reading process will be something completely foreign to most children when they first begin.[19] Consequently it is usually a good idea to start with very familiar material, such as:

1. *Colloquial expressions:* Hello! How are you? What time is it? Is it cold? etc.

2. *Nursery rhymes:* "Jack and Jill," "Peter, Peter, Pumpkin Eater," "Sing a Song of Sixpence," "Little Miss Muffet," "Little Jack Horner," etc.

3. *Familiar categories:* the days of the week; the months of the year; the alphabet, numbers by ones, twos, fives, tens, etc.

Frequently a child will be very much surprised when he realizes, for the first time, that he has understood something that was said, even though he didn't hear it. After the child—or children, if the teacher is working with a group—gains some facility in reading lips using familiar material, new vocabularies for proctice may be grouped in a variety of ways. For example, the first such lesson might be built around animals. In order to add interest, pictures of a cat, dog, horse, cow, elephant, lion, tiger, or other animal, might be used. Ten or twelve pictures are enough to start with. The lesson might follow some such procedure as this:

1. Arrange the group of pictures on the table.

2. Point to each picture, say the word (without voice), and have the child repeat it.

[19] *New Aids and Materials for Teaching Lip Reading,* Washington, D.C., American Hearing Society, 1943; Rose Feilbach, *Stories and Games for Easy Lip Reading Practice,* Washington, D.C., The Volta Bureau.

3. Repeat each word again, this time without oral repetition by the child.

4. Skip around, saying the names of the pictures in random order, having the child identify them. Avoid too much repetition of this step. Speech seldom occurs in single words, but rather in phrases and sentences.

5. Put the names of the animals in such carrier sentences as:
   a. Point to the ...........
   b. Give me the ..........
   c. Where is the ........

6. Devise an interesting sentence for each word pictured. Say it and have the child tell you what was said.

7. Remove the clue words (or pictures) and present a second group of sentences.

8. Tell a short story about one of the animals in the day's lesson. Have the child tell the story or repeat the gist of it.

An informal lip reading lesson comparable to the one just described should take from twenty minutes to half an hour; for a child it should seldom be any longer—his eyes get tired and his attention wanders. He is not only hard of hearing, which makes for a certain amount of strain in trying to understand speech, but he is also still a child, with a comparatively short attention span. The animal lesson is meant to be merely suggestive. Other categories, such as fruits, vegetables, birds, or flowers might be used just as well. The steps in the procedure given in the animal lesson are by no means hard and fast. But some kind of progression from the simple familiar picture to the more complex use of the word in sentences and stories is to be desired. With older children in junior and senior high school the vocabulary can be presented in written rather than picture form.

Another type of lesson that is easily developed is built around a common everyday experience such as a bus trip, the purchase of stamps at the post office, buying groceries, or an expedition to the zoo or art museum. Following is such a lesson built around the post office:

1. Where is the post office?
2. It is across the street from the City Hall.

3. It is a block south of here on the same street.
4. What time does the post office open?
5. It opens at eight o'clock.
6. What time does the post office close?
7. It closes at six o'clock.
8. Did you want some stamps?
9. I'd like six threes, five twos, and four ones.
10. Will this letter go faster by air mail?
11. How much is an air-mail stamp?
12. I'd like to send this letter air mail, special delivery.
13. That will cost twenty-six cents.
14. Will it go out this afternoon?
15. Yes, it will go out at three-thirty.

The situation type of lesson like the above can be handled in a number of ways. One approach might include taking the children to the post office or the grocery store. Upon returning, the teacher and the children might write the lesson coöperatively, including as much of the specific vocabulary common to that experience as possible. The teacher then might read the sentences, one at a time, and ask the children to repeat what she says; or she might ask them questions about the place they have visited and have them give appropriate answers. The lesson could be presented without the first part, but it does add interest.

A slightly more difficult type of lesson might make use of a short story, preferably one that employs a good deal of repetition in the telling. Examples are James Thurber's "Many Many Moons" and the old tale about Epaminondas. Material of this kind must be condensed and cut to the point where it does not require an excessive amount of time in the telling. Sometimes children become a little fearful about their ability to follow a full story when the teacher uses one for the first time. In order to dispel any such feelings a simple outline is sometimes put on the blackboard to show the sequence of events. When the individual or group seems to be having trouble following, it is sometimes a good idea to divide a story into sections. The teacher should tell the first section, then ask questions bringing out the main points, and so on with each part of the story. Then it is a good idea to go back and retell the whole thing from the beginning. One must be careful not to choose a story that is too long, especially at first.

At the beginning of the discussion on lip reading it was suggested that voiceless speech be used in beginning practice periods with a hard of hearing child in order to emphasize or point up the visual stimuli. When the child has progressed to a point where he is able to read voiceless speech with some degree of ease he should be given practice in reading speech that he can partially hear as well as see. This last step is very important because in life situations he will usually have the help of hearing when he attempts to follow conversation.

In city school systems, a number of studies have been done which serve to point up, rather dramatically in some instances, the tremendous help to be found for hard of hearing children in well organized classes for speech reading instruction. In some cases failures have been cut as much as 50 percent. With the advent of smaller and more efficient hearing aids, there has been a trend toward eliminating speech reading in some school systems as being no longer as necessary as it was before the availability of the transistor. Such a trend should be discouraged. It is true that many children receive little, if any, help from the use of a hearing aid. Such a case would be the child with an abrupt, high tone loss. Other children with severe hearing problems, such as a fifteen-year-old boy seen by the writer a month or two ago, are benefited by a hearing aid but still have difficulty in communication. The youngster in question had a loss that had been progressive for several years. When we saw him his speech threshold was about 85 decibels. With a hearing aid his threshold was brought up to approximately 45 decibels. With such a loss he could benefit from lip reading instruction to supplement the help he received from the hearing aid. And there are always those children with borderline losses, that is, those of 20 to 25 decibels, who with the help of lip reading instruction can get along in a normal classroom without difficulty but who, without some special help, will be among those who fail repeatedly because they do not understand the classroom instructions.

## Hearing Aids in the Classroom

Sometimes hard of hearing children are fitted with hearing aids in order that they may continue their school work in the regular classroom rather than being placed in a special school for acoustically handicapped children. The alert classroom teacher will want to know how she can help a child get the most out of such a device.

Hearing aids vary in the degree to which they help different individuals, depending on the extent and type of hearing loss, plus a good many personal factors which seem sometimes to be as varied as the persons wearing hearing aids. At best, a hearing aid is a compensatory device. It is not a substitute for normal hearing and, speaking realistically, there are inconveniences involved which must be considered: batteries have a way of wearing out at inopportune times; cords wear through where they attach to the ear piece or the amplifier case; and the instrument must be taken off if a child wants to join in group games on the playground. But if the child and his teacher learn to anticipate such problems and to accept them, a hearing aid, appropriately placed, can be a great help rather than a nuisance to be tolerated.

Frequently when a hearing aid is suggested as part of a plan for the rehabilitation of a child with a hearing problem, the parents mention concern over curiosity about the hearing aid on the part of other children in the class.[20] Ordinarily this can be handled by the teacher's asking the hard of hearing child to explain the instrument to the children in the room, show it to them, describe how it works, and state briefly why he is going to wear it. Then it might be well if each member of the class is given an opportunity to put it on and try it for himself. Children have little reason to be curious about something they know about, and, in this day of fringe benefits, it might be pointed out that the hard of hearing child himself tends to gain a more thorough acceptance of the instrument by talking freely about it with his classmates.

[20] Eleanor C. Ronnei and Joan Porter, *Tim and His Hearing Aid,* New York, Dodd Mead & Co., 1951.

When a youngster is first fitted with a hearing aid he should not wear it during a full school day. He needs to accustom himself gradually to the earpiece and to the added volume of sound. If he wears the aid a half-hour in the morning and a half-hour in the afternoon daily during the first week, that will probably be long enough. Gradually the time may be increased until the aid is worn during a full school day.

Hard of hearing people often report that the average person, when meeting someone wearing a hearing aid, instinctively raises his voice in order to help him hear. The vocal result of this splendid but misguided impulse to be helpful is sometimes so loud that it is painful to the hard of hearing person. The classroom teacher can prevent this sort of thing from happening, at least in her own classroom, by explaining to her pupils that when John wears his hearing aid it raises their voices for him and this means that they are to speak to John just as they would to anyone else, plus this addition: it is helpful if they try to speak to John when he is facing them, not when his back is turned.

Not every hard of hearing child can benefit from amplification. It is extremely important, therefore, that before parents are urged to provide an instrument for a child they be referred to an oto-audiological center where the situation can be thoroughly evaluated. At such a center his hearing for speech will be tested first without an instrument and then with one. Various types will be tried to determine which aid, if any, gives the child the help that he needs.

It will be the rare child who can put on a hearing aid and enjoy it from the beginning without a period of adjustment. Whether that period is long or short will be dependent on many factors. Probably the first and most important consideration is the attitude of the child and his parents when he first puts on the instrument. His age is another factor, of course, and the duration and extent of the hearing loss are also to be considered. If his is a conductive problem without an inner ear involvement, learning to wear the hearing aid is a matter of becoming accustomed to the instrument itself and the added loudness that it provides. But if the impairment is a nonconductive one the child, in order to benefit most from amplification, should have some training in learning to listen or in what is frequently called "auditory training."[21] During a period of time each day he should be given systematic exercises in learning to distinguish differences among gross sounds, then meaningful sounds of nature, and so on through a series of training experiences until he is listening to conversational speech with a background of noise. Auditory training is usually presented by a teacher who has been specially trained in speech and hearing, but much help can be given by the classroom teacher who realizes that a child with a new hearing aid is likely to need a period of adjustment before his aid can be of maximum benefit to him, and who is therefore patient in her dealings with him.

A hearing aid is probably never an unmixed blessing but when appropriately selected, and when the child is properly trained to use it, it can mean, among many other things, the difference between a child's remaining in the regular classroom or being enrolled in a special class for acoustically handicapped children.

## *Conclusion*

The writer of this chapter has been a public school speech correctionist. As a result of that experience it is her firm belief that most classroom teachers are ready and willing to help any child with an unusual problem if they know how to do it. In this chapter we have first introduced some of the broad concepts concerning the nature of hearing by (1) describing some of the properties of sound, (2) discussing the anatomy of the ear, and (3) describing the degrees and types of hearing loss. After giving the teacher something of a frame of reference in these first three sections, we have gone on to (4) outline general classroom procedures for children with hearing problems, (5) discuss the speech problems that result from impaired hearing and techniques for their correction, and (6) to describe compensatory measures such as lip reading and hearing aids which may be helpful to acoustically handicapped children.

[21] Eleanor C. Ronnei, *Learning to Look and Listen*, New York, Bureau of Publications, Teachers College, Columbia University, 1951.

What the classroom teacher can do for children with impaired hearing aids up to so very much that she may at times wonder how she can possibly accomplish it all and still manage to get her other work done. There would appear to be three main answers to this: First of all, if she can find the necessary time, the teacher will discover that the techniques described in this chapter are as simple as most of the other teaching methods she is using day in and day out with no thought of their "complexity." The second answer is particularly important: much of what is to be done for a child with a hearing handicap takes no time at all. It requires a kind of attitude—and enough information of the sort presented in this chapter to enable the teacher to make the attitude work effectively in her moment-to-moment handling of classroom activities. It is to be appreciated, of course, that everything said in Chapter II applies in the present context with full force.

The third answer leaves more to the teacher's own devices, imagination, and general philosophy of living. It has two parts. One is that occasionally a principal or superintendent will do something about the teaching load that will make it possible for the teacher to work more fully and effectively with the speech correctionist or lip reading instructor, or to use more of her time to do more herself for pupils in her classroom who have hearing problems. The other part is best expressed in the form of an old saying: "Where there's a will there's a way."

# CHAPTER IX

〜〜〜〜〜〜〜〜〜〜〜〜〜〜〜〜〜〜〜〜〜〜〜〜〜〜〜〜〜〜〜〜〜〜〜〜〜〜〜〜〜〜〜〜〜〜

# The Public School Remedial Speech Program

Now comes the relatively pleasant task of explaining how remedial services for children with speech difficulties fit into the public school system and are carried on in this particular type of situation. Although the public school is used as a point of departure, the procedures to be suggested can be adapted easily to the private or parochial school arrangement. They are also usable in hospital, private, university, or service league clinics.

During the past fifteen or twenty years state departments of education, school administrators, parents, classroom teachers, and others have come to recognize that very large numbers of children are affected by speech difficulties. Fortunately for children who have such problems, most states and many schools either have introduced or are contemplating remedial programs. Programs now in operation differ somewhat in organization. Therefore, for the benefit of school administrators who are planning to institute or further develop programs of this kind and for the benefit of speech correctionists and classroom teachers who will work together in elementary and secondary schools, we shall look at representative types of programs in the pages to follow.

As the field of remedial speech instruction has developed, we

406

have learned, along with many other things, that the specialist cannot do the job alone. There are too many children who have speech handicaps. Sufficient numbers of special teachers cannot be trained fast enough. Remedial instruction, in many cases, is a time-consuming process that cannot be hurried or conducted under pressure. In addition, many forces play upon the child which not only are causally related to the speech problem but also obstruct improvement unless they are changed or modified. Consequently, the speech correctionist must go far beyond a direct attack on the speech condition itself and attempt to bring about changes in the behavior of those who make up the child's environment as well as changes in the related behavior of the child himself. Therefore, all of us must accept responsibility for the reëducation of the child, and it is here, in the pages to follow, that we can ascertain our respective responsibilities and get acquainted with one another—superintendents, principals, and supervisors; classroom teachers, speech correctionists, and other special teachers; parents, counselors, and group leaders; teachers in colleges, agency directors, audiologists, psychologists, social workers, physicians, and philanthropists.

As research goes on apace, as creative minds contribute new ideas, techniques, and procedures, as the thinking in one field is incorporated into another, as new knowledge is tested and put to work in the classroom and the clinic, any given field of instruction revises its concepts, changes its procedures, broadens its horizons. This is and has been true of the field of speech correction. And these revisions and expansions, whether they are in a stage of theory and testing or a stage of proved value, indicate alterations that must be made in programs of public school speech correction. To cover the field and its current developments in limited space demands virtually a handbook type of presentation. Illustration and example have been reduced to a bare minimum. Pages of material have of necessity been condensed into paragraphs and even sentences. In spite of these limiting factors, however, we hope that we have here a practical guide for those many individuals who work in the schools, in coöperation with the schools, and outside the schools for the welfare of children who might otherwise go through life reluctantly, haltingly, personally impoverished because of a speech handicap.

It is to be given special emphasis that throughout this chapter we are mindful of those children who are included in the speech correction program by virtue of impaired hearing, as well as speech handicapped children who have normal hearing. Many children with impaired hearing have speech problems that are related to their hearing deficiencies. Some have speech disturbances that are not associated importantly, if at all, with the loss of hearing. Even those who have no speech disorders are given attention, in many school programs, by the speech correctionist, who has the responsibility of administering hearing tests to all children and of referring those who are found to have impaired hearing to appropriate medical and psychological services, and of recommending needed special seating and other attention in furtherance of their educational adjustment. In some schools audiologists are employed to test hearing and serve pupils found to have hearing losses. In other schools hearing tests are administered by the school nurse, or by itinerant hearing survey teams employed by the State Department of Public Instruction. Any speech correctionist, however, should be prepared to do routine audiometric testing and to serve the remedial speech, lip reading, and auditory training needs of pupils who are hard of hearing.

In order to avoid a complex organization of material we shall speak directly to the speech correctionist and, in large degree, talk in terms of what he does as a special teacher. What is spoken in his direction, however, is aimed at the ears of many others, particularly classroom teachers and school administrators, as well as parents, with the hope that all will work together as a team for the benefit of the children who desperately need their help.

## The Public School System

Although there is some variation in the administrative organization of public school systems from city to city and state to state, it is possible to describe a generally representative situation. Usually the control of any local school system is vested in a "school board," a small group of citizens elected or appointed to this important responsibility. The school board employs a "superintendent" as the top administrative officer of the school system. The superintendent, in consultation with the school board, employs a "principal" for each of the elementary schools, junior high schools, and senior high schools. Also, the superintendent, in consultation with the school board and the principal, employs classroom teachers and other personnel. The line of authority and responsibility runs, then, from teacher to principal to superintendent to school board. In large city or county school systems the superintendent frequently attaches to his office certain assistants and supervisors. Usually, these assistant superintendents or supervisors are placed in charge, throughout the school system, of certain rather specialized types of instruction such as music or athletics or speech. In a large system one is likely to find an assistant superintendent in charge of "special services" and under him supervisors of programs in health, hearing conservation, remedial reading, speech correction, etc. These are called special services because they are concerned with children who deviate, in one direction or another, from the "average" or "normal" child and whose instruction requires training that is difficult for the classroom teacher to encompass in her preparation, along with the many other things that she must know, and for which it would usually be hard for her to find sufficient time. Frequently, then, the speech correctionist is directly responsible to a supervisor, and he, in turn, to an assistant superintendent, and he, in turn, to the superintendent. This places the itinerant speech correctionist, when working in any one school, in a position in which he has dual responsibility, both to the principal of that school and to his supervisor.

State departments of public instruction play varying roles in special education. One function of all state departments, of course, is the certification of teachers. To be certified to teach in public schools, the speech correctionist, like any other teacher, must take certain specified college courses in education in addition to courses in speech correction. Certification requirements vary somewhat from state to state and also change somewhat from time to time.[1] The only authoritative source of information about certification in any particular state is the department of public instruction of that state.

Some state departments subsidize and supervise programs of special education in the schools. In Florida, under the Minimum Foundation School Program, any county may apply for one or more units (teachers) in special education; minimum salaries for these units are paid by the state. The various counties may supplement these salaries out of local funds. The program is administered through a Division of Special Education. Somewhat similar plans are in operation in Illinois and Minnesota, as well as many other states. In Iowa the Division of Special Education of the State Department of Public Instruction provides among other things for supervisors, each of whom covers one or more counties, and who survey all pupils in their counties for children with speech difficulties and then supervise the necessary remedial work. Hearing testing is done on a state-wide basis by an itinerant team.

Any individual who desires to know more about the care and education of handicapped children in his state should start his inquiries with the department of public instruction. From this source he will be able to find out what is being done in public schools. No doubt he will also be referred to other state agencies or commissions that work with children. The Florida Children's Commission, for example, in coöperation with the Nemour's Foundation, publishes a directory of all voluntary and public agencies in the state that provide services for handicapped children. The Florida Crippled Children's Commission conducts clinics throughout the state for children suffering from cerebral palsy. On the team that conducts these clinics is a speech correctionist, a pediatrician, a clinical psychologist, an orthopedic

[1] A survey of the requirements for state certification of speech correctionists is presented by Ruth Becky Irwin in "State Certification in Speech and Hearing Therapy," *The Speech Teacher* (March, 1953), 2:124-128.

See also Romaine P. Mackie and Lloyd M. Dunn, *State Certification Requirements for Teachers of Exceptional Children,* Washington, D.C.: Office of Education, U.S. Department of Health, Education, and Welfare, Bulletin 1954, No. 1.

surgeon, and a physical therapist. In other states similar services and agencies are to be found and public school speech correctionists will find it advantageous to be familiar with their programs and policies.

## Types of Programs

The evolving patterns of service for speech handicapped children vary considerably from community to community and from state to state. In spite of a lack of uniformity, however, it is possible to point to certain representative types of programs. Any pattern that has developed in any community is likely to be a combination or adaptation of the six which we shall consider.

### SCHOOLS FOR EXCEPTIONAL CHILDREN

Speech correction is provided in nearly all schools for exceptional children. These specially equipped and staffed schools have been developed as part of regular public school systems in many of our larger cities and more densely populated counties. In these special schools are placed those children who would have great difficulty in following the typical school routine or who might not profit from the usual educational procedures. Among such children are those with severe impairments of hearing or sight, orthopedic handicaps, retardation, cerebral palsy, aphasia, and epilepsy. These schools are distinguished by striking adaptation of instruction to individual differences, by attention to the development of the whole child, by patient, kindly, and understanding teachers, by intense work with the individual child and with small groups of children, by instruction along lines that are most beneficial for specific children, by almost phenomenal accomplishment in many instances with pupils who would not obtain adequate individual attention in the typical overcrowded classroom.

### ITINERANT SPEECH CORRECTIONIST

In many instances remedial speech instruction is provided by an itinerant speech correctionist. Usually the "home" office of such a special teacher is located in the school for exceptional children, in a central administration building, or in a centrally located elementary school. The itinerant speech correction teacher works in from two to four schools, spending two or more half-days in each school each week. The number of schools and the time spent in each is, of course, determined by the number of pupils with speech problems in each school, the nature of the problems, and other factors such as community pressures.

The itinerant teacher faces a few difficulties. One is the matter of transportation. Usually it is convenient for him to own a car; ordinarily, where distances are considerable, he is compensated for the use of it. In one county in Florida a speech correctionist reaches one of her schools by means of a small boat equipped with an outboard motor. Another difficulty is the portage of equipment—the usual "bag of tricks," audiometer, and tape recorder. Other small difficulties center around weather hazards, the handling of class rolls, record keeping, contacting teachers and parents, and becoming a member of the teaching group in each school.

### SINGLE SCHOOL SPEECH CORRECTIONIST

In some cases the speech correctionist is assigned to a single school. This procedure allows him to concentrate his efforts, build a solid program in which he can keep in contact with children as they move from grade to grade, achieve maximum results, and check more readily upon the permanence of the effects of his effort. Also it automatically removes some of the difficulties faced by the itinerant teacher. Any school that approaches a student populaton of 850 will provide more than enough work for a full-time speech correctionist.

### COMBINED SPEECH CORRECTION AND SPEECH IMPROVEMENT

Some administrators and supervisors like to make use of teachers who not only can handle remedial speech instruction but also can direct classroom activity aimed at speech improvement. They attempt to concentrate the efforts of these teachers in single schools. These administrators reason that it is difficult to determine where the need for correction ends and the need for improvement begins. Also they worry about the need of every pupil to improve in the many skills that enter into oral communication. Consequently these teachers are provided time in which they can work with individuals and small groups in corrective effort as well as time, in a typical curricular arrangement, whereby they can teach other fundamentals of speech, such as skill in control of attitude and emotion, skill in reflective and logical thinking, skill in the use of oral language, and skill in organization of thought. Sometimes these teachers also handle enriching activities like the production of school plays. Sometimes, particularly in the elementary school, they visit each class or room in the school two or more times per week to give speech improvement lessons.

CLASSROOM TEACHER PROGRAM

The types of programs explained above are handled by trained specialists who meet the requirements for basic or even advanced certification by the American Speech and Hearing Association. The type of program we will consider at this point is that conducted by the classroom teacher as a supplement to the work of the speech correctionist or, in some instances, as the only remedial speech help available to the child.

Fortunately, many classroom teachers have felt the need to know something about speech handicaps and, in the process of professional preparation for teaching, have taken one or more courses dealing with speech disorders. In some states, teachers are required to take courses in speech correction before they can become certified. Some training institutions expect student teachers to take courses of this kind. In any case, these teachers are able to recognize and evaluate many speech difficulties and to talk effectively to parents about them. They know to whom parents can take their speech handicapped children for special help. They are able to talk with school officials about the need for aid with speech problems. They know, in at least a limited way, what can be done to correct the various kinds of speech disorders. They are able to remedy the less difficult errors of articulation and to make conditions tolerable for those who stutter or for those who have other severe speech deviations, even though they cannot take on the burden of a full speech correction program.

These teachers give a certain amount of speech correction during the course of regular classroom work. Ordinarily they use one or a combination of three procedures which can be adapted to any variation in curricular organization or to any variety of instructional approach. The first is the daily speech period plan. Under this plan, a period is set aside daily for concentration upon the skills of speech. During this period the teacher carries on a highly varied type of speech instruction; she not only attempts to correct speech deviations but also attempts to provide all students with an opportunity to concentrate upon and improve general speech habits. Ways of conducting this speech period will be considered when we turn to an explanation of the methodology of speech correction. The second procedure used by the classroom teacher is called the adaptive instruction plan. Under this plan, remedial lessons are dovetailed with study periods and activity periods in which other children can handle themselves with a minimum of leadership from the teacher. A short corrective lesson with one or a few children can take place while the others are engaged in various projects. In no case, however, should the speech handicapped child feel penalized by this procedure. If he does, it would be better to forget the speech lesson. The third procedure used by the classroom teacher is called the free time plan. Under this plan the teacher takes advantage of breaks in the day's schedule to conduct remedial lessons. Arrangements are made between teachers to free one from the supervision of pupils during recess in order to conduct speech lessons. Advantage is taken of free periods, library periods, individual aid periods, and activity periods to provide speech correction. Some teachers will not mind taking fifteen minutes or so after dismissal to help a student. Here again we want to emphasize that the child must not feel penalized by missing a recess period, being taken from an interesting group activity, or remaining a few minutes after others have gone for the day. Better, again we say, to forget the speech lesson.

The enterprising teacher will find within her daily schedule many opportunities to conduct brief individual and group remedial lessons. These lessons should occur regularly and continuously. They should be carefully planned and highly motivated. They should be closely integrated with and supplemented by other classroom work.

SPECIAL PROGRAMS FOR RURAL AREAS

Either the itinerant speech correctionist type of program or the classroom teacher type, or both, are usable in sparsely settled rural areas in which there are one-room or very small consolidated schools. However, other types of service programs have developed in some of these regions. The mobile speech and hearing clinic is one. The speech correctionists or, as they are sometimes called, speech and hearing consultants (usually a team of two), travel in a panel truck, pulling a house trailer equipped with living accommodations and testing equipment. Arrangements are made with the county superintendents of schools to test children at certain chosen centers. All schools within a distance of perhaps ten to twelve miles around a particular center send their pupils for examination. To aid those children who show speech and hearing handicaps, parents and teachers are provided with reports, longterm recommendations, and suggestions of immediate practical value.[2]

The state-wide demonstration program is another type of speech correction service provided for rural areas. Diagnostic clinics and remedial classes are held weekly, or at other stated intervals, in strategically located cities, each accessible from over a wide expanse of territory. Teachers and parents accompany the children to these clinics and classes. They receive instruction and carry on the remedial program at home and in the school as best they can. In some programs summer residence centers are established in which the children can receive from two to eight weeks of intensive instruction.[3]

---

[2] An interesting program of this kind in North Dakota is described in an anonymous article, "Mobile Speech and Hearing Clinic in North Dakota," *Hearing News*, August, 1949.

[3] A program of this kind in Vermont has been described by Harriet M. Dunn in "A Speech and Hearing Program for Children in a Rural Area," *Journal of Speech and Hearing Disorders* (June, 1949), *14*:166-170.

## The Team

The moving forces that play upon a child and affect the quantity and quality of his speech production are many and diverse. Among these forces are, first, those that operate within the child as of now. It is the child who must do the learning. If he is not ready, if he is not motivated, if he has certain perceptions, evaluations, needs, or standards that tend to interfere with his reëducation, very little can be done for him or with him until these are eliminated or altered.

Second, there are those forces or factors that are the product of relationships between the pupil and the speech correctionist. From the positive side, the correctionist becomes a friendly, attractive, permissive individual who works quietly and objectively in analyzing, planning, releasing, guiding, counseling, motivating. From the negative side, he strives to overcome personal attitudes that show up in authoritarianism, rigidity, tenseness, precipitous reaction, and overgeneralized evaluation.

Third, there are those forces that are the product of the interaction of the pupil with his environment. There is usually a direct connection between the quantity and quality of the child's speech production and his relationships with other individuals. Conversely, these relationships can be changed and modified by speech. In other words, environment has a strong impact upon speech, and speech a strong impact upon environment. Consequently, in many cases speech reëducation is successful only if relevant changes can be induced in the child's environment, or if the important reactions of the child to his environment can be modified. The speech correction teacher attempts to bring about these changes in three ways: first, by leading the child to understand how he can change the reactions of others (environment) by means of his own speech; second, by consultation with those who are significant in the child's environment and whose behavior must be modified—classroom teachers, parents, classmates, relatives, and others; and third, by allowing release of the child's conflicts and frustrations in the hope that he will grow to understand them and take a more objective approach to situations that cause them.

Fourth among the important moving forces are those that stem from certain bodily conditions and processes. Adequate attention has been given in other parts of this book to bodily defects that bear a direct causal relationship, organically or psychologically, to disorders of speech or hearing. These defects, in many cases, must be remedied before speech reëducation can take place. This is accomplished, depending upon the nature of the condition, through orthodontia, prosthesis, surgery, or perhaps the fitting of hearing aids.

Fifth, there are those all-important forces or factors that give the child a feeling of confidence, success, security, independence. These are many and varied. Among them may be listed command of bodily functions, ability to do and to enjoy certain activities (particularly those that are manual), and clear-cut educational and vocational goals. Consequently, there is sometimes a need for psychological counseling, physical therapy, occupational therapy, educational guidance, group participation, vocational guidance-rehabilitation, and, let us not forget, inspiring, easy, appreciative friendships.

All this adds up to the fact that no one individual can do the job alone. Speech reëducation requires the effort of a team, and teamwork. And here, then, we have our team—the child, the speech correctionist, the parents, classroom teachers, social welfare workers, doctors, dentists, nurses, psychologists, physical therapists, occupational therapists, group leaders, vocational and educational counselors—not to mention those many other people who are sufficiently interested in handicapped children to develop and administer programs for the training of teachers, seek legislation, coördinate activities, disseminate information, obtain contributions, and provide money and facilities for essential services. Naturally the team will differ from instance to instance in both size and composition. In one instance the team will be composed only of the child and the speech correctionist. In another instance the team may well be built of all or most of the kinds of individuals we have mentioned.

## THE CHILD

Much has been said in preceding chapters about the child, just as much has been said about classroom teachers, parents, and speech correctionists. Here, therefore, our emphasis will be upon the child as perhaps the most important member of the team that is working for his welfare.

Change of any kind in an individual must come from within that individual. He must be ready for that change, and must want either it or something that will come as a result of it before the change can take place. The principles of readiness and motivation operate here. This is another way of saying that the child must be ready and willing to go along with the speech correctionist before there can be much hope of guiding him into the goal region of improved speech production. The child is not an organism upon which the team operates, but a human being with whom the other members of the team work in partnership. The child is himself a participating member of the team rather than an object to be nagged, bulldozed, coaxed, or pressured in a certain direction.

The principle of readiness insists that when an individual is ready to act in a certain way, to do so is satisfying to him. If he is not ready to act, to do so is annoying and he is likely to resist acting at all. Consequently, any learning activity should be based to the greatest practical extent upon the present needs and interests of the pupil. The more the speech correction teacher knows about his pupils, the better job he is likely to do. We recommend, therefore, concentrated and discerning study of child behavior and development, particularly at those various age levels that mark transitions to new needs and interests. Textbook study should be supplemented by observation and by closely supervised teaching experiences.

Ordinarily, when we speak of motivation we have one of two concepts in mind: either (1) a concept that centers upon the question of why organisms behave as they do; or (2) a concept that centers upon the "circumstances which result in the energizing, selecting, or directing of conduct." Although the two concepts cannot be separated, teachers are primarily concerned with the second as they think of the child as a member of the reëducational team. In order to set up circumstances that will result in the desired conduct, we either make use of extrinsic incentives which get the child to do the desired task irrespective of its inherent satisfaction, or we make use of intrinsic motivation which comes from knowledge or conviction on the part of the child that the task will lead to some desired end. We will have more to say about this under the "conditions of practice."

The child is constantly striving to satisfy bodily needs as well as needs for security, belongingness, status, and independence. When he is able to satisfy these needs in a relatively direct manner, the child develops what we tend to call a well-adjusted personality. When some obstacle interferes with the direct satisfaction of these needs, the child perceives himself and his environment falsely and travels devious paths toward the satisfaction of those needs. He is then said to be maladjusted. Observe, for example, how children bolster their feelings of personal worth. One may do so by striking another. Another may do so by asserting his independence. Still another child may do so by helping others, by participating, by coöperating. Observe the child who acts defensively or aggressively or unconventionally because of social pressures, or lack of recognition, or feelings of inferiority, or false evaluations of himself or his environment. Observe the child who evaluates himself as helpless or superior or worthless because he perceives that individuals in his environment so perceive him. Observe the withdrawing and frustrated child who wants desperately to belong, yet for one reason or another fears that any attempt on his part to enter into activity with his classmates will meet with rejection. Observe, further, how the child reacts toward people or situations which he fears: he runs away from the situation, fights it, or moves toward it. In other words, if the child perceives his environment as threatening to him, he will withdraw or react aggressively or become ingratiating.

In cases of unacceptable behavior the speech correctionist helps the child find more satisfactory ways of meeting his needs and thereby adjusting himself to his environment. At that point, the unacceptable behavior will tend to disappear. In cases of false evaluations of self or environment, the remedial speech teacher provides experiences that will allow the child to revise his perceptions. In cases of fear, the speech correctionist plumbs deep to ascertain the sources of it, encourages the child to talk about it and get it out in the open, attempts to reduce anxiety by demonstrating that situations are not likely to bring on the feared consequences, leads the child into social activity and into doing the thing that he is afraid to do, supports him as long as is necessary but not too long, and sees that he experiences success in his interpersonal relationships.

Connected with all this is the principle of effect. A child will tend to repeat those responses which are accompanied or followed by a satisfying effect. If it is much safer and more satisfying not to talk than to talk, the child will withdraw and avoid oral communication. If refusal to coöperate with his teacher is applauded by his classmates and satisfies the child's desire for status, he will persist in his refusal. On the other hand, if the group refuses to condone such behavior it will not persist; if the group applauds an attempt to coöperate, that kind of activity will tend to be strengthened and will continue.

### THE SPEECH CORRECTIONIST

The speech correctionist, upon first contact with the child, becomes a part of his environment, one of those forces that help to shape and influence his behavior and personality. Each session with the child from the time of his examination to the completion of his reëducation involves an interpersonal relationship that has significance for the child—and the remedial speech teacher. Consequently we have much to say about the speech correction teacher, and to him, throughout this book—much that we hope will be of help to him and to the child. There are a few things, however, that we want to emphasize at this point.

One thing that the speech correctionist must have, and a thing that no textbook can develop, is a deep, warm, and sincere liking for children. The warmth generated by this liking will reach out and encompass the child and bring results that no amount of technique or method could accomplish alone.

Furthermore, the speech correctionist must have a liking for handicapped children. Many of the children with whom he works will not be able adequately to take care of their own personal needs. If he dislikes helping children whose limbs are supported with steel braces or if he dislikes wiping saliva from the chin of a youngster with cerebral palsy, perhaps he should look in another direction for a vocation.

Again, the speech correctionist must like each child as a person even though, at times, he does not like his behavior. One way to avoid entangling the child with his behavior is to delay one's reaction to it, avoid hasty judgments, describe the youngster's behavior to oneself and to others in operational terms, and seek out possible causal factors. Rather than quickly evaluating Johnny as a "naughty" boy, the speech correctionist is likely to tell himself that today Johnny prodded Sammy with a ruler and that probably he was seeking attention. His reaction to Johnny will be determined by the nature of his evaluation of Johnny's behavior.

The speech correctionist should carry on his activities with an optimal degree of tension. The thoroughly relaxed individual will accomplish nothing; activity of any kind requires a certain degree of tension. The overly tense individual, however, is nervous, irritable, quick to take offense, liable to hair-trigger reaction, rigid in patterns of speech and behavior. The speech correction teacher should not be excessively excitable, but rather collected, patient, tolerant, willing to suspend judgment and to consider the many sides to a question. Qualities of this sort can be developed and practiced. If the speech correctionist feels that he has a problem in that direction he might deliberately adopt an easy, thoughtful, slow, quiet pace for a time. As a result, many of his difficulties may be lessened or even disappear.

Of utmost importance to the child is an atmosphere of security and belongingness. The kind of remedial speech teacher of whom we have spoken above will immediately and with little effort establish this kind of atmosphere. He will be permissive but will hold to carefully reasoned limitations and will be consistent in the application of these limitations from situation to situation. He will praise and reward with discrimination. He will manipulate the group in such a way that each child in it feels himself to be an integral part of it.

With individuals or groups, the speech correctionist will exercise leadership primarily through democratic participation. The work of White and Lippitt with ten-year-old boys indicates that, under democratic participatory leadership, work motivation, originality, group-mindedness, and friendliness were greater than under two other forms of leadership. Laissez faire leadership resulted in less work and poorer work. Autocratic leadership resulted in slightly more work over a short period of time but it created discontent, hostility, and aggression.[4]

The speech correctionist should be able to see things through the eyes of the child. How does he perceive himself? How does he perceive his environment and adjust to it? How does he attempt to satisfy his need for status, security, independence? What is his level of aspiration and how concrete is it? How does he bolster his feelings of personal worth? What impact do these perceptions, drives, and aspirations have upon the child's personality and consequently upon his speech?

These things, then, in addition to knowledge of speech handicaps and remedial techniques, as such, make a good speech correction teacher: a liking for children and particularly handicapped children, ability to delay reaction while evaluating the child's behavior and its possible causes, ability to function with an optimal degree of tension in a permissive and democratically handled teaching situation, and ability to see things through the eyes of the child.

### THE CLASSROOM TEACHER

Our schools are paying more and more attention to the spoken word—to both the mechanics of speech production and the im-

---

[4] Ralph White and Ronald Lippitt, "Leader Behavior and Member Reaction in Three 'Social Climates,'" in *Group Dynamics*, ed. Dorwin Cartwright and Alvin Zander, Evanston: Row, Peterson & Company, 1953, pp. 585-611.

provement of its communicative impact, to both the speaker and listener. More speech courses are being added to the regular curriculum, more time is being spent on cocurricular speech activities, and more special teachers for the speech handicapped are being employed. Those who teach courses in methods of teaching are concerned that every teacher, in some way, become a teacher of speech. Why this development? Why this concern? Because at least 75 percent of the communication in our day is carried on through the spoken word. Because much of the learning in any classroom is brought about through oral activities, and because classroom work suffers if children cannot hear or cannot be heard and understood. Moreover, we have learned that the removal of factors that inhibit speech or cause it to deviate will automatically remove factors that are obstacles to other kinds of learning.

Any classroom teacher, in so far as she is able, should attempt, conscientiously, to do something for speech handicapped pupils. If Mary develops a lisp and nothing is done to correct it, she practices a habit which will all too often distract attention from what she is trying to say. If Bob's anxieties cause him to block, repeat, and grimace in oral situations, he will continue to do so— and probably with increasingly severe complications—if nothing is done for him. Habits become fixed, evaluations pile upon evaluations, reticence breeds reticence; something indeed is being done about speech even though nothing, systematically and consciously, is done about it.

What then can the classroom teacher do in terms of correcting faulty speech? The thing that any teacher can do, whether she is trained to teach speech or not, is to utilize the "common denominator" principles that have been discussed in Chapter II. If she does so, her classroom will be characterized by conditions which reduce rather than exaggerate speech difficulties. A free, spontaneous atmosphere will prevail; tension, if it exists at all, will be dispelled by a friendly remark, an interesting exercise, a bit of humor. Hesitancy to speak will disappear under the magic of the teacher's smile. Subtle encouragement will draw individuals into oral activities; once in, they will experience teacher approval.

The teacher will be alert, poised, confident; she will guide young friends, by plans rather than penalties, into exciting oral experiences. Classroom citizens will be so accustomed to speaking that even the visiting parent will not inhibit contributions to classroom discussion. Pupils and teacher will live together in coöperative harmony. Students will enjoy successes; participation will bring rewarding experiences; standards will be high, but not too high.

The great majority of speech deviations are problems of articulation. It has been demonstrated that the incidence of these deviations can be reduced if preschool and primary grade teachers will provide experiences for their pupils in the production of the speech sounds for which they are ready.

If the classroom teacher has a reasonable minimum of training in speech correction, she can adopt one or more of the plans suggested above and make use of many of the techniques which will be explained as we proceed.

If a special teacher of remedial speech is helping with speech problems in the school, how can the classroom teacher become a coöperating member of the team? First, by helping the speech correctionist with "carry-over" activity. Little is accomplished and the remedial process is quite inefficient if the child is allowed to lapse into old habits the moment he leaves the speech correctionist. Here the classroom teacher as well as the parent can be of significant help. There are two techniques that have been used with success in dealing with this matter of "carry-over" from the speech class. One method is for each child to carry a small booklet labeled "My Speech Book." The child is instructed to show it to the classroom teacher and to his parents after every remedial speech lesson. In it the speech correctionist writes suggestions to the classroom teacher and the parent. In it also, she pastes or writes practice material. In the classroom and at home, the child uses this material in speech practice at certain specified times. Another method is to establish "nucleus situations." The speech correctionist and the classroom teacher agree that during some special time (such as the reading period) the teacher will help the child with his speech. The speech correctionist and the parent reach a similar understanding. The child then is encouraged by the remedial speech teacher to request this kind of help from his parents and from his classroom teacher. Under no circumstance is the child pressured into such an arrangement.

A second way in which the classroom teacher may become a coöperating member of the speech correction team is to contribute suggestions, information, and encouragement. She can inform the remedial speech teacher of new students who seem to her to have speech handicaps. She can suggest ways in which to coördinate the speech correction program with the curricular program. If, for example, she will inform the speech correctionist that next week she will introduce a unit of study on "Eskimos," he can plan his work along the same lines and take advantage of the interest and motivation developed in the classroom. The classroom teacher can encourage the child. She can also provide the speech correctionist with information about the child, his parents, his environment, and his educational history; in some cases, information of this kind can change constructively the whole course of the child's progress.

What will the speech correctionist do to encourage the classroom teacher to become a coöperating member of the team? He will take whatever time is necessary to build close-knit relationships. First, he will build what might be called "personal" relationships, the liking of one individual for another. Second, the speech correctionist will build the kinds of relationships that come from understanding and appreciating what the others are trying to do. In line with this he helps the classroom teacher understand the work of speech correction (a) by asking for a few minutes in each of a series of teachers' meetings to explain the nature of speech handicaps and the techniques used in their correction, (b) by setting up a series of short lecture-discussion periods to which all teachers are invited, (c) by extending to the teacher an invitation to visit speech correction class (even though it is necessary to adapt his schedule in order to reach certain persons), or (d) by conducting workshops for classroom teachers when there is a desire and a request for them. Also, the speech correctionist will want to know as much as possible about the classroom teacher's work. Therefore, he will request permission to visit classes, and also will eagerly seek information about classroom activities. Third, the speech correctionist will build the sort of relationship that results from observation of results. If the classroom teacher observes a striking improvement in even one child, she develops respect for the program. Reports of progress sent to the classroom teacher help also. Fourth, the speech correctionist will build the kind of relationship that comes from a clear understanding of mutual obligations. He will confer with the classroom teacher frequently in order to clarify what each can do and will do in order to correct and improve the speech of the child.

## THE PARENT

It has been said that "there are no problem children, only problem parents." Although the statement may be somewhat overdrawn, an accumulating body of research points to its significance. Good speech in the child definitely is in large part the product of certain kinds of parental behavior. It has been demonstrated rather conclusively that both articulatory proficiency and linguistic ability in the child are directly related to reasonable effort on the part of parents to provide the child with speech stimulation and language training in an atmosphere which encourages self-sufficiency, and which is characterized by consistency in regard to discipline. Speech deficiencies in the child also are to an important degree the result of certain kinds of parental behavior. Functional articulatory deficiencies as well as problems which we label "stuttering" and "delayed speech" are to important degrees causally related in some measure to parental maladjustment, standards of fluency, dominance, tension, and over solicitousness.[5]

[5] See Kenneth S. Wood, "Parental Maladjustment and Functional Articulatory Defects in Children," *Journal of Speech and Hearing Disorders* (1946), 11:255-275. Also Frederic L. Darley, "The Relationship of Parental Attitudes and Adjustments to the Development of Stuttering," and Wendell Johnson, "A Study of the Onset and Development of Stuttering," in *Stuttering in Children and Adults: A Report of Thirty Years of Research at the Universty of Iowa*, ed. Wendell Johnson and Ralph Leutenegger, Minneapolis: University of Minnesota Press, 1955.

With this evidence of causal relationship in mind, we can say that evaluating parents, instructing them, and counseling with them are frequently important aspects of speech correction. All this, of course, is aimed at modifying the child's environment. There is considerable evidence that handicapped children whose parents receive this kind of attention make significantly greater improvement than handicapped children whose parents do not.

Relatively few of the parents who have children with speech handicaps need much of this sort of attention, however. Do we then ignore the parents who do not seem to need it? Definitely we do not. Parents are "key people" on the speech correction team. Their responses to the program are all-important, and those responses that we seek to elicit are enthusiasm about the help that the child is receiving, encouragement of the child, and helpfulness to the clinician. Understanding is equally important, understanding of the problem, what the speech correctionist is attempting to do, and why he is doing it in particular ways. Of even greater importance is the willingness on the part of parents to examine and accept their responsibility—responsibility in terms of remedial work.

How then does the speech correctionist go about bringing parents into the team? Through contact with the parents in one or more ways. By requesting permission to take the child out of his regular classroom work for special instruction: a carefully worded permission form to be signed by the parent works well; this is better done, however, by telephone or in face-to-face conference. By home visits: If the speech correctionist knows the parents he will know the child, and both he and the child will profit greatly from the information received, the good will established, the coöperation built, and the kind words spoken about the program. By attending meetings of the Parent-Teacher Association, and making it a point to meet the parents of the children enrolled for remedial speech. By presenting short talks and holding open discussion of speech handicaps with these P.T.A. groups as well as with mothers' clubs and civic-service organizations. By requesting that at least one parent come to school for a conference when the nature of the child's problem indicates that this would be helpful. By asking parents to visit and observe speech correction classes: set a specific date and time; the visit then becomes a responsibility rather than an invitation which can be put off in the press of other affairs. By letters or evaluative reports sent to parents at the beginning of speech instruction: these should explain the problem as well as plans for remedial work; they are to be written in such a way that they can easily be understood by the parents; they should be reassuring and designed so as not to cause great concern or excitement. By progress reports made periodically during the year: these can be made either in the form of a brief letter or by checking a previously prepared and printed form which lists the items upon which you would normally report. By appearances on radio and television. By the preparation of mimeographed or printed materials: these should explain both the nature and causes of speech problems as well as techniques, materials, methods, dynamics, and relationships that are useful in working with them; usually they are prepared for and sent to all members of the team. By carefully planned and organized "home programs"; in projects of this kind the parent receives rather lengthy and thorough preliminary instruction in regard to work to be carried out at home; the speech correctionist and parent, by means of telephone conversations, keep in close contact concerning progress and procedure.

Before moving on to the matter of teamwork with parents, it seems wise to stress a point about initial contacts with parents. Before the correctionist attempts to take a pupil out of regular classwork for periods of remedial instruction, he usually secures permission to do so from the parents. Common sense alone makes this necessary; school statutes rarely require it. Often, however, school administrators insist upon it, because otherwise parents may not understand or may misinterpret the situation.[6] People in

[6] In some schools it is the policy to inform the parents of any child selected for remedial speech instruction that such instruction is to be given the child, and invite them to call or visit the speech correction teacher if they so desire. This serves the basic purpose and avoids delays in starting remedial instruction in cases in which parents are slow to answer requests for permission.

general are still poorly informed concerning speech correction. They may not recognize the increasing importance of skill in oral communication in a society that has developed the telephone, radio, television, and the recording machine. They may not be aware of the importance of good speech habits to people in all walks of life. They may be totally unaware of the undesirable personality deviations brought on by speech difficulties. Parents may have no speech standards or their standards may be too high. They may have become so accustomed to the speech of the child that the suggestion that it requires correction comes as a surprise. They may rationalize, for example, that even though Uncle Harry stuttered, he got along "all right." They may think that Mary will outgrow the difficulty, or they may even think that the way Mary talks is "cute." Even more serious is the fact that parents have been conditioned to believe that something is seriously "wrong" with the child who is placed in a special class. Every parent is acquainted with the "opportunity rooms" in which, in many schools, children are placed because they cannot manage normal classroom work. Likewise, they have, in their own school experience, witnessed the taunting remarks or social ostracism visited upon pupils who somehow were "different"; they do not want their child to suffer that kind of catastrophe. Consequently, if the parent is not reassured, the correctionist may run into difficulty. Parental attitudes vary all the way from indifference to hostility. The most unusual attitude is likely to arise in the most unexpected place. Because the correctionist desires strong parental support of his program, he will take pains to stimulate interest and forestall antagonism. He knows that both he and the program will be discussed over teacups and bridge tables. He hopes that those conversations will be not only intelligent but inspired also by enthusiastic commendation. In order to obtain this response he sees that parents are informed. Once they understand the nature and significance of the program, are convinced of the correctionist's sincere interest in the child, and observe positive results of the training, they tend to give speech correction strong support.

After direct contact has been made with the parent, how does the speech correctionist go about the job of building team spirit? He actively works with parents either individually or in groups. If he prefers to work with parents individually, he may use one or a combination of three techniques: (1) direct instruction, (2) interpretative discussion, and (3) permissive reorientation. *Direct instruction* is provided by the speech correctionist when the parent really wants to know what to do, when the parent lacks adequate information, when the information will not call forth emotional response, and when it does not run sharply counter to the parent's beliefs or attitudes. It deals with such items as the bodily care of the child, the selection of toys or books, the child's activities and the attitude of parents toward those activities, sibling relationships, the importance of not comparing children, and the conduct of remedial speech instruction in the home. *Interpretative discussion* is carried on between the parent and the speech correctionist or between the parent and some other member of the team such as a psychologist or a doctor. Here again the parent must want to know, and must not be too emotionally involved in the child's problem. The parent and the therapist face the situation objectively and openmindedly as a problem to be solved. Free communication is established, with the parent carrying the bulk of the conversation. The therapist guides the parent's thinking with appropriate questions and comments. He interprets and suggests. Gradually the parent gains insight into her behavior toward the child, why she rejected him, why she overindulged him, why the child behaves as he does, what the parents can say and do in an attempt to change that behavior.[7] *Permissive reorientation* is used, ordinarily, when the parent has emotionally charged attitudes toward either the child or the child's problem. It allows the parent to reach her own decision concerning ways to handle the child. The speech correctionist—or doctor or psychologist—creates a permissive situation in which the parent feels free to express her-

[7] For an example of the use of this technique see Martha Turnblom and Julian S. Myers, "A Group Discussion Program with the Families of Aphasic Patients," *Journal of Speech and Hearing Disorders,* (December 1952), 17:393-396.

self, knowing that she will not be penalized by rebuke, condemnation, accusation, attitude, or criticism. In this permissive situation, the parent unburdens herself, gets rid of her negative attitudes, and gradually takes a more objective and constructive approach to the problem. Finally she arrives at decisions which she will attempt to put into practice. After one or more sessions of premissive reorientation, the therapist may feel that he can attempt some interpretative discussion or direct instruction with the parent.

If the remedial speech teacher is so inclined, he will find that working with a number of parents as a group is highly profitable. Group work with parents is particularly practical when direct instruction or interpretative discussion is in order. It is particularly effective with parents who resist individual help but are able and willing to discuss the problems of their children with other parents who have similar difficulties. Usually it is set up as a "study" situation. Sometimes these study groups are held as a part of evening adult education programs. Usually, however, they are held under less formal conditions and as a regular part of the special service program. In smaller school systems, the speech correctionist usually works with a group of parents of the children whom he is personally serving. In larger school systems that enjoy the services of several remedial speech teachers, the program may be arranged so that one of them works with parents of children who stutter, another with parents of children who have organic speech problems, and still another with parents of children who have delayed speech or functional articulatory problems.

Usually it is wise to allow a parent to "carry the ball" in the organization of a parent study group. It is a happy occurrence if the idea for the study group comes from a parent. The seed for this idea may be planted during an individual conference or by means of literature placed in the hands of a parent for a different purpose. With the enthusiasm of the speech correctionist spurring her on, a particular parent approaches the parents of other children who are receiving special help with their speech. The group arranges to meet with the speech correctionist at school or at a parent's home. Usually the responsibility of planning and preparing for meetings is passed from parent to parent, with the assistance and guidance of the speech correctionist. The group meets at hours that are convenient for its members. Midweek morning meetings are preferred in some communities, early afternoon or evening meetings in others. Much depends upon the economic level of the community as well as local social practices, customs, and other factors.

What are the aims of group meetings? They are, essentially, learning situations for the parents. Much good can come to some parents, however, as a result of social interaction, group spirit, and recognition of the similarity between their own problems and those of other parents. Although objectives may well vary from situation to situation, the group meetings should aim (1) to inform parents about the nature, causes, and treatment of speech problems, (2) to help them gain insight into the relationship that exists between their own behavior and attitudes (mental habits, concept of discipline, recreational interests, and so forth) and the speech problems of their children, (3) to help them gain understanding and develop sympathetic reactions to the activities of their children, and (4) to help them face their problems with their children and to utilize a reflective approach in solving them.

How are the meetings planned and conducted? From eight to ten meetings should be held during a school year, ranging in time from one to one and one-half hours each. Topics that might be used for the meetings are (1) Speech Correction—What Is It? (2) Speech Problems—What Are They? (3) Causes of Speech Problems, (4) I Am a Parent (biographical), (5) The Influence of the Parent, (6) Child Behavior and Speech, (7) Discipline and Speech, (8) Parents Can Help, (9) How Speech Problems Can Be Handled, (10) How Children React to Their Speech Problems. These, of course, are offered here only by way of example. They may or may not fit a particular situation.

The first meetings of the group should be particularly interesting, stimulating, and informative for the parents; these first meetings will make or break the study group.

Each meeting should be built upon a formula of (1) catching

interest, (2) involving the parents personally, (3) providing needed information, (4) encouraging discussion, (5) summarizing, and (6) suggesting interim activities. Although this is a typical sequence of events, not every meeting will fall into this pattern. Ordinarily, however, some attention is paid to each of these items in each meeting.

Methods that can be used within this formula are (1) talks by the speech correctionist, (2) demonstrations of speech handicaps, (3) observation of remedial activities, (4) face-to-face discussion, (5) panel or symposium discussion, (6) question and answer sessions, (7) role playing, (8) reports on observations of behavior, (9) reports on techniques attempted, and (10) reviews of articles and books. Materials that can be used are (1) visual aids (films, slides, models, charts), (2) audio aids (recordings, tuning forks, tape recorder), (3) case study books, (4) diagnostic manuals, (5) textbooks, (6) television and radio programs, (7) pamphlets, (8) case histories.

Some speech correctionists like to suggest interim activities or things that parents should do between one meeting and the next. These activities may either follow through on the meeting just concluded or anticipate the next meeting. They can be similar to the following: (1) read certain books, pamphlets, or articles; (2) observe testing and remedial work at the school; (3) make observations needed in order to report on the behavior and problem of a particular child; (4) observe the reactions of children to certain retraining techniques; (5) hold conferences with other individuals providing special services; (6) make changes in the home environment and report on the results of these changes.

Group discussion in these meetings should be handled with care. It should hold to the reflective thinking process in which the group, through the interplay of its members, states the problem in question form, carefully defines terms, tries to discover causes, considers possible solutions, decides upon a preferred solution, and determines how that solution can be put into action. Probably the speech correctionist will exercise leadership in the early discussions; this leadership, however, should as rapidly as possible become distributed among the other members of the group. A different parent might take over the chairmanship of each meeting, introduce and summarize the discussion, help keep it "on the track," help keep it moving ahead, help to draw in the more reticent members of the group, and help to curb or by-pass those who talk too much or attempt to dominate the meeting. Gradually, if possible, the speech correction teacher should become a resource person, active but not too active in the discussion, contributing information, making occasional suggestions, but, by and large, allowing the parents to conduct and handle their own discussion. Some remedial speech teachers have found it helpful to distribute a brief outline of group discussion principles and procedures at one of the early meetings of the group.

Before leaving this matter of teamwork with parents it seems wise to make three observations: the first has to do with speech correction activities in the home; the second and third have to do with differences between programs of speech correction in the schools and in the university clinics, respectively.

The school speech correctionist must decide whether or not she will encourage attempts at speech correction in the home and by parents. Should the parent attempt actual remedial speech work with the child? Is it likely that some parents could and should, while others cannot and should not? Or is the obligation of the parent purely one of providing a happy, secure, ordered, loving world for the child? We suggest that some parents are themselves experienced and capable teachers, temperamentally fitted for this sort of thing. With some instruction they can be of great help. This does not hold true of all parents, however.

The speech correctionist will find some differences between the university clinic situation and the public school situation in regard to relationships with parents as well as parental interest and coöperation. Usually it is the parent who requests an appointment for the child with a university clinic. Concern about the problem and interest in doing something for the child are already present. A quite different situation exists in the public school speech correction program. Usually the first contact is with the child, who has been referred by a classroom teacher or has been discovered in a survey. Perhaps the parents do not realize that the child has a speech or hearing problem; perhaps they feel that something is wrong but do not know what it might be; perhaps, strange to say, they do not care; perhaps they are too busy, too self-conscious, or too prideful to move in the direction of seeing that something is done for the child. It is also to be appreciated, of course, that many children are taken to university clinics by their parents because their speech problems are relatively severe, while many of the children found in speech surveys in the schools have rather mild problems which, for this very reason, have not been taken very seriously by their parents. In any event, it becomes the duty of the school speech correctionist to inform the parents in every case, get them interested in the problem, and enlist their coöperation.

Another difference between the university clinic and the school situation has to do with pressures for service. The university sometimes has more leeway in limiting its case load than does the school speech correctionist. Of necessity the university clinic exists primarily as an institution for training speech correctionists and as a center for research; in spite of the possible existence of a waiting list, it cannot allow demands for service to disorganize its other functions; also the university clinic is somewhat removed from public pressure for clinical service. In the school situation, on the other hand, the primary function of the speech correction teacher is to provide service. The pressures are at his door—pressures from parents, classroom teachers, and administrators, together with powerful self-imposed pressures that stem from sympathy for children who need help and can secure that help only from him. Sometimes these pressures become so strong that it is impossible to hold to a reasonable case load. In the university situation, we might add, much work is absorbed by secretaries and by students in training. In the school situation the speech correction teacher must carry most of the burden unaided.

FUNCTIONING OF THE TEAM

We have said much about the functioning of the team as we have discussed it. However, one thing more remains to be touched upon. That is the "case conference." Essentially it is a round table discussion of the child and his problem. The participants are those members of the team who can make some contribution to an analysis of the child's problem and suggest ways of solving it. It is called by the individual in whose hands remedial work will be centered, and that could be the speech correctionist, or a psychologist, a pediatrician, a counselor, or even a parent. It is held after necessary tests and examinations have been made, and it focuses upon three questions: What is the nature of the handicap? What causal factors are involved? What remedial procedures are to be recommended?

## Relationships

Closely allied with the matter of teamwork is the problem of building strong, friendly, coöperative relationships with colleagues. There are many facets to this problem, if it may be called a problem. It becomes a problem, as such, for the individual who ignores the things that will be considered briefly in this section. The style is direct and personal in the statements that follow. They are addressed to *you*, the individual reader.

YOUR CONCEPT OF TEACHING

The most important thing that we do as speech correctionists is to help others. Our aim is to contribute to the development of socially adequate, vocationally competent, normally strong, creatively adjusted, healthy, reasoning, imaginative, inspired, and happy people. Viewed from this perspective, our responsibilities and duties become broader and more significant than when approached in terms of correcting faulty consonants, nasal voices, or facial grimaces. The speech correctionist who is guided by this broad point of view is likely to expand his professional outlook as well as his remedial procedures. He also is likely to develop attitudes, recognize relationships, and engage in behavior that will allow him to move more easily into programs of instruction in the schools.

## YOUR CONCEPT OF SELF

Basic to the building of good relationships is your view of self in relation to a school program. In the first place, and always, you are a teacher. Failure to regard yourself as a teacher circumscribes contributions that you can make to the development of children, limits your horizons and your potential for professional growth, creates strictures between you and other teachers and administrators, and works to the detriment of your profession. In the second place, no one area of instruction is all-important. The contribution that any one teacher can make to the development of children probably is no greater than that which can be made by any other teacher. Therefore, matters of primacy in instruction, scheduling, and similar problems are approached most effectively from the child's point of view, and with an eye to the fact that these problems revolve exclusively around the child, his needs, his degree of readiness for certain types of instruction, his mental and emotional maturity, and other considerations.

## YOUR RESPECT FOR OTHERS

Another basic requirement is respect for the training, knowledge, skill, and contributions of others. This respect comes only as a result of understanding. It is beneficial to listen actively and attempt to understand the point of view of the speech correctionist whose theories may differ in some respects from yours. By observing him in his work you may learn something. By visiting those who are offering other special services and talking with them, you will understand better how best to work with them. By visiting the classroom teacher, you will come to appreciate her task in handling large numbers of children and to admire the ease with which she does it. There is much to be learned by observing her teaching methods, noting how she motivates desired behavior, how she attends to individual differences, how she lets the pupil learn by doing. You will find her classroom, her techniques of control, and her careful planning instructive.

If you remain alert to the ways in which you can coördinate your efforts with her instruction, you will learn much from her, and if you are wise and considerate, you will tell her so, and let her be aware of your appreciation and good will. Moreover, by visiting the principal you will gain some measure of insight into his philosophy, his problems, his many and varied duties and responsibilities, and through this you will broaden your understanding and improve your attitudes. Finally, you will, of course, visit parents. You will learn that their child is mighty important to them, and you will more than ever realize that what you do for the child is tremendously important, too. You will discover that the parents, in many instances, are truly struggling that the child may benefit from your guidance, and this knowledge can only make you more devoted to your daily work. The better we know each other, the more closely we draw together in mutual respect and support.

YOUR ATTITUDE TOWARD LEADERSHIP

All of us work with a designated leader in the sense that we are responsible to that individual and look to him for certain things, whether it be "paper clips" or "promotion." This leadership is likely to vary in character. In one instance it may be a permissive, democratic type of leadership which encourages you as an individual to accept some of its functions; this you do by contributing your ideas, your energy, and your ability to work with other individuals. In another instance you may evaluate that leadership as somewhat arbitrary and autocratic. In any case, and no matter where the leadership may be located along the continuum from autocracy to democracy, you have certain responsibilities to it. To a very large extent, we get the kind of leadership we ask for. Right or not, the take-it-easy, careless, unimaginative, inefficient teacher is likely to receive some arbitrary orders. Right or not, the inflexible, uncompromising, arbitrary, prejudiced teacher is likely to be the stimulus for equally inflexible behavior. Right or not, that leadership itself may be acting under orders, or have a particular philosophy, or an emergency problem, or a tremendous drive for accomplishment that influences action. If we have difficulties, we have first to look to ourselves. If we are beyond reproach, we will also have developed some tolerance and understanding.

## YOU AS A PERSON

A little self-examination is good for the soul. Sometimes the mirror replies with strong reproach. Are you the well-adjusted individual that you want the child to be? Do you personify the success of education in achieving the ends, with you, that were mentioned above? Do you have strong needs for dependency, status, dominance, aggression, or catharsis that affect your relationships with your students as well as your colleagues? Are you so driven by personal welfare motives that you become obnoxious to others? Are your motivations so completely self-oriented that you resent requests to contribute to tasks, large or small, that are necessary to advance the group? Do you have a genuine liking for the group and an interest in working with other members of it toward a common goal? Are you doing all you can to change yourself into a more constructive and cooperative person?

## YOUR WILLINGNESS TO BECOME A MEMBER OF THE GROUP

This willingness can be demonstrated in many ways, but primarily through active attempts on your part to become acquainted with other individuals in the group and to understand their jobs and their problems.

Get to know your supervisor or the individual to whom you are directly responsible. The ordinary official conference is not always adequate to develop a relationship distinguished by close feeling, complete understanding, and a sense of working together toward mutual goals. Although your immediate superior may open the way, the initiative in advancing this relationship probably will rest with you. A request from him for a conference does not serve to build that relationship. He realizes this. It immediately formalizes personal contacts, and sometimes places a "brake" upon warm, easy, spontaneous interaction. On the other hand, a request from you opens the door. Nothing is more complimentary, and nothing will elicit warmer response than a request for aid in regard to some important matter. A request to confer in regard to a particular child, a request to discuss one of your reports, or a request simply to talk about some of your more general problems provides a good approach.

Get to know the principal of the school or schools in which you work. Here again, it is likely that you will take the initiative. He is the first person you should contact in the school. Ask for an appointment to talk with him about the room where you are to work, about available equipment, about the schedule of the day (what time teachers are expected to be on duty and when they are free to leave, the time of the lunch hour, and so forth). Ask him for copies of each teacher's schedule (usually these are made up in mimeographed form), about the location of boxes through which teachers receive mail and bulletins, about the existence of a handbook (some schools explain many details of procedure in this kind of booklet), about the posting of notices and other information that you should receive. Find out where the cumulative records on students are kept, how these will be made available to you, what they contain. Along the way you will pick up much information about the principal's philosophy of education, his attitudes, his wishes in regard to procedure. The principal, in turn, should be impressed with your desire to move smoothly into the scheme of things in the school, to become an integral part of the teaching force, to find a place for yourself in the lives of students and faculty. If it is necessary for you to evaluate, do it on your own. The supervisor or principal may be a "taskmaster" or a "tyrant" to the individual who isn't measuring up. That does not mean that he will react in that fashion toward you. If you depend upon the possibly warped and colored and overgeneralized evaluations of others, and if you do not press for an "operational report" which is specific in terms of what the individual did or did not do, you are likely to do that individual, and yourself, a grave injustice. And above all, give him a chance to be the helpful, democratic type of principal that he would like to be. He will give you every chance to function as a thinking, dependable, trustworthy person so long as you are that kind of person. He will not shove policy down your throat if you are the sort who can discuss it quietly, objectively, impersonally, in an unprejudiced, intelligent, and far-seeing manner. He will encourage you to help shape policies and procedures if you will think in terms of "what is best for the child and school" rather than in terms of "what I want to do" and "what is best for me." He will not exert undue pressure for changes' or improvements if he knows that you are "on the ball," mentally alive, constantly and intelligently seeking better ways to do things, examining your philosophy, handling your own personal problems rather than carrying them into your work. Under these conditions there would be fewer teachers who provoke conditions which result in their maladjustment.

Get to know as many as possible of the other teachers in the school. This becomes a major task for the itinerant speech correctionist. When you start your program, you should spend at least a day getting acquainted in each of the schools in which you are to work. The principal probably will introduce you to the various teachers but you will want closer contact with them than you can gain in this brief and formal visit. Get to the school early and visit the teachers in their classrooms or in the teachers' lounge. Go out on the playground with them at recess, or use that time to talk and plan with teachers not on playground duty. Have lunch with them. Stay as late after school as necessary to visit and work with them. Have dinner with them. Know them and let them know you as a person, not just as a speech correctionist.

Get to know the school custodian. He can be of tremendous help to you in hanging mirrors, arranging the speech correction room, repairing shades, eliminating noise, and in countless other ways. He can be particularly helpful when you arrive at school with an audiometer or tape recorder that somehow must get from the parking area to a third-floor speech room.

Function under the same expectations that apply to classroom teachers. They are expected to attend and to contribute their best constructive thinking in faculty meetings. They are expected to attend, to show an interest in, and to contribute to meetings of the Parent-Teacher Association. They are expected to perform certain duties on "parents' night," and to help in the observance of certain days or events. One sure way to show your desire to become a member of the group is to volunteer to help the classroom teacher with a May Day program or similar event.

### YOUR WILLINGNESS TO CONFORM

The educational program in any one school is likely to be different from that in another. Sometimes these differences stem from the varying philosophies of education held by the leadership in the various schools. Sometimes these differences have their origin in community characteristics or in type of student. No doubt there are other sources. In any event, if you are an itinerant speech correctionist and move from school to school, some differences will show up in time. It is wise, therefore, to do, while in Rome, as the Romans do. If, for example, you believe in free and easy discipline and can allow it in one school, do not carry that practice into another school where the pattern does not prevail.

The expectations of one community in regard to teachers or the expectations of one superintendent, principal, or supervisor, may vary from those of another. Perhaps it would be wise for you, before accepting a position, and by means of a personal interview, to determine attitudes toward some of your personal habits.

Some persons in administrative positions prefer to stay away from all detail. Others expect to be kept closely informed of changes in program and procedure. Do what is expected.

### YOUR VIGILANCE IN KEEPING CHANNELS OF COMMUNICATION OPEN AND ON AN OPERATIONAL LEVEL

See that you obtain information. Although your immediate supervisor will see that you receive bulletins or announcements that come from his office, principals of schools that you visit once or twice a week are likely to neglect or forget you. If they do, a hint to office staffs usually will provide you with notices and bulletins. Once you receive them, read them. They not only keep you abreast of what is going on in the school but also provide a source of contact with other teachers. Probably your first act upon entering any school is to read notices placed on bulletin boards. If it is necessary to depend upon word of mouth about events in the school, you will soon learn whom you can trust to provide you with a factual, operational report of occurrences rather than a statement compounded of inference, misjudgment, and projection of self. You don't want to wear the dark-colored glasses of another. See that you provide others with information as to what you are doing. The opportunity comes in casual conversation as well as in more formal communicative situations. We have mentioned some of these occasions in our discussion of "the team." We will note others under our consideration of "reports." See that there is some channel through which you can receive criticism; significant changes have often been made in programs of speech correction because other individuals in a school system have heard criticism and have felt that they could safely transmit the information to the speech correctionist, knowing that she would receive it in the proper way. Encourage the reporting of misunderstandings to you. These can be quickly resolved if you encourage and are willing to accept communication that indicates the existence of them. You then can go directly to the source and face the situation squarely in a spirit of attempting to solve a problem.

In connection with this matter of communication, it seems important to suggest that a great deal of it should never take place. A teacher who carries tales from one school to another is likely to find herself in trouble, and soon. So is one who engages in personal and perpetual criticism of others. So is one who chronically complains and, whenever she speaks, builds a spot of decay about herself. So is the one who listens to such a person and allows the viciousness of that person's influence to color her own attitudes and affect her own actions.

## YOUR WILLINGNESS TO EVALUATE THE IMPACT OF YOUR LANGUAGE HABITS

In speech correction, we have grown, perhaps unfortunately, to use a variety of terms that are not guaranteed to arouse pleasure either in parents or in the youngsters whom the speech correctionist is trying to help. This has been discussed in Chapter I, but the matter needs to be emphasized again in the present connection. It is to be constantly appreciated that parents do not like to hear their child called a "case." Neither do they like to hear that the child has been "referred," particularly to a "clinic." Nor do they appreciate the label of "handicapped" or "defective." Barriers between remedial speech teachers and parents are not likely to arise if both are willing to recognize that sometimes words carry unfortunate connotations quite independently of anyone's intentions, and if they are as thoughtful as they can reasonably be in their use of words.

## YOUR DESIRE TO IMPROVE

The first area of activity is in improvement as a person. Unquestionably, an individual's personal needs frequently become mixed up with his professional problems. If you have a personal need for aggression, for example, it frequently will show up in resentment against the actions, no matter how minor, of anyone in authority. Also it is likely to show up in generalized "negativeness." If you have an excessive personal need for status it is likely to expose itself in overconcern about your "title," or in your negative reaction to criticism, or in the way that you make verbal contributions to a group. If you have a personal need for dominance it may show up in subtle or open attack by you upon another or in your persistent attempts to gain acceptance of an idea, or in "social bossiness" on your part, or in your refusal to listen to arguments contrary to a certain position. If you have a personal need for catharsis it may be revealed in verbosity, in emotional involvement in what you are saying, in overly elaborate description, or in the acting out of personal conflicts. Other personal needs are likely to come to the surface in similar fashion and to interfere with your performance of duties or your functioning in a group. Take a look at yourself. Extend your reading, your thinking, your observation, and your discussion to the point where you have gained considerable understanding of yourself and others.

All of us, at times, feel overcome by pressures, frustrated by certain conditions, or depressed by the seeming impossibility of doing an effective job. It usually helps to discuss these problems with our colleagues, learn to limit our activities, seek recreation and release, and accept the fact that it is necessary, at times, to live with imperfections.

The second area of activity is in improvement as a teacher. The further we go in this respect, the more we recognize that we have much further to go. Observe. Observe the techniques used by other speech correctionists in school situations and in the clinic, in parent study groups, in demonstrations at conventions. Participate. Attend workshops of your own group and those of other segments of the teaching profession. You will learn much from discussion sessions on child development, mental health, silent reading, the physically handicapped, and other subjects. Talk. Talk with authorities in these fields. Compare notes with your colleagues. Search for better methods. Draw upon techniques used in choral speaking, creative dramatics, play therapy, radio speaking, group discussion, oral reading, public speaking, sociodrama. Accept evaluations. Accept them from parents, colleagues, administrators, and, if the evaluations are significant, revise your approach, your procedure. Be confident. Have confidence in your own way of doing things but learn to ask questions about it and to evaluate it thoughtfully and objectively. Above all, have confidence in your ability to learn, to improve, to grow.

The third area of activity is in improvement as a member of your profession. Join your professional associations. Read the periodicals published by these associations. Attend their conventions. Engage in graduate study. Examine the new books in your field. Venture out of your own field into the literature on psychology, sociology, education, medicine, dentistry, electronics, recreation, human relations, group dynamics. Read the newspapers and current magazines and be aware of significant fiction and non-fiction. Recognize that research goes on apace—in a dramatically changing world—so rapidly, in fact, that any book written in any field is out of date before it leaves the press. You too will be out of date if you stop with the reading of that book.

## Getting Started

In any endeavor except perhaps a sprint, a slow, careful start (if that is possible) insures a strong finish. We want to emphasize this point for the speech correctionist, whether he is initiating a program or moving into one that is under way. In getting a careful start he needs to (1) do some overall program planning, (2) locate the pupils who have speech problems, and (3) prepare a teaching schedule.

### OVERALL PROGRAM PLANNING

It is easy for the speech correctionist to become so involved with the trees that he cannot see the forest. The need for his services, in terms of both numbers of children and the desperateness of individual cases, can easily press him into a flurry of activity. This precipitous involvement sometimes pays off less well than the giving of more attention, as a preliminary step, to the general program. The point is this: The remedial speech instructor must look at the total job and formulate some overall plan of activity that will fit his particular situation. Planning of this kind will differ from situation to situation. It will differ in relation to the length of time the program has been in operation, the size of the school system, the number and variety of special services offered, the number of speech correctionists employed, whether or not there is an audiologist on the staff, the administrative organization of the program, public attitudes and pressures, and other factors. Overall planning should take into consideration the need to become acquainted with the school system, establish a good climate for speech correction, find and equip proper space, obtain materials, build and train a "team," spend time with classroom teachers, make surveys and retest individual students, prepare case histories, plan schedules, plan the details of day-to-day activity, make referrals, and make reports. We shall deal with "space" and "climate" at this point; other aspects of overall planning will be considered as we proceed.

One preliminary task is a search for adequate space in which to conduct remedial speech activities in each school in which the program is operating. Do not expect this to be easy. The over-crowded condition of most of our schools will work against you. The writer, while visiting speech correctionists interning in public schools, has found them working in book rooms, teachers' lounges, cafeterias, corridors, and, in good weather, under trees. In spite of space difficulties they have been doing good work. We shall hope, however, that you will be more fortunate. Handicapped children, as all other children, should have pleasant and stimulating surroundings in which to grow.

In any event, what you will want for remedial work is a pleasant, well-lighted, easily accessible, quiet, attractively decorated, well-ventilated room. This room should be equipped with a blackboard, large and small mirrors, chairs and tables of varying sizes, a cot, a letter-size file cabinet, a four- by six-inch card file, a speech recorder (tape or disk), and storage space for books, pictures, toys, modeling clay, games, and other instructional equipment. Unless absolutely necessary, the nurse's room or the principal's office should not be used for testing or for special classes. These particular cubicles are too often associated in the mind of the youngster with physical examinations or disciplinary actions which have not always been particularly enjoyable.

Another aspect of overall planning is the important matter of establishing a good climate for speech correction in the community. We shall have more to say about this in various places. It will suffice to say here that the establishment of a program of speech correction in almost any community should be preceded by newspaper publicity, letters to parents, talks at meetings of the Parent-Teacher Association, and talks to various civic service organizations. The purpose of all this activity is to inform parents and the general public concerning the following:

1. The prevalence of speech problems;
2. The fact that they influence the child's educational progress and personality development;
3. The fact that most speech difficulties are not outgrown;

4. The possibility of correcting most types of speech impairments;
5. The desirability of rehabilitation at an early age;
6. The idea that a speech problem is no disgrace and that it is not causally related to mental retardation.[8]

If this job is done well, it will automatically forestall problems that arise from misconceptions, misunderstandings, and lack of adequate information.

LOCATING THE PUPILS WITH SPEECH PROBLEMS

The first essential step in getting a speech correction program under way is to find the children with speech problems. Three procedures may be followed: (1) class visitation, (2) referral, and (3) survey.

*Class visitation,* as the name implies, involves listening in on the oral activities of an entire class and noting those individuals who have speech problems. It is a relatively inefficient method. Considerable time is used in waiting to hear each student read or converse at sufficient length to discover and evaluate difficulties.

The procedure is more reliable and efficient if used by the teacher who is responsible for the corrective work in her own classroom. Over a period of time she hears her students in a variety of oral situations and can record in some detail the speech needs of each student. Before many days have passed she knows the exact nature and severity of each problem. In this case, no special time need be set aside for the administration of prepared tests; the teacher need only focus her attention upon the oral skill of her students during the course of their ordinary activities in the classroom. This assumes, of course, that a considerable amount of oral work is done in the classroom and that the teacher has had some experience in observing speech deviations. Some classrooms, unfortunately, are distinguished by their lack of oral activity and consequent lack of student growth in this extremely important basic skill. Some teachers, unless they have had training and experience in the detection of speech prob-

[8] Ollie L. Backus, *Speech in Education,* New York, Longmans, Green & Co., Inc., 1943, p. 96.

lems, find it difficult to spot specific articulation difficulties in ordinary speech situations although they may realize that "something is wrong."

*Referral* is used quite often in schools that have the services of a speech correctionist. Under this system the clinician relies upon the reports of classroom teachers, parents, the school nurse, or the school psychologist to inform him of pupils with speech problems. Ordinarily, where this procedure is used, the principal or the speech correctionist requests from each grade or homeroom teacher a list of those pupils who are thought to have speech difficulties. In secondary schools that do not have a homeroom arrangement, the request is made of English or social studies teachers; these instructors usually have contact with all students and, moreover, have an opportunity to listen closely to their oral language habits. After the lists are presented, the speech correctionist gives each designated pupil a thorough speech examination to determine more definitely the presence, the kind, and the severity of problems.

The referral method is effective in the degree to which classroom teachers are aware of speech deviations and able to recognize them. It is important, therefore, that the speech correctionist talk to the teachers preceding the request for referral of children. In his talk he should describe and illustrate the various types of speech problems and point out the importance of alleviating or correcting them. Even when this is done, of course, some pupils, particularly those with less severe difficulties, may be missed. Also, some children are referred who do not have speech deviations but who have problems of reading, mental retardation, or adjustment. The method has the great advantage, however, of enlisting the coöperation of each classroom teacher at the outset of the program. As the program goes on and the liaison between clinician and teachers becomes closer, the skill of the latter in detecting significant speech deviations becomes greater. It is unlikely that many pupils seriously in need of remedial attention will be overlooked for long.

The picture is somewhat different in regard to referral for

hearing loss. E. Thayer Curry reports that classroom teachers refer "only 7.4% of the total number of individuals who might be expected to have a hearing loss" and consequently he recommends audiometric tests for all children.[9] This particular weakness of the referral procedure is understandable. Certain types of hearing loss are not easily detectable without instrumentation. Also, few classroom teachers have studied or had significant experience with this type of handicap; with even a little information, their batting average probably would improve.

The *survey* is probably the most thorough procedure in locating children with speech and hearing problems. The survey aims to screen out quickly, by means of a short test of spontaneous and directed speech administered individually, those children who have difficulties; each of these is then given a more thorough examination. The hearing survey is usually conducted by means of group tests, using a multiple audiometer; students who seem to have deficiencies are then tested by the pure tone audiometer (see Chapter VIII).

The teacher who is responsible only for a survey of her own room has but little advance planning to do. She provides her pupils with a seat assignment that requires quiet study or she stimulates interest in an absorbing activity. While the class as a whole is thus engaged, she calls individuals to the back of the room or outside into the corridor and administers the tests.

The speech survey, if used by the speech correctionist to check an entire school, requires careful management and considerable planning to insure efficiency and orderliness. Preliminary arrangements should start with the principal. From him the correctionist wants the necessary authority to proceed, as well as the provision of adequate physical arrangements and guidance in scheduling the survey so that it will not conflict with previously arranged assemblies, demonstrations, or other school activities.

[9] E. Thayer Curry, "The Efficiency of Teacher Referrals in a School Hearing Testing Program," *Journal of Speech and Hearing Disorders* (1950), 15:211-214.

It is usually wise, in making a survey, to start with the youngest group at the particular level at which remedial work is to take place. The correctionist working in the elementary school will ordinarily start with the junior primary or kindergarten and survey it as well as the two or three grades above this level; he will then initiate remedial work with those who need it. Surveys of the remaining grades will be carried out as time and teaching load allow. The remedial speech teacher in the junior high school will usually start with the beginning class in his building and gradually work into the upper classes. In the senior high school, however, one may well begin with the most advanced class in order to give a maximum amount of corrective work to the students who are soon to leave the school by graduation.

We need to digress here in order to explain and to qualify. It has been suggested that the speech survey start in the junior primary or kindergarten and that the teacher begin work immediately, correcting problems discovered at that early age. The reason for usually starting with the youngest group is obvious. Speech problems should be remedied at the earliest age possible. Rarely do pupils beyond the primary grades "grow out of" their acquired speech habits; rather they tend to habituate speech deviations through continued practice of them. The suggestion that remedial work start with the youngest group is a generalization, however, that should be considered in terms of specific difficulties of speech. Undoubtedly something should be done at that early level with pupils who have delayed speech, stuttering,[10] cleft palate speech, or cerebral palsy. Also something should be done about hearing deficiencies. It is not

_____

[10] See Chapter V. In many cases the attention of the speech correctionist is more properly directed to the parents and perhaps the teachers of a child who is said to be stuttering than to the child himself. If a child is acquiring a reputation as a stutterer there is definitely a problem to be handled, even though the child should not be worked with directly, and promptness in dealing with it is to be recommended. For basic policies to be followed in speech surveys so far as stuttering is concerned, see particularly the sections of Chapter V entitled "Definition" and "What Are the Advantages and Disadvantages of Classifying a Child as a Stutterer?" A speech examiner would never be the first to label a child a stutterer.

always necessary, however, to start work in the primary grades with pupils who have certain types of articulatory deficiencies. Although differences caused by delayed physical maturation or relatively unstimulating environment appear, the average girl usually is unable to make certain fricative consonants (*f, v, th, s, z, sh, zh*), semivowels (*r, l, w*) and consonant blends until past the age of six, and the average boy usually does not acquire the ability to make those sounds until the age of seven. The semivowels, *r* and *l*, the fricatives, *s* and *z*, and consonant blends like *lk, str, bl,* and *spr* are, normally, among the last sounds to appear in the child's speech.[11] Omissions, substitutions, and distortions related to the production of late-appearing sounds can as a rule, then, be safely ignored in the primary grades, provided improvement appears to be taking place with general growth and development. No doubt the child should receive help if he is having trouble with other sounds which, in the normal course of things, should have developed by the age of four or five. In general, common sense necessarily determines whether a given child in the kindergarten or first grade should be given speech correction. Intelligibility, or difficulty in understanding the child's speech, and apparent rate of development will be basic considerations in many cases in arriving at a decision.

Now, to return to a consideration of survey problems. The classroom teacher should be consulted well in advance of the survey. She then has an opportunity to arrange classroom instruction in such a way that it will not be unduly hampered by students moving in and out of the room during the survey. The speech correctionist will, of course, be glad to assent to special requests. He will be quite willing to by-pass a particular classroom for a short time, for example, if the teacher is preparing a group for demonstration or public performance. A copy of the class roll may be requested by the speech correctionist at the time of the preliminary consultation. This roster is used to keep a check on pupils as they report for examination. Those who are

[11] Backus, *op. cit.*, p. 59.

absent on that particular day can be examined after their return to school.

At the time of the examination, the class or group is informed of the general purpose of the survey. Considerable flutter and some tension can be avoided by simply telling elementary school youngsters that you are going to ask them to read some sentences or name some objects in pictures; it is better to avoid the words "test" and "examination." In spite of that care, however, some pupils will react tensely to what they size up immediately as an examination situation. A good-natured attitude on the part of the officiating teacher as well as friendly, bantering conversation will help to dispel that tension.

In addition, pupils will be informed of the procedure to be followed. They will be told the exact location of the speech room; they will be asked to coöperate in keeping the building quiet as they move back and forth between this room and the classroom; they will be told exactly in what order they are to report—alphabetically, one after the other up and down rows, or by designation by the classroom teacher.

Because unnecessary time is consumed in asking the name of each child, some economical system of obtaining essential information is usually devised by the correctionist. He may ask the classroom teacher to pin name-bearing slips of paper to the dress or shirt of tiny youngsters. He may ask the classroom teacher to write the names of pupils on cards; each student then carries his card to the examination room. He may request that children come in alphabetical order; it is a simple matter then to check names against the class list in his possession, unless some are absent. In the upper elementary and secondary school grades the correctionist may pass out copies of the form which he will use to record speech errors and ask the student to fill in the blanks that call for name, grade, age, and date; the form is taken up and used by the speech correctionist when each student reports to him for testing.

To start the survey, the correctionist takes two children with him from the classroom; one waits while the other is being tested. As soon as the first pupil is released he returns to his classroom and tells the third, who arrives at the speech room before the second examination has been completed. This procedure continues until the entire group has reported. It allows the correctionist to work rapidly and efficiently without being delayed by the slowness of student traffic. Some correctionists feel that at the primary level it is wise to go after children and return them personally to the classroom.

The speech test used should consist of both spontaneous speech and directed speech. No particular order or arrangement of these two aspects is necessary; the teacher wants to hear spontaneous speech as well as speech that focuses upon particular sounds in as free and natural a situation as possible. The test may start off with a lively conversation about a coming holiday and along the way turn to naming objects on the teacher's desk or to identifying objects in pictures. This procedure will be reversed in some cases. The sole purpose is to obtain speech from the child; to this speech the teacher listens intently in order to detect deficiencies or problems.

Through spontaneous conversation the teacher detects faults of vocal quality, pitch, and loudness as well as rate and fluency characteristics and general inaccuracy in articulation. To stimulate spontaneous conversation, he seizes upon the interests and preoccupations of the pupils; he comments upon classroom projects, displays, and activities, or upon playground incidents or personal interests such as the new dress, the bandaged finger, or the club insignia.

The directed speech test is used primarily to examine articulation. It is so named because it is designed to focus the attention of the examining teacher and the speech of the child upon the individual sounds of the English language. Directed speech tests fall, roughly, into three categories: (1) the test which is set up in the form of a paragraph or story; (2) the test which uses loaded sentences or word lists; (3) the test which makes use of pictures or objects.

The paragraph or story test usually is written to supply the details of some central idea or interesting plot. Sentences and words are carefully selected so that the test contains repetitions of all the sounds of the English language. Because these sounds necessarily are scattered throughout the paragraph or story, the usefulness of the test depends upon (1) the degree of familiarity with these sounds possessed by the examiner, and (2) the examiner's listening experience.

Sentence and word list tests are easier for the inexperienced examiner to use. For each of the English language sounds, a sentence or list of words is provided; the sentence is loaded with words that contain the sound to be tested; each of the words in a word list test contains the sound to be listened to. For example, the sentence, "The ring on her finger has turned green," tests the articulation of *r*, in the initial, medial, and final positions, and in the *gr* blend.

Object and picture tests usually are used to diagnose the articulation of nonreaders and others in the kindergarten and primary grades. Pictures of sail, nest, grass, for example, test the *s* sound in all three positions. Soap, paste, toothpicks are articles that do likewise when named. The teacher may point to objects in the room, personal adornments, or to his teeth, lips, finger, and so forth, to obtain a response that contains the desired sound. Picture tests may be purchased, found in books, or constructed by the examiner. Pictures clipped from magazines and mounted on uniform pieces of cardboard make attractive tests; they can be filed under appropriate headings and used for teaching purposes also.

Material used for testing should be carefully selected. It should be graded to the ability and experience level of the child.[12] The *International Kindergarten Union Word List* or the Gates *Reading Vocabulary for the Primary Grades*[13] will serve as guides for the selection of pictures or objects to test the

[12] See W. Johnson, F. L. Darley, and D. C. Spriestersbach, *Diagnostic Manual in Speech Correction*, New York, Harper & Brothers, 1952, pp. 21-37, for detailed discussion of the problem of preparing and administering tests of articulation. The speech examiner may desire to consult this *Manual* as a whole or equivalent material.

[13] Arthur Irving Gates, Bureau of Publications, Teachers College, Columbia University, 1926; Madeline Horn (chairman), *A Study of the Vocabulary of Children before Entering the First Grade*, Baltimore, International Kindergarten Union, Child Study Committee, 1928.

articulation of primary grade children. Readers used at the various grade levels are also helpful guides. The Thorndike *Teachers Word Book*[14] aids in the preparation of a test for the secondary school levels. Pictures and objects should be selected so that the thing (object, color, shape, action) to be named (1) is within the experience of the pupil, (2) draws the desired speech response, and (3) is attractive and interesting. A picture of a magnet probably is outside the experience of the primary grade pupil; a picture of a basket of apples may call forth either "basket" or "apples"; "gnome" or "gyrate" does not test *g*, nor does "psalm" test *p* or "knot" test *k*; "cat" tests *k*, while "cellophane" tests *s*.

Survey testing may be limited to consonant sounds. Vowels are seldom misarticulated. If the child's speech seems to be fairly clean-cut, the survey articulation test may be further limited to the most frequently misarticulated consonants: *r*ug, *l*eaf, *th*read, *th*at, *s*aw, *z*oo, *sh*eep, trea*s*ure, *wh*ite, *ch*air, *j*ump. Most speech correctionists prefer to test each sound in initial, medial, and final positions in the word. Some, however, suggest that in rapid survey testing it is sufficient, with the exception of *s* and *l*, to test the consonants only in the initial position.

From twenty-five to thirty-five students can be tested in one hour in a speech survey. The purpose is to screen out those who seem to have speech problems, not to give each one a complete speech examination. In this way, classroom instruction is but briefly subjected to slight modification.

Once a speech survey of any one school has been completed, only the new entering class and transfer students need be tested thereafter. Hearing surveys, however, should be conducted at regularly spaced intervals through the student's school career.

### PREPARING THE SPEECH CORRECTION SCHEDULE

Schedule making for the classroom teacher who undertakes speech correction with only her own pupils is a relatively simple task. The speech correctionist or special teacher who takes

[14] Edward Lee Thorndike, Bureau of Publications, Teachers College, Columbia University, 1921.

students out of classroom pursuits in order to provide them with remedial instruction must, on the other hand, consider a number of details. These may be grouped roughly under (1) administrative arrangements, (2) classroom considerations, and (3) student needs. Close coöperation between the classroom teacher, the administrator, and the speech correctionist is essential. As long as all teachers remember that each is attempting to make a contribution to the total growth of the child, there will be few conflicts over minor inconveniences to either the speech correctionist or the classroom teacher.

Ordinarily, after students with speech problems have been located and parents contacted for permission to work with them in special classes, the correctionist arranges for a conference with the principal of the school in which work is to be done. In this conference the correctionist and the principal agree upon matters of policy; these matters usually center upon classes or periods to be avoided and the length and frequency of remedial sessions.

The principal may prefer that pupils not be taken from certain classes or periods. These preferences vary from principal to principal, and probably are based in each case upon a personal philosophy of education or certain conditions which exist in the particular school. Periods for which principals have on occasion requested noninterference are reading, writing, rest, and milk periods.

Short, frequent remedial sessions are to be preferred to relatively long periods, whether frequent or infrequent. Studies investigating time allotments given to the acquisition of motor skills in the elementary school agree that approximately fifteen minutes a day results in as productive work as do longer periods. While it may or may not be possible to generalize fully from these studies to speech correction work, nevertheless experience with public school speech correction has certainly shown that an energetic and skilled teacher with a plan can do a great deal in fifteen minutes. The speech correctionist should make allowances in time schedules so that there will be a minimum of fifteen minutes to work with the pupil after he arrives and before he leaves.

If remedial sessions cannot be held daily, they should be regularly spaced so that youngsters may benefit from both drill and reminder at closely connected intervals. If the classroom teacher is conducting the corrective lessons, it may be possible for her to arrange daily lessons. The speech correctionist, because he works in several buildings or among many classes, often finds it necessary to space remedial sessions further apart. Lincoln School may be visited on Monday, Wednesday, and Friday mornings, Roosevelt School on Tuesday and Thursday mornings, Washington School on Monday and Wednesday afternoons, and Jefferson School on Tuesday and Thursday afternoons.

The amount of time that is allotted to any one school will depend, of course, upon the number of speech handicapped children in that school and the severity of their problems. Also it will depend upon how many classroom teachers have received training in speech correction and the number of cases they can handle.

Wednesday or Friday afternoon or the whole of one of these days usually is scheduled as "coördination day." In the Ohio public schools, this day is used to provide extra time for instruction of children who are not making desired progress, to confer with parents, classroom teachers, and other individuals, to make home calls, to visit classrooms and observe the carry-over of remedial training, to give individual diagnostic speech and hearing tests, to conduct in-service training of teachers, and to work with various agencies.[15] In addition, the day may be used for meetings of parent study groups. Also it may be used for planning, record keeping, and reporting.

Decision as to whether "coördination day" will be one-half or a full day depends upon several factors. One factor is the severity of the speech handicaps that the speech correctionist is handling; if he has many severe cases, it will be necessary for

[15] Ruth Becky Irwin, "Speech and Hearing Therapy in the Public Schools of Ohio," *Journal of Speech and Hearing Disorders* (March, 1949), *14:* 63-68.

him to spend more time in conferences and in the other activities listed above. Another factor is the newness of the program; if it is in a beginning stage, more time must be given to organizational activity and "public relations." As the need for these activities decreases, extra remedial sessions are incorporated accordingly into the weekly schedule.

The next step in schedule development by the speech correctionist is a conference with each classroom teacher. Usually these conferences are quite informal and take place before or after school, during the noon hour, on the playground, or at any convenient time when the classroom teacher is at least semifree from the responsibility of directing and instructing some twenty-five to thirty-five individualists.

In these conferences, the speech correctionist is concerned with four things which will affect the preparation of his correction schedule. (1) He is interested in information concerning each child's particular interests and characteristics. Is the pupil, for instance, likely to be so absorbed in a particular study or activity at a particular time of the day that he would resent being taken from it? That resentment would seriously handicap remedial efforts. (2) The correctionist is interested in knowing the strengths and weaknesses of the child in various subject matter and skill areas. He wants to avoid taking pupils from subjects in which they are weak. Furthermore, he will, if the program of the school makes it necessary, stagger the times at which remedial sessions are held so that a pupil does not miss part of the same class consistently. The pupil's speech sessions under this arrangement, for example, might come at 9 A.M. on Monday, 10:15 A.M. on Wednesday, and 11 A.M. on Friday. (3) The speech correctionist is concerned with the classroom schedule. He does not want to schedule remedial speech immediately following a period of activity which has made similar demands upon the student. (4) He is concerned also with any special requests from the classroom teacher. He will attempt, so far as possible, to tie in his program with that of the classroom.

The third step in preparation of a working schedule is a

study of student needs. Any teacher who is responsible for speech correction will study carefully the needs and characteristics of the pupils to determine which of them he will work with individually and which individuals he will group together for instruction.

In some elementary schools, especially of the platoon type, and in some secondary schools, remedial speech classes are written into the schedule (under a different label, of course, such as "Speech I") and pupils with speech deviations are assigned to or register for them.

As a fourth step, the speech correctionist prepares a tentative schedule and submits it to both the principal and the classroom teachers for a recheck. The final step entails mimeographing the schedule and having it distributed to all teachers from the office of the principal and under his signature.

## Method

"Method" is a word with many referents. Here we use it to include most of the things that a speech correctionist does from the time he first sees a child until he dismisses him from his instruction. It includes such things as an examination of the child, a diagnosis of his problem, and the planning of his program of reëducation. It includes the approach to be used in that program of correction, as well as the adjustive techniques, the practice techniques, and the materials that will be used. Also it includes the use of what we know about interest, learning, and motivation.

### EXAMINATION-EVALUATION

Any good remedial speech teacher, or any good teacher of any sort for that matter, wants to know as much as possible about each child who comes under his instruction. He realizes that he cannot plan intelligently for the child unless he knows something about his needs and interests, his abilities, capacities, and limitations, his drives, ambitions, and personal characteristics. The speech correctionist also realizes that it is impossible to know the child until he understands his environment past and present, and how that environment has affected and is affecting his growth behavior. Moreover, the correctionist knows that information about a child is of little value unless it is brought to bear, by a process of reasoning, upon whatever problem is presented by the child. This process of obtaining information and reasoning from it usually is referred to as "examination" or "evaluation" or "diagnosis." Perhaps "evaluation" is a somewhat better term than "diagnosis," as has been considered in Chapter I. Here we hyphenate the two terms, "examination" and "evaluation," to indicate that the activity suggested by each is part and parcel of the same process. If we were to attempt to distinguish between the two, it might be done in this way. Examination is concerned with the gathering of facts and the recording of those facts as facts (as distinguished from what we call inferences, judgments, conclusions, hypotheses); it reveals the existence and nature of the problem. Evaluation, on the other hand, is concerned with reasoning about and from the facts which have been collected during the examination and, logically, arriving at a tentative decision in regard to the causes of the difficulty and the conditions affecting it—the conditions which need to be eliminated or changed in order to bring about improvement.

Examination-evaluation involves three major activities: obtaining information, recording information, and inference. These activities overlap and go on at the same time. Information is obtained by means of observation, interviewing, and testing. It is recorded in the form of a "case history," using language which presents a clear, precise, objective report. Inference is the process of reasoning in which the facts are assembled and organized, and relationships between the facts noted, and tentative conclusions drawn.

*Obtaining Information.* One thing that we do to obtain information, as we have said, is to observe. We observe what the child does and does not do that interferes with his oral communication. We observe, in so far as possible, the structure and functioning of the vocal organs. We observe the behavior of the child in a variety of situations—with the parents together and with each separately, with other children in both play and social activity, in solitary play, in interaction with the examiner. But we do not just observe at random and without a certain amount of selection. Some behavior may have little relationship to the speech problem; other behavior will have important implications. How do we know what to observe? We observe in relation to what we know in general about the various speech and hearing handicaps, and their causes. Previous chapters of this book have provided you with this essential information. Experience in dealing with these handicaps will increase your power to observe that which is significant. Diagnostic manuals are helpful. Appendix III of this book provides you with a list of things to look for. Do not allow yourself to be circumscribed by any book, however. It could be wrong. It could have neglected something important. Use your head. Profit from experience. Look for behavior or relationships that might have some significant bearing upon the problem.

A second means of obtaining information is through various forms of interviews. Whom do we interview? The speech handicapped child as well as those who know him well. What is an interview? Essentially it is a written or oral exchange prompted by questions or just plain encouragement from the interviewer and carried on with the individual seeking remedial help or those who are rather intimate parts of his environment. Are there different approaches to this matter of interviewing? Yes, the interview, whether written or oral, and viewed from the perspective of the therapist, may extend along a continuum from the completely directive to the completely nondirective.[16]

Written interviews take the form of autobiographies or essays, and may be prompted by the degree of directiveness that the examiner feels is important in any particular situation. Usually the writing of an autobiography is suggested to the individual as a means of getting acquainted with him. It decreases in effectiveness below the upper elementary grades. Some other technique, such as observed play, is used at the lower elementary levels. The individual who is asked to write an autobiography is

[16] See *Diagnostic Manual in Speech Correction, op. cit.,* pp. 3-10.

told that the speech correctionist would like to know as much as possible about his (1) parents, brothers, sisters, other close relatives, (2) teachers, (3) classmates, (4) friends, enemies, (5) shortcomings, (6) achievements, talents, interests, (7) kinds of punishment, from whom, for what, and reaction to them, (8) happy and unhappy experiences, (9) kinds of praise, from whom, for what, and reactions to them, (10) fears and dislikes, (11) main wishes and ambitions. The individual is encouraged to jot down his thoughts as they occur to him, writing as rapidly as he can without revision, and later to put them in some kind of organized form if this seems desirable. Essays differ from autobiographies in that usually they are prompted by suggestion that the individual write upon a single topic such as "People I like best to know."

Interviews, as we have noted, are held with both the pupil and individuals who make up some significant aspect of his environment. The degree of directiveness of the interview will depend upon whether the interviewer seeks (1) to obtain factual information, or (2) to use the interview as a part of remedial instruction and counseling. Interviews aimed at securing case history data usually are strongly but not too strongly directive, and generally fact-finding in nature.

The primary sources of information in regard to the child are parents, particularly mothers, although classroom teachers, physicians, classmates, and others may be able to provide important supplementary information. During the interview, of course, the interviewer is observing. He not only is obtaining factual information about the child as it is reported to him but he is also obtaining factual information about the environment of the child by observing the behavior and attitudes of the parent or other informant.

The directive interview is one in which the interviewer not only assumes full leadership in the interview and full direction of it, but also accepts full responsibility for locating the causes of the handicap and for the prescription of evaluative procedure. The function of the respondent is to provide information which will help the interviewer ascertain those causes and determine that procedure. It is characterized by considerable talking on the part of the interviewer as well as active and direct effort on his part in asking questions, in pointing out problems and causes and implications, and in persuading the person being interviewed to take a certain course of action. In his attempts to persuade, he not only uses his personal influence but also utilizes evidence and sometimes emotional appeal.

The nondirective interview is one in which the interviewer encourages the person being interviewed to do most of the talking. Occasionally the interviewer talks or asks questions for the purpose of obtaining information, or stimulating the respondent in the direction of additional response, or reducing anxieties that create a block to communication between the two. The interviewer does not argue, display authority, give advice, or persuade. Mainly, he listens—and listens actively in a friendly, patient, intelligent manner. He does not respond to fact, reasoning, or other intellectual aspects of what the respondent says. He reflects back, matter-of-factly, and with acceptance, the emotional attitudes expressed by the respondent in somewhat this manner, "You became angry when your son refused to obey your command." Never, in so doing, does his manner, attitude, voice, or bodily expression reflect approval, disapproval, or other reaction. The purpose of the nondirective interview is to bring about self-understanding, self-direction, and self-responsibility by giving the respondent a chance to become more conscious of his own attitudes and feelings, to gain insight into the significance of his behavior, and to accept some of the responsibility for rehabilitation.[17]

In all interview situations the interviewer attempts first to establish rapport and get the other person to talk freely. Rapport is built through mutual respect and trust, honest liking of one

---

[17] For detailed treatment of various interview procedures, including the nondirective type, see Walter V. Bingham and Bruce V. Moore, *How to Interview*, New York, Harper & Brothers, 1941. See also Anne F. Fenlason, *Essentials in Interviewing: For the Interviewer Offering Professional Services*, New York, Harper & Brothers, 1952. A particularly authoritative presentation of the nondirective method is to be found in Carl Rogers, *Counseling and Psychotherapy*, Boston, Houghton Mifflin Co., 1942.

person by the other, and sincere attempts to understand and share problems and experiences. Talk that is quite removed from the task at hand may occupy the first few minutes of the interview; it may focus upon mutual friends or interests or any of those many subjects of conversation which are used in ordinary social situations. A relaxed situation, away from distractions, in which the respondent may smoke if he wishes and not suffer bodily discomfort from a hard chair, poor ventilation, and glaring light is helpful to the accomplishment of these preliminary aims.

In a highly directive interview the speech correctionist explains the purpose of it, and what he and the interviewee are attempting to do for the child. Also, if necessary, he explains that any information will be held strictly confidential. A relatively young interviewer will need to secure the confidence of the informant. This he may do by casual but relevant comments about his training as well as remarks which indicate that he has observed, studied, or worked with similar cases in the past. For the same purpose, he may want to provide information about the views of authorities in the field in regard to the type of problem under consideration. In general, his identification of himself with his profession will be reassuring to the parent or other person whom he is interviewing. General questions should be posed early in the conference, with specific questions coming later when it becomes necessary to tie down, clarify, or elaborate upon a point or when the interviewee tends to "run dry." Questions that are likely to bring refusal to answer or to raise any kind of negativism should not be asked early in the interview. When the respondent seems to be reporting his interpretation of a situation rather than actual fact, the interviewer may ask for specific examples, descriptions, explanations of what was or was not done, said or not said, and so forth. The respondent's evaluations and interpretations of happenings are to be recorded as such, of course; these, coming from a parent, may give valuable insight into a situation; the fact that a parent has a certain attitude or interpretation may itself be a significant fact. Delicate, intimate, emotion-laden questions should not be presented without some preparation of the respondent and never until the interview has gained some degree of friendly warmth and confidentiality; then they should be asked in a matter-of-fact, straightforward manner. Avoid asking questions that are vague, ponderous, and expressed in words of many syllables. Avoid muddled questions in which you hesitate, rephrase, qualify, change direction. Avoid questions that will draw a misleading or insufficient "yes" or "no," and questions that suggest a possible answer or tend to bias the respondent. Ask certain questions that will double-check others, particularly where you have noted inconsistencies or discrepancies. Accept emotional responses, if they come, matter-of-factly and with tact. Establish time-place and individual-to-individual relationships with care. Define terms if necessary, and ask for definitions. Note the reactions, language habits, and attitudes of the respondent. Keep control of the interview at all times.

The speech correctionist, in preparation for an interview, should decide in general what he wants to know, perhaps keeping the outline of a case history in mind. He should make a definite appointment with the interviewee, and see that they have privacy. Enough time should be allowed for the interview; in general it should neither proceed at a breath-taking pace nor drag, although both rapid questioning and painstaking care are at times profitable in obtaining reliable answers. It is wise to keep note-taking within reasonable limits, using a quick method of recording that will not hold up the progress of the interview. Date all important events and write all dates in terms of month, day, *and year*. Note all names and relationships.

A third thing that we do in order to obtain information is to make use of appropriate tests. Hearing tests, of course, should be administered periodically to all children in the school, using a pure tone audiometer for those below the third grade and above five years of age. If the hearing of a child with a voice or articulatory problem has not been tested within recent months or after an ear infection, meningitis, head cold, or similar condition, it should be tested at the time of his speech examination. An intelligence test, in almost every case of speech deficiency of any severity, will be helpful not only in deciding whether low mental ability might be a contributing cause but helpful also in making tentative estimates of how well the child will respond to retraining, barring other complications. Most school systems administer intelligence tests routinely and enter the results of the tests on the permanent record of the student. Achievement tests such as the Unit Scales of Attainment are administered to determine reading skills, and to indicate whether remedial reading lessons should be combined with speech retraining. Personality tests such as the Minnesota Multiphasic Personality Inventory[18] are helpful in detecting anxieties and frustrations, but, of course, special training is needed in order to interpret the results obtained by means of such tests. Autobiographical material as well as observation of behavior will round out this picture. Aptitude tests like the Kuder Preference Record[19] will provide information that is helpful in counseling students who have behavior problems that might possibly stem from unsuitability for certain courses of study that they are following in preparation for a vocation. The speech correctionist will, of course, refer children who require considerable psychological evaluation or counseling to the school psychologist, if there is one, or to a psychologist in a nearby clinic, hospital, university, or other agency.

*Recording Information.* After obtaining information by observing, interviewing, and testing, we attempt to record that information in a tangible, reviewable form. This written account is called a "case history." The kinds of information that should go in it, depending upon the type of problem, will be outlined under "Records and Reports." Here we are concerned primarily, and but briefly, with the language of the report. The case history should be written in clear, precise, specific statements that hang together in a readable, filled-in narrative. Factual information only should be recorded. Quotation marks should be used when you record exact statements that are significant or revealing. If

[18] Psychological Corporation, 522 Fifth Avenue, New York 36, N.Y.

[19] Examiner's manuals may be obtained from Science Research Associates, 57 W. Grand Avenue, Chicago, Illinois.

the factuality of a statement is uncertain, end it with a question mark in parenthesis, (?). Be sure that all time-space and individual-to-individual relationships have been kept clear. If the case history includes information from more than one respondent, be sure that the source of each statement is indicated. Report impersonally, and with an open mind. Anyone interested in developing the ability to report accurately would be well advised to study a short, readable book called *Language in Thought and Action,* by S. I. Hayakawa.[20]

Avoid precipitous labeling of a speech problem. Once the handicap has been labeled as one of stuttering, cleft palate, or cerebral palsy, for example, you tend to (a) overlook items of behavior that might lead to a different diagnosis, (b) read into behavior those things that you have learned to expect in a problem so labeled, (c) fail to make those observations that would seem irrelevant in view of the label, and (d) jump to hasty conclusions about the required type of treatment and retraining. Some speech correctionists would use classifications only rarely for special purposes, or not at all; they argue that any one handicapped individual may be classified in several different categories and that there are significant differences between individuals who might be placed in any one category. They would emphasize the value of simply describing clearly and fully the facts in each case and treating each case on its merits and according to its requirements as a unique individual.

*Inference.* Finally comes the job of inference—the job of reasoning about and from the information you have accumulated. In listing this as a final step in examination-evaluation, we do not intend to imply that you have not been doing this sort of thing all along. You have. You have evaluated the accuracy of the information that you have received in interviews. You have been cautious about your own observations. Whenever you observed or heard something that seemed to be significant in relation to the child and his problem, you looked for other information that would either support or contradict it. You have

[20] S. I. Hayakawa, *Language in Thought and Action,* New York: Harcourt, Brace & Co., 1949.

been much concerned about possible cause-effect relationships. You have thought perhaps of several possible causal relationships and several possible plans of retraining. Your mind has moved from the immediate case to analogous cases that you have read about or observed and then back to the immediate case.

Actually, what you do now is to refine the thinking that you have already done during the process of obtaining and recording information. To do this you ask yourself at least five questions:

1. What kind of person is this child?
2. What kind of environment affects his development?
3. What are the cause-effect relationships involved in the problem?
4. What do clearly analogous cases tell me about the problem?
5. What kind of remedial program is indicated?

Much has been said on preceding pages that helps you to answer all these questions. Consequently, at this point it will be necessary to comment only briefly about the last three questions. Number three, which inquires about cause-effect relationships, is the focal point of your examination-evaluation. Preceding chapters have considered the etiology of various handicaps in adequate detail. But that information simply guides your efforts in attempting to understand any particular case. Now you are working with a unique personality in a unique physical, psychological, and environmental context, with all its complicated and almost inexplicable facets. Consequently, the determination of cause-effect relationships becomes an exercise of logical analysis. Here are some guides for your reasoning: (1) Can you establish definite, clear-cut causal relationships? (2) Is what you think to be a cause adequate to produce the handicap? (3) Is more than one cause operating in producing this effect? (4) Are there other conditions that prevent a possible cause from producing the handicap? (5) Have you verified all the facts that enter into your analysis of causal relationships?

Question 4 suggests that you turn your thinking in the direction of analogous cases and allow these to help you in your reasoning. Remember, however, that case$_1$ is not case$_2$ and that they must be alike in all major respects in order for you to reason that something unknown about case$_1$ will be similar to a parallel condition (or cause or response) in case$_2$.

Question 5 asks what kind of remedial program is indicated. Here it is necessary for you to bridge the gap between your analysis of cause-effect relationships and your knowledge of remedial procedures. In connection with this, it is important to remember two things. The first is the fact that some actual causes cannot be eliminated or even significantly altered. You cannot repair the brain damage that has resulted in cerebral palsy, for example. The thing that you can do in such a case is to change certain of the child's perceptions, behaviors, and adjustive techniques, which in turn may help change the reactions of others—or you may be able to modify directly the attitudes and behavior of these other persons—and in the end bring about better conditions for the child. The second important thing to remember is that you must be selective in regard to remedial procedures. You have received much advice in this book. We hope that it will be most helpful to you. But this advice, or the advice offered in any other book, may not be used without discrimination. It can only provide a general guide. You must select, intelligently select, that which is useful in it in any particular instance. Certain suggestions may be used in working with Billy Jones, others must be discarded and avoided. There can be no substitute for your own judgment.

This completes your examination-evaluation. You have obtained information about the child by observing, interviewing, and testing. You have recorded that information in the form of a case history. As the final step you have reasoned from and about that information, giving particular attention to causal relationships, and as a result of that reasoning you have decided upon a particular course of action. The information to follow will help you plan the resulting program of remedial procedures.

APPROACHES TO RETRAINING

There seem to be three major discernible approaches to the correction of speech handicaps: (1) group work, (2) individualized instruction under group conditions, and (3) individual instruction. These classifications are suggested merely to facilitate explanation. They are not mutually exclusive in that one classification shuts out the other or in that any particular speech correctionist accepts one approach and rejects another. Neither are the approaches necessarily antagonistic to each other. Similarities and differences will become apparent as we proceed.

*Group Work.* Those who conduct remedial instruction by means of group work seem to fall into two categories, (1) those who advocate nonsegregation in regard to type of speech handicap,[21] and (2) those who recommend homogeneity among individuals in the group in regard to age, sex, education, socioeconomic level, and type of speech problem.[22] In general, the group approach to speech correction is based on the theory that improvement in speech behavior is, in certain degree, determined by improvement in ability to handle interpersonal relationships. Treatment starts with "child-in-situation" rather than with speech phenomena which cannot be isolated from either the whole child or his environment. Consequently the first steps in retraining are concerned with those perceptions of self and environment, and those personal needs, standards of value, and adjustive techniques which prevent the child from growing, developing, learning. Rehabilitation is also concerned with social skills—teaching the child how to function with confidence in typical daily social situations, how to win acceptance and support from others, how to share attitudes, how to shift roles. As a part of all this and as the behavior toward which it is aimed, the remedial speech teacher is concerned with both the effectiveness of speech responses in controlling environment and the characteristics of speech production (phonetics, voice, and so forth). Speech correction, in many cases, proceeds more rapidly and efficiently and is more likely to "take" and endure if the psycho-

[21] Ollie Backus and Jane Beasley, *Speech Therapy With Children*, Boston: Houghton Mifflin Co., 1951.

[22] George H. Shames, "An Exploration of Group Homogeneity in Group Speech Therapy," *Journal of Speech and Hearing Disorders* (September, 1953), *18*:267-272.

social needs of the child are adequately met. Furthermore, much more is done for the child as a person.

The Backus and Beasley procedure in speech correction with groups or individuals emphasizes the establishment of a good psychological climate, the use of conversation in social situations, and the occurrence only once, and in context, of the sound to be taught. Good psychological climate is established by the teacher's attitude and manner as well as by (1) encouraging participation, (2) providing a situation in which the child experiences feelings of acceptance and success, (3) permissiveness within certain limits in regard to behavior, (4) accepting the child's feelings, (5) allowing choices, (6) and keeping the situation speech-centered. The remedial lesson, in order to provide for maximum carry-over of the new skill, is built around simple interpersonal situations like getting acquainted, welcoming a friend, giving a party, exchanging toys, asking permission, playing a game, answering and asking questions, choosing, guessing, making inquiries and responding to them, borrowing and lending, giving and accepting apologies, etc. This procedure, which Backus and Beasley recommend for all or most speech handicapped children, is not greatly unlike that usually suggested, in part, for individuals who stutter.[23]

*Individualized Instruction Under Group Conditions.* There seem to be three major differences between group work or therapy and individualized instruction under group conditions: (1) in the emphasis placed on "adjustment" and "social skills," (2) in the directness of attack upon speech production, and (3) in the type of speech activity. Group work or therapy aims at the development of a cohesive group which functions permissively but under rational control. It provides an environment for the child in which he can experience group belongingness and learn social skills. In it he finds acceptance of himself as he is, recognition of his abilities, and a reason to speak. In it he experiences success in his interpersonal relationships and uses speaking both

---

[23] Backus and Beasley, *op. cit.* See also Ollie Backus and Harriet Dunn, "Use of Conversation Patterns to Promote Speed and Retention of Learning," *Journal of Speech Disorders* (1947), 12:135-142.

to create better relationships and to improve speech. Individualized instruction under group conditions is a matter of working with a collection of individuals; it can be called a "group" only in the sense that several children (from two to ten) are gathered together so that each of them may be given remedial instruction in speech. No serious attempt is made to develop group cohesiveness. Social skills are largely ignored, as are many aspects of interpersonal relationship. Leadership, although democratic, is largely centered in the hands of the speech correctionist, and activities are generally controlled and directed by him. The corrective attack is leveled more directly at the production of speech, which is stimulated through games, objects, pictures, and word lists. Remedial work, for articulatory problems, proceeds through a sequence of ear training, producing the sound in isolation, strengthening the sound, producing it in familiar words and then in connected speech.

Successful speech correctionists have developed many techniques which can be used in working with groups. We shall mention several and hope that you will invent equally effective methods of your own.

One exercise makes use of the stimulation method of teaching a new sound and utilizes the other group members to teach one individual. Suppose, for instance, that one pupil in the group has a faulty *s*. Instead of repeating *s* himself for the pupil to imitate, the remedial speech teacher asks all the others in the group to produce the sound. One after the other those who can produce a correct *s* repeat a series of the sound. The pupil with the faulty *s* listens intently and attempts to imitate the sound after each stimulation. In this way all the children actively participate in an effective exercise which they enjoy, and at the same time provide concentrated work on a particular sound for the child who needs it. After a few minutes of intensive work on the *s*, the exercise may shift to some other sound in which another member of the group is deficient. Naturally the instructor will need to vary this procedure if he finds it necessary to combine the phonetic placement method or some other technique with the stimulation method in order to teach the sound, or if he finds it necessary to make other adaptations to individual differences.

A variation of the method just described is used by many teachers. The group is broken up into two or three pairs of children, each pupil paired with another who can properly produce the sound in which he himself is deficient. A youngster who can produce a good *s* but has difficulty with the articulation of *r*, for example, may be paired with one who can produce a good *r* but makes an incorrect *s*. The children then take turns in stimulating each other with the sound each is attempting to learn. The teacher moves from pair to pair demonstrating and lending aid whenever necessary. Often this exercise carries over into other situations. It is not unusual to discover two pupils spontaneously and carefully doing the exercise during the noon hour or at recess time. The technique may be used for almost any step in the corrective process.

Still another variation is an echo game in which the teacher stimulates and the group in unison imitates him. Interesting variations of many kinds may be invented. One is the "firecracker" game which may be used when working on the *s*. Immediately after stimulation by the teacher the pupils produce a sustained *s*. The teacher listens carefully and then points to the pupil who seems to be making the best *s*; this pupil says "Boom!" and then the procedure is repeated. Once a good *s* is obtained the same method may be used to combine the sound with vowels and to use the sound in phonetically simple words. Each child, some time during the lesson, should have an opportunity to say "Boom!"

Elementary school pupils like to and do imitate sounds they hear. Some develop quite a repertoire of imitations. To obtain a desired language sound, the teacher may ask the group to imitate some sound which closely resembles it. Then, through repeated practice, he attempts to move the group from the imitation to the desired sound, usually in combination with a vowel. Many teachers, in attempting to teach *r*, ask the group to growl like a dog, and then upon a signal from the teacher to say *ra* or some other *r*-vowel combination. From this preliminary step it is usually not too difficult to move on to simple words like rat, rut, and run.

The "simultaneous talking-and-writing" technique explained by Van Riper can also be used very handily in group work.[24] Members of the group are seated about the room so that they do not interfere with each other. Each articulates the new sound, its combination with a vowel, and finally the whole word at the same time that he is writing the symbols for the sound, the sound-vowel combination, and the word. One member of the group may be writing "s s s s su su su su suit" while another is talking-writing some other combination that represents his particular problem. The teacher moves from pupil to pupil providing help.

Exaggerated speech sessions may be held with the group on occasions. The pupils read aloud in unison, exaggerating the speech movements. Individual speech problems are pointed out and worked on as they are heard and observed, considering, of course, the kind of problem and the psychological impact upon the pupil of doing or not doing this kind of thing. If the instructor feels it wise, each pupil may speak alone at times, continuing to exaggerate.

Whisper sessions may be used now and then. For several short lessons the pupils and teacher will communicate only by means of whisper. Short talks delivered in a whisper may be included in these sessions. Speech problems will be pointed up by this process, and corrective practice can follow.

*Individual Instruction.* Our concern, even when working with groups, is with the individual in the group, and, as we have seen and as any teacher knows, there is a good deal of attention to be given to each child on an individual basis even though he is a member of a group. When we talk of individual instruction as such, however, we are thinking of a stiuation in which the remedial plan is structured around one child working alone with the speech correctionist. The interpersonal relationships involved in this lesson situation are largely those between teacher and child. The procedures that the instructor uses to bring about

[24] Charles Van Riper, *Speech Correction: Principles and Methods,* Third Ed., New York, Prentice-Hall, Inc., 1953.

emotional adjustment, for example, are necessarily those that can be used with a single child. Sometimes they take the form of catharsis through play; the child may perhaps form a clay model and with a blow of his fist release the aggression that has been building up within him; or the child and the speech correctionist may throw darts at a caricature drawn upon paper, which to the child represents an authority figure; or the child may "talk it out of his system" to a hand puppet which he manipulates as his feelings urge. Attention to social skill is concentrated in the direction of an adult-child relationship, unless other children are at some time incorporated into the instructional plan. The attack upon the speech problem, once inhibiting emotional forces have been released, is direct and concentrated, as in individualized instruction in a group situation.

### ADJUSTIVE TECHNIQUES

There are a number of techniques that the speech correctionist can use to bring about changes in the feelings and behavior of the child. These techniques aim, of course, to free the child from emotional blocks and conflicts which prevent him from making a satisfactory adjustment to his environment. To bring about these changes, the correctionist may deal with the environment of the child, with the child himself, or with both environment and child.

The two most important aspects of the environment of the child are the home and the school. In the home the strongest influence upon the child is, of course, that of the parents. Sometimes sibling rivalry enters into the picture. Ways in which the remedial speech teacher and the parent can work together have been considered in the section of this chapter headed "the team." In the school the strongest influences upon the child are those of his classroom teachers and his schoolmates. These influences also have been considered under "the team." We will repeat here only the frequently observed fact that the best school environment is one that provides a friendly, relaxed atmosphere in which the child engages in meaningful and satisfying tasks which are within his capacity to achieve and which provide him with a sense of accomplishment. A special school is the answer, in some cases of severe degrees of handicap, where it is extremely difficult or impossible for either the home or the regular school to provide a proper environment.

Changes in the behavior of the child, as has been said, also can be brought about by action directed specifically at the child himself. This action may be taken in one or a combination of four ways: (1) by direct problem solving; (2) by group activity inside or outside the school; (3) by expressive activities like role playing in sociodrama, psychodrama, creative dramatics; and (4) by catharsis, individually or in a group.

*Direct Problem Solving.* This technique is used with the older child who is generally well adjusted but who has a specific problem which is causing some conflict and tension. With the speech correctionist the child approaches the problem situation frankly and objectively, isolating the central problem, attempting to get at reasons for it, evaluating consequences to himself and his family, looking at the pros and cons of possible solutions, and arriving at a decision concerning the best course of action.

*Group Activity.* For some children with behavior problems group activity seems to be the best answer. It is indicated (1) when the child's problems center around social adjustment to schoolmates, people in authority, or siblings, (2) when the child reverts to infantile behavior, (3) when the child cannot be reached through individual attention but will respond to group activities and pressures, and (4) when one of the child's great needs is for independence and responsible self-direction.

Group activity outside the school can be obtained in summer speech camps, in the Y.M.C.A. or Y.W.C.A., in the Scouts, in church groups, in clubs. Before recommending activity of this kind for any child, however, the speech correctionist will consider the aims and procedures of the group, the character of the leadership of the group, the age and interests and social maturity of the child, the intellectual level of the child and that of active members of the group, and marked differences in the child that might be penalized by the group.

Group activity within the school can follow a number of patterns. One such is the pattern developed by Backus and Beasley which we have previously considered. Another is that used typically by psychotherapists, and which can be adapted to the remedial speech situation. Ordinarily the members of the group are of one sex, between the ages of five and ten and with no more than two years' difference in individual ages. Usually the children are similar in degree of social maturity, and usually a mixture of withdrawing and aggressive "types. Ordinarily the children are not known to one another before the start of group activity. They are taken into a room equipped with tools and materials for handicrafts. In using these tools and materials the individual child directs his aggression toward objects rather than his companions. An air of permissiveness and acceptance tends to develop, and this allows for release of emotion and wears down hostility. Communication develops between the children. They talk about their projects and praise each other for work well done. In time there is no longer a significant need to engage in antisocial acts in order to gain status or assert independence. The group exerts its own discipline, to which the individual child tends to conform. After a time, group experiences are expanded to include picnics and tours. In these the child encounters new social problems and gradually develops more realistic reactions to his environment. He discovers limitations and controls, but to the degree that permissiveness is present and hostility is absent, resentment is not aroused and the individual brings himself under control. The amount of direction and suggestion provided by the leader or instructor depends upon his own point of view and the nature of the group.[25]

[25] The following are excellent sources of supplementary information: Amy Bishop Chapin and Margaret Corcoron, "A Program for the Speech Inhibited Child," *The Journal of Speech Disorders*, (1947), 12:373-376; Margaret W. Gerard, "Treatment of the Young Child," *American Journal of Orthopsychiatry*, (1948), 17:414-421; Robert G. Hinckley and Lydia Hermann, *Group Treatment in Psychotherapy*, Minneapolis, University of Minnesota Press, 1951; Otto Pollak, *et al.*, *Social Science and Psychotherapy for Children*, New York, Russell Sage Foundation, 1952; S. R. Slavson, *An Introduction to Group Therapy*, New York, The Commonwealth Fund, 1943; S. R. Slavson, *The Practice of Group Therapy*, New York, International Universities Press, 1947; S. R. Slavson, *Child Psychotherapy*, New York, Columbia University Press, 1952.

*Role Playing.* The term "role playing" is used to represent a variety of activities. Here, however, we shall use it to indicate the part an individual takes in impromptu dramatic skits which are designed to provide insight into his own behavior and that of others. These impromptu dramatic performances are variously labeled "psychodrama," "sociodrama," and "creative dramatics." Although the labels are sometimes used interchangeably and "role playing" is common to all, there are some who insist upon sharp distinctions. Special, and in some instances intensive, training is required for the use of many of the techniques presently to be described. It is assumed that speech correctionists will acquire the necessary training before attempting to use play therapy or psychodrama, for example. In the meantime, these methods involve basic principles that can be and are applied by all good teachers, pediatricians, speech correctionists, and others who work professionally with children. Moreover, it is very desirable that speech correctionists be familiar with these techniques, not only in order to cultivate within practical limits the attitudes which they require, but also in order to be able to refer certain children to professional workers and clinics that make use of these procedures.

Psychodrama is a psychiatric technique in which chronically frustrated neurotic and psychotic individuals are given an opportunity to act out and express their fantasies, thus securing release similar to that obtained by less emotionally disturbed people through culturally provided outlets. Usually it concentrates upon the unique problems and needs of a particular individual, and should be conducted only by a psychiatrist or psychologist.[26]

Sociodrama, on the other hand, deals with problems that are not uncommon to most of the members of a group. It is designed to be helpful in relieving the more ordinary tensions, frustrations, and conflicts which, although common, have strong in-

[26] The individual who is interested in additional information concerning psychodrama would do well to consult J. L. Moreno, *Psychodrama*, New York, Beacon House, 1946; Robert Bartlett Haas, *Psychodrama and Sociodrama in American Education*, New York, Beacon House, 1949; Edwin M. Lemert and Charles Van Riper, "The Use of Psychodrama in the Treatment of Speech Defects," *Sociometry* (May, 1944), 7:190-195.

fluence upon the behavior of children—and their parents, therapists, and teachers.

Sociodrama makes use of a briefly outlined situation in which two or more individuals spontaneously act out their designated roles. Either the members of the group or the instructor may structure (outline) the situation and select those who are to take part. No value is placed upon skill in acting. It is hoped that those who play roles will be able to become completely absorbed in them. The scene is allowed to run from two to five minutes. The person in charge of the scene (it may be either the speech correctionist or a member of the group) calls "cut" when it becomes apparent that further participation will not be profitable. The role players and their audience then discuss the situation. Usually this discussion is conducted by the instructor and is stimulated by questions directed at the participants as well as the audience.

Sociodrama proceeds through eight well-defined steps: (1) defining the problem, (2) establishing a situation covered by the problem, (3) casting, (4) explaining the situation to the actors and the observers and warming them up to their various roles, (5) acting out the situation, (6) cutting the action, (7) analyzing and discussing the situation as well as the behavior of the actors, and (8) either planning further testing of the insights which were gained or deciding how new behaviors can be put into practice. Almost any parent-child, teacher-pupil, child-sibling, child-classmate problem can be acted out, analyzed, and possibly changed through this technique.[27]

Creative dramatics is a much used teaching device which aims primarily to develop the child's faith in his creative power, to help him become independent in his thinking, and to allow him to experience teamwork, democratic participation, and group

[27] For more extensive discussions of sociodrama, see Norman R. F. Maier, *Principles of Human Relations*, New York, John Wiley & Sons, Inc., 1952, Chapters 4 and 5; Staff of the Educator's Washington Dispatch, eds., *Portfolio of Teaching Techniques*. New York, A. C. Croft, 1951; Bert Strauss and Frances Strauss, *New Ways to Better Meetings*, New York, The Viking Press, Inc., 1951, Chapter 11; Grace Levit, "Learning Through Role Playing," *Adult Leadership* (October, 1953), *11*:9-16.

membership. However, it has tremendous possibilities for use in the constructive adjustment of behavior as well as in the improvement of speech skills per se. It is designed to allow the release of strong emotional feeling and, if necessary, the direction of that feeling into more healthful channels. It can help children understand how others think and feel, help them to understand themselves better, and help them to enjoy feelings of security, belongingness, and success.

In this form of group activity, children act out meaningful experiences, creating their own dialogue and action. Usually, the experiences are carefully planned or chosen by the instructor with the needs of individual children in mind. Potentially valuable experiences are countless. They may revolve around classroom or playground activities like "helping teacher" or "organizing a baseball team." They may touch upon simple social activities like "going calling with mother." They can enable the child to anticipate and prepare for situations like "going to the dentist." They may center upon personal attributes like those required in "helping other children to be liked." Also these experiences may be built around Mother Goose rhymes, fairy tales, poems, riddles, legends, myths, and adventure stories that contribute to the instructor's purpose. Again they may center upon "dreamed-of-experiences" or "wished-for things." The possibilities are limited only by the range of imagination.[28]

*Catharsis.* This fourth adjustive technique allows for uninhibited release of tension, insecurity, fear, aggression, confusion, and frustration. One way in which the remedial speech teacher allows for catharsis, of course, is to listen with understanding to children and to accept their feelings whenever they boil to the surface. Another way to encourage catharsis is through play therapy. In using this technique, the child is encouraged to bring to the surface or "play out" his feelings. The play therapist, if using a directive approach, helps the youngster face and control his feelings by interpreting and guiding. If using a nondirective

[28] Ruth Gonser Lease and Geraldine Brain Siks, *Creative Dramatics*, New York, Harper & Brothers, 1952; Winifred Ward, *Playmaking With Children*, New York, Appleton-Century-Crofts, Inc., 1947.

approach, he reflects back the feeling and lets the child assume full responsibility for his own self-direction.

The nondirective approach to play therapy, as developed by Axline,[29] and based upon the therapeutic technique of Dr. Carl R. Rogers, rests upon four assumptions (if we may risk misinterpretation): (1) growth is constant change which results from the interaction of the individual with his environment; (2) there is a force or drive within each individual that causes him to strive for maturity, independence, self-direction, self-realization; (3) when progress toward self-realization is blocked, the drive toward it gains momentum because of "the generative force of tensions created by frustrations" and is satisfied vicariously by withdrawal, compensation, daydreaming, identification, projection, regression, repression; (4) play therapy allows the child to expose, face, and control his feelings if (a) the therapist has established a warm, friendly relationship with the child, (b) the child is accepted completely without a show of impatience, criticism, reproof, tension, threat, or attempt at control, (c) there is established an atmosphere of complete permissiveness which is devoid of both suggestions and questions as well as praise, encouragement, and approval, (d) the child's feelings are "reflected back" to him in such a way that he gains insight into his behavior, (e) the child is allowed to assume responsibility for his behavior and no attempt is made to direct either his actions or his conversation, (f) the therapist has complete confidence in the ability of the child to solve his own problems, (g) if the process is not pushed, hurried, or forced, and (h) if the therapist is consistent in imposing a few necessary limitations upon the child, limitations that stop him from destroying materials, damaging the room, attacking the therapist, or engaging in acts that might bring harm to himself.

Play therapy may be used with one child or with groups of children. Axline reports interesting possibilities in the method for speech correction. Also she suggests that it can be used by the classroom teacher (with limitations, of course, upon complete expression of feelings). The teacher of English may encourage

[29] Virginia Mae Axline, *Play Therapy*, Boston, Houghton Mifflin Co., 1947.

children to write autobiographies, placing emphasis upon their thoughts and feelings. In going over the papers the teacher can "reflect back" these feelings, allow them to pour out more fully, and in this way help the child to gain insight into his attitudes and to control them. Other "therapeutic" writing experiences may center upon "Things that make us angry," "Things I hate," "Things I would like to do," "Things I am afraid of." The teacher of art may also give children an opportunity to get their feelings out in the open. Rather than impose art activities, she may allow the child to use his clay, chalk, or paints to obtain emotional release. Once negative feelings are released, the child will tend to move on to more positive feelings and constructive activities.

FORMS OF PRACTICE

The correction-improvement of speech must come about, of course, through speaking. Singing can also be used in certain ways. Singing is used by speech correctionists, on occasion, to determine normal pitch level, obtain wider mouth opening, eliminate nasality, and also to attack other speech problems. Also it is used frequently to provide interesting variations in method. Usually, however, speech correction-improvement is accomplished through speaking. But what kind of speaking? There are many types or forms that can be used. At the same time that the child is using them to correct or improve his speech, he can learn something about the various forms. The speech correctionist or classroom teacher must use judgment, of course, in selecting the particular form that will materially assist the corrective process at any particular stage of retraining.

*Perceptual Reorganization.* Essentially speech correction is a process of replacing old habits with new, whether they be habitual ways of reacting to situations or habitual ways of producing a phoneme or habitual ways of using the voice. This process of change involves a high degree of perceptual reorganization. This, in essence, is a term that covers the retraining procedures explained in previous chapters. To change his speech habits the individual goes through an auditory-intellectual-kinesthetic process of recognition, discrimination, differentiation, restructuring, solidifying, transition, and use.

In order to get a start in the correction of any handicap, assuming that there are no emotional complications, the individual must recognize and accept the fact that he has a problem and also must want to do something about it. Moreover, he must learn to discriminate and differentiate between that which he does and that which would be better. Then he restructures the situation in order to produce the sound (or achieve the pitch level or do whatever he is attempting to do) either in isolation from its use in connected speech or in relatively simple communicative acts. The process of restructuring requires that he think, verbalize, feel, and finally perform the new pattern. The stutterer, for example, revises his perceptions and works upon an easy pattern of nonfluency. Then comes the transition into acts of speaking for a purpose. All this is accomplished in context, so to speak—as part of and in relation to normal communicative activity.

*Naming.*    This form of speaking is used extensively in speech correction. Usually the child names either objects or pictures of objects. These objects or pictures frequently are selected and arranged so that, when named, the sound to be corrected occurs in initial, final, and medial positions in phonetically simple and familiar words. Sometimes this process is expanded in such a way that a simple sentence is repeated over and over again, naming a different object each time, "Sing the song to Sammy," "Sing the song to Simon," and so forth.

*Oral Reading.*    This form of speaking also is used extensively. The child reads the words aloud from specially prepared or selected material. Word lists and paragraphs frequently are used. Short poems and bits of prose are useful, particularly if they are inherently interesting to the child. Reading readiness books, regular classroom readers, and supplementary classroom reading materials are excellent. In using these readers, the speech correctionist may feel reasonably certain that the words and sentences are graded to the educational level of the child. It goes without saying that the material used for oral reading must be selected or prepared for the immediate purpose at hand.

*Conversation.* It is suggested by some remedial speech teachers that there is a chance for greater carry-over outside the speech room if conversation is used as the vehicle for correction, particularly if it centers on normal, daily activities of the child. Conversation is stimulated by the instructor in a number of ways: by casually remarking about something that the child is wearing or carrying; by leading him into a report on his playground activity, his hobbies, his studies; by planning the lesson around normal social or recreational activities such as "welcoming guests to a party," "going fishing," "introducing others."

*Radio Speaking.* The simple fact that the child is speaking into a microphone "like the radio announcers" has a motivating effect. If the microphone is attached to a tape recorder there is the added advantage of emphasizing problems of speech, to the extent that small deviations are noticeable even to the untrained ear. There is no better way to convince a pupil that he has a speech problem (if it is the psychologically proper thing to do) than to use a tape recorder and play back the recording to the child or the group. Some correctionists use their "Train Ear" equipment as a public address system for this type of lesson if other apparatus is not available. The child may read, or tell a story, or speak extemporaneously into the microphone.

*Group Discussion.* This type of speaking activity aims at solving a problem. It teaches children to make use of reflective thinking, and frequently this kind of analysis (problem, causes, possible solutions, preferred solution) can be turned upon perplexing conditions that face the group, such as "the boy who always trips us on the playground." Research conducted with college students indicates that oral, coöperative attempts to solve a problem produce better results in terms of voice and diction than do platform speaking exercises.[30]

*Storytelling.* Some speech correctionists like to stimulate this kind of speaking by means of pictures. They use fairly large cards

---

[30] Alma Johnson, "Teaching the Fundamentals of Speech Through Group Discussion," *Quarterly Journal of Speech* (October, 1939), 25:440-447.

upon each of which is glued a colored picture that depicts some simple action situation within the experience of the youngster. These are presented one by one, and the child tells a story about each picture. If this technique is used with a group, the children may take turns in telling others in the group a story, in supplementing the story told by one child, or in picking out things in the picture that the first child failed to noice. Another use of this kind of speaking is to allow children to tell stories to each other, stories that they have made up, heard, or read. Also the well known procedure of allowing one pupil to start a story and the next to add to it and so on through a group sometimes works well.

*Choral Speaking.* This is sometimes called verse speaking. It involves the oral interpretation of poetry or poetic prose by several voices speaking in unison or in smaller segments of the larger group. Also, in some arrangements, individuals speak some lines alone. With older groups, voices are arranged according to pitch, quality of tone, and volume. Types of choral speaking that are particularly well adapted to younger children are: (1) the refrain, in which one child reads the narrative and the group joins in on the refrain; (2) two-part or antiphonal speaking, in which the group is divided and use is made of "question-and-answer" as well as other types of poetry; (3) line-a-child reading, in which each child is given a chance to speak one line alone and then all speak the last line in unison. Books containing choral speaking arrangements for various grade levels are available in almost any library.[31] This type of speaking has been used in psychotherapy as well as remedial work with voice, articulation, and stuttering problems. It allows a considerable amount of concentration on individual difficulties and, at the same time, provides an interesting oral activity that improves the speech of the group in general. The poem "Spin, Lassie, Spin" by Lady Strachey, for example, is adaptable to arrangements that provide motivating practice situations for pupils who are attempting to

---

[31] Three usable little books are Carrie Rasmussen, *Choral Speaking for Speech Improvement*, 1953; Louise Abney and Grace Rowe, *Choral Speaking Arrangements for the Lower Grades*, 1953; Louise Abney, *Choral Speaking Arrangements for the Upper Grades*, 1952, all published by The Expression Company, Magnolia, Massachusetts.

strengthen the use of the *s* in words. For example, the line, "Spin, lassie, spin," in each stanza, may be read in unison by the pupils with newly developed *s* sounds, while the remainder of the group speaks the other lines of each stanza. The poem also provides good practice material for the *m, n,* and *ng* sounds.

*Public Speaking.* Although most speaking is done in some kind of public or group situation, the expression "public speaking" has come to denote the preparation and delivery of speeches to audiences on more or less formal occasions. Usually these speeches have a well-defined purpose—to inform, interest, stimulate, or persuade. Public speaking in the classroom provides the child with a practice situation in which he may not only correct and improve his speech as well as his speaking, but also build confidence in his ability to face and communicate with audiences in situations that contain many unknowns and consequently strike fear. The "telling hours," stimulating to elementary school children, are simple forms of public speaking.[32]

[32] Representative books which contain information about all these forms of speaking at the elementary school level are Mardel Ogilvie, *Speech in the Elementary School*, New York, McGraw-Hill Book Co., 1954; Lorna Shogren Werner, *Speech in the Elementary School*, Evanston, Illinois; Row, Peterson & Company, 1947; Virgil A. Anderson, *Improving the Child's Speech*, particularly Chapter 12, "Integrating Speech Training with the School Curriculum," New York, Oxford University, Press, 1953. Elementary Committee of the National Association of Teachers of Speech, *Guides to Speech Training in the Elementary School*, Magnolia, Massachusetts, The Expression Company, 1943; Letitia Raubicheck, Grace V. Dooley, and Leontine A. Murtha, *Toward Better Speech: A Manual for Teachers of All Grades*, New York City, Board of Education, Curriculum Bulletin Series, Number 5, 1953. Representative texts for the junior high school level are W. Kirtley Atkinson and Theodore F. Nelson. *Speech and Your Personality*, Chicago, Benj. H. Sanborn & Co., 1955; Alice Evelyn Craig, *The Junior Speech Arts*, New York, The Macmillan Co., 1942; Gladys Louise Borchers, *Living Speech*, New York, Harcourt, Brace & Co., 1938. Representative texts for the high school level are Harry B. Gough *et al., Effective Speech*, New York, McGraw-Hill Book Co., 1948; Letitia Raubicheck *et al., Your Voice and Speech*, New York, Prentice-Hall, Inc., 1953; Wilhelmina G. Hedde and William Norwood Brigance, *American Speech*, Chicago, J. B. Lippincott Co., 1954; Andrew Thomas Weaver and Gladys Louise Borchers, *Speech*, New York, Harcourt, Brace & Co., 1946; Loren D. Reid, *Teaching Speech in the High School*, Columbia, Mo., Artcraft Press, 1952; Willard J. Friederich and Ruth A. Wilcox, *Teaching Speech in High Schools*, New York, Macmillan Co., 1953.

MATERIALS

In every chapter of this book something has been said about materials that can be used for examination and evaluation as well as for instructional purposes. Consequently there is no need here to duplicate these many suggestions. If the reader desires to order speech correction materials a list may easily be prepared by reviewing the various chapters.

PLANNING

Any attempt to outline a program of reëducation for the child who has a serious speech handicap should be based upon a thorough examination-evaluation. A clear-cut analysis of the nature of the speech problem and its possible causes is essential to good planning. It indicates a general approach and makes possible the definition of specific goals at which to shoot. A shotgun fired into the air and over the shoulder, with or without the aid of mirrors, is not likely to bring down much game.

*Long-Range Planning for the Individual or Group.* As his first act after examination-evaluation, the remedial speech teacher outlines, at least in his mind, a long-range program for each child. This program aims, first, to lead the child from his present condition into a certain "goal region" in regard to oral communication. This "goal region" is a flexible and elastic concept that must be defined in terms of the child. It recognizes a child's limitations as well as his potentialities. Some can arrive at "intelligibility," some at "adequacy," some at well-nigh "perfection." It recognizes the impracticality and impossibility of establishing a standard of phonetic precision, complete fluency, perfect speech for every—if, indeed, for any—child. The long-range program aims, second, at self-realization for the individual. In other words, it aims to develop a mature, self-directing, responsible individual who feels some degree of security, belongingness, and acceptance. The long-range program aims, third, toward the development of the child as a member of a family and community group, as a producer and consumer, and as a good citizen. Undoubtedly the reduction of a speech handicap improves oral communication, and this in turn contributes to the youngster's capacity to function in these various roles. How much better for the individual, however, if the correctionist keeps these other aims specifically in mind and uses materials and techniques which contribute to their achievement as well as to the improvement of speech as such. The long-range program aims, fourth, to provide a progression of experiences for the child which are designed to lead him from his present condition into the goal area of improved communication. This progression of experiences is planned in terms of the individual child rather than in terms of children in general or in terms of a speech handicap, narrowly considered. It differs somewhat for each child, depending on whether he is working alone with the correctionist or as a member of a group. This progression of experiences almost always starts with those that satisfy the psychological needs of the individual and proceeds toward those that contribute to the more minute aspects of communicative skill, such as phonetic accuracy. The long-range program aims, fifth, to lay out, for use when needed, what seem to be the most effective procedures, adjustive techniques, practice techniques, and instructional materials for each particular child with his particular speech problem. A most important part of the job is the selection of the proper tools.

*Lesson Planning.* The remedial lesson provides one experience for the child in that progression of experiences which make up the long-range program. It is an integral part of that program and should move the child a little closer to his goal region. It should be carefully planned in advance of actual instruction.

Lesson planning is helpful in a great many ways. It enables the remedial speech teacher to move with sureness and confidence into each instructional situation. If he is definite and confident, the child will feel secure and confident. Lesson planning enables the teacher to be efficient, to know exactly where he is going with the child, what procedures and materials he will use, and how he will evaluate the effectiveness of the lesson. There is less waste motion, uncertainty, and marking of time. It allows the instructor to focus his reasoning powers, insights, and creative imagination upon the child and his problem in the quiet of his office or room, and away from the distractions that thrust themselves into the daily schedule of instruction. It allows him to anticipate unacceptable behavior and to organize the situation so as to make its occurrence less likely.

Plans once made can be and often should be abandoned for the inspiration of the moment. When this occurs planning has not been unnecessary or unprofitable. "Inspiration" or "spur-of-the-moment" ideas that are worth anything are usually the product of careful preliminary thought; the mind that has not played with a problem rarely, if ever, strikes suddenly upon a method of solution.

Planning need not necessarily be done on paper; written plans, however, serve to remind the teacher of his insights and to reassure the administrator. But, whether written or mentally noted, they should not stand in the way of sensible changes and adaptations to the child's responses or to other conditions, as they occur during the week.

Lesson plans should be reviewed and evaluated. Once a lesson has been taught, the planning of it should be reviewed with a critical eye. What were its strengths? What were its weaknesses? What, if anything, was not anticipated? Additional questions to be asked about planning will arise in individual cases.

A well prepared lesson plan should contain the answers to seven questions. The questions, of course, are always asked about a child who has a problem.

1. What is my major objective? The major objective is the ultimate end in view for a particular pupil, the final outcome desired from corrective procedures. It is a rather clear outline of the goal region toward which the child is advancing. It is not limited to the development of adequate fluency or phonetic accuracy, for example, but usually includes or implies the achievement of a sufficient measure of self-realization, social skill, group membership, and citizenship. Here are some typical major objectives: "To help the child develop self-confidence in social situations which include authority individuals." "To help the child attain a feeling of status in groups of his classmates." "To develop ability to use the *t* sound in all positions in connected speech in

school and home situations." "To teach the child to adopt an easy, simple pattern of nonfluency when talking to his friends outside the speech room." Major objectives, or kinds of improvement, for stutterers and for children with speech problems of other types are presented in Chapters III through VIII.

2. What is my lesson objective? A lesson objective is one of the activities or experiences intended to lead the child closer to the major objective. Sometimes the lesson objective is formulated as a result of psychological considerations; sometimes as the logical next step in the planned sequence. Usually this sequence moves from lessons that emphasize personal and social adjustment of the individual toward lessons that place emphasis on details of speech production. At this stage of planning the correctionist asks two questions: What is the immediate next step that must be taken in order to move the child closer to the major objective? Does it seem likely that the child, with some effort, will be able to achieve this objective? Lesson objectives usually are stated in such terms as these: "To allow release of aggressive tendencies," "To produce *s* in isolation," "To secure transfer of *s* into commonly used words," "To eliminate the stutterer's eye-closure habit," "To improve activity of the soft palate," "To teach the child to discriminate between *w* and *wh*," "To strengthen the production of *s*," "To teach the child to imitate his own stuttering," "To have the child engage in negative practice of his defective *s*."

3. What will be the pupil's immediate objective? The pupil's immediate objective and the teacher's lesson objective become the same when (a) the student is aware of his need, (b) he is impelled for one reason or another to improve, and (c) he recognizes that the accomplishment of the day's lesson is a necessary and important step toward the series of subgoals which he and the teacher have established to guide their work. Ordinarily, however, the child's immediate objective is not nearly so clean-cut. His only desire may be to please the teacher, and if this is so, he is more likely than he might otherwise be to perform activity that results in accomplishment of the lesson objective. To the teacher, the immediate next step might be to combine the *l* sound with vowels. For the child, the immediate need is to achieve a

feeling of success. Therefore the correctionist ties his perception of need together with the child's perception of need and tells the group, "We will give Mary a chance to earn the first gold star today." Mary is successful. She receives the star and the applause of the group. The needs of both the child and the instructor are met, and the child moves forward, happily, toward the major objective.

In this phase of planning, the teacher is concerned with the drives, motives, and wants of the child which are likely to impel him in a desired direction. Once he has determined these forces he is in a position to turn them in the direction of speech reëducation. A desire on the part of the child for recognition and status, for example, might be met by appointing him "teacher's helper" for the period. The consequent stimulation is likely to carry over into his practice efforts in speech.

4. What procedures shall I use? The procedures used in the corrective session will depend, of course, upon the immediate objectives of both the teacher and the child. If the immediate objective is concerned with some phase of ear training, the teacher devises or adapts techniques to accomplish that purpose. If the immediate aim is to revise the pupil's evaluations of his stuttering, methods are invented to achieve that end. Should the immediate objective be to strengthen the expulsion of breath through the mouth by a child who has had a cleft palate repaired, the teacher may have the pupil blow a ping-pong ball about a table, blow light feathers into the air, fill balloons with air, blow a horn or whistle, blow water from one bottle into another through connecting tubes, blow the wheel of a toy windmill, or imitate a siren by whistling.

The procedures used in teaching any skill or subject are devised by inventive minds which have been stimulated by study and experience. Although in this book we have attempted to provide the teacher with observations drawn from the most recent research in speech correction and the experience of successful teachers, it is impossible to supply specific procedures for every one of the varied problems he will meet. If, however, the reader has secured a grasp of the nature of speech disorders and an understanding of the basic principles and methods of correction, he can use his inventive powers to devise specific techniques for accomplishing his immediate and major objectives.[33]

The following questions may be suggestive of those that the teacher will ask in planning the procedure for a particular session. What school or extracurricular activity is the child engaged in at the present time that is of great interest to him? Does he have other strong immediate interests? If so, how can I tie in the remedial lesson with those activities and interests? What is the attitude of the child toward his speech lessons? If the attitude is negative or apathetic, how can I relate the lesson to his normal drives and wants? What was the previous lesson? Is a review of it necessary? Will the child recognize the relationship between this activity and the activities that he normally engages in on the playground and in the classroom? Will he profit by an explanation of the probable causes of his problem and the steps proposed to correct it? Should he listen to a recording of his speech? If so, what precisely is he to listen for? Will it help him to observe the movements of his lips in a mirror in attempting to produce a particular sound? What game can be devised that will result in getting Bob's hands away from his mouth? Should John read in chorus with Betty? How can I get Jim to help plan his next lesson? How can I get considerable variety of procedure and material in this lesson? What will I do if the interest of the child wanders away from the lesson? How will I summarize or clinch the lesson? What can I do to get the child to anticipate and look forward with eagerness to the next lesson?

5. What materials should be used? The materials used in

[33] See the most recent edition of *Bibliography of Books for Children,* Literature Committee, Association for Childhood Education, Washington, D.C., for available children's publications containing a wealth of practice material. The Association for childhood Education also publishes a compilation of imitative games, guessing games, etc., under the title *Games Children Like.* For up-to-date lists of speech correction drill and practice books and related materials for use with children consult the National Society for Crippled Children and Adults, 11 South LaSalle Street, Chicago, Ill., or write direct to major publishers.

speech correction depend on the nature of the problem as well as upon the ability, maturity, and interests of the youngster. A highly important consideration is that they be drawn from his ordinary interests and activities. Practice on sounds, words, and sentences used in asking and answering questions, asking and giving directions, carrying messages, telephoning, expressing appreciation, conversing, asking favors, extending and accepting and declining invitations, greeting others, shopping, and reporting is much more effective than practice on word lists and sentences that have little relationship to ordinary activities. Typed transcripts taken from a recording of the student's own conversation, or sentences taken from his comments, make good practice material. If play is the basis of training, the natural choices of children should be considered. Kindergarten play equipment, for example, "should include raw materials (e.g., clay, large floor blocks, wood, printing materials); pattern toys; housekeeping or dollcorner equipment, locomotor toys; and simple picture books." Collections of children's poems and stories, illustrated dictionaries, mail-order catalogues, and collections of mounted pictures are useful materials. Reading selections used for retraining purposes should conform to the natural interests of the youngster at his particular level of maturity. Boys twelve years of age, for example, are interested in biography and history as well as stories of adventure, athletic prowess, inventions, mechanics, scientific research, and industrial processes. Girls of the same age are interested in biographies of women, as well as stories of home life, school life, and nature.

6. What means of evaluation can be used? How can the pupil and the teacher arrive at an evaluation of his performance? Should the group comment on the progress of individual members? Should the pupil attempt to evaluate his own performance? Should today's lesson be recorded and compared with a recording made previously? Should some kind of tabulation be made of the correct responses in today's lesson in an attempt to surpass the number counted last time?

7. What should the pupil do between this meeting and the next? An interim "assignment" should be short as a rule and

always specific and accomplishable. It may be decided upon at any opportune time during the remedial session. If it is a practice assignment, it should be checked and evaluated by a parent, classroom teacher, or friend. If the pupil, for example, is to make a certain sound each time he goes through a particular door at home, a parent, brother, or sister should listen for correct and incorrect productions of the sound. If it is an experience assignment, it should be reported specifically and objectively at the next session. If a stutterer, for example, decides to make two telephone calls before his next lesson, he should make a report concerning them.

THE CONDITIONS OF PRACTICE

Beyond the removal or minimization of certain causes, the basic principle used in speech correction is that of guided practice. Even the primary consideration of improving the pupil's personal and social adjustment entails practice: practice by the child in doing the things he is afraid to do, practice in discovering the falsity of his evaluations, practice in reacting objectively to his difficulty. Practice is a condition of learning whether it be of speech, writing, reading, computing, or the development of attitudes or moral standards. By practice, however, we do not mean the sheer repetition often called "drill." Practice of that nature is relatively useless as a learning device.

It is only under certain conditions that practice results profitably in learning. Although many of these conditions have been mentioned at one place or another in this book, it will be well to summarize them briefly and generally as a part of this particular discussion of method in general, and in their close relationship to planning. Plans are formulated to guide the process of learning; consequently they must consider the conditions of practice in learning.

1. Perhaps it has become trite to repeat the phrase, "We learn by doing." Nevertheless, it is a significant principle of methodology and the basic idea behind that of guided practice. The lesson must allow the child to *do* the thing that will change his perceptions, change his adjustive techniques, satisfy his needs,

revise his standards of value, and develop adequate skill in speech production. Obviously, however, the *doing* must not amount to repetition of a bad habit. It must replace old habits with new; no correction is obtained by the repetition of a lateral *s*, for example. The doing must involve a conscientious effort to change, accompanied by an understanding of *why* and *what* and *how*.

2. Practice, if it is to be accompanied by insight, and if it is to result in maximum transfer, should take advantage of those natural and normal speaking situations in which the child participates from day to day. A great many of these situations have been mentioned from place to place in this book. Among them were listed the asking and answering of questions. Studies have revealed that the average three-year-old child asks approximately 375 questions during a day and the average four-year-old approximately 400. Any mother would probably attest to this fact without having to be informed of the experimental evidence. The point is that we have in this natural inquisitiveness the basis for an important type of practice activity which is meaningful to the child. The same comment could be made concerning the other situations already listed. For purpose of example, however, we shall limit this discussion to an illustration of how the teacher can take advantage, in remedial teaching, of this natural inclination to ask questions.

It is not enough that the activity of the remedial session be generally planned to center about a natural type of activity in an ordinary socialized situation. If questions are asked, for example, they are asked about something. The remedial lesson should not only take advantage of a natural speaking activity but it should also involve the needs, interests, and preoccupations which are the stimuli for that oral activity. Suppose, for example, that a field trip to a farm is impending for an elementary school class of city youngsters. Excitement runs high as the children anticipate the trip. What are they likely to see on the farm? Teacher and pupil make a list. On this list appear the words "cows," "cats," "kittens," "chickens," and so forth. Can the guide understand the child who asks questions about these and doesn't make the *k* sound correctly? Teacher and pupil set to work industriously on the sound at whatever stage the remedial work has reached. If no work has been done on the sound before that time, the list of words containing the *k* sound is used as a basis for ear training. If the child can distinguish between the *k* and the sound he is substituting for it, the correctionist attempts to teach the sound. So it goes—the remedial work is related to the immediate need and interest of the youngster.

This naturally motivated practice can be strengthened by what Backus and Dunn designate as "reinforcement on one response rather than many."[34] Remedial work is concentrated on one word in which the sound occurs once. This one word is used in a variety of socialized situations. In this way a correct speech sound response tends to become automatic and then to spread to many words. It is to be remembered, however, that the pupil must be able to discriminate between his error and the correct production of the sound, as well as to make the sound in isolation, before using this reinforcement practice with one or more frequently used words.

Furthermore, the correctionist and the pupil can work out a series of questions about the farm animals which the pupil is going to see—questions the child will want to ask the guide during the trip about the farm: "Do the chickens crow at night?" "Do the cats like the cows?" "Do the cows bother the chickens?" The pupil can then read these questions to his classmates during "planning and telling" time, concentrating, of course, on the use of the new sound.

Procedures of this kind have numerous advantages over practice on words and sentences which have no relationship to the pupil's immediate needs and interests. The pupil learns the new sound in the way he is going to use it. Advantage is taken of his intrinsic motivation. He understands the significance of his remedial work. He has encountered a problem and has an incentive to solve it. His practice has a purpose. He works with zest and enthusiasm.

3. Retraining practice should follow a progression of experiences which are dictated by the nature of the problem and the

[34] Ollie Backus and Harriet Dunn, *op. cit.*

individual needs of the child. In other words, the teacher studies the child and the nature of his difficulty and, on the basis of that study, decides what should be done first and, so far as possible, step by step thereafter. His study of the child starts with specific errors and other speech reactions and proceeds backward to possible causes; his retraining procedure starts with the elimination or minimization of causes and moves forward to new habits. Psychologically, the correctionist asks what needs to be done to increase the security of the child, to give him a sense of achievement, to make him want to improve, to provide conditions that will lead to his reëvaluation of his ability or increase his sense of belonging. Logically, he asks what is the present state of the difficulty? What causes need to be removed or mitigated? What specific changes in speech need to be effected? What is the first step in remedial procedure? What is the next step? What is to be done if a particular technique does not succeed?

There seem to be strong differences of opinion among practicing speech correctionists with regard to the learning of motor skills.[35] Some advocate a progression of steps which proceed from (a) ear training to (b) production of the sound in isolation to (c) strengthening of the sound to (d) the use of the sound in familiar words to (e) the use of the sound in connected speech. Some argue, however, that there seem to be no clear-cut steps, that it is first necessary for the individual to develop an awareness of the difference between what he is doing and what he is attempting to learn to do, and that this awareness or understanding and consequent change in behavior must combine evaluative, sensory, and motor learning. Probably it is the combined action of these different modes of learning that sometimes suddenly produces the sound overnight. Neither view has been subjected to adequate experimental analysis, and of course they are not mutually exclusive in nature. No doubt much is to be said for a combination of the two approaches.

There seem to be differences of opinion concerning the order in which consonant sounds should be introduced into lessons having to do with articulatory handicaps. Some advocate that

[35] This discussion may be supplemented by reference to Chapter III.

sounds should be introduced into remedial lessons in the order in which they normally develop in the child's language. Others suggest that it would be more relevant to the retraining situation to start with those sounds most easily learned by a particular child or group of children at a specified time. By starting with sounds that are easy to produce (such as the *th* sound) the child can experience success almost immediately and at the same time learn the basic procedure to be used in the retraining program.

Another relevant consideration in this connection has to do with improvement in intelligibility of the child's speech. If the learning of a particular sound, even though somewhat more difficult than others, will make a striking improvement in the child's speech he is likely to receive the praise of others, along with other satisfactions, and thus be spurred to greater effort.

The remedial speech teacher, whatever his point of view concerning method, must also deal with the problem of transfer—the problem of getting a child to use new speech habits in ordinary speaking situations. A few suggestions are in order. It is wise to set standards at a fairly low level in the beginning and then gradually to raise them as remedial training continues. Transfer of a new sound into words should progress from phonetically simple and much used words to those that are more complex and less often used. Transfer of the new sound into connected speech should follow a similar progression. It is far better to introduce *l*, for example, into connected speech in a simple response like "a ball" (when naming an object in a picture) than in a phonetically complex sentence like "All the little lasses licked lollipops." Some correctionists insist that new sounds, when introduced into words, should be used first in the final position, next in the medial position, and last in the initial position; others prefer to proceed from the initial to the final to the medial position. In Chapter III the problem of transfer has been dealt with in considerable detail.

4. The practice situation must be simple. It should not require elaborate verbal explanation; rather, it should be suitable for quick presentation, and by *showing*: For example, "Each time you make the sound correctly, you get to move your car to the

next square (showing the movement)." The child should be able to grasp the total pattern of activity and understand his role in it—"At our party each of us will take turns in welcoming a guest." It should be possible for each child in a group to help one or more other children.

5. The child should be allowed to participate in decisions concerning practice. Fundamentally this becomes a matter of allowing the child to make choices among activities or procedures or materials previously determined by the instructor, any one of which will contribute to the lesson objective. The choice is offered without implied preference. If an unexpected choice is made from outside those planned by the instructor, he should accept the decision and quickly bend it in the direction of the lesson objective. If the response is negative, it is to be accepted in a matter-of-fact way and other choices offered. If responses continue to be negative the correctionist may accept the fact that the child doesn't want to do anything, and then turn to an activity that he feels will interest the child, and even engage in it by himself until the child (through both boredom and interest) is drawn in. Freedom of choice establishes an atmosphere of permissiveness in which the child gains release from frustration brought on by restraint. It serves as an outlet for aggressive needs and also gives him a feeling of participation.

6. The attention of the child (or each child in the group) should be kept focused on the purpose of the lesson. Almost invariably the beginning speech correctionist falls somewhat short in this respect; he frequently loses the attention of one or more children in a group and does not notice the fact. The duration of a child's effective attention is very short, in fact only a few seconds. Consequently the instructor needs to plan the lesson so that the participation of any one individual in a group is not only short, but frequent. He needs to plan also for a variety of activities for the pupil who is taught on an individual basis.

Attention can be caught and held by a variety of methods: by activities that are of normal interest to the child; by suspense, competition, coöperation, and novelty. It can be held by the seating arrangement of the group; if the most attentive and active children are placed on the fringes of the group and the least attentive in the middle, the instructor can encompass the least attentive in the activity of the group and also more easily observe and do something about them. Attention also can be kept fastened upon the lesson in a group situation by expecting each child to "notice how Sarah does it," "help John make the sound," or "tell the others what you like about what Joe does." Some correctionists use a "good speech chair" which is won when a child detects an error and is lost when he makes an error.

7. The pupil should be strongly motivated to develop the skill being taught. Ordinarily, he should be made aware that he has a problem and also furnished with a reason for wanting to do something about it. If conditions in general are good for the child, if he feels secure and successful, no harm will result from making him aware of his problem. If he is aware of no reason for wanting to remedy the condition he should be supplied with reasons. Sometimes a simple comment such as "I like the way John made that *s*" supplies all the motivation needed. Acts which satisfy a motivating drive are practiced and strengthened whether that motivation stems from an intrinsic drive toward self-improvement or from a desire to please the teacher, to speak as plainly as Tom, to be cast in a puppet show, or to receive a star on an achievement record. The instructor will continuously be on the alert to strengthen motivation by the use of inherently interesting materials, self-competition, wholesome group competition, praise, judicious and essentially good-humored reproof, or knowledge of results.

8. Practice should be concentrated on the particular aspect of the activity being learned. In general, each step in the retraining process should be thoroughly accomplished before going on to the next. It frequently happens that, in his eagerness to do something for the child, the speech correctionist slights ear training, or the process of strengthening a sound in isolation, or some other step in the process of remedying an articulation fault, and discovers that he must return to that particular phase of retraining if he is to accomplish his major objective. Furthermore, even when a particular phase of corrective procedure is well

taught, it may be forgotten. It is well to include a review of previously taught skills along with practice on a more advanced skill. We do not mean to suggest, either, that it is unwise, if the correctionist is working on articulation, to include some total word responses containing the new sound as it is being worked on in isolation or in nonsense syllables. These total responses help to keep the pupil oriented to the significance of his practice. What we are trying to emphasize is the importance of thorough, concentrated learning which secures, during the remedial session, as many of the desired responses as it is possible to obtain and which firmly fixes one aspect of a skill before another is attempted.

In connection with these comments, it is in order to offer a word of caution. The game or activity devised to make a lesson interesting sometimes requires so much time that practice of the desired response is reduced to a minimum. Guided practice of desired responses is the end in view; techniques and devices are simply means to that end, and they should be used accordingly.

9. In the guidance of practice sessions the speech correctionist should consider the varying needs of pupils. In the first place, he should be sensitive to the tensions, attitudes, and reactions of each particular child on each particular day, and adapt the materials as well as the procedures of instruction to them. After all, children are human beings and are likely to have pains, worries, and problems as acute to themselves as are those of the teacher to himself. In the second place, the correctionist must move at the pace of the child. Differences in ability and insight from youngster to youngster will determine individual rates of progress. Attempts to go too fast or to accomplish too much may not only stifle learning but also result in tension and frustration for the child. Making the pupil overanxious to see results may create or make worse the very condition that the teacher should be trying to eliminate. In the third place, the length and frequency of remedial sessions should have some relationship to the progress of the child. They should be frequently and regularly scheduled at the start of retraining; toward the end, practice may be distributed in diminishing amounts and at longer intervals. In

connection with this point it seems important to say that the pupil should not be completely dismissed from corrective work until results have been checked outside the speech room, in the classroom, and in the home, as well as on the playground.

10. Practice should be as interesting as it is possible to make it. Ideally, of course, it should be positively fun. Both the materials and the procedures can contribute to that end. The speech room and the classroom should be equipped to stimulate creative and spontaneous expression. Construction materials, toys, pictures, tools, plants, decorations, museum articles, and books help to bring this about. These materials, of course, must be appropriate for the particular level at which teaching is being done. Many kinds of games can be devised which add zest to profitable practice. The various seasons and holidays should be exploited for teaching purposes. The introduction of a picture of a Christmas scene into the remedial session near that time of year will provoke spirited practice. The speech correctionist, of course, is the most important element in creating an interesting remedial session. His enthusiasm, congeniality, and eagerness are "catching." The cheerful, human, friendly, helpful teacher gets results where the discontented, impatient, uninspired, humorless teacher using the same book knowledge and the same corrective procedures consistently fails.

11. Practice periods should be relatively short and should not follow periods in which great demands have been made on the use of the same or similar skills. Remedial speech sessions probably should not follow immediately after vocal music practice, oral reading classes, or "telling times."

12. Practice sessions, as we have said before, should be highly varied. Several kinds of activities and exercises should be used in even a fifteen-minute remedial period. It is important to change the activity or the material just before the child begins to tire of it. The point of emphasis, however, should remain the same. The lesson aim should remain constant although the methods of reaching that end are greatly varied.

13. All pupils in group sessions should be kept profitably busy. If one individual is singled out for brief emphasis on his

particular difficulty, others in the group should be actively listening, observing, responding, or in some way getting benefit from work with the individual being instructed. Exercises should allow each member of the group to participate as frequently as possible. Games should include all, or each should have his own game. The teacher should be constantly on the alert for any sign of restiveness or disinterest and immediately draw the individual exhibiting such signs into active participation. The wise teacher will sometimes, in group sessions, allow individual youngsters to do what he himself would normally do in an individual session. Thus a child who can produce a particular sound correctly may be used to stimulate a youngster who misarticulates that particular sound.

Participation by each child in a group can be stimulated by building a group standard of active participation, by leading off the lesson with an individual who is eager to participate and whose enthusiasm is infectious, by praising a child who just precedes one who is less interested and willing, by positive expectation on the part of the instructor that all will participate (this expectation is shown in both attitude and language), by firm and positive yet unemotional acceptance of hesitancy or refusal with replies similar to "We will help you," or "We know you will be ready when your turn comes again."

14. Allow the child to experience feelings of success. Again at the risk of triteness we should remind ourselves that "success breeds success." Moreover, it helps to give the child a feeling of security and acceptance. If the child is to experience success, the lesson or experience must be appropriate for him, within his immediate capacity. It must be sufficiently simple, and yet challenging. It must be a lesson for which the child is ready, in which he has some interest, and is motivated to accomplish. Feelings of success are made more probable also when the instructor encourages and accepts attitudes and comments and by a relaxed, easy, congenial situation. Honest, sincere praise, used discriminatingly, tends to lead the child to greater growth. Praise, however, should put no undue pressure on the child. It should reward behavior that can be repeated somewhat suc-

cessfully. Approval of the child's accomplishments by other children, parents, and teachers—and especially by his peers—is to be judiciously encouraged.

15. The child's progress may be made clear and meaningful to him by the use of scores or charts. A chart of a child's development encourages him not only to compete with himself but also to study his own progress. If he made the *s* sound correctly four times on Monday, he will be aiming for at least five correct responses in his next lesson. If he stuttered well on two occasions Monday, he will want to do it well on at least three occasions Tuesday. Much motivation results from a gradually rising line on a chart, or a gradually increasing score on a record form. Basically, charts and scores are visual symbols of success.

16. In working with groups, there is sometimes an advantage in experimenting with coöperative projects rather than competitive activity. There is reason to believe that for some children competitiveness results in greater personal insecurity than does coöperative activity. Also there is reason to believe that coöperative projects sometimes stimulate greater desire for achievement, more attentiveness to the activity of others in the group, greater productivity per unit of time, more friendly responses, and more favorable evaluations of the group and its work by individual members of it. There seem to be no significant differences in the amount of interest, or involvement, or in the amount of learning that takes place in the two types of activity.[36]

17. In working with groups, it is important to develop group cohesiveness. Cohesiveness increases as the members of the group come to feel a genuine liking for each other, and if the activities of the group are interesting and rewarding. If a cohesive group is dominated by children who are eager to learn and have developed certain standards of accomplishment and conduct, they will exert strong pressure on other children in these directions. Lessons in which children tell each other something they like about each other help to build friendliness, a feeling of belongingness, and, as a result, cohesiveness.

[36] Morton Deutsch, "The Effects of Cooperation and Competition upon Group Process," *Human Relations* (1949), 2:129-152, 199-231.

These, then, are some of the more important conditions which tend to make remedial speech practice effective in producing learning. The good speech correctionist will do his best to observe them constantly.

## Records and Reports

Essential record keeping is not busy work imposed on overburdened teachers by a perfectionistic administrative staff. It is a necessary detail that makes for good speech correction as well as for good school administration. Record keeping is important from a speech correction point of view because (1) adequate information must be assembled concerning each pupil who has a serious speech problem, and (2) many speech difficulties require a long period of reëducation, during which time there is constant need to review what has been done in the past and to evaluate progress. Record keeping is important from an administrative point of view because (1) there is a rapid turnover of teachers because of marriage, the attractiveness of higher paying positions in other vocations, and other reasons, and good record keeping allows a new remedial speech teacher to take over where another has left off; (2) the school population is somewhat mobile, and it is important that a child's records go with him to his new school so that he may quickly be placed in the proper room and with the right teachers; and (3) public school administrators and supervisors find it necessary to make periodic reports to school boards, state departments of education, legislatures, and other bodies; in order to do this they must have reports from individual instructors, who must keep records in order to prepare these essential reports.

Reporting is as essential as record keeping in a continuing program of speech correction. Through reports administrators are informed of the need for corrective work; armed with these reports, they are able to secure necessary financial support. Even more important, however, is the fact that reports are a direct means of helping individual children; through them, parents and teachers are informed of the nature, causes, and consequences of speech problems, and all are drawn into activity which makes conditions better for each handicapped child.

The task of keeping records and making reports need not be too grueling. Much of it can be done in time that ordinarily might be wasted—before school begins in the morning, after dismissal at night, during recess periods, when a pupil is absent from school and his appointment time is left free, and when assembly programs, pep meetings, or movies interrupt the schedule. The efficient teacher will take advantage of these opportunities.

RECORDS

The record-keeping system of the speech correctionist should include (1) individual "case" folders, (2) individual "case" cards, and (3) individual "recordings" cards. The "case" folders are necessities. The "case" cards frequently save time and effort. The "recordings" cards are useful if disks or tapes are preserved.

*Individual Case Folders.* Speech correctionists find it convenient to keep an individual, letter-size, heavy duty manila folder for each pupil; most classroom teachers are similarly inclined. The name of the child is printed on the tab in ink, last name first. The name of his school is printed in pencil so that it can be erased in case of transfer. His grade also is printed in pencil so that it can be changed as he advances.

In the individual case folder, in the order listed, are kept the following seven kinds of records:

1. A cumulative record;
2. A case history (if one has been considered necessary);
3. Medical and dental reports;
4. Psychological, audiometric, and other test records;
5. Records of conferences with parents, classroom teachers, and others;
6. Carbons of reports to parents, classroom teachers, and others;
7. Lesson plans (kept in sequence).

The cumulative record and case history will be considered immediately below. Lesson plans have been discussed above. Here there is need for only a few comments about the other records. Some speech correctionists like to carry a loose-leaf notebook in which is inserted a page for each child and upon which can be written several lesson plans; whenever desired, the page can be transferred to the child's folder. In asking the school doctor or dentist for a report, the information wanted should be specified; if the parents are asked to obtain these reports, they should have either a letter specifying the information desired or a form to be filled out by the medical person; in all cases it is wise to work through the school nurse in obtaining medical reports. Most psychological and other tests have their own summary or report forms. Audiograms have been considered in Chapter VIII. It is wise to keep carbon copies of all reports for frequent reference. Notations should be made about all but the most incidental conferences with parents, classroom teachers, and classmates; a conference about a child which seems to result in nothing important may nevertheless be significant.

The cumulative record, which is the first in the sequence of records in the child's case folder, contains items which provide at quick glance a complete summary of work with the child from the time of his first speech examination up to the time of his dismissal from remedial work or up to the end of any particular school year. Usually these items of information are grouped into six divisions:

1. Identification:
    Name, sex, date of birth, names of parents, home address, telephone number.
2. Education:
    School, room number, grade, name of teacher (space should be allowed for a year-by-year record over a period of years).
3. Speech Tests:
    Brief description of problem or problems (written in terms of what the pupil does or does not do). Name of examiner.
4. Other Tests and Observations:
    Bodily abnormalities (those that have some relation-

ship to the speech problem; those that possibly have some impact upon other behavior). Results of audiometric, intelligence, personality, reading, scholastic achievement tests. Autobiography. Observations of behavior, environment.

5. Speech Recordings:
   Type, date, file number.

6. Remedial Record:
   Semester or year, number and length of lessons, types of remedial procedure, results, remarks, signature of speech correctionist.

At the end of a school year, these records are checked for both completeness and logical sequence and then stapled together.

One other matter should be mentioned here. Most school systems keep a complete record of personal data, grades, attendance, test results, illnesses, and activities of each pupil from the time he enters school until he is graduated. This collection of information also is called a "cumulative record." From it is taken information requested by universities and colleges, prospective employers, and the armed forces, as well as by individuals, agencies, and institutions that need confidential information about the student. Upon this record should be noted not only the nature and severity of speech problems of the student, but also the general results of corrective work. Incidentally, the school cumulative record for a child can be an invaluable aid to the speech correctionist in the preparation of his case history.

The case history has been considered in this as well as in preceding chapters.[37] For obvious reasons, it appears next in sequence in the individual case folder. In preparation of the case history, consideration should be given to items that fall roughly into eleven categories:

1. Identification: (Same as on cumulative record.)
2. Complaint: (As stated by the individual or by the referral source.)
3. Referred by: (Self, other individual, agency.)
4. Speech problems: Brief description of problem (written in

[37] See also *Diagnostic Manual in Speech Correction, op. cit.,* pp. 1-12.

terms of what the pupil does and does not do). History of the speech difficulty. Attitude of child toward the difficulty. Attitudes of others toward it.

5. Personal habits: Attitudes toward others, self, situations. Coöperation. Temperament. Delinquency. Social traits. Work habits. Leisure activities. Play. Sleeping and feeding habits.

6. Environment: Socioeconomic status of family (estimate from occupation, education, vocation, home of parents). Neighborhood. Parents' interests and activities. Parent-child and sibling relationships. Discipline practices. Bilingualism in home. Companions. Relatives.

7. Mental and educational development: Present school and grade. Previous schools. Age entered. Past progress and achievement. Attendance record. Subjects causing difficulty. Language problems. Playground problems. Teacher-child relationships. Parent-teacher relationships. Special talents. Special interests.

8. Family history: Names and ages of parents. Occupation of parent or parents. Siblings. Family deficiencies (speech, hearing, reading, mental, emotional). Family traits. Attitude toward child. Attitude of parents toward each other. Previously attempted speech correction. Same information on immediate relatives.

9. Medical history: Diseases. Injuries. Inoculations. Health problems.

10. Developmental history: Birth data. Breast or bottle fed? Bladder and bowel control. Toilet training. Sleeping and feeding problems. Height and weight gain. Age of sitting up, walking, talking, teething, dressing, and feeding self. Dental care. Handedness. Coördination.

11. Interview observations: Rapport. Emotional reactions. Language behavior. Rationalization. Expressive movements. Unconscious projection.

The individual case folder remains, ordinarily, in the correctionist's files until the child has been dismissed permanently from special speech work. The folders are finally stored where they can easily be examined. They become valuable sources of information for the beginning speech correctionist who is developing his ability to work with speech handicapped children.

A somewhat different procedure is followed by the classroom teacher who works with speech handicapped youngsters in her own room. At the end of each school year, the classroom teacher deposits each child's folder with the school principal who passes it on to the proper teacher at the beginning of the next school year. If the folder has been kept as suggested, the new teacher will be able to review quickly the status of the problem and continue remedial work without delay.

*Individual Case Cards.* A file card for each child sometimes saves time and energy for the remedial speech teacher. Such cards allow for quick counting in making reports, and they are convenient sources of names, addresses, telephone numbers, and other information.

Individual case cards may be printed or mimeographed. The following form has been found convenient and practicable:

Name ........................ School ...... Grade ....
Home Address ......................................
Telephone .... Birth Date .... Date of Examination ....
Description of Problem ..............................
..................................................
Recordings: Date, File Number, Type: ..................
Disposal of Case: Referred to .........................
Receiving Correction ..... Corrected and Dismissed .....
Corrected, Follow-Up ................................
Other Disposition ..................................

There are various methods of organizing the card file. Ordinarily, the cards are filed alphabetically under three divisions: (1) Active Cases, (2) Follow-Up Cases, and (3) Inactive Cases. Correctionists who work in several schools often partition the file into sections for each school; each of these sections is then subdivided into the active, follow-up, and inactive divisions. A distinctively colored card may be used for each school.

*Individual Recordings File.* This file is helpful if speech recordings are made and stored. A card is prepared and filed alphabetically (by last name) for each child's speech recording. It contains the following information: Name: filing number of record; date of recording; kind of record (disk, tape, wire); speed of recording (and direction, if a disk). On each recording is pasted a label on which is written its file number, the name of the child, the date, the speed and direction of recording. The recordings are then stored in numbered sequence.

REPORTS

The speech correction program, in order to function at its highest level of effectiveness, requires the enlightenment and coöperation of all those involved in it. The speech correctionist helps to bring about these conditions by reporting findings, activities, results, and recommendations, whenever the need or opportunity arises. The correctionist's reports may be grouped into two categories: (1) instructional reports, and (2) administrative reports.

*Instructional Reports.* Reports of this type are directly concerned with the reëducation of particular children, and they are of two kinds: (1) evaluative reports, and (2) progress reports. The evaluative report, as the name indicates, is prepared as soon as the speech examination has been completed and the findings have been evaluated. It is sent to parents, classroom teachers, and others who will coöperate with the speech correctionist in one way or another. It should contain four kinds of information: (1) the usual items of identification; (2) an explanation of the child's problem, stated in terms of what he does and does not do that interfere with his oral communication; (3) a general explanation of remedial procedure (this explanation should indicate judiciously what parents, classroom teachers, and others can do to help with remedial work); and (4) a prognosis or brief statement of eventual results that can be expected from remedial work. This prognosis or prediction cannot be stated exactly and is never, under any conditions, to be given the sense of a guarantee. It is useful, however, as a reasonable indication of the time and work likely to be required and the results to be expected, so far as can be predicted, "other things being equal" and "circumstances permitting."

The progress report has two aims: (1) to report on the child's progress in speech reëducation to date, and (2) to indicate to the parent and classroom teacher the ways in which they can help the child further. This report is ordinarily sent in the form of a note which may be as informal or confidential as the correctionist feels it should be. Usually copies of the report go to parents and classroom teachers, and sometimes copies are sent to other individuals who are working with the child and who know the plan of retraining. In general these progress reports are issued at the times at which classroom teachers issue what are commonly called "report cards." In some cases, however, the speech correctionist may want closer and more frequent contact with parents and classroom teachers.

Before leaving this topic we want to emphasize the point of view that "grade" reports of progress in remedial speech work are certainly not advisable. Even the "satisfactory" or "unsatisfactory" type of report is questionable. It is to be strongly emphasized that marks or grades are definitely not to be given for speech correction work. They do not provide the kind of motivation desired; rather, they tend to weaken or distort the desired type of motivation.

*Administrative Reports.* Ordinarily, speech correctionists make three types of reports to their administrative officers: (1) survey reports, (2) periodic reports, and (3) annual reports. Other types may be necessary, but these are representative.

The typical procedure in starting a program of speech correction in a school or school system is for the correctionist to conduct a survey to determine the number of children who have various kinds of speech problems. The results of the survey are important, first, because they tell the administration something about the number of persons who should be employed to handle the job, and second, because they tell the speech correctionist where the most pressing problems are located and how he should plan the overall aspects of his work. For his own benefit, then, as well as for the benefit of others who are concerned, he prepares a tabulation of findings which is called a survey report. The procedure is as follows. For each room surveyed, an alphabetical list of pupils is prepared. Alongside each name is typed an appropriate comment such as "no speech problem," "stuttering," "*th* for *s* substitution." Occasionally, the correctionist will include notations concerning other difficulties such as problems in hearing, vision, or reading that he has observed in the child Three copies of the report for each grade are prepared. The third carbon copy is retained in the correctionist's files. The second is presented to the classroom teacher most vitally concerned in coöperating in the program. In most elementary schools this will be the room teacher. In secondary schools, it may be the homeroom, speech, English, or social studies teacher. The original copies of the reports for the various rooms in the school are stapled together with a summary sheet on top; these are submitted to the principal; they provide him with an overall picture of speech conditions in his school. To provide the superintendent, assistant superintendent, or supervisor of special education with a statistical summary which tells him at quick glance the need for remedial work in the system at large, the correctionist gathers together copies of the summary sheets prepared for the principals and to these he staples a composite summary. The summary sheet for each school as well as the composite summary sheet for the school system as a whole (or the grades surveyed) itemizes:

I. Total number of pupils examined;
II. Total number of speech handicapped children discovered;
III. Percentage of pupils having speech problems;
IV. Breakdown of total problems into the numbers of cases to be classified, respectively, as
    A. Articulatory
    B. Voice
    C. Stuttering
    D. Retarded Speech
    E. Cleft palate
    F. Cerebral palsy

    G. Hearing loss

    H. Other.

Another type of administrative report is commonly called a periodic report. This is brief and covers a four-week, six-week, or nine-week period of instruction. Usually when administrators need a report of this kind they are mainly concerned with some or all of these nine items:

    I. Number of pupils receiving corrective work at the beginning of the period;

    II. Number of pupils receiving corrective work at the end of the period;

    III. Number of pupils dismissed as corrected during the period;

    IV. Number of pupils discontinuing corrective work during the period, their names, and reasons for dropping;

    V. Number of pupils added during the period, their names, and types of problems;

    VI. Number of pupils aided by welfare or service organizations or clinics during the period, their names, and kind of help received by each;

    VII. Number of home calls during the period;

    VIII. Number of conferences with parents at school during the period;

    IX. Number of meetings with parent study groups during the period.

The third type of administrative report is that made at the close of each school year. This annual report is especially important. It is designed to provide the superintendent with an exact picture of the nature and progress of the program. It contains information which he needs in order to justify the cost of the program to the board of education or to secure financial aid from the state. In it are included requests which will involve expenditures that the superintendent can include in the estimated budget for the year to come. Even if the superintendent does not request an annual report, he should be given one. The report should be sent, of course, through proper channels and should be signed or approved by each person in line. It should contain at least six major items:

I. An introductory page which explains the nature and purposes of the program.

II. A statistical tabulation of corrective work which itemizes:

A. Total number of pupils examined for speech deficiencies (and the number given hearing tests, with findings, if included in program);

B. Total number of pupils receiving help from the program;

C. Breakdown of the total number into the numbers of cases to be classified, respectively, as:

1. Articulatory
2. Voice
3. Stuttering
4. Retarded speech
5. Cleft palate
6. Cerebral palsy
7. Hearing loss
8. Other;

D. Breakdown of the total number of hearing loss cases (if included in program) into the numbers receiving:

1. Lip reading instruction
2. Hearing aid instruction and auditory training
3. Speech training
4. Classroom aid (specify);

E. The total number of cases corrected but needing follow-up;

F. The total number of cases corrected and dismissed;

G. The numbers of cases referred to

1. Speech clinics
2. Hearing clinics
3. Reading clinics
4. Dentists
5. Physicians
6. Psychologists
7. Other specialists or agencies.

    H. Number of pupils receiving aid from welfare or service organizations (explain the kinds of aid).

III. Statistical tabulation of supplementary work which itemizes:

    A. Number of speeches delivered to community groups

    B. Number of faculty meetings at which discussions or demonstrations were held

    C. Number of home calls

    D. Number of parent conferences held at school

    E. Number of parent study groups conducted during the year and number of meetings held by each group

    F. Number of visits by parents to remedial classes

    G. Number of visits by classroom teachers to remedial classes

    H. Number of conferences held with doctors, dentists, welfare supervisors, etc.

IV. An explanation of progress made and difficulties encountered in conducting the program.

  V. Recommendations concerning the organization and administration of the program in the future.

VI. Requests for assistance, equipment, teaching aids, and supplies for the year to come (list of items and estimated cost of each).

## A Final Word

Although this book has been addressed primarily to the prospective as well as the working speech correctionist and classroom teacher, it has been written for many other readers, too— the school administrator, social worker, psychologist, dentist, physician, and parent. It could not be otherwise; the efforts and objectives of one are the labors and aims of all. Each is dedicated to the task of safeguarding and teaching American children and youth, and all are in firm agreement that, in our program of education for all, handicapped children must not be ignored and neglected. When they are neglected, each knows that he has failed, first, in his duty to see that every child is attuned as happily as possible to the way life is lived in our time, and second, in realizing his opportunity to increase the creative and productive capacity of individuals who can make significant contributions to the society in which they live.

From the first page to the last this book has pleaded for principles of teaching—"common denominator" principles—that are good for all pupils. Pupils are people. As people, they need to live and work and play under conditions which encourage natural and normal growth in skill, attitude, appreciation, and understanding. As people they are engaged in a constant search for security, a sense of belonging, and pride of achievement. It is important that the home and the school satisfy this continuous quest. Pupils as people are individually different in background and ability and need. These differences will be recognized and provided for in the school that exists for the sake of children rather than for the convenience of teachers or the rigidity of the curriculum. As people, pupils have needs that cannot be satisfied by learning the formula for hydrochloric acid or the date on which Balboa discovered the Pacific. The teacher who feels an obligation to the child as a person rather than to some specialized area of knowledge cannot fail to be sensitive to these needs and to teach with due regard for them.

The superior remedial speech teacher learns more and more about the human resources with which he works and bends himself as well as his materials in the direction of the child he is trying to instruct. He combines the use of good method with a personality that is attractive to the youngster. He begins his instruction on the level of the child's experience, interests, and needs. He uses techniques that allow for friendly, varied, socialized individualized, and guided learning. He is purposeful, prepared, clear, helpful, and patient. He adds to teaching method those human, companionable, and sympathetic traits which make of learning an exciting event for children and give free rein to their creative expression.

The superior speech correctionist increases his insight into the whys and wherefores of human behavior. He recognizes the signs of fear and repression and tension and loneliness. He appreciates the futility of trying to help pupils achieve significant growth of any kind while they are suffering from serious feelings of inferiority or anxiety or inadequacy. He understands that the child who stays in at recess or sits rigidly in the back row is as needful of attention as the pupil who is overaggressive or belligerent. He searches long and deeply for causes of unfortunate and handicapping behavior. He longs to do and he does do something constructive for those pupils who seem always on the perimeter of classroom activity and are never drawn into the exciting adventure of working and playing with their fellows. He knows, on the one hand, that inadequacies in speech may cause unfortunate behavior patterns and, on the other, that withdrawal from the group may result in speech difficulties.

Through all this he makes of himself a vital and enriching force not only to the children with whom he works but also to the people of his community. The best of instruction is achieved through teaching by example, and the kind of teacher here described is one who, by example, teaches the most treasured personal qualities that any child may acquire in or out of school.

*Appendixes*

Appendices

# APPENDIX I

## Projects for Students

1. Make a speech survey of an elementary or secondary school classroom and submit a typed report on the speech problems discovered in that room.

2. Observe six speech correction lessons and, on the basis of a set of criteria drawn up for yourself, report upon your observations.

3. Visit a speech clinic. Before the visit prepare a list of the equipment, procedures, types of problems, etc., which you wish to see demonstrated. After the visit make an oral or written report of your more important observations.

4. Visit an elementary school classroom. During your visit note (a) teacher personality, (b) classroom atmosphere, (c) methods used to enhance learning, (d) methods of motivation, (e) classroom "management," (f) teacher-pupil relationships, (g) opportunities for remedial work in speech. Report upon your observations.

5. Prepare a list of what you think are "common denominator" principles of classroom teaching. Visit an elementary school classroom, observe the teaching being done, and prepare a written report which explains how these principles were fostered or violated in that classroom.

6. Select the names of six pupils with speech problems from an elementary school enrollment. Confer with the principal and teachers, if they are willing, about conditions which would affect the scheduling of these pupils for special speech classes.

7. Make a thorough investigation of the speech correction program in your state, covering (a) a description of the state program, including the activities of State-supported and private agencies, (b) a descrip-

tion of the services provided by college and university clinics, and (c) a list of the communities providing speech correction in the schools, or under some other auspices.

8. Prepare a series of lesson plans covering some phase of the re-training process for a particular child who has a speech difficulty. Your instructor will probably designate some specific aspect of retraining which you should outline. The lesson plans should be prepared for an actual case, but if necessary a hypothetical case may be set up.

9. Interview the superintendent of schools in your county or city and prepare an informative report of services offered to speech handicapped children.

10. Interview an in-service speech correctionist. Obtain advice concerning a program of studies which will adequately prepare you for active service in a school system.

11. Looking toward future study and activity, draw up a plan which will enable you to obtain a thorough knowledge of children. Your plan should include courses that you will take, books that you will read, observations that you will arrange, and vacation activities in which you will engage.

12. Set up a "truth session" with a group of your fellow students. Quietly, objectively, and unemotionally talk about your personal strengths and weaknesses as potential speech correction teachers.

13. Visit a public school class in which you are likely to find considerable speech activity. From your observations, write a short paper in which you expound upon the opportunities for remedial speech work in the ordinary classroom.

14. Prepare the following for evaluation by your instructor:

*a.* A form letter which requests permission of the parent to take a child out of regular classroom work for remedial speech instruction.

*b.* A letter which asks a parent to visit the school for a conference about a speech handicapped child.

*c.* A twelve-minute radio talk which explains to parents the nature of the public school program of speech correction.

15. Arrange to listen in upon and observe a speech correction teacher's conference with a parent. Write a report in which you explain the techniques used, the strengths and weaknesses of the conference, and apparent results.

16. Do the necessary library research and other investigation and prepare a paper in which you offer:

*a.* Suggestions for the conduct of face-to-face group discussions for parents of speech handicapped pupils.

*b.* Suggestions for the conduct of a panel or symposium discussion involving parents.

*c.* A list of audio-visual aids (including essential data on the producer and the cost) which can be used with parent study groups.

*d.* A list of pamphlets, manuals, case study books, textbooks, and articles that could be recommended for use by parent study groups. Remember that they must not be too technical and that they must contain adequate orientational information.

17. Observe several "case conferences" involving a speech correctionist, classroom teachers, psychologists, and others. Report on the special services represented and the contribution of each to an understanding of the child's problem.

18. Interview a public school speech correctionist and obtain information in regard to problems and procedures in overall program planning, locating the student with a problem, and preparing a schedule of remedial work.

19. Observe an instance of examination-evaluation of a speech handicapped child. Provide the class with a "play by play" report in which you resist any tendency to interpret, infer, or evaluate. At the conclusion of your report, engage in group discussion in which the class as a whole arrives at reasonable interpretations, inferences, and evaluations.

20. Prepare a list of tests that might be used by a speech correction teacher for the purpose of examination-evaluation. Include essential information that would be needed in obtaining copies of these tests. Under each test, write a paragraph explaining its purpose and use. Keep in mind the matter of age levels.

21. Observe an instance of examination-evaluation. On your own, do the job of "inference." Compare your work with that of the clinician who conducted the examination. Report on the entire process, laying stress on what you learned.

22. Read a textbook which explains in some detail the process of group therapy. Report to the class on the major premises that might well guide the thinking of speech correction teachers in using this technique.

23. Read at least six selected articles or a selected book and report on the use of one of the following in speech therapy:

*a.* Group activity.

*b.* Psychodrama.

*c.* Sociodrama.

*d.* Creative dramatics.

*e.* Play therapy.

24. Select one of the remedial procedures mentioned in this book. After considerable supplementary reading, prepare a report in which you explain, with examples, how it can be used by the speech correction teacher.

25. Select a particular child who is attempting to remedy his speech. Study the records on the child. Prepare a plan for each of his next six lessons or remedial sessions.

26. Build a speech correction kit in which you include books, tests, games, and other materials which you will want to have immediately available for work with elementary school children. Don't forget items like cleansing tissue.

27. Make a thorough study of the information contained in a "case folder." Report upon the strengths and weaknesses of the records kept in this particular instance.

28. Observe nonfluencies in the speech of several nonstutterers— classroom lecturers, professional public speakers, members of panel or round-table discussions, and speakers randomly selected in ordinary dinner-table situations, conversation, class discussions, in stores, shops, etc. Observe spontaneous or essentially extemporaneous speech. Oral reading, or speeches delivered from detailed notes, will not be relevant, except possibly for comparative purposes.

The nonfluencies will occur in the form of interjections, such as ah, er, um, throat clearings, etc.; repeated parts of words; repeated whole words; repeated phrases; prolonged sounds, usually initial or final sounds of words; revisions; incomplete phrases; and broken words. You may also want to count conspicuous pauses.

Tabulate, as you listen, the number of nonfluencies per minute. This can be done easily by counting on the fingers. Fold under one finger of the right hand for each nonfluency observed; five will make a "fist." For each "fist" fold under one finger of the left hand; one left hand "fist" thus stands for 25 nonfluencies. Observe for ten minutes. Record the total and divide by ten to find the average number of nonfluencies per minute. By using a tape recorder you can make a more detailed analysis.

In *Diagnostic Manual in Speech Correction* (W. Johnson, F. L. Darley, and D. C. Spriestersbach, New York, Harper & Brothers, 1952), Appendix D is entitled "Observation of Nonfluencies in Normal Speakers," and it contains a detailed assignment together with a "Recording Sheet for the Observation of the Nonfluencies of Normal

Speakers." These may be used or adapted for the present purposes, of course.

29. Two or more students, or even the entire class, are to listen to a stutterer speak for five to ten minutes. Each student, independently, makes a tally mark each time he thinks he hears the speaker stutter. When the speaker finishes, each student reports the total number of tally marks recorded, and the instructor writes the numbers, from lowest to highest, on the blackboard. Note the range, the average, and the nature of the distribution. What does the average mean, if anything? How do you account for the extent of disagreement? Does the stutterer himself tend to agree with the lowest number, the highest, or the average? How many stutterings were there "really"? See C. E. Tuthill, "A Quantitative Study of Extensional Meaning, with Special Reference to 'Stuttering,'" *Speech Monographs* (1946), *13* (No. 1): 81-98. Use this article as the basis of a comprehensive class discussion in connection with this project. Students familiar with general semantics will be especially interested in this discussion.

30. Go into three stores—or use other suitable situations, such as conversation at the dinner table, on the bus, etc.—and pretend to be a stutterer. Do it with a straight face, and don't explain what you are doing. Try to make the stuttering look real. Stutter on at least three words in each situation. Describe the reactions of each listener. Account for them, as best you can, in terms of the listener's attitudes, information or lack of it about stuttering, educational level, personal insecurities or good adjustment, or in terms of your own attitudes and behavior while doing the faked stuttering. Describe your feelings and reactions before, during, and after the performance in each case. What did you learn from this assignment about stuttering and what it means to be a stutterer? In connection with this project the following articles will be extremely interesting: Eugene T. McDonald and James V. Frick, "Store Clerks' Reaction to Stuttering," *Journal of Speech and Hearing Disorders* (1954), *19*:306-311; Oliver Bloodstein and Annette Bloodstein, "Interpretations of Facial Reactions to Stuttering," *Journal of Speech and Hearing Disorders* (1955), *20*:148-155.

Appendix E of the *Diagnostic Manual*, referred to above in No. 28, deals with the simulation of stuttering, and may be used or adapted to the purposes of the present assignment.

31. Do assignment 30 again, but this time pretend to be a lisper. In your speaking substitute the voiceless *th* for *s*, as in *thockth* for *socks*, *yethterday* for *yesterday*, etc.

32. Repeat assignment 30, pretending you have a very nasalized voice.

33. Repeat assignment 30, pretending to be seriously hard of hearing. In each situation ask at least twice to have statements repeated; at least once pretend not to hear some particularly important remark; and at least once show that you definitely "misunderstand" by giving an obviously wrong or irrelevant answer or comment.

34. If there is a surgeon in the vicinity who has performed cleft palate operations, it would be highly desirable to consult him. Many surgeons make a plaster cast of the palate before operating. If the instructor could borrow some of these for class demonstration, it would be possible to convey to the students an excellent idea of the extent and variety of clefts.

35. In many parts of the country there are boarding or day schools for crippled children, public or private. As a rule, a large proportion of the children attending such schools have cerebral palsy. Almost all have speech correction work, and in some the speech program has been developed to a high degree of excellence. If such a school is nearby, it would be well worth while for the instructor to arrange to take the class to visit it for a day. Firsthand observation of speech and physical therapy of cerebral palsied children would acquaint the students with some of the problems involved in this sort of work.

Inquiries about such schools should be made of state or local medical societies, state societies for crippled children, the National Society for Crippled Children and Adults (11 South LaSalle Street, Chicago 3, Illinois), local Easter Seal organizations, or other such agencies.

36. There is an increasing amount of audio-visual material that can be used to good advantage in the study of speech and hearing problems. Most movies need a bit of explanatory introduction by the instructor, and their value is usually enhanced considerably by class discussion after they have been viewed. The American Speech and Hearing Association has made available *A Guide to Audio-Visual Materials on Speech and Hearing Disorders,* by Albert O. Weissberg, Ph.D., as Monograph Supplement No. 2, 1952, of the *Journal of Speech and Hearing Disorders.* This publication contains a well-ordered and annotated listing of films, filmstrips, slides, charts and diagrams, models, photographs, recordings, radio program scripts, and anatomy test sheets. Primary sources and rental and loan sources are listed, and commentary and suggestions concerning the utilization of these audio-visual materials in teaching are included.

For information about films and other materials that have become available since this Monograph was published, inquiries may be addressed to the sources listed by Dr. Weissberg. In 1954-55 the Columbia Broadcasting System presented a TV series entitled "The Search" which included programs dealing with laboratory and clinical studies of hearing problems at the University of California at Los Angeles and at Johns Hopkins University, and of stuttering at the University of Iowa. Films of these CBS-TV programs are available on a rental basis from many audio-visual departments in colleges and universities, or on a purchase or rental basis from Young America Films, 18 East 41st Street, New York 17, N. Y.

NOTE: Further assignments are to be found in the *Diagnostic Manual in Speech Correction*, referred to above in Nos. 28 and 30. This *Manual* contains thirty-two sections that are concerned with taking the case history, voice and articulation tests, examination of the speech mechanism, measures of speech development and retardation of development, procedures for observing and evaluating stuttering, tests of handedness, report writing, and various related activities. Practical assignments are to be found at the end of each section of the *Manual;* they can be used as they stand or adapted to the instructor's or the student's specific circumstances and purposes.

# APPENDIX II

wwwwwwwwwwwwwwwwwwwwwwwwwwwwwwwwwwwwwwwwwwwwwwwwwwwwwwwwwwwwww

## Suggested Topics for Term Papers

1. The speech correction program in ———— school.
2. Speech correction training programs in American universities.
3. State programs for speech handicapped children.
4. The program for the speech handicapped in your state.
5. The speech correction needs of ———— (city, county, state).
6. The National Society for Crippled Children and Adults: its national program and its organization in your own state and county.
7. The American Hearing Society.
8. The International Council for Exceptional Children.
9. The American Speech and Hearing Association.
10. The Speech Correction Fund. See "The Speech Correction Fund: Objectives, Policies and Operating Procedures," *Journal of Speech and Hearing Disorders* (1954), *19*:158-260.
11. State certification regulations for speech correction teachers. (Address inquiries to U.S. Office of Education, as listed in Appendix IV.)
12. Federal agencies which minister to the needs of the speech handicapped. (Investigate particularly your own state division of services for crippled children, and its affiliation with the federal government.)
13. A critical review of a textbook in speech correction or audiology.
14. An evaluative summary of the work of some particular speech pathologist or audiologist.
15. A critical evaluation of some particular theory of a speech disorder.
16. A critical evaluation of some particular clinical or remedial method.
17. The anatomy of the larynx.

18. The role of the soft palate in speech and speech disorders.
19. Factors contributing to the retardation of speech development.
20. Case study of a child with delayed speech development.
21. Personality problems of the cerebral palsied.
22. Handicapped persons who have made outstanding achievements.
23. The speech development of the normal child contrasted with the speech development of the deaf child.
24. Residential schools for the deaf.
25. Day school classes for the hard of hearing.
26. Approaches to the teaching of lip reading.
27. Employment opportunities for the hard of hearing.
28. A critical review of studies of speech sound discrimination.
29. Methods of testing articulation correctness.
30. Stuttering viewed as learned behavior.

# APPENDIX III

~~~~~~~~~~~~~~~~~~~~~~~~~~~~~~~~~~~~~~~~~~~~~~~~~~~~~~~~~~~~~~~~~~~~~~~~~~~~~~~~~

# Class Demonstrations of Problems

In many situations it will be possible to present class demonstrations of children with speech or voice problems, or hearing impairments. While instructors vary more or less in their preferred ways of conducting such presentations, the following suggestions may be of value in many instances:

## General

1. Students should be prepared for a demonstration by advance discussion of the type of speech problem to be presented, and by suggestions of just what to look for in observing the particular child they are to see. It goes without saying that they are to be courteous and matter-of-fact in their reactions to the individual being demonstrated. They are to treat the problem presentation as confidential and not as a subject of indiscriminate conversation outside the classroom. Customary professional ethics are always to be observed.

2. The individual to be presented to the class should likewise be prepared in advance. He should not be presented if he is definitely opposed to it or seems to be overly apprehensive. Certainly his permission is to be obtained. He should be told in some detail about the class and the professional training purpose of the demonstration. Most persons, children or adults, are quite willing, even eager, to coöperate if they understand that they will be helping prospective teachers to understand better how to help others with similar problems. They should be encouraged to look upon the demonstration as an opportunity to "tell them what they ought to know" about children with impaired speech and to be of genuine service generally in a good

cause. The individual should be told just what to expect, precisely what he will be asked or expected to do or to talk about, and when to arrive and to leave.

3. A brief summary of the problem should be given to the class by the instructor before the individual is brought into the room. (Unit 1, "The Case History," Unit 22, "The Examination Report," and Appendix I, "Remedial Case Summaries," of the *Diagnostic Manual in Speech Correction*, previously referred to in Appendix I, contain relevant forms and discussion.) Then the individual should be presented, according to the suggestions given below, or according to the instructor's own preferred procedure. He should then leave, and after he is gone there should be relevant class discussion of the problem and possible ways of dealing with it.

4. It will almost always—and so far as most teachers and most schools are concerned it will always—be unwise to demonstrate a child with a speech handicap to a lay audience made up of his parents and their neighbors. *If* it is done in precisely the "right" way, with thorough appreciation on the part of everyone concerned as to the purpose of the demonstration, it might not be objectionable, and it might even have value, but the *if* is so large as a rule that it overshadows all other considerations. Now and then a child—one who stutters, for example— might reach the point in his training where he genuinely desires to tell a P.T.A. audience, perhaps, about his own stuttering, and stuttering in general. Having done this sort of thing in his classes, he might feel that he would gain something for himself and do a good turn for others by talking to a group of parents. Certainly he should have his parents' permission, and the teacher in charge should be fully capable of making clear to the audience what the youngster is going to do, why he wants to do it, and what the purpose is. In case of doubt, however, it should not be attempted.

Demonstrating children to people, even laymen, who do not know them or their families is something else again, of course. It can be a most effective educational procedure. Problem demonstrations can also be presented before teachers' meetings with good effect.

5. The usual presentation should be well planned, brief, and to the point. Discussion before and after may, of course, be as detailed as seems profitable. The same child may be brought before the class several times, but each presentation should be pointed up purposefully.

6. The instructor should feel no concern about his ability to answer all the questions that might possibly be asked about a child he has demonstrated. Problems presented to classes are to be discussed and

pondered. They serve to raise far more difficult questions than easy answers.

7. Demonstrations are to be conducted matter-of-factly, with due respect shown to the child as a person, with no embarrassing show of sympathy, and in a spirit of professional observation and study. The child being presented is to be regarded as a partner in a learning situation.

### Stutterers

**WHAT TO LOOK FOR**

1. General adjustment to the speaking situation. Evidence of poise, or lack of it. Tendency to be apologetic, self-effacing, to alibi, to boast, to exhibit self-pity, or to be matter-of-fact, objective, and good-natured.

2. General quality of speech and voice aside from the stuttering.

3. Apparent physical condition or state of health.

4. Approximate percentage of words stuttered. It will be instructive for the members of the class to make independent estimates and see how well they agree or how widely they disagree. In general, until sufficient experience has been gained, there will be a tendency to pitch these estimates too high. (See Units 16 and 17, *Diagnostic Manual*.)

5. Phenomena to be observed during stuttering. (Unit 15, *Diagnostic Manual*, contains a "Check List of Stuttering Phenomena" that can be used in this connection.)

6. The stutterer's ability to modify or eliminate specific features of his stuttering.

7. The stutterer's ability to reduce the tension in his stuttering.

8. The stutterer's ability to imitate his own stuttering, with or without a mirror, and to stutter in other specific ways in response to instructions to do so.

9. The stutterer's ability to sing, whisper, talk very fast, very slowly, in a monotone or singsong, to speak with a dialect, in time to rhythms, to read in chorus with another person, even another stutterer.

10. Any types of speaking or reading which the stutterer can perform with little or no difficulty or with which he has unusual difficulty.

11. The stutterer's own beliefs, assumptions, or theories regarding the causes of his stuttering, especially his ability to marshal scientifically acceptable evidence of the soundness of his views.

12. The stutterer's ideas as to what he should do to overcome his speech difficulty and his ability to outline specific techniques and to provide sound reasons for his recommendations.

13. Conditions that tend to make the stuttering worse or better, so far as these can be reliably reported by the stutterer.

14. Specific problems of adjustment in home, school, or community, and in relation to educational and vocational planning, in dating and other social situations, as these can be described by the stutterer.

15. The stutterer's suggestions as to what he should do about these adjustment problems, and his ability to defend the soundness of his suggestions.

16. The stutterer's main abilities and personality assets.

## QUESTIONS FOR SUBSEQUENT CLASS DISCUSSION

1. What general impression did the stutterer make on the various members of the class? Did he seem intelligent? Dull? Average in mental ability? Why did he seem so? How would each of the students rate the general severity of his stuttering on the 7-point scale to be found in Unit 17 of the *Diagnostic Manual?* What specific features of his stuttering were most prominent? Would the students judge him to be popular? Withdrawing? Good-natured? Sensitive? Tough-minded or objective? What particular jobs would he have difficulty getting or holding? What kinds of jobs could he probably handle satisfactorily or even in a superior manner? How would he probably get along on a date? What special adjustments should be made for him with respect to oral work in his classes? Would he be pleasant to work with in a speech correction situation? What specific difficulties would probably arise in trying to improve his speech? Why?

2. In undertaking to improve the stutterer's speech, what specific changes should be attempted first? What are the next two or three things that might be attempted?

3. Should he be referred to a doctor, psychologist, or to other specialists or clinics? For precisely what purpose?

4. What changes should be made in the stutterer's home conditions, school arrangements, study habits, recreational program, daily routine, vocational plans, social activities?

5. Should conferences be held with his parents, teachers, roommate, employer, or other persons? For precisely what purpose? Who should talk to these individuals? Should the stutterer do it himself?

6. Has he had any speech correction in the past? What was the nature of it? How did he respond to it?

7. In what important ways does he differ from other stutterers the

students have seen in class or elsewhere? What probably accounts for these differences?

8. If he is not receiving remedial instruction, what course should he be advised to follow?

NOTE: It is not to be expected that all of these questions, or even most of them, will be answered satisfactorily in any given case. It is not intended that they should necessarily be answered. Often the best answer will be, "I don't know. I don't think I should try to answer the question until I get to know the stutterer better, and until I have had more training and experience." The things to look for and the questions for class discussion listed above are presented simply for their value in suggesting directions that observation and study might well take.

### Children with Cleft Palates

In presenting a child with a cleft palate to a class, often no attempt should be made to show the students the child's palate, whether it is repaired or not. In order for anyone to get any notion of the actual condition of the palate, it is necessary to examine it with the use of a flashlight and tongue blade. This means that only one or two students can look at a time. It would usually not be wise to subject a child to close observation by each member of a class of any size. It will often be best, therefore, not to try to demonstrate the palate.

The child should first be introduced to the class. Then if he has prepared some remarks, he may proceed to make them. Otherwise the teacher may ask him questions. Following this he may answer questions from the class.

WHAT TO LOOK FOR

Is there any abnormality in facial appearance? Is there a scar of a repaired harelip? Is the upper lip sunken or tightly drawn? Is the voice unusual? In what respects? Is the speech clearly understandable? Are any sounds misarticulated? Which ones? What sort of articulatory imperfections occur—omission, distortion, or substitution? What manifestations of attitude and adjustment are to be observed?

### QUESTIONS FOR DISCUSSION

1. What sort of impression does the child make? (See Question 1 under "Stutterers.")

2. If any abnormal facial appearance was noted, in what way might the cleft be related to it?

3. Is the voice nasal? Is it free from nasality at times or on certain words? Does it carry well?

4. What were the impaired sounds? Could the cleft be held responsible for each of these? What other factors might explain any faults in articulation which probably are not caused by the cleft?

5. What sort of speech correction techniques should be used to improve the speech of this child? Why? Describe the goals and the means that might be used to reach them.

6. What assets and abilities does the child seem to have? Are these more or less important than the cleft? What is gained by regarding the child as a "cleft palate case"? What is lost or overlooked?

## Children with Cerebral Palsy

If the child wishes to make a little prepared talk, that is a good way to start the presentation. Otherwise, he may be interviewed by the instructor. It is desirable for him to answer questions from the class—provided, of course, that he willingly agrees to this in advance. He should write his name on the blackboard, if he can, so that the class can observe his writing.

Throughout the presentation, the attitude of the instructor should be friendly, encouraging, good-humored, and calm. The incoördinations of such a child are made worse by excitement, and the child is likely to be excited when he appears before the class. One must not be misled into thinking that his willingness to appear in class will prevent his being excited. Often such a child will be eager to talk to the class. His desire to do a good job and to tell others how a spastic or an athetotic person feels will frequently result in a high pitch of excitement. This clearly means that it is important to discuss the class appearance with the child—and with the class—well in advance of the date set for it. The child should understand clearly what he is to do. His overeagerness and anticipation should be calmed as much as possible. If he has not achieved relative calmness and relaxation in other situations, it might be harmful to use him in a class demonstration. He could easily become so excited and tense as to be unable to function adequately at all. Even if he has made considerable progress in controlling his reactions of excitement, it can be expected that he will in some degree react to the appearance before the class.

WHAT TO LOOK FOR

What is the general appearance? Observe the walking and other movements. What differences from normal do you see? Describe the handwriting. Is the voice unusual? In what way? Is the rate of speaking slow? Estimate the number of words per minute. Does speaking seem to be labored and effortful? Is the flow of speech jerky and hesitant? Is the speech clearly understandable? Are any sounds misarticulated? What sounds? How are they misarticulated?

## QUESTIONS FOR SUBSEQUENT CLASS DISCUSSION

1. What sort of impression did the child make? (See Question 1 under "Stutterers.")

2. How much are walking, writing, etc., affected? How much handicap does this create?

3. Which of the characteristics of the speech may be ascribed to the cerebral palsy? Which may not? How does the palsy operate to produce the deviations observed?

4. What speech correction problems does the case present? What means might well be used to attack these problems?

5. What is gained by regarding this child as a "cerebral palsy case"? What is lost? How should one regard him?

### Children Who Are Hard of Hearing

In presenting a child with a hearing deficiency the general rules previously outlined should be followed. In addition, the audiogram should be shown and discussed, results of the speech examination should be reviewed, the child's ability to read lips should be demonstrated, and the advisability of a hearing aid is to be considered. The medical history, general physical examination, and the ear, nose, and throat findings should be summarized. The school history and the results of mental tests should also be presented. It will usually be desirable to have the examining physician, audiometrician, and psychologist present to give their reports in person whenever this can be arranged.

This general procedure is followed in the hearing clinics conducted at the University of Iowa by the Department of Oral Surgery and Otolaryngology with the coöperation of the Speech Clinic and the Department of Psychology, and the Iowa State School for the Deaf. In each of these clinics a number of cases are reviewed and discussed, the required services for each one are agreed upon, and procedures for obtaining these services are outlined. Otologists, speech correctionists, the workers responsible for audiometric and hearing aid tests, psychologists, social workers, and the superintendent and other members of the staff of the State School for the Deaf participate in the presentations and discussions. The parents of the children are present. County welfare workers, physicians, teachers, and other professionally interested persons frequently attend the clinics. Students enrolled in courses in speech pathology and audiology, nursing, occupational therapy, physical therapy, clinical psychology, and special education also attend.

This is an arrangement that might not be possible in some situations. The above brief description of it may, however, serve the purpose of suggesting the basic principle of teamwork in making a desirably comprehensive attack on the total problem presented by a hard of hearing child. Problem presentations in any training class can be conducted, of course, in the essential spirit of this principle.

WHAT TO LOOK FOR

Try to ascertain the degree to which a given hearing loss is socially handicapping. For example, one might be demonstrating a child with a 35-decibel loss in the speech range (512, 1024, and 2048 c.p.s.). Have him turn his back or close his eyes, and then talk to him in a normal tone of voice. Show how much speech he is able to understand without the aid of lip reading. Then show the facility with which he understands when he can see as well as hear. Point out the necessity of having a child's attention when giving him instructions in the classroom.

Show a child whose hearing loss is of recent occurrence. Point out the fact that there is little if any speech deterioration, although it may be expected to occur eventually unless "speech insurance" training is given.

Demonstrate a child with a perceptive or inner ear type of loss which has existed for a long time. Contrast his speech with that of a child whose loss is of the middle ear or conductive type.

Point out and emphasize the most effective way of addressing the hard of hearing child—without exaggerated lip movement and without shouting.

## QUESTIONS FOR SUBSEQUENT CLASS DISCUSSION

1. What were the overt characteristics which indicated difficulty in understanding speech?

2. How would you obtain a rough estimate of a child's lip reading ability?

3. For the child with a hearing loss of recent occurrence, in what ways would you expect speech to deteriorate with respect to voice, articulation?

4. To what extent was any observed articulatory impairment probably due to the hearing loss?

5. Would a hearing aid be advisable, if the child does not have one? What sort of instruction and training would he need in learning to use a hearing aid most effectively?

6. What recommendations should be made with respect to educational provisions and vocational counseling for the individual?

### Children with Articulatory Problems

It will usually make a good presentation if the speech of the child can be observed on two kinds of material: (1) ordinary connected speech which can be either an oral reading of a paragraph, a short talk, or a conversational situation in which he is interviewed by the instructor; (2) lists of words containing the sounds on which he tends to make errors. These words may be elicited by means of pictures, especially if the child is young. If he is able to produce some of the sounds correctly in isolation or in words, especially in response to auditory stimulation by the teacher, a demonstration of his ability in this respect will add effectively to the presentation.

WHAT TO LOOK FOR

What sounds are misarticulated? What types of errors does he make —substitutions, distortions, or omissions? How consistent are the errors? How much is his ordinary speech affected? Unintelligible? Partly unintelligible? Intelligible but with numerous errors so that it seems severely impaired? Intelligible with only a few errors, so that it seems only slightly impaired? Are there any observable characteristics, such as dental irregularities, which may be related to the speech problem? How responsive is he to auditory stimulation? How does he adjust to the speaking situation?

## QUESTIONS FOR SUBSEQUENT CLASS DISCUSSION

1. What errors were observed?

2. What organic, emotional, or environmental factors may be related to the speech problem? In what way?

3. To what extent may these factors be remediable? How can they be

corrected and should speech retraining be deferred until after the correction has been made?

4. What is the probable prognosis? What favorable factors would point toward good progress? What unfavorable factors would tend to impede progress?

5. How much of a handicap does the speech present?

6. What special speech correction problems does the child present, if any?

### Children with Voice Problems

Observation of the usual speaking voice can ordinarily be made by having the child read aloud or present a short talk. He can also be interviewed by the teacher. Individuals who have improved with training can sometimes be most effectively presented if during a part of the presentation they simulate the voice which they used prior to retraining in a sort of "before and after" demonstration. Recordings made at the beginning of remedial work and from time to time thereafter can also be used in presenting such cases.

#### WHAT TO LOOK FOR

What is the most noticeable unpleasant or deviant feature of the voice? In what additional ways is the voice significantly faulty? Does the pitch level seem suitable for the individual? Can he produce adequate loudness? How would you classify the voice quality? Normal? Nasal? Breathy? Hoarse? Harsh? Is there any evidence of excessive strain or tension? What is the individual's general adjustment to the speaking situation?

### QUESTIONS FOR SUBSEQUENT CLASS DISCUSSION

1. What seemed to be the most noticeably faulty characteristic of the voice?

2. In what other respects was the voice faulty?

3. What factors are known to exist—organic, emotional, environmental, etc.—which might possibly be related to the problem?

4. What is the probable relationship of these factors to the voice problem?

5. To what extent are these factors remediable? How can they be remedied?

6. What sort of program of voice retraining would be suitable for this child?

# APPENDIX IV

〜〜〜〜〜〜〜〜〜〜〜〜〜〜〜〜〜〜〜〜〜〜〜〜〜〜〜〜〜〜〜〜〜〜〜〜〜〜〜〜〜〜〜〜〜〜〜〜〜〜〜〜

# Agencies and Organizations

The student of speech and hearing problems has need to be aware of the agencies and organizations that are designed to be of service to him and to the children and adults whose problems are of professional concern to him. They can provide him with a wealth of statistical information, answers to specific questions, publications, audio-visual materials, and professional counsel of various kinds. Many of the organizations publish journals and magazines. He will be particularly interested, of course, in the *Journal of Speech and Hearing Disorders* of the American Speech and Hearing Association, the professional organization of speech correctionists and audiologists in the United States.

## International Agencies

International Council for Exceptional Children, 1201 16th Street, N.W., Washington 6, D.C. International Society for the Welfare of Cripples, 127 East 52 Street, New York 22, N.Y. United Nations International Children's Emergency Fund, United Nations Building, New York 17, N.Y. World Federation for Mental Health, 19 Manchester Street, London, W. 1, England.

## Federal Agencies

The following federal agencies are units within the United States Department of Health, Education, and Welfare, Washington 25, D.C.
Bureau of Public Assistance.
Children's Bureau.
Interdepartmental Committee on Children and Youth.

542

Office of Education.
Office of Vocational Rehabilitation.
Public Health Service.

### Voluntary and Professional Organizations

American Academy for Cerebral Palsy, Inc., 4743 North Drake Avenue, Chicago 25, Illinois.

American Academy of Pediatrics, 610 Church Street, Evanston, Illinois.

American Association for Cleft Palate Rehabilitation, Pennsylvania State University, University Park, Pennsylvania.

American Association of Mental Deficiency, Inc., P.O. Box 96, Willimantic, Conn.

American Association of Psychiatric Clinics for Children, 1790 Broadway, New York 19, N. Y.

American Foundation for Mental Hygiene, Inc., 1790 Broadway, New York 19, N.Y.

American Hearing Society, Inc., 817 Fourteenth Street, N.W. Washington 5, D.C.

American Medical Association, 535 Dearborn Street, Chicago 10, Illinois.

American Occupational Therapy Association, Inc., 33 West 42 Street, New York 36, N.Y.

American Physical Therapy Association, 1790 Broadway, New York 19, N.Y.

American Psychological Association, 1333 Sixteenth Street N.W., Washington 6, D.C.

American Rehabilitation Committee, Inc., 28 East 21 Street, New York 10, N.Y.

American Speech and Hearing Association, Inc., Wayne University, Detroit 1, Michigan. (May also be reached through Speech Correction Fund, 11 South LaSalle Street, Chicago 3, Illinois.)

Audiology Foundation, Box 21, Glenview, Illinois.

Child Welfare League of America, Inc., 345 East 46 Street, New York 17, N.Y.

National Association for Mental Health, Inc., 1790 Broadway, New York 19, N.Y.

National Association for Retarded Children, 129 East 52 Street, New York 22, N.Y.

National Association of the Deaf, Inc., 2495 Shattuck Avenue, Berkeley 4, California.

National Committee on Sheltered Workshops and Homebound Programs, 15 West 16 Street, New York 11, N.Y.

National Congress of Parents and Teachers, 600 South Michigan Boulevard, Chicago 5, Illinois.

National Education Association, 1201 Sixteenth Street N.W., Washington 6, D.C.

National Foundation for Infantile Paralysis, Inc., 120 Broadway, New York 5, N.Y.

National Publicity Council for Health and Welfare Services, Inc., 257 Fourth Avenue, New York 10, N.Y.

National Rehabilitation Association, Inc., Room 614, 1025 Vermont Avenue, N.W., Washington, D.C.

National Society for Crippled Children and Adults, Inc., 11 South LaSalle Street, Chicago 3, Illinois.

National Society for the Study of Education, 5835 Kimbark Avenue, Chicago 37, Illinois.

Shut-In Society, Inc., 221 Lexington Avenue, New York 16, N.Y.

Social Legislation Information Service, Inc., 1346 Connecticut Avenue, N.W., Washington 6, D.C.

Speech Correction Fund, 11 South LaSalle Street, Chicago 3, Illinois.

Toy Clinics of America, Inc., Lakewood Drive, Stamford, Connecticut.

United Cerebral Palsy Association, Inc., 369 Lexington Avenue, New York 19, N.Y.

Volta Speech Association for the Deaf, Inc., 1537 Thirty-fifth Street N.W., Washington 7, D.C.

# APPENDIX V

~~~~~~~~~~~~~~~~~~~~~~~~~~~~~~~~~~~~~~~~~~~~~~~~~~~~~~~~~~~~~~~~~~~~~~~~~~~~~~~~~~~~~

# Some Basic Features of Speech Sound Articulation

The purpose of this section is to present a brief discussion of the sounds of English speech, especially as spoken by the majority of Americans, which may be helpful in understanding how these sounds are articulated. By no means is the short discussion which follows to be considered more than a brief introduction to the subject of phonetics.

To understand and appreciate what follows the reader will need to have some acquaintance with the sound system of American English. Accordingly, the following list of common vowels, diphthongs, and consonants is presented. This list does not include all of the sounds that occur in every dialect of American English. It does present the sound system of the dialect which is spoken, with some variations to be sure, throughout most of the United States, exclusive of the East and South. In particular, certain vowels which are found in the dialects of those regions are not included, and the list includes the "r-colored" vowels for words like *work* and *butter,* which are regular in the General American dialect, but absent from the speech of most persons who are native to the Southern and Eastern dialect regions.

Speech sounds can be classified in a number of different ways. One distinction which is useful to this discussion is that between vowels (including diphthongs which are made up of vowel elements) and consonants. These two rather distinct kinds of speech sounds differ in a number of ways. In this discussion we shall be concerned mainly with physiological differences in the articulation of vowels and consonants.

## Vowels

| Orthographic Symbols | Phonetic Alphabet Symbol | Key Words |
|---|---|---|
| ē | [i] | cheese, beat, brief |
| ĭ | [ɪ] | chip, myth, built |
| ā | [e]¹ | face, play, eight |
| ĕ | [ɛ] | deck, friend, feather |
| ă | [æ] | black, plaid, trap |
| ä | [ɑ] | father, calm, arm |
| ô | [ɔ] | caught, lawn, awful |
| ō | [o]¹ | coat, go, own |
| ŏŏ | [ʊ] | book, pull, could |
| ōō | [u] | blue, chew, fool |
| ŭ | [ʌ]² | mother, cup, bubble |
| ă | [ə]³ | about, connect, sofa |
| ûr | [ɝ]² | work, burst, certain |
| ẽr | [ɚ]³ | butter, persuade, actor |

¹ These vowels when prolonged tend to become diphthongs: [e] tends to become [eɪ] and [o] tends to become [oʊ]. In English speech this difference is not distinctive, i.e., we may pronounce the word *face* as either [fes] or [feɪs], without changing the meaning of the word spoken.

² These vowels occur only in stressed syllables. Hence, in the word *above* [əbʌv], only the second syllable, which is stressed, is transcribed as [ʌ]. Likewise in the word *murder* [mɛdɚ], only the first syllable is transcribed as [ɝ].

³ These vowels occur only in unstressed syllables.

## Diphthongs

| Orthographic Symbol | Phonetic Symbol | Key Words |
|---|---|---|
| ī | [aɪ] | kite, try, buy |
| ou | [aʊ] | cow, doubt, round |
| oi | [ɔɪ] | boil, toy, oyster |

These are not the only diphthongs which occur in English speech. They are the ones which need to be especially noted because they occur as distinctive sound units. In addition to these and the diphthongs [eɪ] and [oʊ], which have previously been noted, there are the diphthongs formed with the unstressed vowel [ɚ]. Examples are: *card*, [kɑɚd], *tear*, [tɛɚ], *steer*, [stɪɚ], etc.

## Consonants

| Orthographic Symbol | Phonetic Symbol | Key Words |
|---|---|---|
| p | [p] | *p*eople |
| b | [b] | *b*a*b*y |
| t | [t] | *t*as*t*e |
| d | [d] | *d*an*d*y |
| k | [k] | *k*i*ck* |
| g | [g] | *g*a*g* |
| m | [m] | *m*ai*m* |
| n | [n] | *n*oo*n* |
| ng | [ŋ] | ri*ng*i*ng*, i*n*k |
| f | [f] | *f*ood, *ph*oto |
| v | [v] | *v*ase, lea*v*e |
| th | [θ] | *th*irst, ba*th* |
| th | [ð] | *th*is, ba*th*e |
| s | [s] | *s*in*ce*, *sc*ent, pa*ss* |
| z | [z] | bu*zz*, bu*s*y, lo*s*e |
| sh | [ʃ] | *sh*ow, *s*ure, o*c*ean |
| zh | [ʒ] | u*s*ual, a*z*ure, bei*g*e |
| h | [h] | *h*ome, *wh*ole |
| ch | [tʃ] | *ch*ew, bat*ch* |
| j | [ʒ] | *j*oke, ba*dg*e |
| hw | [m] | *wh*y, *wh*ere |
| w | [w] | *w*ill, *w*ear |
| l | [l] | *l*ook, ba*ll* |
| r | [r] | *r*oad, *r*eel |
| y | [j] | *y*ellow, *y*awn |

### SHAPING OF RESONANCE CAVITIES FOR VOWELS

Vowels are produced as a result of movements of the lips, jaws, and tongue which produce characteristic shapings of the vocal resonance cavities during the utterance of a vowel. The sound vibrations for the vowels originate in the *larynx*[5] and the distinctions among the various vowels result from the selective action of the resonance cavities which

[4] This is true whether the vowel is spoken as a voiced sound (with vocal fold vibration) or whether it is whispered. In the latter instance the breath stream is modulated by being forced through a narrow opening in the larynx, rather than by vocal fold vibration.

modify this laryngeal sound in characteristic ways for each different vowel. It is an important feature of vowels that the only place where the breath stream is set into vibration is the larynx. This is true because there is so little constriction of the vocal tract during vowel production that the vibrating breath stream passes freely outward without being further modulated.

CONSONANTS CHARACTERIZED BY NOISE GENERATION

On the other hand, it is characteristic of consonants that the vocal tract is constricted or obstructed in a particular way at some location above the larynx. As a result the breath stream is constricted, or diverted, or obstructed momentarily. For many consonants this constriction or obstruction of the breath stream becomes the source of noise vibrations which are therefore added to any sound vibrations which have originated from the vocal folds in the larynx. Consonant sounds consisting of vibrations from the vocal folds, to which noise vibrations produced by a constriction or obstruction of the vocal tract may be added, are called voiced consonants. Others for which there is no vocal fold vibration may be classified as voiceless consonants. For these latter consonants the only source of sound vibration is the modulation of the breath stream by the constriction or obstruction of the vocal tract. For example, the consonants [s] and [z] are both produced by a narrow channeling of the breath stream between the tongue and the gum ridge behind the upper front teeth. The jet of air produced by forcing the breath through this narrow opening is directed across the cutting edges of the teeth so that a hissing noise is produced. In the case of [z], the breath stream has already been set into vibration by the vocal folds and this hissing noise is therefore added to the voice vibrations so that a voiced sound is produced. For [s] the only source of vibration is the jet of air directed against the cutting edges of the teeth and it is a voiceless sound.

VOWEL-LIKE CONSONANTS

For a few consonant sounds the breath stream is not constricted or obstructed sufficiently to generate additional sound vibrations. These sounds are like vowels in that they are given their unique sound characteristics as a result of the particular way the complex vibration from the vocal folds is modified by the vocal tract resonators. For example, the nasal consonants are produced by diverting the vibrating breath stream through the nasal passages. This nasal emission of sound occurs because the oral channel is completely obstructed by the tongue or lips while at the same time the soft palate is sufficiently relaxed to permit air to pass through the velopharyngeal port into the nasal cavities. As a consequence of the special resonance characteristics of the nasal cavities, these sounds have a common kind of quality. Each nasal consonant has its own special characteristics, also, which result from the particular way the oral cavity is shaped for it. Thus for [m] the oral cavity is closed by the lips and is therefore much larger than for [n] on which the tongue produces the obstruction of the oral cavity by making contact with the upper gum ridge.

In spite of the fact that these sounds are like vowels in that their special characteristics result from resonance, rather than generation of noise vibration in the vocal tract, they are usually classified as consonants because of the constriction or obstruction of the oral channel which is required for their articulation. However, these vowel-like consonants are often put in a special class of consonants and given the label, semi-vowels.

## HOW VOWELS ARE CLASSIFIED

Because vowels are produced as a result of the way the vocal tract is shaped, and because the tongue plays such an important role in shaping the vocal tract, phoneticians commonly classify vowels according to the tongue position which is most typical for the articulation of each vowel. Thus [i], the vowel in the word *meat*, is classified as a high, front vowel, since the front of the tongue is high in the mouth during the utterance of [i] and the whole tongue is quite far forward. On the other hand, [ɑ] as in *father* is classed as a low back vowel because the tongue is retracted and low within the mouth. Following is a table which classifies the vowels primarily on the basis of tongue position. For the vowels produced with retracted tongue positions, the presence or absence of lip-rounding is also noted and the feature of [r] coloring is considered in distinguishing among the central vowels.

|  | Front | Central with [r]-coloring | Central, no [r]-coloring | Back unrounded | Back rounded |
|---|---|---|---|---|---|
| High | i |  |  |  | u |
|  | ɪ |  |  |  | ʊ |
| Mid | e | ɝ |  |  |  |
|  | ɛ | ɚ |  | ʌ | o |
| Low | æ |  |  | ɑ |  |
|  |  |  | ə |  | ɔ |

CLASSIFICATION OF CONSONANTS ACCORDING TO
PHYSIOLOGICAL FEATURES

In cataloguing consonants according to physiological features of
articulation, as shown in Table A, it is common practice to employ a
three-fold system of classification in which consideration is given to
the following:

(1) *Place of Articulation.* This basis for classification takes special
note of where in the vocal tract the breath stream is constricted
or obstructed and what articulatory structures function to narrow
or close the passageway. Thus, [p] and [b] which are produced
by contact between the lips are classed as bilabial sounds, and
[s] and [z] which require contact of the tongue against the gum
ridge (alveolar ridge) behind the upper front teeth are classed
as alveolar, or post-dental, sounds.

(2) *Manner of Articulation.* This dimension of articulation refers to
the particular way the articulatory structures act to produce the
characteristic sound pattern of the consonant. Different phoneticians use somewhat different classes to denote this aspect of
consonant articulation. The ones which are employed in this discussion are: fricative, stop-plosive (sometimes shortened to
*stop*), affricate, nasal, glide.
*Fricatives* are sounds produced by narrowing of the vocal tract
so that the air stream is set into vibration by forcing it through a
restricted opening. Because the characteristic noises of these consonants are produced as a result of friction between the air stream
and the constricted articulatory structures the name fricative describes quite well the manner of their production. It should be
noted that some pressure is required to force the breath through
the constriction, and so the closure between the soft palate and
pharyngeal walls must be relatively complete if these sounds are
not to be produced with an abnormal emission of air through the
nose.
*Stop-plosives,* also called stops, are produced by momentary
complete obstruction of the vocal tract, which dams up the
breath stream and creates increased pressure, followed by a sudden release of the breath pressure which often produces an
audible, explosive puff of air or aspiration. There are thus two

phases for the complete stop-plosive consonant: (a) the stop phase in which the appropriate articulatory structures are brought into contact and complete obstruction of the vocal tract is produced, and (b) the explosion, or release, phase which is the sudden release of the air pressure which been built up behind this occlusion. Particular examples of stops, as they occur in running speech, do not necessarily have both phases as audible components of the sound. Which phases of the sound actually occur will depend on what sounds precede and follow the stop. Like fricatives, stops require closure of the nasal port; that is, the soft palate and pharyngeal walls must come into contact to prevent air from escaping through the nose.

*Affricates.* Some phoneticians do not include this as a separate classification, since the affricates may be thought of as consisting of stops followed by frictional release of breath. Thus, they combine some of the features of stops with certain features of fricatives.

*Nasals* are sounds in which there is complete obstruction of the oral cavity, but the air is not blocked, since the nasal port is not closed. Hence, the vibrating breath stream is diverted through the nasal passages.

*Glides* are a class of consonants which are characterized by movement. They do have a place of articulation, in the sense that they begin with a characteristic placement of the tongue or lips. However, this placement is very transitory. The structures move immediately toward the placement for the sound which follows. Hence, the most significant characteristic of these sounds is the movement which is denoted by the class name, glide.

(3) *Voicing.* The third aspect of consonant articulation which is employed in the three-fold classification is the presence or absence of vocal fold vibration. For certain pairs of sounds this characteristic is the only significant feature which distinguishes one member of the pair from the other. Thus [s] and [z] differ only because [s] is voiceless while [z] is voiced. As previously noted, for the voiced sounds there are really two sources of sound generation, the laryngeal vibration and the place of constriction or obstruction. For the voiceless sounds all of the sound generation takes place at the constriction or obstruction of the vocal tract. Table A classifies the consonants of English according to this three-

TABLE A.  Classification of Consonants According to Principal Physiological Features of Articulation

| | Stop-plosive | | Fricative | | Affricate | | Nasal | Glide | |
|---|---|---|---|---|---|---|---|---|---|
| | Voiced | Voiceless | Voiced | Voiceless | Voiced | Voiceless | Voiced | Voiced | Voiceless |
| Bilabial (lips) | b | p | | | | | m | w | ʍ |
| Labio-dental (lip-teeth) | | | v | f | | | | | |
| Lingua-dental (tongue-teeth) | | | ð | θ | | | | | |
| Alveolar (tongue-gum ridge) | d | t | z ʒ | s ʃ | dʒ | tʃ | n | l | |
| Palatal (tongue-hard palate) | | | | | | | | r j | |
| Velar (tongue-soft palate) | g | k | | | | | ŋ | | |
| Glottal | | | | h | | | | | |

fold system. Close study of this table will help the reader to understand a good deal concerning how particular consonants are produced. It is strongly urged that as this table is studied the reader experiment with articulating the various consonants and attempt to observe introspectively the various features of the consonants which are denoted by the way in which they have been classified.

# APPENDIX VI

~~~~~~~~~~~~~~~~~~~~~~~~~~~~~~~~~~~~~~~~~~~~~~~~~~~~~~~~~~~~~~~~~~~~~~~~~~~~~~~~~~~~

# *Estimating Natural Pitch Level*

The most satisfactory method for estimating a person's natural pitch level that has yet been devised is that given by Fairbanks.[1] An adaptation of Fairbanks' instructions for carrying out this procedure and his table for interpreting results are reproduced below.

> Estimate the subject's natural pitch level as follows. Have the subject sing down to his very *lowest* tone. Letting this tone be *do* of the musical scale, have the subject sing up the scale to his very *highest* note including *falsetto*. Repeat this several times to be sure that the maximum range is being covered. (If the subject has difficulty in singing a scale it may be necessary for the teacher to sing it with him.) Count the notes as the subject sings from his lowest to his highest note. Research has shown that, following these instructions, superior speakers have average total singing ranges, including falsetto, of approximately 22 to 24 notes, or 18 to 20 musical tones. Refer now to the accompanying table and locate the highest note by number in column 2. The number opposite this in column 3 is the *number of musical tones* in the total singing range. Now move directly across to column 4 which states in musical tones approximately how far the natural pitch level lies above the lowest tone. In other words, this last value is a measure of the subject's *natural* pitch level in musical tones above the lowest note of his range. If a piano is available it will be possible to locate exactly the various pitches used in this process.

[1] Grant Fairbanks, *Voice and Articulation Drillbook*, New York, Harper & Brothers, 1940, pp. 168-171.

The procedure just stated will serve very well provided the individual is able to sing a scale and has a pitch range that is not too severely restricted. If either of these latter conditions is not satisfactory, it will be necessary to modify the procedure somewhat.

When a person seems to be completely unable to sing a scale, even with the teacher singing at the same time, determination of the total pitch range becomes difficult. Usually a reasonably good determination can be made, however, if a piano is available, if the individual is coöperative, and if the teacher has a reasonably good ear for pitch.

Often a person can sing a pitch glide, either upward or downward, when he cannot sing the spaced steps of the musical scale. If he can do this have him sing the vowel *ah* and glide slowly downward in pitch to the lowest tone he can produce and hold that tone for a moment. The teacher should listen carefully for that lowest tone, remember it, and find the note on the piano which most nearly matches it. This procedure should be repeated several times to make sure that the lowest note has been located as accurately as possible. A similar procedure is then followed, employing an upward glide in pitch, to locate the highest note. The number of notes on the piano keyboard between these lower and upper limits may then be counted and this number used in entering column 2 of the table. The person's singing range will then be given by the corresponding number in column 3 and the location of the natural pitch level may be found in column 4.

Sometimes an individual will have difficulty even with this pitch glide procedure. However, he may still be able to produce an upward or downward inflection of pitch, if one suggests an actual word to him and how it is to be spoken. Have the subject speak the word "No" with a downward inflection suggesting a decisive declaration. If possible, it should be spoken so that the lowest pitch reached is sustained for a moment to make sure it is really a tone which he can prolong. Research has shown that we sometimes inflect downward to pitches below those that the voice can sustain. This possibility will be minimized if the subject prolongs the lowest tone for a few seconds. Following determination of the lowest pitch, the word "No" may be spoken as a question with a long upward inflection. If possible the highest pitch reached should be sustained briefly. As before, the procedure should be repeated a number of times to make sure the maximum range is covered. The teacher will have to listen particularly closely in this procedure to hear and remember the lowest and highest

TABLE A. Calculation of Natural Pitch Level in Tones Above Lowest Note, by Determining 25 Per Cent of Total Range

| Name of Highest Note | Number of Highest Note | Range in Musical Tones | Natural Pitch Level in Tones | Name of Natural Pitch Level |
|---|---|---|---|---|
| do | 1 | 0 | | |
| re | 2 | 1.0 | | |
| mi | 3 | 2.0 | | |
| fa | 4 | 2.5 | | |
| so | 5 | 3.5 | | |
| la | 6 | 4.5 | 1.1 | re |
| ti | 7 | 5.5 | 1.4 | re |
| do | 8 | 6.0 | 1.5 | mi |
| re | 9 | 7.0 | 1.8 | mi |
| mi | 10 | 8.0 | 2.0 | mi |
| fa | 11 | 8.5 | 2.1 | mi |
| so | 12 | 9.5 | 2.4 | fa |
| la | 13 | 10.5 | 2.6 | fa |
| ti | 14 | 11.5 | 2.9 | fa |
| do | 15 | 12.0 | 3.0 | so |
| re | 16 | 13.0 | 3.3 | so |
| mi | 17 | 14.0 | 3.5 | so |
| fa | 18 | 14.5 | 3.6 | so |
| so | 19 | 15.5 | 3.9 | so |
| la | 20 | 16.5 | 4.1 | la |
| ti | 21 | 17.5 | 4.4 | la |
| do | 22 | 18.0 | 4.5 | la |
| re | 23 | 19.0 | 4.8 | la |
| mi | 24 | 20.0 | 5.0 | ti |
| fa | 25 | 20.5 | 5.1 | ti |
| so | 26 | 21.5 | 5.4 | ti |
| la | 27 | 22.5 | 5.6 | ti |
| ti | 28 | 23.5 | 5.9 | do |
| do | 29 | 24.0 | 6.0 | do |

pitches until they can be matched on the piano. Because there is likely to be more uncertainty in locating these tones with this procedure, not less than ten measurements should be made of each. Any that are decidedly out of line with the majority should be discarded, and the average of the remainder should be taken as the final estimate.

A second difficulty in estimating a person's natural pitch level arises because individuals with voice disorders sometimes have restricted pitch ranges. The procedure described by Fairbanks was worked out with superior speakers and seems to work very well for those with average or greater pitch ranges. However, when a person has a very restricted pitch range the procedure of estimating his natural pitch level as 25 percent up his total singing range from his lowest tone is likely to result in estimates that are consistently too low. For example, if this procedure is followed strictly with an individual who has a range of only one octave, his natural pitch level will be estimated as being only one and one-half tones above his lowest pitch. This is so low that there is very little chance for pitch inflections to occur below this level. It is necessary, therefore, to compensate for this systematic error. The following procedure is recommended:

1. Use the Fairbanks table reproduced here to estimate the natural pitch level for any person who has a pitch range of two octaves or more.

2. For individuals having pitch ranges between one and two octaves take as the estimate of natural pitch level the pitch which is three musical tones above the lowest note that the subject can produce.

3. For those few individuals who may have pitch ranges of even less than one octave, the mid-pitch of the range should be chosen as the one to be made habitual.

Lastly, it is to be emphasized that a method such as that outlined can be employed too rigidly. One should check the results obtained by careful observation of the result. The pitch level chosen should be that at which voice can be produced most easily and efficiently, and from which easy natural inflections can be produced, in both an upward and a downward direction. One should experiment with it to see whether or not it does produce any improvement in voice.

# APPENDIX VII

∿∿∿∿∿∿∿∿∿∿∿∿∿∿∿∿∿∿∿∿∿∿∿∿∿∿∿∿∿∿∿∿∿∿∿∿∿∿∿∿∿∿∿∿∿∿∿∿∿∿∿∿∿∿∿∿∿∿∿∿∿∿∿∿∿∿∿∿∿∿

# An Open Letter to the Mother of a "Stuttering" Child[1]

My dear Mrs. Smith:

I thoroughly appreciate your concern over the speech difficulty of Fred, your four-year-old boy. You say that he is in good health, that he is mentally alert, and is generally normal by any standards you know about. I note that you have been careful not to change his handedness, and that he is now generally right handed. But you feel that, in spite of all this, he stutters.

It will interest you to know that the majority of four-year-old children regarded as stutterers by their parents just about fit that description. I want to say to you very nearly the same things I should say to the mothers of thousands of other "Freds."

Toward the end of this letter I am going to make a few suggestions

[1] This is a revision of an article which was published in its original form in the April, 1941, issue of the magazine *You and Your Child,* and reprinted in the *Journal of Speech and Hearing Disorders* (1949), *14*:3-8, and in *Crippled Child Magazine,* October, 1950. The "Open Letter" is included in this book because many speech correctionists, physicians, psychologists, teachers and others who work professionally with children have reported that they have found it suitable for parents whom they serve. Anyone wishing to make it available to parents or students may obtain copies from the Interstate Printers and Publishers, Danville, Illinois, printers of the American Speech and Hearing Association's *Journal of Speech and Hearing Disorders,* or from the National Society for Crippled Children and Adults, 11 South LaSalle Street, Chicago 3, Illinois.

which I believe might prove helpful. If you are like other mothers, however, you will want to have these recommendations explained so that you might understand clearly what is back of them. For that reason, I shall introduce the suggestions by giving you certain information.

This information has been obtained in the course of several years of research. Certain investigations of very young children regarded by their parents as stutterers have been particularly revealing. In summarizing the main findings of this research, I shall try to emphasize those points which will help you most to understand Fred's problem.

First of all, I want to put you at ease if I can by stressing that the most recent studies have tended strongly to discredit the popular view, which perhaps you share, that stutterers are generally abnormal or inferior in some very fundamental sense. Concerning this point, I should like to make as clear a statement as possible—and I make it on the basis of some 200 scientific studies of stuttering in older children and adults, and several recent investigations involving approximately 700 young children, stutterers and non-stutterers.

The statement is this. About one per cent of school children are classified as stutterers. I think any expert can be quite safely challenged to examine 1000 children who have not yet begun to speak, and to pick out the ten or so among them who will be regarded as stutterers five years later. In fact, I should be willing to let the expert examine the children after they had begun to speak but before any of them had come to be labeled as stutterers. And if he were asked to pick out the ten to twenty who would later be known as stutterers, my best judgment is that he could do little better than make pure guesses. I should not want him to talk with the parents, but he could examine the children as much as he liked in search of the abnormalities that are supposed to cause stuttering.

I should be willing to go even further. I believe any expert can safely be challenged to go into a room in which there are 100 adult men and women and pick out the ten stutterers whom we shall include in the group. He may use any tests whatever, except that he may not hear anyone speak, nor may he obtain any information about each individual that relates in any way to the question of how the person speaks or used to speak. I should be surprised if the expert could make better selections with his tests than he could by means of eenie-meenie-minie-moe.

In fact, I do not know of any way of examining a child so as to determine, with any degree of certainty, whether he will ever come to be regarded as a stutterer. So far as I know, stutterers generally are not significantly different from non-stutterers aside from their speech, and aside from the way they feel about their speaking experiences. So far as I know, in fact, even the speech of young children who are thought by their parents to be stutterers is quite normal until their parents begin to think of them as stutterers.

This last point is particularly important. I mentioned above that recently several studies have been made, involving over 700 young "stutterers" and "normal speakers." I have had a hand in these studies, and I must say that as the results began to come in we were frankly puzzled. We soon discovered that it was very difficult in most cases— apparently impossible in many cases—to tell the difference between "normal speaking" children and *newly diagnosed* "stuttering" children.

We found, for example, that two-, three-, and four-year-old children in a large nursery school, somewhat better than average children by most standards, spoke, on the average, with 35 to 50 repetitions per 1000 words. They repeated s-s-sounds like that, or or words, or two or two or more words. We found no child who never did this sort of thing and the most repetitious did it slightly more than 100 times per 1000 words. These are figures for normal children—the norm.

Now, what puzzled us particularly was the fact that, so far as we could determine, the youngsters whose parents believed they were stuttering were speaking as fluently as that. They were, that is, at the particular moment of the particular day when their parents first thought of them as stutterers. We were forced to conclude that these children were not only apparently normal in general, but also that their speech itself was apparently normal at the moment they were first regarded as stutterers. We simply could not escape the fact that, to all appearances, most of these parents had applied the label "stuttering" to the same types of speech behavior that other parents apparently take to be "normal speech."

Then the question came up as to whether this could make any difference. Doesn't a rose by any other name smell just as sweet?

Investigation seemed to show that a rose by any other name doesn't smell the same at all. If you call a child a "stutterer" you get one kind of speech—and personality—development, and if you call him a "normal speaker" or a "good speaker" you get another kind of development—within limits, but they seem to be rather wide limits.

I can illustrate what I mean by telling you briefly about two cases. The first case is that of Jimmy, who as a pupil in the grades was regarded as a superior speaker. He won a number of speaking contests and often served as chairman of small groups. Upon entering the ninth grade, he changed to another school. "A speech examiner" saw Jimmy twice during the one year he spent in that school. The first time she made a recording of his speech. The second time she played the record for him, and after listening to it, told him he was a stutterer.

Now, if you have ever tried to speak into a speech recording machine you probably suspect what is true. In the studies to which we have already referred all children who have done this have shown hesitations, repetitions, broken sentences, etc. It is easy to see how the apparently untrained teacher misjudged Jimmy who was, after all, a superior speaker as ninth-graders go.

He took the diagnosis to heart, however. The teacher told him to speak slowly, to watch himself, to try to control his speech. Jimmy's parents were quite upset. They looked upon Jimmy's speech as one of his chief talents, and they set about with a will to help him, reminding him of any little slip or hesitation. Jimmy became as self-conscious as the legendary centipede who had been told "how" to walk. He soon developed tense, jerky, hesitant, apprehensive speech—the kind that any speech pathologist would call stuttering of at least average severity.

The second case was Gene, a three-year-old boy. His father became concerned over the fact that now and then Gene repeated a sound or a word. Gene didn't seem to know he was doing it, and he wasn't the least bit tense about it. But the father consulted the family doctor and told him that Gene was stuttering. The doctor took his word for it. (Practically all original diagnoses of stuttering are made by laymen—parents nearly always and occasionally teachers—and it is a very serious matter when their diagnoses are not challenged.) He told the father to have Gene take a deep breath before trying to speak. Within forty-eight hours Gene was practically speechless. The deep breath became a frantic gasping from which Gene looked out with wide-eyed, helpless bewilderment.

These are real cases, and they seem to be fairly representative of such cases generally. We were exceedingly mystified as our investigations went on and such results as I have sketched kept coming in. Not only were practically all of the so-called stuttering children, *at time of diagnosis*, speaking as well as the normal children, but we could also find no evidence that they had suffered more injuries and diseases, including birth injuries, than had the normal children. Moreover, in spite of the traditional theory that stuttering usually begins as the immediate result of serious illness, severe fright or shock, and the like, we found that just as an amazing proportion of automobile accidents occur on dry, straight highways, in daylight, in the country, in good automobiles, so most stuttering develops in ordinary homes, under conditions that are not very dramatic, in children who are apparently normal and quite able to speak as well as other youngsters of their age.

These so-called stuttering youngsters were so puzzling just because they were so normal—until we decided to give up the assumption that they should necessarily be abnormal. Then the mystery began to lift. Slowly we saw more and more clearly what was staring us in the face. I suspect that we had overlooked it so long—for centuries, in fact— just because it was so obvious.

What we had overlooked, and what we now noticed, was simply that in case after case stuttering, as a serious speech and personality disorder, developed *after it had been diagnosed.* The diagnosis of stuttering is one of the causes of stuttering, and apparently one of the most potent causes.

I believe I can make this clear and also help you toward an understanding of Fred's problem, if I sketch for you what I should regard as a good method for making practically any child into a stutterer. It is the method used by parents themselves in bringing about the problem in their own children—not only unintentionally, of course, but because of a tendency to be overly conscientious. Broadly considered, it is the method commonly used—unintentionally, and out of a strong desire to get children to be good and to grow up rapidly—to make children awkward, or timid, or finicky about food, or afraid of the dark or of "doctors, dogs, deluges and demons."

Briefly, the method consists of calling a spade a spatula, and then using it as if it were one. In order to do this, one must steadfastly ignore the fact that it is more effectively used as a spade, but this does not seem difficult for most of us. Applying this principle then, as the parent of a normal child, you will first of all listen closely for the interruptions in his speech. You will hear many of them.

You must be impressed by these interruptions. Therefore, there are five things that you must quite completely overlook. First, you are not to pay attention to the circumstances in which the interruptions occur, because if you do the interruptions will seem to be perfectly natural. Second, you are to overlook the fact that for quite some time the child has given ample indication of his ability to speak normally for his age. Third, you must fail to notice that except for the occasional hesitations or repetitions his speech is apparently all right. Fourth, you are not to be impressed by his comparatively normal health, intelligence, and social development. And finally, above all, you are not to observe carefully the way other children of the same age speak under various conditions, for if you do your child will seem to be doing nothing out of the ordinary.

It is essential, you see, that you be impressed by what your child seems to be doing wrong. This will make it possible for you to focus your attention more or less completely, not upon the child and not upon his speech, but upon the interruptions in his speech. The next step—*and this is extremely important*—is to select a name for these interruptions. You want to select a name which implies a profound but mysterious abnormality, a name that will fill you with worry and dread every time you utter it or think it. "Stuttering" is just the name you want.

Having labeled the speech interruptions "stuttering," you will react to them as if they were all that the label implies. This will not be difficult. In fact, you will do it quite naturally, without realizing that you are doing it at all. By your very facial expression and your tone of voice, as well as by what you tell your child, you will easily convince him that he is not able to speak normally, or at least that he does not know how to do so, and that you disapprove of his natural best efforts to speak. In your zeal to control what you now call his "stuttering," you might even convince your child—without meaning to at all, of course—that you no longer love him, or at least that you are disappointed in him as a person.

For the label "stuttering" implies that your child needs help and you, of course, will respond eagerly to the task of helping him, because you love your child very deeply. If you are like other parents, you will conscientiously show the child how to inhale and how to exhale, how fast or slow to speak, how to breathe "with the abdomen" or "with the chest," how to place the tongue for certain sounds. You will urge him—perhaps with considerable urgency—to stop and start over, or to "think out" what he intends to say before he tries to say it. You wouldn't, of course, but some parents might, shall we say, scold him if he does not speak smoothly after all these "helpful" instructions. By such means you would succeed readily in setting up in the child your own attitude of anxiety and disapproval when his speech does not proceed smoothly.

As soon as he has acquired this attitude from you he will promptly supplement your feelings about him and his speech and your efforts to help him with his own particular feelings of uneasiness and self-disapproval and his own ingenious attempts to speak according to the standard of fluency which you appear to demand. He will try hard. He will so want to do the thing properly—so you will smile again, and tell him he is a fine boy. Naturally, he will strain. Of course, he cannot strain without holding his lips together tightly, or holding the tongue against the roof of the mouth, or constricting the muscles of his throat. He cannot strain in certain ways without holding his breath.

The fact that all this will interfere still more seriously with his speech and make him appear to be "stuttering" much worse—this fact will only spur him on to greater effort, and encourage you to be even more generous with your suggestions. You will tell your friends about it and they will also try to help.

In some cases the child finally reaches the point where he is straining practically all the time and so becomes quite speechless. In other cases, however, in spite of all that is done, the child still speaks fluently much of the time.

In saying all this, I have not meant to be at all facetious. On the contrary, I am most serious. I have simply outlined for you what may be regarded as the usual story of how "stuttering" begins and develops into a serious condition. I believe this information might help you to understand better the problem which you face with Fred. Other factors may be operating in Fred's situation and, if so, the problem will be different accordingly.

In saying all this, moreover, and in putting it in this particular way, I have by no means intended to say that you have done something for which you are to be criticized. On the contrary, you have acted from the finest of human motives—the great love you feel for your child. Your child knows this, you know it, and I feel very sure of it. You have done the best that you have known how to do. My sole purpose in writing as I do is to help you if I can to know how best to help Fred, which is what you want so very much to do.

If I have outlined then, in the main essentials at least, the problem with which you have to deal, I believe the following suggestions will prove helpful:

1. It is far from likely, according to your own statements, that the

speech difficulty is due to any physical cause. This does not mean that you might not have other reasons for taking Fred to see a physician. If he has any need for medical attention it should be provided for him. This will certainly not do his speech any harm. It might make him feel better in general and this is likely to be reflected favorably in his speech as well as in his other behavior.

2. Do nothing at any time, by word or deed or posture or facial expression, that would serve to call Fred's attention to *the interruptions* in his speech. Above all, do nothing that would make him regard them as abnormal or disgraceful. If he has begun to notice his own interruptions do all you can to convince him they are normal and perfectly acceptable. In this, however, do not make the mistake of "protesting too much." You can make him self-conscious about his speech even by praising his speech—if you praise it to excess. Err, if you must, on the side of approving it a bit more than is justified. I am not suggesting that you "pay no attention to his stuttering." If he is normally non-fluent he is not doing any stuttering. He is normal. If he is more hesitant in speech than most children, look about him, and at yourself, and try to find out the reasons. Then remove them.

3. In order to help you see Fred and his speech in relation to the things about him and to develop for yourself the necessary insight and a proper sense of proportion about Fred's speech interruptions, you should observe carefully (*a*) the conditions under which they occur; (*b*) the fact that most of his speech is fluent and always has been so; (*c*) the fact that he is, generally speaking, a comparatively normal child; (*d*) the fact that other youngsters of his age are, on the whole, just about as hesitant and repetitious in speaking as he is, especially under certain conditions (when they are "excited" or talking "over their heads," for example); and (*e*) the fact that even when he does not speak altogether fluently he does not as a rule fail utterly or "go to pieces"—even his repetitions and "uh-uh-uh's" are spoken more or less smoothly (or were before and at the time that you first regarded him as a stutterer).

4. Do not label Fred a "stutterer." If you do, you will have an almost irresistible tendency to treat him as if he were as defective and unfortunate as the label implies. It is foolish to risk the probable consequences of this. Instead of saying that he "stutters," say exactly what you mean, that under certain conditions (and *describe these specific conditions*) he repeats sounds or words, says "uh-uh-uh"—or whatever it is he does. This is a matter of such profoundly fundamental

importance that I could not possibly emphasize it too much. The way you classify Fred will determine very largely the way you react to him. This is as true of his speech as it is of everything else about Fred. If we label a boy a thief, no good will come of it. If we frequently call a youngster stupid, it will be hard for us to see how smart he is. Just so, if we think of a child as a stutterer we will worry about him and literally not hear how well he speaks.

5. There are certain conditions under which practically any child tends to speak smoothly and other conditions under which he tends to speak hesitantly. You will find it wise, therefore, to observe the following simple rules:

First of all and above all, try to be the kind of listener your child likes to talk to. You know how to be this kind of listener, but it may be that no one has ever helped you to realize how tremendously important it is to your child—and to you, and to the two of you together —that you be such a listener whenever he talks to you.

See that his brothers and sisters are not always "bossing" him, or not always talking when he wants to talk.

Read to him whenever you can. In reading or speaking to Fred, enunciate clearly, be interested in what you are reading, and avoid a tense voice. Make this reading fun and companionable. Do some of it every day, preferably just before bedtime, if possible.

Avoid asking Fred to "speak pieces" for company or to "show off" in other ways.

He should never have reason to doubt that you love him and that you enjoy hearing him talk.

Don't say, "No, you can't" or "Don't do that" when it really wouldn't matter if he did go ahead and do what he wanted to. Try to keep "Stop that" and "Don't do that" kind of remarks down to 25% or less of all the things you say to Fred.

Say "That's fine!" to Fred much more often than "Don't be so careless and awkward in the way you do things!" Rewards are far better than punishments.

Don't keep him in a state of excitement by too much teasing, nagging, bullying, or too much "running and jumping."

When you take him to strange places or ask him to do something that is new to him, prepare him for it by explaining ahead of time.

When he is talking "over his head," be very patient and now and then supply him with a new word which he has not yet learned but which he needs at the moment. To a reasonable extent and in meaningful ways help him add to his vocabulary.

In general, try to avoid situations that are unduly frustrating, exciting, bewildering, tiring, humiliating, or frightening to the child.

As for "discipline," so far as possible help Fred to discipline himself. Help him to understand how others feel and to be considerate of them. To borrow a mighty bit of wisdom from the poet Ovid, if Fred is to be loved he must be lovable. Help him to learn how to be.

My last suggestion may sound quite drastic, but I believe it is within the bounds of reason: Try as a rule to be as friendly and considerate toward your own child as you would be toward a house guest.

Unless Fred's speech difficulty is in some way exceptional, or has developed into a truly serious condition, the suggestions I have outlined should prove genuinely helpful. Do not expect a miracle to happen "overnight"—and remember that Fred is human. He—and you, or I, or anyone else—will never be as fluent as a faucet. Even the most silver-tongued orator makes an occasional bobble. But if within six months you feel, for any reason, that Fred is not showing as much improvement as he should, I hope you will consult a good speech correctionist, preferably one who holds Basic or Advanced Certification in the American Speech and Hearing Association.[2]

Yours very sincerely,<br>Wendell Johnson

[2] The American Speech and Hearing Association is the recognized professional organization of audiologists and speech correctionists in America. The Secretary-Treasurer of the Association (1956) is Dr. George A. Kopp, Wayne University, Detroit, Michigan. The Association may also be addressed through the Speech Correction Fund, 11 South La Salle Street, Chicago 3, Illinois.

# INDEX OF NAMES

# INDEX OF SUBJECTS